SECURITY AND ARMS CONTROL

SECURITY AND ARMS CONTROL

Volume 2:
A Guide to International Policymaking

Edited by Edward A. Kolodziej
and Patrick M. Morgan

Greenwood Press
NEW YORK • WESTPORT, CONNECTICUT • LONDON

Library of Congress Cataloging-in-Publication Data
(Revised for volume 2)

Security and arms control.

Includes bibliographies and indexes.
1. National security.   2. Security, International.
3. Arms control.   I. Kolodziej, Edward A.   II. Morgan,
Patrick M., 1940–   .
UA10.5.S38   1989   355'03   88–7224
ISBN 0–313–25257–2 (lib. bdg. : v. 1: alk. paper)
ISBN 0–313–25258–0 (lib. bdg. : v. 2: alk. paper)

British Library Cataloguing in Publication Data is available.

Library of Congress Catalog Card Number: 88–7224
ISBN: 0–313–25258–0

First published in 1989

Greenwood Press, Inc.
88 Post Road West, Westport, Connecticut 06881

Printed in the United States of America

The paper used in this book complies with the
Permanent Paper Standard issued by the National
Information Standards Organization (Z39.48–1984).

10 9 8 7 6 5 4 3 2 1

Contents

Preface

This two-volume reference series is organized around the notion that national and international security and arms control studies are an interdisciplinary field of study. It seeks to give more precise form and profile to this emerging area of study than now exists in the literature. Volume 1 is concerned with the broad analytical perspectives that are relevant to security and arms control considerations of any national government. Volume 2 attempts to clarify and define selected current issues and problems from an international perspective.

These volumes seek to fill three needs. First, through the topics that have been identified for each volume, they attempt to define the scope of the emerging interdisciplinary field of security and arms control studies as a serious field of systematic inquiry. The chapters identify major problems, key concepts, methods, disciplinary approaches, intellectual styles, and data sources associated with the principal sub-fields of international security and arms control studies. It is very difficult to coherently order the multiple literatures and disciplines appropriate to the study of security and arms control. These volumes present one way—by no means the only one—of organizing this scattered material and diverse activity.

Second, the chapters of both volumes provide a critical review and evaluation of the most important literature associated with each sub-field to assist more extended analysis by interested students and policymakers than can be attempted in these brief evaluative surveys. Contributors were recruited specifically because of their acquaintance with a broad range of interdisciplinary literature relevant to each sub-field and, where appropriate, because of their experience in policymaking.

Third, the volumes can be used as texts for courses in international and national security and arms control. Each may be used as the framework for a year-long, two-semester course or used separately as need dictates. The literature or sources evaluated in each chapter may be used to supplement these volumes.

In meeting these needs, these volumes seek to achieve several objectives. They can assist the further development of courses and programs in international and national security and arms control at universities and colleges. A liberal education implies knowledge of the world around us, not simply those of bygone eras. The possibility of war, nuclear holocaust, or terrorist attacks now weighs so heavily on human consciousness that serious and systematic study of the determinants of force and the mechanisms to control it needs to be part of the formation of the educated citizen in an open society, as much as history, art, or science. How else can the imperatives of using, threatening, and controlling force be reconciled with those imperatives associated with democratic norms, requiring broad public consent and informed support of governmental strategic policies?

Next, policy analysts and decision-makers will be aided in their effort to extend their special areas of responsibility to include concepts, methods, criteria, and data used in other fields. They should also find the volumes helpful in learning about the broader dimensions of the specific security and arms control problems which they are responsible for managing or resolving.

Finally, the volumes provide a provisional agenda for further research and analysis by indicating where more work needs to be done to advance security and arms control studies and policymaking.

These volumes reflect two conflicting assumptions arising from the strategic problems confronting national decision-makers: that force and coercive threats are fundamental features of the behavior of states and that the utility of force, given the increasing lethal power in the hands of nations, has never been more questionable and problematic. There is no reason to believe that in the immediate future states will eschew force or threats in pursuing their objectives. Yet, thoughtful analysts and decision-makers are aware of the costs and risks of arms races and the danger of prodigal and improvident use of force in supporting a nations's aims and interests. We need to understand the problems associated with making national and international security and arms control policy and how states are attempting to relax, if not resolve, the dilemmas posed by organized violence today.

Rationalizing the use of force has never been as difficult or as fraught with danger as it is today. Not only the nuclear arsenals of the superpowers, but also the sustained and unremitting development of centers of military power around the globe threaten to envelop the world community in war. If states demonstrate little interest in rejecting force in support of their political objectives, they are no less confronted with the imperatives of determining how their assembled military power can be prevented from toppling their regimes and of calibrating its use to ensure its subordination to legitimate political and moral purpose. Using and controlling war as an instrument of state policy are, therefore, only different aspects of a single imperative confronting national decision-makers. The nation's response to this imperative constitutes its strategic policy.

Two important caveats are in order. First, these volumes cannot hope to cover all the relevant topics, literature, and approaches appropriate to the study and practice of national and international security and arms control. They are designed only as a start toward shaking down and synthesizing some of the major components of this vast, sprawling, and still uncharted field. They are an initial and provisional inventory of what is known, what is not known, and what needs to be known about the behavior of states as they seek, alternatively, to use, threaten, and control force. The editors expect that others will be stimulated to improve on our effort in clarifying the parameters of strategic studies and the methods and approaches relevant to them. The editors freely admit that much has been left out as a consequence of funding shortfalls, space limitations, the availability of analysts, and the exigencies of cloture and publication schedules, to mention only some of the constraints under which these volumes were produced.

Second, the editors have stressed problems and problem-solving. We believe that theory-building in international relations must proceed in part by concentrating on what decision-makers are concerned about and about what they say and do. For students of international relations, the task is to describe, explain, and ultimately predict the behavior of states and decision-makers. One way to approach this problem is to begin with *their* problems and to assess whether or not they see them clearly rather than simply substitute our own paradigms in the dubious hope that they are relevant to serious human concerns.

The division between national and international security and arms control problems is a convenient distinction, though hardly the only one that could be employed. The perspective of Volume 1 is that of the decision-maker who is obliged to develop strategies for the use, threat, and control of force to support national objectives. He or she has an interest in determining the outcomes of conflict relations in favorable ways where coercion or violence acts as arbiter. The second volume assumes more the perspective of the analyst who is interested in defining security and arms control issues from a global perspective. The problems are by and large system-wide in their impact and assume some level of international cooperation if they are to be managed or resolved. Volume 2 concludes with an extensive bibliography covering works vital for a core reference library in the field, part of the effort to have these volumes define and promote the development of the field. This contribution, by Stephen Atkins, is as important as any in these works. We hope the volumes complement each other since the problems addressed in Volume 2 will be solved, if at all, by policymakers responsible for strategic policies rather than by analysts who can warn, criticize, or cajole but who cannot take initiatives to strike workable, albeit tenuous, balances between the competing requirements of national and international security. Through these volumes, analysts can speak but cannot dictate to power.

Edward A. Kolodziej
Patrick M. Morgan

Introduction

EDWARD A. KOLODZIEJ AND
PATRICK M. MORGAN

Military conflicts among nations are as old as nations themselves. Indeed, they have had much to do with the creation and development of nations. Early in the history of the nation-state system, thoughtful analysts were intrigued by the problem of war and began suggesting ways to do something about it. However, this early interest did not give rise to an intensive and systematic intellectual effort in security studies; even international relations as a recognizable field is a twentieth-century development. Apart from military history, extended academic study of conflict and security in international politics is relatively new. Confined largely to this century, it has been growing at an enormous rate since 1945. Initially the offspring of the general, and itself emerging, field of international relations, there has been such an accumlation of specialists, effort, information, and analysis on security matters that it now approaches the status of a field on its own. It is busily acquiring all the trappings: innumerable specialties and sub-specialties, an immense literature complete with specialized journals and technical publications, important clusters of theory, degree programs promising impressive levels of competence, and a proliferating jargon. If security problems could be solved by studying them to death, we would now be on the verge of success.

For most of the history of international politics war was a regular, sometimes useful, and quite legitimate tool of statecraft. In some respects it still is. As an absorbing and technically complex enterprise, it primarily attracted and preoccupied specialists in the profession of arms. Systematic study was most often undertaken in a professional mode, the subjects of scrutiny reflecting concerns of those in the business—how to organize men for combat, how to lead, how to advance and retreat, how to make and employ arms. Other fields were drawn on in a utilitarian way—engineering for fortifications, mathematics for navigation, medicine for the wounded. As an eminently

practical activity, war seldom attracted abstract analysis and scholarly investigation.

Carl von Clausewitz was a remarkable exception, providing an early bridge
from the professional study of war to the abstract exploration of the phenomenon of war. Late in the nineteenth century another true pioneer, Ivan
Bloch, mounted a social science effort (largely neglected) to depict what
modern warfare would be like and to uncover its implications for the pursuit
of national and international security. Both men were moved by the perception that warfare had reached a point, in terms of its destructiveness as well
as its socio-economic and political disruptions, that required steps to tran-
scend the treatment of it on a narrowly professional level. They were groping
toward a perspective that placed war, for purposes of analysis, within the
broad political pursuit of national security precisely because the thoughtless
use of force had become so costly and dangerous.

What acute observation and sustained reflection can do for giants, bitter
experience must do for lesser men. Insufficient appreciation of what Clausewitz and Bloch had to offer allowed the catastrophe of World War I, a grinding
slaughter to the point of exhaustion that Bloch had predicted, with dimensions
and adverse consequences far exceeding the value of the political objectives
for which it was initiated. The war had the effect of directing much more
attention to concerns and ideas that had been raised prior to 1914 and that
have since become (with the help of World War II) central preoccupations
in the field—the problem of devising an effective and stable deterrence
system, the fear of weapons of mass destruction, deep concern about arms
racing and arms transfers, systematic efforts at arms control, and suggestions
that the decaying utility of force necessitated devising a less war-prone international system.

The intellectual effort after World War I that all this involved was, in the
end, futile. Solid links between the dimly perceived dynamics and implications of what was happening and the complex processes that shaped national
security policies could not be forged on a sufficient scale within the very
limited time allowed. It is a failure with which we can sympathize, for the
forging of those links is still incomplete. As the theme in the opening chapter
of Volume 1 puts it, although "force and coercive threats are fundamental
features of the behavior of states ... the utility of force, given the increasing
lethal power in the hands of nations, has never been more questionable and
problematic."

World War II and the onset of the nuclear age galvanized efforts to study
the emerging subject of security. The major initial steps came in the United
States which exploited the resources and flexibility of its universities while
generating a new structure, the "think tank," to direct intellectual efforts at
theory and research. In a process that is still continuing, the effort eventually
spread, with important centers and able analysts appearing in a number of
other nations. Today the field is global in its dimensions, with members

immersed in intricate networks of communication and interaction. It serves as a three-way bridge between the actual practice of warfare, the immediate concerns of the policymaker, and the empirical and theoretical findings of the natural and social sciences. This permits much coming and going in all directions, but not without tension at the intersection and ambiguity about where we are headed and in what order to proceed.

The complex, delicate, and dangerous matter of security shows few signs of diminishing in importance, and the scale of the work being done, usefully or not, continues to mount. Thus, it seems appropriate to survey the state of the field and summarize its key features. This two-volume collection was designed for that purpose. Together, these volumes provide:

A quick introduction to a great many aspects of the field for those who are just coming to it or who need to dip into it for some particular purpose.

Surveys of much of the work that has been done that should be of interest to the specialist in the field, including outlines of leading perspectives, theories, and schools of thought.

Summaries of a good deal of factual information pertaining to security matters.

Extensive bibliographies pertaining to the various sub-fields.

Volume 1 is divided into four broad parts. The first introduces the field by identifying those characteristics of the international system that currently condition the use or threat of force and that prompt the need to control violence and discipline its use to national purpose. It also stipulates the major functions of strategic policy when approached from a national perspective. Many of these functions are then addressed in the second section where chapters review key facets of the use or threat of force. Other functions are taken up in the third section, where the focus is on contriving internal and external controls to limit the adverse feedback arising from organizing, threatening, and using military power. The final section reviews ways that nations might move beyond violence and threats in order to better cope with their conflicts.

The predominantly national perspective in the first volume gives way, to some extent, to an international one is this volume. Contributors have tried to apply a regional or global view or to treat specifically national experiences and practices on a comparative basis, while emphasizing the continuing development of a field that embraces both national and international levels of analysis. The opening section offers a survey and critique of efforts to specify the relationship between the nature of the international system and the conflicts among states. A second section reviews many aspects of nuclear deterrence in theory and practice. Its concluding chapter on extended deterrence moves the focus of attention toward problems that arise in the use of conventional military strength and in the flourishing business of arms transfers, the broad topic of Part III. The next part then turns to the application of force and attendant issues that can be located at the sub-conventional war level. As with Volume 1, the final section is devoted to examining certain types of remedies, that is, arms control and the better understanding and management of crises.

Surveying the field by perusing these chapters will invite the observation that a number of matters are omitted or touched on too briefly. It would not have been difficult to envision three volumes or more. Largely untapped is the burgeoning literature on intelligence as a component of national security policy making. Far less is said than it is possible to say about many facets of arms control. The economic and technological dimensions of security-oriented statecraft are not fully covered, and the logistical side of modern warfare gets uneven attention. What might be termed the sociology of military forces in today's nations is somewhat neglected.

This catalog could continue. In short, the field is more immense than this collective effort could encompass. We can only hope that these two volumes take us down the road to defining the core and main parameters of the field and provide something like a benchmark from which to measure future progress. With respect to the latter, the impression that these volumes evoke is that a considerable amount of work has been done and that there is plenty left to do. In fact, the authors provide suggestions for further research and analysis.

VOLUME 2: AN OVERVIEW

One of the more appealing ways to explain international conflict and war is to trace it to evil men and bad policies. Replace "evil men" with human nature, personality disorders, or cognitive limitations, and "bad policies" with distortions in decision-making introduced by factors such as group dynamics, organizational processes, internal politics, and the like and we arrive at the modern social science equivalents. However, the awful persistence of war and the threat of war have fostered a recurring suspicion that the nature of international politics itself is at fault. William R. Thompson in Chapter 1 carefully and comprehensively reviews efforts to give this suspicion a theoretically rigorous expression. His discussion makes it evident that this portion of the field is currently characterized by stimulating theoretical work of an innovative sort taking place alongside the vigorous recasting of traditional perspectives, realist and Marxist.

One of the disturbing aspects of tracing the problem of security to the international system by finding that the system drives states to behave in dangerous ways is that this considerably narrows our options. In the broadest sense, either the system must be significantly altered, or some way must be found to suspend or cancel its normal effects. There are those who think that the international system is currently undergoing substantial modification, but they are more than offset by others who doubt this is true. When it comes to policy, analysts in security studies have generally displayed little confidence that the system can be deliberately and effectively refashioned; statesmen normally display even less. Attention and effort have therefore concentrated on preventing political conflicts from culminating, as they so often have in the past, in war. This is reinforced in policymaking by an inclination to trace threats to security not to the system but to particular governments that need to be compelled to keep the peace.

Accordingly, whereas some analysts see the dynamics of the system as also responsible for the periodic absence, not just the occurrence, of major wars, great states place their trust in nuclear deterrence. With so much at stake, it has received a great deal of attention in the field and several chapters have been devoted to it here. One chapter deals with the development and current status of the theory of nuclear deterrence (Patrick M. Morgan, Chapter 2) tracing the way in which its classical version is being supplemented by historical and empirical studies. The endless complexities of assessing the nuclear balance have provoked intense debates in and out of policymaking circles, not simply out of strictly military considerations but because, as a psychological relationship, deterrence has been believed to be affected by images and perceptions which the balance helps to shape. William H. Baugh (Chapter 3) offers a tour of relevant considerations, methods, and debates as well as figures, casting illumination on an often dim corner of the field.

Built into nuclear deterrence by the weapons and delivery systems involved is the problem of stability, the possibility that the weapons could, in a crisis, either incite a preemptive attack or arouse such a fear of one that policymakers would be stampeded into war. Fear of vulnerability to Soviet preemptive attack has led to a long series of "gap" controversies in Western, particularly American, defense policymaking. The latest of these concerns is C^3I, the alleged disruptions in communications, command, control, and intelligence pertaining to retaliatory forces in the event of an attack. C^3I vulnerability also bears on the possibilities for the precise and extended conduct of a nuclear war as envisioned in current American strategic planning, a highly controversial matter. Stephen J. Cimbala (Chapter 4) reviews the state of the field on this matter, covering one of the most swiftly developing bodies of literature on security in this decade.

Several other nuclear-armed states besides the superpowers see themselves as practicing nuclear deterrence, and in doing so they bring to bear their particular security concerns, strategic perspectives, and resources. Edward A. Kolodziej (Chapter 5) identifies the factors that produced their nuclear forces and that are now shaping their further development, such as regional and superpower conflict and accord, internal technological-economic progress, and the evolution of national military doctrines. He also analyzes the emerging multilateral character that these forces are imposing on nuclear deterrence, that is to say, on a subject that has been traditionally studied largely as a bilateral superpower relationship.

As early as NSC-68 in 1950, it has been understood that to the extent that mutual nuclear deterrence is in place for the superpowers, extended nuclear deterrence declines in credibility and conventional forces rise in importance. Under such circumstances, alliances have to be managed amidst quite understandable doubts about their cohesion in the face of extreme provocations Such doubts have contributed to both the development of regional nuclear forces and large-scale peacetime deployments of conventional forces. David Schwartz (Chapter 6) probes the theory and practice of extended deterrence, in which nuclear and conventional forces interact in an uneasy tangle affecting budgets, policies, deployments, strategies, and alliance politics. His analysis of what the field has to offer on this provides a point of departure to the issues and uncertainties involved in conventional military forces, where many of the same problems reappear in other guises.

Conventional forces are seemingly more usable and useful than nuclear weapons, yet they remain exceedingly difficult to employ effectively at acceptable cost. Richard J. Kugler (Chapter 7) considers many facets of this matter via what is, in effect, an extensive case study of NATO. His approach differs from that of most of the other chapters; typically, they examine basically civilian/academic security studies, while he takes us inside the ongoing development of analytic efforts by military professionals. This important source of expert input into security policymaking is traced within the politico-military interactions of the alliance, and its action-reaction relationship with the Warsaw Pact, complementing the two preceding chapters.

Robert S. Wood (Chapter 8) covers contemporary findings about the exercise of conventional military power on, and from, the sea. Here, too, conventional and nuclear forces coexist on uneasy terms. Naval power is a highly controversial subject to which attention has been drawn by its application from the South Atlantic to the Middle East in this decade and by the impressive superpower investments in their respective navies. Naval strength is at once potent, fragile, and highly visible, a volatile mixture in policymaking.

For most nations, important conventional weapons systems—naval, land, and air—must be imported or produced under license. One of the more striking features of contemporary security affairs is the continuing trade in arms which is contributing to the steady diffusion of military power. This is Michael Brzoska's topic in Chapter 9. For most states, arms transfers are nearly always an important segment of their security policies and a major contributor to their security problems. Suppliers and recipients are immersed in endlessly complicated relationships reflecting a welter of motives, based on conflicting priorities, and having uncertain consequences. Numerous efforts have been made to monitor and assess what has been happening, producing a scholarly labyrinth for which Brzoska supplies a map.

Arms transfers and the diffusion of conventional military power have had some bearing on the phenomenon of subconventional military activity, both as cause and effect. All major states have recently found themselves directly involved with instances of "low-intensity conflict," Richard Shultz's topic in

Chapter 10, either while contributing to the defense of governments they like or promoting the demise of governments they dislike. Numerous other states are similarly involved, while low-intensity conflict has become a significant arena for nonstate actors in the international system. Shultz compares the experience, doctrines, and organizational responses of several states to the challenges posed by something that is now so ubiquitous that it can no longer be termed an "irregular" form of warfare. Still further down the scale of deliberate violence in the system but near the top in current visibility and concern is international terrorism. In one sense it closes the circle: nuclear deterrence holds ordinary citizens hostage, conventional and low-intensity warfare have eroded the distinction between military and civilian targets, and now terrorism puts people in harm's way with violent, sometimes random intrusions into daily life. This is another highly controversial subject. In Chapter 11 Martha Crenshaw's thorough review of a rapidly accumulating literature lays out the ongoing debates about everything from how to define terrorism to whom to blame and what to do about it.

When examining the field as a whole, we see that it has always had, and retains, a strong orientation toward contributing not just to an understanding of security matters but also to the better management and resolution of security problems. A number of the chapters trace this inclination toward policy relevance, while the concluding ones give it particular attention. Strategic arms control is best understood as a management effort. It emerged as an adjunct to nuclear deterrence, designed to make deterrence more bearable, via a logical extension of deterrence theory. Patrick M. Morgan (Chapter 12) summarizes the current state of the field on strategic arms control and finds it in some disarray. However, recent developments in the direction of major agreements promise to lift the gloom that settled over the arms control community at the start of the decade. If their promise is fulfilled, this topic may soon be one of the most exciting around.

An awkward feature of nuclear deterrence is that it tends to invite the diffusion of nuclear weapons in the international system, in imitation and due to the limitations on extended deterrence or the specific security needs of regional powers referred to earlier. In theoretical terms, it can be difficult to explain why nuclear deterrence is stable and reliable for great states, whereas lesser states cannot be trusted with it. Nonetheless, arms control has been summoned to impede proliferation, and William C. Potter offers a truly comprehensive survey of this subject in Chapter 13. Potter not only reviews the work that has been done, but also indicates where the weight of the evidence now falls among competing explanations as to when and why proliferation occurs.

The final chapter, by Charles F. Hermann, deals with the unevenly rewarding but always interesting study of crisis, where force, politics, strategy, and decision-making intersect. One of the grand themes of the modern study of security is that the dynamics of crisis may overload national decision-making systems, leading to failures in perception, assessment, and communication that can result in unwanted and unnecessary wars. His application of multiple levels of analysis and elucidation of conceptual/definitional problems provide a way of distinguishing and then integrating the many kinds of crisis studies that have been undertaken. Hermann makes it clear that we cannot now supply a complete guide to successful crisis management.

In concluding this introduction, the editors want to note the many debts we have accumulated as this project has developed, debts we will never fully be able to repay. We want to take this opportunity to thank the contributors for their willingness to add one more, rather demanding, chore to their already overcrowded agendas. The caliber of their offerings confirms their well-deserved reputations in the field, and we have been honored by the chance to work with them. In the course of the project, the editors alone have drawn on secretarial support from four universities on two continents, quite apart from the assistance of this sort which the other contributors have had, and we are very grateful to have been so well served. Finally, praise is due to Greenwood Press and, in particular, editor Mildred Vasan for appreciating the need to survey an amorphous and vital field and for the patience to outwait the inevitable delays in such an undertaking.

PART I

CONFLICT AND THE INTERNATIONAL SYSTEM

On Systemic Sources
of Conflict

WILLIAM R. THOMPSON

In a volume concerned with security and arms control, it goes without saying that the international system is not very peaceful. Conflict has certainly been the rule and not the exception. Quincy Wright (1942/1965, p. 653) once observed that eight European states were at war from nearly one-fourth to one-third of the years between 1450 and 1900 (Spain, 33 percent; Turkey, 30.5 percent; Russia, 30 percent; Austria, 27.5 percent; Great Britain, 25 percent; France, 23.5 percent; the Netherlands, 22 percent). On a more collective note, Jack Levy (1983, pp. 97, 99) states that

[t]here can be no doubt regarding the pervasiveness of interstate war involving the Great Powers. The Powers have been involved in interstate wars for roughly 75 percent of the 481 years of the system [1495–1975], and in 60 percent of these years they have been involved in Great Power war [wars involving at least one great power on both sides]. On average, a new war begins every four years and a Great Power war every seven or eight years. In the typical year . . . , slightly over one war involving the Great Powers and slightly less than one Great Power war is underway, two and a half Great Powers are at war, there are nearly three nation-years of war, and 6,500 deaths.

It also goes without saying that great power warfare is something less than the whole of systemic conflict. If the aggregate amount of international conflict (as opposed to all conflict) were viewed as a systemic property, we would need to include non-great power warfare, interventions in internal warfare, border skirmishes, and several varieties of terrorism, to say nothing of a host of diplomatic wrangles and disputes. Yet when the question of conflict in the system is raised, we often are really referring to the most dramatic, expensive, and deadlier manifestations—warfare between the system's major state actors. As a consequence, much international relations theory is oriented toward this very subject. This chapter will not deviate from that practice. Conflict and warfare between the system's major powers is a worthy preoccupation and one that is not particularly difficult to justify.

How are we to account for this long history of disputes and bloodletting? The theoretical literature offers a bewildering variety of avenues to explore. Biological instincts, decision-maker misperceptions, national attributes (such as type of economic system, business cycles, number of borders, or internal pressures to be diverted through external outlets or scapegoats), the surprise and pace of crisis management, the reflexive reactions of arms racing, or simply the number of major powers in the system—to name a few—represent plausible and worthwhile explanatory paths to pursue. Yet it is difficult to pursue all of these simultaneously, and absolutely impossible to do so in a brief chapter. This author also suspects that many of these more conventional explanations are secondary to more fundamental processes.

Given these considerations, this chapter will focus strictly on systemic sources of conflict and war between and among the system's principal actors. Just what is "systemic" in international relations is not entirely clear. Some analysts view most activities pertaining to the interaction of states as systemic (e.g., McClelland, 1966; Choucri and North, 1975), For others, systemic behavior entails the aggregation of all behavior. Systemic conflict thus equals all of the conflict taking place anywhere in the world in some period of time. Still others regard only the state as real and any talk of an interstate system as unrealistic.

Neither the interactional nor the aggregation perspective is utilized here. In this chapter, "systemic" will refer to the patterned interactions and attributes of the modern world system that began to emerge around 1500 and that has continued to evolve since. Systemic structures and properties thus refer to the ways in which the world's collective relationships are patterned and to their emergent characteristics.

The justification for the narrowed focus on systemic sources is as follows. Aside from their indisputable significance to world politics, a good reason for looking only at the "systemic" sources is that they are so frequently overlooked or at least partitioned off as a delimited category of limited explanatory power (Waltz, 1959; Singer, 1961). In this chapter, it will be argued that the systemic sources of major power conflict should not be compartmentalized as one of several analytical clusters of hypotheses or alternative levels of analysis. Instead, it will be suggested that the systemic sources need to be more closely integrated with the other forms of interpretation. Without them, the other forms (e.g., misperception, arms races, crises, and so forth) constitute unanchored, context-free explanations and are therefore inherently restricted interpretations.

Examples of restricted, context-free explanations are not particularly difficult to find. The war models of Blainey (1973) and Bueno de Mesquita (1981), for instance, provide strong illustrations. Whether or not states choose to fight depends, subject to various caveats, on whether decision-makers believe they are likely to win or lose. Their calculations on the probability of winning, in turn, hinge on relative strength assessments. Yet from a systemic point of view, actors are embedded in historical structures and therefore are rarely, if ever, entirely free to do precisely as they wish. These historical structures do not necessarily determine actor choices, but they are likely to channel them. As a consequence, actors will be constrained from pursuing some ends just as systemic structures may encourage or facilitate the pursuit of other goals.

Even the interests that actors pursue have been shaped and conditioned by structures and by the actors' positions within the structures. Relative strength remains an important factor, not for telling us that the weak are usually reluctant to attack the strong, but for alerting us to the changes that occur in relative positions within structural networks and the accompanying changes in actor incentives for seeking to improve or defend these relative positions.

Of course, not all conflicts and wars may be explained equally well by an emphasis on systemic structure. But then perhaps we should not expect all conflicts and wars to be accounted for by a single, "one-size-fits-all" model. The alternative—viewing all conflict from a single lens—can certainly lead to serious distortion as in Blainey's (1973) and Bueno de Mesquita's (1981) tendency to view the cases of World Wars I and II as disputes between Austria-Hungary versus Serbia and Germany versus Poland, which happened to ex-pand into wider conflicts. In contrast, it will be argued that there is an un-derlying structural rhyme and reason to major power disputes that is critical to making sense of these confrontations.

To suggest this does not imply that all historical-structural analysts agree exactly on what the underlying pattern is. Yet there is considerable overlap. To demonstrate this point (and to introduce quickly some of the available points of view), the next section will briefly sketch five models pertaining to major power conflict and confrontation. Then the stage will have been set for specifying some of the structural common denominators and for considering their implications.

Five Historical-Structural Approaches to Systemic Conflict

The Power Transition Model

The power transition model (Organski, 1968; Organski and Kugler, 1980) stratifies the system into two primary classes: the relatively weak, small/middle powers and the stronger great powers. A third special category is reserved for the strongest great power, the system's dominant power. This state is responsible for establishing or acquiring control over the system's distribu-tion of privileges. As the primary beneficiary, the dominant power is likely to be the most comfortable or satisfied with the international status quo.

Other members of the great power class are linked to this dominant power in various ways (usually through past and present alliances) and, over time, can be considered relatively satisfied with their respective niches in the systemic order. Newer arrivals to great power status, however, are less likely to be receiving what their decision-makers perceive to be a fair share of the system's benefits. Their capabilities may have expanded, but the older, more established elite states are less than eager to yield some portion of their resources and privileges without a fight. Dissatisfied great powers are thus portrayed as frustrated with an inflexible, zero-sum status quo that does not accommodate significant changes in the system's distribution of power.

Given this milieu, the parameters of systemic conflict and peace are quite clear. Peace should prevail when the powerful, satisfied great powers remain much stronger than the powerful, dissatisfied great powers. The probability of systemic warfare increases as the aggregated capabilities of the dissatisfied approach some approximation of the satisfied. The threat of war increases even more dramatically when a single dissatisfied great power's positional or capability improvements facilitate its catching up to or passing the position of the traditional dominant power. As this power transition occurs, the challenger sees an opportunity to defeat the protectors of the status quo and establish a new order more to its liking. The system's once dominant power, now in relative decline, not surprisingly perceives the same opportunity for radical system change but one that is entirely unwelcome. A major war fought over dominance in the system is therefore likely to ensue.

A half dozen factors are thought to be important in elaborating this perspective. War becomes less probable if the dominant power is flexible and adjusts to the challenger's improved capability position. The historical pattern of relations between the two potentially confrontational states could make some difference. A history of cooperation presumably makes war less probable. The extent to which the challenger proposes to revise the international order should also influence the dominant power's degree of threat perception. A more radical challenger therefore increases the likelihood of war. It may also make some difference whether the conventional pattern of economic gains leading to enhanced state effectiveness is reversed by an ascending challenger. Just how novel the industrial policies of catch-up oriented states are is debatable, but it is conceivable that the pace of the catch-up process can be accelerated (or slowed) by state intervention.

The speed with which a challenger approaches the dominant power's position can be important. A rapid ascendancy on the part of a challenger is viewed as more dangerous than a slow rise. Rapid change leaves little time for adjustment by either the challenger or the dominant power. Challenger decision-makers may be more likely to become impatient in such contexts. They may also tend to exaggerate their own capability advances, leading to overconfidence and a misperception of relative standings. There is also the possibility that the economic changes and dislocations underlying the challenger's positional gains will cause domestic stress that may be tempting to alleviate or divert through external scapegoating and adventures.

Finally, some consideration is given to the challenger's potential power. If this potential is so obviously great that all observers predict that the challenger will some day be the system's dominant power, the likelihood of conflict is less because the probable battlefield outcome should be equally obvious. On the other hand, a limited growth potential should serve to constrain the challenger's conflictual impulses. Between these two alternatives lies the most dangerous situation. If a challenger sees that the best it can hope for is a rough approximation of the waning dominant power's position, the temptation to seize the dominant role may be all the greater. Meanwhile, the dominant power is less likely to be convinced that it needs to peacefully surrender its position. Nor can the challenger afford to outwait the status quo coalition until the relative power pendulum swings clearly toward the anti-status quo coalition. The development of structural ambiguity thus points to a high risk of war.

The Power Cycle Model

Power cycle theory (Doran and Parsons, 1980; Doran, 1983a, 1983b, 1985) begins with the observation that absolute growth in state capabilities (population, industrial production, armed forces, and urbanization) tends to be positive, roughly linear, and perhaps even exponential. However, the capability growth relative to other states tends to be non-linear. Relative power tends to rise, to plateau, and then to decline. Several reasons have been posited for this phenomenon. Variations in resources mean that larger, better endowed states will ultimately supplant smaller states in the power hierarchy. Later industrializers have tended to replace the early industrializers. But, at the same time, increases in organizational size and age ultimately lead to rigidities in how institutions cope with change. Productivity declines, bureaucracies overdevelop and stagnate, and societal creativity is discouraged. Development and growth rates decay. Population and capital migrate to new centers of growth. In the end, newer states catch up with and bypass older states which have attained their maximum relative capability position.

As states pass through the cycle of ascent, maturity, and decline, adjustments have to be made to the shifts in systemic position. Four points in particular— the two inflection points on the rising and falling sides and lower and upper turning points—are believed to be especially dangerous. It is at these critical points that psychological adjustments must be made to conform to the relative capability changes. At the inflection points, new states enter the system's core group and older declining states may drop out. At all four points, strategic and foreign policy options are altered. Systemic roles (e.g., leader versus follower) change. New rivalries and threats emerge. All of these changes are most unsettling and stressful for both the decision-makers and the country's population at large. Consequently, the probability of misperception and outright error is greatest at the cycle's critical points. The interaction of decision-making pathologies and power shifts renders these critical points especially prone to warfare between the major powers.

This perspective emphasizes the destabilizing vertical movement of states. Vertical mobility also threatens systemic order that, viewed on a horizontal plane, depends for stability on balancing against the possibility of hegemonic expansion. When one state threatens to dominate through expansion, other states are expected to realign in hopes of creating an anti-hegemonic alliance with sufficient resources to suppress the threat to the system's equilibration. Since this process depends a great deal on intelligently calculated diplomacy that neither overreacts nor underreacts, the destabilizing nature of the vertical mobility spills over into the horizontal balancing process. Alternatively put, upward and downward mobility tends to interfere with the multiple adjustments needed to maintain the equilibrium of the horizontal plane. Serious warfare between major powers can be seen as a failure of the central system to cope with the rise and fall of its most important players. The more widespread, rapid, and unanticipated the changes in relative position, the more difficult it is for the key players to adjust to the structural changes. The more extensive the positional changes and the associated difficulties in responding to them, the more likely is extensive conflict and war.

The Hegemonic Cost-Benefit Model

The hegemonic cost-benefit model (Gilpin, 1981) contends that international political systems are characterized by government, authority, property rights, and law just as domestic political systems are. Government is provided by the dominance of a hegemonic leader and other great powers. Authority is predicated on the prestige hierarchy established among the major powers. Property rights are similar to territorial divisions, and law is reproduced through the rules of the system.

The problem is that these systemic rules, hierarchies, and institutional structures are created for the purpose of benefiting and protecting the interests of the most powerful actors. As the distribution of power changes over time, a disjuncture emerges between the older political structure and newly powerful actors who would benefit from a change in the existing political-economic arrangements. The greater the change in the balance of power, the greater the level of systemic disequilibrium and crisis. Until structures are realigned to accord with the capability distribution, the structural crisis persists.

Thus, there are states that have improved their relative capability positions. They have incentives to work toward changing the operational rules of the system. On the other hand, there are states that were once dominant and able to shape the system. All states are assumed to seek territorial, political, and economic expansion. Those states with relative capability advantages, among other facilitating factors, are the ones that are most likely to be successful at expansion. Indeed, the state with the system's greatest capability advantage is the most likely candidate to dominate the system.

Nevertheless, expanding states eventually reach a point at which the costs of further expansion are escalating faster than the perceived benefits. These costs could rise for a variety of reasons. Geographical and logistical barriers are compounded by increasing competition and opposition. Increasing protection costs coupled with tendencies to consume more at home over time lead to falloffs in investment and productivity. Diminishing marginal returns are thereby accentuated and aggravated by a tendency to undercut the once successful state's comparative advantages.

Older states decline and newly powerful states emerge. The once dominant states are no longer in the superior position needed to underwrite the system's governance. The newly powerful states have little reason to see the older governance patterns continued. To resolve the resulting systemic disequilibrium, hegemonic wars are fought to decide how the system should be governed. A decisive victory by one side will create a new post-war prestige hierarchy. The accompanying peace settlement will create a new status quo that reflects the current power distribution. The more pronounced the dominance of the winners, the more likely it is that systemic conflict will be minimal. A victory in the last hegemonic war clearly demonstrates the winner's capabilities and enhances the dominant state's prestige and legitimacy. As the system's most efficient and technologically advanced economic power, the hegemonic leader also has the most to gain from a smoothly functioning world political economy. In return, the hegemon acts as a systemic governor, providing order and stability as long as its dominant position remains unchallengeable.

The Systemic Leadership Long Cycle Model

The long cycle of world leadership perspective (Modelski, 1978, 1981, 1983, 1987; Modelski and Thompson, 1987; Thompson and Rasler, 1988) focuses primarily on the global political system. Patterns of interaction are viewed as layered—local, national, regional, and global. The global layer is concerned principally with macroscopic issues of order and security, territorial rights, and the stability of commodity exchanges. The effectiveness of political management at the global layer, however, is non-constant and depends on a cyclical governance mechanism.

The leadership long cycle begins with a global war fought over the way in which authority is to be arranged in the global layer. A state, referred to as the system's world power, emerges from the war as the principal victor. It enjoys, at least initially, preponderance in terms of the resources most suitable for global order keeping. Sea power historically (and more recently aerospace power) has been especially critical for developing and maintaining a global reach capability. Complementing its military advantages, the world power also tends to possess the most dynamic national economy—one characterized by high industrial productivity, economic growth, and investment/ trade centrality. Since the newly emergent world power controls at least one-half of the global reach resources, it becomes the system's principal supplier of security and the principal author of the post-war global order as reflected in international organizations and international economic relations.

The world power is not hegemonic in the sense that it dominates all the activities that go on in the various layers. There may very well be areas where its influence is not very impressive, but it does possess the lead position in the global layer and therefore is most likely to be influential in intercontinental and oceanic transactions.

The world power's influence is temporary. Its preponderance declines relative to the capability gains made by allies and rivals alike, especially by elite states (the global powers in this model) which must meet minimal capability standards to remain competitive in the global layer. This deconcentration of the power process is compounded by a tendency for the coalition of global powers that won the previous global war to fracture. Repeatedly, a former member of the winning coalition switches sides and becomes the primary challenger in the next leadership succession/constitutional struggle.

The decay of the world power's order and influence passes through four successive stages of roughly generational length. Global layer power concentration peaks in the *post-global war phase* of world power. The decay of the world power's relative position continues through the intermediate phases of *delegitimation* and *deconcentration*. During these periods, challengers work toward improving their own relative positions, but they do not tend to catch up sufficiently to be able to successfully defeat and supplant the old world power. The attempt to establish a new global order takes place in the *global war phase*.

One of two things tends to occur in the global war. Either the old world power reestablishes its global preponderance and defeats the challenger(s), or the old world power and its successor in combination defeat the challenger(s). A third possibility—a challenger defeating the former system leader—has not yet occurred. In any event, the global war phase "switches" the global political system from the relative anarchy of oligopolistic competition among the global powers to a systemic condition of power concentration, a monopolistic world power leader, and a new or reinvigorated semblance of global order. And the cyclical process of concentration and deconcentration continues.

The World-Economy Model

While it is possible to describe world-economy models (Wallerstein, 1974, 1980, 1984; Chase-Dunn, 1981, forthcoming; Bergesen, 1985) as interested primarily in the capitalist world economy's division of labor and capital accumulation patterns, an important segment of the world-economy model addresses actor mobility and conflict within the world system. The *core, peripheral,* and *semi-peripheral categories* outline the system's basic stratification structure. Core states are characterized by considerable advantages in production efficiency and complexity, centralized and effective state bureaucracies, military strength, and integrated national cultures. They also monopolize much of the system's capital accumulation. As a consequence, core states reap more than their share of the system's benefits.

Peripheral states are relatively weak, highly penetrated, and culturally divided. Their role in the system's division of labor is to specialize in the provision of raw materials and labor. Semi-peripheral states constitute an ambiguous category in between the exploiters and the exploited. They engage in some of the activities found in both the core and the periphery and function as intermediate collection points for the system's exchange processes.

Some movement to and from each of the three categories is not only possible but also likely. Nonetheless, the primary focus of the mobility activities is reserved for movements into, within, and from the core. From time to time, a single state becomes dominant within the core by developing a superior position in agro-industrial productivity, commerce, and finance. When these superior positions overlap, the leader of the core is accorded hegemonic status.

Hegemonic dominance has proven to be a transitory phenomenon. The productivity advantages tend to diffuse. The other core states are working to improve their positions by narrowing the gap in competitive capabilities. The hegemon is also burdened by increasing overhead costs, taxes, and wage levels. As its core rivals catch up, the hegemon is gradually reduced to the status of but one of several powerful core states. Systemically, this process of hegemonic decline translates into irregularly alternating phases of power concentration and diffusion, accompanied by corresponding fluctuations in the freedom of maneuver permitted other states in the system.

Compounding the rise and fall of the hegemons are alternating phases of economic expansion (A phases) and stagnation (B phases). Although the reasons for stagnation are eventually overcome, the B phases increase the incentives to minimize the vicissitudes of economic contraction by expanding and intensifying their exploitation of the periphery. Expansion in the periphery, then, reflects increases in competition within the core and leads to a higher probability of intra-core conflict and warfare.

World-economy analysts have in fact combined the expansion/stagnation process with the process of hegemonic ascent and decline to produce a set of predictions about the level of conflict in the system (Research Working Group, 1979; Bousquet, 1980; Vayrynen, 1983b). The period of genuine hegemony, labeled hegemonic maturity, is an A phase that plays itself out in a generally open, low-conflict system. In the next phase, declining hegemony, core states seek to carve out exclusive control zones in the periphery in response to the onset of a B phase. Conflict between the declining hegemon and its aspiring successors becomes acute, but the succession issue remains unresolved. The acute conflict and rivalry between the aspirants to hegemony continues into the next A phase, called the phase of ascending hegemony. But it is not until the subsequent B phase that a hegemonic aspirant finally bypasses the previous hegemon.

Some Common Denominators

These five models have been described in such a way that their similarities and areas of overlap are accentuated while their divergences are downplayed.[1] The divergences are certainly there and include fundamental disagreements about the epistemological assumptions in international relations (realist versus neo-Marxist for instance); the basic behavioral motors (for example, territorial expansion versus capital accumulation) driving the systemic models; the cast of elite players (great powers, core powers, global powers); the capability base on which relative position is founded (gross national wealth, population size, military power, or the global reach capabilities of sea power and lead economies). All of this is to say that they are very much five different models.[2] Yet they do share emphases on relative capability positions, upward and downward mobility, and the conflictual consequences of structural change.

Suppressing the idiosyncrasies associated with each model, a skeleton conflict model based on a form of elite circulation emerges. The world system is composed of actors with different resource bases and varying levels of ambition. As in other political systems, there is a power hierarchy or pecking order that is wide near the bottom and narrow at the top. Accordingly, many system members play only marginal roles. A few elite actors, however, possess great influence, and, from time to time, one of these elite actors enjoys a sufficiently commanding lead after a bloody struggle over the nature of the system's constitution that it climbs to the top as the system leader.

World politics, in this view, can hardly be said to be characterized by persistent randomness or anarchy. Structures, order, rules, and some degree of regulative capability affect foreign policies and transactions. To the extent that a structural set of rules influences who gets what, when, and how, systemic orders are inherently biased. Some actors win (lose) more than others. Older power contenders, especially if they fought on the winning side of the last succession struggle, have the opportunity to shape international interactions and relations in their own favor. Since the benefits are allocated before latecomers have achieved significant positions in the pecking order, the prevailing order tends to discriminate against their goals and aspirations. Improvements in relative capability position for some actors thus go hand in hand with structural constraints on goal attainment—a situation that is rendered all the more frustrating because the goals are apt to become more ambitious as well. In the absence of some type of cooptation by established elites, latecomers are prone to become challengers of a systemic status quo which they see as biased against them. To eliminate or at least modify many of the structural constraints imposed on them by a previously established order, challengers are encouraged to attack the prevailing order.

A good many domestic political systems normally handle structural reforms, elite circulation, and leadership succession struggles through legislative, judicial, and electoral formats. The same procedures often require more forceful approaches in the external systemic arena. Declining elites are unlikely to surrender their positions and their advantages without a struggle. Ascending challengers are equally unlikely to obtain all of their goals entirely peacefully. Challengers are not only confronted with elite intransigence, but systemic custom also dictates that they demonstrate their claims to movement up the pecking order. A perceived improvement in relative capability position simply will not suffice. What needs to be demonstrated is the ability to effectively mobilize capability and to apply it successfully. Such rites of passage can be accomplished by defeating weaker opponents in the regional neighborhood. The Germans (Prussians) fought Denmark twice and Austria once before taking on France in 1870. Japan defeated China in 1895 and, in some respects, did the same to Russia a decade later. The 1898 Spanish-American confrontation represents still another manifestation of the graphic demonstration of status mobility at the expense of a weaker neighbor.

Hence, systemic conflict is characterized by occasional and very intensive warfare involving many, if not all, of the elites fighting over who and whose rules will govern the system. A second type of conflict behavior is displayed by upwardly mobile states that become embroiled in disputes with their neighbors and downwardly mobile powers. A third, not completely mutually exclusive, type of conflict behavior is represented by elite powers probing and testing the positional claims of other elite actors.[3] This form of conflict may take the form of bilateral crises that end with one or both sides backing away from full-scale warfare. If the probes suggest weaknesses that might be exploited, more extensive tests may be forthcoming which, in turn, may lead to the first two types of systemic conflict. Alternatively, the outcomes may be less than fully conclusive as in the three Anglo-Dutch wars of the seventeenth century or the repeated Anglo-French confrontations of the eighteenth century. One side may do better than the other side in the combat but not quite well enough to suppress the likelihood of subsequent tests and probes.

To equate the systemic sources of conflict with structural shifts in the hierarchy of relative power and position may seem both presumptuous and reductionist. Whether it is truly presumptuous depends on whether this focus is capable of encompassing many of the rival explanations that appear to be given short shrift—a subject to which we will return shortly. Just how reductionist the approach is hinges in part on the degree to which it can coopt and subsume the older approaches to explaining the systemic sources of conflict.

But it is also worth pointing out that the structural change interpretation encompasses a considerable amount of complexity. If we go beyond the briefly noted disagreements implicit and explicit in the five models surveyed earlier, we see that a host of factors have been put forward as variables influencing the probability of conflict. How flexible/intransigent are the established elites to the claims of rising newcomers? How radical are the claims of these *nouveaux* powerful? How quickly are the upwardly mobile catching up? To what extent can rising challengers be expected to catch up? How likely are the variously positioned actors to misperceive the structural shifts going on around them? Most fundamentally, why do the relative positions of states rise and fall? Is this process cyclical? Is it subject to recurring phases that operate like systemic conflict seasons? These questions hardly exhaust the queries that deserve answers. But they also constitute an extensive research agenda that belies the charge that an emphasis on structural change oversimplifies the problem at hand.

IMPLICATIONS FOR OTHER SYSTEMIC ARGUMENTS

Earlier, it was suggested that it is a mistake to segregate systemic from non-systemic explanations. We very much need to begin integrating levels of analysis if for no other reason so that individual, group, national, and inter-national explanations can be situated in their appropriate systemic contexts.[4] This chapter, however, is not the place to attempt the formidable task of multi-level synthesis. Instead, the remainder of this chapter will be focused on topics that have received little attention to this point—the more conven-tional systemic arguments on conflict behavior. Even so, some selectivity is in order. The topics that will receive attention include the balance of power, preponderance versus parity, polarity and system stability, polarization and alliance configurations, and status inconsistency.

Other topics might have been selected. Dependence structures and ine-quality as a systemic property might have been examined. But these topics seem to divert attention somewhat from the present preoccupation with conflict among the major powers.[5] Geopolitics, long of interest to students of international relations, is a quasi-systemic subject that deserves some attention in the sense that Mahan (1890), Mackinder (1904), Spykman (1942), and others were (and are) advocating strategies for getting ahead in the system or for defeating challengers. Brzezinski (1986) is a recent contribution along these lines.

Still another line of inquiry involves topics usually associated with levels of analysis below the systemic level that have been examined with some consideration for systemic context. Crisis decision-making (Snyder and Diesing, 1977; Brecher and James, 1986), deterrence (Modelski and Morgan, 1985), military doctrine (Posen, 1984), trade restrictions (Krasner, 1976; Ellings, 1985; Frederick, 1987), and arms races (Vayrynen, 1983a) come readily to mind. These interactional phenomena, it is argued, work differently in different systemic contexts. Crises in periods of high-capability concentration may be less serious than crises that take place in periods of low-capability concentration. Or, as Modelski and Morgan (1985) suggest, it may be quite difficult to assess whether or to what extent nuclear deterrence is responsible for the absence of warfare between the major powers when much the same result may be attributed to a high degree of capability concentration or unipolarity. Regretfully, space considerations require that the first priority be given to the contextual changes per se—a choice that leaves little room for a thorough review of all their consequences.

The Balance of Power

Without doubt, one of the more venerable systemic explanations of conflict is the balance of power. Over the centuries that the concept has been around, it has taken on a number of different meanings (Haas, 1953; Kaplan, 1957; Claude, 1962; Zinnes, 1967). Given its inherent flexibility and downright slipperiness, one may be tempted simply to set the idea(s) aside as a conceptual quagmire that might best be avoided. Yet there is a classical balance of power interpretation that fits well with the notion of vertical movement up and down the systemic hierarchy. The classical version (Wight, 1978, pp. 168–85) was focused on European regional politics. Should one European state seek to dominate the continent, the other European powers, whose own positions were clearly at risk, should unite to resist the would-be regional hegemon. A second feature of the classical version involves the role of balancer—that is, a state that could be expected to add its weight to whatever coalition was necessary to resist the threat of continental expansion. Implied is the assumption that extra-regional assistance might be needed to successfully suppress the attempt to establish regional dominance.

This conceptualization of the balance of power is an important systemic argument because the European region has long been a, if not *the*, central region of the world system. Moreover, much of the most important systemic combat has been fought in the name of preserving the balance of power. What this means is that the balance principle was invoked repeatedly to rally coalitions opposing the intermittent systemic challenges advanced by Philip II, Louis XIV, Napoleon, and the two German bids of the twentieth century. The principle also helped to justify English/British participation in what were ostensibly regional affairs with much wider implications should continental dominance be imposed successfully as a platform for further expansion.

As a doctrine justifying coalition formation to defend the systemic status quo, the balance of power concept has some explanatory value. The concept becomes more problematic, however, when it is tied to the concentration of power in the system. Because the concept's emphasis is placed on resisting regional expansion, a number of analysts have inferred the corollary principle that a system populated by several states of roughly equal power is less conflict prone than a system in which one (or some) state(s) is (are) more powerful than others and therefore more tempted to seek regional dominance.

What this corollary overlooks is that the balance of power concept was restricted somewhat one-sidedly to coalitions against ascending challengers—not all increasing concentrations of power. It did not, for instance, apply to the deteriorating concentration of power against which the challengers were rebelling. In other words, a procedure designed to preserve the systemic status quo is not likely also to explain how the taken-for-granted status quo came into being in the first place. Yet in the process of suppressing a rising challenger, one or more members of the winning coalition also improved their relative positions. In this sense, the balance of power was never a process to combat the concentration of power per se. Its operation tended to improve or safeguard the relative positions of some winners, while at the same time it penalized the positions of the ultimate losers.

Preponderance Versus Parity

Putting aside the balance of power concept, analysts have disagreed on whether the level of conflict is positively or negatively associated with the degree of capability concentration. One of the more influential studies, Singer, Bremer, and Stuckey (1972), has sought to summarize much of this debate by linking three variables: capability concentration, decision-maker uncertainty, and war. In this formulation, analysts on both sides of the debate expect an increase in uncertainty to accompany capability deconcentration. As power diffuses, relative capability positions become less clear-cut. Coalitional propensities also are thought to become less predictable. Where analysts are said to diverge is over the link between uncertainty and war.

Parity proponents see an increase in uncertainty as encouraging decision-makers to be more cautious and therefore less conflict prone. Advocates for the pacifying effects of preponderance are described as equating an increase in uncertainty with increases in misperceptions, miscalculations, and other decision-making errors that increase the probability of war outbreaks. If it is assumed that the three variables are the most appropriate factors, both camps cannot be equally correct. Movement away from preponderance toward parity or vice versa should either increase or decrease conflict tendencies.

Historical-structural models are apt to side with the preponderance camp's point of view. Conflict should be least likely when the system's capabilities are highly concentrated and most likely after some amount of deconcentration has been experienced. Whether we should expect the relationship to be perfectly linear with conflict increasing as the level of concentration moves from high to low is less clear (see Modelski and Thompson, 1987). Equally unclear is whether decision-maker uncertainty is linearly related to deconcentration. For example, the relative decline of a system leader's position may increase the collective level of uncertainty. At some point, however, a showdown between the declining leader and an aspiring successor will become increasingly probable. To the extent that this showdown is anticipated, one would think that the level of uncertainty about whether a fight will take place should begin to ebb—even though there may be some continuing uncertainty about who will align with whom.

Finally, historical-structural analysts are quite familiar with periods of preponderance. Periods of genuine parity are less easy to identify in eras in which the system's elite strata consist of more than two states. This observation raises the possibility that we need to control for the concept of polarity. The arguments for preponderance may fit systems with different numbers of poles. The merits of parity may in fact be restricted to a specific kind of capability distribution—namely, bipolarity.[6]

Polarity and System Stability

Closely related to the discussions of balance of power mechanisms and the consequences of concentration/deconcentration is the relationship of polarity and system stability. Polarity is a different way of assessing the nature of the system's distribution of power. If the system is dominated by a single state, the situation is considered to be a unipolar power distribution. Two roughly equal powerful states represent a bipolar distribution. Three or more elite states would be counted as a multipolar system. Polarity thus refers to the number of elite states (above some capability threshold) or the number of poles or centers of power in the system. System stability, on the other hand, can mean a variety of things, but in the polarity context it usually refers to the absence of major or significant structural change. Presumably then, a war-torn multipolar system could be viewed as stable as long as it remained multipolar in structure.

The principal debate on the connection between system stability and polarity concerns the stability merits of bipolar versus multipolar systems. The advocates of multipolarity (Deutsch and Singer, 1964) stress the complexity of a system with several centers of power. If a finite ability to monitor one's environment is assumed, the more primary actors there are, the less possible it is for any actor to fixate on another actor. There are simply too many possible sources of threat and opportunity. A pluralist distribution of power is also expected to be associated with cross-cutting pressures. State A may be in a dispute over issue X with states B and C, but A and C's agreement on issue Y makes it less likely that the X dispute will be allowed to escalate (for fear of losing the advantages derived from the Y agreement).

On both counts, bipolarity, it is argued, is less attractive. With only two powers closely monitoring every move the other power makes, a dispute over issue X is likely to spill over into issue Y as well. Multipolarity is therefore preferred because conflict cleavages tend to be blurred, whereas in a bipolar world they are apt to be augmented and reinforced. The probability of destabilizing conflict is accordingly greater in a bipolar system than in a multipolar system.

Bipolarity has its advocates as well (Waltz, 1964, 1967, 1979). Much of the argument for the benefits of bipolarity hinges on the perceived drawbacks of multipolarity and the relative simplicity of a two-power system. Environmental monitoring becomes an easier and less uncertain task when there is only one primary opponent. The process of balancing gains made by the opposition should also be more reliable in the less flexible and more limited opportunity two-power case. In both respects, decision-maker uncertainty, and therefore the probability of error, should then be lower in a bipolar system than in the more complex, less rigid multipolar world. In a sense turning the pluralist argument on its head, moreover, multipolar systems are associated with greater levels of interdependence and competition. Interdependence is assumed to make conflict more probable, whereas competition renders cooperation more difficult. Neither tendency bodes well for the stability of a system with multiple poles. In contrast, bipolar systems may be more prone to crisis brinkmanship, but it is also brinkmanship that is moderated by the stark clarity of the system's structure.

Of course, a number of questions could be raised about the underlying assumptions of these models. How significant are cross-cutting cleavages in multipolar systems? Are decision-makers really any more likely to spread their environmental scanning energies across the board in a system with several powerful actors as opposed to a system with only two principal elite states? Is alignment flexibility beneficial or detrimental to reducing decision-maker levels of uncertainty? These generalizations represent critical assumptions. Only rarely are they the object of investigation. Usually, analysts have been much more interested in comparing patterns of warfare in systems with different numbers of poles with the equally usual mixed results.[7]

Rather than pursue the amount of empirical support available for the polarity model assumptions here, however, two observations stemming from the elite circulation perspective (Thompson, 1986) seem particularly pertinent. First, the overriding emphasis on comparing bipolarity and multipolarity is unduly restrictive. Omitted altogether is an important third possibility—unipolarity—which has tended to be dismissed as a category with no real-world examples. Yet, most historical-structural models are clearly predicated on intermittent unipolarity. If historical-structural analysts are right, the arguments over the relative advantages of multipolarity and bipolarity are strangely stilted.

A second way in which the polarity debate seems to have misinterpreted structural history is found in the static nature of the arguments. Systems are said to be either bipolar or multipolar. The possibility that a bipolar system could become multipolar or vice versa is not ruled out. But such transformations are not viewed as part of a normal process of structural change. Historical-structural models, in marked contrast, tend to view structural shifts in the distribution of power as an almost routine, certainly normal, ongoing process. Unipolarity gives way to bipolarity and/or multipolarity. In this respect, there is not much incentive to discuss the stability merits of one type of distribution as opposed to another. Since the power distribution categories are fairly temporary phenomena, it is the overall process of structural change that ultimately is destabilizing. One may find the least major power conflict in a unipolar period, but, eventually, power tends to diffuse and conflict propensities are altered as a consequence. As long as systems regularly move from one type of distribution to another, the relative stability of any single category must remain rather transitory.

Polarization and Alliance Configurations

A great proportion of the literature on alliances and conflict is non-systemic in nature.[8] The work that could be described as systemic falls into two subcategories: polarization patterns and alliance formation/disintegration behavior. Although the distinction is not made nearly often enough, polarization processes need to be distinguished from polarity (Modelski, 1974; Rapkin, Thompson with Christopherson, 1979). Polarity refers to the number of power centers. Polarization refers to the tendency of weaker states to cluster around the poles. One might expect some level of covariance. For instance, there is some probability that a bipolar system will exhibit some level of bipolarization. But this should not be a constant expectation. Bipolarity may persist even as the bipolarized pattern of interaction decays as in the post–1945 experience. Alternatively, a multipolar system could become bipolarized as the major powers choose sides for a systemic war. World War I provides a good example of this phenomenon.

Given the extreme variety in conceptualization and measurement exhibited by analysts of polarization (compare, for instance, Wallace, 1973a; Healy and Stein, 1973; Goldmann, 1974; Bueno de Mesquita, 1981; McDonald and Rosecrance, 1985), it is nearly impossible to provide anything resembling an overview of the work done in this area in a short space. For our purposes, it suffices to note that analyses on polarization are closely, and perhaps inevitably, intertwined with the arguments on polarity, concentration, and the balance of power. A prototypical example is the "invisible hand" model put forward by J. David Singer and Melvin Small (1968). Overlapping with the Deutsch-Singer preference for multipolarity, Singer and Small contend that a system's pluralistic stabilizing mechanisms are strongly and positively influenced by the aggregate freedom of maneuver enjoyed by the major powers. The greater the opportunity to interact with other actors as interests dictate, the more likely it is that multiple issue areas will lead to cross-cutting pressures and compensating trade-offs. Alliances reduce opportunities for interaction and thereby interfere with the system's stabilization procedures. An increase in the number of alliance commitments should therefore lead to increased instability and conflict. Any movement toward a few mutually exclusive coalitions or blocs will only exacerbate the behavioral restrictions imposed on the key actors by their alliances.

Despite the popular impression that World War I was made highly probable because the main actors were trapped by a rigid alliance network, the empirical evidence for systemic alliance configurations acting as an independent casual agent is not very impressive (Moul, 1973; Ostrom and Hoole, 1978; Thompson, Rasler, and Li, 1980). Yet it is certainly true that much of this analysis has been conducted outside of historical-structural points of view. It may very well be that alliance configurations are simply reflections (not unlike what is sometimes said about arms races and crises) of more fundamental elite tensions and antagonisms. As such, they would have to be considered fairly superficial causes of conflict. There is also the problem of disentangling polarization patterns from the other aspects of systemic structure such as the distribution of power. We still have not determined how autonomous polarization tendencies and polarity patterns really are. More fundamentally, however, not much has been done yet to consider the casual role of alliances in the upward and downward movements of the system's major actors.[9]

Much the same observation can be made about the questions of alliance formation and disintegration processes. Here, the systemic emphasis has been twofold. One cluster of work has pursued the implications of changing structure for alliance behavior. Whether alliance formation is a relatively random process in a presumably flexible, multipolar, balance of power era and nonrandom in less flexible eras constitutes one visible set of questions within this cluster (Job, 1973; McGowan and Rood, 1975; Li and Thompson, 1978). A much different emphasis on alliance formation and cohesion has to do with the role of threat in forming and sustaining alliances. To what extent do states make and maintain their commitments as a response to a variable level of perceived threats?[10] What gives this research thrust a systemic flavor is that the empirical applications are frequently focused on the contemporary, bipolarized confrontation of the Soviet Union and the U.S. led blocs (Liska, 1962; Holsti, Hopmann, and Sullivan, 1973; Thompson and Rapkin, 1981). Implicitly at least, the questions being raised by this line of research pertain to assessing the reasons for persistence and decay in certain structural patterns. As usual, more work needs to be done—ideally along more explicitly historical structural lines of inquiry.

Status Inconsistency

A popular approach to systemic analysis in the late 1960s and early 1970s (Galtung, 1964; East, 1972; Wallace, 1973b; Ray, 1974; Midlarsky, 1975) that evidently has lost much of its appeal is status inconsistency. The basic argument is that states, like individuals, have ascribed and achieved status. To the extent that these two types of status do not correspond very well, as in the case of ascribed status (e.g., wealth, population size) being greater than achieved status (e.g., diplomatic rank), an actor is expected to display aggression in response to the frustration brought about by the status inconsistency. The greater the system's level of status inconsistency (the greater the number and intensity of actors with disequilibrated status), the greater will be the level of systemic conflict.

One reason for the decline in popularity of this approach relates to the less than impressive empirical results associated with testing the status inconsistency argument. However, the empirical results undoubtedly are closely related to the tremendous conceptual and measurement problems involved in applying the ideas of ascribed and achieved status to nation-states. For example, is wealth an ascribed or achieved attribute? How well does an index that counts the number of diplomats sent to a state's capital tap the idea of external status validation? There is also the problem of whether all states in the system should be expected to respond in similar fashion to their status disequilibrium.

Nonetheless, the point to be made is the general congruence between the status inconsistency argument and the historical-structural models of elite circulation. Is not status inconsistency a possible metaphor for rising challengers and declining powers? Challengers perceive that they do not receive the political-economic treatment that their improved capability position deserves. Declining powers can be portrayed as enjoying better treatment than their actual positions would predict. The points of conceptual overlap, when the notion is applied selectively, are at least encouraging. But one might well raise the question of whether we need the status inconsistency metaphor when the phenomenon can be explained more straightforwardly from a historical-structural point of view.

CONCLUSION

The ultimate systemic source of conflict is the manner in which the system is organized to deal with political problems. Political-economic power is concentrated in a small, oligopolistic group of states. Intra-elite competition and conflict are affected primarily by the degree and pace of flux in the group members' relative positioning. A high level of capability concentration is critical for establishing a foundation for systemic leadership and some level, albeit intermittent, of systemic governance. Perversely, intensive systemic warfare also seems to be necessary to bring about the conditions that permit leadership and governance. The subsequent erosion of the system leader's relative capability position fosters leadership decline which, in turn, facilitates an intensified jockeying for position among the elite contenders. A basic structural axis or fault line of conflict emerges between the declining system leader and the system's primary challenger(s) for leadership succession. However, positional probes and tests occur throughout the elite subset as the system's most powerful actors reconnoiter one another's credentials for, and claims to, elite status in the world's political economy.

An emphasis on structure is distinctively different from the more atomistic approaches to interpretation. The first stresses context and pattern, whereas the second sacrifices both of these ideas in favor of an exceedingly narrow version of the decision-making calculus. Nevertheless, structural interpretations of international conflict are not novel. Balances, preponderances, polarities, polarizations, and inconsistencies are all terms that have been around for some time. In part because these terms have been around for awhile, they have taken on a variety of meanings. To best harness their explanatory value, the theoretical assumptions and conceptual language of systemic analysis will require and deserve careful evaluation and cautious integration into the recently emerged and evolving perspectives on historical-structural interpretations of world politics.

NOTES

1. The critical literature is in fact expanding rapidly. See Skocpol, 1979; Zolberg, 1981, 1983; Rapkin, 1983; Thompson, 1983a, 1983b, 1983c, 1983d; Chase-Dunn and Sokolovsky, 1983; Levy, 1985; Holsti, 1985; Rosecrance, 1987.

2. The array of different models might have been expanded even further if Toynbee (1954), Dehio (1962), Farrar (1977), Goldstein (1985), and Midlarsky (1986) had been reviewed as well.

3. Tilly (1975) applies these same structural conflict principles to domestic systems.

4. In this respect, one could argue that the "systemic sources of conflict" are all-inclusive. Systemic sources have sub-systemic roots and vice versa.

5. The obvious exceptions to this observation are the several variants on what has come to be known as Lenin's theory of imperialism (see Brewer, 1980).

6. Situations involving dyadic or less than systemic preponderance/parity I regard as ostensibly a completely different topic and will not be discussed here. See Siverson and Sullivan (1983) for a review of the dyadic literature.

7. See Sabrosky (1985) for recent examples of this literature.

8. Very useful overviews of the alliance literature may be found in Job (1981) and Ward (1982).

9. At the same time, it should be noted that the role of alliances does surface explicitly in a variety of ways in various historical-structural works (Organski and Kugler, 1980; Vayrynen, 1983a; Modelski, 1987).

10. For an extremely different orientation to the primary motivation underlying alliance relations, the process of controlling allied behavior, see Schroeder (1976).

REFERENCES

Bergesen, Albert. 1985. Cycles of War in the Reproduction of the World Economy. In Paul M. Johnson and William R. Thompson, eds., *Rhythms in Politics and Economics*. New York: Praeger.

Blainey, Geoffrey. 1973. *The Causes of War*. New York: Free Press.

Bousquet, Nicole. 1980. From Hegemony to Competition: Cycles of the Core? In Terence K. Hopkins and Immanuel Wallerstein, eds., *Processes of the World-System*. Beverly Hills, Calif: Sage.

Brecher, Michael, and Patrick James. 1986. *Crisis and Change in World Politics*. Boulder, Colo.: Westview Press.

Brewer, Anthony. 1980. *Marxist Theories of Imperialism: A Critical Survey*. London: Routledge and Kegan Paul.

Brzezinski, Zbigniew. 1986. *Game Plan: How to Conduct the U.S.-Soviet Contest*. Boston: Atlantic Monthly Press.

Bueno de Mesquita, Bruce. 1981. *The War Trap*. New Haven, Conn.: Yale University Press.

Chase-Dunn, Christopher K. 1981. Interstate System and Capitalist World-Economy: One Logic or Two? *International Studies Quarterly* 25:19–42.

————. forthcoming. *The Structure of World-Systems*. Berkeley: University of California Press.

————, and Joan Sokolovsky. 1983. Interstate System, World-Empires and the Capitalist World-Economy: A Response to Thompson. *International Studies Quarterly* 27:357–67.

Choucri, Nazli, and Robert C. North. 1975. *Nations in Conflict: National Growth and International Violence*. San Francisco: W. H. Freeman.

Claude, Inis L., Jr. 1962. *Power and International Relations*. New York: Random House.

Dehio, Ludwig. 1962. *The Precarious Balance: Four Centuries of the European Power Struggle,* translated by C. Fullman. New York: Alfred A. Knopf.

Deutsch, Karl W., and J. David Singer. 1964. Multipolar Power Systems and International Stability. *World Politics* 16:390–406.

Doran, Charles F. 1983a. Power Cycle Theory and the Contemporary State System. In William R. Thompson, ed., *Contending Approaches to World System Analysis*. Beverly Hills, Calif.: Sage.

————. 1983b. War and Power Dynamics: Economic Underpinnings. *International Studies Quarterly* 27:419–41.

————. 1985. Power Cycle Theory and Systems Stability. In Paul M. Johnson and William R. Thompson, eds., *Rhythms in Politics and Economics*. New York: Praeger.

————, and Wes Parsons. 1980. War and the Cycle of Relative Power. *American Political Science Review* 74:947–65.

East, Maurice A. 1972. Status Discrepancy and Violence in the International System: An Empirical Analysis. In James N. Rosenau, Vincent Davis, and Maurice A. East, eds., *The Analysis of International Politics*. New York: Free Press.

Ellings, Richard J. 1985. *Embargoes and World Power*. Boulder, Colo.: Westview Press.

Farrar, L. L., Jr. 1977. Cycles of War: Historical Speculations on Future International Violence. *International Interaction* 3:161–79.

Frederick, Suzanne Y. 1987. The Instability of Free Trade: Power, Order and Trade Policy Patterns in the World System. In George Modelski, ed., *Exploring Long Cycles*. Boulder, Colo: Lynne Rienner.

Galtung, Johan. 1964. A Structural Theory of Aggression. *Journal of Peace Research* 1:95–119.

Gilpin, Robert. 1981. *War and Change in World Politics*. Cambridge: Cambridge University Press.

Goldmann, Kjell. 1974. *Tension and Detente in Bipolar Europe*. Stockholm: Scandinavian University Books.

Goldstein, Joshua S. 1985. War and the Kondratieff Upswing. *International Studies Quarterly* 29:411–41.

Haas, Ernst B. 1953. The Balance of Power: Prescription, Concept or Propaganda? *World Politics*, 5:442–77.

Healy, Brian, and Arthur Stein. 1973. The Balance of Power in International History: Theory and Reality. *Journal of Conflict Resolution* 17:33–61

Holsti, K. J. 1985. The Necrologists of International Relations. *Canadian Journal of Political Science* 18:675–95.

Holsti, Ole R., P. Terrence Hopmann, and John D. Sullivan. 1973. *Unity and Disintegration in International Alliances: Comparative Studies*. New York: John Wiley.

Job, Brian L. 1973. Alliance Formation in the International System: The Application of a Poisson Model. Paper presented at the annual meeting of the International Studies Association, New York.

———. 1981. Grins Without Cats: In Pursuit of Knowledge of International Alliances. In P. Terrence Hopmann, Dina A. Zinnes, and J. David Singer, eds., *Cumulation in International Relations Research*. Denver: University of Denver Monograph Series in World Affairs.

Kaplan, Morton A. 1957. *System and Process in International Politics*. New York: John Wiley.

Krasner, Stephen D. 1976. State Power and the Structure of International Trade. *World Politics* 28:317–47.

Levy, Jack. 1983. *War in the Modern Great Power System, 1495–1975*. Lexington: University Press of Kentucky.

———. 1985. Theories of General War. *World Politics* 37:344–74.

Li, Richard P. Y., and William R. Thompson. 1978. The Stochastic Process of Alliance Formation Behavior. *American Political Science Review* 72:1288–1303.

Liska, G. 1962. *Nations in Alliance: The Limits of Interdependence*. Baltimore: Johns Hopkins University Press.

McClelland, Charles A. 1966. *Theory and the International System*. New York: Macmillan.

McDonald, H. Brooke, and Richard Rosecrance. 1985. Alliance and Structural Balance in the International System. *Journal of Conflict Resolution* 29:57–82.

McGowan, Patrick J., and Robert M. Rood. 1975. Alliance Behavior in Balance of Power Systems: Applying a Poisson Model to Nineteenth Century Europe. *American Political Science Review* 69:859–70.

Mackinder, Halford J. 1904. The Geographical Pivot of History. *Geographical Journal* 23:421–44.

Mahan, Alfred T. 1890. *The Influence of Sea Power upon History, 1660–1783*. New York: Hill and Wang.?

Midlarsky, Manus I. 1975. *On War: Political Violence in the International System*. New York: Free Press.

———. 1986. *The Disintegration of Political Systems: War and Revolution in Comparative Perspective*. Columbia: University of South Carolina Press.

Modelski, George. 1974. *World Power Concentration: Typology, Data, Explanatory Framework*. Morristown N.J.: General Learning Press.

———. 1978. The Long Cycle of Global Politics and the Nation-State. *Comparative Studies in Society and History* 20:214–35.

———. 1981. Long Cycles, Kondratieffs and Alternating Innovations: Implications for U.S. Foreign Policy. In Charles W. Kegley, Jr. and Patrick J. McGowan, eds., *The Political Economy of Foreign Policy Behavior*. Beverly Hills, Calif.: Sage.

———. 1983. Long Cycles of World Leadership. In William R. Thompson, ed., *Contending Approaches to World System Analysis*. Beverly Hills, Calif.: Sage.

———. 1987. *Long Cycles in World Politics*. Seattle: University of Washington Press.

———, and Patrick Morgan. 1985. Understanding Global War. *Journal of Conflict Resolution* 29:391–417.

———, and William R. Thompson. 1987. *Sea Power and Global Politics, 1494–1993*. Seattle: University of Washington Press.

Moul, William B. 1973. The Level of Analysis Problem Revisited. *Canadian Journal of Political Science* 6:494–513.

Organski, A.F.K. 1968. *World Politics*. New York: Alfred A. Knopf.

———, and Jacek Kugler. 1980. *The War Ledger*. Chicago: University of Chicago Press.

Ostrom, Charles, Jr., and Frank Hoole. 1978. Alliances and Wars Revisited: A Research Note. *International Studies Quarterly* 22:215–36.

Posen, Barry R. 1984. *The Sources of Military Doctrine: France, Britain, and Germany Between the World Wars*. Ithaca, N.Y.: Cornell University Press.

Rapkin, David P. 1983. The Inadequacy of a Single Logic: Integrating Political and Material Approaches to the World System. In William R. Thompson, ed., *Contending Approaches to World System Analysis*. Beverly Hills, Calif.: Sage.

———, William R. Thompson with Jon A. Christopherson. 1979. Bipolarity and Bipolarization in the Cold War Era: Conceptualization, Measurement and Validation. *Journal of Conflict Resolution* 23:261–95.

Ray, James L. 1974. Status Inconsistency and War Involvement in Europe, 1816–1970. *Peace Science Society (International) Papers* 23:69–80.

Research Working Group on Cyclical Rhythms and Secular Trends. 1979. Cyclical Rhythms and Secular Trends of the Capitalist World-Economy: Some Premises, Hypotheses, and Questions. *Review* 2:483–500

Rosecrance, Richard. 1987. Long Cycle Theory and International Relations. *International Organization* 41:283–301.

Sabrosky, Alan N., ed. 1985. *Polarity and War: The Changing Structure of International Conflict*. Boulder, Colo: Westview Press.

Schroeder, Paul W. 1976. Alliances, 1815–1945: Weapons of Power and Tools of Management. In Klaus Knorr, ed., *Historical Dimensions of National Security Problems*. Lawrence: University Press of Kansas.

Singer, J. David. 1961. The Level-of-Analysis Problem in International Relations. In Klaus Knorr and Sidney Verba, eds., *The International System: Theoretical Essays*. Princeton, N.J.: Princeton University Press.

———, Stuart Bremer, and John Stuckey. 1972. Capability Distribution, Uncertainty, and Major Power War, 1820–1965. In Bruce Russett, ed., *Peace, War and Numbers*. Beverly Hills, Calif.: Sage.

———, and Melvin Small. 1968. Alliance Aggregation and the Onset of War. In J.

David Singer, ed., *Quantitative International Politics: Insights and Evidence*. New York: Free Press.

Siverson, Randolph M., and Michael P. Sullivan. 1983. The Distribution of Power and the Onset of War. *Journal of Conflict Resolution* 27:473–94.

Skocpol, Theda. 1979. Wallerstein's World Capitalist System: A Theoretical and Historical Critique. *American Journal of Sociology* 82:1075–90.

Snyder, Glenn, and Paul Diesing. 1977. *Conflict Among Nations*. Princeton, N.J.: Princeton University Press.

Spykman, Nicholas. 1942. *America's Strategy in World Politics*. New York: Harcourt, Brace.

Thompson, William R. 1983a. Succession Crises in the Global Political System: A Test of the Transition Model. In Albert Bergesen, ed., *Crises in the World-System*. Beverly Hills, Calif.: Sage.

————. 1983b. The World-Economy and the Long Cycle of World Leadership: The Question of World System Time. In Patrick J. McGowan and Charles W. Kegley, Jr., eds., *Foreign Policy and the Modern World-System*. Beverly Hills, Calif.: Sage.

————. 1983c. Cycles, Capabilities and War: An Ecumenical View. In William R. Thompson, ed., *Contending Approaches to World System Analysis*. Beverly Hills, Calif.: Sage.

————. 1983d. Uneven Economic Growth, Systemic Challenges and Global Wars. *International Studies Quarterly* 27:341–55.

————. 1986. Polarity, the Long Cycle and Global Power Warfare. *Journal of Conflict Resolution* 30:587–615.

————, and David P. Rapkin. 1981. Collaboration, Consensus and Detente: The External Threat-Bloc Cohesion Hypothesis. *Journal of Conflict Resolution* 25: 615–37.

————, and Karen A. Rasler. 1988. War and Systemic Capability Reconcentration. *Journal of Conflict Resolution* 32.

————, Karen A. Rasler, and Richard P. Y. Li. 1980. Systemic Interaction Opportunities and War Behavior. *International Interactions* 7:57–85.

Tilly, Charles. 1975. Revolutions and Collective Violence. In Fred I. Greenstein and Nelson W. Polsby, eds., *Handbook of Political Science: Macropolitical Theory*. Reading, Mass.: Addison-Wesley.

Toynbee, Arnold J. 1954. *A Study of History,* vol. 9. London: Oxford University Press.

Vayrynen, Raimo. 1983a. Economic Cycles, Power Transitions, Political Management and Wars Between Major Powers. *International Studies Quarterly* 27:389–418.

————. 1983b. Economic Fluctuations, Technological Innovations and the Arms Race in a Historical Perspective. *Cooperation and Conflict* 18:135–59.

Wallace, Michael D. 1973a. Alliance Polarization, Cross-Cutting and International War, 1815–1964. *Journal of Conflict Resolution* 17:573–604.

————. 1973b. *War and Rank Among Nations*. Lexington, Mass.: D. C. Heath.

Wallerstein, Immanuel. 1974. *The Modern World-System: Capitalist Agriculture and the Origins of the European Economy in the Sixteenth Century*. New York: Academic Press.

————. 1980. *The Modern World-System: Mercantilism and the Consolidation of the European World-Economy, 1600–1759*. New York: Academic Press.

————. 1984. *The Politics of the World-Economy.* Cambridge: Cambridge University Press.

Waltz, Kenneth N. 1959. *Man, the State, and War.* New York: Columbia University Press.

————. 1964. The Stability of a Bipolar World. *Daedalus* 93:881–909.

————. 1967. International Structure, National Force, and the Balance of World Power. *Journal of International Affairs* 21:215–31.

————. 1979. *Theory of International Politics.* Reading, Mass.: Addison-Wesley.

Ward, Michael, D. 1982. *Research Gaps in Alliance Dynamics.* Denver: University of Denver Monograph Series in World Affairs.

Wight, Martin. 1978. *Power Politics.* Hedley Bull and Carsten Holbraad, eds. New York: Holmes and Meier.

Wright, Quincy. 1942/1965. *A Study of War.* Chicago: University of Chicago Press.

Zinnes, Dina A. 1967. An Analytical Study of the Balance of Power Theories. *Journal of Peace Research* 4:270–88.

Zolberg, Aristide R. 1981. Origins of the Modern World System: A Missing Link. *World Politics* 35:253–81.

————. 1983. "World" and "System": A Misalliance. In William R. Thompson, ed., *Contending Approaches to World System Analysis.* Beverly Hills, Calif.: Sage.

PART II

NUCLEAR DETERRENCE

2

On Nuclear Deterrence:
Determining What It Takes
to Deter

PATRICK M. MORGAN

As a coherent body of ideas pertaining to central elements of the subject, a "theory" of nuclear deterrence did not emerge until 1953. However, the modern predicament with which nuclear deterrence contends and of which it is an integral part had its origins well back in the nineteenth century. The onset of industrialization allowed governments to draw heavily on science and technology for military purposes. With this change came the necessity of trying to anticipate, dictate, and adjust to the militarily relevant products of labs and factories (Pearton, 1984). The prodigious growth in destructive capabilities that resulted became increasingly difficult to encompass within traditional military practices and strategic thought. New technology outmoded old tactics, altering the conduct of war. Attention fell, of necessity, on large initial battles that would bring decisive victories (and defeats) and thus on the use of technological breakthroughs and strategic surprise to gain a critical early advantage. This shaped the Prussian approach to war, and it soon spread through Europe. It is visible in British and German naval strategies after 1890 and in the planning of states for what became World War I. (See Snyder, 1984.) Airpower theorists emphasized it after the war, and it played a major part in German and Japanese military strategies in World War II.

Thus, strategic thought and military planning during this period faced two problems: the capacity for destruction was reaching terrible proportions, and the physical ability of states to win a war quickly appeared to be growing. This is precisely what we confront today. In 1890–1941 we see much that is familiar, including patterns of thinking that foreshadow nuclear deterrence theory (Quester, 1966). Nonetheless, despite early elucidation of key elements by Bernard Brodie, Jacob Viner, and William Liscum Borden, an intellectual framework encompassing the use and implications of nuclear weapons was not in place until the 1950s (see Freedman, 1981; Kaplan, 1983).

Deterrence was not a new idea. Indeed, it is inherent in political-military relations among sovereign states (Cohen and Lee, 1986a, pp. 6–9). But nuclear weapons changed this phenomenon, and by explaining why and how they did so, deterrence theory was meant to provide a guide for policy makers on the requirements for successful deterrence. However, the theory emerged *after* the weapons. The first use of nuclear weapons and the initial development of national nuclear arsenals, including early development of the hydrogen bomb, occurred without benefit of theory. Hence, at its inception the theory was an effort at rationalization. It tried to explain what had been deployed and was meant to serve as a guide to rational behavior for governments given those deployments. It was also devised to assist policymakers to set force levels and define weapon systems for the future in a context of continuing technological change, varying resource constraints, and a severe international conflict.

The theory's golden age (roughly 1953–1963) has been followed, many analysts insist, by stagnation. Mandelbaum sees the years after 1963 as "a series of footnotes to the Kennedy Administration" (1979, p. 191). Freedman says nuclear strategy has gone nowhere, except in circles, for years. "What is impressive is the cyclical character of the debates. Much of what is offered today as profound and new insight was said yesterday; and usually in a more concise and literate manner" (1981, p. xv). A critic of the Reagan administration's notions about fighting a nuclear war traces their inadequacy to deterrence ideas that have been around so long they seem real. Thus, "it was easy to forget that there was nothing more in the real world to substantiate them in 1982 than there had been in 1952, when the ideas first took form" (Kaplan, 1983, p. 390).

This chapter summarizes our understanding of what is necessary for nuclear deterrence. It provides a chance to evaluate Freedman's conclusion but will take us further. We must review not only "nuclear strategy" but also research bearing on deterrence.

DETERRENCE THEORY

Deterrence is an effort by one state to prevent another from launching an attack, on itself or others it wishes to protect, by threatening a harmful response. A more elaborate definition would specify that in a deterrence situation one party is thinking of attacking, the other knows it and is issuing threats of a punitive response, and the first is deciding what to do while keeping these threats in mind (Morgan, 1983, pp. 33–42)

What does it take to deter? The proper initial step would be to determine which variables that shape attackers' decisions can be manipulated by deterrence threats. Deterrence theorists ignored this problem or skirted around it by the assumptions they employed. For instance, the international context might have much to do with whether an attack is made; if deterrence threats cannot affect the context or its impact, then the likelihood that deterrence will work, and what we would say it takes to deter, varies with the environment (Modelski and Morgan, 1985). Deterrence theory said nothing about this.

Instead, the theory adopted, as given, the bipolar superpower rivalry present at its creation. Occasional suggestions that the decline of bipolarity requires a new theory (see Rosecrance, 1975) have not led to one. Context is also slighted because nuclear weapons are said to dominate it. (Situations that used to cause wars do not do so now because of nuclear weapons.) Thus, nuclear deterrence was analyzed largely on its own, without reference to the environment. The closest analysts normally come to citing contextual factors is to suggest that states stay out of crisis situations.

Alternatively, deterrence might be strongly affected by the *nature of the governments* involved. Deterrence theorists typically exclude this notion from consideration as well. One way to do this is to assume rationality, usually for a unitary actor. This leaves no variations in governments to which one must attend. Another procedure is to assert that nuclear weapons force governments and statesmen to be rational. (See, for example, Brodie, 1973, pp. 313–34.) Accordingly, governments are all the same.

Deterrence theory therefore markedly simplifies the problem of determining what it takes to deter. The critical variables are those the deterrer can manipulate: what the attacker hears from the deterrer and how this is interpreted. Hence, in a deterrence relationship a severe political conflict has brought (at least) one party to the point of contemplating an attack. The deterrer makes a careful assessment of what he has at stake and wishes to protect. He then devises and effectively communicates appropriate threats, which are evaluated in terms of credibility, feasibility, and potential consequences by the potential attacker in the course of his cost-benefit calculations. When deterrence works it is because the attack looks unrewarding, *primarily because of the deterrer's threats,* in comparison with other alternatives; when it fails it is because the payoff from attacking looks best.

Thinking in this way about deterrence eventually allowed analysts to deduce prerequisites for success: (1) the deterrer needs a capacity to impose unacceptable costs on the attacker via defense, retaliation, or a combination of the two; (2) that capacity must be survivable in event of attack; (3) the deterrer must be able to establish a commitment to do unacceptable damage and deliver a perceptible threat; (4) the threat must be credible; (5) the deterrer must have sufficient control not to inflict the threatened costs by accident or inappropriately; and (6) the deterrer's military posture must not be provocative, inciting a war. There has been no basic change in these prerequisites since the 1950s. Disagreements *within* this theoretical perspective have concerned the relative importance of those six elements and how to achieve or maintain them. On an abstract level, analysts in the USSR and China would probably agree on the necessity of these elements. In this sense, there really is a single theory of nuclear deterrence. If we want to know what it takes to deter, what does this theory tell us?

The Capacity to Do Unacceptable Damage

Surprisingly enough, deterrence theory is of no help on this. There are two ways to proceed: employ an *absolute* standard or a *relative* one. The first descends from Bernard Brodie who suggested that the deterrent effect of possessing additional nuclear weapons rose steeply at first but then flattened out well below 100 (Brodie, 1959a, pp. 177–78). McGeorge Bundy asserts that political leaders would view one nuclear weapon detonated on one of their cities as awful, and ten weapons on ten cities as an incomparable catastrophe and an utter failure of policy (Bundy, 1969). Some have suggested that the ability to destroy the Soviet Union's 50, or 100, largest cities is a simple and adequate measure. The ultimate in absolute standards is "assured destruction." Since 1965, this phrase has been taken to mean the capacity to destroy 50 to 75 percent of Soviet industry and kill at least 25 percent of the population outright (Enthoven and Smith, 1971, p. 207). Some versions of it take the form of a "minimum deterrence" posture. The USSR adopted one in the 1950s, and the Navy advocated another at that time as an alternative to Massive Retaliation. In short, the approach says that some specified very high level of destruction will be "unacceptable" for *any* government and thus is sufficient to deter.

For the relative approach, what it takes to deter depends on the situation, the opponent, and the opponent's military might. A standard view since 1945 has been that the Soviet government is not like others—it is indifferent to its people's welfare and willing to bear enormous casualties to achieve its ends. (See Wohlstetter, 1983.) Thus, what it takes to reach "unacceptable damage" against the USSR is much greater than that for other states.

What it takes has also been said to vary with the situation. Some insist that Moscow would accept huge losses to achieve a payoff amounting to global domination. Deterrence could also fail, many have feared, in a situation in which war seems unavoidable and the outcome of attacking first, no matter how bad, looks better than absorbing the first blow. Deterrence can also fail when a nuclear response looks inappropriate because the stakes are too low. Thus, capabilities to fight at lower levels are also required to deter. The most important "relative" approach appears in the assertion that deterrence can be undermined if the Soviet Union has more nuclear war options or can inflict more damage at some or all levels of hostilities, that is, if the Soviets have escalation dominance and can "win." In effect, whether the war's costs are acceptable depends partly on the *results,* and the results partly consist of relative damage.

Devotees of an absolute approach believe that what it takes to deter virtually anyone under almost any circumstances was available years ago. Therefore, nuclear deterrence is very effective; "the chances of war between the United States and the USSR are very slight" (Jervis, 1984, p. 14). Attempts to escape from this situation, so that nuclear weapons can carry more political weight and be militarily more useful, regularly reappear but with no chance of success. From this perspective those so misguided as to treat nuclear weapons as just like other weapons embody a dangerous intellectual lag—seeking "superiority" where there is none, in pursuit of "winning" when everyone would lose (Jervis, 1984, pp. 47–63; Bundy, 1986).

Critics of the absolute approach emphasize that military strength is power. A state with weaker forces and fewer options will look inferior and feel inferior. It will have trouble holding allies, be expected to give way in confrontations, and be less able to deter. Military force at all levels remains the true currency of international politics. Moscow sees this point perfectly well, and so must the West (Martin, 1979).

The dispute among analysts has had only a modest effect on policies. The McNamara criterion of assured destruction had nothing to do with any careful calculation of Moscow's threshold of "unacceptable damage." Rather, it reflected the point of diminishing returns (in potential destruction) in projected increases in American strategic forces. In the same way, the dispute helped shift declared policy or operational doctrine, but the character and targeting of U.S. strategic forces were actually designed—contrary to public pronouncements—as a damage-limiting system strongly inclined toward a first-strike capability (Betts, 1986–1987). Setting the eventual number of U.S. missiles was done by reference to domestic and bureaucratic politics rather than either conception of what it takes to deter. We have good reason to suspect that Soviet nuclear forces have been similarly designed (Lee, 1986).

Each superpower resolved the conflict between the absolute and the relative approaches in roughly the same way. Each decided years ago to construct a greatly redundant assured destruction capability, beyond what any absolute standard would suggest. Superpower military establishments—with periodic approval from civilian superiors—applied a *relative* approach by the 1960s. Deterrence, it was said, depends on who is "ahead," but it is not clear that this view was due to deterrence theory. Politicians eyed the domestic political implications of being "behind" more than the supposed implications for deterrence, whereas the military establishments used almost any criterion for defining who is "ahead" that could boost appropriations.

The superpowers, therefore, arrived at their nuclear force levels in ways that were only marginally related to deterrence theory. One reason was that the dispute over the absolute and relative conceptions of what it takes to deter cannot be resolved by reference to the theory. This applies even to whether possession of an assured destruction capability is the minimum necessary for superpower deterrence. The conclusion that it is has enjoyed wide support in the United States. One reflection of it is the assertion that very large nuclear arsenals are good for deterrence, whereas deep cuts would be quite dangerous (Intriligator and Brito, 1984b; Quester, 1986) Yet the idea is not inherent in deterrence theory and cannot logically be derived from it.

Why, then, did assured destruction become the bedrock, the bare minimum necessary for deterrence? Partial responsibility goes to the image of Stalin's Russia as the epitome of evil, an image of Moscow nurtured in some circles ever since. Then there is the theory as rationalization. We said a capacity for total destruction was necessary because that was what we had already built and planned to use. Also relevant is the absence of any way to operationally define "unacceptable damage," any logical way to calculate it. (The closest anyone has come to devising one is Bueno de Mesquita's expected utility approach—1981, 1985, and 1986.)

Thus, we have no idea what constitutes a minimum level of unacceptable damage in the nuclear age. Available explanations are speculative, nothing more.

Survivable Forces

Maintaining survivable forces is one of the core problems of nuclear deterrence, and it is an area in which deterrence theorists have made some of their most important contributions. Survivability has been a mounting problem in this century, as military forces have gained greater range and destructive power. Modern weapons carried forward that trend.

In the early post-war years, American military planners greatly feared a surprise attack in Europe by Soviet ground forces and saw no ready way to cope with it at the point of attack (Etzold and Gaddis, 1978). Despite this, plus the legacy of Pearl Harbor, plus the obvious fact that a nation cannot deter if its forces can be crippled or erased in an attack, U.S. officials were slow to appreciate the true nature of the problem in the nuclear age. Albert Wohlstetter and others only slowly convinced officials that a Russian strategic surprise attack could destroy any U.S. strategic forces that were not suitably dispersed, hardened, and alert. (See Kaplan, 1983.) Concern about survivability appeared in the "bomber gap" and then the "missile gap." In the 1970s it was the "hard-target-kill" gap. In the 1980s came a concern about C^3I vulnerability (Ball, 1981; Bracken, 1983; Ford, 1985; Blair, 1985). Immense effort has gone into coping with such "gaps."

On the Soviet side it appears that the national security hierarchy was deeply concerned about Soviet vulnerability to nuclear attack by 1953, which spurred a sharp shift in military thought after Stalin's death. The survivability problem also shaped the Soviet strategic buildup after Khrushchev's ouster. Recent deployments of mobile missiles, intermediate and strategic, suggest that serious concern about survivability continues.

The problem is inherent in modern technology. It is not just weapons, but the vast improvements in surveillance and gains in guidance systems that make precise targeting possible. In addition, the training and orientation of armed forces dictate aiming to destroy enemy weapons, offensively or via defenses, so there is an inherent institutional pressure toward making enemy weapons vulnerable. Each side thus exacerbates the other's survivability problem.

American analysts in the 1960s asserted that reciprocal threats to the survivability of retaliatory forces could be contained by arms control. To avoid the futility and expense of seeking a preemption capability and having the opponent frustrate the effort, governments could cooperate to mutually sustain the survivability of their deterrents. Thus far, this cooperation has been very difficult to achieve. Technology has outrun arms control negotiations and agreements, in part because the military establishments were so intent on building damage-limitation capabilities. It may also be, as some charge, that Moscow has never truly accepted the idea of mutual vulnerability because its military leaders have had too much influence over national security policy. In any event, the survivability problem is a recurring one. It has affected the debate over MX and is reflected in the attention given today to C^3I vulnerabilities.

Establishing a Commitment

It is relatively easy to promise to respond to an attack on one's territory, though even this is problematic in the nuclear age. But difficulties mount when the attack could be just on one's forces abroad (the marines in Lebanon), or on one's friends or allies (South Vietnam), or on an area considered strategically sensitive (Iran). Establishing commitments is often discussed in terms of credibility, a subject we take up shortly. Here we examine the definition and expression of commitments.

The Korean War called attention to this matter (in the debate over whether Secretary of State Dean Acheson had virtually invited the attack) and led to the Eisenhower administration's desire for formal pacts specifying U.S. commitments. Then came Thomas Schelling's clever analysis stressing that commitment meant physically, politically, or psychologically eliminating one's alternatives. He also provided an unmatched analysis of the techniques for signalling a commitment (Schelling, 1966; 1980).

The last major advance was provided by George and Smoke (1974), who stressed that a commitment is often difficult to define and convey because the exact national interest at stake is unclear. Even established commitments are rubbery because governments and circumstances change and induce recalculation. Commitments are often fuzzy at the margins, which is unfortunately just where challenges often arise. Finally, commitment is not just a matter of signalling technique. Citing Maxwell (1986), George and Smoke described commitments as political evaluations of what the national interest requires. Where the interest is slight, no signalling technique will convince sophisticated opponents to take the commitment seriously. Conversely, where the interest is large and obvious, commitment will be assumed despite absence of formal expression of it. (See Jervis, 1979, pp. 314–22.) No further development of the *theory* has taken place. (American officials, in *practicing* deterrence, do not display a clear grasp of the theory even as it stands).

Credibility

According to the literature, nuclear deterrence is inherently incredible and unavoidably credible! Credibility as a problem has several facets. One is that in Western statecraft war is supposed to involve a balanced relationship between means and ends. Nuclear weapons are out of proportion to nearly any sensible political objective. Therefore, a nuclear weapon is not something "with which one readily springs to the defense of one's friends" (Kennan, 1982, p. 7). Nuclear threats against lesser opponents look like threatening to dynamite a neighbor's house because he dumped garbage in the yard; the threats are so gross as to be incredible.

A second aspect is that nuclear threats are even less credible when the opponent can respond in kind. The third facet of the problem arises in extended deterrence. The autonomy of states has always made alliance commitments less than completely credible, given the reluctance of states to bear severe costs on behalf of others. Nuclear weapons multiply this problem for alliances enormously.

Concern about the credibility of American commitments was expressed as early as NSC-68 and played an important role in the U.S. decision to intervene in Korea. Since 1957 there has seldom been a time when Europeans were not questioning the American commitment, Americans were not worrying about their credibility in the eyes of the Russians, and people were not casting about for remedies (Morgan, 1985).

The striking advances provided by theorists consisted mainly in calling attention to credibility and elucidating why it is so hard to achieve. They pointed out that it is indispensable—deterrence threats must be believed to work. They then developed a spectrum of ways to try to bolster credibility, all of limited utility in the nuclear age.

At one end of the spectrum is making retaliation rational, a view espoused by Herman Kahn and now associated with Colin Gray. Retaliation is incredible if it is irrational, and it is irrational if the deterrer cannot bear the consequences. Therefore, the key to credible nuclear deterrence is being prepared to fight, survive, and win a nuclear war. This calls for damage-limiting offensive forces, civil defense, strategic defenses, and multiple options for nuclear war. When you can fight successfully, people believe your threats. (See Kahn, 1960; Gray, 1979). The Reagan administration has been accused, with some justification, of having been interested in a nuclear-war-winning capability in its early years.

Making threats credible by making it rational to carry them out is also the theoretical taproot of "Flexible Response," which is usually considered to stop short of a nuclear-war-winning posture. Its point of departure is the assumption that to be credible a threat must be linked to *employable* forces. Nuclear weapons are not easy to employ, so one must be able to respond to non-nuclear attacks in non-nuclear ways. Where nuclear weapons are necessary, the more carefully and narrowly they can be used the more readily a decision to use them can be taken and thus the more credible the threat. This stance can eliminate enemy incentives to attack, constrict enemy incentives to escalate should war break out, and remove pressure on the deterrer to escalate. It was foreshadowed by NSC-68, developed in the late 1950s, installed as declaratory U.S. policy in the Kennedy administration, and revived under James Schlesinger in the Nixon administration as an operational posture that has lasted to the present. The most extreme version, one Moscow is accused of having adopted, is seeking a pronounced military superiority at every level, a condition the United States enjoyed (for nuclear weapons) when this doctrine was first developed.

At the opposite end of the spectrum, the credibility problem is minimized by asserting that governments do not risk total catastrophe. Nuclear deterrence is credible with only a small possibility of retaliation; it even restricts lesser provocations because the possibility of escalation cannot be discounted. Normally, this is linked to an operational definition of "catastrophe" that requires only a few nuclear explosions, so that even a modest number of weapons can provide a credible threat.

Between these extremes lie other proposed solutions. As noted above, Schelling (1966, 1980) treated credibility partly as a matter of technique. Steps to strip away options, develop a reputation for upholding commitments, or convey an image of irrationality can contribute greatly to credibility. Schelling also offered another solution, which is to call attention to the imperfections of governments. Leaders can be irrational, especially in crises or once fighting begins. Governments cannot fully control their soldiers, and bureaucracies do not always send, read, or receive messages clearly. Thus, even an irrational deterrent threat may be quite credible. Elements of this view can be found in recent work as well (Brams and Kilgour, 1986—see the Bibliography it contains; Brams and Kilgour, 1985; Zagare, 1985).

Over the years, advocates of Massive Retaliation and mutual assured destruction (MAD) have generally relied either on the notion that possible catastrophe makes governments very hesitant or on Schelling's second solution, that governments are not fully in control. This is true of Bundy's "existential deterrence" and of the Jervis rejection of Flexible Response at the strategic nuclear level (Jervis, 1984). Even those who dismiss MAD sometimes slip into this perspective as when Harold Brown cites (as contributing to deterrence) Soviet uncertainty about whether the United States would resort (quite irrationally) to launch-on-warning in an attack, or when Colin Gray says that "objectively" the U.S. commitment to NATO lacks credibility but Moscow must respect it anyway because who knows what a president might do. (See Brown, 1980, p. 80; Gray, 1982, p. 291.)

NATO's strategy, called Flexible Response, is really a variant of MAD. NATO's conventional forces, it is widely believed, cannot defeat a massive attack, so NATO promises to escalate. The nuclear balance at each higher level either favors the USSR or no one, so escalation is not a rational option. Correctly understood, Flexible Response is geared to not having to escalate, whereas NATO's posture reflects a perceived need to do so. Flexible Response makes escalation unlikely—NATO tries to make it look certain. As Gray suggests, the basis of NATO's credibility is that Moscow cannot be sure NATO members will not be silly enough or scared enough, or even angry enough, to escalate. This is far from Flexible Response.

A final approach to credibility has been associated with Flexible Response over the years, though there is no necessary connection. This is the emphasis on *image* (not just reputation). Its foremost exponent has been Paul Nitze. In this view, credibility requires an image of toughness, readiness, and will. In a psychological relationship like deterrence, perceptions of these things are critical. As Schlesinger, Brown, and Weinberger have insisted, a state that *appears* ahead in various aspects of strategic arms may become overconfident, too pushy in a crisis. Hence, the concern for "perceived equivalence" has arisen, which has played a part in justifying the GLCM (ground launch cruise missile) and Pershing II deployments in Europe, the M-X program, and others.

What, then, do we know for sure about credibility by consulting deterrence theory? Not much. We do not, for instance, know whether a degree of uncertainty about the deterrer's potential response is good or bad. In addition, each of the above solutions to the credibility problem has serious limitations. To assert that nuclear deterrence is credible because no one willingly risks catastrophe is to dismiss the lessons of the 1930s. Hitler's Germany and Tojo's Japan were willing to do just that. Jervis (among others) has asserted that once assured destruction forces exist deterrence grows enormously compelling. A crisis becomes a competition in taking risks of disaster. But it is not clear why the deterrer should win such a competition. Hitler was able to exploit British and French reluctance to revisit World War I to overturn the status quo and ultimately ignore their efforts at deterrence. Why would such a ruthless success story be impossible today? This clashes with Jervis's suggestion that the psychological edge in confrontation under nuclear deterrence necessarily goes to the deterrer who is oriented to the status quo (Jervis, 1979).

A logical extension of the view that nuclear deterrence is inherently credible and induces prudence would be that more nations should practice it. Kenneth Waltz expresses exactly this thought, but few MAD advocates are prepared to go so far (Waltz, 1982). (See also Intriligator and Brito, 1982; Bueno de Mesquita and Riker, 1982; Berkowitz, 1985.) Another logical extension, widely endorsed, is that cutting nuclear arsenals can be destabilizing. Intriligator and Brito (1984b) urge that strategic arms controllers devote less attention to cutting arsenals and concentrate instead on preventing crises, barring accidents, and improving crisis management. This may be going too far in making a virtue of a necessity. It almost finds nuclear weapons good for us!

Those who claim war must be made rational to achieve deterrence credibility do not convincingly relate the potential destruction to what most people will accept as meaningful political purposes. It is also difficult to pay the financial costs of this deterrence posture, especially when the other side has every incentive to frustrate the effort. It may be rational to want strategic superiority, but it is difficult to explain how a nation is to achieve it unilaterally in a system of rational actors or even just highly suspicious ones.

We have already noted the George and Smoke critique of credibility-by-technique. Credibility via the threat that leaves something to chance, while plausible, leaves us in a quandary. Deterrence theory assumes rationality, yet now we explain credibility by retreating from that assumption—deterrers may sometimes be irrational or lose control. If so, then this may be true of attackers as well—they may be too irrational to be deterred. What comfort is there in having potentially incompetent states in charge of capacities for catastrophic destruction?

The notion that Flexible Response lends credibility rests on dubious assumptions. Does fighting for one commitment enhance the credibility of others? Certainly not always, as Vietnam indicates. Will options make a state more willing to fight? Logically, this is true only if it is clear that escalation is quite unlikely or, better yet, something the deterrer can fully control. Otherwise, the Cuban missile crisis is an example of statesmen scared stiff at the thought of using even a very low level of military force because of the possibility of escalation. It is entirely possible that European critics are correct—Flexible Response is an invitation to discount the threats it is supposed to sustain. If so, credibility ultimately derives not from options but from the lurking possibility that MAD will occur in the end, a view often offered by those who think a controlled war is a physical, emotional, and political impossibility (Ball, 1981).

Theoretically, the trouble with escapes from the credibility problem is that no single way of characterizing decision-making holds consistently across governments over time. Under MAD a government may be too foolish, or too rational, to be deterred; a defender may be too rational to carry out his threat. With a threat that leaves something to chance, some governments may be too risk-acceptant to be deterred, and some may be too controlled to credibly threaten loss of control. Under Flexible Response a government may be too willing to risk escalation to be deterred because it counts on the rationality of the defender. And so on.

Sufficient Control

Deterrence theory provided a great service by calling attention to the importance of controls over forces and weapons, pointing out how a loss of control or a misleading action could provoke a war. Since the 1950s the United States (and other nuclear powers, one hopes) has paid great attention to development of barriers to unathorized use of nuclear weapons. Many analysts now judge the probability of an accidental firing of U.S. weapons to be nearly zero. Flexible Response has also led to attention to the command and control necessary to provide viable options.

Where does the field stand on the larger problem of accidental war? There is a modest division of opinion. Michael Howard dismisses the problem:

However inchoate or disreputable the motives for war may be, its initiation is almost by definition a deliberate and carefully considered act and its conduct...a matter of very precise central control. If history shows any record of "accidental" wars, I have yet to find them (Howard, 1983, p. 12).

Others, however, are deeply concerned about the growing technological and organizational complexity of military forces even as the available reaction time, if something goes wrong, shrinks. Bracken sees the superpowers' forces as complex organizations that together constitute a gigantic interlocking system in which disturbances in any one part reverberate throughout. The danger is not war via technical failure itself, but war as a result of accident or breakdown amidst a grave crisis when weapons are on alert, forces are primed for quick reaction, and so on (Bracken, 1983).

On maintaining sufficient control for Flexible Response, the Reagan administration has sought a capacity to conduct limited, controlled nuclear war for as long as two months. Critics insist communications will dissolve, command centers will vanish, and stress will overwhelm leaders. Fear of decapitation will mean preprogrammed devolution of authority to fire, inviting a spasmodic war. (See Ball, 1981.)

A Non-provocative Posture

There is considerable tension between the goal of credibility and that of sustaining stability. The first encourages building a usable military superiority that undermines the second. Perhaps this is why the mismatch between the dictates of deterrence theory and the behavior of the superpowers has been at its greatest here.

The theory emphasizes that deterrence can be unstable in a crisis because certain kinds of forces may give governments an incentive to attack. The incentive arises if one has a capacity to preempt, fears the opponent has such a capacity, or fears doing much worse in a war by going second rather than first. Thus, for stability a government should avoid having vulnerable forces, avoid developing a first-strike capability of its own, make sure the results of its retaliating or attacking first will be much the same, and *cooperate with the opponent* to preclude threats to deterrence stability.

Alas, the hostile relationship that makes deterrence necessary makes cooperation unlikely. Military services plan for the *failure* of deterrence and inherently prefer a damage-limitation (to the point of first-strike) capability. It is also difficult to cancel every possible benefit of going first when war seems unavoidable. (One attraction of the "nuclear winter" thesis is that it would make a nuclear war equally bad for attackers and defenders.)

We can see the results. For years the United States maintained a huge nuclear superiority, and SAC (Strategic Air Command) doggedly sought a first-strike capability. When Nikita Khrushchev announced Soviet missile progress, he chose the most provocative way to do so. When the Kennedy administration discovered the true missile gap was markedly in its favor, this did not curb its planned missile buildup. In those days it was regularly asserted that the United States was deliberately not seeking a first-strike capability. We now know that the United States—in terms of actual military plans—was far less interested in stability via mutual vulnerability than it claimed. (See Rosenberg, 1986; Ball, 1986.) Even Defense Secretary Robert NcNamara's shift to MAD was apparently undertaken in part because the services persistently tried to convert limited counterforce targeting into a first-strike capability.

Along the same lines, once the Soviets reached a non-provocative strategic parity, they promptly went right past it to SS-18s and 19s with good damage-limitation capabilities. The Pentagon maneuvered to keep MIRVs out of SALT I, to allow a larger U.S. counterforce capability. The services in both nations have also pressed for strategic defenses that could be quite provocative. Most analysts will accept limited defenses as non-provocative (for example, see Lodal, 1980). But they usually dismiss a comprehensive national defensive system as technically impossible and strategically provocative. Debates continue about what is the acceptable trade-off between a greater counterforce capability (for various objectives) and a non-provocative posture.

Deterrence Theory—A Summary

Modest spurts of activity notwithstanding, deterrence theory is not a flourishing intellectual arena. Over almost thirty years the theory has experienced no big changes or breakthroughs and leaves numerous problems and puzzles unresolved. It has guided thinking, research, and, to a point, policy. Yet it has problems, dilemmas really, which seem ineradicable. The credibility problem is a good example; explaining why deterrence threats are convincing is very tough when the weapons are nuclear and governments are said to be rational (Morgan, 1983). As Jervis says, "A rational strategy for the employment of nuclear weapons is a contradiction in terms" (1984, p. 19). Postulating governments as unevenly rational eases the credibility problem, but only by making it more difficult to explain how deterrence is stable.

Examples of other "puzzles" which the theory seems unable to resolve include, is it better to issue clear or ambiguous threats? Is it necessary for both sides to hold the same conception of "stability" and share the same strategic perspective? Does deterrence operate almost automatically or must there be great attention paid, and cooperation invoked, to keep it stable? What kind of, and how much, rationality is required of the attacker? Of the defender? This has led to people criticizing the theory for many years. (For a good list of criticisms, see Roberts, 1983.)

The criticisms have never taken hold, however. Thomas Kuhn's perspective suggests why (Kuhn, 1970). Theories can always be criticized. The crucial step in discarding a widely held theory is the emergence of a better alternative. Where the subject is important and the existing theory is workable, to propose its abandonment will not do—there must be something to put in its place. Indeed, even when a substitute is available, Kuhn emphasizes, replacement can be a difficult step.

We have been pursuing nuclear deterrence for years without a clear answer from the theory as to what it takes to deter. Most criticisms of the theory simply reject it. They offer no compelling substitute. If deterrence were not necessary, the theory might be discarded. However, a belief that deterrence is necessary is very widespread and may even be an inherent feature of international politics. If we need to be deterring, then we need a theory. Once one is in hand, we will not readily give it up.

The only alternative theory *of* deterrence available goes as follows (Morgan, 1983). Deterrence does not involve upping the perceived, quite specific, costs of the opponent's cost-benefit calculations. Instead, it seeks to convince an opponent that the consequences of a war can be awful, and that those consequences are unpredictable and uncontrollable. To attack would be to leap into the unknown when the results could be grave. When a government is "sensible," it has a healthy respect for its own and others' infirmities and avoids leaps into the unknown. It anticipates that misunderstandings will occur, estimates will miss the mark, events may get out of hand, emotions may distort perception and action, and so on.

The trouble is, *governments are not always sensible.* Sometimes they are overconfident, see destiny on their side, or see no choice but to run great risks. Then they may be impervious to deterrence threats. Sometimes domestic political conditions can create exactly these sorts of governments. On the other hand, sensible governments may be caught in an incrementally building conflict, a war neither would have launched precipitously but that cannot now be evaded (or halted) without exactly the precipitous and risky departures from present policy that sensible governments rarely take.

Thus, some factors that determine whether deterrence works have nothing to do with the design and delivery of deterrence threats, and relatively little to do with the scale of the destruction promised or whether one pursues MAD or Flexible Response. The key is the nature of the government one is trying to deter. What works for one opponent may not work for another.

This stresses the *limitations* of nuclear deterrence, and of deterrence theory, as a guide to action. But policymakers and the rest of us need guidelines for the nuclear age, something on how to survive in safety. The sensible decision-maker approach works reasonably well as a descriptive theory, but less so as a policy-relevant theory.

The alternative to the theory of deterrence would be a theory of international influence that encompassed deterrence and other measures as well, which explained in an intellectually, psychologicallly, and politically satisfying way how security could be sustained and war avoided. George and Smoke pointed to the need for this theory some years ago as part of their critique of deterrence theory. We do not have such a theory, and it is unclear whether anyone is even working on this subject in the field.

EMPIRICAL ANALYSIS

What does it take to deter? Attempts to explore this problem empirically developed very slowly. Only in recent years has a significant body of literature emerged. Deterrence theory developed without examination of available evidence from other contexts (evidence on deterrence with animals, children, criminals) and from the past history of international politics. The theory was created in an ahistorical, non-empirical fashion, and it was some time before analysts tried to change that.

We should start by noting some intrinsic limitations of any historical/ empirical approach. The most obvious is that it is difficult to know when deterrence has worked. Absence of attack is insufficient evidence; the absence may be due to something other than deterrence. If we cannot list deterrence "successes," it is hard to detect correlations between success and selected conditions or tactics, or to test hypotheses about what it takes to deter. Less obvious is the fact that detecting a *failure* of deterrence is also difficult. For example, was the North Korean attack on South Korea a failure of American deterrence, or a failure on the part of Washington to seriously practice deterrence?

A second difficulty with historical studies is that most examples or cases of deterrence involve conventional, not nuclear, forces. A standard assertion in the literature is that nuclear weapons create a qualitative difference in state behavior (for example, see Nacht, 1986). If so, lessons from such cases do not apply. (See the response in Bueno de Mesquita, 1981, pp. 133–35.) This problem interacts with the first one. If we had a long list of nuclear deterrence successes and failures, we would not need to examine cases of non-nuclear deterrence, or we could get a better sense of whether the two are basically the same. (The best discussion of this topic is Snyder and Diesing, 1977, pp. 450–62.)

A third problem is access. Deterrence is a psychological relationship, so a penetrating empirical investigation requires getting inside the thoughts of potential attackers. Although it is not impossible, it is certainly not easy. Governments resist being penetrated in this fashion. Even in historical cases, accurately reconstructing the perspectives, feelings, and calculations of decision-makers is an uncertain endeavor.

In spite of these difficulties, analysts have devised two broad types of empirical studies. One is quantitative, using modern data collections to search for patterns in state behavior that would confirm the usual notions about deterrence. The other uses historical case studies, either singly or via comparative examination of multiple examples, to trace in detail the behavior of states in deterrence situations.

If we look at the principal "requirements" for deterrence, we find that these empirical studies are concerned with only a few. They say little about what constitutes a capacity to do "unacceptable damage," about survivability of forces, or about how forces can be non-provocative. For the most part, empirical analyses have shown no interest in the problem of controlling forces. The remaining requirements receive all the attention—establishing commitments and the *credibility* of commitments, as well as the matter of whether commitments and their credibility are important for preventing war.

Does Nuclear Deterrence Work?

The most important topic taken up by these empirical studies is whether nuclear deterrence really works, whether (in effect) nuclear deterrence even exists. That it does exist and has prevented wars among great powers since 1945 is usually taken for granted. (See, for example, Allison et al., 1985, pp. 7–9.) Empirical studies have called this matter into question but not conclusively so.

Organski and Kugler boil deterrence theory down to the following propositions:

that the nuclear threat will change the behavior of the threatened nation; that a nation threatened with nuclear retaliation will change her mind about committing aggression; that leaders have become more cautious in their dealings with one another because of the danger of a nuclear holocaust (Organski and Kugler, 1980, p. 177).

They survey international conflicts since 1945 and examine specific cases in which nuclear weapons were a factor. They find no evidence that any one of those propositions is true. As far as they can determine, the military factor most important in the resolution of those conflicts was the *conventional* military balance. If anything, nuclear weapons deter their owners more than the opponent. This conclusion fits the findings of Blechman and Kaplan that, in conflicts short of war since 1945 involving the United States, outcomes were relatively unaffected by the strategic nuclear balance (Blechman and Kaplan, 1978, pp. 127–29).

Organski and Kugler also argue that if deterrence rests on perceptions, a state must pay close attention to its rival's military strength to ensure that a

Table 2.1
Constraints on Conflict: Evidence for Nuclear Deterrence

Presence of Nuclear Constraints	Conflict Type		
	Threat	*Intervention*	*War*
Nuclear Power versus Nuclear Power	4	2	0
Nuclear Power versus Nation with Nuclear Ally	7	6	0
Nuclear Power versus Non-nuclear Power	8	13	2
Non-nuclear Power versus Non-nuclear Power	10	31	17

military balance suitable for deterrence is maintained. In turn, this means an arms race—each arms with the other's arms in mind. They find little evidence of this thinking in American-Soviet military spending since 1945, which they take to mean that nuclear deterrence is absent. Kugler (1984) adds the finding that great powers possesssing a wide nuclear advantage over rivals have not attacked, which contradicts the idea that it is nuclear deterrence that prevents war. Lebow has used analysis of numerous case studies to raise the same point, arguing more broadly that at both nuclear and conventional levels states do not seize on "windows of vulnerability" to attack. He concludes that any explanation of the absence of war must go well beyond deterrence (Lebow, 1984).

Other studies do not confirm these findings. It may be that, contrary to Organski and Kugler, a superpower arms race exists if we use the right measure (Ward, 1984). If so, nuclear deterrence may also exist. Blechman and Kaplan find that when the United States brandished a nuclear threat in a conflict there was an increased chance of a successful outcome (1978, pp. 95–101). Weede examined the behavior of states in 1962–1980 and found a small but statistically significant change. The incidence of war was less than one would expect, particularly among states allied to the superpowers (Weede, 1983). Bueno de Mesquita and Riker (1982) find that the presence of an explicit or implied nuclear threat greatly reduces the incidence of escalation just as nuclear deterrence is supposed to (see Table 2.1). Other quantitative studies have concluded that nuclear deterrence makes a difference, that it increases peace and security. Usually, they do so by examining cases of conventional as well as nuclear deterrence (Bueno de Mesquita, 1981; Russett, 1963; Huth and Russett, 1984). Tillema and Van Wingen (1982) find that since 1945 the major states have avoided military interventions in places where any one of them had a clear commitment. That is, extended deterrence has worked.

On the other hand, we must not neglect contrary findings. An early cross-cultural survey found little statistical support for the idea that preparation for war reduces the incidence of it (Naroll,1969). Various studies note that, from the perspective of deterrence theory, a disturbingly high percentage of arms races have ended in war. These studies are by analysts who see the super-power relationship as an arms race (Smith, 1982; Wallace, 1979, 1980, 1981; Weede, 1980). Unfortunately, these studies are inconclusive. Arms races in the years since 1945 have not frequently culminated in disputes that led to war. It may be that arms races result in war only under certain conditions, and that nuclear weapons—suitably deployed—make arms races much safer. (See Intriligator and Brito, 1984a.)

What Makes for Success?

Another subject of empirical investigation has been the conditions associated with the success or failure of deterrence. Organski has long argued that the condition most associated with the outbreak of great power warfare—and thus with failures of deterrence—is a "power transition" in which one state (the challenger) is rapidly gaining on the dominant power(s) and is about to, or already has begun to, pass it (them) by (Organski and Kugler, 1980). Thus, clear military superiority for the status quo state is the best basis for deterrence. There are elements of this viewpoint in Gilpin (1981) as well as Smith (1982), and a survey of relevant studies finds most support for the view that a significant power disparity breeds peace (Siverson and Sullivan, 1983) Obviously, some versions of classic deterrence theory would support this position, but we now bet on parity instead. Under nuclear deterrence conditions, superiority is seen as breeding instability through first-strike inclinations and fears.

Some empirical studies find that local conventional military superiority is the key to success in crisis. The Cuban missile crisis is often cited as an example. Mearsheimer has suggested that for modern conventional war among great powers the key is whether the potential attacker has a strategy and capacity to win quickly, that is, a blitzkrieg capability. If he does, deterrence is likely to fail (Mearsheimer, 1983). Thus, the relevant "superiority" must be measured in a dynamic, not static, way.

Russett initiated the empirical study of deterrence with an effort to inductively identify the conditions associated with successful extended deterrence. His article "The Calculus of Deterrence" examined seventeen cases to compare the outcome with the presence/absence of nine conditions: defender strategic superiority, a prior formal commitment, and so on. Only one factor, a high degree of economic interdependence (measured by trade) between deterrer and client, was found to be closely related to deterrence "success," with indicators of political interdependence as the next most important (Russett, 1963). Fink attacked this study for imprecision in defining "success," for its failure to demonstrate the direction of causation in the correlations, and for not limiting the potentially relevant variables and theoretical explanations by employing a deductive approach (Fink, 1965).

Huth and Russett recently returned to the "calculus" of deterrence. Analyzing forty-four cases, they used a carefully drawn conception of a deterrence situation and a deductive expected utility model. Their findings, however, were not much different from those of the earlier study.

[Deterrence] success is most often associated with close economic and political-military ties between the defender and its protege. Local military superiority for the defender and its protege also helped. Only marginal contributions were made by the possession of nuclear weapons and by not having a history of earlier abandonment of a protege. Existence of a formal military alliance played no significant role (Huth and Russett, 1984).

With these findings, the list of useful conditions for successful deterrence is broadened to include political–military ties and, as Organski and Kugler found, local military superiority. Schelling's stress on reputation was not confirmed, but the suspicion of George and Smoke, and Jervis, that the presence of a formal alliance is not significant was supported. What is important is a web of economic–political–military ties.

The historical case study approach has been used not so much to define the prerequisites for successful deterrence as to enrich our understanding of what actually occurs in deterrence situations. Russett initiated this with a study of Pearl Harbor that questioned the utility of statistical studies alone. It emphasized the danger to deterrence if the opponent is deeply dissatisfied with all the other alternatives to war (Russett, 1967). Alexander George has sought to develop a rigorous analytical approach to comparative case studies. In an examination of deterrence cases after 1945 in American foreign policy, George and Smoke stressed the importance of *context* in low-level (i.e., crisis and sub-conventional war) deterrence and the complex nature of the decision-making required. It is hard to clarify commitments and convey clear threats, whereas an attacker is likely to limit his risks and contain escalation by trying to design around a commitment or erode it at the margins. They find deterrence too complicated and too limited; other tools of statecraft need more attention.

They employ the assumption of rational decision-making *for the attacker,* who is depicted as carefully calculating risks and opportunities. But the deterrer (the United States) is seen as uncertain, internally divided, and so forth, and thus not overly rational in responding to situations.

Later efforts using the same research technique try to demonstrate that these conclusions apply equally well to strategic nuclear deterrence—that it is context-dependent, very complex to apply, and of limited utility. They do so primarily by piling up evidence that participants in deterrence situations have not been particularly perceptive, calculating, or rational. These studies fall in with Jervis's view that the thinking of governments and officials conforms to standard cognitive processes, which lead to distortions in communication, perception, and understanding (Jervis, 1976). This suggests that rational decision models are inappropriate, casting doubt on the theoretical structure of deterrence.

The role of rationality in deterrence is itself unclear. To begin with, rationality on the part of the attacker is not required for successful deterrence. Creatures we do not consider rational can sometimes be dissuaded by the threat of painful consequences. Rationality was assumed for purposes of theory; its behavioral accuracy is irrelevant (Bueno de Mesquita, 1981, pp. 81–82). Or is it?

It seems reasonable to expect the assumption of rationality to bear some resemblance to the world the theory explains. Bueno de Mesquita himself says that governments are, in fact, pretty rational when making decisions about war (1981, pp. 32–33). Brams also sees deterrence as an extension of the rationality found in politics (1985). We would not expect deterrence to work—at least not in the same way—if governments were often irrational. The question is: how rational must they be for deterrence? Quester argues that decision-makers only need enough sense to fear the consequences of nuclear war (Quester, 1986, pp. 81–82), which is roughly the view held by MADvocates. But many analysts depict a deterrence that requires detailed or intricate calculations, such as in the "counterforce gap" literature or the descriptions of controlled attack and retaliation scenarios. There is also the rationality of the deterrer to consider. What if rationality erodes the credibility of threats? As we noted earlier, theorists have reached no consensus on this subject. They do not even agree about whether it would ever be rational to retaliate. It has long been said that superpower retaliatory threats would be irrational to carry out, but some philosophers assert that it is rational to do so nonetheless (Gauthier, 1985; see also Brams, 1985).

The case study literature joins the discussion by demonstrating that governments are imperfectly rational, at best, and that their imperfections contribute directly to failures of deterrence. Studies of strategic surprise find that, although attacks were usually planned with great care, the attackers' strategic perspectives were frequently in error, ignoring the available evidence. Attackers often misperceived things that affect the impact of deterrence threats—relative military strengths, necessity for war, and so on (see Knorr and Morgan, 1983). Lebow finds that those who provoked crises by challenging another state's commitments usually had unrealistic assessments of the probable response. The challenges were initiated "in the absence of any good evidence suggesting that the adversary lacked the resolve to defend his commitment. In many cases the available evidence pointed to just the opposite conclusion" (Lebow, 1981, p. 184).

The Snyder-Diesing (1977) survey of crises concluded that actor conceptions are often incorrect and that states differ widely in openness to new information or flexibility under pressure. Some are quite rigid, overconfident, and so on. This is not a promising milieu for deterrence. Smoke's study of escalation finds that failures of perception and analysis by policymakers are frequent, particularly "fundamental failures to comprehend how the world looked to others" (Smoke, 1977, p. 252). Escalation was usually the result of failures of interpretation and analysis, not lack of information.

Stein's reconstruction of Egyptian decisions on whether to attack Israel on five occasions in 1969–1973 finds that the Egyptians did little to assess the relative balance of interests, wrongly estimated the military balance despite abundant evidence, and deviated grossly "from norms of rational procedure" by not comparing estimated gains from war with those of other options and by ignoring the calculation of probabilities (Stein, 1985). Lebow's summary of the Falkland Islands case stresses the compelling domestic political need behind the Argentine junta's attack, its serious misreading of Britain's probable response, and its wishful thinking about how a war would go. As the crisis developed, psychological factors bred reluctance to face facts. Lebow also stresses that Britain's behavior illustrated how deterrers frequently misread situations and opponents, leading to failures to clearly signal commitments and convey threats (Lebow, 1985).

In effect, these studies produce markedly more complex pictures of how deterrence works (or fails), with deterrence as only one of many factors that determine whether war occurs. A recent study emphasizes that each of the factors—organizational, psychological, and so forth—must be studied in tandem with others. For example, the organizational rigidities in deterrence capabilities on the eve of World War I which helped bring about the collapse of deterrence must not be examined in isolation; their existence and impact grew out of systemic, psychological, and other factors (Levy, 1986). In effect, explaining the absence of World War III in our times becomes steadily more complicated, more multi-faceted. Nuclear deterrence looks less important even as it looks less reliable. (See Morgan, 1986; Gaddis, 1986.)

CONCLUSION

It seems fair to say that a gap has opened up between the "field" and the practitioners. Superpower rhetoric continues to display an image of nuclear deterrence as it emerged in the heyday of the classic theorists. Even most public critics of contemporary security policies would continue to rely on nuclear deterrence as it was classically conceived. Meanwhile, in the field the whole conception of nuclear deterrence has been steadily changing. Its effects are debated, and its reliability is challenged. The explanations as to what actually happens in deterrence situations reach far beyond the theory. The theory itself is beset by seemingly intractable problems, only some of which are reviewed here. (Omitted is the debate about whether nuclear deterrence can be morally acceptable.)

Too much can be made of this gap, however. It has often been suggested that rhetoric does not mirror practice and that statesmen do not take seriously the abstract elements of the theory. Thus, the statesman is more attuned to the subtleties and complexities than official postures would suggest.

In any event, this corner of security studies is in flux. Clearly, more studies—quantitative and historical—of behavior in international conflict situations are called for to continue enriching our information base. At the same time, we are badly in need of new theoretical tools to order and refine this information. We need a new theory of deterrence, or a larger theory that encompasses deterrence, to make sense of the materials, insights, and arguments piling up in the field. Such a theory would be of great assistance in the management of U.S.-Soviet affairs in the rest of this century.

We also need to better integrate the concerns of the classic theory and recent research. For instance, a mathematical explanation as to why "enough" nuclear weapons to ensure a mutual second-strike capability will guarantee stability is inadequate if the credibility of nuclear threats is in serious doubt. Correlational studies and related ways of checking the effects of nuclear deterrence (looking at arms races, etc.) have only an oblique impact unless they are somehow linked to the *process of decision,* which is really what deterrence theory purports to describe. Historical case studies are rich in details but neglect the central problem that gave rise to deterrence theory—the need for abstracting from the details a theory simple and accurate enough to assist policymakers.

A matter that should be receiving greater attention is whether nuclear deterrence is dispensable. Can we do without it? The question arises in several different ways. Until the Strategic Defense Initiative (SDI) proposed by President Reagan, suggestions that nuclear deterrence should be done away with came almost entirely from outside the field. That proposal has at least created some debate about whether it would ever be possible to achieve nuclear disarmament, about how—if at all—this could be done and whether it could be done safely. The response of most people in the field is highly skeptical, but this does not seem to rest on any profound analysis of the idea of nuclear disarmament or any appreciation of the full implications of the empirical research findings reviewed earlier. Many in the field are also not sure that we should *want* to put nuclear deterrence aside, fearing that it is all that protects us from a renewal of great power wars. Surely we should be trying to assess as accurately as we can just what nuclear deterrence has (or has not) done for us, and not be swept along by the inertia behind the events and assumptions of the nuclear age.

REFERENCES

Allison, Graham, et al. 1985. *Hawks, Doves, and Owls: An Agenda For Avoiding Nuclear War*. New York: W. W. Norton.

Ball, Desmond. 1981. Can Nuclear War Be Controlled? *Adelphi Papers* No. 119. London: International Institute for Strategic Studies.

――――. 1986. The Development of the SIOP, 1960–1983. Pp. 57–83 in Desmond Ball and Jeffrey Richelson, eds., *Strategic Nuclear Targeting*. Ithaca, N.Y.: Cornell University Press.

Berkowitz, Bruce D. 1985. Proliferation, Deterrence, and the Likelihood of Nuclear War. *Journal of Conflict Resolution*. 29, no. 1:112–36.

Betts, Richard. 1986–1987. A Nuclear Golden Age? The Balance Before Parity. *International Security* 11, no. 3:3–32.

Blair, Bruce. 1985. *Strategic Command and Control: Redefining the Nuclear Threat*. Washington, D.C.: Brookings Institution.

Blechman, Barry, and Stephen Kaplan. 1978. *Force Without War*. Washington, D.C.: Brookings Institution.

Bracken, Paul. 1983. *The Command and Control of Nuclear Forces*. New Haven, Conn.: Yale University Press.

Brams, Steven. 1985. *Rational Politics: Decisions, Games, and Strategy*. Washington, D.C., Congressional Quarterly Press.

――――, and D. Marc Kilgour. 1986. Is Nuclear Deterrence Rational? *PS* 19, no. 3 (Summer 1986):645–51.

――――, and D. Marc Kilgour. 1985. The Path to Stable Deterrence. In Urs Lauterbacher and Michael D. Ward, eds., *Dynamic Models of International Conflict*. Boulder, Colo.: Lynne Rienner.

Brodie, Bernard. 1959a. *Strategy in the Missile Age*. Princeton, N.J.: Princeton University Press.

――――. 1959b. The Anatomy of Deterrence. *World Politics* 11, no. 2.

――――. 1973. *War and Politics*. New York: Macmillian.

Brown, Harold. 1979. *Department of Defense Annual Report Fiscal Year 1980*. Washington, D.C.: Department of Defense, 1979.

Bueno de Mesquita, Bruce. 1981. *The War Trap*. New Haven, Conn.: Yale University Press.

――――. 1985. The War Trap Revisited. *American Political Science Review* 79:157–76.

――――, and David Lalman. 1986. Reason and War. *American Political Science Review* 80, no. 4:1113–29.

――――, and William H. Riker. 1982. An Assessment of the Merits of Selective Nuclear Proliferation. *Journal of Conflict Resolution* 26, no. 2:283–306.

Bundy, McGeorge. 1969. To Cap the Volcano. *Foreign Affairs* 48, no. 1:1–20.

――――. 1986. Risk and Opportunity: Can We Tell Them Apart? Pp. 27–36 in Catherine Kelleher et al., eds., *Nuclear Deterrence: New Risks, New Opportunities*. Washington, D.C.: Pergamon-Brassey.

Cohen, Avner, and Steven Lee, eds. 1986. *Nuclear Weapons and the Future of Humanity*. Totowa, N.J.: Rowman and Allenheld.

Enthoven, Alain, and K. Wayne Smith. 1971. *How Much Is Enough?* New York: Harper and Row.

Etzold, Thomas, and John Lewis Gaddis, eds. 1978. *Containment: Documents in American Policy and Strategy 1945–1950*. New York: Columbia University Press.

Fink, Clinton. 1965. More Calculations About Deterrence. *Journal of Conflict Resolution* 9, no. 1:54–95.

54   PATRICK M. MORGAN

Ford, Daniel. 1985. *The Button: The Pentagon's Strategic Command and Control System*. New York: Simon and Schuster.
Freedman, Lawrence. 1981. *The Evolution of Nuclear Strategy*. New York: St. Martin's Press.
Gaddis, John Lewis. 1986. The Long Peace: Elements of Stability in the Postwar International System. *International Security* 10, no. 4:99–142.
Gauthier, David. 1985. Deterrence, Maximization, and Rationality. In Russell Hardin et al., eds., *Nuclear Deterrence: Ethics and Strategy*. Chicago: University of Chicago Press.
George, Alexander, and Richard Smoke. 1974. *Deterrence in American Foreign Policy: Theory and Practice*. New York: Columbia University Press.
Gilpin, Robert. 1981. *War and Change in World Politics*. Cambridge: Cambridge University Press.
Gray, Colin. 1979. Nuclear Strategy: The Case for a Theory of Victory. *International Security* 4:63–87.
———. 1982. NATO's Nuclear Dilemma. *Policy Review,* no. 22:97–116.
Howard, Michael. 1983. *The Causes of Wars*. London: Unwin Paperbacks.
Huth, Paul, and Bruce Russett. 1984. What Makes Deterrence Work Cases from 1900 to 1980. *World Politics* 36, no. 4:496–526.
Intriligator, M. D., and D. L. Brito. 1982. Nuclear Proliferation and the Probability of Nuclear War. *Public Choice* 37:247–60.
———, and Dagobert Brito. 1984a. Can Arms Races Lead to the Outbreak of War? *Journal of Conflict Resolution* 28, no. 1:63–84.
———, and Dagobert Brito. 1984b. Non-Armageddon Solutions to the Arms Race. Stockholm: Nationalekonomiska Foreningen.
Jervis, Robert. 1976. *Perception and Misperception in International Politics*. Princeton, N.J.: Princeton University Press.
———. 1979. Deterrence Theory Revisited. *World Politics* 31, no. 2:289–324.
———. 1984. *The Illogic of American Nuclear Strategy*. Ithaca, N.Y.: Cornell University Press.
Kahn, Herman, 1960. *On Thermonuclear War*. Princeton, N.J.: Princeton University Press.
Kaplan, Fred. 1983. *The Wizards of Armageddon*. New York: Simon and Schuster.
Kennan, George, 1982. *The Nuclear Delusion*. New York: Pantheon Books.
Knorr, Klaus, and Patrick Morgan. 1983. *Strategic Military Surprise: Incentives and Opportunities*. New Brunswick, N.J.: Transaction Books.
Kugler, Jacek. 1984. Terror Without Deterrence. *Journal of Conflict Resolution* 28, no. 3:470–506.
Kuhn, Thomas. 1970. *The Structure of Scientific Revolutions,* 2nd ed. Chicago: University of Chicago Press.
Lebow, Richard Ned. 1981. *Between Peace and War*. Baltimore: Johns Hopkins University Press.
———. 1984. Windows of Opportunity: Do States Jump Through Them? *International Security* 9, no. 1:147–86.
———. 1985a. Deterrence Reconsidered: The Challenge of Recent Research. *Survival* 27, no. 1:20–28
———. 1985b. Miscalculation in the South Atlantic: The Origins of the Falklands War.

Pp. 89–127 in Robert Jervis et al., eds., *Psychology and Deterrence*. Baltimore: Johns Hopkins University Press.

Lee, William T. 1986. Soviet Nuclear Targeting Strategy. Pp. 84–108 in Desmond Ball and Jeffrey Richelson, eds., *Strategic Nuclear Targeting*. Ithaca, N.Y.: Cornell University Press.

Levy, Jack. 1986. Organizational Routines and the Causes of War. *International Studies Quarterly* 30, no. 2:193–222.

Lodal, Jan. 1980. Deterrence and Nuclear Strategy. *Daedalus* 109, no. 4:155–75.

Mandelbaum, Michael. 1979. *The Nuclear Question*. Cambridge: Cambridge University Press.

Martin, Lawrence. 1979. The Role of Military Force in the Nuclear Age. Pp. 1–29 in Lawrence Martin, ed., *Strategic Thought in the Nuclear Age*. Baltimore: Johns Hopkins University Press.

Maxwell, Stephen. 1986. Rationality in Deterrence. *Adelphi Papers,* No. 50. London: International Institute for Strategic Studies.

Mearsheimer, John. 1983. *Conventional Deterrence*. Ithaca, N.Y.: Cornell University Press.

Modelski, George, and Patrick Morgan. 1985. Understanding Global War. *Journal of Conflict Resolution* 29, no. 3:391–417.

Morgan, Patrick. 1983. *Deterrence: A Conceptual Analysis,* 2nd ed. Beverly Hills, Calif.: Sage.

———. 1985. Saving Face for the Sake of Deterrence. Pp. 125–52 in Robert Jervis et al., eds., *Psychology and Deterrence*. Baltimore: Johns Hopkins University Press.

———. 1986. New Directions in Deterrence Theory. Pp. 169–89 in Steven Lee and Avner Cohen, eds., *Nuclear Weapons and the Future of Humanity*. Totowa, N.J.: Rowman and Allanheld.

Nacht, Michael. 1986. Why Nuclear Deterrence Will Not Go Away. Pp. 118–28 in Catherine Kelleher et al., *Nuclear Deterrence: New Risks, New Opportunities*. Washington, D.C.: Pergamon-Brassey.

Naroll, Raoul. 1969. Deterrence in History. Pp. 150–64 in Dean Pruitt and Richard Snyder, eds., *Theory and Research on the Causes of War*. Englewood Cliffs, N.J.: Prentice-Hall.

Nitze, Paul. 1976. Assuring Strategic Stability in an Era of Detente. *Foreign Affairs*.

Organski, A.F.K., and Jacek Kugler. 1980. *The War Ledger*. Chicago: University of Chicago Press.

Pearton, Maurice. 1984. *Diplomacy, War and Technology Since 1830*. Lawrence: University Press of Kansas.

Quester, George. 1986. *Deterrence Before Hiroshima*. New York: John Wiley.

———. 1986. *The Future of Nuclear Deterrence*. Lexington, Mass.: Lexington Books.

Roberts, Adam. 1983. The Critique of Nuclear Deterrence. *Adelphi Papers,* no. 183. London: International Institute of Strategic Studies.

Rosecrance, Richard. 1975. Strategic Deterrence Reconsidered. *Adelphi Papers,* no. 116. London: International Institute for Strategic Studies.

Rosenberg, David Alan. 1986. U.S. Nuclear War Planning, 1945–1960. Pp. 35–36 in Desmond Ball and Jeffrey Richelson, eds., *Strategic Nuclear Targeting*. Ithaca, N.Y.: Cornell University Press.

Russett, Bruce. 1963. The Calculus of Deterrence. *Journal of Conflict Resolution* 7, no. 2:97–109.

————. 1967. Pearl Harbor: Deterrence Theory and Decision Theory. *Journal of Peace Research,* no. 2 (1967):89–106.

Schelling, Thomas. 1966. *Arms and Influence.* New Haven, Conn.: Yale University Press.

————. 1980. *The Strategy of Conflict,* 2nd ed. Cambridge, Mass.: Harvard University Press.

Siverson, Randolph, and Michael Sullivan. 1983. The Distribution of Power and the Onset of War. *Journal of Conflict Resolution* 27, no. 3:473–94.

Smith, Theresa. 1982. *Trojan Peace: Some Deterrence Propositions Tested.* University of Denver Graduate School of International Studies Mongraph Series. Vol. 19, Book 2. Denver: Graduate School of International Studies.

Smoke, Richard. 1977. *War: Controlling Escalation.* Cambridge, Mass.: Harvard University Press.

Snyder, Glenn, and Paul Diesing. 1977. *Conflict Among Nations.* Princeton, N.J.: Princeton University Press.

Snyder, Jack. 1984. *The Ideology of the Offensive: Military Decision Making and the Disasters of 1914.* Ithaca, N.Y.: Cornell University Press.

Stein, Janice. 1985. Calculation, Miscalculation and Conventional Deterrence I: The View From Cairo. Pp. 34–59 in Robert Jervis et al., eds., *Psychology and Deterrence.* Baltimore: Johns Hopkins University Press.

Steinbruner, John. 1976. Beyond Rational Deterrence: The Struggle for New Conceptions. *World Politics* 28:223–45.

Tillema, Herbert, and John Van Wingen. 1982. Law and Power in Military Intervention. *International Studies Quarterly* 26, no. 2:220–50.

Wallace, Michael. 1979. Arms Race and Escalation: Some New Evidence. *Journal of Conflict Resolution* 23, no. 1:3–16.

————. 1980. Some Persisting Findings: A Reply to Professor Weede. *Journal of Conflict Resolution* 24:289–92.

————. 1981. Old Nails in New Coffins: The Para Bellum Hypothesis Revisited. *Journal of Peace Research* 18:91–95.

Waltz, Kenneth. 1982. The Spread of Nuclear Weapons: More May Be Better. *Adelphi Papers,* no. 171. London: International Institute of Strategic Studies.

Ward, Michael Don. 1984. Differential Paths to Parity: A Study of the Contemporary Arms Race. *American Political Science Review* 78, no. 2:297–317.

Weede, Erich. 1980. Arms Races and Escalation: Some Persisting Doubts. *Journal of Conflict Resolution* 24, no. 2:285–87.

————. 1983. Extended Deterrence by Superpower Alliance. *Journal of Conflict Resolution* 27, no. 2:231–54.

Wohlstetter, Albert. 1974. Is There an Arms Race. *Foreign Policy,* no. 16:48–81.

————. 1983. Bishops, Statesmen, and Other Strategists on the Bombing of Innocents. *Commentary,* June.

Zagare, Frank C. 1985. The Pathologies of Unilateral Deterrence. In Urs Lauterbacher and Michael D. Ward, eds., *Dynamic Models of International Conflict.* Boulder Colo.: Lynne Rienner.

3

On the American-Soviet Strategic Nuclear Balance

WILLIAM H. BAUGH

WHAT IS A STRATEGIC NUCLEAR "BALANCE," AND HOW WOULD WE RECOGNIZE ONE?

The accepted state of the nuclear strategic "balance" is the result of a political debate about issues that are inexorably both political and technical. Assertions about that balance have been increasingly prominent in major political deliberations in the 1980s, including those about desirable levels of Soviet and U.S. defense spending; goals to be sought in possible new arms control agreements; what new types of strategic weapons to build, such as the MX and Midgetman missiles, or the B-1B bomber; and whether to pursue the Strategic Defense Initiative (SDI or "Star Wars"). Despite this increasing attention, the concept of strategic "balance" remains ambiguous because there is little agreement either within or between governments and polities on how it should be measured. Disagreements arise in part from technical and methodological issues in policy assessment, and in part from the practice of staking out politically advantageous positions, but also from the fact that doctrines for the use of strategic weapons are themselves ambiguous. Those ambiguities, in turn, exist because we have never fully resolved the political questions about what to do with the weapons we already have, let alone with the weaponry we can envision (Baugh, 1984). Yet despite widespread sloppiness and biased usages, assertions about the strategic "balance" have played an increasing role in the political debates of the past decade, and thus in deciding the very weapons programs, doctrines, and deployments that are perceived to determine that balance.

In this chapter, "strategic" will refer to offensive weapons systems that have intercontinental range either directly [Inter-Continental Ballistic Missiles

—The author expresses thanks to his Oregon colleagues David Jacobs and Kenneth K. Wong, and to the editors, for extremely helpful comments in the preparation of this chapter.

(ICBMs) and intercontinental bombers] or indirectly [Submarine-Launched Ballistic Missiles (SLBMs)], and defenses against them. This is consistent with both Strategic Arms Limitation Talks (SALT) usage, in which attention was confined to so-called central strategic systems capable of reaching the heartland of one party from the home territory of the other (Barton and Weiler, 1976, pp. 180–81), and U.S. Department of Defense usage, which follows an extensive definition, simply listing the classes of weapons considered to be strategic (Brown, 1980, pp. 71–72, 77; Weinberger, 1986, p. 213). "Balance" will refer to a comparison of the strategic nuclear force levels or capabilities of the two superpowers, which may or may not be in equilibrium or rough parity at any given moment. It thus refers to a changing, dynamic quantity, endowed with high political salience, and the measurement of which is subject to considerable controversy.

It may be argued that the SALT definition of strategic weaponry has always had more political than physical meaning, and that it means less today than at the time of the 1972 SALT I agreements. Soviet agreement to exclude European-based Intermediate Nuclear Forces (INF) from consideration in SALT I and II was a major concession, since a Pershing II Intermediate-Range Ballistic Missile (IRBM) based in West Germany can threaten Moscow as seriously as a Minuteman II ICBM based in Montana. This fundamental geopolitical asymmetry between the superpowers was not formally recognized in their arms control negotiations until the 1983 START (STrategic Arms Reduction Talks). By the eve of the ultimately unproductive 1986 Reykjavik summit meeting, it appeared that the two sides were close to agreement on eliminating most INF and reducing to equal numbers of strategic warheads (Cannon, 1986). The United States would have had to give up roughly as many more strategic warheads as the Soviets would have given up on INF, implying that INF are really equivalent to strategic forces, as the Soviets have long contended. This raises serious questions about how separable and significant the "strategic" balance remains. Those questions have been compounded by increased INF deployments in Europe, including Soviet SS-20 IRBMs and U.S. Pershing IIs and Ground-Launched Cruise Missiles (GLCMs), and also by increased numbers of "gray area" systems, such as Sea-Launched Cruise Missiles (SLCMs) on surface ships.

Much of the SALT II debate, circa 1979, hinged on perceptions of the statics and dynamics of the U.S.-Soviet strategic nuclear balance, and many measures of balance were suggested. Numbers of missiles, numbers of warheads, size of warheads, payload or "throw-weight" of missiles, and "hardness" of missile silos against blast effects were frequently cited. Some analysts even went so far as to compare the *number of such measures* on which one side or the other excelled. For example, Donley (1979, p. 40) presented a chart of time lines for thirteen strategic balance measures, divided each line into periods of "US Advantage," "USSR Advantage," and "equality," and drew dire conclusions from the fact that the number of indices on which the United States led declined steadily over the period 1960–1983. Similar practices continue today (see, e.g., U.S. Department of Defense, 1984a, p. 23), and it is routine for analysts and politicians to cite "balance" measures chosen to support their own policy conclusions.

Classes of Strategic "Balance" Measures

Simple Counts. The most facile measures of strategic balance are direct counts of specific types or classes of weapons, the material resources available as inputs to a nuclear exchange. The simplicity of such static measures has led many analysts to refer to their use as "bean counting." A count of ICBM warheads, for example, gives a rough measure of the gross number of targets that could be attacked with fairly high accuracy, but implies that all such warheads have roughly equivalent characteristics, such as explosive yield, accuracy, range, reliability, and availability for time-urgent launch. This is manifestly untrue within the arsenal of either superpower, let alone in comparisons between U.S. and Soviet forces.

Similar difficulties beset other simple measures, such as comparisons of weapon system reliability; numbers and characteristics of defensive systems; and performance parameters such as missile throw-weight and accuracy, or silo hardness. In general, the simple counting measures are crude and oversimplified to the point that they may well mislead, primarily because of inaccuracies in aggregating individual weapons and targets into a composite picture of total military force capability. They continue to be very widely used, however, precisely because of their simplicity, which makes them easily understood, often fairly readily obtainable, verifiable with fairly high degrees of confidence, and, for all these reasons, highly politically salient (Schelling, 1960, ch. 2). Within the political debates about strategic weapons and policy, simple counts often play important symbolic roles. In the SALT I debates and the following years, for example, supporters of the agreements typically pointed out that the United States had more nuclear missile warheads, while opponents argued that the Soviets were allowed more missiles. (See, e.g., *New York Times,* 1976.)

Composite Measures. In the search for more accurate assessments of what might happen under wartime conditions, numerous composite measures have been developed. These are calculations on or transformations of the simple counts, according to simple theories, in order to overcome some of the difficulties inherent in aggregating the properties of individual weapons across entire arsenals. For example, a simple count of total available explosive yield (megatonnage) can be used to give a rough indication of the total soft-target (e.g., city) area destroyable, but it fails to take account of the fact that the same area can be destroyed with fewer megatons if more but smaller warheads are used. The calculation of "equivalent megatonnage" (EMT), one of the best known composite measures, is fairly straightforward [EMT =

aYexp(2/3), where Y is yield and a is a constant]. It gives a more accurate measure of soft-target destructive capability than does total megatonnage and can be calculated from the same raw input data; a one megaton (1 MT) warhead would only destroy about 63 percent of the area destroyable with four quarter-MT warheads. In general, the composite measures form a bridge between static counts and dynamic effects measures. They are more detailed and subtle than the simple counts, give more accurate information about aggregate capabilities of arsenals of weapons, and are less subject to the difficulties of the simple counts, although they require additional calculation. Because they are less straightforward, they have a lower political saliency, and their use is often confined to the technically trained policy elite.

Outcome or Effects Measures. The most accurate, though most complex, class of strategic balance measures is dynamic outcome or effects measures, derived from simulations of hypothetical war scenarios by means of nuclear exchange models, asking in effect, "What would result if a war were fought with this targeting plan and these arsenals of weapons?" Such simulations solve the aggregation problems of simpler measures by allowing higher levels of disaggregation, sometimes even to the level of individual warheads and targets. All relevant target and warhead parameters may then be taken into account in highly sophisticated targeting plans, at the cost of considerable complexity. As policy analysis tools, one may then apply desired figures of merit, including any of the simple or composite indices, to the arsenals expected to result from a hypothetical nuclear exchange. Secretary of Defense Harold Brown, for example, used U.S. warheads expected to survive a Soviet first strike as an effect measure (1980, p. 87), as well as surviving warheads and EMT expected under two different alert conditions (1980, p. 125). His successor used surviving hard-target kill capability (Weinberger, 1986, p. 47).

Such effect measures automatically take account of asymmetries between the arsenals, strategic doctrines, and political structures of the competitors, presuming that they are known. The application of Monte Carlo simulation techniques can even allow us to determine a range of expected outcomes. In such a simulation, values of key parameters are randomly chosen from their known or anticipated probability distributions, so that the effect measures calculated over many runs should show a reasonable probability distribution. The benefits of effects measures cost significantly in time, complexity, and information, however, and the requirements of the most highly disaggregated nuclear exchange models far exceed the limits of open literature data. Measures of the results are not always as readily understood and communicated as the simpler indices, particularly to the uninitiated, because the simulation results depend critically on large sets of assumptions about the planning and execution of strategic nuclear exchanges. That dependence may force greater clarity about uncertainties regarding performance parameters, and about ambiguities in doctrine and targeting plans; but it also forces greater reliance on the expertise of a technically trained elite. Even though Harold

Table 3.1
Features of Different Classes of Strategic "Balance" Measures

Class of Measures	Advantages	Disadvantages
Simple ("Bean") Counts (Static)	Easily understood Highly politically salient Readily obtainable Most easily verifiable	Static Crude Oversimplified May be misleading
Composite Measures	More subtle and detailed More information on effects Less subject to problems of the simple counts	Cannot handle all aggregation problems Less politically salient than the simple counts
Effects Measures (Dynamic)	Dynamic Automatically handle asymmetries in arsenals, doctrines, political systems Allow application of simple or composite measures Allow evaluation of ranges of uncertainty in outcomes	Time/cost/detail trade-offs High information requirements Intelligible primarily to the technically trained

Brown's effects measures were readily understandable, few individuals could knowledgeably challenge the assumptions and calculation procedures, which were (in the event) not published. Finally, there are many reasons to doubt that an actual nuclear exchange would or could follow the simulation plan in complete detail (Baugh, 1984, p. 161; Steinbruner and Garwin, 1976, pp. 141, 148–49). The advantages and disadvantages of the different classes of measures are summarized in Table 3.1

Perceptions and Actualities

The enormous information demands of simulations to calculate effects measures highlight another, and perhaps more fundamental, difficulty: determining the relative salience of perceptions versus actualities in evaluating the strategic "balance." It is a truism of behavioral science that we act on our perceptions of the world around us, and many politically salient perceptions are later discovered to be counterfactual. An asserted "missile gap" between the number of Soviet and U.S. ballistic missiles played a major role in the 1960 presidential election campaign. Later it was learned that, although the Soviets had possessed a lead in numbers of IRBMs, the United States had actually had a small lead in numbers of ICBMs. (See Baugh, 1984, pp. 149–51, and Freedman, 1977, p. 102). Yet within two years the Minuteman program, promoted in part because of the "missile gap" fears of 1960, had given the United States a significant, though transitory, lead in numbers of ICBMs. This case highlights the fact that, to the extent that political decisions about strategic weapons building are reactions to an adversary's weapons programs, they are only as sound as our own intelligence estimates.

Those estimates are themselves crucially tied to perceptions. Producing a United States National Intelligence Estimate (NIE), for example, can involve an extended and intense political debate in the attempt to reach a consensus among the representatives of the various agencies involved. In an outstanding example of the political uses of estimates, President Gerald Ford in 1976 accepted a recommendation from the Foreign Intelligence Advisory Board (FIAB) that an outside panel of experts, more pessimistic about Soviet plans than advocates of the rough parity thesis, be appointed to compete with the regular CIA team in preparing an NIE on Soviet strategic objectives over the next ten years. The two groups, referred to as "Team A" and "Team B," produced substantially different estimates of overall Soviet strategic capabilities and objectives. After the two competing estimates had been argued before the FIAB, it was said that the conservative outside estimate contributed greatly to adoption of a majority view much more somber than past NIEs, stating in sum that the Soviet Union was seeking superiority over U.S. forces (Binder, 1976). That conservative judgment was then used in arguments for increases in real U.S. military spending, which had been trending downward with the winding down of the Vietnam War.

There has long been concern in the United States about how the perceived strategic balance affects the U.S. or Western image abroad; its counterpart is Soviet attention to the international "correlation of forces" (about which more is said below, in the subsection Soviet Perspectives). Concern about image was also part of the justification for "perceived equivalence" as the minimally acceptable U.S. goal, as it emerged in the 1970s. If one seeks only to maintain what McGeorge Bundy (1984) has termed "existential deterrence," massive increases in strategic investment are manifestly unnecessary—for either superpower. Yet both continue to express concerns about falling behind their opponent's asserted drives for superiority. Since the United States entered the nuclear age with a monopoly, its position relative to the Soviet Union could only deteriorate over time; but neither state is willing to accept a position of strategic inferiority, a point repeatedly emphasized both by U.S. presidents and Soviet general secretaries. Thus, only rough balance or parity or essential equivalence is mutually acceptable, but both sides continue to express fears of a strategic "breakout," while pursuing programs that evoke reciprocal fears. (See Talbott, 1984.)

Secretary of Defense Robert McNamara in 1965 institutionalized a process for considering the "greater-than-expected (GTE) threat" (Freedman, 1977, pp. 85–86). There is some range of uncertainty in any intelligence estimate, but how far is it prudent to go out on the tails of the distribution of uncertainty, either toward optimism with the risk of underestimation, or toward pessimism with the risk of overestimation? Responding to the GTE threat implies a consistent pattern of overreaction which is at least inefficient and expensive, and at worst will trigger an excessive counterreaction and increase the risk of the very war one seeks to avert. There seems to be no single solution to this difficulty, and it is tempting to adopt the stance taken by the physicist Freeman Dyson (1984, p. 24) when he considered the survivability of nuclear war and dogmatically declared it "undecidable." And yet we must come to *some* decision in setting levels of military expenditures.

Dyson also suggested a more fundamental problem of perception that affects the whole gamut of political decisions about arms and arms control. Although it involves many aspects of styles of thought and action, it hinges on which of two broad sets of issues an individual considers to be more significant and tractable. In this chapter it is referred to as the "two communities" problem. Dyson writes of the two "worlds" of the "warriors" and the "victims." Warriors "share a common language and a common style" (Dyson, 1984, p. 4), and, whatever their differences of political position or specific policy recommendations, they seek to apply the tools of objective factual analysis to help produce incremental improvements in world conditions. This outlook leads naturally to questions about the state and management of political and military balances. The question, "What is the U.S.–Soviet strategic nuclear balance?" is meaningful to warriors, and whatever their political differences, most readers of this chapter probably belong to this group. Victims, however, tend toward a personalistic, anecdotal, non-technical, and humanistic style of argument; they are likely to focus strongly on the human tragedy of war and to seek revolutionary rather than incremental change. Those holding that outlook naturally raise questions about reforming the international system and disarming nuclear weapons.

Dyson worries that the two communities speak different languages and consequently regard each other's concerns as irrelevant to the "real" problems. His concept provides a metaphor for an undeniable difficulty that plagues this subject area, among others: fundamental disagreements on the questions we should be asking, and even more on the methods we should adopt to answer them. Echoes of the two communities problem can be found even within the ranks of the warriors, who tend to divide between those—often, but by no means necessarily, political conservatives—who worry about maintaining the strategic balance in order to make deterrence work and preserve the peace, and those—often, but again not necessarily, political liberals—who seek to reduce arms levels and prevent action–reaction arms–racing processes, again to preserve the peace. (See Wallace, 1982.)

This is a fundamental political argument about strategic doctrine, and one that has profound implications for how we interpret data regarding the strategic balance. One important continuing manifestation of that argument is the controversy between doctrines of nuclear "warfighting" or "damage limitation" (hereinafter, DL), and "assured destruction" or "mutual assured destruction" (hereinafter AD or MAD). The DL view was well set out by Secretary of Defense Harold Brown in the following statement:

> I am not at all persuaded that what started as a demonstration . . . could be kept from escalating to a full-scale thermonuclear exchange. But . . . there are large uncertainties . . . and . . . it should be in everyone's interest to minimize the probability of the most destructive escalation and [to] halt the escalation before it reach[es] catastrophic proportions. [In general, the U.S. aims] . . . to make a Soviet victory as improbable (seen through Soviet eyes) as we can make it, over the broadest possible range of scenarios (1980, pp. 65–67).

Thus, making deterrence fully credible requires convincing our opponents that we can preserve options for prosecuting and prevailing in any war that might be forced on us. In particular, this leads to requirements for limited nuclear options (LNOs; see Synder, 1977) and for the hardening of command, communication, control, and intelligence (C^3I) facilities, to convince an attacker of the futility of beheading strikes. The typical contrasting view holds that escalation will be unstoppable once the nuclear threshold is crossed, so that the existence of LNOs makes nuclear war more likely. In the author's own county, after vocal public protests, Senator Mark Hatfield intervened in 1986 to prevent construction of an Air Force Ground Wave Emergency Network (GWEN) tower as part of a network to ensure radio communications during any nuclear exchange (Flanigan, 1986). This view ties policy firmly to a belief that only all-out nuclear exchanges are possible; we might do well to remember that the acronym "MAD" was coined by *opponents* of assured destruction doctrine.

Where Do We Find the Data?

If we can agree that it is meaningful to ask what the strategic balance is, we must still decide where to look for appropriate data. Relying strictly on open-literature data raises major difficulties, among which are (a) the ease with which those having access to classified data can retreat behind a screen of inaccessibility to shield their political conclusions from scrutiny, and (b) the tendency of insiders to discount the critical perceptions of those who do not work full-time, on-site with the data. Both insiders and outsiders are engaged in ongoing debates within and between their groups in the attempt to reach a consensus about the technical data, knowing that those data have significant political ramifications. Thus, there may be major disagreements even among analysts who concur on the raw data values.

Much more attention is paid in the open literature, and a much stronger consensus is reached, on weapons *quantities* than on weapons *qualities* or *performance parameters,* a natural consequence of the greater ease with which quantities can be verified. Among the most widely accepted open-literature sources are the publications of the International Institute for Strategic Studies (IISS) in London, especially its annual publication *The Military Balance* and its *Adelphi Papers* series (typically commissioned on current topics from recognized experts); publications of the Stockholm International Peace Research Institute (SIPRI), especially its annual *Yearbook* of *World Armaments and Disarmament;* the weekly trade journal *Aviation Week and Space Technology,* sometimes referred to in Washington circles as "Aviation Leak" because of its frequent use for the divulgences of political infighting; and the English Jane's publications such as *Jane's Weapon Systems*. Although there are differences of emphasis and perspective—SIPRI, for example, has a strongly pro-arms control bias, whereas information leaked to sources such as *Aviation Week* is much more likely to support program-building options than arms control—there are few major disagreements among these sources, or between these sources and classified data, on such current data as missile quantities, models, and numbers of warheads. (See further comments in the subsection Strategic Program Scope.)

Data on weapons performance characteristics are more problematic and less readily obtainable. They are more likely to appear in Jane's publications and *The Military Balance,* for example, than in SIPRI publications. We are largely reduced to depending on the open-literature writings of experts who have access to the classified literature (e.g., Steinbruner and Garwin, 1976; Gray, 1977), and on occasional congressional and governmental "leaks" (e.g., Downey, 1976). Annual summaries of statistical trends in the U.S.–Soviet military balance published in recent years by John M. Collins of the Congressional Research Service of the Library of Congress are highly regarded. His 1985 version (Collins and Cronin, 1985, p. 12), for example, included unclassified data on warhead yield, missile throw-weight, CEP (accuracy), and range. Yet, even a compilation of open-literature data by an informed person with classified data access can be subject to security classification.

As a consequence of all these limitations, establishing accepted weapons performance parameter values in the open literature leads to a continuing dialogue characterized by limited new information input and relatively slow changes in accepted values. Although technical analyses, like any others, can always be skewed toward desired conclusions, a careful evaluation of technical possibilities and political realities can be one of the most objective unclassified data sources. One must determine the distribution of technical possibilities and then make a political judgment about how far out on the tails of that distribution it is prudent to move.

Soviet Perspectives

Each superpower must take the other's strategy and doctrine, to the extent they are known, into account in formulating its own plans. Societal differences make it considerably more difficult and speculative to evaluate Soviet plans and attitudes than those of the United States, but there are still substantial Soviet and Western literatures on Soviet views. (See Arnett, 1979; Kolkowicz and Mickiewicz, 1986.) The greatest Soviet contribution to the measurement of the strategic balance is the concept of the international "correlation of forces." Official Soviet statements lay considerable emphasis on that concept, a comprehensive frame of reference that encompasses global military, political, economic, and moral balances (Holloway, 1984, pp. 81–83). Within the military sector, the correlation of forces comprehends both strategy and tactics at levels from theatre to global. Although partly grounded in the Soviet version of Marxist political doctrine, it is more comprehensive and less compartmentalized than typical U.S. views. Soviet–American differences over whether INF and intercontinental nuclear weapons should be dealt with in the same negotiations exemplify their contrasting perspectives.

Contrasts may also be found between the superpowers' military doctrines. Although there is some tendency to quote whichever Soviet authorities support one's own view (see Baugh, 1984, p. 40), both sides appear to embrace the use of nuclear forces to "prevail" in war or to perform damage-limitation (DL) tasks. U.S. authorities, however, are much more likely to embrace the notion that DL implies having LNOs, whereas Soviet military writings are closer to the MAD perspective. Arguably, Soviet military equipment design, which tends to avoid maintenance-intensive high technologies, is better suited to fighting a war and prevailing, especially in a context of all-out war. Soviet military organization seems better structured to maintain operations when central communications are disrupted, although the Soviets are widely believed to have invested much more heavily than the United States in "hardening" C^3I facilities against attack.

THE U.S.–SOVIET STRATEGIC NUCLEAR BALANCE

Even if we cannot achieve closure on all the issues of measurement and interpretation, it is still meaningful to ask what the U.S.–Soviet strategic nuclear balance is, both currently and prospectively, according to various measures. Many statements about that balance have been vague and undiscriminating, such as President Reagan's 1984 claim that his predecessors had managed "a decade of neglect" that left the United States "struggling not to regain the superiority we once enjoyed, but simply to restore the military equivalence we need to keep the peace" (U.S. Department of Defense, 1984b, p. 33). Navy Secretary John Lehman, echoing a phrase popularized by Reagan, charged that the administration's defense programs were preceded by "nearly a decade of unilateral disarmament" (1985, p. 272). Colin Gray, among other analysts, concurs:

The core of the ["decade of neglect"] thesis is about the fit between strategy and policy, given the evolution in the estimated net military prowess of the U.S. and U.S.–

allied arms. It is our contention that U.S. grand strategy and defense policy were permitted, intentionally or not, to come unraveled over the period from the mid-1960s to the early 1980s (Gray and Barlow, 1985, p. 46).

Not surprisingly, Carter administration officials rejected such charges out of hand. Defense Secretary Harold Brown, for example, while concerned about the long-term effects of different U.S. and Soviet military spending levels, particularly on strategic arms (1981, p. 16), asserted that "by most relevant measures, we remain the military equal of or superior to the Soviet Union" (1981, p. 52). Exemplary of the more liberally optimistic analysts, the Center for Defense Information has consistently argued that the United States is superior to the Soviet Union on most relevant measures of national and military power. (See *Defense Monitor,* 1984.)

Statements regarding the overall U.S.–Soviet military balance have often been tied to long-term budgetary trends. There is little disagreement that total Soviet military outlays rose while U.S. outlays shrank during the 1970s (see, for example, Brown, 1981, p. 14), although Soviet military spending increases had slowed or stopped by the end of that decade. The relatively few key issues regarding trends in the strategic nuclear balance, however, include (a) relative scope and potential effects of U.S. and Soviet weapons-building programs; (b) overall goals of strategic programs; (c) growing vulnerability to a disarming first strike, owing to ever-increasing missile accuracies ("ICBM vulnerability"), whether or not in some particular time "window"; and (d) alleged Soviet violations of the SALT arms control treaties, which raise the broader issue of the degree of confidence one can have in verifying adherence to such agreements. These issues will be considered seriatim in this section.

Strategic Program Scope

Although there is increasing agreement that "no single measurement can give a full representation of the strategic nuclear balance" (IISS, 1985, p. 178; see also Gray and Barlow, 1985, p. 39), there is relatively little disagreement that Soviet strategic weapons-building programs have outstripped those—admittedly non-trivial—of the United States since the early 1970s. Using numbers of strategic nuclear warheads as a measure illustrates both U.S. and Soviet building trends, and the degrees of difficulty and consensus in counting. Warhead counts for the period 1972–1986, obtained from the several sources discussed above in the subsection Where Do We Find the Data, are summarized in Table 3.2.

Methodologically, Table 3.2 illustrates the relatively high agreement between different major open-literature sources and analysts; the fact that certain quantities are more easily counted or estimated than others; discrepancies caused by different authorities choosing different reference times of year during periods when building programs yield non-trivial year-to-year

Table 3.2
Alternative Simple Counts of U.S. and Soviet Strategic Nuclear Warheads

Measure and Source[a]	1972 USA	1972 USSR	1982 USA
Warheads on ICBMs			
CDI			
CRS	1,474	1,547	2,149
IISS	1,254	1,510	2,152
MT&Z, 1986			
SIPRI			2,152
Warheads on SLBMs			
CDI			
CRS	2,384	497	4,800
IISS	2,096	440	4,688
MT&Z, 1986			
SIPRI			4,800
ICBM + SLBM Warheads			
Gray & Barlow, 1985	3,700	2,000	7,000
CDI			
CRS	3,858	2,044	6,949
IISS	3,350	1,950	6,840
MT&Z, 1986			
SIPRI			6,952
Warheads on Bombers			
CDI			
CRS	1,820	145	2,626
IISS			
MT&Z, 1986			
SIPRI			2,588
Total Strategic Warheads			
CDI			
CRS	5,678	2,189	9,575
IISS			
MT&Z, 1986			
SIPRI			9,540

[a]Sources:
CDI: *Defense Monitor*, 1985, p. 5.
CRS: 1972, 1982: Collins and Glackas, 1983, p. 27.
1985: Collins and Cronin, 1985, p. 20.
IISS, 19nn: IISS, *The Military Balance 19nn–19nn + 1*.
MT&Z, 1986: Medalia, Tinajero, and Zinsmeister, 1986, p. 10.
SIPRI, 19nn: *SIPRI Yearbook 19nn*.

1982 USSR	1985 USA	1985 USSR	1986 USA	1986 USSR
	2,124	6,250		
5,862	2,130	6,420		
5,554	2,118	6,420	2,110	6,420
	2,107	6,420		
7,152			2,117	6,515
	5,728	2,178		
1,865	5,344	2,122		
969–3,275	5,536	2,787+	6,656	3,216
	5,760	2,704		
1,238			5,760	2,300+
7,500				
	7,852	8,428		
7,727	7,474	8,542		
6,523–8,829	7,654	9,207+	8,766	9,636
	7,867	9,124		
8,390			7,877	8,815+
	3,614	780		
345	3,296	1,052		
	2,520	680	4,080	1,080
	3,772	800		
412			<5,093	<930
	11,466	9,208		
8,072	10,770	9,594		
	10,174	9,987+	12,846	10,716
	11,639	9,924		
8,802			<12,970	<9,745

Quantities as of:
July 1985

January 1, 1985
(Autumn) 19nn
December 31, 1985
Mid-year

changes; and the ranges of uncertainty or disagreement. There is least contention about ICBMs and their warhead loadings, especially for the United States. The Soviet practice of deploying several models of some missiles, with different numbers of warheads on each, leads to greater uncertainties. This problem is more difficult for Soviet SLBMs and still more severe in estimating bomber loadings for both superpowers. Some authorities detail their assumptions about loadings, while others do not, give only ranges, or, in the case of SIPRI (1986), tabulate total warhead stockpiles, including reload capability. The values in Table 3.2, however, are for warheads deployed on launchers.

The sources consulted in compiling the table demonstrate a significant change in ideas about the appropriate and accepted unit of account. Although SALT I and II focused on launchers or delivery vehicles, attention has shifted increasingly to warheads as a better measure of strategic balance—one unconstrained under SALT I, and only imperfectly constrained since SALT II. The 1972 sources generally tabulate launchers, so that warhead counts must be calculated by looking up loadings per launcher in other tables. More recent sources, however, prominently tabulate warheads as well as launchers.

Substantively, Table 3.2 illustrates the very different mixes between ICBMs, SLBMs, and bombers deployed by the two sides, and their significant increases in numbers of pre-attack missile and bomber warheads since 1972. Also shown are Soviet increases in ICBM warheads that outstripped U.S. increases to move from rough parity in 1972 to about three-to-one superiority by 1985; a five- to sixfold increase in Soviet SLBM warheads while U.S. SLBM warheads roughly tripled, reducing U.S. superiority from about 4.8:1 to less than 2.5:1; a more than sevenfold increase in Soviet warheads carried by long-range bombers, reducing U.S. superiority from better than 12:1 to roughly 4:1; and a shift from U.S. superiority in total strategic warheads of 2.59:1 in 1972 to no more than 1.33:1 in 1986. Soviet gains resulted from strategic offensive procurement expenditures estimated to have exceeded those of the United States from 1966 until at least 1985, in amounts cumulating to $85 billion over the two decades, including $50 billion between 1975 and 1985 (U.S. Department of Defense, 1984c, II-13 and II-15). Medalia, Tinajero, and Zinsmeister (1986), while crediting the United States with an advantage of 1.17:1 in total strategic warheads at the end of 1985, forecast that advantage to be reversed under each of four scenarios examined for the period 1985–2000.

As noted earlier, simple static counts may be highly misleading, and pessimists tend to argue that static measures understate the extent of the shift from U.S. advantage circa 1972 to Soviet advantage today. Counts of warheads or delivery systems or strategic procurement budgets do not adequately measure the effects of programs such as the hardening of missile silos to increase their resistance to blast (assertedly much more extensively pursued by the Soviets than by the United States); comparable hardening of C^3I facilities; and improvements in missile accuracies, another area in which the significant U.S. lead around 1972 is believed to have been largely erased.

Strategic Program Goals

Compounding the problem of determining the significance of such trends is the difficulty of deciding how they affect probable *operational* plans. As Colin Gray reminds us,

The prospective performance of U.S. strategic forces must be judged in the light of the objectives specified in U.S. policy guidance and plans. Can U.S. forces do what the U.S. government requires of them, regardless of their static quantitative or qualitative standing *vis a vis* Soviet forces? (Gray and Barlow, 1985, p. 32).

He then goes on to assert that

SALT I and SALT II focussed public attention upon the static indices of strategic power—the ever-ambiguous "launchers," missiles, and warheads—and helped structure debate, even among the supposed cognoscenti, in such a way that the strategic purposes and prospective political utility of U.S. strategic forces were grossly neglected (Gray and Barlow, 1985, p. 40).

The SALT agreements and subsequent negotiations indeed tended to focus political attention ever more strongly on simple static counting measures and away from effects measures that better measure operational capabilities. While that was happening, the always ambiguous U.S. strategic doctrine was evolving away from emphasis on retaliatory attacks on cities and other "value" targets, as would be stipulated by MAD doctrine, and toward increased emphasis on capabilities to attack military targets with high accuracy, offering options for protracted but limited nuclear warfighting, as stipulated in NSDM (National Security Decision Memorandum)-242 of 1974 and PD (Presidential Directive)-59 of 1980. Thus, while political attention shifted increasingly to quantities of weapons, strategic doctrine placed increasing emphasis on the qualities or performance characteristics of those weapons, demanding higher levels of technical performance in hopes of achieving the inherently difficult tasks of high-accuracy, limited-force attacks against hardened military targets.

The technical demands of such counter-military attacks lead to massive budget requests, as President Kennedy's secretary of defense, Robert Mc-Namara, discovered when he attempted to implement a strategic doctrine of second-strike counterforce (SSCF), under which an attack against U.S. military targets would be met with retaliation principally against Soviet military targets. Thus, we should not be surprised either that Soviet gains in such technical performance capabilities as MIRVing and ICBM accuracies have required massive levels of strategic investment, or that the Reagan administration considered major increases in strategic spending essential to maintaining a U.S. technological lead. Although not all investments yield payoffs, we probably should not be surprised that the Soviets continue to match most U.S. technical military capabilities, albeit often with less advanced technologies and usually with lag times of several years.

ICBM and Other First-Strike Vulnerabilities

Many fears have been raised about vulnerabilities to attack initiation ("first strikes") directed toward paralyzing C^3I capabilities ("beheading" strikes) or wiping out significant portions of the potential retaliatory forces. In particular, concerns about the vulnerability of fixed-location ICBMs have been raised for at least the last decade. For example, a House Armed Services Subcommittee report (1978) asserted that "it has been decisively shown that the ICBM element of the U.S. strategic triad is becoming increasingly vulnerable to a Soviet attack." Not all authorities agree, however; as Steinbruner and Garwin (1976, p. 138) note, "Vulnerability of the land-based missile forces, to paraphrase Wolfgang Panofsky, is far more a state of mind than a physical condition; but, nevertheless, it is an extremely important state of mind, worthy of the most exacting analysis."

In theory, land-based missiles are becoming vulnerable to a disarming first strike because increasing accuracy of attack is outstripping the passive defense capability of fixed targets, while active defenses, pending possible deployments under the U.S. Strategic Defense Initiative (SDI) and/or a Soviet counterpart, remain essentially prohibited by the 1972 SALT I ABM Treaty and, for space-based defenses using nuclear weapons, by the 1967 Outer Space Treaty. A major debate developed during 1986–1987 over whether development and operational testing of SDI mobile or space-based "exotic ABMs" were permitted by the ABM Treaty. In the traditional or "narrow" interpretation, such development and testing, as well as deployment, were banned; only fixed, land-based exotics could be developed and tested, at ABM test ranges only, and they could not be deployed. Authorities such as Senator Sam Nunn (1987) found this view to be supported by the record of Nixon administration representations to the Senate at the time of ABM Treaty ratification in 1972, by subsequent practice of the parties, and by the negotiating record. In contrast, under the broad or "legally correct" interpretation put forward by the Reagan administration, although deployment was banned unless the treaty were renegotiated, development and testing of mobile exotic ABMs were permitted even though U.S. negotiators had intended to ban them. (See Nitze, 1987, p. 2.)

Pending resolution of this controversy, there is increasing attention to composite and effects measures of the strategic balance, several of which are summarized in Table 3.3. Since Soviet missiles typically have higher throw-weights than their U.S. counterparts, they can carry more warheads, often

Table 3.3
Some Composite and Effects Measures of the U.S.–Soviet Strategic
Nuclear Balance

Measure and Source[a]	1973 USA	1973 USSR	1985 USA	1985 USSR
Relative Deliverable EMT				
—From Missiles				
IISS, 1985			1.0	2.39
—From Missiles + Bombers				
US DOD, 1984a	1.05	1.0		
IISS, 1985			1.0	1.61
Relative time-urgent (missile)				
hard-target kill				
US DOD, 1984a	2.25	1.0	1.0	2.5

[a]*Sources:* IISS, 1985:   IISS, *The Military Balance 1985–1986*, p. 179.
          US DOD, 1984a: U.S. Department of Defense, 1984a, p. 23.

with higher explosive yields, giving Soviet strategic forces an advantage in (hypothetically) deliverable equivalent megatonnage (EMT). Increases in Soviet missile accuracies, together with increases in numbers of Soviet ICBM warheads, typically with larger explosive yields, and a Soviet silo-hardening program more extensive than that pursued by the United States, have led the U.S. Department of Defense (1984a, p. 23) to assert that the mid-1970s U.S. advantage in time-urgent hard-target kill potential has been almost exactly reversed to favor the Soviet Union by a factor of better than 2.5:1.

Although many U.S. officials are intensely concerned about a possible "ICBM vulnerability gap," believers in pure MAD doctrine dismiss such gaps as unimportant. The present author's Nuclear Exchange Model (NEM) analyses of a wide variety of ICBM-building and defense scenarios through the 1980s and into the 1990s suggest that first strikes could leave as few as 200 surviving ICBM *warheads* (Reentry Vehicles, or RVs) on either side (Baugh, 1984, pp. 170–84). Yet it remains unclear whether any great political or military advantage would result from such attacks; many of them would use up almost as many warheads as they would destroy, non-trivial numbers of bombers and missile-carrying submarines (SSBNs with SLBMs) could survive, and 200 ICBM RVs targeted on cities would still be a formidable retaliatory force. As numbers of expected surviving RVs decrease, however, the range of uncertainty in the outcome becomes an important consideration, an issue rarely addressed (but see Steinbruner and Garwin, 1976).

ICBM vulnerability might be solved by some combination of strategic defense; dropping ICBMs from the "triad" of ICBMs, SLBMs, and bombers; concealment; and missile mobility. Of these options, giving up ICBMs seems least politically likely. Concealment shades into mobility, which may take many different forms. The Carter administration's Multiple Protective Shelter (MPS) basing scheme was designed (a) to make the MX ICBM land-mobile among enough shelters that a disarming first strike would be impossible if quantities of ICBM RVs were held to SALT II limits, while (b) still allowing the numbers of MXs to be verified by the Soviets. The Soviet SS-X-25 ICBM, generally believed to be land-mobile, represents a different solution with greater verification problems. Missile submarines provide yet another form of mobility, conceived from the start as a means of preserving a deterrent from the eventually expected ICBM vulnerability. The Trident D-5 SLBM is designed for sufficient accuracy to accomplish a silo-killing mission, and thus appears to be the U.S. Navy's means for performing all the traditional ICBM missions. In addition, the newer SLBMs of both superpowers have almost intercontinental range, further aiding concealment and allowing SSBNs to operate closer to protective land-based air cover.

Minimizing C^3I vulnerability may present even greater problems than dealing with ICBM vulnerability. The many potential threats to C^3I raise technical issues that make the overall threat very difficult to assess. The degree of warning available about an attack is critically dependent on the nature and scope of that attack, as well as on the shifting balance in availability of reconnaissance and other warning satellites. In recent years this concern has led to a rather desultory competition in anti-satellite (ASAT) weaponry. The Soviets are generally accepted as having a rather crude operational ASAT, whereas the United States' more sophisticated ASAT was tested against a rather passive target satellite in 1985, and thereafter was subject to an on-again, off-again congressionally imposed testing ban intended to curb ASAT competition. (See SIPRI, 1986, pp. 132–33.) In some respects, the hardening of C^3I assets has been even more controversial than ASATs. Many reports credit the Soviets with major programs to protect military and political command centers and lines of control, and the Reagan administration accelerated programs to enhance U.S. C^3I. Yet, as noted above, some of those programs have produced intense domestic controversies, again raising the underlying argument between nuclear "damage limitation" and "mutual assured destruction."

Arms Control Compliance and Noncompliance

Further assessment difficulties are presented by opposing claims regarding alleged Soviet violations of the arms control agreements thus far reached, especially the SALT II and ABM Treaties. The Reagan administration consistently charged the Soviet Union with violations of the 1972 SALT I ABM Treaty, which remained in force, and of the SALT II Treaty, which although unratified remained a legal obligation of both governments until 1981, when the United States formally notified the Soviets of its intent not to ratify, and continued as an expressed political obligation by agreement of both parties. Political agreement regarding SALT II and the SALT I Interim Agreement on numbers of ICBMs, SLBMs, and SSBNs (missile submarines) ended in 1986, when President Reagan announced a revised U.S. policy of "interim restraint" under which the United States would base future "decisions regarding its strategic force structure on the nature and magnitude of the threat posed by Soviet strategic forces and not on standards contained in the SALT structure" (USDS, 1986, p. 2). Under that policy, the United States exceeded SALT II limits on bombers carrying air-launched cruise missiles (ALCMs) late in 1986 (*Washington Post,* 1986). President Reagan raised numerous charges of Soviet non-compliance in a series of special reports to the U.S. Congress, beginning in 1984 (U.S. Department of State [USDS], 1985, 1987). Those charges are considered below, in order of increasing controversy within categories.

SALT II. In the March 1987 report, the Reagan administration claimed that "we have put the Interim Agreement and the SALT II Treaty behind us" (USDS, 1987, p. 4) and did not report SALT violations. Previous reports, however, had alleged some seven violations of SALT or related strategic weapons agreements. (1) There seems little doubt that the Soviets encode at least some data transmitted from their ballistic missile test flights, making it more difficult to determine the nature and results of those tests. Whether the extent of such encryption is so great as to pose a serious impediment to verification, thus violating SALT II, is debated, but it cannot make verification easier. (2) SALT II limited each side to testing and deploying one "new" type of ICBM and set technical limits on the extent of changes allowed in modernizing older types. The Soviets declared their SS-X-24 the allowed new ICBM; the U.S. government labeled the SS-X-25 a prohibited second new type, while the Soviets called it a modernized version of an earlier type. If the Soviet claim is correct, testing of the SS-X-25 appears to violate the SALT II provision against testing an existing ICBM with a single reentry vehicle whose weight is less than 50 percent of the throw-weight of the ICBM, a provision intended to prevent the rapid MIRVing of single-warhead missiles. In addition, the United States has charged that encryption of SS-X-25 test data has impeded resolution of the claims. Deployment plans are not yet entirely clear. (See IISS, 1985, p. 21.) The Soviets were also accused of (3) "concealment of the association between a missile and its launcher during testing" and (4) "exceeding the permitted number of strategic nuclear delivery vehicles (SNDVs)" (USDS, 1987, p. 3).

Charges of other SALT-related violations are more controversial. (5) Under SALT II, production, testing, and deployment of the SS-16 ICBM were prohibited, but "somewhat ambiguous" evidence "indicates that the [SS-16] activities at Plesetsk are a probable violation" (USDS, 1985, p. 5). Two other charges concerned the Backfire bomber, long a subject of controversy. The Soviets were accused of (6) giving the Backfire an intercontinental capability by Arctic basing, despite their refusal to count it under SALT II limits; and of (7) exceeding politically agreed limits on Backfire production (USDS, 1987, p. 3).

ABM Treaty. Under the Reagan administration, the U.S. "judge[d] that the aggregates of the Soviet Union's ABM and ABM-related actions *suggest* that the USSR *may be preparing* an ABM defense of its national territory," prohibited under the ABM Treaty (USDS, 1985, p. 6; author's emphasis). Some five specific charges were involved. (1) Construction of a new, large, phased-array radar near Krasnoyarsk in central Siberia was challenged by the United States as a violation of the ABM Treaty, which limits such large radar installations in order to prohibit the construction of ABM systems, or the rapid conversion of air defense systems, for territorial defense. Although the Reagan administration "judge[d] ... that the ... radar ... constitutes a violation" (USDS, 1985, p. 5), the issue remains debatable. Other charges were more controversial. (2) Evidence on "Soviet actions with respect to ABM component mobility" was said to be "ambiguous." (3) Numerous incidents were interpreted as indicating that "the USSR probably has violated the prohibition on testing SAM [air defense Surface-to-Air Missile] components in an ABM mode." (4) Evidence regarding possible upgrade of SAMs to ABMs was found to be "insufficient to assess compliance," and (5) evidence regarding possible rapid reload of allowed ABM launchers was declared "ambiguous" (USDS, 1987, pp. 4, 5).

Assessing the Alleged Violations. There is little controversy about the raw data underlying some items on these lists of alleged Soviet violations, such as the Krasnoyarsk radar and the SS-X-24 and SS-X-25 ICBMs. Arms control optimists argue that at worst the Soviets are, as usual, pushing interpretation of agreements to the limit, whereas their disputed actions cannot seriously affect the balance of strategic capabilities; pessimists argue that Soviet violations demonstrate untrustworthiness and the need for more effective means of verification. Reagan administration claims discussed in the open literature are admittedly judgments based on often ambiguous evidence, and suggest that those determined to find violations will find them, while arms control optimists will find the Soviets to be in essential compliance with existing agreements. Taken as a group, the asserted Soviet violations raise more questions about the future of arms control than about the present and middle-term future of the strategic nuclear balance. None of the weapons quantities involved is large relative to those allowed under SALT. The U.S. decision in 1986 to substitute "interim restraint" for strict adherence to SALT II, however, may be a watershed event. Given five to ten years of further deployments, and in the absence of further arms control agreements or with a breakdown of the SALT/START process, there could be substantial changes in the strategic balance according to many of the commonly accepted indicators.

STATE OF THE ART: AN ASSESSMENT OF STRATEGIC BALANCE MEASUREMENT

Given the increased political emphasis on perceptions of the strategic nuclear balance in recent years, how has our grasp of this subject progressed among students of national and international security? Until the early 1970s, essentially all of the detailed technical analyses—and concomitant use of the more advanced, simulation-based effects measures—were confined to the defense analysis community and the classified literature. In 1973, a key article by Davis and Schilling publicized methods for calculating the hard-target kill capability of missiles. In a 1974 SIPRI monograph, Kosta Tsipis applied crude composite measures to assessing the U.S.–Soviet nuclear balance. His 1975 article in *Science* regarding calculations for hard-target kill prompted an exchange with Department of Defense official John B. Walsh and others (Tsipis, 1975a, 1975b; Walsh, 1975). Steinbruner and Garwin (1976), in a seminal article in the first issue of *International Security,* utilized effects measures and raised critical issues about the feasibility of massive, disarming first strikes. In that same year, in an article in the *American Journal of Political Science*, the author utilized effects measures calculated by using a simple nuclear exchange model (NEM) to assess some arms control possibilities. In its own way, each of these articles represented a "first" for these journals; yet each also represented a bit of "rediscovering the wheel," in that all of us were re-creating in the open literature, more or less on our own, what had already been much more highly refined and far more extensively utilized in classified research. Many analysts working with classified data, however, continue to dispute the value of quantitative studies in general and nuclear exchange modeling in particular.

By the late 1970s, many of the composite measures had become fairly well known among social scientists and others outside government interested in national security policy, and some effects measures had attracted attention. Some of this work was even published in general-circulation journals (e.g., Tsipis, 1975c). Interest was spurred by the SALT II debates of 1978–1979, which led to additional articles on specific problems of strategic balance measures (Richelson, 1980, 1982) and on their applications to such policy problems as ICBM vulnerability and MX basing (Richelson, 1979; Baugh, 1980). Articles from that period show increasing closure on the technical problems of strategic measurement outlined above. They have also stimulated an intensifying dialogue between researchers working in the open literature and the social science journals, and others working in government and the contract policy analysis establishment, including some individuals with regular access to classified data. Effects measures have yet to be completely accepted, although they are now increasingly utilized in government publications, as discussed above. Elsewhere (Baugh, 1984, ch. 4) the author has dealt with the case for employing such measures in policy studies.

On the Recycling of Issues and Views

Are we making progress in resolving basic issues concerning the strategic nuclear balance and its measurement, or do those issues keep reoccurring?

There is a growing consensus that no single measure of strategic balance is sufficient. Relative to the state of knowledge within the social sciences ten to fifteen years ago, there is much wider knowledge of possible measures and reasonable closure on their uses and shortcomings, although effects measures are still rarely utilized. Moreover, although many more social scientists are involved in this research today than in the early 1970s, their numbers remain relatively small. Yet, to a degree that could be both surprising and disheartening, many strategic weapons issues continue to be fought over decade after decade. For example, every time some practical issue of "retargeting" for limited nuclear options (LNOs) comes up, it raises anew the dispute over whether a nuclear war can be fought and kept limited, or whether LNOs are required for fully credible deterrence. Arguably, similar "recycling" happens regarding views of the U.S.–Soviet strategic nuclear balance. Whenever the state of the strategic weapons regime is in flux, and particularly when we perceive ourselves to be at a disadvantage, there is renewed interest in the *state* and *significance* of that balance, and a tendency to investigate new methods for its measurements.

In 1972, the Nixon administration argued that greater numbers of U.S. missile warheads more than offset greater numbers of Soviet missiles allowed under SALT I, although new weapons-building programs were still proposed in the categories not constrained by SALT. Within a few years, as the Soviets began MIRVing and thus began to erase U.S. superiority in numbers of warheads, the wisdom of the 1972 agreements began to appear more doubtful, and political attention shifted increasingly to (a) concepts and measures of "balance," for example, whether the SALT II formula of "equal aggregates with freedom to mix" really met the 1972 Jackson amendment stipulation requiring numerically balanced ceilings, and (b) concerns about the adequacy with which we could verify adherence to arms control agreements. This was a time of increasing attention to balance measures in the social science literature, and the above-noted progress in measurement.

Interactions Between Intellectual Analysis and Policymaking

The difficulties of analyzing national security policy questions using open-literature data remain substantial. A case in point is the use of nuclear exchange models (NEMs) to generate effects measures under alternative arms control proposals. Steinbruner and Garwin (1976) worked with NEMs using classified data; the present author and other social scientists essentially had to rediscover that approach independently in the 1970s. To date, no work with NEMs in the open literature has reached the complexity and subtlety of the classified research, both because government and contract researchers can bring an intensity of focus to work with such models over extended periods of time and because the highly disaggregated NEMs require data at a level of detail that demands classification. (See Baugh, 1984, pp. 143–45.)

Classified and unclassified data often differ very little, but there is a widespread belief within the government that classified access is necessary to "really" know what is going on. This makes it difficult for analysts to have policy impact simultaneously in academia, while working in the open literature, and in government, using classified data. In its own way, this is a different sort of "two communities" problem. Current political concerns and preoccupations tend to dominate government and contract research, contributing to the sense of separation from academia. Of course, it is virtually impossible to assess the impact of Western strategic policy research on Soviet doctrine and activity.

Limitations Faced by Analysts

Analysts in both communities face a number of other limitations. Since there is no consensus on any single measure of the strategic balance, those who work with the more detailed measures may be perceived as excessively preoccupied with narrow technical aspects of the problem. A nuclear exchange simulation can be no better than the detailed data and assumptions utilized as input, and the larger NEMs have required full-time staffs of highly skilled computer programmers for their development and operation (Baugh, 1984, p. 143). In 1985 the U.S. Arms Control and Disarmament Agency (ACDA) ordered a new NEM featuring a user-friendly, menu-based operation, to be run on a medium-sized in-house computer; that action could be justified as easily on grounds of bringing end-users closer to the detailed analysis, as on grounds of lower cost and improved security. Certainly, some of the "rediscovery" of strategic balance measures by open-literature social scientists during the 1970s—for example, hard-target kill computations—was a highly technical and esoteric debate, although the parties were open and definite about their end goals of more effective arms control and a reduced probability of war.

Another, partially opposing charge is that analysts have been caught up in abstract questions with little policy relevance, because they have lacked adequate understanding of actual war plans and the true characteristics and effects of pertinent weaponry and military forces. The literature on formal models of arms racing, to which the author has occasionally contributed, is undeniably abstract and has done little to advance policy formulation beyond the rhetorically useful concept of an action–reaction–process "arms race." Less abstract studies are open to the charge that data at the required level of detail are classified. In recent years, however, a considerable body of information about the history and formulation of U.S. nuclear strategic doctrine and operational plans has become available in the open literature, partly because crucial documents from the 1950s have been declassified. (See Fried-berg, 1981; Rosenberg, 1979.)

AN AGENDA FOR RESEARCH

In the continuing debates about strategic policy, doctrine, and balance, some things have never changed—and probably cannot be expected to change. A full assessment of the strategic nuclear balance continues to require multiple and often rather complex measures. Political temptations to use measures favorable to one's own position are extremely powerful, particularly when dealing with complicated technical issues. The very complexity of those issues tends to invite oversimplification and helps make the simplest measures of strategic balance most politically salient, even though they may also be the most misleading. As long as a security system is needed, it tends to limit the policy impact of analysts outside government, keeping some valuable data from them and bolstering the exclusivity claims of insiders. Indeed, the very concept of a strategic nuclear balance has only limited meaning outside the context of assumptions about strategic doctrine and operational plans, which are necessary to carry out any nuclear exchange simulation and to give op-erational meaning to composite measures or even simple counts.

If such factors seem immutable, logically inherent in the physical and political processes involved, other factors may yet be changeable. Among them are the divergences between adherents of AD and DL doctrines, a split as readily characterized by the term *two communities* as is the gulf between Dyson's warriors and victims. Some convergence on improved measures of the strategic balance, particularly effects measures, can be detected over the last decade. Consequently, our present need is not so much for improved measures, as for greater agreement on which measures to use under what circumstances. Yet because the appropriateness of specific measures depends at least in part on policy and doctrinal goals, the resolution of issues regarding the strategic balance depends in no small part on the resolution of other issues. Hard-target kill capability, for example, is critical to DL plans but relatively less important to AD, under which the ability to destroy military targets is less vital. The technical issues of strategic balance measures, in-cluding effects measures, are now largely solved, and are increasingly known in the open literature. What remain are the enduring political disputes of policy and doctrine; extending understanding of and "selling" the use of the best measures; and closing some of the "two communities" gaps.

Social science has a good deal to say on such issues, and many types of research may speak to these concerns. The question of whether arming leads to peace through deterrence or to war through action–reaction–process arms racing is a subject for empirical historical study. A variety of settings, ranging from historical case studies to laboratory experiments, may allow us to ex-amine decision-making under risk and uncertainty when stakes are very high.

More complete and accurate knowledge of Soviet military doctrines and internal decision-making processes could help us improve the war and arms control scenarios studied by means of NEMs, and refine our concepts of the minimum mutually acceptable bargaining set. Promoting dialogues between differing belief communities, whether they be warriors and victims, or AD and DL adherents, may help reduce polarization and encourage closure on some of the questions that underlie any meaningful attempt to assess the strategic balance. This might be undertaken both by seeking to forge a common language of analysis and discourse on strategic issues, and by striving to identify and extend areas of agreement. Finally, we should continue to apply our most refined and appropriate measures of strategic balance, in hopes of increasing both the policy and the educational impacts of our analyses.

POLITICAL SIGNIFICANCE OF THE STRATEGIC NUCLEAR BALANCE

In light of all the above considerations, how should we assess the present and prospective political significance of the strategic nuclear balance? Perceptions of that balance are clearly important in American domestic politics. We see that impact in widespread concerns about the United States' image abroad, as during the 1980 presidential campaign. In internal bureaucratic politics, we see measures of strategic balance used as political tools in budgetary battles. It is more difficult to assess the role of strategic balance perceptions in Soviet politics, but "balance" as understood in the West is necessarily part of the correlation of forces, and the Soviet Union has long placed great emphasis on its own image abroad.

What of the general political utility of strategic balance measures in international politics? Can they be reliable indicators of shifts in nation-state power and international leverage, modernized indices akin to the classical balance of power? The Soviets profess the belief that the international correlation of forces has profound implications for the ability of states, even superpowers, to project power abroad. Yet, whatever the operational military plans, there is a substantial decoupling of nuclear from conventional forces, based on a widespread belief in the political salience of a "nuclear threshold," essentially a belief that LNOs will not work and that any use of nuclear weapons will escalate uncontrollably. If so, the nuclear *strategic* balance does not measure usable political leverage. Vivid examples are provided by the May 1987 Iraqi attack on the frigate U.S.S. *Stark* in the Persian Gulf, and by the inability of the United States to put together a workable plan to rescue the Teheran embassy hostages in 1980. In both cases, usable capabilities were determined by relative strengths in conventional weaponry that could be brought to bear in the immediate problem area.

Serious strategic force imbalances, however, should still count. It can be argued that U.S. global strategic superiority was decisive in persuading the Soviets to yield to U.S. local conventional superiority in the 1962 Cuban missile crisis, and the Soviets determined that they would never again allow such an imbalance. Indeed, so serious an imbalance seems extremely unlikely in the foreseeable future, barring the always elusive, enticing, and scary strategic "breakout." Thus, new strategic arms control agreements should be possible, provided that rough parity or essential equivalence is maintained—which depends in part on what measures are used and how they influence perceptions. Such agreements could extend to balanced deep cuts, again given no breakouts, which the Soviets profess to fear from SDI. It thus seems essential to maintain an approximate, if perhaps declining, balance in strategic nuclear weaponry, so that those weapons remain largely irrelevant in the conduct of the rest of international politics.

REFERENCES

Arnett, Robert L. 1979. Soviet Attitudes Towards Nuclear War: Do They Really Think They Can Win? *Journal of Strategic Studies* 2:172–91.

Barton, John H., and Lawrence Weiler, eds. 1976. *International Arms Control: Issues and Agreements.* By the Stanford Arms Control Group. Stanford, Calif.: Stanford University Press.

Baugh, William H. 1976. Arms Control Possibilities for the SALT II Negotiations and Beyond: An Operations Analysis. *American Journal of Political Science* 20:67–95.

———. 1980. Deceptive Basing Modes for Strategic Missiles: An Exercise in the Politics of an Ambiguous Nuclear Balance. *Western Political Quarterly* 33:247–59.

———. 1984. *The Politics of Nuclear Balance: Ambiguity and Continuity in Strategic Policies.* New York: Longman.

Binder, David. December 26, 1976. New C.I.A. Estimate Finds Soviet Seeks Superiority in Arms. *New York Times,* p. 1.

Brown, Harold. 1980. *Department of Defense Annual Report, Fiscal Year 1981.* Washington, D.C.: U.S. Government Printing Office.

———. 1981. *Department of Defense Annual Report, Fiscal Year 1981.* Washington, D.C.: U.S. Government Printing Office.

Brzezinski, Zbigniew. 1986. *Game Plan: A Geostrategic Framework for the Conduct of the U.S.–Soviet Contest.* Boston: Atlantic Monthly Press.

Bundy, McGeorge. 1984. Existential Deterrence and Its Consequences. Pp. 3–13 in Douglas MacLean, ed., *The Security Gamble: Deterrence Dilemmas in the Nuclear Age.* Totowa, N.J.: Rowman and Allanheld.

Cannon, Lou. October 13, 1986. Reagan-Gorbachev Summit Talks Collapse as Deadlock on SDI Wipes Out Other Gains. *Washington Post.* Pp. A1, A29.

Collins, John M., and Thomas Peter Glakas. 1983. *U.S./Soviet Military Balance: Statistical Trends, 1970–1981 (As of January 1, 1983).* Washington. D.C.: Congressional Research Service, Report No. 83–153 S (August 1, 1983).

———, and Patrick M. Cronin. 1985. *U.S./Soviet Military Balance: Statistical Trends,*

1975–1984. Washington, D.C.: Congressional Research Service, Report No. 85–83 F (April 15).

Davis, Lynn E., and Warner Schilling. 1973. All You Ever Wanted to Know About MIRV and ICBM Calculations But Were Not Cleared to Ask. *Journal of Conflict Resolution* 17:207–42.

Defense Monitor. 1984. U.S.–Soviet Military Facts. Washington, D.C.: Center for Defense Information. (Vol. 13, No. 6.)

———. 1985. U.S.–Soviet Nuclear Arms: 1985. Washington, D.C.: Center for Defense Information. (Vol. 14, no. 6.)

Donley, Michael B., ed. 1979. *The SALT Handbook.* Washington, D.C.: Heritage Foundation.

Downey, Thomas J. 1976. How to Avoid Monad—and Disaster. *Foreign Policy* 24:172–201. A more complete form is given in *Congressional Record—Senate,* September 20, S16210–S16218.

Dyson, Freeman J. 1984. *Weapons and Hope.* New York: Harper and Row.

Flanigan, James C. September 20, 1986. Air Force Drops Tower Plan. *The [Portland] Oregonian.* p. E [A1].

Freedman, Lawrence David. 1977. *U.S. Intelligence and the Soviet Strategic Threat.* Boulder, Colo.: Westview Press.

Friedberg, Aaron L. 1981. A History of U.S. Strategic "Doctrine"—1945 to 1980. *Journal of Strategic Studies* 4:37–71.

Gray, Colin S. 1977. *The Future of Land-Based Missile Forces.* London: International Institute for Strategic Studies, Adelphi Paper, no. 140.

———, and Jeffrey G. Barlow. 1985. Inexcusable Restraint: The Decline of American Military Power in the 1970s. *International Security* 10, 2 (Fall):27–69.

Holloway, David. 1984. *The Soviet Union and the Arms Race.* 2nd ed. New Haven, Conn.: Yale University Press.

House Armed Services Subcommittee. 1978. U.S. Congress, House, Committee on Armed Services, Subcommittee on Intelligence and Military Application of Nuclear Energy, Staff Study, *Land-Based ICBM Forces Vulnerability and Options,* 95th Cong., 2nd Sess., October 5, HASC Report No. 95–69.

International Institute for Strategic Studies [IISS]. Various Years. *The Military Balance 19nn–19nn + 1.* London: IISS.

Kolkowicz, Roman, and Ellen Propper Mickiewicz, eds. 1986. *The Soviet Calculus of Nuclear War.* Lexington, Mass.: Lexington Books.

Lehman, John. 1985. The Soviet Strategic Advantage. *International Security Review* 5:272.

Medalia, Jonathan, Al Tinajero, and Paul Zinsmeister. 1986. *Strategic Nuclear Forces: Potential U.S./Soviet Trends With or Without SALT 1985–2000.* Washington, D.C.: Congressional Research Service, Report No. 86–135 F (July 15).

New York Times. 1976. Aspin Rebuts Data on Soviet Defense. April 5, p. 34.

Nitze, Paul H. 1987. Interpreting the ABM Treaty. U.S. Department of State Current Policy No. 936, April 1.

Nunn, Sam. 1987. Interpretation of the ABM Treaty. *Congressional Record—Senate,* March 11, S2967–S2986; March 12, S3090–S3095; March 13, S3171–S3173.

Richelson, Jeffrey T. 1979. Multiple Aim Point Basing: Vulnerability and Verification Problems. *Journal of Conflict Resolution* 23:613–28.

———. 1980. Evaluating the Strategic Balance. *American Journal of Political Science* 24:779–803.

———. 1982. Static Indicators and the Ranking of Strategic Forces. *Journal of Conflict Resolution* 26:265–82.

Rosenberg, David Alan. 1979. American Nuclear Strategy and the Hydrogen Bomb Decision. *Journal of American History* 66:62–87.

Schelling, Thomas C. 1960. *The Strategy of Conflict*. Cambridge, Mass.: Harvard University Press.

Snyder, Jack L. 1977. *The Soviet Strategic Culture: Implications for Limited Nuclear Operations*. Santa Monica, Calif.: RAND Corporation Report R–2154–AF.

Steinbruner, John D., and Thomas M. Garwin. 1976. Strategic Vulnerability: The Balance Between Prudence and Paranoia. *International Security* 1, 1 (Summer):138–81.

Stockholm International Peace Research Institute [SIPRI]. Various Years. *World Armaments and Disarmament: SIPRI Yearbook 19nn*. Oxford and New York: Oxford University Press, 19nn.

Talbott, Strobe. 1984. *The Russians and Reagan*. New York: Vintage Books.

Tsipis, Kosta. 1974. *Offensive Missiles*. Stockholm: SIPRI Stockholm Paper No. 5 (August).

———. 1975a. Physics and Calculus of Countercity and Counterforce Nuclear Attacks. *Science* 187:393–97.

———. 1975b. Response to Walsh. *Science* 190:1119.

———. 1975c. The Accuracy of Strategic Missiles. *Scientific American,* July:14–23.

U.S. Department of Defense. 1984a. Organization of the Joint Chiefs of Staff, *United States Military Posture for FY 1985*. Washington, D.C.: U.S. Government Printing Office.

———. 1984b. Selected Statements. *Current News,* January-June.

———. 1984c. Under Secretary for Research and Engineering, *The FY 1985 Department of Defense Program for Research, Development and Acquisition*. Washington, D.C.: U.S. Government Printing Office.

U.S. Department of State [USDS]. 1985. *Soviet Noncompliance with Arms Control Agreements*. Washington, D.C.: USDS Special Report No. 122, February 1.

———. 1986. *U.S. Interim Restraint Policy: Responding to Soviet Arms Control Violations*. Washington, D.C.: USDS Special Report No. 147, May 27.

———. 1987. *Soviet Noncompliance with Arms Control Agreements*. Washington, D.C.:USDS Special Report No. 163, March.

Wallace, Michael D. 1982. Armaments and Escalation: Two Competing Hypotheses. *International Studies Quarterly* 26:37–56.

Walsh, John B. 1975. Strategic Arms Debate. *Science* 190:1117–18.

Washington Post. 1986. Democrats on Hill Denounce U.S. Violation of SALT II. November 29, p. A2.

Weinberger, Caspar W. 1986. *Report of the Secretary of Defense to the Congress on the FY 1987 Budget, FY 1988 Authorization Request and FY 1987–1991 Defense Programs*. Washington, D.C.: U.S. Government Printing Office.

4

On the Command and Control of Nuclear Forces

STEPHEN J. CIMBALA

In the past, many debates about U.S. deterrence strategy have been conducted without reference to operational war plans or "employment policy" as it is known to students of military strategy (Ball, 1986). As a result, issues that are very abstract and theoretical dominate discussions of deterrence policy to the frequent exclusion of issues that have more to do with the real likelihood of success or failure in war. Exclusion of issues that influence the actual probability of losing or winning wars, in turn, feeds back into deficient deterrence theories.

Illustrative of this self-deceiving feedback loop is the treatment of command and control issues in writing about U.S. nuclear strategy for most of the nuclear era. However, since the mid-1970s more has become known about actual U.S. war plans, and Soviet doctrine and strategy have been compared more closely with U.S. and allied doctrine and strategy. The result has been some clarification of how far, and in what directions, declaratory and operational strategies for nuclear war and deterrence deviate from one another. One of the discoveries apparent from this growing knowledge base about U.S. operational policy is that U.S. strategic command, control, and communications (C^3), or C^3I in the commonly used abbreviation when "intelligence" is included, has been less capable than commonly supposed. It has also barely supported, as discussed below, U.S. strategies calling for the largest and least complicated retaliatory strikes.

The issues discussed below are not only theoretical; they have imminent policy implications. The Reagan strategic program continues the search begun by its predecessors in the Nixon/Ford and Carter administrations for C^3 which can support additional targeting flexibility, control of escalation, and discrimination in the employment of strategic nuclear forces (Weinberger, 1986, pp. 247–54). One need not question the motivations of U.S. planners who sought options between massive countersocietal destruction and acquiescence to Soviet demands. However, limited nuclear wars between super-powers are difficult to choreograph, and no secretary of defense has ex-pressed optimism that, once begun, U.S.-Soviet strategic nuclear exchanges could be limited. Flexible nuclear response is one of those ideas that appear attractive in principle, especially when the alternative is considered. In prac-tice, flexible response is difficult to apply to strategic nuclear forces, which would be used only in response to threats against vital interests if they are used deliberately at all. The need for flexibility, in order to reassure civilian policymakers that their control over military activities extends beyond de-terrence failure, contrasts with the improbability of obtaining flexibility given C^3 constraints on implementing actual war plans.

SCOPE AND METHOD

The technical cast of U.S. writing on command and control issues is most apparent in the use of military acronyms like "C^3I" as bureaucratic shorthand. Abbreviations symbolize perceptions of larger realities, and the perceptions are common to academic faculties and Washington bureaucrats. By combining the characteristics of "command," "control," "communications," and "intel-ligence" under one rubric, we are in danger of losing sight of some very important trees in creating an artificially homogeneous forest.

First, there is the concept of command, which military traditionalists will find abusively treated in the C^3I literature. The functions of "command" and "control" are not synonymous. Command has to do with the conduct of military operations in order to accomplish the objectives established by pol-icymakers, or by higher level military commanders for their subordinates. (See Van Crevald, 1985, pp. 5–16.) Control is a related but distinct phenom-enon, which is why commanders have staff officers and totalitarian countries have political officers interspersed within the military chain of command. As Samuel P. Huntington pointed out many years ago, there are two generic approaches to controlling the military on the part of their civilian superiors: subjective and objective control. The subjective refers to the inculcation of the moral values and political aspirations of the state within its officer corps. The objective asks that the officer corps be experts in the art of war and totally obedient to its political masters regardless of ideology (Huntington, 1957). Now this issue is extremely important in the context of the command and control over nuclear forces, given the consequences of deterrence failure. It is brushed up against by C^3I studies under other guises and, for want of recognition, bypassed. Instead, the matter of "control" becomes a question of technology and wiring, with some passing mention of delegation and devolution of authority in crisis.

The status of "communications" and "intelligence" in the C^3I lexicon is murkier still. Communications are the contents of messages and the pathways through which they are processed. They also involve the location and tasking of centers and persons who are authorized to record, process, and evaluate information. This spills over into "intelligence," although this function as a component of C³I is frequently included with little or no reference to the large body of literature on that subject. Intelligence traditionally understood was what the commander needed to know in order to win the battle, and what he wanted the enemy not to know in order to maintain any advantage. Military history is rich in accounts of deception and surprise attack which might also have assumed pride of place in discussions of the implications of C³I. Again, for the most part, any in-depth recognition of the nuances of intelligence collection, processing, and evaluation is missing from the policy and academic studies of C³I, for the very good reason that intelligence expertise is a substantial commitment in itself[1] (Godson, 1983). It is not that aspects of communications and intelligence matters do not appear in the C³I discussions, but they appear in other forms because they are intended to serve the agendas of the academic and policy analysts doing C³I studies.

This discussion is not merely splitting hairs about terminology. The distinctions are fundamental and have operational implications. Consider, for example, the difference between "command" and "control." The frustration which has been expressed within the ranks of our armed forces over failure to observe this distinction is summarized very well by Lieutenant Colonel Frederick W. Timmerman, Jr., former editor of the official journal (*Military Review*) of the Army Command and General Staff College: "In daily operation, the Army has become one of controllers rather than commanders. In the process, more managerial attributes than leadership behaviors are exhibited. This is, perhaps, satisfactory until commanders have to perform on the battlefield" (Timmerman, 1985, p. 55).

Were this phenomenon only found in the Army and not service-wide, it might be too specific for our consideration. But it is, according to the widely quoted study of the Pentagon by Edward Luttwak, pandemic. He is one among many investigators of the U.S. military command structure who have found the ratio of controllers to commanders too unfavorable to the latter. Too many commanders also confuse their mission with controlling, a separate but related issue. The consequences are real enough; documentation at the level of tactics and operations is abundant. As Edward N. Luttwak writes:

But it cannot seriously be argued that today's peacetime forces require almost as much leadership, command, and administration as the vast armed forces of the Second World War, which fought in both Europe and Asia on a dozen widely separated fronts, whose air and naval operations spanned the globe, and which had many duties that are now quite absent, from the military government of tens of millions of civilians in occupied areas to the upkeep of hospitals in India, airfields in Central Africa, and clandestine weather stations in Mongolia (Luttwak, 1984, p. 19).

One has to be careful not to identify command/control confusion *only* with the problem of "micromanagement," about which Luttwak inveighs at great length and which the Congress, in the midst of scorched earth investigations of Pentagon tactical and procurement incompetence, continues to confuse with oversight.[2] Pressures for defense reorganization have resulted from procurement scandals such as the $600 hammer and from the desire of members of Congress to assume the mantle of self-appointed strategist. The confusion between command and control has special implications for nuclear forces, however disruptive it is of general-purpose forces and their effective employment.

As Paul Bracken notes in his thought-provoking study, *The Command and Control of Nuclear Forces,* U.S. strategic nuclear forces provoked the development of command and control organizations built specifically for those forces (Bracken, 1983). Although tactical nuclear weapons were commingled within preexisting conventional force structures, U.S. strategic forces were thought to require a unique set of organizational arrangements. These arrangements went through various phases in their evolutionary development, which Bracken reviews chronologically. His evaluation is that the U.S. command and control system for strategic nuclear forces has developed incrementally but successfully in response to unprecedented environmental challenges. Bracken would not contend that there are no remaining problems, but his overview of command/control system development suggests that the arrangements with regard to U.S. strategic forces, viewed in isolation, have become progressively more dependable, although not without risk entirely.

Even so, the command system and the control system for strategic nuclear forces are at loggerheads in several areas, and one has only to follow the examples developed by Bracken (1983), Bruce G. Blair (1985), Desmond J. Ball (1981), and John Steinbruner (1981–1982) to see how this is so. Essentially, the early stages of the control problem were focused on the prevention of accidental or inadvertent war.[3] This problem has now been, relatively speaking, solved, according to the estimates of these and other C^3 experts, although complacency is certainly not warranted. It might be more appropriate to say that purely accidental war is a very remote possibility and inadvertent war not improbable. As Bracken explains, accidental war would involve war that "starts without explicit decisions by responsible leaders, perhaps through misunderstanding, equipment or system failure, or a subordinate's unauthorized action." He also states that accidental/inadvertent war "flows from an escalation process in which each side keeps seeking an edge until the unintended eruption occurs" (Bracken, 1985 p. 29).

ASSESSMENT AND PERFORMANCE

The details of the U.S. strategic and tactical C^3I systems are now better known than even one decade ago. Assessment of the performance of the strategic command and control systems varies with the focus of the analyst. There are several requirements that the U.S. strategic command system might be expected to fulfill: (1) not to invite attack on itself; (2) to respond to surprise attack on tactical warning and inflict devastating societal retaliation; (3) to respond to surprise attack and carry out a coherent retaliation against a comprehensive military target set; and (4) to allow for flexible response and escalation control in order to limit the consequences of theatre or strategic nuclear warfare, and to make possible bargaining toward eventual war termination (Carter, 1987).

According to Ashton B. Carter (1987), the U.S. command system can be expected to fulfill the requirements for no. 2 and no. 4, above, because there are really two different kinds of command systems involved. The first is the one that must be survivable against worst-case surprise attacks and allow for devastating counter-societal retaliation. The second, according to Carter, is the system that would permit flexible nuclear response during a war that was less than total. If war were total, flexible response would be irrelevant; if it were limited, then the central U.S. command system would survive. Thus, the major concern about U.S. capabilities following a surprise attack is whether the Strategic Integrated Operating Plan (SIOP) requirements for retaliation against a comprehensive target set can be accomplished.

This might seem reassuring, but the possibility of errors in decision-making in anticipation of deterrence failure is still strong. Given very little time in the case of tactical warning that attack is possibly under way, political and military leaders will have to optimize between the possibility of Type I and Type II errors (Carter, 1987a). A Type I error is a failure to launch or retaliate when an attack is actually in progress, and Type II is a launch or "retaliation," although no attack is actually taking place. There is no escape from marginal costs which must be paid during alerting procedures in crises. Electronic locks that can be removed only by National Command Authority instructions, as authenticated by the proper codes, control the use of all U.S. nuclear weapons except those based at sea. The system is designed to do nothing unless it is otherwise stimulated, and even then numerous checks and balances are built into it to prevent response. Blair terms this procedure "negative control" in contrast to what he calls "positive control" procedures in which the bureaucratic and electronic "locks" are removed and the forces move from day to day to "generated" alert in which they are poised to retaliate. In other words, the system is turned off most of the time and can only be turned on under very specified conditions, and then not very rapidly as these times are measured in the nuclear age.

The forces themselves can be readied for immediate retaliation if they are land-based missiles, and bombers, given appropriate warning, can disperse and take off. Submarines on patrol would not be vulnerable to Soviet anti-submarine warfare for the foreseeable future. So it is not the case that the forces themselves need more reversible momentum during crises. It is the commanders for those forces whose behavior and expectations it may be more difficult to turn around.

When we say "commanders" we are reminded, of course, that the president of the United States is the constitutional commander-in-chief and would, under normal conditions, give the orders for retaliatory strikes. The problem is that nuclear crisis and war will be anything but "normal conditions," and a well-designed Soviet first strike might take out the president, the secretary of defense, and other Washington principals in the civilian line of succession and military chain of command. Whether these principal commanders, including the president, can be provided with the wherewithal to survive well-planned Soviet surprise attacks is doubtful. The arrangements for the president, for example, have an Alice-in-Wonderland quality: he is to be whisked from Washington aboard a helicopter to a meeting place for transfer to his National Emergency Airborne Command Post (NEACP), which will have taken off from Grissom Air Force Base, Indiana, for the rendezvous (Ford, 1985, pp. 136–37). Neither the NEACP aircraft nor its alternates might escape Soviet submarine-launched ballistic missiles (SLBM) fired off the Atlantic coast against inland targets, including bomber bases.

Destruction of the president and other principals will result, in the midst of attack, in a search for an authenticated successor who will give orders to retaliate. While this search is going on, SAC is either absorbing a Soviet nuclear bombardment without reacting or is, under certain understandings that are not discussed explicitly, retaliating against pre-programmed targets stored in the SIOP. Officials in every administration skirt around this matter because it seems legally dubious to acknowledge that someone other than the president might order the firing of retaliatory forces under certain conditions, but everyone involved understands that it cannot be otherwise. Were it otherwise, the entire system could be locked into inaction by the loss of the head of state. The "control" system must provide for logical and de facto devolution of the capacity to respond to attack, whatever the status of the legal search for a constitutional successor (Bracken, 1987).

The uncertainty surrounding U.S. strategic nuclear devolution adds to its deterrent credibility in Soviet eyes. Because Soviet planners cannot know the exact nature of command devolution and the control arrangements that unlock access to retaliatory forces, they cannot plan with confidence any "decapitation" against the U.S. command and control system. Bracken suggests an analogy between the command/control system and a pistol: the president and National Command Authority (the president, the secretary of defense, and/or their successors in the military chain of command) are the safety catches that hold back retaliation, and their destruction would guarantee that lower level commanders, most probably the commanders-in-chief (CINC) of the various major unified and specified commands, would automatically take control (and the deputies of the CINCs in the case of their destruction, and so forth) (Bracken, 1983, p. 196).

However deterred the Soviets might be, Blair is less sanguine about the probable performance of the command/control system. He argues that we have consistently overrated its survivability by emphasizing force structures, modernization, and traditional deterrence theory. Blair's indictment of deterrence theory bears on later arguments about C^3I and strategy. His pessimism is of immediate concern, and it follows from his assessment that the U.S. strategic command system, not just its physical architecture, has been vulnerable to destruction for some time. Blair is not given to understatement: "Deficiencies in U.S. C^3I systems have been so severe for so long that developments in the size and technical composition of the superpowers' arsenals have been practically irrelevant to the nuclear confrontation" (Blair, 1985, p. 4). Whether deterrence will hold depends in part on Soviet crisis incentives for attacking the U.S. command structure. Pessimism about Soviet interest in early destruction of the U.S. command system is shared by many American analysts, although it would not necessarily be easy for the Soviets to accomplish this against generated or highly alerted U.S. forces. Not only do USSR planners apparently envision counter-command attacks in the early stages of global nuclear war, but also they appear not to recognize any very strong possibility of limiting that war once nuclear weapons have been exchanged against targets in superpower homelands (Ermarth, 1981). Of course, it may well be that we are comparing the perspectives of Soviet military writers, in their "military technical" or operational cast, with U.S. civilian defense analysts who are more concerned with the issue of nuclear diplomacy and escalation control. Nevertheless, some Soviet reciprocation is assumed necessary in foregoing attacks explicitly designed to trump the command system, or, according to the expert assessments of many analysts, the system will probably fail.

The Soviets might believe that we believe our system to be vulnerable, and so conclude that we will preempt rather than wait to strike back. Persuaded of this, the USSR would attempt to preempt our (assumed) preemption, in the fashion of Western gunfighters beating one another to the draw. The problem is not that U.S. policymakers or military leaders are planning for preemptive attacks. Nor is the command/control system so poorly constituted that it cannot provide for Massive Retaliation. The real problem is that one Massive Retaliation against the broadest possible array of targets may be all that the system can do, or that policymakers, given their knowledge of the limits of the system, may want to do.

This last statement contradicts orthodoxy and also has implications for the later discussion of C^3I and strategy, of which more is said below. At this point, it must be noted that every president since John F. Kennedy has called for more numerous, and more fine-tuned, options for the SIOP, in order to escape the proverbial dilemma of "suicide or surrender." It has been U.S. declaratory policy since 1974 that flexible strategic options pre-established in the SIOP will allow for discriminating targeting assignments with low collateral damage, escalation control, and withholding of strategic forces for later tasking if need be (Ball, 1981a). The expectations of policymakers have become more demanding, although the C^{3}I system has had enough to do to meet the basic requirements of assured destruction, involving as is thought primarily large-scale attacks against the USSR economy, industrial infrastructure, and capacity for social recovery. This capability to inflict "unacceptable damage" on Soviet society was once quantified by the Department of Defense as a "metric" to be used for force sizing under McNamara; McNamara's successors, though more reluctant to posit specific numerical criteria, have nevertheless included assured destruction among their necessary conditions for deterrence (Sloss and Millot, 1984).

According to Blair, policymaker's expectations about the capabilities of the command/control system are far removed from its actual capabilities. The gap between expected capabilities and actual capabilities has the potential to turn command misdemeanors into felonies. As Blair explains:

U.S. reaction (to Soviet nuclear attack) could hardly be rational in either the subjective or objective sense. Subjective rationality, in its simplest version, is an attempt to specify objectives, calculate expected payoffs for alternative choices, and select the alternative with the highest payoff. Under conditions of nuclear attack, there would not be enough time and information for a subjectively rational decision process to run its course. The decision process is also unlikely to produce an objectively rational choice. Regardless of what calculations political leaders might make at the time, they would come under intense pressure to choose without delay an option that would provide for all that they would ever expect to accomplish in retaliation to an attack of uncertain dimensions (Blair, 1985, p. 233).

The attack would be of "uncertain dimensions" because U.S. attack assessment capabilities are lacking in peacetime and would be seriously disrupted under the stress of nuclear combat. Bracken discusses at length the differences between peacetime and wartime assessment systems, and Blair notes flatly that

The United States also lacks the capability to perform an independent accurate assessment of the scale and character of a Soviet attack. A selective counterforce attack could not be reliably distinguished from a comprehensive attack because of deficiencies in the U.S. tactical warning and attack assessment system (Blair, 1985, p. 223).

So small attacks cannot reliably be distinguished from large attacks, especially given the abbreviated time lines within which policymakers will have to select a retaliatory option and order the forces to fire. The capabilities–objectives gap has thus widened to the point at which something more sinister than total system failure could occur (sinister, at least, from the standpoint of the tidy world of the analyst). Instead of failing totally, the system could be transformed into some hybrid that would break down and then reestablish itself in unpredictable ways. As Bracken explains:

Disruption of command systems does not necessarily lead to marginal losses in effectiveness; it can lead to a radical transformation of the controllability of a war. In an informationally decentralized nuclear war, authority too will be decentralized. The course of action that will be taken will depend on behavioral details of the isolated players, their weapons, alert status prior to attack, and many other microscopic features of the tactical wars being fought (Bracken, 1983, p. 128).

Disconnected islands of retaliatory capability might be responding to Soviet attacks rather than a centrally directed mechanism. The result might preclude termination of war on any conditions other than exhaustion of the inventories of the participants. Long before then, war would have ceased in the sense of being responsive to policy guidance, and destruction for its own sake would have taken over. This situation is not the result of poor planning or technical stupidity; it is, according to Bracken, inherent in the character of large and complex organizations of certain kinds, which are prone to what Charles Perrow has termed "normal accidents"(Perrow, 1984). Normal accidents are those which system complexity and system-environment relations, under certain conditions, make inevitable, although we can only see this after the fact (nuclear power plants providing an excellent illustration). Notice how this concern differs from the classical concern, noted earlier, of "accidental" war, which results from the more simplistic failure of individual components (in the case of NORAD computers, a failed computer chip which provoked temporarily false warnings of attack) (Pringle and Arkin, 1983). Perrow's concept, applied to Bracken's, Blair's, and Ball's descriptions of the strategic C³I system, is more subtle. The system may be unknowingly "designed " to fail given the right combination of unexpected and simultaneous perturbations.

SOVIET AND U.S. STRATEGY

Presumably, the business of war has something to do with strategy, and strategy, with objectives and methods of the opponent. With rare exceptions, the Soviet adversary appears in very amorphous or stylized garb. This is not because major effort is not being expended by government and other analysts to unravel Soviet strategic approaches. Instead, it is in the nature of Western culture not to appreciate the subtleties of others, especially as this lack of appreciation relates to questions of strategy (Booth, 1979). Some very important work at the RAND Strategy Assessment Center is now attempting to introduce modular "Ivans" and "Sams" into models of competitive interaction under varying conditions of superpower conflict (Davis and Stan, 1984). Until this and other avant garde work is developed further, we will have to do with stereotypic Soviets (although some stereotypes are more convincing than others).

Soviet "military doctrine" conveys the party-political authoritative guidance about the kinds of wars the USSR would expect to fight and about who its opponents are likely to be. This military doctrine moves in surface and sub-surface currents, much in the manner of ocean tides. The surface movements have to do with "high politics" as we might say in the West, while the sub-surface movements have a military-technical cast. This contrast between the political and military-technical levels of Soviet writing on military affairs creates problems of interpretation for Western analysts. To mention one very pertinent problem, it has led to spirited debates in the United States over whether the USSR, as Richard Pipes has alleged, thinks that it can "fight and win" a nuclear war (Pipes, 1977; see also Arnett, 1979). Raymond L. Garthoff puts this concern into a broader perspective:

In its political, or war versus peace, policy dimension, military doctrine was thus moving *away* from questions of waging war to place greater stress on preventing war, although its military-technical or war-fighting component continued to emphasize preparedness to wage war decisively, and with a particular accent on offensive operations and on being prepared to wage all-out warfare if nuclear war should come (Garthoff, 1985, p. 780).

Garthoff is summarizing recent trends in the development of Soviet military thinking and pointing toward what is apparently inconsistent from the Western perspective, but actually consistent when perceived through Soviet lenses. The political leadership is expected to attain Soviet objectives without war if it can; if it cannot, the USSR will prosecute the war omnivorously until the enemy coalition is defeated.

Should they perceive that war might be forced on them, the Soviets prefer, according to Stephen M. Meyer, a combination of preemption with active and passive defenses in order to obtain as much damage limitation as possible (Meyer, 1985a). They are realistically pessimistic about what happens after deterrence fails. According to John Erickson, "there is implicit recognition that rapid and total escalation is the most likely contingency arising from any so-called 'limited' war, speedily involving the full range of U.S. strategic capabilities" (Erickson, 1986, p. 174). This might be a very logical conclusion for them to draw, given NATO strategy of relying on extended nuclear deterrence to compensate for NATO-Pact disparities in conventional forces. Further pertinent to the interaction of the U.S. and Soviet command systems, Soviet and American views on the matter of surprise attack are based on very different frames of reference. Most U.S. analysts and policymakers have preferred models of deterrence and arms control, which emphasize offensive retaliation as the necessary and sufficient condition for stability. The Soviet perspective is that one cannot rely on offenses alone; active and passive defenses are prudent hedges against the failure of deterrence (Sienkiewicz, 1981).[4] Above all, cautions John Erickson, "after the near catastrophe of June, 1941 when German armies were launched against the Soviet Union, it is inconceivable that any Soviet leadership will countenance absorbing any initial strike" (Erickson, 1986, p. 173).[5]

This brings us to the question of what, given these Soviet perceptions, the

U.S. strategy ought to be, and where the command and control system fits into plausible U.S. deterrence and denial capabilities. Unfortunately, life has not been fair to U.S. strategic planners. Especially since the promulgation of NSDM-242 in 1974 and until the present, U.S. policy planners and secretaries of defense have struggled to create multiple and more subtle options for the use of U.S. strategic offensive forces. But all of this has apparently rested on a command and control system that cannot support it. Such a verdict would produce immediate disagreement from the Reagan administration, which has invested substantial sums in improvements which may be welcome if they improve the near-term survivability of the U.S. strategic C^3I system. But they will not change the improbability of the system supporting controlled or protracted strategic nuclear war (Blair, 1985, p. 287). This seems "unfair" because former Secretary of Defense James R. Schlesinger and others made very strong cases, at the level of logical abstraction, for more numerous and more refined strategic options, in order to improve the probability of terminating nuclear war before it escalated out of control.

Improved strategic logic will not change the limitations on the command system, and neither will technical fixes alter it fundamentally. For the system is required to do very different things which, in times of crisis, might be contradictory. It is supposed to prevent accidental or unauthorized launch of the strategic forces when policymakers want them leashed, and it is supposed to guarantee prompt Flexible Response when called on to do so. But no system can be designed that gets around human beings and their limitations in trying to decide which of these very important goals to optimize during the twilight zone of a crisis. Under two very different circumstances, there is no tension. The first is normal peacetime conditions and the second a premeditated Soviet "bolt from the blue" with no immediate provocation. As different as these conditions are in their historical and political consequences, they are similar in that neither stresses the command system in the most important way. Neither unambiguous peace nor unambiguous war requires that the system *synthesize* rather than *optimize*. A crisis involving the *possibility* of a Soviet attack but one that is far from a certainty, and one that depends partially on what *we* do, maximizes the push me–pull you which can tear the system, and its highest level commanders, apart. This is how commanders of nuclear forces differ from commanders of other forces in the past: they are equally desirous of avoiding war and not being defeated in war because the consequences of superpower nuclear war so heavily outweigh any foreseeable benefits.

The command system is not built for synthesizing under these conditions. It has had no experience with sustained high-level alerts, or with mutual Soviet and American alerts. It cannot rob Peter to pay Paul without endangering both. Bracken explains this dilemma effectively: "What is ironic, however, is that the price paid for the redundancy of checks and balances intended to dampen the strong dynamics within the forces has been a corresponding increase in the system's peacetime vulnerability to surprise attack" (Bracken, 1983, p. 73). The implications for U.S. strategy can be seen if we presume four generic types of strategy for the deterrence of strategic nuclear war: retaliation only; countervailing strategies; prevailing strategies; and defense-dominant strategies. It might be worthwhile to consider which, among these generic options, the command system could most plausibly support. This will allow us to draw final conclusions about the implications of C^3I for U.S. strategy and force posture.

With some necessary injustice to the nuances, we may say that *retaliation only* strategies correspond to reliance on countervalue retaliatory capabilities which are survivable against enemy preemption and capable of inflicting "unacceptable" damage to the opponent's society. *Countervailing* and *prevailing* strategies are more demanding. Countervailing strategies, as they were described during the Carter administration, call for denying the opponent his objectives by deploying counterforce capabilities sufficient to match, or overmatch, his own. The United States should be able to avoid being disarmed in counterforce exchanges and to preserve enough residual power to hold at risk Soviet military and command targets (Slocombe, 1981; for an opposing view, see Jervis, 1984). Both the capacity to fight the prompt counterforce war and the capacity to preserve residual capacity to hold at risk the social and economic assets of the opponent are presumed.

Prevailing strategies are more demanding still. Prevailing strategies would require U.S. offensive capabilities sufficient to "win" counterforce exchanges (ending up with favorable firepower ratios) and to deny Soviet attackers access to important U.S. and NATO allied targets, including retaliatory forces and command centers.[6] Prevailing strategies require more capable strategic offensive forces than we now have, as well as some active defenses for retaliatory forces and (perhaps) portions of the society (Office of Technology Assessment, 1985). *Defense-dominant* strategies would, following the "strategic concept" of the Reagan administration, gradually substitute very competent defenses for reductions in strategic offenses until deterrence stability was based on mutual assured survival rather than offensive retaliation (Nitze, 1985).

These alternative strategies may be more hypothetical than real, from the perspective of what the command and control system can be expected to do. The countervailing strategy was the declaratory strategy of the Carter administration, but Carter lacked the forces or the C^3I to implement it. By the time he left office, the United States had a de facto strategy which was "retaliation only" combined with flexible targeting.[7] The Reagan administration initially made noises in the direction of prevailing strategies, or at least prevailing slogans. The actual Reagan strategy was to attempt to provide the forces and other components for the Carter countervailing strategy, although the U.S. Congress made its own decisions about MX/Peacekeeper deployment which left the actual strategy unclear. Since March 23, 1983, the Reagan declaratory strategy has been defense dominance, although there is some evidence that this strategy falls short of enthusiastic reception among Pentagon planners who must focus on near-term threats and budgets.

Now the irony is that, among these strategies, only the defense-dominant strategy, if it could be made to work, might improve the survivability and performance of the strategic C^3I system so that it could fulfill the minimum requirements of assured destruction (retaliation only). Comparatively weakened offensive forces, stronger and presumably non-nuclear defenses, and improved space-based reconnaissance and warning which would follow any Ballistic Missile Defense (BMD) deployments might all combine to provide survivability for U.S. (and Soviet) strategic C^3I systems.[8] For this to take place, more elaborate U.S.-Soviet arms control agreements than heretofore possible will be required. Short of that, one can imagine various "confidence-building measures" which would, in the near term, reduce the risks of accidental or unintended superpower war, such as the Nuclear Risk Reduction Centers proposed by Senators Sam Nunn and John Warner (Betts, 1985; Appendix A, 1985).

The difficulty with this prescription for defense-dominant command survivability, is that there is no such thing as a defense-dominant world except in a tautological sense. Neither superpower can do without any forces for offensive retaliation, so the real issue will be the balance of offensive forces remaining under the defensive umbrellas. Here we confront a paradox. The smaller the absolute number of offensive weapons on both sides, the more precarious the balance of relative capabilities, because very small changes can make a great deal of relative difference. Now proponents of defenses might object that all the calculations change when defense is stronger than offense, and that post-attack balances of offensive warheads no longer matter. But it will be hard to convince military planners and statesmen of this, especially those in Moscow, because the defense systems will never be tested realistically until war actually occurs.[9] Thus, the expectation that the USSR can be talked into doing away with a substantial investment in offensive retaliatory forces is misplaced, and it is probably misplaced for the United States as well, unless the U.S. Air Force is somehow reorganized out of business (Meyer, 1985b).

The low likelihood of superpower offensive disarmament in favor of defensive supremacy is due not only to lack of trust and experience with a defense-dominant world, but also to the difference in their defense requirements. The United States is the principal alliance partner in a heterogeneous coalition of NATO governments which rely at least partially on our willingness to *initiate* the use of nuclear weapons to deter conventional war in Europe. This coupling among U.S. strategic, U.S./NATO theatre nuclear, and NATO conventional forces is the essence of Flexible Response strategy. The command and control problems attendant to crisis stability for war in Europe make those which we have so far been discussing seem comparatively innocuous. Nuclear forces in Europe are interspersed with conventional general-purpose forces and are not in the hands of commanders and command organizations specifically designed for nuclear forces. Bracken's discussion of the consequences of this arrangement is guaranteed to keep any reader attentive. Although NATO depends on European and U.S.-based nuclear forces to deter Soviet aggression and to help defeat any attacks if need be, it is unlikely that NATO can control the forces it has deployed during crisis, and almost impossible after war begins. NATO nuclear use may seem plausible to the Soviets not because they have faith in our control but because they anticipate our loss of it:

> If it is desirable to ensure that a nuclear war is triggered, a fully controllable, invulnerable force may be positively undesirable, because employment of such a force would depend upon a rational decision to execute the threat. In the face of the suicidal consequences of a war in Europe, it is easy to see why a rational political leader would never take steps leading to devastation. What is needed instead of a rational procedure for going to war is a posture that is so complex that war could be triggered in any of a number of different ways without rational control (Bracken, 1983, pp. 163–64).

Bracken is articulating the European perspective on theatre nuclear warfare via his own insights into the command system. What it amounts to is: since we cannot control it, the Russians will be afraid of it. Perhaps they will, but this is surely an ironical destination for the C^3I improvement programs of the past decade. The potential for loss of control may not be deterring to the Russians, but provoking, or inviting to them.

In this regard, it is noteworthy that the latest issue of the Pentagon's threat assessment, *Soviet Military Power,* contains the following carefully crafted statement about Soviet views of nuclear war: "However, Soviet military forces have taken actions and exhibited behavior which indicate that they believe a nuclear war could be fought and won at levels *below general nuclear war"* (U.S. Department of Defense, 1986). This may have something to do with greater U.S. appreciation of nuances in Soviet doctrine, including some more explicit recognition by them of the consequences of a U.S.-USSR strategic war (see the last section of this chapter).

It is even more likely that the Office of Net Assessment and others have been looking carefully at Soviet conventional and nuclear capabilities for theatre warfare in Europe, and that what they are discovering is not reassuring for NATO. Soviet capabilities for a short, decisive conventional attack against West Germany, the Low Countries, and/or Denmark and Norway have grown considerably during the past decade. Rapid Soviet and Pact advances would be made possible by "a massive air operation to paralyze NATO's air, air defense, theater nuclear, and command and control capabilities and by an amphibious operation to secure the Danish straits" (U.S. Department of Defense, 1986, p. 60; see also Donnelly, 1983, Hines and Peterson, 1983, and Dick, 1985). The same Soviet attackers would have the benefit, in wartime, of what the Pentagon estimates to be "a robust and survivable command system featuring numerous hardened, fixed and mobile command posts; a dense communications network providing redundant channels between command posts; and extensive camouflage, concealment, and deception" (U.S. Department of Defense, 1984, p. 60; see also Hemsley, 1982).

Certainly, the Pentagon is in the business of making the Soviets appear very well prepared for all kinds of wars, but other analyses confirm the growth of Soviet conventional capabilities for war in Europe and the increased sophistication of their doctrines for using those capabilities.[10] Moreover, Soviet forces are apparently prepared for rapid transition to theatre nuclear warfare, and for preemption of NATO short- or long-range theatre nuclear forces should they perceive preparations for launching those forces (Hampsen, 1985). Complicating things further, NATO defensive measures taken to assure survivability of its theatre nuclear forces and C^3I assets might provoke the preemption they are designed to prevent. In other words, the problems of command vulnerability in Europe are so acute that NATO C^3I may be destroyed by Soviet conventional attacks and NATO escalation deterred by superior Soviet theatre nuclear forces, and equivalent (to U.S.) strategic forces.

If NATO is indeed vulnerable to C^3I suppression by Soviet conventional forces, then the balance of firepower ratios on the Central Front may matter less than the balance of command vulnerabilities. U.S. strategic command and control may be the residual rather than the central problem. Not only U.S. retaliatory forces are "coupled" to defense of Western Europe, but also the command and control system for guaranteeing responsive use of those forces. Under current conditions flexible and responsive use of those U.S. strategic forces cannot be assumed. Meanwhile, NATO's C^3I system is perhaps vulnerable to imminent destruction without nuclear weapons, and NATO has lost the "escalation dominance" needed to compensate for that, if any compensation is possible.

Thus, the final chapter of the C^3I *Lord of the Rings* could be a defeat if the system solves the wrong problem (of Soviet strategic surprise attack disconnected from conflict elsewhere). Inadequate conventional forces and dubiously survivable theatre C^3I could bring down the entire house. Worse still, NATO weaknesses in conventional forces could invite the attacks against the U.S. strategic C^3I system which would otherwise not occur; once war in Europe began, it would be difficult for policymakers to impose any limitations on it. As war in Europe escalated, superpowers desperate for a way out could reason that a *coup de main* against the brain of the enemy was their only hope. Vulnerable strategic command and control systems would make both sides take this possibility more seriously, and thus encourage a crisis slide toward mutual preemption.[11]

Instead of searching for C^3I technologies that can endure for protracted nuclear wars, we might better invest our money in protecting theatre C^3I in Europe and in improving those conventional forces which at the moment only delay Soviet attackers until nuclear detonations can be authorized. The distinction between "command" and "control" seen from this perspective could not be more important. Without credible conventional denial forces at their command, NATO planners are depending on a fragile system of control in order to terminate any war before it expands into unlimited countersocietal destruction. This creates the gap between deterrence and reassurance to which Michael Howard has so effectively pointed:

The object of deterrence is to persuade an adversary that the costs to him of seeking a military solution to his political problems will far outweigh the benefits. The object of reassurance is to persuade one's own people, and those of one's allies, that the benefits of military action, or preparation for it, will outweigh the costs (Howard, 1984, p. 256).

Fixing the technical components of the C^3I problem receives no dissent here; it is the attainment of alliance consensus on conventional denial capabilities necessary for credible deterrence that is in doubt. The United States neither commands nor controls in an alliance of democratic societies, only bargains.

UNFINISHED BUSINESS

The foregoing discussion suggests a future research agenda. Broadly speaking, the following general areas need further study and explication, if the above arguments are taken as indicative of underformulated issues.

First, it would seem that U.S.-Soviet crisis behavior is dependent not only on the efficacy of U.S. C^3I but also on the Soviet command and control system. This is so in the physical sense that attacks on the Soviet control system might render it more difficult for them to prosecute the war, or to seek war termination on terms favorable to the West. There is a perverse interaction between Soviet and U.S. C^3 capabilities here, of two sorts. First, the physical destruction of either side's command network could make continued warfighting impossible, thus creating a temptation to do so in the event that deterrence fails. Second, destruction of the opponent's command structure and strategic communications is to be avoided if U.S. or Soviet policymakers hope to establish post-attack control over their military forces and war termination (see Bracken, 1983; Gray, 1979, 1984).

This dilemma is related to the expectation of the decision-makers on each side during crises about the reliability of "positive" versus "negative" control over nuclear forces and commanders, as previously noted. It would be counterproductive to lock the U.S. nuclear response system too tightly, but it must be locked sufficiently so that it cannot be unlocked by accident or by inadvertence. Nuclear alerts should not cause nuclear wars, but they should contribute to deterrence by convincing our opponents that we mean what we say. The willingness to move forces to higher levels of alert is part of the bargaining process in which nuclear weapons are some of the components, along with alerts of conventional forces, diplomatic signals, and public pronouncements with hidden agendas that are to be picked up and understood by the other side.

We know distressingly little, however, about how Soviet C^3 operates in peacetime, and even less about how it would operate during a serious U.S.-Soviet nuclear crisis (see Ball, 1983, 1985). The Kremlin if faced with a crisis it had not anticipated, such as an outbreak in Eastern Europe which haphazardly spilled over into NATO territory, might be improvising.[12] Soviet behavior during and prior to the invasion of Czechoslovakia in 1968 and in Poland in 1980–1981 showed great reluctance to implement the "Brezhnev doctrine" as well as extreme sensitivity to the possibility of Western overreaction. It would be reasonable to suppose that Soviet C^3 hardware and software lag behind those of the United States, which may not be a blessing given the interdependency of the superpowers' control systems during serious crises. But offsetting the Soviets' apparent inferiority on the technical side is their serious commitment to protect their political and military leadership from the effects of war, including nuclear war.[13] Whatever Soviet expectations about "fighting and winning" nuclear wars may be assumed to be, they are not expecting to rely for the survival of their leadership on reciprocal targeting restraint. This may be prudent given the purported tasking of U.S. SIOP forces to attack Soviet command targets.

The above leads naturally enough into a second set of matters. This second set might be termed the Soviet understanding, compared to the Western one, of crisis management, escalation control, and intrawar deterrence. We are using the Western terminology in each case, for which there may exist no explicit Russian transliteration. Colin S. Gray, among others, has charged that U.S. concepts of crisis management and escalation control are ethnocentric and have little or no meaning to those in the Politburo or the *Stavka* who will make war and peace decisions. In addition, his judgment about the results of U.S. policymaking, having allegedly profited from the infusion of crisis management concepts, is not favorable:

Although there should be policy value in wisdom derived from the careful historical study of statecraft and from a high-level theory of crisis management, the fact remains that the U.S. record of crisis management prior to the enunciation of crisis management theory was not obviously inferior to the postenunciation record (Gray, 1986, p. 180).

Even if we assume that the United States has its act together on crisis management and the control of escalation after war begins, it is not clear that the Soviet leadership will understand its crisis or wartime objectives in the same way. Now this needs to be carefully stated, since there is substantial evidence that the USSR is extremely cautious about getting into wars and relies on the competent diplomacy of its politicians to avoid war without sacrificing vital interests. However, once engaged in a U.S.-Soviet war, even a conventional war, the USSR would be unlikely to express optimism that it could be controlled and would prepare for the worst. It would be imprudent for U.S. planners to assume that the USSR would observe thresholds or restraints on escalation which seemed obvious or "salient" to their Western counterparts, unless it were advantageous for the Soviet leadership to do so for reasons of tactical or strategic advantage (Lambeth, 1984; see also Meyer, 1987).

As Fritz W. Ermarth has pointed out, Soviet military doctrine does not suggest to their planners that post-war outcomes can necessarily be inferred correctly from pre-war force balances alone. The "correlation of forces" before and during war as perceived by the Kremlin includes a more elaborate matrix of perceptions and expectations about both sides' economic potential, social cohesion, and other variables (Ermarth, 1981). Having decided on war, under the assumption that Soviet leadership (through its conceptual lenses) felt that war was forced on them, Soviet pessimism about escalation control can be safely assumed. War between NATO and the Warsaw Pact would, after all, be about the post-war balance of power in Europe, at a minimum. It is difficult to conceive of a Soviet leadership that would view such a conflict through a prism of Marxist-Leninist concepts as anything other than compulsively pessimistic about keeping nuclear weapons out or limiting their use once they were introduced.

Fundamental to the assumptions that Soviet leaders might make about the controllability of nuclear alerts or limited strategic or theatre nuclear war is the Soviet view of the relationship between war and policy. At this level of grand strategy, the USSR might envision a coupling between deterrence and warfighting policy which is at variance with the Western tendency to separate the two.[14] Of course, it must be remembered that Western nuclear strategy is more frequently the product of civilian analysts, whose writings are then compared with those of Soviet marshals in order to arrive at the remarkable discovery that they differ. U.S. military writers discussing military operations are as frequently disinterested in the refinements of escalation control and crisis management theory as are Soviet military writers.

However, there is the significant difference between the Soviet expectation that wars are not politically meaningless, including nuclear wars, and the Western assumption that nuclear war between superpowers would have no political purpose. The difference between these modal points of view can be misstated. Soviet leaders are not optimistic about the consequences of nuclear war should it occur, nor about its controllability. But they do not believe that wars have *apolitical causes*. Thus, a U.S.-Soviet major conventional or nuclear war, especially in Europe, will be "about" something, and Kremlin leaders may well conclude that it is "about" the post-war survival of their imperial control.

Thus, U.S. and other NATO assumptions about distinct firebreaks between conventional, theatre nuclear, and strategic nuclear force engagement may not be perceived as important by Soviet antagonists, compared to other lines of demarcation. The first of these, from the Soviet perspective, is the outbreak of war in *Europe,* as opposed to war outside Europe, however menacing to other Soviet assets. Conflict in Europe, East or West, poses an implicit (and perhaps explicit) threat of German unification under unfriendly auspices and the rebirth of revolt in Eastern Europe. The second threshold which may be more important to the USSR is whether its own homeland, compared to assets of its allies, is attacked. Some analysts have suggested that the USSR might conceive of a theatre nuclear war which did not escalate into a strategic exchange, provided weapons exploded on European rather than Soviet soil. Soviet interest in limited nuclear options for war in Europe has been one result of their growing capabilities in strategic and theatre nuclear forces, according to some studies.[15]

A third matter of unfinished business is war termination. After a long period of disinterest, this subject is now receiving renewed attention (see Ikle, 1971; Cimbala, 1986; Cimbala and Dunn, 1987). The U.S. Maritime Strategy as publicly proclaimed in the January 1986 issue of *Proceedings of the U.S. Naval Institute* elevates war termination to the status of principal objectives (Watkins, 1986). However, few have contended that war termination of a superpower nuclear exchange can or should be expected. The issue will not go away, because the alternative to strategic war termination, after deterrence fails, is unprecedented societal destruction. The Kremlin cannot view the prospect of societal destruction very favorably regardless of the fate of its military forces and commanders. A "successful" series of exchanges with the United States would leave the Soviet Union as the second most important economy in the Communist orbit, at best, and no longer the cynosure of Marxism. Soviet capabilities for the wartime survival of their leadership and heavy industry might also provide some incentive to save what they could before leadership control disintegrated and resources were reduced to rubble. Although U.S. commentators have for the most part failed to notice it, the USSR's most acute vulnerability is the possibility of an end to its food supply. Western post-attack leverage in this regard might be substantial (as it was following World War I).

These judgments are admittedly speculative. The alternative to war termination, on the other hand, is all too clear. It is the mutual exhaustion of both participants and the destruction of two ways of life. But making the abstract case for war termination does not make it easier to bring about. The survivability of U.S. and Soviet C³I through the early phases of war is judged doubtful by many experts. Although much as been made of the probable cohesion of wartime Soviet leadership and plans for its survival, this cohesion and planning must be seen in perspective. A so-called limited strategic war, which was then terminated, would offer the Kremlin some substantial dividends for having made such thorough preparations, assuming for purposes of discussion that this "limited strategic war" might be fought against the Chinese as well as NATO. A protracted nuclear war against the West is another matter. No convincing evidence has been presented that either superpower can sustain a protracted nuclear war for many months; statements in U.S. declaratory policy to this effect are merely fig leaves to cover the real deficiencies in C^3I for survivability (Blair, 1985, p. 181). Although the USSR might according to Marxist dogma insist that all wars, including nuclear wars, can be fought to victory, Soviet political leaders have shown marked propensity for taking the risk-averse advice of their military planners. On the occasions when they did not, history has not been kind.

A fourth and final matter of unfinished business reminds us that the subject of command and control is not limited to the arcana of nuclear strategy. This topic is the application of command and control to amorphous wars in the Third World. This writer has suggested the term *amorphous wars* to describe those that commingle conventional and unconventional military and paramilitary tactics; political and military objectives that might shift during the course of the conflict; and a process of escalation during which the crossing of a boundary from one stage to another is not clear. Vietnam was an example of an amorphous war; the protracted struggles between Israel and its state and state-less opponents is another. Perhaps the problem of terrorism fits the description of an amorphous war, seen from the U.S. perspective when that perspective avoids the worst excesses of ethnocentrism. Various wars which fall into the category of low-intensity conflict fit the description of amorphous wars.

If Vietnam is illustrative, and it may be a worst case, the problems of command and control could not have been more acute. Although the United States had all the technological advantages compared to its opponents, it could not bring them to bear in order to achieve anything resembling a sensible political objective. Information was dumped in large quantities on policymakers and field commanders but was infrequently subjected to the kinds of analysis that would be useful to them. The age of automation made the problem worse. Proliferation of computerized data bases resulted in clogs in communication channels and confusion between management and command (Van Creveld, 1985). As Robert Komer has noted, what was missing in Vietnam was either theatre or strategic unity of command. As Komer explains:

Looking back, one is struck by how often we Americans in particular did the thing that we had the most readily available capability to do, whether or not it was the most relevant. Whatever overall policy called for, the means available tended to dictate what we actually did (Komer, 1986, p. 16).

Thus materialized a gap between policy and performance; the policy could not be implemented, whatever its character. Elsewhere in his study, Komer illustrates that we have much to learn about the issue of command and control for low-intensity and other wars. North Vietnam had unity of command and the United States and South Vietnamese ran separate political and military conflicts, within and between their command hierarchies. In other words, the North Vietnamese understood that command is something more than C³I technology or management. It is fundamentally strategic, and its test of success or failure is in combat or in deterrence of combat.

Hence the most inclusive research agenda requires that we keep straight the topics of command, leadership, and management. Command is charged with the performance of military combat missions or war preparedness in peacetime. Political leadership should provide clear objectives for commanders and not task them for "missions impossible" given their resources and the character of the American political process. Management has to do with the control of resources and their cost-effective use in support of command and leadership objectives. Keeping all of this straight on paper is easier than doing it in practice, and armchair strategists do not carry the burdens of combat commanders and force planners. Nevertheless, there is nothing wrong with thinking clearly on the basis of good and bad historical experience, while admitting to past mistakes (academic and applied) and getting on with the job.

NOTES

1. For important studies of surprise, see Knorr and Morgan, 1983.

2. This is acknowledged by Senators Goldwater and Nunn in *Armed Forces Journal International,* 1985.

3. Accidental war results from technical failure of individual components of a system or unpredictable human error. Inadvertent war is the result of a process in which crises escape control. See Bracken, 1985.

4. The survival of second-strike forces was the decisive issue for most U.S. strategists; stability depended on preserving the capability for offensive retaliation. The Soviet perspective emphasized defenses in case deterrence failed. Thus, the United States drew more of a distinction between deterrence and defense than the USSR, primarily because of the influence of civilian strategists. See Kaplan, 1983.

5. Western pragmatic strategists may not always appreciate the richness of Soviet military thought. Consider the Soviet view on whether wars can have *apolitical causes* (they cannot) and the Soviet view of the political utility of war (it depends on the war). Thus, a war that is politically caused may have no political utility. This apparent contradiction is actually quite consistent with the Aristotelian distinction between formal and efficient causes.

6. The Office of Technology Assessment distinguishes between strategies of (1) retaliation only; (2) countervailing; (3) prevailing; and (4) defense dominance. They see the Reagan strategy as countervailing, once defined by Harold Brown as ensuring for the USSR that "no course of aggression by them that led to the use of nuclear

weapons, on any scale of attack and at any stage of conflict, could lead to victory, however they may define victory" (Office of Technology Assessment, 1985, p. 77).

7. Colin Gray (1984a, pp. 71–72) describes current U.S. policy as "counterforce and countercontrol preeminence with recovery denial."

8. Even primitive BMD systems can be anti-satellite weapons (ASATs), and ASATs could attack other ASATs which would make them defensive anti-satellite weapons (DSATS). See Office of Technology Assessment, 1985.

9. Especially problematical is reliance on software untested under realistic conditions. See Lin, 1985.

10. Of course, there is a gap between technically possible capabilities and those achieved in combat. The Soviet forces at the tactical level may not be up to the demands of high-speed, fluid operations.

11. In addition, cognitive processes in crisis are vulnerable to a variety of pathologies. See Jervis, 1984b.

12. My favorite scenario is a defecting platoon or squad from Soviet forces in Germany that crosses the border and resists attempts to forcibly return it.

13. The Soviets emphasize using surprise during conventional war in Europe to disrupt NATO command and control. See Betts, 1982, p. 208.

14. In the United States, warfighting capabilities have been seen as prompt counterforce capabilities. The USSR knows that warfighting involves more than silo busting. See Erickson, 1986.

15. I am grateful for having been able to review an unpublished paper on this topic by Notra Trulock III.

REFERENCES

Appendix A: A Nuclear Risk Reduction System. 1985. In Barry M. Blechman ed., *Preventing Nuclear War*. Bloomington: Indiana University Press.

Armed Forces Journal International. 1985. October.

Arnett, Robert L. 1979. Soviet Attitudes Toward Nuclear War: Do They Really Think They Can Win? *Journal of Strategic Studies* 2, no. 2 (September):172–91.

Ball, Desmond J. 1981a. Can Nuclear War Be Controlled? *Adelphi Papers*, no. 169. London: International Institution for Strategic Studies.

———. 1981b. Counterforce Targeting: How New: How Viable? *Arms Control Today* (February), as reprinted with revisions in John F. Reichart and Steven R. Sturm, eds., *American Defense Policy*. Baltimore: Johns Hopkins University Press, pp. 227–34.

———. 1983. Soviet Strategic Planning and Control of Nuclear War. Reference Paper No. 109, Strategic and Defense Studies Centre, Australian National University.

———. 1985. *The Soviet Strategic Command, Control, Communications and Intelligence (CI) System*. Canberra: Strategic and Defence Studies Centre, Australian National University.

———. 1986. Toward a Critique of Strategic Nuclear Targeting. Pp. 15–32 in Desmond Ball and Jeffrey Richelson, eds., *Strategic Nuclear Targeting*. Ithaca, N.Y.: Cornell University Press.

Betts, Richard K. 1982. *Surprise Attack: Lessons for Defense Planning*. Washington, D.C.: Brookings Institution.

————. 1985. A Joint Nuclear Risk Control Center. Pp. 65–85 in Barry M. Blechman, ed., *Preventing Nuclear War,* Bloomington: Indiana University Press.

Blair, Bruce G. 1985. *Strategic Command and Control: Redefining the Nuclear Threat.* Washington D.C.: Brookings Institution.

Booth, Ken. 1979. *Strategy and Ethnocentrism.* London: Croom, Helm.

Bracken, Paul. 1983. *The Command and Control of Nuclear Forces.* New Haven, Conn.: Yale University Press.

————. 1985. Accidental Nuclear War. Pp. 25–53 in Graham Allison et al., eds., *Hawks, Doves and Owls: An Agenda for Avoiding Nuclear War.* New York: W. W. Norton.

————. 1987. Delegation of Nuclear Command Authority. Pp. 352–72 in Ashton Carter et al., eds., *Managing Nuclear Operations.* Washington, D.C.: Brookings Institution.

Carter, Ashton B. 1987a. Assessing Command System Vulnerability. Pp. 555–610 in Carter et al., eds., *Managing Nuclear Operations.* Washington, D.C.: Brookings Institution.

————. 1987b. Sources of Error and Uncertainty. Pp. 611–39 in Carter et al., eds., *Managing Nuclear Operations.* Washington, D.C.: Brookings Institution.

Cimbala, Stephen J., ed. 1986. *Strategic War Termination.* New York: Praeger.

————, and Keith A. Dunn, eds. 1987. *Conflict Termination and Military Strategy.* Boulder, Colo.: Westview Press.

Davis, Paul K., and Peter J. E. Stan. 1984. *Concepts and Models of Escalation.* Santa Monica, Calif.: RAND.

Dick, Charles J. 1985. Soviet Operational Concepts: Part 1. *Military Review* 65, no. 9 (September):29–45.

Donnelly, Christopher N. 1983. Soviet Operational Concepts in the 1980s. Pp. 105–36 in *Strengthening Conventional Deterrence in Europe: Proposals for the 1980s,* Report of the European Security Study Group. New York: St. Martin's Press.

Erickson, John. 1986. The Soviet View of Deterrence: A General Survey. In John B. Harris and Erik Markusen, eds., *Nuclear Weapons and the Threat of Nuclear War.* New York: Harcourt Brace Jovanovich.

Ermarth, Fritz W. 1981. Contrasts in American and Soviet Strategic Thought. In Derek Leebaert, ed., *Soviet Military Thinking.* London: Allen and Unwin.

Ford, Daniel. 1985. *The Button.* New York: Simon and Schuster.

Garthoff, Raymond L. 1985. *Detente and Confrontation.* Washington, D.C.: Brookings Institution.

Godson, Roy, ed. 1983. *Intelligence Requirements for the 1980s: Elements of Intelligence.* New Brunswick, N.J.: Transaction Books.

Gray, Colin S. 1979. Nuclear Strategy: A Case for a Theory of Victory. *International Security* 4, no. 1 (Summer):54–87.

————. 1984a. Warfighting for Deterrence. In Stephen J. Cimbala, ed., *National Security Strategy.* New York.: Praeger.

————. 1984b. *Nuclear Strategy and Strategic Planning.* Philadeliphia: Foreign Policy Research Institute.

————. 1986. *Nuclear Strategy and National Style.* Lanham, Md.: Hamilton Press.

Hampsen, Fen Osler. 1985. Escalation in Europe. Pp. 80–114 in Graham Allison et al., eds., *Hawks, Doves and Owls: An Agenda for Avoiding Nuclear War.* New York: W. W. Norton.

Hemsley, John. 1982. *Soviet Troop Control: The Role of Command Technology in the Soviet Military System*. Oxford: Brassey's Publishers Limited.

Hines, John G., and Philip A. Peterson. 1983. The Warsaw Pact Strategic Offensive: The OMG in Context. *International Defense Review* (October):1391–95.

Howard, Michael. 1984. *The Causes of Wars*. Cambridge, Mass.: Harvard University Press.

Huntington, Samuel P. 1957. *The Soldier and the State*. Cambridge, Mass.: Belknap Press for Harvard University Press.

Ikle, Fred Charles. 1971. *Every War Must End*. New York: Columbia University Press.

Jervis, Robert. 1984a. *The Illogic of American Nuclear Strategy*. Ithaca, N.Y.: Cornell University Press.

———. 1984b. Deterrence and Perception. Pp. 57–84 in Steven E. Miller, ed., *Strategy and Nuclear Deterrence*. Princeton, N.J.: Princeton University Press.

Kaplan, Fred. 1983. *The Wizards of Armageddon*. New York: Simon and Schuster/ Touchstone Books.

Knorr, Klaus, and Patrick Morgan. 1983. *Strategic Military Surprise*. New Brunswick, N.J.: Transaction Books.

Komer, Robert W. 1986. *Bureaucracy at War*. Boulder, Colo.: Westview Press.

Lambeth, Benjamin S. 1984. On Thresholds in Soviet Military Thought. Pp. 173–82 in William J. Taylor et al., *Strategic Responses to Conflict in the 1980s*. Lexington, Mass.: D.C. Heath.

Lin, Herbert. 1985. The Development of Software for Ballistic Missile Defense. *Scientific American* 253, no. 6 (December):46–53.

Luttwak, Edward N. 1984. *The Pentagon and the Art of War*. New York: Simon and Schuster.

Meyer, Stephen M. 1985a. Soviet Perspectives on the Paths to Nuclear War. Pp. 167–205 in Graham Allison et al., eds., *Hawks, Doves and Owls: An Agenda for Avoiding Nuclear War*. New York: W. W. Norton.

———. 1985b. Soviet Views on SDI. *Survival* 27, no. 6 (November/December):274–92.

———. 1987. Soviet Nuclear Operations. Pp. 470–534 in Ashton B. Carter et al., eds., *Managing Nuclear Operations*. Washington, D.C.: Brookings Institution.

Nitze, Paul H. 1985. On the Road to a More Stable Peace. *Current Policy,* no. 657, U.S. Department of State.

Office of Technology Assessment. 1985. *Ballistic Missile Defense Technologies*. Washington, D.C.: U.S. Government Printing Office.

Perrow, Charles. 1984. *Normal Accidents: Living with High-Risk Technologies*. New York: Basic Books.

Pipes, Richard. 1977. Why the Soviet Union Thinks It Could Fight and Win a Nuclear War. *Commentary* (July):21–34.

Pringles, Peter, and William Arkin. 1983. *SIOP*. New York: W. W. Norton.

Sienkiewicz, Stanley. 1981. Soviet Nuclear Doctrine and the Prospects for Strategic Arms Control. Pp. 73–91 in Derek Leebaert, ed., *Soviet Military Thinking*. London: Allen and Unwin.

Slocombe, Walter. 1981. The Countervailing Strategy. *International Security* 5, no. 4 (Spring).

Sloss, Leon, and Marc Dean Millot. 1984. U.S. Nuclear Strategy in Evolution. *Strategic Review* (Winter):19–28.

Steinbruner, John. 1981–1982. Nuclear Decapitation. *Foreign Policy,* no. 45 (Winter): 16–28.

Timmerman, Frederick W., Jr. 1985. Of Command and Control and Other Things. *Army* (May).

U.S. Department of Defense. 1984. *Soviet Military Power: 1986*. Washington, D.C.: U.S. Government Printing Office.

Van Creveld, Martin. 1985. *Command in War*. Cambridge, Mass.: Harvard University Press.

Watkins, James D. 1986. The Maritime Strategy. U.S. Naval Institute, *Proceedings* (January).

Weinberger, Caspar W. 1986. *Annual Report to the Congress: Fiscal Year 1987*. Washington, D.C.: U.S. Government Printing Office.

5

On Multilateral Deterrence and Regional Nuclear Powers

EDWARD A. KOLODZIEJ

The size and sophistication of nuclear capabilities in the hands of states other than the superpowers and their spread to other states have critical implications for the theory and practice of deterrence and for the preservation of regional and global stability. Currently, there are three announced regional nuclear powers—France, Great Britain, and China; one nuclear state—India—which exploded a nuclear device in 1974 but which has yet to deploy a weapons system; and an unannounced nuclear power—Israel—which, if various published sources are reliable (*London Times,* October 5, 1986; Harkavy, 1977), has nuclear weapons of an undisclosed number and explosive magnitude as well as aircraft and missile systems capable of delivering them against regional adversaries.[1]

Because of the superpower nuclear balance and the globalized nature of the superpower conflict and the real or implied political and strategic alliance or conflict patterns between these smaller nuclear states and one or the other of the superpowers, neither superpower can be indifferent to the military doctrines and nuclear policies of these states. Although American and Soviet thinking remains primarily focused on their bilateral nuclear balance, the doctrines and practices of these regional nuclear powers make nuclear deterrence and arms control policies progressively more multilateral at a global level and differentially defined at a regional level as a function of the divergent aims and nuclear capabilities of local actors, the scope and intensity of their rivalries, their variable security relations with the superpowers, and their unequal and differing economic, military, and technological capabilities.

---

[1]I will use the terms *nuclear powers* and *states* interchangeably throughout this chapter. The context should make clear, however, that India is more a nuclear state than a power, whereas, paradoxically, Israel may be considered an incipient nuclear power but not officially a nuclear state. The behavior of both countries warrants examination for the insights they can furnish with respect to the theory and practice of deterrence.

An understanding of how deterrence works in regulating interstate conflict at global and regional levels requires closer attention to the strategic doctrines and arms control policies of the current nuclear powers. These five cases provide an introduction to the problems posed by multilateral deterrence for the creation and maintenance of stable security regimes and to the difficulties encountered in attempting to prevent nuclear war as the number of states and their divergent security and political interests are multiplied in an international framework that is becoming progressively multilateralized.

Multilateral deterrence has received most attention in France's development of its nuclear forces. The nuclear debate in France has proceeded almost without interruption over a period of almost thirty years since the formation of the Fifth Republic in 1958 and the nuclear striking force by the de Gaulle regime. (For a review, see Kohl, 1971; Harrison, 1981.) It continues until today without abatement (Yost, 1985a and 1985b). In contrast, the development of a body of doctrine for the use or threat of nuclear weapons by other actual or incipient nuclear powers is all but non-existent, the British case representing a partial exception. Explanations for this uneven pattern vary according to the case. What principles of deterrence are being practiced must be deduced from experience based on what states do (e.g., India's explosion ostensibly of a peaceful nuclear device) or do not do (Israel's and Pakistan's refusal to admit to the possession of nuclear arms).

This chapter is divided into three parts corresponding roughly in descending order to the explosive potential of the nuclear capabilities under examination and the degree of explicit governmental pursuit of a nuclear deterrence strategy. The first part focuses on deterrence in Europe. It sketches evolving French doctrine and reviews British debates and practice in developing a nuclear deterrent. In the absence of a fully articulated official doctrine, domestic critics of the British deterrent have largely filled the vacuum left by successive governments which have been reluctant for differing reasons over time to explicate official thinking (Gowing 1974; Simpson, 1986). British and French behavior is then examined to identify their respective operational deterrent codes. Their nuclear policies are aimed at influencing the behavior simultaneously of the common adversary (the Soviet Union), the guarantor ally (the United States), and other allies (including each other) in preferred ways.

The second part contrasts deterrence in Europe with Asia principally from the perspectives of China and India. China, once a formal ally of the Soviet Union, appears now to have adopted a long-term security strategy which, while even-handed toward the superpowers on the surface, currently favors the West and the United States over the Soviet Union. India, officially a nonaligned state, remains heavily dependent on the Soviet Union for conventional arms and implicitly on the superpowers to restrain a nuclear China and emerging nuclear Pakistan. As superpower leverage declines, India appears increasingly pressured to rely on its own capabilities to strengthen deterrence against China and Pakistan. Meanwhile, Pakistan, if it should acknowledge possession of nuclear arms, would have to confront a host of questions, now pending, about the size of its forces, their future development, the strategic doctrine to rationalize and control them, and the likely and potentially countervailing reaction of India, its principal regional opponent (Cohen, 1984, pp. 152–161, and 1987).

The third part reviews the unique considerations affecting the practice of multilateral nuclear deterrence in the Middle East. Israel, closely allied with the United States, although bound by no treaty comparable to the NATO alliance, purportedly has nuclear weapons but officially pursues a policy of deliberate ambiguity. At the same time, Israel, as its destruction of Iraq's nuclear facilities in 1981 suggests, appears to have adopted a policy of regional nuclear hegemony, opting for direct, national controls of regional proliferation rather than rely on the international regime created by the non-proliferation treaty.

MULTILATERAL DETERRENCE IN EUROPE

Nuclear Weapons and Alliances

In the late 1950s when France's nuclear strike forces were formed, three divergent schools of thought arose in France over the question of the feasibility and utility of an independent nuclear deterrent. The first contended that even a small nuclear force was sufficient to deter a more powerful nuclear adversary if one could inflict greater damage on the adversary than could be gained in attacking one's homeland. This strategy of proportional deterrence was carried to its logical conclusion in the contention that no state could rely on another to protect its vital interests if it risked annihilation itself (Gallois, 1961; for an elaboration of this argument, see Poirier, 1983). Conversely, no state could tolerate alliance with another state if it were drawn into a nuclear war not of its own choosing. Otherwise, it would relinquish its responsibility for national security, viz., the decision to decide the question of war and peace.

This early version of French doctrinal thinking addressed the set of complex issues associated with the impact of nuclear weapons on alliance commitments. Would the guarantor ally risk its own existence in meeting its alliance obligations? Would it resist the temptation to compromise with the common adversary at the expense of a weaker ally's security and foreign policy interests? Given the destructive character of nuclear war, how could one isolate oneself from conventional wars that might erupt in Europe or from a superpower nuclear exchange? Similarly, how could one be insulated from provocative initiatives by an ally that might lead to war outside one's region of primary interest? These concerns led to a line of reasoning that tended to equate adversary and ally, since either, alone or in combination, threatened the state's involvement in an undesired nuclear war. An independent national nuclear force ostensibly quieted these concerns by yielding several alleged benefits. Nuclear weapons, based on proportional deterrence, were sufficient for national defense. They also provided a sanctuary from conventional or nuclear wars since belligerents presumably had no incentive to attack a weaker but nuclear state, like France, for any conceivable gain would be offset by the latter's nuclear destructive capability. Allies, therefore, were not needed, nor would they be a risk if they collided or compromised their differences with the common adversary at the presumed expense of their abandoned nuclear ally.

This narrowly focused nationalist position was indirectly associated with a systematic French attack, launched by the regime of President Charles de Gaulle on the bipolar system arising from World War II. Superpower hegemony was faulted on two counts: as destabilizing, that is, as leading to war, and as illegitimate (Kolodziej, 1974, pp. 69–175). Bipolarity was unstable either because both sides were locked in an arms race leading to war from which they could not extricate themselves or because their global struggle risked leading to a confrontation in an otherwise marginal area of concern, a crisis prompted by the aggressive expansion by either or both superpowers or by the initiative of a client. A bipolar system was also illegitimate. It confined states within an international regime, defined by the superpowers and bloc politics, and insulated the United States and the Soviet Union from the influence of third states seeking to shape the operating rules and structure of their security environment.

In direct contradiction to the position advocating autonomous national nuclear capabilities and a depreciation of alliances, there emerged an argument favoring an independent nuclear deterrent as a mechanism for strengthening alliances as well as deterrence (Beaufre, 1966). The presence of three nuclear powers—two in alliance and the remaining power as the common adversary—was alleged to have created an entirely different calculus of deterrence than a strictly bilateral system. Nuclear states now had to take the interests, capabilities, and behavior of all nuclear states into account in making their nuclear moves. The relationships were fundamentally triangular and influence patterns ran simultaneously, though with differential impact, along the sides of a triangle whose three points were occupied by the two principal nuclear states and the minor nuclear power. (The triangle would presumably become a rectangle or pentagon as the number of allied nuclear powers increased.)

In an alliance, based on the mutual commitment of partners to defend each other, a major nuclear power might well have an incentive to abandon an ally in a confrontation between the ally and the common adversary. The stakes involved would be marginal to the major ally, and the risk of nuclear war would caution against intervention. But under conditions of multilateral deterrence, *within an alliance,* the minor ally, in threatening a nuclear war, would *ipso facto* transform an otherwise marginal interest of its stronger alliance partner into a high stake for both. A potential zone of instability, created by the asymmetry of nuclear capabilities between a small and large nuclear state and the marginal stake at issue for the stronger ally, would be presumably stabilized by the stronger ally's support of the weaker nuclear ally against the common nuclear opponent as a matter of alliance obligation and as a strategic requirement both to avoid war and to preserve the alliance. The major ally could not be indifferent to the calculations of damage that the common antagonist would have to make if it were to be engaged in a nuclear exchange with the smaller nuclear ally and the inferior position in which it would be placed, given the damage that could be inflicted by the smaller nuclear power in its confrontation with its principal adversary.

A third school of opinion found neither polar position plausible. An independent nuclear deterrent was rejected on several grounds: as unfeasible and lacking in credibility (too small and vulnerable); as damaging to extended deterrence (as the major ally had incentive to decrease its commitment); as a stimulant for nuclear proliferation (i.e., other non-nuclear states in the alliance would seek nuclear weapons); and as prone to accident or unauthorized use and provocative to an adversary, raising the incentives to preempt in time of crisis (Aron, 1965). Lacking a credible nuclear force and faced with national annihilation, there appeared little likelihood that a French president would be able to win a war of nerves with his Soviet counterparts (Aron, 1965, pp. 107, 138).

Evolving French Nuclear Strategy

French governmental practice of multilateral deterrence has steered unevenly between these three schools. To retain its political independence, the de Gaulle government withdrew from the integrated command structure of NATO in 1966 but remained within the Atlantic Alliance. It assumed a position somewhere between national military autonomy—the Gallois thesis—and the stance of a faithful ally entitled to be consulted on nuclear policy and the protection of extended deterrence of the superior nuclear ally—the Beaufre counter-proposal. Meanwhile, France's access to American nuclear support was indirectly tied to its bilateral treaty with West Germany and to its membership in the Western European Union, which included Britain, a country that retained, as described below, a special political and nuclear relationship with the United States within the Atlantic Alliance. France's nuclear superiority on the West European continent was also implicitly ensured in West Germany's pledge under the West European treaty to renounce efforts to acquire nuclear weapons. Britain's entry into the European Community during the Pompidou government reinforced implicit U.S. nuclear protection of France by its guarantee to Britain and West Germany. France could enjoy U.S. and allied support, yet purport to base its security policies on alliance-eroding principles of non-belligerency and non-automaticity in an armed confrontation between the superpowers or between NATO and the Warsaw Pact blocs.

The deliberate contradiction of the French position—as independent nuclear actor and as faithful ally—is highlighted by successive doctrinal reformulations of deterrence doctrine to guide the operational use and control of conventional, tactical, and strategic nuclear forces. In the early development of the French force, French Chief of Staff, General Charles Ailleret (1967), adopted a stance closest to the Gallois thesis of national autonomy. Ailleret advocated a nuclear strategy capable of protecting France from all directions (*tous azimuts*). Blurred in this exposition was the traditional distinction between enemy and ally as the source of threat. Slighted also were the use of tactical nuclear and conventional forces or cooperation with allies in resisting foreign attack.

Ailleret's extreme doctrinal position was subsequently relaxed (Fourquet, 1969) with the admission that the Soviet Union was France's principal threat. In a confrontation with the Eastern bloc, two battles were envisioned. In the first, outside France's borders, French conventional and tactical nuclear forces might participate in a forward battle in support of NATO's forward defense posture. Tactical nuclear weapons were viewed as a useful means to test the intentions of an aggressor, although their extensive battlefield use was not envisioned. Conventional forces were to be designed primarily to contribute to nuclear deterrent moves and not as military forces with a strategic mission independent of France's nuclear systems. Whether France would take part in this first battle would depend on circumstances of the moment. Non-automaticity was still the rule and non-belligerency an option. Cooperation with allies was contingent on their contribution to the preparation for the second battle, viz., for France itself.

In the mid-1970s, French Chief of Staff, General Guy Méry (1976), challenged the notion of two battles. A single field of battle was substituted for the artificial distinction of two battles. France's national perimeter of defense was defined as extending from the Rhine to the Mediterranean. French forces could be engaged at the onset of hostilities. They would remain fully under national control, and the decision to use tactical or strategic arms would in no way be delegated to another power or to an allied command. Cooperation with allies was possible—even desirable—but only on French terms; non-automaticity was explicitly affirmed, while non-belligerency was implied. What had significantly shifted in French thinking was France's need to influence the outcome of the conventional engagement in Europe before escalating to tactical and strategic nuclear weapons.

Although French regimes continue to underline the political independence and strategic autonomy of French nuclear forces, the trend in French military policy has been to equip and organize its conventional and tactical nuclear forces for prompt deployment in support of the forward battle for Europe if the French president decides to cooperate with allied forces in meeting an attack. A new Rapid Action Force, designed for greater mobility and firepower, has been created. Equipped with 200 helicopters for anti-tank, troop protection, and attack purposes, it is expected to enter battle quickly. At the same time, plans have been laid to replace the Pluton tactical nuclear system with Hadès, which is more mobile and lethal (10 to 60 kiloton (kt.) warheads versus 15 to 25 kt.), more accurate, and of greater range than its predecessor (350 km. versus 120 km.) (Yost, 1985a, pp. 48–64; IISS, 1986, p. 202).

Pluton's short range makes it risky to use since its warheads are likely to land in West Germany on allied forces and civilians. Hadès missiles are an improvement since they can reach targets in Eastern Europe, provided they are fired far enough eastward. Allied control over French escalation to nuclear levels remains a major problem. The French refuse to share either their plans for Pluton, Hadès, or air-delivered tactical weapons deployed with Air Force and Navy units. Under crisis or combat conditions, France retains the option of non-belligerency and, if engaged, of autonomous use of its nuclear forces. In either instance, but especially in the case of autonomous use, France positions itself to impose its preferred strategy on its allies, potentially to their disadvantage. These are serious impediments in efforts by post-Gaullist France to strengthen bilateral military ties with NATO and its European allies, principally Germany.

Evolving British Nuclear Strategy

In contrast to France, Britain has sought to influence the strategic behavior of its principal ally (the United States) and adversary (the Soviet Union) by attempting to integrate its nuclear forces as closely as possible with those of the United States. The decisions to build an atomic bomb and later to develop a thermonuclear device, aside from Britain's desire to remain a great power, were aimed principally at encouraging the United States to share its nuclear technology with Great Britain and to gain a place for Britain in U.S. strategic planning. From the outset it was assumed that Britain would have to rely on the United States in any war on the continent (Gowing, 1974; Simpson, 1986). Whereas France, since the accession of Charles de Gaulle to the presidency in the newly formed Fifth Republic in 1958, sought to influence U.S. deterrent and larger foreign policy aims and strategy through opposition to the United States, Britain insisted on its utility and on its moral and political claims as a trusted and reliable ally to inflect U.S. policy in preferred ways.

Although Britain was denied access both to American nuclear technology and to planning as a consequence of the McMahon Act of 1946, its nuclear policies were still based on the assumption of Britain's supplementary contribution to American strategic bombardment. Britain would hit targets that American forces might ignore or consider of secondary value. Its possession of the bomb and advanced delivery systems—principally V-bombers by the late 1950s and into the 1960s—was expected to prompt American nuclear decision-makers to coordinate their targeting with British planners. If the United States could not be engaged, Britain would still possess its own nuclear forces to deter an aggressor (Freedman, 1985a). What Britain sought, therefore, was national control over nuclear forces but not necessarily self-sufficiency in their development (considered in the long run beyond Britain's means), nor independence from American and NATO planning. Whereas France sought to shape American and Soviet behavior by maintaining its distance and by insisting on national self-sufficiency (a sentiment all the more reinforced by American refusal to share its nuclear technology with France), on the operational autonomy of its nuclear forces, and on the option of non-belligerency, Britain cast itself in the role of America's principal ally within the Atlantic Alliance and strove to nurture a special nuclear relationship with Washington (Simpson, 1986; Baylis, 1984; Pierre, 1972).

Britain's persistence was rewarded with the amendment of the McMahon Act in 1954 and 1958, permitting Britain's access first to Polaris submarine and missile technology in the 1960s and then to Trident and D-5 long-range missiles in the later 1970s and 1980s. Britain's present nuclear force includes four Polaris submarines, with 16 A-3 missiles. Each is armed with the British-developed MRV Chevaline, which is reportedly capable of delivering three warheads, with accompanying decoys, to a single target. British nuclear forces are pledged to NATO and are planned for use as part of the alliance's response to aggression in Europe. The British government may, however, withdraw and employ these forces "where Her Majesty's Government may decide that supreme national interests are at stake" (quoted in Freedman, 1985a, p. 118).

British tactical nuclear forces, principally deployed in Germany, are also assigned to NATO. These include Lance missiles and artillery whose warheads are under dual-key control with the United States. British Vulcan, Jaguar, Buccaneer, and Tornado aircraft are also nuclear capable. The Tornado is designated as Britain's principal nuclear-capable fighter-bomber. Work is underway to replace its ordinance of British-made free-falling bombs with a stand-off missile to enhance the aircraft's survivability and penetrability. It would appear that these forces can also be conceivably withdrawn from battle or used independently by Britain in an emergency, although neither possibility has been publicly acknowledged as an option.

British planners have attempted to turn this ambiguity to a virtue. They advance the notion that a second center of decision adds uncertainty to an aggressor's calculations, while assuring allies, especially the United States, that these forces are dedicated to alliance purposes. There has been little penchant in official British circles to go much beyond the reassertion of this view or to articulate publicly a fully developed strategy for the use of its tactical and strategic forces. To follow the French lead might prompt second thoughts in Washington about sharing nuclear know-how and plans. It might also intensify public debate over the independent nuclear program, threatening further, as described below, its existence since British public opinion, unlike French public opinion, is deeply split on the issue (Freedman, 1981). Whereas French leaders joined the issue of an independent nuclear force and gradually shaped a supportive consensus favoring the maintenance and modernization of France's nuclear forces, British leaders have preferred to make these decisions largely in camera, relying on ad hoc committees of key cabinet ministers (McInnes, 1986, pp. 1–41). A low-profile and behind-the-scenes tactic in developing nuclear weapons was adopted for several mutually reinforcing reasons: continued American assistance and commitment to Europe's defense; management and mollification of domestic critics; deterrence of Soviet hostile behavior; and, through the promotion of arms control accords, mutual superpower restraint.

Modernization and Multilateralization

The nuclear arsenals of France and Britain are expected to grow so large in the 1990s that neither ally nor adversary can be indifferent to these forces, the doctrine guiding their use or threat, or the strategic and political contingencies under which they might be employed. Either European state will theoretically be able to inflict damage on the Soviet Union at least equal to the crude standard for minimum deterrence relied on by U.S. nuclear planners in the 1960s. The latter was equated to an attack capable of destroying roughly two-thirds of the Soviet Union's industrial plant and one-third of its population. The British Trident program, if implemented, will be composed of four submarines, each carrying sixteen D-5 missiles (contrasting with twenty-four for the U.S. Trident subs). At full payload, the D-5 has a range of 7,000 kilometers, approximately twice that of the current Polaris fleet, and will be more accurate. Although each MIRVed missile can carry eight to fourteen warheads, along with decoys, penetration aids, and coverings hardened to blast and electronic failure, the Thatcher government, to disarm critics and promote arms control has announced that it will restrict the British D-5 to a maximum of eight warheads per missile. In any event, the payload of each missile will also increase dramatically depending on the number of warheads and kilotonnage assigned to the reentry vehicles.

Since the D-5's explosive potential and accuracy approach land-based systems, they conceivably could be used for silo-busting missions. The Trident system could possess somewhere between 384 and 512 warheads, depending on how many submarines were fully armed at any one time. Since at least one Trident submarine will always be on patrol, one can count on 128 warheads at sea. Their number would double if two submarines were on patrol, which would likely be the case in a crisis. A British Trident system, even with only 384 warheads, will transform the so-called Moscow criterion that has guided British nuclear planning until now and that led to British development of the Chevaline warhead to ensure penetration of Moscow's ABM defenses (Freedman, 1980, pp. 41–51).

Similarly, France will expand its submarine nuclear forces in the 1990s, approximating British capabilities, and will do so almost entirely through its own national effort. At the core of its strategic forces will be at least six nuclear submarines, three always on patrol, and each carrying initially sixteen M-4 missiles, later to be replaced by a more advanced M-5 missile. Each missile will be fitted with six 150 kt. warheads for a total 576 warheads, at least half of which must be assumed to be on station, perhaps more during a crisis. Currently, France has six strategic nuclear submarines. Five of these will be fitted with M-4 missiles over the next several years. One will retain its sixteen M-20 missiles, each armed with a one-megaton warhead. These forces are supplemented by eighteen Intermediate Range Ballistic Missiles (IRBMs) armed with one-megaton warheads and approximately eighteen Mirage IV strike aircraft, some of which are being converted from their present bomb delivery configurations to an air-to-surface missile stand-off capability. These ASMPs will have a range of 100 to 300 kilometers and carry 150 kt. warheads (IISS, *Military Balance, 1986*, pp. 202–203). In the 1990s, Britain and France could conceivably deploy nuclear systems with a combined force approaching 1000 warheads. Viewed from another angle, British and French submarine forces may comprise over 25 percent of Western sea-based strategic systems, a discernible increase over the current 3 percent, if the superpowers agree on deep cuts in their strategic forces.

Incorporating either or both of the European nuclear systems into a superpower arms control regime will be difficult. France continues to stress national autonomy and proportional deterrence; Britain rationalizes its nuclear forces by incorporating them into NATO planning, while retaining the right to withdraw them for national use in an emergency. Both countries insist that three conditions must be met before they will even contemplate entering into discussions about modifying their projected nuclear plans: (1) substantial reductions in superpower offensive nuclear forces; (2) no substantial change in superpower defensive capabilities (Grove, 1985; Kolodziej, 1987a); and (3) substantial decreases in Soviet and Warsaw bloc chemical weapons and conventional forces. A word about each condition may clarify their significance for what is perceived as the minimum requirements of a credible nuclear force.

The vertical proliferation of the superpowers, especially since the late 1970s, overshadows both European nuclear systems. Strategic warheads of the two superpowers already exceed 24,000 and, unless arrested by an arms accord, promise to increase further. Both European governments reason that they cannot be expected to make the first move toward decreasing the size of their systems since the superpowers are racing faster than either of them. This position places the British in a somewhat contradictory position based on a previous adherence to a Moscow criterion. British notions of nuclear deterrence appear to be expanding to fit the number of warheads available. The Trident system is too large to be confined to the Moscow criterion of the Polaris system (Freedman, 1985a). The longer range, greater warhead load, and accuracy of the D-5 missile potentially place all of the Soviet Union's twenty-two cities with a population of one million or more within the targeting capability of a single British submarine. The potential silo-busting capability of the D-5 missile also raises questions about its possible first-strike uses. The close working relation between British and American nuclear planners gives additional point to concerns that increased British capabilities extend American warfighting potential through NATO.

French policy is no less reluctant to decrease its strategic offensive forces or reduce the size of their planned modernization unless superpower arsenals are sharply cut. Targeting plans have apparently been enlarged to include not only major cities but also so-called vital works—*oeuvres vives*—of the Soviet Union (Yost, 1985a). As in Britain, deterrence requirements parallel the expansion of nuclear capabilities. Neither Britain nor France appears prepared, however each defines "substantial" superpower cuts in offensive forces, to reduce their respective arsenals unless corresponding limits are placed on superpower defenses against nuclear attack. Overloading Soviet defenses by increased striking power is the simplest way to retain a credible deterrent.

The prospect of improved superpower antiballistic missile (ABM) or anti-submarine warfare (ASW) defensive capabilities would seriously tax both European nuclear systems. The attention of British and French strategists is now focused on advances in Soviet ballistic missile defenses that might degrade the penetrability of their nation's nuclear forces. Soviet nuclear forces already threaten their ground-based nuclear forces as well as their sea-based forces in port. In addition, an unregulated arms race in nuclear defensive systems would place great pressures on already tight British and French defense budgets to keep pace with superpower developments. Increased spending would also exert potentially severe strains on the political support structures in both countries for an independent nuclear deterrent. This is an especially acute problem in Britain where the social compact on nuclear weapons appears to be in serious disrepair. It is not an exaggeration to argue that British nuclear force development since World War II has been closely calibrated to Soviet defense systems. As Soviet air defenses improved, the V-Bomber force of the 1950s gave way to the Blue Steel, Blue Streak, and Skybolt missile programs and, finally, to Polaris as the replacement for the V-Bombers. Subsequently, when the Golash system around Moscow appeared to threaten the Moscow "criterion," Chevaline was developed. Now Trident is supposed to assure the reliability, penetrability, and survivability of the British nuclear force.

The French will face similar budgetary and political strains. Demands for increased welfare are unabated. Since the late 1960s, France's political parties have tacitly agreed to a cap of approximately 4 percent of gross national product (GNP) on defense spending (Kolodziej, 1987b, ch. 3). There is little likelihood that the French five-year military equipment plan adopted in 1987 will meet its goals. It purports to develop a new follow-on missile for the M-4 and a new ground-based mobile missile, to begin replacing an aging nuclear submarine force, to lay the keel of a new aircraft carrier, and to launch, without allied support, a new fighter (Rafale) to replace the Mirage 2000 as well as a combat helicopter with German support while supplying tactical or pre-strategic nuclear weapons to all of the services. There is little likelihood of reaching these goals under current spending limits (Heisbourg, 1986, 1987).

It is not surprising then that the British and French share concern about superpower progress in anti-ballistic missile defense systems (Yost, 1988). Of equal interest is their support of the ABM treaty as well as carefully crafted and verifiable restrictions on research, development, and testing. On this score, both appear to be closer to the Soviet position on the Strategic Defense Initiative (SDI) and the ABM treaty than to the position of the Reagan administration. In supporting the SDI initiative, Prime Minister Margaret Thatcher attached several conditions to British cooperation that sharply contrast with U.S. administration expectations. In December 1984, a joint Anglo-American communiqué affirmed that "the U.S. and western aim is not to achieve superiority but to maintain balance, taking into account Soviet developments; SDI-related deployments would, in the view of treaty obligations, have to be a matter of negotiations, the over-all aim is to enhance, not undercut, *deterrence;* and East-West negotiations should aim to achieve security within reduced levels of offensive systems on both sides" (quoted in Howe, 1985). In keeping with traditional French practice, Paris directly challenged the destabilizing features of SDI. As a backfire, it also launched its own civilian-based Eureka program to provide an alternative for European cooperation in advanced aerospace systems (Fenske, 1986).

One final dimension of multilateral deterrence in Europe should be mentioned: the deployment of American-controlled theatre nuclear forces. In the late 1970s, with increasing evidence of a Soviet strategic buildup, Europeans began to fear that the rough strategic balance struck between the superpowers might be upset. Even if maintained under SALT II, there was the even greater concern that the United States would be self-deterred in coming to the assistance of its European allies. Particular attention was drawn to the modernization of Soviet theatre nuclear forces capable of destroying NATO facilities and threatening the military forces, including nuclear systems, of the European states.

In December 1979, NATO ministers agreed to a "two-track" approach to the Soviet expansion. The United States would deploy 464 cruise missiles in several European states, including Britain, and 108 Pershing II IRBMs in West Germany. These systems would be capable of striking targets in Eastern Europe and in western Soviet Union. This deployment would purportedly assure U.S. allies that American and European security interests would be "coupled." Deployments, however, would be contingent on Soviet willingness to dismantle its SS-20 and Backfire bombers. For the first time, the United States consented not only to a European role in deploying nuclear systems in Europe, but also to allied consultation over U.S. arms control policy to the degree that European-based systems within NATO were involved. This was an indirect mechanism for the European states to oversee, however tentatively and tenuously, superpower theatre nuclear arms control talks (Bertram, 1982, 1986).

What is also of interest about the NATO decision is the reversal of European and American positions toward Pershing II and the cruise missile. Under the pressure of widespread domestic opposition to U.S. deployments, European governments, including Britain, wavered about accepting U.S. missiles, only to have the United States insist on deployment to underline alliance cohesion and deterrence vis-à-vis the Soviet Union (Talbott, 1985). Western governments found themselves in conflict with large segments of their own populations; many of whom considered the United States more a threat to peace than the Soviet Union. Under these confused circumstances it became difficult to discern against whom deterrence was being directed; whether to restrain an ally or to contain the common adversary, or both.

These reversals in allied expectations about mutual commitments to nuclear deterrence were given yet another reverse spin when President Reagan was reported to have agreed to the elimination of ballistic missiles over a decade at the Reykjavik summit in the fall of 1986. Read against the President's persistent disparagement of nuclear deterrence, underlying his determined support of SDI, the apparent Reykjavik concession prompted Prime Minister Thatcher to elicit the president's pledge to restrict the U.S. negotiating position at Geneva to 50 percent cuts in superpower weapons inventories and to reaffirm the West's primary reliance on nuclear deterrence for its collective security (British Embassy, 1986).

Once superpower medium- and short-range nuclear weapons are dismantled in Europe and Asia, increased pressure will inevitably grow to integrate British and French forces into the superpower-negotiated nuclear regime for Europe. Not only do Anglo-French conditions with regard to deep cuts in offensive systems and limits on R and D work and deployments of defensive systems have to be met, but also both states insist on asymmetrical reductions, greater for the Warsaw Pact than NATO, of non-nuclear forces as a part of their consideration even to enter into strategic arms talks. Even with the elimination of superpower regional nuclear forces in ranges between 300 and 3,200 miles (the approximate ranges, respectively, of Soviet SS-23 and SS-20 missiles), superpower arsenals together would still be ten times greater than those of Britain and France if 50 percent cuts were made. Whether these reduced levels would be enough to entice London and Paris to negotiate a new multilateral nuclear regime for Europe remains uncertain. National nuclear weapons are perceived in both European capitals as equalizers of superpower military strength, as insurance policies against an uncertain future, and, implicitly, as a status symbol and lever in big power negotiations (not to mention a special standing within NATO and the Western European Union vis-à-vis Germany). Neither European nuclear power has the conventional capabilities or the will to expand them at the expense of retaining and modernizing their nuclear forces simply for the sake of bolstering Western conventional defenses. Both prefer nuclear deterrence cum (conventional) defense to the U.S. preference for defense cum deterrence, guided by NATO's Flexible Response strategy.

NUCLEAR DETERRENCE IN ASIA

The nuclear deterrent postures of China and India contrast with each other and differ sharply from those of the Western powers and the Soviet Union. Both states, while aligned with one or the other of the superpowers, have been largely compelled to rely on their own resources in developing nuclear capabilities and in meeting their perceived need for nuclear weapons. The Soviet Union refused to share its nuclear technology or warhead design with China after some initial assistance. India's explosion of a "peaceful" nuclear device in 1974, while assisted materially, if not wittingly, by Canada and the United States, was produced by indigenous scientific and engineering personnel.

Unlike the European states, neither India nor China can count on a superpower for protection. In China's case, the Soviet Union is the principal threat, and, until recently, the United States was of equal or even greater concern. India's signature of a treaty of friendship with the Soviet Union in 1971, at the height of the Bangladesh crisis and the Indo-Pakistan War, has some residual security implications, but it has neither the deep historical nor the organizational and material dimensions of those between the Soviet Union and its Warsaw Pact allies.

Adding to the exposure of China and India is their mutual suspicion of each other. India's nuclear policies were initially shaped—and still continue to be influenced—by Chinese nuclear developments. Before the 1962 Sino-Indian War, New Delhi pursued a policy of non-alignment and an announced policy of unilateral renunciation of nuclear weapons (Rao, 1981, p. 156). The Sino-Indian War in 1962 and the Chinese explosion of an atomic device in 1964 prompted a reevaluation of Indian nuclear policy. New Delhi resisted the extremes of moving quickly to a bomb or of unequivocally affirming its nuclear renunciation position. Instead, India has left open the question of whether it would or would not exercise a military nuclear option (Thomas, 1986, p. 325). Several considerations advised a deterrent strategy of deliberate ambiguity: an Indian explosion would likely spur Chinese efforts and increase the threat to India; both superpowers, at odds with China in the 1960s, could be counted on to restrain Beijing; and the absence of long-range Indian delivery vehicles capable of striking Chinese population and industrial centers made a bomb decision somewhat moot. Pakistan did not figure in these early calculations since its nuclear program had not yet reached a threatening state of development.

An Indian decision to move from the status of a nuclear state to a nuclear power by developing nuclear arms and delivery systems would inevitably have implications for Chinese strategic calculations. Whereas China is a vastly weaker nuclear power vis-a-vis the superpowers, it is currently superior to India. Its status as a nuclear power, however vulnerable, is viewed as a strategic asset by Beijing (Pollack, 1981, p. 139) as well as a mark of big power stature (Lin, 1988). Having to share this status with India, which might well be a long-term threat to China, would present the Communist regime with hard choices: to engage India in a nuclear arms race which Pakistan would almost inevitably join (Spector, 1984, pp. 70–110; Cohen, 1984, pp. 152–61), lending a triangular synergism to the efforts of each (Chari, 1986); to develop regional arms control strategies to halt or hinder Indian nuclearization; or, following the superpower lead, to adopt some variant of both.

In exploding a nuclear device in 1974, India modified, but did not abandon its open options approach. Several conflicting considerations appeared to have prompted Delhi to decide on a peaceful nuclear explosion (PNE). The PNE was a compromise between nuclear renunciation and a weapons program. It signaled India's determination to acquire nuclear weapons if its dominant regional position were to be undermined. This fear had been reinforced by the rapprochement between the United States and China, weakening perceived international restraints on China, and by their separate but equally sharp criticism of India's intervention in Bangladesh and its crushing defeat of Pakistan. India recoiled from going further, apparently apprehensive about Chinese and Pakistani nuclear counterreactions. There was the added worry of whether a stable deterrent regime could developed with Pakistan given centuries of communal animosity. In crossing the nuclear threshold with the PNE, however, India appears to have given impetus to Pakistani development of a Muslim bomb (Thomas, 1986, pp. 326–329) The upshot is that India faces the prospect of two nuclear powers—a stronger nuclear China and an emerging nuclear Pakistan, both in uneasy alignment with the United States. India's concerns are bolstered by the U.S. supply to Pakistan of F-16 fighters that could be modified to carry nuclear weapons (Naim, 1987, pp. 250–281) and by China's vigorous space program that has produced rockets capable of delivering nuclear warheads on Indian targets (Lin, 1988, pp. 37–62).

Although both superpowers have been alternately perceived in Beijing as China's principal foe, China's deployment of almost all of its forces against the Soviet Union indicates that Moscow is considered the primary threat today. What is less certain is the strategic doctrine guiding Chinese military forces and modernization. Observers differ widely (Lin, 1988; Wang, 1984), ranging from those convinced that conventional forces are assigned top priority to those who argue that tactical, warfighting nuclear capabilities (Segal, 1981) or strategic nuclear weapons are being given primary emphasis (Wong-Fraser, 1981).

The paucity of hard data about Chinese military priorities and the controversial and problematic character of what is known seriously hamper efforts to define Chinese deterrent strategy. What is clear is that the Chinese understanding and practice of nuclear deterrence differs markedly from Western and Soviet practice (Lin, 1988). Deterrence has been adapted (1) to China's traditional approach to war, defined by its massive population, dependence on large ground armies, and geographical extension, (2) its militarily inferiority in modern nuclear and non-nuclear weapons relative to the superpowers and its resulting vulnerability to long-range nuclear attack, and (3) the fragility of its economic base and the scarcity of its techno-scientific resources.

China cannot match superpower arsenals, nor adopt their nuclear warfighting postures. China's major strategic advantages remain its masses and land mass. Chinese deterrence blends, therefore, Mao's notion of a people's war with a military modernization program that is steadily improving the quality of Chinese nuclear and non-nuclear arms. The upshot of the evolution of Chinese military capabilities since China first exploded a nuclear device in 1964 (the intervening Cultural Revolution notwithstanding) would appear to be a strategy aimed at presenting a would-be aggressor—identified today as the Soviet Union—with a set of unpalatable options. On the one hand, growing Chinese nuclear capabilities would hold the Soviet Union hostage to nuclear attack. Although China might not be able to inflict as much destruction on the Soviet Union as the latter could in reverse, the gradual development of a Chinese second-strike force will increasingly discourage a preemptive Soviet strike since the damage to the Soviet Union would presumably outweigh any rational strategic or political advantage in attacking first. Moscow would also expose itself to Western, specifically U.S., counteraction. At a minimum it would seriously disrupt the nuclear regime that has crystallized over decades of bargaining and testing and on which the superpowers rely to stabilize their competition.

On the other hand, if the Soviet Union chose to attack Chinese forces with conventional arms or even with tactical nuclear weapons, its forces would be confronted by the daunting problem of holding large areas of Chinese territory inhabited by a hostile population and defended by large Chinese armies. To this degree Mao's notion of a people's war is still cited although with decreasing force and relevance as Chinese conventional forces are modernized and deployed to absorb the first shock of a possible (though progressively implausible) Soviet attack. An attacker would be faced either with being drawn into an unwinable conventional war or of being forced to escalate to nuclear weapons, with all their attendant costs and risks, without the assurance that China would be defeated (Wang, 1984, p. 1048). China's consistent pledge of no-first use appears also designed to conceal Chinese weakness and to place the burden of choice of crossing the nuclear firebreak squarely in the hands of the attacker.

While Beijing continues to deprecate the importance of nuclear weapons as strategically decisive (Segal, 1985, pp. 245–249), China's conventional deterrent posture is slowly but steadily being reinforced by the development of tactical, theatre, and strategic nuclear arms. Several tests have been conducted since 1977 at levels below 20-kiloton (kt) yields, suggesting a Chinese miniaturization program. Meanwhile, progress is reported to have been made on developing delivery vehicles for tactical nuclear arms, including aircraft, missiles, artillery, and atomic demolition munitions (ADMs). The latter, which fit perfectly with China's defensive posture toward the Soviet Union, would be used to hinder the advance of an invading army by destroying mountain passes, disrupting waterways, or raising widespread havoc. In conjunction with these efforts, tactical aircraft, armed with nuclear weapons, would assume theatre missions. They would supplement China's estimated 50 medium-range ballistic missiles (MRBMs), each armed with a 20-kt warhead that have been deployed since the 1970s (Lin, 1988, pp. 90–92).

Chinese strategic forces are based on a triad of bombers and a small but gradually expanding number of land- and sea-based missiles. There appear to be a modest number of nuclear-capable bombers and fighter-bombers in China's inventory of over 5,000 largely aging jet aircraft (Pollack, 1981, p. 138; IISS, 1986, p. 142) The long-range bomber force is composed of approximately 120 Tu-16 Badgers, built in the 1950s, and of a portion of China's 500 Ilyushin IL-28 Beagles, a light bomber. The Tu-4 has been retired and a new bomber, the Hong-8, is being developed (Lin, 1988, pp. 47–48). These forces are supplemented by 60 intermediate-range ballistic missiles, armed with 2-megaton (mg) warheads as well as 5–10 limited-range and 5–10 long-range ICBMs carrying, respectively, 3-mg and 5-mg warheads. China is also reportedly working on MIRVing. In 1981, it successfully launched three satellites with one missile, and in 1985 it was alleged to have tested its first multiple warhead missile (Lin, 1988, p. 55).

Beijing also has a program underway to develop sea-based delivery vehicles, including ballistic and cruise missiles. In 1982, the Chinese successfully tested a sea-launched ballistic missile and reportedly have two missile-carrying submarines, each with twelve ballistic missiles (IISS, 1986, pp. 142–3; Jacobs, 1985). If a fleet of such submarines can be built and deployed with long-range missiles, the Chinese will have the kernel of an invulnerable second-strike force and confront the Soviet Union with a four-sided strategic nuclear threat—three from the West and one from its own forces. Since sources differ about the size and composition of Chinese nuclear forces, the analyst should be cautious about relying on any one source for force levels, or in equating warhead and delivery data with operational capabilities. (Contrast, e.g., Lin, 1988, which is the most comprehensive, with Fieldhouse, 1987; IISS, 1986, pp. 142–43; and Segal and Tow, 1987.)

As India observes the inexorable expansion of China's nuclear arsenal and as Pakistan draws nearer to a nuclear detonation, pressures mount on New Delhi to abandon its posture of deterrence by ambiguity. India can already attack Pakistan with Anglo-French Jaguar aircraft. This delivery capacity will be enhanced by the introduction of Mig-29s and French Mirage 2000s into India's inventory (Naim, 1987, pp. 251–82). India's well-developed civilian missile program also positions it to develop IRBM and ICBM capabilities comparatively rapidly if this is deemed necessary. The prospect of growing Chinese nuclear forces (Lin, 1988; Bhatia, 1985), a Pakistani nuclear explosion, and a reactive Indian decision to develop a nuclear weapons systems promises to spark an Asian nuclear arms race, with potentially damaging effects not only on regional stability but also on the superpower balance (Chari, 1986). Strategies to promote regional nonproliferation will recede in relevance as new and untried deterrence strategies assume their place. The peculiar resource constraints of South Asia, the special circumstances of its regional balances and rivalries, and the singular dynamics of its internal politics strongly suggest that the experience of the superpowers or the European nuclear powers will provide only a tenuous, even misleading, guide to the future of Asian nuclear deterrence.

NUCLEAR DETERRENCE IN THE MIDDLE EAST

As the focus shifts from Europe and Asia to the Middle East, the players and rules of deterrence also change. At least four novel elements are present. First, there is no formally recognized nuclear state or power in the region. Israel officially pursues a deliberate policy of denial, an approach that, only on the surface, appears similar to that of India and Pakistan. Since 1965, Israeli governments have relied on the formula that "Israel does not have nuclear weapons and will not be the first to introduce them into the region" (quoted in Beres, 1986, p. 191). In contrast to South Asian deterrence practice, however, Israel appears to have an undisclosed but impressive number of nuclear arms and means of delivering them (*Sunday Times,* London, October 5, 1986; Steinberg, 1986; Harkavy, 1977). Israel is therefore something more than a nuclear state, but not a full-fledged nuclear power.

Second, the number of regional opponents to be deterred are multiple. Twenty-one members of the Arab League are opposed in varying degree to the existence or to the territorial and strategic policies of the Israeli state (Aronson, 1984; Yaniv, 1986, 1987). Over the past forty years, these states, in various combinations, have been at war with, or have supported armed hostilities against, Israel. In no other region is the spectrum of threats facing a (potential) nuclear opponent as wide, diverse, or intense. Conversely, Israeli exercise of its nuclear option or, in the aftermath of public avowal, its threat to use nuclear weapons will very likely have a variable impact on the governmental leadership of its Arab adversaries who are at odds with themselves, including some who confront determined domestic opponents. Their reactions will be conditioned by their hostility to Israel, the material resources at their disposal to counter Israeli nuclear forces, and their own inner-Arab and internal differences that bar a united stance. These differing responses cannot be understood solely in current action-reaction models of arms races or superpower bilateral deterrence theory.

Third, the internal stability of regional adversaries is more uncertain in the Middle East than in Europe or Asia. It is not always clear which rival faction contesting for governmental power is to be deterred or by whom. Therefore, deterrence works under far more fluid and diffuse conditions than between the superpowers or in other regions.

Fourth, the pattern of security commitments of the superpowers to regional opponents in the Middle East differs from the patterns in Europe and in Asia. U.S.-Israeli ties are as close as any between the United States and its NATO allies, although no formal treaty binds the two states together. In contrast, the mutual security commitments between the superpowers and the Arab states and Iran have varied over time in scope, durability, and reliability. Whether and to what extent superpower nuclear deterrence behavior has had an impact on regional powers or whether Israel's own ambiguous nuclear deterrent practices have had a desired effect on its opponents are questions that receive contradictory replies from analysts. Some contend that in the Yom Kippur War, Israel's ambiguity "helped secure the Arabs a conventional war game, safe from Israel's nuclear threat, of which Israel herself was more afraid than her foes" (Aronson, 1984, p. 139). Others dispute the view that Israeli ambiguity eased the Arab decision to attack Israel in 1973 (Evron, 1984).

Israel's current policy of deliberate ambiguity is alleged to have three benefits: retention of a strong and reliable U.S. security guarantee; discouragement of the Soviet Union's extension of its nuclear deterrent and security commitments to its Arab clients; and inhibition of a "dangerous Arab-Israeli and . . . Middle Eastern . . . nuclear arms race" (Yaniv, 1986, p. 59). In contrast to British and French nuclear strategies, which are aimed as much at the United States as the Soviet Union, Israel's non-nuclear posture assures Washington that close security ties with Israel do not increase the threat of regional nuclear war or a nuclear confrontation with the Soviet Union as a byproduct of possible Israeli nuclear threats aimed at Arab clients of the Soviet Union. Whereas Britain has sought to ensure the American nuclear guarantee by acquiring nuclear weapons through a special cooperative relationship with the United States, Israel has attempted to strengthen the American security commitment by publicly eschewing nuclear weapons or their pursuit. There is also little sentiment in Israel for the French approach, which is partially aimed at imposing its preferred strategy on the United States through the manipulation of nuclear threats.

There are also divided views in Israel about what military form an announced nuclear option might assume either as a credible second- or first-strike posture. In the former instance, Israel would have been destroyed, and in the latter, it might visit nuclear destruction upon itself either in provoking an Arab or Soviet nuclear response or in having to cope with the radioactive fallout of its own weapons explosions against nearby Arab opponents. Nuclear weapons appear to be accepted as a measure of last resort. A policy of ambiguity presumably retains the deterrent effect of nuclear weapons without having to exercise the option with a potentially damaging impact on the American security guarantee and on badly needed economic and political assistance which depends on the U.S. commitment.

Those opposed to an open nuclear policy for Israel also contend that a nuclear Israel will not intimidate the Soviet Union but will prompt extension of its nuclear shield to its Arab allies. Larger British or French nuclear capabilities than those that are possibly in Israeli hands have neither cowed the Soviet Union nor precluded Moscow from brandishing its nuclear weapons in Middle Eastern conflicts, alternately against France and Britain in the Suez crisis or at different times, more implicitly than explicitly, against the United States. Israel does not possess delivery vehicles capable of reaching the Soviet Union's major population centers, although advances in missile technology, including the range and accuracy of the Jericho missile, may place cities in southern Russia at risk. Israel would still confront formidable penetration problems in attempting to reach targets in southern Russia against alerted and formidable Soviet defenses. A deliberate and announced Israeli nuclear deterrent policy would pressure the Soviet Union to support its interests in the Middle East by confronting Israel directly, by greater military aid and commitment to its Arab clients, or both. Meanwhile, Soviet and American efforts to discourage Arab or Pakistani and Indian nuclear programs would be fundamentally undermined.

The stimulation of a Middle Eastern nuclear arms race would be particularly disturbing in light of the multiple number and instability of Israel's regional opponents. As several commentators observe, and as terrorist behavior in the region suggests, Israel's adversaries are not necessarily motivated by a desire for their own self-preservation or that of their states—an assumption presumed to underlay the deterrence behavior of the major nuclear powers. The goal of a liberated Palestine or simply of a destroyed Israel could conceivably prompt a breakdown in deterrence. Notions of rational control of nuclear weapons shift as the political and psychological context for deterrence changes. What then would be considered "rational" behavior would vary widely if one were speaking about the patterned behavior of the superpowers or about deeply seated emotional and historically sanctioned Arab-Israeli antagonisms. The nuclear thresholds and punishment-absorptive capacities of Middle Eastern opponents are also likely to be very different from those of other nuclear powers. Nuclear Middle Eastern states are likely to be more willing to take greater risks in threatening or in using nuclear weapons. Perceptions of self-defense, given opposed military forces at a high state of alert, may invite a preemptive strike. "The objective of such a strike would not be conquest per se, but rather national security through prophylaxis" (Beres, 1986, p. 5).

The political strife within many Arab states raises the prospect of nuclear weapons falling into the hands of increasingly radical elements, even terrorist groups who may not be deterred by the same considerations of cost, risk, and punishment associated with the way deterrence is expected to be played among developed nuclear powers and responsible governments. Deterrence then becomes entwined with domestic turmoil, *coups d'état,* and terrorist activities.

The material conditions under which nuclear deterrence would be played in the Middle East also pose serious problems for the maintenance of a stable deterrence regime. Asymmetrical strategies are likely to be more the rule than the exception. Nuclear adversaries in the region would differ widely in their nuclear capabilities, their delivery systems, the vulnerability of their nuclear facilities and deployed weapons, the quality of their safety mechanisms, and their C^3I systems. The probability of greater accidental, unintentional, and unauthorized nuclear firings would also very likely rise, possibly triggering a regional holocaust. The likelihood of these occurrences increases as one examines the diverse systems of political and military authority within the region. The chances of "authorized" use of these weapons may actually increase. The incentives for preemption may also be enhanced not only as reactions to what are perceived as hostile moves by an opponent, but also in response to internal threats. The lack of safe and sophisticated nuclear capabilities and C^3I systems exacerbates the instabilities already inherent in the multiple levels of conflict between rival factions within a state and between states (Beres, 1986; Dowty, 1986).

Opposed to this line of reasoning are a group of analysts who argue that an avowed Israeli nuclear state, with advanced weapons systems, or, more generally, a nuclear Middle East would actually be a source of regional stability. There are those, like former Defense Minister Moshe Dayan, who pointed to repeated breakdowns of conventional deterrence in the Middle East and to the increasing costs and perceived risks of a non-nuclear posture (Steinberg, 1986). A nuclear Israel is said to compensate for the deficiencies of conventional deterrence and Israel's long-term vulnerability confronted by a vastly larger Arab population, possessed of greater geographic extension and resource capabilities. Dispelling ambiguity is viewed as a strengthening of deterrence, a precondition for the development of doctrine and safe practices for the creation, deployment, and control of nuclear forces, and as a check on opponent miscalculation. The experience of the superpowers in stabilizing their arms competition is transported to the Middle East where each adversary's commitment to destroy its foe would be offset by the fear of its own annihilation (Feldman, 1982).

Other analysts go further and allege that a nuclear Israel might actually strengthen the hand of Arab leaders in their attempt to answer domestic critics who insist on Israel's destruction or isolation. A nuclear Israel would weaken the expectation that Israel can eventually be defeated without the Arab states risking their own self-destruction (Aronson, 1984). In addition, a nuclear Israel would make Israel less dependent on the United States, freeing it of the uncertainties and vicissitudes of the American security guarantee (Tucker, 1975).

These supporting arguments for a nuclear Israel are offset not only by the considerations sketched earlier, but also by specific rejoinders to the alleged benefits of explicit Israeli avowal of nuclear weapons. Conventional deterrence may actually have worked if one focuses on the "calculus" of expectations of Arab states over time, and not narrowly on the outbreaks of hostilities in the region. Over the past forty years, several Arab states have abandoned the aim of Israel's destruction. Egypt, with the largest military forces of the Arab states, has signed a peace treaty with Israel. Both states, along with several other moderate Arab regimes, are essentially contained within an American-led security system. Israeli announcement of a nuclear capability and, by inference, a more independent military stance, would possibly damage the international framework on which its security depends by forcing a reexamination of the American guarantee; by encouraging, as noted already, greater Soviet military intervention in the region (already signalled, for example, in treaty commitments to Syria); and by stimulating Arab and greater Islamic efforts to acquire nuclear weapons (Yaniv, 1986).

Regional proliferation potentially destabilizes the superpower management of their global arms race and deterrence regime; Israeli conventional capabilities will decline as a function of scarce resources being devoted to nuclear weapons; ironically, Israel is likely to be self-deterred by its own weapons; and its diplomatic isolation will be reinforced. The transition to a nuclear Middle East would itself be destabilizing in light of the differential military and technological capabilities of opponents. These potentially damaging consequences of a nuclear Israel and Middle East would not be offset by any measurable enhancement of Israeli security which is not otherwise already attainable by continued pursuit of a policy of nuclear ambiguity (Yaniv, 1986, 1987).

THE FUTURE OF MULTILATERAL DETERRENCE: FUTURE RESEARCH AGENDA

There is ample room for new theory-building and empirical research to describe and explain the workings of multilateral deterrence. Compared to the literature bearing on bilateral deterrence between the superpowers or on specific national programs, such as French or British nuclear behavior, there are serious gaps in our knowledge that need to be filled and new questions need to be posed about the stability of regional and global nuclear deterrence systems and how, if at all, they mutually interact.

This brief review has identified several characteristics of deterrence that need examination. First, there is the issue of numbers. The so-called N-country problem needs to be reexamined in light of the modernization programs of Britain, France, and China, the possible transformation of India from a nuclear state to a nuclear power, and the possibility of Israel's and Pakistan's emergence as nuclear powers. The implications of these possible developments for regional and global nuclear deterrence and stability, as well as an increase in the number of new nuclear states or powers, remain to be fully explored. It is by no means clear whether regional and global stability, that is, regimes inhibiting the use of nuclear weapons, would be strengthened by increased proliferation. (For one such effort, see Jones, 1984; an earlier work that is still relevant is Kemp, 1974a and 1974b.)

Second, depending on the region under examination, threat patterns and the role assigned to nuclear weapons or even the decision to exercise such an option vary widely and do not conform to the expectation of behavior arising from our knowledge of superpower deterrence. For India and Israel, regional neighbors present more of a security problem than either superpower. Yet one or the other or both superpowers are expected to support, partially through their nuclear policies, regional security regimes on which these incipient nuclear states depend. The differential and divergent expectations of superpower support are highlighted by the British and Israeli cases where exercise of a nuclear option by Britain is supposed to reinforce the U.S. nuclear guarantee, while the same strategy is viewed by most (but not all) analysts as a weakening of the U.S. guarantee for Israel.

Third, the domestic determinants of deterrence policies are also more clearly exposed in regional behavior. China appears to have placed a lower priority on nuclear modernization than one might have expected. It has instead been assigning greater resources to long-term social reform, economic growth, industrialization, and techno-scientific development. These priorities have apparently slowed the rate and scope of nuclear and conventional arms modernization. Moreover, as a weak nuclear power relative to the superpowers, Beijing has apparently put more emphasis on diplomacy than on military deterrence to relax the imperatives of its security needs. Meanwhile, China's low nuclear profile but steady, if gradual, nuclear weapons modernization program would appear to have a restraining effect on any Indian decision to assume a nuclear power status. Any shift in Chinese priorities toward a faster paced nuclear modernization might well tilt Indian internal opinion toward a nuclear weapons option. This trend could be reinforced either if China assists in Pakistan's nuclear development or if

Pakistan goes nuclear on its own accord. From an opposed angle, Israeli domestic opinion is split on the question of the exercise of its nuclear option. This division is not likely to be repaired if Israel becomes an announced nuclear power. The implications for regional stability of a divided Israeli consensus on deterrence practice which is aimed at shifting factional elements competing for power within rival Arab states are by no means clear.

Equally uncertain are the long-term repercussions of internal opposition to Britain's Trident program and, more generally, to its possession of nuclear weapons. With less than 50 percent of the vote, the Thatcher government has won a majority of seats in three successive parliamentary elections (1979, 1983, and 1987). However, it confronts a Labour party officially prepared to renounce nuclear weapons or bargain them away. The Alliance, composed of Liberals and Social Democrats, has opted for a smaller deterrent than Trident, but support for this option is weak, especially among many Liberals whose opposition to an independent British nuclear deterrent parallels that of the Labour party. Even France's consensus on nuclear weapons may be more brittle than has been assumed (Yost, 1985a and 1985b; Harrison, 1981). The Gaullist policy of the empty chair appears to have been overtaken by new strategic imperatives and by internal economic, technological, and political constraints which have inhibited France from keeping pace with the superpowers (Heisbourg, 1987).

The material dimensions of deterrence also vary widely as one moves from Europe to Asia and the Middle East. Exploding a nuclear device is only a partial resolution of the problem of creating a credible deterrent. A working weapons system requires reliable and invulnerable delivery vehicles, testing facilities, and a dependable and invulnerable C^3I infrastructure. Little is known about how these systems might look and how they might operate (Karp, 1984–1985). From an arms control perspective, the superpowers may have to contemplate sharing their C^3I technology with smaller nuclear powers if their efforts to stop proliferation fail.

Analysts are already positing the need to adjust to a proliferated world (Dunn, 1982). It follows that assisting nuclear states to stabilize their regional deterrence systems may be the next logical, if unpalatable, measure that may have to be taken by advanced nuclear powers to ensure that stable deterrence prevails between and among them and that smaller states are able to manage their emerging nuclear deterrence regimes or to relax the requirements for erecting them in the first place. This latter concern focuses renewed interest in fostering conventional deterrence strategies and in providing non-nuclear arms to states to decrease the incentives to go nuclear—the so-called "dove's dilemma." But before deterrence can be "engineered" to work better regionally and globally, we will need to know more than we know now about how the superpower experience applies (if at all) to the regional security needs of actors and how regional nuclear states and powers impact in what appear to be novel and significant ways on the superpower nuclear competition. Maintaining deterrence under different regional strategic and political conditions is more difficult and hazardous than some analysts imply (Waltz, 1981).

Like hanging, nuclear weapons focus attention. They provoke caution against risk taking. Witness Israeli and Indian and Pakistani prudence in developing nuclear forces or in announcing their aims in pursuing their nuclear policies. But viewed as a socio-political system rather than just a collection of force capabilities, deterrence in more complex and volatile than a narrowly conceived analysis of destructive capabilities implies. Rules for stability vary widely across regions, and need to be better understood and observed. In addition, supporting accords and political constraints need to be devised and appropriately engineered to regional specifications if nuclear deterrence is to work, that is, not lead to a nuclear attack or exchange.

REFERENCES

Ailleret, Charles. December 1967. "Défense 'Dirigée' ou Défense 'Tous Azimuts' " *Revue Défense Nationale*, pp. 1923–33.

Aron, Raymond. 1965. *The Great Debate: Theories of Nuclear Strategy*. Trans. Ernst Pawel. New York, N.Y.: Doubleday.

Aronson, Shlomo. 1984. "The Nuclear Dimension of the Arab-Israeli Conflict: The Case of the Yom Kippur War." *Jerusalem Journal of International Relations* 7:107–42.

Baylis, John. 1984. *Anglo-American Defence Relations: 1939–1984,* 2nd ed., London: Macmillan.

Beaufre, André. 1966. *Deterrence and Strategy*. Trans. from the French by R. H. Barry. New York, N.Y.: Praeger.

Beres, Louis René. 1986. *Security or Armageddon*. Lexington, Mass.: Lexington Books.

Bertram, Christoph. 1982. "Implications of Theatre Nuclear Weapons in Europe." *Foreign Affairs* 60:305–26.

———. 1986. "Strategic Defense and the Western Alliance." Pp. 279–96 in Franklin Long, *et al.,* eds., *Weapons in Space*. New York, N.Y.: W. W. Norton.

Bhatia, Anita. October 1985. "India's Space Program: Cause for Concern." *Asian Survey* pp. 1013–30.

British Embassy, November 15, 1986. News Release. Washington, D.C.

Chari, P. R. 1978. "China's Nuclear Posture: An Evaluation." *Asian Survey* 18:817–28.

———. 1985. "How to Prevent a Nuclear Arms Race between India and Pakistan." Pp. 120–63 in Bhabani Sen Gupta, ed., *Regional Cooperation and Development in South Asia*. New Delhi: South Asia, Vol. I.

Cohen, Stephen P. 1984. *The Pakistan Army*. Berkeley, Calif.: University of California Press.

———, ed. 1987. *The Security of South Asia*. Urbana, Ill.: University of Illinois Press.

Dowty, Alan. 1986. "Going Public with the Bomb." Pp. 15–28 in Louis René Beres, *Security or Armageddon*. Lexington, Mass.: Lexington Books.

Dunn, Lewis. 1982. *Controlling the Bomb*. New Haven, Conn.: Yale University Press.

Evron, Yair. 1984. "The Relevance and Irrelevance of Nuclear Options in Conventional

Wars: The 1973 October War." *Jerusalem Journal of International Relations* 7:143–73.

Feldman, Shai. 1982. *Israeli Nuclear Deterrence: A Strategy for the 1980s.* New York: Columbia University Press.

Fenske, John. 1986. "France and the Strategic Defense Initiative: Speeding Up or Putting on the Brakes?" *International Affairs* (London), 62:231–46.

Fieldhouse, Richard. 1987. Chinese Nuclear Forces. Pp. 255–68 in Carl Jacobsen, ed., *Weapons Without Hope? Military Technologies of the Future,* London: Oxford University Press.

Fourquet, Michel. May 1969. "Emploi des différents systèmes de forces dans le cadre de la stratégie de dissuasion." *Revue de Défense Nationale,* pp. 757–67.

Freedman, Lawrence. 1980. *Britain and Nuclear Weapons.* London: Macmillan.

———. 1981. "Britain: The First Ex-Nuclear Power?" *International Security* 6:80–104.

———. 1985a. "British Nuclear Targeting." *Defence Analysis* 1:81–99.

———. 1985b. "Role of Third-Country Nuclear Forces." Pp. 113–40 in Jeffrey Boutwell et al., eds., in *Conflict in Europe.* London: Croom Helm.

Freeman, J. P. G. 1986. *Britain's Nuclear Arms Control Policy in the Context of Anglo-American Relations, 1957–1968.* London: Macmillan.

Gallois, Pierre. 1961. *The Balance of Power.* Trans. Richard Howard. Boston, Mass.: Houghton Mifflin.

Gowing, Margaret. 1974. *Independence and Deterrence: Britain and Atomic Energy, 1945–52.* 2 vols. London: Macmillan.

Grove, Eric J. 1985. *Where and When? The Integration of British and French Nuclear Forces with the Arms Control Process.* Faraday Discussion Paper, No. 5. London: Council for Arms Control.

Harkavy, Robert E. 1977. *Spectre of a Middle Eastern Holocaust: The Strategic and Diplomatic Implications of the Israeli Nuclear Weapons Program.* Monograph series in World Affairs. Denver, Colo.: University of Denver Press.

Harrison, Michael M. 1981. *The Reluctant Ally: France and Atlantic Security.* Baltimore, Md.: Johns Hopkins University Press.

Heisbourg, Francois. Spring 1986. "Europe/Etats-Unis: Le couplage stratégique menacé." *Politique Internationale,* pp. 111–27.

———. 1987. "Défence française: L'Impossible Statu Quo." *Politique Entrangère* 36:137–53.

Hernu, Charles. December 1983. "Equilibre, dissuasion, volonté: La voie étroite de la paix et de la liberté." *Défense Nationale,* pp. 15ff.

Howe, Sir Geoffrey. March 15, 1985. *Speech of Rt. Hon. Greffrey Howe,* Secretary of State for Foreign and Commonwealth Affairs.

International Institute for Strategic Studies (IISS), 1986. *The Military Balance: 1986–1987.* London.

Jacobs, G. February 1985. "China's Submarine Force." *Jane's Defence Weekly.* pp. 220–24.

Jones, Rodney W. 1984. *Small Nuclear Forces and U.S. Security Policy.* Lexington, Mass.: Lexington Books.

Karp, Aaron. 1984/1985. "Ballistic Missiles in the Third World." *International Security* 9:166–95.

Kelleher, Catherine McArdle. 1981. "The Present as Prologue: Europe and Theater-Nuclear Modernization." *International Security* 5:150–68.

Kemp, Geoffrey. 1974a. *Nuclear Forces for Medium Powers: Part I: Targets and Weapon Systems.* Adelphi Paper, no. 106. London: IISS.

———. 1974b. *Nuclear Forces for Medium Powers: Part II and III: Strategic Requirements and Options.* Adelphi Paper, no. 107. London: IISS.

Kohl, Wilfrid L. 1971. *French Nuclear Diplomacy.* Princeton, N.J.: Princeton University Press.

Kolodziej, Edward A. 1974. *French International Policy Under De Gaulle and Pompidou: The Politics of Grandeur.* Ithaca, N.Y.: Cornell University Press.

———. 1987a. "Modernization of British and French Nuclear Forces: Arms Control and Security Dimensions." Pp. 239–254 in Carl Jacobsen, ed., *Weapons Without Hope? Military Technologies of the Future.* London: Oxford University Press.

———. 1987b. *Making and Marketing Arms: The French Experience and Its Implications for the International System.* Princeton, N.J.: Princeton University Press.

Lin, Chong-Pin. 1988. *China's Nuclear Weapons Strategy: Tradition within Evolution.* Lexington, Mass.: Lexington Books.

Malone, Peter. 1984. *The British Nuclear Deterrent.* London: Croom Helm.

McInnes, Colin. 1986. *Trident: The Only Option?* London: Brassey's Defence Publishers.

Méry, Guy. June 1976. "Une Armée pour quoi faire et comment." *Défense Nationale,* pp. 16–27.

Naim, S. Rashid. 1987. Asia's Day After: Nuclear War Between India and Pakistan? Pp. 250–81 in Stephen P. Cohen, ed., *The Security of South Asia.* Urbana: University of Illinois Press.

Pierre, Andrew. 1972. *Nuclear Politics: The British Experience with an Independent Nuclear Force, 1939–1970.* London: Oxford University Press.

Poirier, Lucien. 1983. *Essais de Stratégie Théorique.* No. 22. Paris: Fondation Pour les Etudes de Défense Nationale.

Pollack, Jonathan. 1981. "The Evolution of Chinese Strategic Thought." Pp. 137–52 in Robert O'Neill and D. M. Horner, eds., *New Directions in Strategic Thinking.* London: Allen and Unwin.

Rao, R.V.P. Chandrasekhara. 1981. "Strategic Thinking in India in the 1970s: Prospects for the 1980's." Pp. 153–168 in Robert O'Neill and D. M. Horner, eds., *New Directions in Strategic Thinking.* London: Allen and Unwin.

Segal, Gerald, and William T. Tow, eds. 1987. *Chinese Defense Policy.* Urbana, Ill.: University of Illinois Press.

Segal, Gerald. 1981. "China's Nuclear Posture in the 1980s." *Survival* 23:11–18.

———. 1982. "China's Security Debate." *Survival* 24:68–77.

———. 1985. *Defending China.* London: Oxford University Press.

Simpson, John. 1986. *The Independent Nuclear State: The United States, Britain, and the Military Atom,* 2nd ed. London: Macmillan.

Spector, Leonard S. 1984. *Nuclear Proliferation Today.* New York, N.Y.: Vintage.

Steinberg, Gerald M. 1986. "Deliberate Ambiguity: Evolution and Evaluation." Pp. 29–44 in Louis René Beres, *Security or Armageddon.* Lexington, Mass.: Lexington Books.

Sunday Times (London) 5 October 1986. Revealed: the Secrets of Israel's Nuclear Arsenal.

Talbott, Strobe. 1985. *Deadly Gambits.* New York, N.Y.: Vintage.

Thomas, Raju G. C. 1986. "India's Nuclear and Space Programs: Defense or Development?" *World Politics* 382:315–42.

Tucker, Robert. 1975. "Israel and the United States: From Dependence to Nuclear Weapons?" *Commentary* 60:29–43.

Waltz, Kenneth N. 1981. *The Spread of Nuclear Weapons: More May Be Better.* Adelphi Paper, no. 171. London: IISS.

Wang, Robert S. 1984. "China's Evolving Strategic Doctrine." *Asian Survey* 24:1040–55.

Wong-Fraser, Agatha S. Y. 1981. "China's Nuclear Deterrent." *Current History* 80:245–49.

Yaniv, Avner 1986. "Israel's Conventional Deterrent: A Re-Appraisal." Pp. 45–60 in Louis René Beres, *Security or Armageddon.* Lexington, Mass.: Lexington Books.

———. 1987. *Deterrence without the Bomb: The Politics of Israeli Strategy.* Lexington, Mass.: Lexington Books.

Yost, David S. 1985a. *France's Deterrent Posture and Security in Europe;* Part I: *Capabilities and Doctrine.* Adelphi Paper, no. 194. London: IISS.

———. 1985b. *France's Deterrent Posture and Security in Europe;* Part II: Adelphi Paper, no. 195. London: IISS.

———. 1986. "French Nuclear Targeting." Pp. 127–56 in Desmond Ball and Jeffrey Richelson, eds., *Strategic Nuclear Targeting.* Ithaca, N.Y.: Cornell University Press.

———. 1988. Western Europe and the U.S. Strategic Initiative. *Journal of International Affairs* 41:269–324.

6

On Extended Deterrence

DAVID N. SCHWARTZ

As long as alliances between stronger and weaker nations have existed—that is, as far back as Ancient Greece—one of the great problems of statecraft has been how to use the power of the strong to guarantee the security of the weak. At its root, the problem we know today by the name of extended deterrence is only the most recent manifestation of this much older problem. But if NATO's political leaders in the nuclear era face the same basic problem as that which faced the leaders of the Athenian alliance in the fifth century B.C., it must be conceded that the strategic environment in which this problem must be solved is vastly different.

- The leader of each alliance has the capacity unilaterally to destroy the leader of the other alliance, a capacity against which there is no current (or for that matter, the Strategic Defense Initiative notwithstanding, any likely future) defense.

- The use of such a capacity cannot prevent the other leader from exercising its own destructive capacity in retaliation. Hence, mutual suicide is a possible and perhaps likely outcome of any nuclear attack by one superpower against the other.

- Both the United States and the Soviet Union are global powers, whose interests (and vulnerabilities) extend well beyond the confines of the alliance systems they respectively lead.

This chapter will explore the concept of extended deterrence as applied to the problems facing NATO, and by inference the Warsaw Pact. It will begin with some analytical considerations; elaborate on the strategic environment in which the two alliances operate; review recent history to put some of these

The author wishes to acknowledge the research assistance of Randall Poole in the preparation of this chapter.

analytical debates into a meaningful perspective; and, finally, suggest directions for further thought.

ANALYTICAL FRAMEWORK

It would be impossible to understand the debate over extended deterrence, as it has developed in the West, without first understanding the basic concept of deterrence. This topic has been touched on by other authors in this volume. In short, deterrence is thought to rest on the ability to credibly threaten to impose such high costs on a would-be aggressor that aggression becomes an irrational act; that is, there is no possible gain that is worth the likely cost of aggression to the aggressor.

Since the 1960s, the United States has attempted to maintain a robust, secure "second-strike" retaliatory capability to inflict unacceptable damage on the Soviet Union even after absorbing a full-blown nuclear onslaught by the Kremlin. As the Soviet arsenal has grown, so have the perceived requirements imposed on U.S. planners to maintain a credible deterrent. Exactly how much is required to deter an attack on the United States has been a subject of intense debate.

Some have viewed the requirements as relatively small. Surely (they argue) the possibility of the destruction of Moscow, Leningrad, Kiev, and five or six other major urban areas in the Soviet homeland should be enough to deter even the most irrational Soviet leader from attacking in the first place. We will call these the "minimal deterrence" advocates.

Others have viewed the requirements as more demanding. They argue that the Soviet leadership must be persuaded that U.S. forces must be sufficiently numerous, varied, accurate, and powerful as to pose the threat of effective retaliation, not against Soviet population centers but against the infrastructure of Soviet military capabilities. If the Soviets are really to be deterred, they argue, it is not sufficient to threaten to blow up their cities. Such a threat carries no strategic purpose other than killing millions of Russians. What is needed is to convince Soviet leaders that any such attack will result in the destruction of their capability to continue to wage war. We will call this "robust deterrence."

Yet another group in this debate has argued that even this objective is not sufficient; that Soviet leaders can only be deterred from attacking if the United States can pose a retaliatory threat to "win" in some militarily meaningful sense as a result of a direct attack by the Soviet Union.

This is, admittedly, a caricature of the debate about superpower deterrence. For example, most thoughtful observers understand that a direct, "bolt-out-of-the-blue" attack by one superpower on the other is most unlikely, given the extraordinary risks involved; that conflict between the superpowers is likely to continue, at varying degrees of intensity, at a political level; that in a political crisis leaders may not be capable of fine-tuned strategic calculations of cost and benefit in a nuclear war; and that they are more than likely to assume the absolute worst outcome in any nuclear conflict. There is also general agreement that a situation wherein it was obvious that one superpower could gain decisive advantage by attacking the other with impunity would hardly be conducive to international harmony, even were it not to lead directly to such an attack. Political coercion and blackmail could well be the result.

Politicians, in contrast to strategic analysts, tend to measure the strategic deterrence equation from a political perspective. Rather than think through the consequences of one side or the other using its nuclear weapons first in various more-or-less well-defined scenarios, they look to see if there is a "rough equivalence" between the two superpowers. Most would agree that there is; both sides have tens of thousands of nuclear weapons aimed at each other and have active, ongoing modernization programs designed to maintain large, powerful arsenals well into the twenty-first century.

The analytics become a bit more complicated when one begins to factor in the requirement to deter attack against allies as well as against oneself. What one is willing to do in response to a direct attack on oneself, when the interests at stake are rather obvious, is nevertheless a matter of some uncertainty. What would the actual response of the United States be to a "first strike" by the Soviet Union? Most people take some sort of response for granted, but what kind of response, and to what end? When one poses the same question with respect to an attack on America's allies, the uncertainties become even murkier.

The central analytical problem is often posed this way: is it possible for one country credibly to threaten suicide in defense of another country, in order to extend its deterrent over that country?

One solution, theoretically, would be to make it manifestly impossible for the guarantor not to respond to an attack on one of its allies with nuclear weapons, that is, to create a technical "tripwire" which would, for example, unleash the nuclear might of the United States against the Soviet Union in the event of a Warsaw Pact attack on West Germany even if U.S. leaders did not want to do so. Even if such a system were technically possible, however, it would seem most unwise to take such an awesome decision out of human hands. Not all attacks are the same, and not all would merit the same kind of response. Indeed, in most situations one might imagine, an attack on a NATO ally would occur only after a prolonged period of political tensions arising out of particular political issues, which are almost impossible to foresee. In such an environment, it may be extremely difficult to understand which side initiated the fighting; what kinds of military operations were in fact taking place; how well NATO forces were coping with the attack; and so on. Yet surely all this information would be essential input into any decision by U.S. leaders to initiate the use of nuclear weapons. What might be good for extended deterrence, then, would be profoundly bad for statecraft and global survival.

Another solution would be to create a situation wherein it was viewed as extremely likely—though not certain—that aggression against an ally would eventually result in the use of strategic nuclear weapons to attack the aggressor. In such a case, an aggressor would be most careful in weighing the various pros and cons in any premeditated attack, trying to think through the likely outcome of each action and weighing the likelihood of nuclear response against the potential gains in the absence of a nuclear response. In the event of accidental, or unpremeditated, aggression, both sides would have significant incentives to bring the hostilities to an end as early as possible, given the prospect of nuclear war resulting from continued military operations. In this instance, we would not only have created a strong deterrent against any kind of war breaking out; we would have established a basis for *intra-war* deterrence as well.

Such a view of extended deterrence is, as we will see, one that is widely adhered to in the West, and in some measure informs the elaboration of NATO's central doctrine of Flexible Response. Those who agree that this is the most sensible route toward achieving an extended deterrent disagree, however, on the appropriate resources and capabilities required to make it a reality.

A third way of pursuing extended deterrence is really a variant of the second one above. This entails establishing not the likelihood, but merely the possibility, that nuclear weapons would be used to defend against an attack on an ally. In some sense, the mere existence of nuclear weapons, along with the political commitment of the alliance leader to come to the defense of the ally, may be deemed sufficient to establish a possibility that would deter any but the most irrational aggressor.

There is a fourth view, of course: that extended deterrence is impossible. Some have argued, more or less articulately, that there are no conceivable circumstances in which the threat to respond with the use of strategic nuclear weapons to aggression against one's allies could be viewed as credible. For those who believe this, and who believe themselves to be threatened by another nuclear weapons state, the only logical route is to develop a deterrent of one's own.

These, then, are the four analytically complete solutions to the problem: making nuclear retaliation certain; making it probable; making it possible; and accepting it as impossible. Since, as we have argued, making it certain is neither technically possible nor politically desirable, we will find that most discussions of extended deterrence throughout the past thirty years have focused on the last three solutions. Before these approaches can have any real-world meaning, however, it is important to understand the strategic environment in which they have developed.

THE STRATEGIC ENVIRONMENT

The strategic environment relevant to understanding extended deterrence today is largely one defined by the superpower blocs. Two mutually antagonistic blocs of allies face each other across the borders of Central Europe. On one side, the North Atlantic Treaty Organization consists of sixteen nations, whose most powerful member, the United States, is separated by the Atlantic Ocean from the rest of its allies (except Canada). Every NATO member contributes a military contingent to NATO; along the central region, where the greatest threat is posed, West German forces are supported by British, Dutch, Belgian, and over 300,000 American forces. With such a large standing force, and with an extensive infrastructure for adding even more forces in time of mobilization, the United States' contribution to NATO's conventional forces is more than token. Yet it must be stated that, at least initially, U.S. forces were seen mainly as hostages, insuring that U.S. forces would be directly engaged in any initial fighting between NATO and the Warsaw Pact. This would make it more probable that U.S. nuclear weapons would eventually be used to defend NATO allies.

The U.S. contribution to NATO's defense on the continent extends beyond conventional forces. Over 3,000 U.S. nuclear weapons are stationed in Europe, for a variety of military roles and missions. All of them, however, carry with them the implicit but obvious possibility of use in any direct conflict. They were originally placed in Europe in the 1950s and early 1960s in order to bolster NATO's conventional firepower in the face of an apparently overwhelming Warsaw Pact conventional force advantage. In this sense, they were seen by military planners as just another weapon in the NATO arsenal, necessary to repel an enemy advance. Political leaders saw in their stationing a signal to the Warsaw Pact that America's commitment to their defense involved nuclear weapons; that any attack on Europe would raise the specter of nuclear war; and that, once initiated, nuclear war would very quickly lead to an intercontinental exchange between the superpowers.

In the 1950s and early 1960s, of course, this may have been comforting to European leaders and publics who saw the United States as having a rather obvious and decisive advantage over the Soviet Union in strategic nuclear power. The number of U.S. strategic bombers was overwhelmingly superior to that of the Soviet Union and could have responded to aggression with truly "Massive Retaliation," as the argument went, with little to fear in the way of reprisal. Extended deterrence was not seen as problematic, at least in this sense. When, in the mid-1960s, the Soviet Union began to pull even with the United States in the numbers and capability in its strategic nuclear arsenal, the comfort provided by the so-called tactical nuclear weapons stationed in Europe was appreciably reduced. But even then they were retained, as an additional factor in an ever more complex deterrence equation and as an important part of military contingency planning. Few today doubt that their presence adds to NATO's overall deterrent, and complicates Warsaw Pact military planning in useful ways.

Finally, the United States' immense strategic arsenal, pledged in part to the defense of NATO territory, poses an awesome threat to the Soviet Union directly. While U.S. forces could not execute a "disarming" strategic attack on the Soviet Union, few serious analysts today would argue that the Soviet Union could effectively limit damage from U.S. retaliation to such acceptably low levels as to make aggression against the United States, or any of its allies, particularly tempting.

The NATO alliance is, of course, more than a collection of military forces committed to the common defense by a solemn treaty. The member states by and large have a common political and cultural heritage, and benefit immensely from strong economic and social ties as well. All military aspects aside, this fact adds, perhaps imprecisely but certainly undeniably, to the strength of the alliance itself. The countries of Western Europe which rely on the U.S. nuclear guarantee are precisely those countries whose political, cultural, and economic relations with the United States make that guarantee plausible.

One additional element of the strategic environment worth noting here is that NATO has two other nuclear weapons states as members—Britain and France. Both have strategic nuclear weapons in part as the result of a political decision that nuclear status is what separates great powers from lesser powers in the post-war world. These arsenals are, in this sense, political statements as much as anything else. But they have from time to time been justified, particularly in France, on the grounds that extended deterrence is impossible; that U.S. nuclear guarantees cannot possibly prevent an attack on France or Britain because no American president would willingly risk Chicago for Paris.

That the Soviet Union shares, at least in post-war history, the same intimacy of relations with its Warsaw Pact partners cannot be denied. The Warsaw Pact may not resemble NATO in many ways, but its history suggests that the Soviet leadership places a particular strategic value in having these countries as a friendly strategic buffer against the armed might of the NATO allies. Soviet troops are stationed throughout the Pact, in some areas (such as Czechoslovakia) more as a reminder to the local populace of the perils of straying from the Soviet will than as a defense against NATO troops. But in East Germany, where the Soviet presence is most concentrated, the Red Army is clearly designed as a fighting machine to bring the fight to Western European territory, should it come to that. Soviet forces are equipped with nuclear as well as conventional capabilities, and the Soviet strategic nuclear arsenal is fully equal to the challenge of the Western strategic arsenals.

There are several crucial differences, however. No other Warsaw Pact state possesses its own nuclear weapons. We may never know whether Warsaw Pact allies are confident of the strategic guarantee offered by the Soviet Union, but no ally has ever been in the position of challenging the guarantee with a capability of its own. In addition, Eastern Europe itself is of very different strategic value to the Soviet Union than is Western Europe to the United States. For the United States, Western Europe's importance lies in its political and cultural heritage, and in economic resources vital for U.S. prosperity. The Soviet Union shares, to some extent, a cultural heritage with some of its

Eastern European allies, but historically very little political heritage is shared. Certainly, the Soviet Union had little confidence, at least during the immediate post-war period, in Eastern Europe as a source of economic resources vital for Soviet prosperity. What is so vital to Soviet security is the fact that the plains of Eastern Europe have historically provided the most important avenue for Russia's invaders over several hundred years, from Napoleon on down to Hitler. An attack from east to west, if successful, ends at the shores of the Atlantic, behind which sits the United States; an attack from west to east, however, ends in the Soviet heartland, with results that the current Soviet leadership remembers well.

THE DEVELOPMENT OF FLEXIBLE RESPONSE

This analysis suggests that in a changing strategic environment, what constitutes effective extended deterrence might be expected to evolve as well. Indeed, what NATO has considered necessary to feel comfortable under the strategic umbrella of the United States has changed in important ways over the past thirty years.

In the immediate post-war period, up to the late 1940s, the U.S. commitment to the defense of Western Europe was mainly declaratory. The United States had substantially demobilized, and few political leaders felt the need to consider direct military support for Western Europe. The major task facing the West was not one of deterrence, after all, but rather one of rebuilding. Even after the crucial 1947–1948 period, when Soviet actions in Eastern Europe made it clear that post-war cooperation between East and West would be impossible, the United States was reluctant to send troops back to Europe. The philosophy guiding U.S. policy at the time was straightforward. The best way to guarantee the viability of strong Western European democracies was to nurture economic recovery and to rehabilitate the major industrial strength of the West, particularly in Germany. The shift, beginning in 1948 and carrying over into the creation of NATO in 1949, from a strategy of economic development and political containment to a strategy of politico-*military* containment through the deployment of military forces was slow and difficult. Even in 1950, as the United States began to deploy a relatively small military force in Western Europe as the backbone of its NATO commitment, many in the United States viewed the arrangement as temporary. As soon as the Western European countries were back on their feet economically, the burden of military security would shift from the United States to the European partners.

In these early days, when the United States had unquestioned nuclear superiority over the Soviet Union, most NATO leaders were content with a general declaration that the United States would use its massive nuclear superiority in their defense if needed. U.S. troops in Europe were seen as more or less a tripwire (although their number and role in actual war plans have always implied more than a tripwire function). Critiques notwithstanding—and there were several very trenchant ones during the mid- to late 1950s—NATO relied on a unilateral U.S. declaration of a Massive Retaliation doctrine, which was seen not as an ideal solution to the problem of extended deterrence, but as the only affordable solution in the circumstances.

If a single event can be identified as having changed the general level of comfort with this situation, it would have to be the launching of the Sputnik satellite by the Soviet Union in 1957. Sputnik drove home, in a particularly dramatic way, that the days of U.S. invulnerability to Soviet attack, an invulnerability that underlay the credibility of the U.S. nuclear guarantee, were numbered. It was, in fact, many years before the Soviet Union could pose a threat to the U.S. homeland equal to the U.S. threat to the Soviet homeland. But the launch of Sputnik immediately touched off a debate within NATO as to the best way to ensure the continued viability of the U.S. guarantee.

One immediate reaction was to accelerate the development and deployment of U.S. intermediate-range nuclear missiles, known as Thor and Jupiter, to Europe. The deployment of these missiles provided, for the first time, a direct way of attacking the Soviet homeland with missiles from bases in Western Europe. The deployments were not without controversy, however, as Western European publics were for the first time made aware that their homelands could be targets for Soviet nuclear attack. The controversy over the deployment of these new weapons, however, led directly into another political debate—namely, whether the United States could provide extended deterrence of any kind in an environment in which it was itself directly at risk from Soviet nuclear missiles.

France, which had been trying for several years to develop its own independent nuclear deterrent, was the most vocal proponent of the proposition that deterrence could not be extended to others in an environment in which the superpowers were mutually vulnerable. In the Gaullist argument, the only country that could ultimately guarantee France's security was France—hence, the strategic argument for pursuing its own deterrent capability.

Other countries may have been sympathetic to the argument but could hardly afford the enormous expense of any national commitment to develop nuclear weapons of their own. West Germany, the newest member of NATO at the time, had expressly committed itself never to develop a nuclear capability of its own. The initial response to this dilemma was to create a NATO nuclear stockpile, controlled by the United States but available to other NATO armies upon release by the U.S. president.

Officials of the Kennedy administration felt a longer term solution was needed. One response, promoted by the Kennedy administration in the early 1960s, was the idea of a NATO multilateral nuclear force (MLF). This was to have been a jointly manned, jointly controlled fleet of nuclear-armed vessels (both surface and submarine variants were explored) which foundered on technical problems related to command and control, and political concerns over the role of West Germany in any alliance nuclear force. If the allies were nervous about the credibility of an American finger on the nuclear trigger, these concerns, it turned out, could not be allayed by placing four or five fingers on the trigger, one of which would inevitably be a German finger.

The NATO nuclear stockpile scheme, of which the MLF was perhaps the most cumbersome (and final) manifestation, was not particularly attractive to men like Robert McNamara or Maxwell Taylor, who felt that it would be extremely difficult to impose centralized control on the use of nuclear weapons by NATO; that in most imaginable military scenarios the use of nuclear weapons in the European theatre would result in the destruction of the territory NATO was trying to defend, without decisively bringing hostilities to an end; and that any long-term solution to the problem of extended deterrence had to take into account the probability that war might evolve not out of any deliberate massive assault, but out of a political crisis that got out of control, and the desirability to preserve as many options as possible for political decision-makers on both sides even after hostilities began.

What eventually developed, over a period of five or six years, was a strategic concept known as Flexible Response, formally adopted by NATO in 1967. Flexible Response held that the most effective way for the United States to extend its deterrent over the rest of its allies would be to ensure that the alliance had the capability to respond appropriately to aggression at any level at which it was initiated, holding in reserve the option to use nuclear weapons as called for by circumstances. Flexible Response envisioned three levels of response to aggression:

1. *Direct Defense:* NATO would be prepared to defend itself against a conventional assault using conventional means at first, with the goal of forcing the enemy to cease his attack and withdraw.

2. *Deliberate Escalation:* NATO would also be prepared to escalate its response, in terms of intensity and geographic scope, in order to impose costs and risks that outweighed any conceivable military or political objectives held by the Warsaw Pact. Once again, the goal would be to cause the enemy to cease hostilities and withdraw. Deliberate escalation might—although not necessarily—involve the use of nuclear weapons on the battlefield, or even behind enemy lines.

3. *General Nuclear Response:* U.S. strategic nuclear response would be an ultimate option if efforts to contain and roll back Warsaw Pact forces had failed. Such a threat would be perhaps the last desperate act of political leaders, but would certainly be considered a live prospect by Warsaw Pact leaders committed to full conquest in Western Europe.

The beauty of the concept of Flexible Response was that it was vague enough to paper over the very real differences in political perspective which drove the debates over extended deterrence during the 1960s. By not spelling out in any great detail the relationship between the three levels of response above, Europeans who were reluctant to see their homelands become another conventional battlefield akin to World Wars I and II—not to mention a nuclear battlefield of unimaginable destruction—were able to maintain a kind of hope that if hostilities ever were to erupt, they would very quickly involve inter-continental nuclear exchanges between the superpowers which would leave most of Europe intact. American leaders who were eager to avoid ever having to make a decision to use nuclear weapons were able to argue for greater conventional forces for NATO, on the grounds that both direct defense and deliberate escalation required more effective conventional forces. Military planners who had become accustomed to the availability of nuclear firepower in the theatre in order to bolster conventional force weaknesses were able to continue to rely on such weapons in the name of deliberate escalation.

At the same time, however, the adoption of Flexible Response in 1967 did indicate fundamental agreement on the part of all NATO members (except France) on a number of propositions. First, everyone accepted the notion that the U.S. strategic nuclear guarantee, uncertain though it might be in some eyes, did in fact undergird the overall NATO deterrent. Second, everyone agreed that, difficult though it might be to implement in practice, the U.S. president had to be placed in a position where he did not immediately face the dilemma of trading New York for Hamburg, or Chicago for Paris. Such a choice, difficult as it may seem, would be easier to make if it were clear that all other options had been pursued and had failed. Third, most agreed that improvements to NATO's conventional forces were essential if there was to be any meaning in the notions of direct defense and deliberate escalation.

These agreements took place in part as a result of intensive consultations in new forums within the alliance set up to develop more intimate dialogue among high-level alliance officials regarding nuclear weapons policy. Spe-cifically, the NATO Nuclear Planning Group, in which defense ministers and officials from throughout the alliance regularly meet to discuss important matters of nuclear policy, was established in the late 1960s to respond to a recognition that at least part of the nervousness over U.S. credibility had to do with the fact that alliance political leaders and officials had little regular insight into the nuclear planning process of the United States. This forum, and other institutions that have grown up around it, continue to play an important role in alliance deliberations, most recently in the development and implementation of the December 1979 intermediate range nuclear forces (INF) decision.

CONVENTIONAL FORCE ISSUES

The understanding of the late 1960s suggested that the role of conventional forces would remain a central concern of NATO doctrine, and indeed it has. The debate over what level of conventional forces is required to perform the function defined by the doctrine of Flexible Response, and over the relationship between conventional and nuclear forces, has been as intensive, wide ranging, and ultimately indecisive as any within the alliance. From the point of view of *extended deterrence,* however, the issues are a little narrower. As one might imagine, they center on the role of American forces in the conventional force structure of the alliance.

The contribution of U.S. forces to conventional defense of the front line is substantial, and has been ever since the late 1950s. Today, some 310,000 military personnel are stationed in Europe. Of this total, the vast majority are stationed in West Germany, where 205,000 soldiers serve alongside 41,000 Air Force personnel, organized in four Army divisions, several additional regiments and brigades, and two Air Force divisions. All in all, roughly 25 to 30 percent of all U.S. conventional forces are deployed in peacetime in the European theatre. In addition, during mobilization a substantial portion of the balance stationed in the United States would be brought over to the European continent. In U.S. general war planning, the "NATO contingency" is by far the most important in terms of resource planning and allocation. These are the simple facts which give teeth to U.S. efforts to support the conventional force requirements of extended deterrence.

There are two levels of debate over this commitment, one military and the other political. The military debate centers, naturally, over whether such a force, combined with the sizable contributions of the West German armed forces and the somewhat smaller contributions of other NATO members, is sufficient to perform conventional deterrence functions against the might of numerically superior Warsaw Pact forces. The analysis brought to bear on this question is fairly complex, and no attempt will be made to examine the arguments in detail. The main parameters to consider involve the amount of warning NATO would have in advance of an attack; the speed with which the two opposing military blocs could mobilize; and the general adequacy of military strategy and tactics in an environment in which technology is rapidly outstripping traditional modes of planning. Those who are fairly comfortable with the level of military resources on NATO's side argue that the fighting effectiveness of NATO forces, which would be defending their own territory, would be greater than that of the Warsaw Pact; that warning time would be sufficient to mobilize effectively against the oncoming threat; that Warsaw Pact military operations would likely be hamstrung by generally inferior technology and more complex logistical problems; and that these factors, combined with the ever-present possibility that NATO might escalate to the use of nuclear weapons, would result in an effective deterrent to all but the most desperate aggression.

On the other side are those who argue that warning time might not be as great as NATO planners assume; that mobilization across the Atlantic is bound to be more cumbersome and inefficient than assumed; that the lower tech-nology relied on by the Warsaw Pact is likely to be more robust, and more reliable, than the fragile and complex high technology on which NATO generally relies; and that Warsaw Pact armies are generally more flexible when it comes to command, control, and communications than are NATO armies.

Another theme of the military debate focuses on whether the best way to deter aggression is to be able to defend and hold at the front line, by applying the maximum firepower at the point of contact between the two armies, or alternately to concentrate firepower toward the rear of enemy operations, disrupting mobilization and command and control nodes which support Warsaw Pact operations at the front. NATO planners have gradually come to the conclusion that some shift in emphasis away from the front lines, and toward the enemy's rear echelons, is required to provide an effective deterrent against enemy attack. But the technical and fiscal requirements to make such a shift are substantial, and whether NATO can muster the resources required to achieve such a shift remains to be seen.

On the political level, the role of U.S. conventional forces has been subject periodically to intense debate within the United States. The themes of this debate are familiar: Can the United States afford to maintain such a significant commitment to the conventional defense of Europe, in light of its ongoing budgetary difficulties and demanding worldwide security commitments? Should the NATO allies contribute more to their own defense? Although these questions are somewhat amenable to quantitative analysis, the problems are at their heart political. Those who press for a greater contribution on the part of NATO allies are by and large reflecting general political frustrations that NATO allies sometimes do not see eye to eye with Washington on U.S. foreign policy objectives unrelated directly to Western European security, including such disparate matters as the Middle East, Central America, international trade and economic policies, and the response to international terrorism. But behind the general frustrations over these difficulties lies a more profound political impulse, born of 180 years of U.S. history in which the United States stood apart, quite deliberately, from the security problems of the European powers. Even after forty years, the mantle of international leadership sits uncomfortably on the American electorate. This discomfort is often felt by U.S. politicians who are required to vote for the funding of America's most important security commitment. The old isolationist impulses of the past have not been definitively put to rest, and one should expect them to resurface periodically.

The implications for extended deterrence are obvious. Intensive public debate in the United States over the political wisdom of the NATO commitment inevitably erodes perceptions of the strength of the commitment, in the eyes of both European leaders and, equally important, Warsaw Pact political leaders. Naturally, actual withdrawals of U.S. troops from Europe in the aftermath of such a debate would do more than erode these perceptions; they would fundamentally shake the confidence of European leaders in the American commitment, and change the politico-military calculations of risk and reward which shape Warsaw Pact planning.

That said, until now these debates have rarely produced the effect feared by those who believe that the U.S. commitment, both militarily and politically, must remain the centerpiece of the NATO deterrent. In part, this is because the debates have been carefully orchestrated and controlled; the major, and perhaps healthy, result has been a periodic realization among the U.S. partners that they must do more for their own defense. But one must not forget that an important reason that the debates have not resulted in reduced U.S. commitment is that the basic premise of the U.S. commitment—that it is essential in terms of narrowly construed U.S. security interests—has been sustained at the end of every such debate. As long as political sensitivity is demonstrated on both sides of the Atlantic, one might hope that this state of affairs will continue into the foreseeable future.

INTERMEDIATE RANGE NUCLEAR FORCES (INF)

The adoption of Flexible Response was in part an acceptance of the new strategic reality of a vulnerable United States. Nevertheless, changes in the strategic environment continued to alter the perceived validity of the U.S. extended deterrent. In the early 1970s, these changes were primarily political in nature, as the United States and the Soviet Union began to engage in SALT negotiations which codified a central strategic relationship without direct involvement of the allies. Most NATO political leaders were pleased that nuclear tensions between the superpowers were eased in the context of detente. Some, however, began to worry that politics and strategic self-interest might eventually lead the United States to cut a deal with the Soviet Union which would neglect the specific security interests of the NATO allies.

These fears became more real during the negotiations over SALT II. For as these negotiations developed, new Soviet systems were being deployed which seemed to some to alter the strategic equation on which extended deterrence rested. Yet SALT II did not seem to acknowledge these changes. Foremost among these was the SS-20, an intermediate range Soviet missile that began deployment in 1977. Some saw it as a fundamentally new capability; others viewed it as an evolutionary upgrade of capabilities that the Soviet Union had possessed since the 1960s, when it deployed SS-4 and SS-5 medium range missiles against European targets. But in the context of the debate over the extent to which U.S. and European strategic interests were being treated separately, its sole purpose appeared to be to target European and Asian allies, while not posing a threat to the continental United States. From the point of view of negotiators in Geneva, these systems fell outside the scope of central strategic systems which were on the table in Geneva. From the point of view of many influential European leaders, particularly Helmut Schmidt of West Germany, the U.S. neglect of these new strategic factors illuminated a new danger—namely, that imbalances in the central strategic relationship might be rectified without parallel rectification of regional imbalances. This fear, expressed by Schmidt in a well-publicized address to the International Institute for Strategic Studies in London, but obviously shared by leaders and strategists throughout the alliance, had both a political and a strategic aspect.

The political aspect was that extended deterrence would be weakened to the extent that the American president, Jimmy Carter, would be seen as neglecting major security concerns of his allies as he pursued a SALT II agreement for the United States. From a strategic aspect, however, the intro-duction of the SS-20 into the Soviet arsenal posed, in some minds at least, a direct challenge to the strategic underpinnings of Flexible Response.

The SS-20 gave the Soviet Union the ability to threaten strategic targets throughout Europe from the Soviet homeland. In this it gave Soviet leaders a new avenue for escalation of an East-West conflict. In the terminology of the strategic analyst, the Soviets had established a new "rung" on the "escalation ladder." To respond, NATO's only alternative would be to threaten the Soviet homeland with U.S. (and British) central strategic systems, since there were no theatre-based capabilities to strike Soviet territory. NATO strategists came to view this as creating a "gap" in the "spectrum of deterrence," enabling the Soviet Union, in the context of U.S.-Soviet strategic parity, to hold Western Europe hostage from the sanctuary of its homeland, confident in the knowl-edge that the only response left open to the West would be a highly incredible U.S. central strategic attack.

So went the logic behind the deliberations that eventually led NATO, in December 1979, to respond by deploying cruise missiles and Pershing II missiles in Western Europe capable of striking Soviet territory. The fact that an arms control "track" was added to the decision, allowing for the possibility of a negotiated outcome in which deployments on both sides would be lower than they might otherwise be, did not detract from the basic message. Ex-tended deterrence had been placed in jeopardy by the combined effects of SALT II, strategic parity, and deployments of threatening new Soviet missiles.

(It should be remembered that adding to widespread perceptions of de-clining U.S. strategic advantage was the beginning of the debate over a new generation U.S. ICBM to replace Minuteman. Influential U.S. analysts began to argue that U.S. strategic forces were becoming increasingly vulnerable to a disarming first strike, arguments that did little for allied confidence in the U.S. strategic guarantee.)

It is easy to criticize the logic behind the decision. It was, for one thing, hard to imagine the Soviets fine-tuning their response to a nuclear attack on their own territory on the basis of the source of that attack. In this case, the notion that cruise and Pershing missiles provided a new rung on the escalation ladder was probably illusory; their use would almost certainly trigger a central strategic exchange, and hence was no more nor less credible than the use of U.S. central strategic systems in the same circumstances. In addition, ex-tended deterrence ultimately rested not on the certainty that NATO could respond and prevail at any level of aggression the Warsaw Pact pursued, but on the inherent possibility of the use of nuclear weapons at some point in a sustained Warsaw Pact–NATO conflict, with the ultimate possibility that U.S. central strategic systems would eventually be used. The deployment of the SS-20 did not fundamentally alter any of this.

But such decisions are, in the end, the product not of pristine strategic logic, but of more compelling political arguments. The United States was faced with a damaging political debate within NATO over the credibility of U.S. leadership and the effectiveness of the nuclear guarantee, stemming from a series of inept political decisions. In order to resolve the debate, some sort of leadership was necessary; that U.S. decision-makers chose to respond by leading NATO to the two-track decision probably reflects less on their assessment of the logic of escalation dominance than it does on their assessment of the political costs of not responding at all.

At the December superpower summit in Washington, the two superpowers agreed to eliminate this entire class of weapons on both sides—the so-called zero option. Whether the zero option will, in the end, improve extended deterrence depends entirely on one's strategic and political perspectives. Here it is possible only to highlight the major lines of argument.

Those who believe that the zero option will improve extended deterrence from a strategic point of view will claim that this outcome eliminates the most important source of the problem raised in the first place—the threat posed by the SS-20 force. The Soviets will no longer be able to threaten Europe with this missile; a rung on the escalation ladder will have been removed for both sides, and we will have effectively established the status quo ante. From a political point of view, advocates of the zero option will argue that extended deterrence is strengthened not only because it represents a new level of strategic cooperation between East and West, but also because it shows that NATO was able to withstand the political pressure against deployment, move forward with deployments as scheduled, and hold out until the Soviets came around to a negotiated solution that reduced the threat to both sides substantially.

Those who oppose the zero option on strategic grounds will no doubt argue that it undermines extended deterrence because the gap in the spectrum of deterrence which was plugged by the cruise and Pershing deployments was not created by the SS-20, but was a function of a gap in NATO's capabilities. In other words, the deployments were necessary whether or not the Soviets deployed new theatre capabilities of their own. On political grounds they might oppose it because it once again shows U.S. willingness to negotiate away NATO security interests in pursuit of narrow political objectives.

In the end, however, it should be remembered that the problems that prompted NATO to decide on INF deployments in December 1979 were as much the result of political doubts over the strength of American commitment to NATO as they were the result of strategic problems surrounding escalation dominance and control. The period from 1979 until 1983, when NATO made good on its threat to deploy in the absence of a negotiated agreement to the contrary, was an extraordinary example of strong U.S. leadership and coherent alliance response in the face of concerted political opposition to the deployments. In effect, one might conclude that the process of deployment has resolved many of the doubts NATO might have harbored in the 1977–1979 period of U.S. inconsistency and policy weakness. A negotiated result that eliminates deployments on both sides, by demonstrating the political strength of NATO's INF initiative, can only strengthen extended deterrence even further.

STRATEGIC DEFENSE

If the December 1979 INF decision, and its subsequent implementation in both deployments and arms control agreements, serves unambiguously to strengthen the U.S. extended deterrent, the debate over strategic defense initiated by the 1983 U.S. Strategic Defense Initiative (SDI) is more troublesome. Although SDI has had a wide-ranging impact on NATO generally, it is appropriate to focus here only on the impact it has had on arguments about extended deterrence. Does SDI strengthen or weaken extended deterrence?

Not surprisingly, the answer depends entirely on what one defines as SDI. If SDI is seen, as President Reagan's initial speech indicated, as a step toward the elimination of nuclear weapons and the transcending of nuclear deterrence, then SDI is bound to have a very different impact on extended deterrence than if it is seen, as the president's advisers in the Pentagon seem to wish, as a means of enhancing nuclear deterrence by complicating Soviet attack planning.

For SDI to provide complete defense against nuclear missile attack—technical complexities aside—would be to render the United States invulnerable to the kind of concerted, precision first-strike attack that is seen as most dangerous and most essential for the United States to deter. NATO allies might view the United States as more likely to commit its own nuclear forces to their defense from behind a truly protective shield. This would, superficially, replicate the situation in the immediate post-war period, when U.S. invulnerability was supposed to give its nuclear guarantee greater credibility. But given the immensely greater nuclear might of the Soviet Union today, unless such a shield protected the allies as well, such assurances would hardly be comforting and would most likely be seen as eroding extended deterrence. A shield that protected the United States but left Europe vulnerable to attack would immediately transfer all nuclear risk to the allies, fundamentally undercutting extended deterrence. In effect, a fully protective shield would have to defend the allies against missile attack to the same extent that it defended the United States.

The fully protective variant of SDI becomes even more troublesome if one extends the logic to include SDI-type defenses for the Soviet Union. A fully protective shield for the Soviet Union would have even greater impact on extended deterrence, because it would fundamentally alter the range of threats the West could pose to deter aggression on Western Europe. The great danger, seen by as many U.S. as European analysts, is that with fully protective shields around both the United States and the Soviet Union both superpowers would be spared the ultimate consequences of war between the two blocs. Hence, war might become more likely. If war were in fact to occur, fully protective shields for each superpower could mean only one thing—that the war would be fought, both conventionally and with nuclear weapons, on European soil.

So far we have been analyzing the logic of the possibility of fully protective shields, without examining technical or financial realities. The technical realities are far more constraining than the logic would have us fear. The actual prospect of a fully protective defense—that is, if by fully protective one means a shield that can limit damage to the United States or the Soviet Union to acceptable levels irrespective of the intensity and scope of the attack—is so remote as to be unworthy of serious discussion (advocates' claims to the contrary notwithstanding). The more technically realistic prospects have more to do with defenses that are designed against certain highly structured, limited attacks to destroy specific U.S. or NATO military capabilities in a first strike. Here, traditional and more exotic technologies may combine in the future to provide effective defenses against these attacks, and to some degree might actually enhance the survivability of second-strike deterrent capabilities as well as command, control, and communications facilities necessary to carry out military operations. Point defense of airfields, for example, may provide useful protection against certain types of missile attacks, hence enhancing deterrence. It should be stressed, however, that such relatively traditional focuses for SDI are not at all what President Reagan has in mind for the program. It is clear that his interests, and those of his closest advisers, lean far more toward the more comprehensive objectives set for SDI in the initial flurry of policy pronouncements on the subject in 1983. To the extent that high-level political figures still believe these goals to be attractive, European allies should remain concerned about the political implications for extended deterrence. To the extent that such objectives are completely without technical foundation (not to mention financial wherewithal), European allies need not take dramatic action to underscore their concern.

CONCLUSIONS

Extended deterrence, as we have seen, is not merely a subject of some academic interest; it has been the focus of serious policy debate for over thirty years. These debates continue today and are likely to persist as long as NATO survives as an alliance. Its evolution has been, and will remain, a function of two interrelated factors: the political confidence of the NATO allies in the ability and willingness of the United States to commit its full military resources to the defense of its allies; and the technical/strategic balance of power between the United States and the Soviet Union, and between NATO and the Warsaw Pact. Both factors, politics and technology, will evolve over the next decade, and with it the debate over whether the extended deterrent inherent in the U.S. security guarantee to its NATO allies remains credible.

Areas for Further Work

Requirements for Conventional Defense

As noted above, there has been sustained debate during the 1980s as to the adequacy of NATO's conventional force posture. The work of analysts such as William W. Kaufmann and John J. Mearsheimer has brought our understanding of these requirements substantially further than they were a decade ago. However, two points are worth further attention. First, the nature of the conventional threat has changed and will continue to change; for this reason a force structure analysis must be an ongoing project. Second, it is increasingly apparent that, whatever the policy desires of future American administrations, fiscal prudence may impose a substantial rethinking about allocation of resources in the U.S. economy. The United States can probably survive the long-term effects of running $150 to 200 billion federal deficits for the past seven or eight years; it probably cannot survive another seven or eight years at the same pace. Something has to give, and cutbacks in government spending, including defense spending, cannot be ruled out. Important work must be done to consider the type of U.S. conventional forces consistent with total military spending cut back from the current 6 to 7 percent of GNP to 3 to 4 percent of GNP.

The Role of NATO's Other Nuclear Powers

Both Britain and France are in the process of modernizing their independent strategic deterrents. Britain, however, faces severe financial pressures stemming from the expense of a modern strategic submarine force. Much work has already been done to study the alternatives to the current program of Trident submarines and missiles; placing these studies more directly in the context of alliance nuclear planning would be a useful direction.

As for France, the most interesting developments have had to do with Franco-German security cooperation, and the extent to which this cooperation will or should extend to the nuclear area. This area remains potentially the most fruitful one for further study, not merely for its strategic implications but for its profound political ramifications.

BIBLIOGRAPHICAL NOTES

Extended deterrence has been the subject of an immense literature over the past four decades. The following bibliographical essay can give only a brief survey of sources for further reading.

Perhaps the best starting point can be found in one of two books: Lawrence Freedman, *The Evolution of Nuclear Strategy* (New York: St. Martin's Press, 1984), or David N. Schwartz, *NATO's Nuclear Dilemmas* (Washington D.C.: Brookings Institution, 1983). The first is perhaps the most thorough intellectual history of nuclear thought to date, and certainly should be a basic reader in every subject touched on in this chapter. The second is more focused on issues relating strictly to NATO, seen from an American perspective.

Classic treatments on the logic of deterrence, which still provide food for thought since the logical/analytical issues remain much the same as they were in the beginning, are Thomas Schelling, *The Strategy of Conflict* (Cambridge Mass: Harvard University Press, 1960), and Bernard Brodie, *Escalation and the Nuclear Option* (Princeton N.J.: Princeton University Press, 1966). Morton H. Halperin's *Limited War in the Nuclear Age* (New York: John Wiley, 1963), is also relevant today, and has a superb annotated bibliography for use in delving into the historical debates.

The best treatment on the origins of NATO remains Robert E. Osgood, *NATO: The Entangling Alliance* (Chicago: University of Chicago Press, 1957). Most of the historical episodes touched on in this chapter have at least one superb treatment of them in the literature. On the debate over Massive Retaliation, see John Foster Dulles, "The Evolution of Foreign Policy," *Department of State Bulletin* 30 (January 25, 1954), and the classic critique by William W. Kaufmann, "The Requirements of Deterrence" in Kaufmann, ed., *Military Policy and National Security* (Princeton, N.J.: Princeton University Press, 1956). On the introduction of Thor and Jupiter missiles post-Sputnik, see Michael H. Armacost, *The Politics of Weapons Innovation: The Thor-Jupiter Controversy* (New York: Columbia University Press, 1969). On the MLF, see John D. Steinbruner, *The Cybernetic Theory of Decision* (Princeton, N.J.: Princeton University Press, 1974). On the origins and development of Flexible Response, there are three excellent treatments, two from the Kennedy period and one more recent: Alain C. Enthoven and K. Wayne Smith, *How Much Is Enough? Shaping the Defense Program, 1961–1969* (New York: Harper and Row, 1969); William W. Kaufmann, *The McNamara Strategy* (New York: Harper and Row, 1964); and Jane Stromseth, *The Origins of Flexible Response* (New York: St. Martin's Press, 1988).

Historical surveys on developments in the major NATO allies are also readily available; the ones cited here are the best available from U.S. authors, and no doubt are rivaled in the domestic literature in each country. For West Germany, the best source is Catherine McArdle Kelleher, *Germany and the Politics of Nuclear Weapons* (New York: Columbia University Press, 1975); for France, Wilfrid L. Kohl, *French Nuclear Diplomacy* (Princeton, N.J.: Princeton University Press, 1971); and for Britain, Andrew J. Pierre, *Nuclear Politics: The British Experience with an Independent Strategic Force, 1939–1970* (London: Oxford University Press, 1972).

On conventional force issues, see John Steinbruner and Leon V. Sigal, eds., *Alliance Security: NATO and the No-First-Use Question* (Washington, D.C.: Brookings Institution, 1984); and John Mearsheimer, "Why the Soviets Can't Win Quickly in Central Europe,"

International Security 7 (Summer 1982). These are admittedly written from the point of view of those who believe NATO's conventional force problems are solvable, but they give an excellent introduction to the debate. On strategic defense, a good starting point is Ashton B. Carter and David N. Schwartz, eds., *Ballistic Missile Defense* (Washington, D.C.: Brookings Institution, 1984); see also Richard I. Brody, *Strategic Defences in NATO Strategy,* Adelphi Paper no. 225, International Institute for Strategic Studies, 1987. Finally, a good recent overview of issues relating to NATO nuclear problems can be found in Catherine McArdle Kelleher, "Managing NATO's Tactical Nuclear Operations," *Survival* 30, no. 1 (January/February 1988).

PART III

CONVENTIONAL WARFARE

7

On Land Warfare: NATO's Quest for Vision, 1962–1987

RICHARD L. KUGLER

Lord Salisbury, the late-nineteenth-century British prime minister, once said that, while he felt burdened by the task of weighing policy options before him, he was less worried about the actual consequences of his choices. This was true, he said, even in matters of war and peace. Evidently, he either felt confident about his decisions or doubted that they mattered much. Although this view may have been appropriate then, Salisbury probably would feel differently if he were alive today and responsible for NATO's conventional forces. The impact of his decisions likely would cause him fully as much stress as the difficulty of making them. This, at least, is their effect on modern statesmen on both sides of the Atlantic, even those with Salisbury's self-confidence and knowledge about foreign affairs.

What sets these decisions apart is, in part, the amount of money involved: each year, the alliance spends fully $250 billion on these forces. Beyond that, these decisions not only shape the military quality of NATO's forces, but also affect the alliance's vital security interests. They influence NATO's internal cohesion and peacetime security affairs in Europe, including relations with the Soviet Union. They help determine whether deterrence is preserved in Europe, and they would have a bearing on the outcome of a NATO-Warsaw Pact war there, should it occur. Above all, they might well influence whether a war can be contained at the conventional level, or instead would escalate into a nuclear conflagration that could destroy Western civilization.

Since these decisions are too important and complex to be taken lightly, NATO's leaders depend heavily on formal planning and analysis to help make them. In this context, this chapter undertakes a general examination of NATO's ability to analyze the important subject of land warfare in Central Europe. Although it focuses primarily on ground forces, it also considers the impact of air forces on the land battle. Together, these forces consume roughly two-thirds of NATO's defense spending and play a major role in the alliance's military strategy. Because decisions on how these forces are configured to wage land warfare are among the most critical and difficult ones facing NATO, the alliance especially requires a good capability to analyze them.

This appraisal does not devote major attention to institutional matters. When formal defense analysis was first adopted, some twenty-five years ago, many civilian and military leaders were ignorant of analysis and distrusted it. Moreover, the United States, the West European allies, and NATO head-quarters lacked adequate professional staffs even to perform it. But this situation has changed since then. Large staffs have been established throughout the alliance, and senior officials today normally are willing to listen when analysis has something to say. Indeed, defense analysis, albeit not preeminent, often has major influence on NATO's plans. Thus, the key issue in assessing defense analysis is not institutional, but rather competence and performance. Can analysis adequately deal with the major defense issues at stake and produce results that materially contribute to better decisions?

To help answer this question, this chapter focuses on the quality and impact of analysis itself. Rather than simply assess analysis and its methodologies by technical criteria, it examines them in their historical context. Since defense analysis is an applied, not pure, science, it can best be judged pragmatically: whether it has aided NATO's decision-making over the years. This judgment can be made only by considering the issues and the ways in which analysis has been used. The chapter addresses three distinct but overlapping phases, from the 1960's to the present, in which analysis was called on to examine different NATO land warfare issues. These issues include the NATO-Warsaw Pact conventional balance in Central Europe, NATO's force improvement plans, and maneuver warfare. For each phase, it illustrates how the policy setting shaped the agenda facing analysis, and how analysis responded to help U.S. and NATO officials make the defense choices facing them.

The following pages contend that the historical legacy of analysis, both substantively and politically, has been a positive one. Over the years, analysis has helped NATO gain a better understanding of the Center Region balance and its own priorities. Equally and perhaps more important, analysis has helped the alliance bridge strategy and politics. Beyond simply enabling NATO to clarify its views on military strategy, analysis has regularly aided in the politically demanding task of helping the alliance forge consensus on decisions regarding this critical security issue. Consequently, NATO's defense policies have been guided by greater coherence and stronger cohesion than is commonly realized, especially by critics who see only drift in the alliance.

This central theme, which is articulated below, is not meant to imply that analysis has fully resolved all of NATO's disagreements and produced co-herent policies in all areas. As well as being transparently wrong, any such claim would naively misinterpret NATO's essence. Simply stated, NATO has always been a political alliance of sovereign nations joined together by parallel strategic interests but not always identical policies. Its sometimes turbulent history is ample evidence that not all of its problems can be solved by dialogue, especially when the interests of its members are not fully aligned. But just as the presence of politics is not antithetical to rational decision-making, not all, or even most, of the defense issues facing the alliance fall outside the realm of common interests and combined planning. Within this realm, where cooperation historically has been the glue that binds the alliance together, analysis has decidedly made a difference for the better. Because of its presence, the alliance has been better informed and has decided more intelligently and effectively than otherwise would have been the case. To some important, albeit unmeasurable, degree, NATO owes its undeniable success to the positive role that analysis has played.

At the same time, neither analysis nor NATO can afford to rest on its laurels. The challenges ahead, especially the threat of maneuver war posed by the ongoing Warsaw Pact buildup, will compel the alliance to intensify its efforts to plan well and spend wisely. They will also compel analysis to stay attuned to the policy agenda facing NATO's leaders and to continue creating new and better techniques for analyzing it.

In addition to assessing the quality of NATO's analyses, this chapter, in keeping with the purpose of this volume, also seeks to summarize the "state of the art" with regard to our knowledge of land warfare. By reviewing the history of analysis on this subject, it endeavors simultaneously to identify how our knowledge of land warfare has evolved and where it stands today. This approach is possible for the simple reason that this field's analytical methods and its substantive body of knowledge have evolved closely together, in mutually reinforcing fashion. By accounting for the history of the methods, it is possible, indeed unavoidable, to assess the status of the knowledge.

In this context, it is important to note that we cannot hope to cover the entire subject of land warfare simply by studying the Central European military balance. Land warfare has occurred in many other regions, and future conflicts there could take quite different shapes than a NATO-Warsaw Pact war. Hence, what applies in Europe might not apply elsewhere, and vice versa. While generalization is accordingly difficult, a major conventional war in Europe nonetheless would be the ultimate form of land warfare. It is the frame of reference that many nations, including the superpowers, use to make decisions regarding forces and strategy for other theatres and contingencies. For this reason, planning for defense in Europe has a major spillover effect elsewhere. Thus, while the subject of this chapter is narrowly limited to one region, the implications are broader.

THE CONVENTIONAL FORCE BALANCE AND NATO'S DEFENSE STRATEGY

The first serious phase of defense analysis in NATO traces its origins to the transatlantic debates that began in the 1960s over the role of conventional forces in NATO's military strategy. At the time, the United States, led by Secretary of Defense Robert McNamara, was seeking to reduce NATO's heavy dependence on nuclear weapons, as embodied in its official military strategy (MC 14/2). The U.S. goal was to replace MC 14/2 with a new strategy that called for a combined posture of nuclear and stronger conventional forces. Many West European allies, led by France and Germany, initially preferred MC 14/2 and resisted this demarche. NATO's need to forge consensus on its military strategy left the alliance facing a long and difficult dialogue over the fundamentals of its defense planning.

To an important degree, this debate stemmed from differing strategic goals and priorities. U.S. officials believed that, because the Soviets were building their own nuclear posture, NATO's nuclear forces no longer credibly could be relied on to deter or defend against a Soviet conventional attack on West Europe. They were also concerned that nuclear escalation, once initiated, might be uncontrollable. They wanted to improve NATO's conventional posture in order to bolster deterrence as well as provide broader options short of escalation. Aware that West European economic recovery was making rapid progress, they figured that the time had arrived for the alliance to pursue more ambitious defense plans than before.

Many allies, by contrast, believed that nuclear weapons should remain the backbone of NATO's deterrent posture. Initially unwilling to concede that nuclear weapons were losing their deterrent power, they feared that a strategy change would lead to the "decoupling" of U.S. nuclear forces from Western Europe. Moreover, they were concerned that NATO, by signalling that a war might not automatically escalate, would weaken deterrence by implying a willingness to fight a long conventional war. Their preference was to continue living under the seemingly safe and inexpensive umbrella of U.S. nuclear coverage.

Eventually, the West Europeans began acknowledging that the idea of greater conventional strength had merit on grounds of not only transatlantic harmony, but also military strategy. They still questioned its affordability. Their doubts were anchored in NATO's longstanding assumption, going back to the 1952 Lisbon Force Goals, that the Warsaw Pact enjoyed a major preponderance in military strength. As long as this assumption went unchallenged, arguments in favor of a force buildup were moot because the gap appeared too great for NATO to close at affordable cost. The United States, its plans for strategy reform in abeyance, was faced with the task of trying to refute this view.

It was at this juncture that defense analysis entered the debate. McNamara had established a Systems Analysis staff in his office, and he began using it to examine the force balance in Central Europe. This was a subject that, albeit widely discussed, had not been researched in depth and was not well understood. Recognizing this situation, McNamara directed his staff to determine whether, and exactly to what degree, the Warsaw Pact's forces, in fact, were decisively superior to NATO.

McNamara's actions triggered a major U.S. and NATO analytical effort on the NATO–Warsaw Pact conventional force balance that lasted several years and, in many ways, continues today. Although the analytical tools initially available were primitive, major progress was made in improving them and gradually providing a more sophisticated understanding of the force balance. As it unfolded, this effort, while reaffirming that the Soviets pose a serious military threat to Europe, also showed that NATO's forces were stronger than commonly realized and that conventional defense was a feasible goal.

Defense analysts began studying the military balance by developing a more discriminating appraisal of how many divisions and tactical combat aircraft each side would commit to a Center Region war. The appearance of massive enemy superiority, to some degree, had stemmed from the conservative practice of counting nearly all forces in the Warsaw Pact inventory while including only those NATO forces that already were deployed in Central Europe. This practice produced a skewed picture. It credited the Soviets with many units that would not be used in Central Europe because they were needed elsewhere, while excluding forces based in the continental United States that would be deployed to Central Europe in a war.

In order to provide a more accurate picture, analysts instead began to employ symmetrical counting rules that reflected the forces that the two sides actually would deploy in a war. This technique had the effect of deflating the enemy threat to more manageable levels, while adjusting upward the forces that NATO would have at its disposal. The net result was the portrayal of a closer force balance. Over the years, analysts eventually agreed on a likely Warsaw Pact threat of about 90 ground divisions and 4,000 combat aircraft. In forces already deployed in Central Europe, NATO, even with France, was credited with only about 40 division-equivalents (counting independent brigades) and 3,000 aircraft. But full U.S. reinforcement brought NATO's posture up to about 60 divisions and 4,000 aircraft. This count left the Soviets with a 1.5:1 lead in ground forces—a worrisome margin, but far less than the 5–6:1 advantage assumed earlier.

Partially offsetting this more reassuring picture, however, was the realization that the military balance would depend not only on total forces committed by each side, but also on their buildup rates at the inter-German border. During peacetime, both sides kept few forces directly on the border. Forces based in Germany itself typically were deployed back by some 100 to 200 kilometers, whereas large reserves were kept at even longer distances. For example, about thirty Soviet divisions were deployed in the western military districts of the USSR, and about twenty U.S. division-equivalents were based across the Atlantic Ocean. In a crisis, each side would have to move its forces to the battle area; the balance, at any moment, would depend on how many units from each side had arrived.

It quickly became apparent that geography and the ability to initiate mobilization conferred important buildup advantages on the Soviets. At issue then, as now, is whether and to what degree the Soviets could employ these advantages to win a buildup race against NATO. Defense analysts examined the ability of both sides to conduct this race. Computer models were built for analyzing respective buildup rates, and the major determinants (e.g., lift needs, mobilization processes, and transportation systems) were studied in detail. This analysis initially produced the troublesome conclusion that, whereas the results were highly sensitive to enemy performance, the Soviets quickly might be able to deploy large forces to the forward areas. It suggested that, after only a few days, they could launch a short-warning attack with their highly ready forces in East Germany and Czechoslovakia. Alternatively, and depending on their ability to mobilize less ready divisions in the rear areas, they plausibly could launch a full ninety-division attack after only a few weeks.

The analysis suggested that, although this buildup rate would stress NATO's posture, the alliance would not be outclassed at all stages. Although the threat of a short-warning attack clearly was serious, NATO, provided it kept its own forces in Europe at high readiness and reacted promptly to warning, had enough already-deployed forces to blunt it. NATO's ability to meet the fully mobilized, ninety-division attack, however, seemed less secure. The United States then lacked adequate mobility programs to speed the deployment of its forces to West Europe. As a result, the Soviets, by achieving a quick buildup, appeared able to gain a large 2:1 lead in ground forces that would not be reduced for many weeks: until after U.S. forces had arrived in strength. Moreover, because of their armor-heavy posture, the Soviets' lead in tanks and artillery would be even greater: about 2.5:1 or more. Should the Soviets attack in this period (as seemed likely), this disparity appeared to pose a serious threat to NATO's security.

This assessment was quickly challenged by critics who pointed out that Soviet buildup rates might be slower than assumed. They argued that the Soviets' need to train their less-ready divisions in the USSR could elongate their buildup. The original analysis had assumed that the Soviets would spend little time on training and would need only to move their forces to the forward areas. Although the movement process itself might be brief, owing to the large rail network in East Europe, the training process, these critics said, could take several weeks. A careful review of the Soviet posture, which showed that these divisions were manned largely by reservists who likely would need further training before entering combat, lent credibility to their arguments.

Unfortunately, the possibility that the Soviets might take longer, as other analysts pointed out, was no guarantee that NATO would profitably use the extra time to prepare itself. Indeed, NATO's cautious reaction to the Soviet invasions of Czechoslovakia and Hungary was a sobering reminder that, in a crisis, NATO might delay its decision to mobilize until after enemy forces had completed their training and began approaching the inter-German border. For this reason, this critique did not invalidate the original buildup analysis. NATO's plans continued to employ a prudently conservative scenario that postulated NATO mobilization only a few days or weeks before a full, ninety-division attack. Nonetheless, this critique showed that a real crisis might be less severe than this scenario and that NATO, simply by reacting promptly, might be able to give itself valuable time to prepare.

Meanwhile, in-depth analysis of the force structures on both sides raised further questions about the aura of Soviet invincibility. The Soviets' 2.5:1 lead in tanks and artillery would be offset partially by NATO's qualitative edge in these weapons as well as by its large inventory of other systems, such as modern anti-tank missiles, helicopters, and infantry weapons. Development of static scoring techniques that aggregated the various weapon categories into a single index suggested that the Soviet advantage in weapons was no greater than its lead in maneuver units: about 2:1 at M + 15 in the planning scenario.

Analysis further showed that the balance would be affected not only by weapons but also by manpower: a factor working more in NATO's favor. For example, analysis found that NATO's soldiers trained more than Soviet soldiers and should be able to fight better. Equally important, it also showed that NATO's divisions typically had more soldiers than Soviet units and enjoyed greater rear area support. As a result, they would receive better help in such important areas as command and control, intelligence, communication, engineering, maintenance, and resupply. Finally, analysis showed that NATO's large and better quality air forces would also help offset the firepower disparity on the ground. The net effect of these insights was to suggest that, although the balance was too complex to measure easily, it clearly was closer than a simple count of divisions and major weapons alone would suggest.

Beyond that, analysis raised insightful questions about the yardsticks by which NATO's defense capability should be judged. It pointed out that, although the Soviets would gain the initiative by attacking, NATO would enjoy all the classical advantages of being on the defense. Among other things, NATO would be able to preselect and prepare the terrain, and to fight in the coordinated way that employs its weapons and logistics to full effect. As a result, NATO should be better able to slow the enemy's advance and extract favorable exchange rates. Analysis was not able to predict exactly the effect of these advantages. But it was able to show that, though no guarantor of victory, they could, within limits, help an outnumbered defender rebuff a powerful attacker. This, research showed, also was history's verdict.

For this reason, analysis suggested that NATO's posture did not need to precisely match the Soviets in divisions, weapons, and combat power. To some degree, NATO safely could tolerate a force disparity. In assessing the balance, analysis concluded, the important issue was not the initial force ratio, but whether NATO's posture met the requirements of its defensive strategy, which might be less than the Soviets needed for their offensive strategy. These requirements, it pointed out, derive not only from the enemy threat, but also from terrain, density, force-to-space, doctrinal, training, and mission considerations. They particularly demand that the defender deploy sufficient forces for a strong front line and sizable operational reserves. But they did not necessarily require the defender to match the attacker in size or structure. NATO's posture, the analysis concluded, should be judged according to the standards they imply.

Subsequent analysis was unable to pinpoint precisely NATO's requirements. Indeed, it showed that the force needs themselves could vary from small to large, depending on the battlefield performance of NATO's forces and other intangibles. Nonetheless, static analysis suggested that, although NATO's posture did not fully meet the requirements that seemed most likely to prevail, neither was it grossly deficient. This conclusion was borne out by dynamic analyses, employing computer-based wargaming systems, that examined the performance of NATO's forces during the full course of a war. These analyses showed that, although results were sensitive to imput data and assumptions, NATO's forces were able to conduct a staunch forward defense in the early stages. The risk of being overwhelmed arose later, only after they had absorbed major losses and were compelled to retreat. The outcome of a war, dynamic analyses concluded, would be driven more by sustainability than by Soviet superiority at the onset. NATO's forces, to the extent they were weak, seemed to lack staying power rather than initial capability.

To be sure, these static and dynamic analyses did not imply that NATO enjoyed a high-confidence defense posture. To the contrary, they suggested that the Soviets, owing to their large forces, probably would prevail after several days or weeks and that NATO faces uncomfortably high risks in Central Europe. But they also showed that the existing military balance was not hopelessly adverse in basic assets and that NATO likely would not be defeated quickly and easily. Equally important, they also suggested that the balance could be improved tangibly if NATO were to take moderate and affordable steps to strengthen its posture. They showed that an adequate posture for a purely defensive strategy, rather than being well beyond NATO's grasp, was definitely within reach.

By jarring the prevailing assumption about NATO's military inferiority, this message, in turn, had a major impact on the debate over the alliance's military strategy. Defense Secretary McNamara promptly employed this new appraisal to help persuade doubtful West Europeans about the merits of the U.S. position. His efforts were carried forth by U.S. defense secretaries in the 1970s, especially James Schlesinger and Harold Brown. In the face of this drumbeat, most West European governments, although initially skeptical, began to warm to the U.S. view, or at least softened their opposition to it. Gradually, a consensus on the feasibility of conventional defense began to grow in NATO civilian and military circles. As it took hold and gained strength, it began influencing NATO's strategy choices themselves.

Its impact was manifested most importantly in NATO's landmark decision in 1967 to change MC 14/2 to MC 14/3, the "strategy of Flexible Response."

Although this new strategy did not abandon reliance on nuclear weapons, it did call on NATO to build a more ambitious "initial" conventional defense as part of a "triad" posture. The specific aim that it posited, for the near term, was modest: a conventional posture strong enough to provide national leaders the time and clarity needed for making a decision to escalate. But it also committed NATO to the demanding concept of forward defense along the inter-German border, and it left open the prospect of elevating NATO's goals as time passed by and the forces improved. In doing so, it sent NATO down the path toward a stronger posture. In the years immediately following 1967, the alliance became firmly and perhaps irrevocably wedded to conventional defense as a major, not minor, pillar of NATO's triad.

NATO's adoption of MC 14/3 did not mean that all West European doubts about conventional defense had faded. To some degree, MC 14/3 was a compromise between U.S. and allied positions. Indeed, France earlier had expressed its opposition by withdrawing from NATO's integrated military structure, thereby weakening (albeit not fatally) the alliance's conventional posture. As a result, MC 14/3 remained ambiguous about exactly where conventional defense was to leave off and a nuclear response was to begin. It left this critical issue open and gave the alliance flexibility to review its position from year to year in response to new conditions. Since then, the alliance's position has evolved slowly and steadily in the direction of stronger conventional defenses. But the issue was never finally resolved, and even today NATO has not yet reached a firm consensus.

Even so, MC 14/3 did more than merely paper over competing transatlantic positions. It represented adoption of a new, internally coherent military strategy based on a genuine alliance consensus. Moreover, this consensus, fledgling in 1967, has matured and grown stronger over the years. A key indicator is the expensive modernization programs being pursued by West Germany and other allies. Another is France's growing efforts to establish stronger connections with NATO's conventional improvement efforts.

Today's debates have an entirely different tenor than those of the 1960s. The earlier debates focused on the very feasibility and desirability of conventional defense. Now, disagreements over military strategy are less fundamental, more concerned with programmatic and fiscal issues: whether NATO's nations are willing to pay the price and undertake the cooperative efforts required to execute the strategy. The U.S. commitment to conventional defense has grown stronger over the years, and though allied doubts linger, they are much less powerful than before. The idea that NATO both needs and plausibly can build a conventional deterrent, rather than being a source of serious discord, has become a common basis of discourse.

In evaluating the impact of analysis on this historic development, it must be noted that influence is difficult to measure. This is especially the case for something as intangible as analysis in a setting as complex as NATO. Nonetheless, it seems clear that analysis played a role in NATO's strategy shift that was as powerful as it was diffuse. Obviously, analysis was not solely responsible for the strategy decisions that NATO made from 1967 onward. These decisions were inherently political and institutional, and could not have been made in the absence of a strong alliance consensus. At the same time, these decisions probably would not have been made in the absence of analysis. It is hard to imagine how, or why, the alliance would have moved so decisively in this direction had analysis not successfully demonstrated that conventional defense was a goal worth pursuing. Without this, the U.S. effort to reform NATO's strategy probably would have died aborning, or at least fallen far short of its goals.

NATO'S CONVENTIONAL FORCES: IMPROVEMENT EFFORTS AND THE LTDP

The second phase of analysis spans the 1970s, a period in which debate over the military balance gradually gave way to a dialogue on how NATO could best improve its conventional posture. It began in 1970, when the alliance adopted AD-70, but did not intensify until the mid-1970s when the United States, then emerging from Vietnam, began focusing heavily on Europe. Accelerating in the Carter years, it reached its peak when NATO, at the 1978 Washington Summit, adopted the Long Term Defense Plan (LTDP), a major, U.S.-backed effort aimed at improving its posture in ten areas. It ended in 1981, when a transition to a new phase began as NATO increasingly focused on maneuver warfare. In this section, we will focus on the key 1975–1981 period.

During this time, NATO's concern for its conventional defenses was heightened by the major military buildup the Soviets were undertaking in Europe. Having decided to bolster their conventional posture, the Soviets embarked on a massive modernization program in which they deployed thousands of new tanks, artillery pieces, combat aircraft, and other weapons. In addition, they began reconfiguring their armor-heavy forces for combined arms operations by adding more infantry, logistic support, and other assets. As the 1970s unfolded, this buildup steadily gathered momentum and soon reached the point where Warsaw Pact forces were being improved more rapidly than NATO's forces. If unmatched, it began threatening to alter fundamentally the military balance in Europe. It left NATO no alternative to accelerating its own improvement efforts.

Alarmed by this trend, NATO turned to its military authorities to design an appropriate response. Drawing on U.S. Army concepts and the 1973 Mideast war, they crafted a new operational doctrine that was designed to counter the Soviet buildup and fulfill MC 14/3. Labeled the "active defense," this doctrine called on NATO's ground forces to establish a strong linear defense line along the entire inter-German border. Its objective went beyond merely delaying the Soviet advance. By committing most of NATO's forces forward in positional defenses, it aimed first to halt the enemy advance and then to wage a classical war of attrition designed to denude the Soviets' offensive power. Its ultimate goal was to establish a forward defense that was unyielding.

This doctrine not only gave rise to new employment concepts, it also profoundly affected plans for force improvements. For obvious reasons, wars of attrition are normally sought by the side with the largest forces. Unable to match the Soviets in numbers of maneuver units and weapons, NATO's commanders attempted to compensate by increasing the ability of their forces to generate massive firepower. Their hope was to use this firepower, supported by air and logistics, to destroy the enemy's larger combat formations before NATO's forces themselves were worn down. Firepower thus became the key ingredient in NATO's doctrine to "fight outnumbered and win," and a central goal of its future plans.

Albeit outnumbered, NATO's ground posture had grown in strength since the 1960s owing primarily to the German Army's emergence and the reorientation of the U.S. Army to Europe. As a result, it now was large enough to form an adequately dense front line for executing this concept. But its weapons were aging and required replacement with modern, highly lethal systems that could fight intense armor and artillery-dominated battles. The posture suffered further from less obvious but important deficiencies, such as inadequate depth owing to a lack of reserves, vulnerable airbases, poor interoperability, maldeployments, training shortfalls, and insufficient stocks. These problems also needed correcting if NATO was to fight an "active" forward defense anchored on firepower.

This need for widespread force improvements confronted the alliance with formidable problems in management and planning. Although NATO's defense spending was rising, sufficient funds still were not available for all the modernization, readiness, and sustainability measures needed. NATO's planners were compelled to make the best use of the limited resources that would be available. In turn, their need for analytical help confronted analysis with a new, quite different task. Whereas analysis previously had been called on only to assess the military balance, now it was required to go beyond this by helping NATO manage intelligently. It was being asked to help NATO identify high-leverage programs, to set priorities, and to forge a balanced investment strategy that senior officials could employ to guide the multiyear force improvement effort that lay ahead.

Because the techniques that had been used to assess the balance were not suited for making investment decisions, pressure was placed on analysts to create new methodologies. For the most part, they seem to have responded effectively. During this period, for example, defense analysts developed better data bases on NATO's force requirements and improvement programs. They reconfigured their static scoring systems by developing a capacity to forecast how alternative NATO investments would affect the future military balance. They also built better dynamic wargaming systems by creating improved ways to link resource inputs to simulation results. This step enabled dynamic models to weigh the impact of different weapons and programs on such tangible output measures as exchange rates and terrain loss in Europe. Finally, they created improved economic models of choice that could better handle the problems of multiple objectives and cross-program analysis inherent in forming coherent investment strategies.

This response led to the emergence of analysis as an influential participant in NATO's planning during this period. This trend was especially pronounced in the Carter administration, whose senior DoD officials were prone to employ analysis on NATO issues. Analysis also began making serious inroads at NATO's headquarters and among the allies, who began establishing their own analytical staffs. Furthermore, NATO's military commanders, originally hostile to analysis, began making use of the Shape Technical Center and other analytical staffs at their disposal. The net effect was an increased willingness by senior NATO policymakers to use analysis to inform their judgments.

During this period, analysis evidently played its most helpful role not in supporting specific programs, but rather in encouraging the steady deepening that took place in NATO's policy commitment to improved conventional defense. Whereas most member nations entered this period committed to MC 14/3 only as a strategy, by its end they had begun to forge the actual plans and programs needed to give this strategy life. The Long Term Defense Plan (LTDP) marked the high point of this evolutionary process by formally ratifying a NATO scheme for a stronger posture that could fully execute MC 14/3 and the active defense doctrine. Although only partially implemented, the LTDP goaded NATO's efforts in 1978–1981 and set the stage for the alliance's adoption of similar policies and goals in the 1980s.

The LTDP, and the chain of events leading up to it, were most directly a product of U.S. political leadership. Analysis helped support this effort by underwriting the strategic direction that the United States was urging on NATO. For example, it validated the controversially ambitious resource guidance and force goals that the LTDP posited. It showed that annual defense spending increases of about 3 percent (in real terms) were needed to permit an adequate rate of improvement, and that the LTDP's force goals were required to forge a better military balance. Analysis thus gave the LTDP greater legitimacy as a strategic plan, and thereby helped build the alliance consensus that made its adoption possible.

With respect to impact on actual programs, analysis evidently did not have comparable influence on NATO's major, costly decisions to buy new weapons for its forces. This pattern holds true at least for the M-1 and Leopard II tanks, the Bradley fighting vehicles, and the F-15, F-16, and Tornado combat aircraft. These weapons were the centerpiece of NATO's plan for a firepower-oriented defense and, consequently, were designed to employ advanced technology and meet demanding performance standards. For example, the design features for NATO's new main battle tanks featured such revolutionary improvements as larger guns, better munitions, laser range finders, solid state computers, improved shock absorbers, more powerful engines, and laminated armor. Advanced design features like these, rather than analysis, primarily determined NATO's modernization plans during this period.

This emphasis on quality discouraged the alternative of lower cost weapons bought in greater quantity than analysis traditionally supported. Nor was analysis needed to advance the cause of these weapons: they enjoyed major constituencies, and the military requirement for them was undisputed. As a result, analysis did not play a dominant role in the research, development, and deployment decisions for these systems. Exceptions to this rule, of course, did occur; the A-10 aircraft is an example in which analysis helped advocate the system itself. But for the most part, analysis was limited to influencing decisions when budgetary constraints mattered: the total number of weapons produced and the rate at which they were acquired. Although these decisions affected the pace of NATO's efforts, they did not determine their nature, direction, or ultimate magnitude.

Analysis, however, had a relatively greater, and sometimes decisive, impact on the lower cost but equally important measures that NATO undertook to enhance readiness and sustainability. It also helped broaden NATO's planning beyond favoring only qualitative improvements in its weapons. It encouraged a greater emphasis on quantity, even at the expense of relying on less sophisticated weapons. In addition, it helped drive NATO in the direction of deploying not only new, high technology weapons, but also the entire support systems needed to employ these weapons properly.

For example, analysis played a dominant role in the decisions to speed the deployment of U.S. ground combat forces to Europe. At the time, the United States lacked adequate mobility forces to airlift promptly the six U.S.-based divisions that were needed to meet its ten-division goal there. Analysis showed that this goal could be achieved, in a cost-effective way, by prepositioning equipment in Europe (POMCUS) for these divisions and by undertaking low-cost improvements to U.S. airlift forces (e.g., CRAF upgrades). Although initially not enjoying widespread backing, this idea gradually gained greater U.S. and allied support and was approved in the late 1970s. This program was particularly important to the LTDP. In addition to clearly signalling U.S. resolve, it made a major military contribution by providing earlier arrival for U.S. forces that were badly needed to provide greater depth to NATO's posture.

Furthermore, analysis helped channel this U.S. rapid reinforcement effort into the NORTHAG area in Germany, where it was most needed. Since NORTHAG's forces faced open terrain and lacked operational reserves, they were relatively more vulnerable than CENTAG. Analyses of their vulnerability led directly to the decision to deploy a heavy U.S. brigade there and to preposition POMCUS sets for three U.S. heavy divisions nearby. This decision helped correct one of NATO's most critical deficiencies.

Analysis had a similar impact on the important host nation support (HNS) program that was negotiated in the late 1970s and signed in 1982. This program was designed to provide U.S. combat forces the improved support they needed. At the time, the U.S. Army, having emphasized combat forces, lacked adequate service support units for wartime operations. This deficiency, a subject of mounting concern, had led to charges that the U.S. Army in Europe was "hollow" by virtue of being unable to provide the tail needed to give its teeth real bite. However, NATO's doctrinal emphasis on firepower made equally unpalatable the alternative of converting its teeth back to tail. NATO was therefore faced with a serious dilemma that had no obvious solutions.

Supported by analysis, U.S. planners developed the innovative idea of using German reservists to solve this problem. Although the Germans had ample reserve manpower for providing this support, costs were a major inhibitor and, beyond that, logistic support was regarded as a national responsibility in NATO. This idea thus required not only program development but also major coalition planning. After prolonged negotiations, in which detailed analysis demonstrated the feasibility of this concept, agreement was reached with West Germany and other allies to execute this program by sharing costs. This coalition program attracted little public notice, but it bolstered NATO's defenses by providing a low-cost way to build an adequate wartime support tail without reducing the U.S. Army's teeth.

Analysis also had a significant impact on NATO's efforts to derive full military value from its expensive tactical air forces. Although NATO was investing heavily in a major modernization program for these forces, it lacked an adequate airbase structure to operate them. Their performance in a war would have been sharply constrained by this critical limitation. Analysis helped address this problem by calling attention to three important programmatic initiatives: Co-located Operating Bases (COBs), aircraft shelters and airfield hardening, and sortie surge. The COBs program aimed to provide a number of allied bases to absorb large U.S. reinforcements and resources to operate effectively in a war. The shelter program funded construction of additional shelters to protect aircraft, while hardening measures improved airfield survivability. The sortie surge program tried to improve the ability of the air forces to operate at a high tempo. These three low-cost programs, albeit not yet fully implemented, materially strengthened the ability of NATO's air forces not only to win the air war, but also to contribute to the ground battle.

Other examples could be cited, including interoperability and programs to increase NATO's ammunition stocks and war reserves, but need not be detailed here. In each case, a similar pattern prevailed. One feature, common to all programs that analysis influenced in this period, is worth noting: analysis was not singularly responsible for any of them. None could have been agreed on in the absence of strong U.S. leadership and allied cooperation in pursuing a true coalition defense. At the same time, all of these measures, important militarily and generally inexpensive, originally lacked major constituencies.

They also were politically controversial and ran against the grain of NATO's proclivities. In each case, analysis played a major role in their survival by identifying their importance, bringing them to the attention of senior officials, and monitoring their progress. In contrast to modernization programs that enjoyed large constituencies, most of these measures would probably have gone unnoticed or died as a result of fiscal stringency. The fact that their implementation was often prolonged, and not always completed, indicates the barriers to their success even when supported by senior officials. The major progress made on them reflects the positive impact that analysis had on these low-visibility but high-payoff pillars of NATO's defense preparedness.

CONVENTIONAL DEFENSE AND MANEUVER WARFARE

In many ways, the third phase of analysis, which began in 1981 and has not yet culminated, has been similar to that of the 1970s. The differences, which derive from a change in operational doctrine rather than basic NATO policy and strategy, are sufficiently subtle to escape detection by casual observers. Yet they have been important enough to bring about alterations in NATO's assessment of the military balance, as well as its force plans and program priorities. They have also created major new demands and pressures on analysis to which it has not yet fully responded.

During this period, NATO's policy commitment to MC 14/3 and an improved conventional posture has remained undiminished. If anything, it has grown stronger in response to growing doubts about the deterrent power of nuclear weapons and to the course of arms control negotiations. Although the LTDP, as such, was deemphasized shortly after the Reagan administration assumed office, the alliance continued to pursue similar policy and strategy goals. The LTDP had not institutionally meshed well with NATO's planning machinery, and its abandonment represented only a U.S. desire to work more directly through Brussels and Mons. There was no accompanying downturn, or redirection, of U.S. defense plans and programs in Europe.

Early in 1981, the Reagan administration decided to continue pursuing the NATO defense programs that had been started in the 1970s and to urge the allies to do likewise. During the next two years, the United States was preoccupied with the debate over deploying the Pershing II and GLCM missiles. But once this decision had been made, it began switching its attention back to the conventional balance. Secretary of Defense Caspar Weinberger, other DoD officials, and SACEUR publicly began discussing several different concepts for improving NATO's conventional posture. After alliance deliberations, these ideas were combined and folded into NATO's Force Goals. In 1985, they gave rise to the CDI (Conventional Defense Improvement) plan, which was submitted by NATO Secretary General Lord Carrington for guiding future conventional force improvements. The CDI called for Resource Guidance and Force Goals aimed at steady force improvements for fulfilling MC 14/3.

It thus pointed NATO in a similar policy and strategy direction as the LTDP: toward enhanced conventional defense and less undue reliance on nuclear weapons.

The role of analysis followed a similar pattern of continuity and gradual growth during these years. In particular, NATO took important steps further to institutionalize analysis in its planning process. In the U.S. Defense Department, efforts were made to strengthen SACEUR's voice in the Planning Programming Budgeting System (PPBS) process and to achieve better recognition of NATO's requirements. In Europe, this period saw the steady maturing of NATO's analytical staffs as well as the development of "performance measures" for assessing NATO's Force Goals. These important steps provided senior NATO civilian and military officials with improved mechanisms for charting the future course of alliance force improvements. As a result, NATO was better able to assess the military balance, to monitor member nations' efforts to implement their programs, and to calibrate their likely impact on the alliance's security.

What distinguishes this phase is the growing attention that maneuver warfare has commanded in NATO's planning circles. This originated when military experts become aware that the Soviets did not intend to fight the linear attrition war that NATO's operational doctrine envisioned. Since the 1960s, the Soviets themselves had been engaging in their own innovations in strategy and force structure. Their activities were partly a response to NATO's actions and partly a product of their own planning. Originally committed to an exclusively nuclear strategy, they began taking conventional war seriously at about the same time that NATO adopted MC 14/3. From then on, they made a massive commitment to building their conventional posture and configuring it to defeat NATO.

In World War II, they had gained extensive experience in fighting a conventional war, defensively and offensively, against the Germans. This background led them to conclude that once NATO's force improvements had gone beyond a certain point, the Warsaw Pact would be hard-pressed to win if it attacked in an unimaginative way. Evidently realizing that this type of war would work to NATO's advantage, the Soviets began crafting a new military strategy, based on their World War II experience, aimed at bypassing NATO's strengths. Rather than conduct a broad frontal attack that would lead to a prolonged attrition struggle, their new maneuver strategy called for the concentration of large forces at selected points along NATO's front line. Attacks by these forces would be designed to gain breakthroughs that would then allow fast-moving exploitation in NATO's rear areas. The goal of this strategy was to win quickly and decisively by using maneuver to shatter NATO's cohesion, unravel its forces, and then defeat them in detail. In essence, this envisioned the same type of victory that the Germans gained over the French and British in May 1940 and that the Soviets eventually turned against the Germans on the Russian front.

Military studies showed that the Soviets clearly were building a posture, with modern tanks and artillery pieces, that was ideally suited to this strategy's emphasis on mobility and violent meeting engagements. More worrisome, these studies suggested that NATO's posture was disturbingly vulnerable to this strategy. History suggested that the concentrated fury of an armor-heavy breakthrough attack would be difficult to contain under the best of circumstances. While NATO's forward corps were capable of stiff resistance in the early stages, they could be worn down and stretched thin by sustained enemy pressure. In the event of a rupture, NATO would have to rely on its operational reserves to contain the enemy advance. But NATO's reserves seemed dangerously small. Even after a month of mobilization, they would include only U.S. III Corps, the French First Army, and a few German units. Although these forces might be adequate for awhile, studies suggested, they would be hard pressed to handle the multiple breakthroughs that could occur in a lengthy fight.

In the event of their failure, NATO could find itself unable to prevent large Soviet forces from reaching the open rear areas. Studies further showed that, once able to move freely there, the Soviets might be able to inflict the decisive defeat on NATO that their strategy sought. In a swirling maneuver war in the rear areas, NATO's smaller combat forces, unable to take advantage of positional defenses, could be swamped by the enemy's larger numbers. If things went poorly, the result could be an explosive destruction of NATO's posture similar to what happened in 1940.

In many NATO circles, this realization brought about a rebirth of pessimism about the military balance. It suggested that the Soviets had found a way to employ their larger combat forces that NATO could not readily offset with assets and advantages in other areas. It also triggered a major reappraisal of NATO's operational doctrine. Senior NATO military authorities concluded that the active defense, while effective against a broad front advance, could not confidently checkmate an expertly conducted breakthrough attack. Indeed, it seemed to exacerbate NATO's problems by committing so many forces along the front line that inadequate reserves were left available in the rear. Beyond that, the active defense's emphasis on modernizing weapons and improving firepower in the forward areas no longer seemed to be a proper basis for developing new programs. It simply improved NATO's forces in areas where they were already strong, while not remedying the critical deficiencies that were making them vulnerable to the Soviet maneuver strategy.

Recognizing this fact, NATO's military leaders developed a new operational doctrine aimed at giving NATO a defensive maneuver strategy of its own. This doctrine made no alterations in the size or disposition of NATO's forward corps sectors. AFCENT continued to have eight corps sectors with similar boundaries and forces as before. The new doctrine thereby eschewed a mobile defense that would have pulled entire corps to the rear in order to fight the major battles there, while leaving a thin forward crust that could not be defended intensely. It also rejected the idea of large cross-border attacks deep into East Germany in hopes of taking the fight to the enemy. It thus reaffirmed MC 14/3's call for a stalwart forward defense at the inter-German border.

The new doctrine, however, made a definite departure from the previous doctrine by calling for aggressive employment of the operational art in fighting the forward corps battles. No longer were these corps expected to commit all of their forces to static positions directly on the FLOT. Instead, they were now expected to withhold sizable forces in corps reserve and to use them in mobile counterattacks aimed at unhinging the enemy's advance. Moreover, NORTHAG and CENTAG operational reserves were no longer intended exclusively for eventual commitment along the front line. Instead, their employment plans now envisioned early corps-sized counterattacks into enemy salients in order to disrupt and destroy advancing Soviet tank armies.

This new doctrine thus marked a shift away from the concept of massing all NATO forces on the front line and trying to win a set piece war of attrition purely by deluging the enemy with lethal firepower. While still planning to retain strong positional defenses, it intended to supplement them with maneuver operations conducted in synchronized fashion by its reserves at corps and Army Group. This doctrine stopped short of viewing maneuver as the primary mechanism for defeating the enemy; firepower continued to perform this function. Rather, it used maneuver defensively for the limited but high priority task of controlling breakthroughs. Maneuver was its way of preventing the enemy from fracturing NATO's cohesion and bypassing its forward defenses, thereby forcing the Soviets to face the destructive inferno of firepower that the forward defenses could deliver.

Although NATO planners felt satisfied that this doctrine would improve NATO's defenses, they concluded that it alone would not suffice to defeat a Soviet attack. Accordingly, they began examining two other broad alternatives for improving NATO'S posture: Follow-On Forces Attack (FOFA) and reserve mobilization. FOFA recognized that, although NATO's forces could probably handle the initial onslaught, they would be vulnerable to subsequent attacks by the enemy's "second echelon" reinforcements that would arrive shortly thereafter. Accordingly, FOFA sought to develop a system of command and control, aircraft, and missile forces that, by firing deeply into the enemy's rear, could delay and destroy these forces as they approached the battlefield. This would give NATO's beleaguered ground forces more time to reconstitute while reducing the enemy reinforcements that they later would be required to fight.

FOFA was endorsed largely by the technical community, which argued that technological progress was rapidly making this idea militarily feasible. By contrast, the idea of reserve mobilization was advanced by planners who preferred to solve NATO's breakthrough problems by more traditional means.

Skeptical that FOFA would effectively degrade the enemy's massive reinforcements, they sought to add greater depth and staying power to NATO's ground posture itself. Believing that NATO's primary deficiency was its chronic lack of operational reserves, they endorsed programs to add several allied reserve ground divisions and brigades. They also offered related measures that would have a similar effect: preparation of the terrain and procurement of larger war reserves and ammunition stockpiles. They believed that these measures would make unnecessary the pursuit of expensive long-range firepower in the hope of destroying the enemy before NATO's ground posture collapsed. If done in sufficient magnitude, they contended, these measures would prevent the posture from collapsing in the first place.

These two approaches presented NATO officials with seemingly competitive programmatic alternatives based on different operational premises. Closer inspection, however, revealed that they actually were highly compatible because they would provide each other with synergistic support if undertaken jointly. For example, FOFA would help take enemy pressure off the new ground reserves, thereby enabling them to fight more effectively. These reserves, in turn, would help NATO's ground posture survive longer, thus giving FOFA valuable time to work its magic on the enemy's second echelon. The result would be a stronger posture than either approach alone could provide.

Partially for this reason, NATO's officials decided to incorporate both approaches, along with programs to support the new maneuver doctrine. This reflected a judgment that a combination of programs in all three areas ultimately should be bought. They left open, however, future decisions on the exact mix. Recognizing that fiscal constraints would limit the resources that could be applied in each area, they called for intensive study of NATO's options. In the next few years, some difficult choices regarding the various trade-offs will be required.

The complex nature of these issues clearly creates a premium on analysis to help guide NATO's future decisions. Until recently, whether analysis would be able to respond seemed highly problematic. The reason is that maneuver war and its new doctrines caught analysis unprepared. Because static methods were not useful for evaluating maneuver combat, it was compelled to rely on dynamic wargaming systems as its principal tool. Unfortunately, its dynamic models themselves were not adequate for this task. Analysis thus found itself in a position akin to scientists who, having mastered Newtonian physics, discovered that reality could best be explained by quantum mechanics. In order to conduct meaningful inquiry, it first faced the difficult task of retooling its core methodologies.

Its dynamic models suffered from the drawback that, in response to 1970s doctrines, they were built to portray land warfare as a slugfest between a NATO linear defense and a broad Soviet frontal attack. They assumed that combat was driven not by maneuver dynamics, but by sheer physical attrition:

the interaction of mass and weapons with lethality calculated by the Lanchester equations. They measured combat results according to the grim statistics of attrition war: relative losses, exchange rates, and survivors. They treated control of terrain as a byproduct of the attrition process and resulting force ratios. Therefore, they predicted victory or defeat on the basis of whether NATO could wear down Warsaw Pact forces before NATO's own exhaustion. Not surprisingly, they pointed NATO's improvement efforts at programs that would enhance firepower. Other considerations, such as mobility, agility, and depth, were secondary.

Although these models were well suited for analyzing the active defense doctrine, they were ill equipped for studying the maneuver war that both sides were now preparing to fight. They could not adequately model enemy breakthrough attacks, and were completely unable to portray the classical envelopment tactics that Soviet strategy envisioned after a breakthrough. Nor could they model NATO's use of its maneuver doctrine to contain breakthroughs. Limited to portraying combat along a linear front, they could model only defensive tactics aimed at introducing reinforcements into the front line. NATO's new doctrine, however, intended to use its reserves in precisely the opposite fashion: mobile counterattacks in fast-moving meeting engagements.

Further magnifying this limitation were weaknesses in the core assumptions that these models made about the determinants of combat power in a maneuver war. In particular, they assumed that combat power is primarily a function of mass and firepower and that movement merely determines which forces are present in engagements. Maneuver doctrine, however, assumes that combat power is a mutually reinforcing product of mass and movement. In maneuver doctrine, the military use of movement encompasses far more than cross-country mobility. It involves timing, momentum, and tempo: the ability to synchronize and choreograph the combat operations of many units in order to achieve maximum leverage and effectiveness. Although attrition remains the final arbiter of battle, movement plays the all-important role of shaping the operational setting in which the attrition fight takes place. In essence, movement determines an army's ability to mold the fluid maneuver battlefield to its advantage by focusing its power at decisive points while forcing the enemy off balance.

History shows that, although stationary wars may have been shaped primarily by attrition dynamics, maneuver combat has been driven largely by this art of movement. Armies that have shown mastery of it typically have done well in maneuver warfare. Indeed, this art has often enabled smaller forces to inflict major defeat on larger armies. For this reason, the new doctrine sought to employ rapid, synchronized movement in order to gain the "force multiplying" effects that history shows it offers. Unfortunately, the dynamic models, by virtue of their physical character, were unable even to portray the tactical impact of this use of movement, much less assess its multiplying effects.

Beyond that, these models implicitly assumed that combat across an entire theatre was a simple aggregate of a series of individual battles. As a result, they were unable to assess the impact of force cohesion, or its loss, on combat power. Yet the lessons of history suggest that cohesion—the ability of an entire posture to fight in a combined, coordinated way—is critical on the maneuver battlefield. Armies that preserved it typically won, whereas armies that lost it normally were defeated. Aware of this reality, both sides now aimed at winning the key breakthrough battles not simply by bludgeoning each other to death. Instead, they intended first to use maneuver to break the other's cohesion, and only then to destroy by firepower and attrition. This was a subtle and complex use of military force that NATO's dynamic models could not measure, much less analyze. Unable to analyze maneuver warfare, these models perforce offered no insights on NATO's future program priorities.

This quandary touched off a major ferment in analysis. Over the next four years, analysts set about the complex task of improving their dynamics models to portray maneuver. By 1984, this effort had begun to produce payoffs as maneuver-oriented wargaming systems began cropping up in the United States and Western Europe. Over the next two years, the models showed a promising ability to capture the rhythms of maneuver war. Initial studies confirmed the risks that a maneuver war posed to NATO and validated the new doctrine. They also highlighted the military payoffs deriving from FOFA and reserve mobilization measures, insights that influenced NATO's decision to incorporate these measures.

While a long distance remains to be covered, this progress provides grounds for optimism that analysis has recovered from its belated response to maneuver warfare. Whether it now will advance rapidly enough remains to be seen. What can be certain is that it faces a demanding agenda. Now that analysis can model the war that both NATO and the Warsaw Pact intend to fight, it faces the challenge of building the intellectual capital needed to aid the defense planning decisions that lie ahead.

NATO'S FUTURE AGENDA AND THE KEYS TO RELEVANCE

Analysis has not made the study of land warfare a science, or removed uncertainty and the need for judgment from NATO's planning. Nor should it have been expected to do so. But analysis has consistently helped NATO think more clearly about the military balance and defense strategy in Central Europe. It has also contributed tangibly to important alliance decisions and helped build consensus for them. It has helped bridge strategy and alliance politics, and has reduced the tensions between them. In the process, it has helped NATO strengthen its security by enabling the alliance to perform more effectively in crafting its strategy and building its forces. Above all, it has helped solidify NATO's policy commitment to MC 14/3 and a stronger conventional defense. Although it has had less impact on specific weapon systems and modernization plans, it has helped broaden NATO's planning beyond a narrow fixation on high technology. It has particularly helped foster some "nuts and bolts" programs that, in its absence, might not have been pursued at all. In the process of aiding NATO's senior leaders, it has also matured. In this practical sense, it has passed the test of relevance.

Whether its past will be prologue remains to be seen. But since the alliance clearly faces complex issues and difficult decisions in the future, the need for analysis will continue. In this regard, analysis will be required not only to refine NATO's military plans, but also to help continue bridging politics and strategy. It will be needed to help ensure that alliance political debates are constructive, rather than destructive, and that they are conducted along the disciplined and focused lines that lead to sound decisions. *Ceteris paribus,* to know more is to be more, in action as well as thought. Because of analysis, the alliance is better able to plan for land warfare today than two decades ago. If analysis continues to grow, NATO can only be rendered more capable of pursuing the defense goals critical to its security in the 1990s and beyond.

The analytical agenda ahead exactly parallels the policy and strategy agenda facing NATO. Perhaps the most fundamental policy issue is that the United States and the allies will face a continuing need to harmonize their force presence in Europe with pressing fiscal constraints, arms control, and military requirements in other theatres. For powerful military and strategic reasons, no major changes in NATO's military strategy of reductions in its conventional force posture seem likely, or desirable. Nonetheless, NATO's members will need to address these issues. In addition, individually and collectively, burden sharing looms as a problem that, if not managed properly, could weaken the alliance. The principal risk is that some U.S. forces might be unilaterally withdrawn out of frustration with allied sluggishness in their defense efforts. This might well trigger a parallel allied downturn in defense efforts, rather than the upturn which advocates of this U.S. step seek. Inevitably, the result would be a weaker NATO conventional posture and a greater reliance on nuclear weapons at a time when the credibility of the U.S. nuclear guarantee was itself growing weaker.

Because these issues pose risks to the alliance's cohesion, NATO and its member nations must handle them carefully. Analysis alone cannot solve NATO's problems in these areas. Clear strategic vision, continuing commitment, recognition of common interests despite competing priorities, and a willingness to compromise will be needed to an even greater degree if NATO is to maintain its cohesion. Conversely, the lack of these ingredients could cause NATO's unraveling even in the presence of vigorous, insightful analysis. Nonetheless, analysis can help in a limited way. In particular, it can help calibrate and articulate the adverse consequences of unsound politics, and it can help separate fact from fiction in the debates about force commitments and burden sharing. It should be used accordingly.

With respect to the Center Region military balance, NATO's defense planning seems destined to evolve along the broad lines suggested above. This implies a growing need for analysis to ascertain how NATO's forces can best be strengthened, through a complex set of initiatives, to defend in a maneuver war. In addition to program issues currently on its plate, the alliance will eventually be confronting major decisions on new weapon systems and its basic force structure that will also be affected by maneuver warfare. In order to address these issues, further progress will be required in developing dynamic wargaming systems that can model maneuver dynamics, assess the interaction of ground and air forces, and portray the subtle interplay between motion and firepower. Progress will also be needed in developing analyses of cross-program investment strategies that can coordinate the combined impact of disparate programs in achieving the common goal of improved conventional defense. This will require progress not only in substantive analyses themselves, but also in the discipline's underlying methodologics and paradigms of war.

Beyond that, analysis will likely be increasingly called on to assess how NATO can best intensify coalition planning in order to reduce costs. Because of fiscal constraints, NATO will almost inevitably need to adopt such difficult measures as armaments cooperation, multinational logistics, and greater specialization along "division of labor" lines. All three areas offer major opportunities to cut spending, as well as formidable problems and complexities.

Armaments cooperation, for example, offers the prospect of decreasing redundancy in research and development, as well as enabling greater economies of scale in production. But competition among national defense industries poses a major barrier to quick progress. Multinational logistics planning offers the prospect of reduced redundancy and greater efficiency, but the principle of national responsibility for logistics is firmly embedded in NATO's history. "Division of labor" concepts offer reduced costs and greater effectiveness by having each nation concentrate in areas of comparative advantage. For example, the United States might focus more heavily on air and naval forces while West Germany and other allies would concentrate more on ground forces. But this concept, for obvious political and military reasons, has drawbacks too.

Because of these problems, progress in all of these areas will be constrained by political barriers and will not easily be achieved. Yet the alliance must make major progress on them if it is to erect a robust conventional posture. The task facing analysis will be to identify practical, high-leverage, and politically achievable measures that can be pursued in the coming years. This will require further progress in analysis. At present, most methodologies are oriented toward enhancing combat power rather than reducing expenditures and achieving a more efficient, less redundant coalition posture.

If it is to continue being relevant, therefore, analysis cannot afford to be inattentive or static. Interests, as Winston Churchill said, are fairly permanent.

But policy issues change from year to year, and methods created to solve past problems often are not able to solve new ones. For this reason, analysis did best in the 1960s and 1970s precisely because it kept closely attuned to NATO's leaders and innovatively created new techniques to respond to their needs. But when it embraced its own methods at the expense of losing contact with evolving policy and doctrine, its relevance flagged. Its initial failure to keep pace with maneuver warfare is a sobering reminder of how analysis can be susceptible to this fault. In this regard, the past almost certainly is prologue.

At the same time, history also shows that analysis cannot prosper if ignored. It has performed effectively only when senior leaders have paid attention to it, channeled it properly, and used its results. Hence, the future of analysis depends not only on its own performance, but also on the wishes of NATO's leaders. They must decide whether analysis is to play a major, or minor, role in their efforts. Although management styles differ, all future leaders could profit, in this regard, from Salisbury's example. An effective prime minister in similarly troubled times, he justifiably felt confident about his decisions precisely because he insisted on thorough analysis and planning in advance. His exemplary record in guiding Great Britain in its glory years reaffirms the wisdom of thinking carefully before acting.

APPENDIX: THE OFFICIAL AND ACADEMIC LITERATURE

Although many official studies on NATO's defenses are classified, the U.S. government publishes a large volume of unclassified documents that are a valuable primary source for research in this area. Among these documents are the *Annual Department of Defense Report to the Congress,* DoD's annual *Report on Allied Contributions to the Common Defense,* and DoD's *Soviet Military Power.* Also worthy of careful scrutiny are various official publications from allied governments, such as the defense "white paper" published regularly by the Federal Republic of Germany. NATO also publishes documents that describe alliance plans and programs, and appraisals of the Warsaw Pact military threat.

Although NATO's quest for vision is guided primarily by internal studies and analyses, NATO defense strategy has also been studied by others, particularly in the academic community. A significant academic literature mirrors many official debates and periodically has influenced them. This literature bears close study, especially by those without access to official documents. Space does not permit a complete citing all of this literature, but it is possible to identify a representative sample.

One book that covers NATO's nuclear debates is *NATO's Nuclear Dilemmas,* written by David N. Schwartz (1983). Stanley M. Kanarowski's *The German Army and NATO Strategy* (1982) covers the evolution of NATO's conventional strategy through the early 1960s. The issues surrounding Flexible Response are addressed in William W. Kaufmann's *The McNamara Strategy* (1964). Henry A. Kissinger's books on NATO also are important: *Nuclear Weapons and Foreign Policy* (1959), *The Necessity for Choice* (1961), and *The Troubled Partnership* (1965). The U.S. and NATO appraisal of the NATO–Warsaw Pact conventional military balance is addressed by Alain C. Enthoven and K. Wayne Smith's *How Much Is Enough: Shaping the Defense Program, 1961–1969* (1971). The classic study of Soviet strategy and forces in this period is Thomas W. Wolfe's *Soviet Power in Europe, 1945–1970* (1970).

Unfortunately, the academic study of NATO's defense strategy suffered a major hiatus in the 1970s. Henry Kissinger's memoirs, *White House Years* (1979) and *Years of Upheaval* (1982) provide a valuable reference source on NATO policy debates during 1969–1976. The Annual DoD Reports issued by Secretary of Defense James Schlesinger in the mid-1970s address NATO's defense strategy then. Former Secretary of Defense Harold Brown's book, *Thinking About National Security, Defense, and Foreign Policy in a Dangerous World* (1983), discusses the Carter administration's defense policy in Europe. Other useful books include Lawrence and Record's *U.S. Force Structure in NATO: An Alternative* (1974); William D. White's *U.S. Tactical Air Power: Missions, Forces, and Costs* (1975); and Jeffrey Record's *Sizing Up the Soviet Army* (1976).

The 1980s have seen a rebirth of academic literature on NATO that covers current defense strategy issues. Among these writings, the Steinbruner and Sigal book, *Alliance Security: NATO and the No-First-Use Question* (1983), provides good articles on NATO nuclear and conventional issues. William P. Mako's *U.S. Ground Forces and the Defense of Central Europe* (1984) provides a quantitative assessment of NATO's force requirements. Richard Betts' *Surprise Attack* (1984) assesses NATO's ability to respond to a Soviet attack with little warning. Robert W. Komer's *Maritime Strategy or Coalition Defense* addresses U.S. strategic options regarding NATO, whereas William W. Kaufmann assesses U.S. defense priorities in *A Reasonable Defense* (1986). Zbigniew Brzezinski's *Game Plan* (1987) articulates a case for withdrawing U.S. forces from Europe, and John Mearsheimer, in *Conventional Deterrence* (1986), argues that conventional defense in Europe is feasible.

An academic literature is also emerging on the important subject of maneuver warfare and NATO's response to it. The author's article, "Warsaw Pact Forces and the Conventional Military Balance in Central Europe: Trends, Prospects, and Choices for NATO" (1986), addresses Soviet strategy for maneuver war. Richard E. Simpkin's *Race to the Swift* (1986) covers the theory of maneuver warfare. Andrew Pierre's edited volume, *The Conventional Defense of Europe: New Technologies and New Strategies* (1986), analyzes technology options for enhancing NATO's defenses against maneuver war. In addition, several journal articles, too numerous to cite here, have been written in recent years on other ways to strengthen NATO in this regard.

In evaluating this literature, it is noteworthy that no complete history has been written of NATO's defense planning and preparations since MC 14/3 was adopted. This gap in the literature badly needs to be filled. A major study could help in the debate over whether NATO's progress in preparing for land warfare has been meager or substantial. Similarly, the literature provides no thorough appraisal of the conventional military balance in Central Europe, including forces and strategy on both sides. A study of this topic could help resolve the debate over whether conventional defense is a viable goal for NATO. Finally, there is no study on long-range alternatives for enhancing NATO's conventional defenses through intensified coalition planning, or for readjusting burden-sharing arrangements in the alliance. An examination of these important topics could also contribute both to the academic literature and to NATO's internal planning.

References

Betts, Richard. 1984. *Surprise Attack;* Washington D.C.: Brookings Institution.

Brown, Harold. 1983. *Thinking About National Security, Defense, and Foreign Policy in a Dangerous World.* New York: Little and Brown.

Brzezinski, Zbigniew. 1986. *Game Plan: How to Conduct the U.S.-Soviet Contest.* New York: Atlantic Monthly Press.

Enthoven, Alain C., and K. Wayne Smith. 1971. *How Much is Enough: Shaping the Defense Program, 1961–1969.* New York: Harper and Row.

Kanarowski, Stanley M. 1982. *The German Army and NATO Strategy.* Washington D.C.: National Defense University Press.

Kaufmann, William W.; 1964. *The McNamara Strategy;* New York: Harper and Row.

———. 1986. *A Reasonable Defense.* Washington D.C.: Brookings Institution.

Kissinger, Henry A. 1969. *Nuclear Weapons and Foreign Policy;* New York: W. W. Norton.

———. 1982. *The Necessity for Choice.* Westport, Conn.: Greenwood Press.

———. 1982. *The Troubled Partnership: A Re-Appraisal of the Atlantic Alliance.* Westport, Conn.: Greenwood Press.

———. 1982. *White House Years.* New York: Little and Brown.

———. 1982. *Years of Upheaval.* New York: Little and Brown.

Komer, Robert W. 1986. *Maritime Strategy or Coalition Defense.* Cambridge, Mass.: Abt.

Kugler, Richard L. 1986. Warsaw Pact Forces and the Conventional Military Balance in Central Europe: Trends, Prospects, and Choices for NATO. *Jerusalem Journal of International Relations* 8, nos. 2–3.

Lawrence, Richard, and Jeffrey Record. 1974. *U.S. Force Structure in NATO: An Alternative.* Washington, D.C.: Brookings Institution.

Mako, William P. 1984. *U.S. Ground Forces and the Defense of Central Europe.* Washington, D.C.: Brookings Institution.

Mearsheimer, John. 1983. *Conventional Deterrence.* Ithaca, N.Y.: Cornell University Press.

Pierre, Andrew, ed. 1986. *The Conventional Defense of Europe: New Technologies and New Strategies.* New York: Council on Foreign Relations.

Record, Jeffrey. 1976. *Sizing Up The Soviet Army.* Washington, D.C.: Brookings Institution.

Schwartz, David N. 1983. *NATO's Nuclear Dilemmas.* Washington, D.C.: Brookings Institution.

Simpkin, Richard E. 1985. *Race to the Swift.* London: Brassey.

Steinbruner, John D., and Leon V. Sigal. 1983. *Alliance Security: NATO and the No-First-Use Question.* Washington, D.C.: Brookings Institution.

White, William D. 1976. *U.S. Tactical Air Power: Missions, Forces, and Costs.* Washington, D.C.: Brookings Institution.

Wolfe, Thomas W. 1970. *Soviet Power in Europe, 1945–1970.* Baltimore: Johns Hopkins University Press.

8

On Warfare at Sea and Naval Forces

ROBERT S. WOOD

The period since World War II has been one of turbulence for naval forces and thought—especially for the United States which emerged from the war as effectively *the* naval power. The end of the colonial empires, the enormous cost of naval systems in an age when the deadliness of weapons was in some respects as impressive on the conventional as on the nuclear level, and the problematical uses of navies in a general war—each of these developments drove most traditional maritime states toward a more modest definition of naval power and further limited the already modest reach and defensibility of smaller maritime nations.

On the other hand, Soviet naval forces, though clearly the junior partner in the armed forces of this continental power, showed impressive, if at times fitful, growth, not only in attack and ballistic missile submarines and land-based naval aviation, but also in longer range surface vessels. Although sustained by the Mahanian arguments of Admiral S. G. Gorshkov, the Soviet Navy was primarily based in this period on protection of the army's flanks and approaches to the homeland, as well as on the development and protection of a submarine nuclear capability. As the Soviet empire began to extend its political reach, however, the construction of a truly impressive merchant marine and a surface combatant force began to develop apace. Given the general growth of Soviet power and the nature of the U.S.-Soviet competition, as well as the fundamental character of the USSR as an extended land empire, none of these developments is particularly surprising.

It is the course of U.S. naval forces and thinking that provides the most interesting and revealing development. As a maritime nation with global interests and as the fly wheel of the Western alliance, the changes, uses, and strategic perspectives of the U.S. naval services provide the clearest insights into the promise and peril of naval power in the contemporary era. Assessment of these matters depends on a clear understanding of the role of strategic

thinking and the influence of geography and technology on strategic conceptions. To be effective, strategy must not only link, in some general sense,
resources to ends, but must also provide the conceptual basis for developing
and exercising a variety of operations or campaign options. The conditions
of political influence and deterrence and the requirements of victory depend
on time, space, and circumstance. The meaning of time and space and the
nature of circumstances are, however, not static. Not only are the nature of
one's adversary and the character of his forces important, but so too are
general political and technological trends. Clausewitz observed that everything in strategy is simple in theory and extremely complex in practice. It is
to both the conceptual simplicity and the circumstantial complexity we must
turn if we are to grasp the state of naval warfare in general and U.S. naval
developments in particular.

MILITARY STRATEGY AND NAVAL WARFARE

Strategy, in its broadest terms, involves more than the threat or application
of force (Wood, 1987). It entails an interlinked set of concepts through which
we seek to relate ends to means. It reflects all of those interests, values,
assumptions, principles, and guides to action that go under the name of
policy. Moreover, international conflicts of interest are endemic, and it is
sometimes difficult to divide time into periods of peace and periods of war.
The spectrum of conflict is continuous and any point on the spectrum requires
that we bring to bear the relevant panoply of national capabilities from psychological to economic to cultural to military.

It is also patent that any national strategy must harmonize with the strategic
culture of the people it seeks to serve. Strategic culture refers to generally
shared attitudes in the society concerning the nature and requirements of
external security, the conditions of peace, the cause of war, and the utility
and restrictions on force. These attitudes are in turn most decisively shaped
by geography, civic culture and political order, economic status, and technology.

Thus, military strategy and, concomitantly, naval warfare analytically and
in practice reflect the political objectives and strategic culture of the state. At
its most basic, military strategy is a plan of action designed to achieve policy
objectives and to meet the threats and seize the opportunities identified by
policy. Ideally, military plans of action will not only flow from policy but will
also be consistent with the diplomatic, economic, and other plans of action
designed to serve policy. If military strategy links forces with ends, it must
also provide the conceptual basis not only for raising and organizing forces
but for developing and exercising a variety of operational or campaign options
as well. Strategy must be executed at a particular time, in a particular place,
and under particular circumstances. The translation of strategic concepts into
force deployments and employments in time, space, and circumstances con-

stitutes military operations and campaigns. Campaigns are a connected series of military operations designed to attain the result defined by political judgment and the strategic concept. Campaign plans, in effect, provide the guidance for a battle force commander to reach the strategic objective. As campaign plans are developed and exercised, strategic concepts may in turn be refined or even altered to take into account operational experience. On occasion, even policy presuppositions are modified.

Needless to say, the actual relationship among policy, strategy, and campaign options is never this tidy. America's best known strategic thinker, Alfred Thayer Mahan, grasped how far practice may diverge from reality when he wrote in December 1896:

Preparation for war involves many conditions, often contradictory one to another, at times almost irreconcilable. To satisfy all of these passes the ingenuity of the national treasury, powerless to give the whole of what is demanded by the representatives of the different elements, which in duly ordered proportion, constitute a complete scheme of national military policy, whether for offense or defense. Unable to satisfy all, and too often equally unable to say, frankly, "this one is chief; to it you others must yield, except so far as you contribute to its greatest efficiency," either the pendulum of the government's will swing from one extreme to the other, or, in the attempt to be fair all round, all alike receive less than they ask, and for their theoretical completeness require. In other words, the contents of the national purse are distributed, instead of being concentrated upon a leading conception, adopted after due deliberation, and maintained with conviction (Mahan, 1897).

However confused the process of strategic and force structure development, it is important to understand the hierarchy of policy, strategy, campaigns and operations, and force structure, if only to critique actual circumstances.

Whatever the defects in the practice of states, Mahan was surely correct: national strategy and resources should be "concentrated upon a leading conception, adopted after due deliberation, and maintained with conviction." In the first instances, this leading conception must emanate from the nature of a state's regime, its geographical position, and the location, importance, and vulnerability of its external interests and alignments—as well as the character and direction of the threats to those values. To the point of this chapter, the role of naval forces for a particular state can only be adequately evaluated by reference to the "leading conception" arising from these considerations. This approach is at the heart of the distinction between a "continental" and "maritime" approach to strategy (Barnett, June 1987; Dunn and Staudenmaier, 1984; Gray, 1986).

CONTINENTAL AND MARITIME STRATEGIES

In simple terms, continental perspectives are shared by states that for geographical and historical reasons feel particularly vulnerable either within their own direct domains or on their borders, or both, and whose survival and most vital interests may be directly affected by the movement of their forces across land and the airspaces above it. Those states animated by a maritime perspective feel relatively secure within and on their frontiers, have a large number of vital interests that can only be affected by the movement of force across the seas and the airspace above it, and are particularly dependent on the convergence of their interests with many distant allies whose behavior they may influence but can seldom control as effectively or economically as they might should they share a common border.

It should be quickly noted that, while it may be obvious that naval power may play a more vital role in the strategy of a maritime than a continental power, the actual structure and size of naval force relative to other elements is not so obvious. The latter will be determined by the actual character of one's objectives and of one's enemies, the type of warfare possible and projected, and the state of technology. Nonetheless, a clear understanding of whether a particular strategy arises from a continental or a maritime perspective will go a long way toward answering the critical strategic questions posed by the late strategist-logistician, Admiral Henry E. Eccles:

What to control,
For what purpose,
To what degree,
When to initiate control,
How long to control (Eccles, 1979).

The continental-maritime distinction is particularly applicable to great powers; for lesser powers, fewer capabilities may make the security of their immediate frontiers and the ability to secure and defend distant interests dependent on the protection or good will of one great power or another and on the general character of the balance of power. In practice, this means that the strategies of these lesser powers will be shaped by their proximity to or association with great powers whose circumstances dictate continental or maritime strategic orientations. The strategic issues and indeed dilemmas of, say, a lesser power, on the one hand, threatened by a great continentalist power and, on the other hand, aligned with a great maritime power, should be manifest. Much of the strategic dialogue in NATO is animated by this simple configuration of power.

STRATEGY, TECHNOLOGY, AND POLITICS

Having established the general strategic orientation of a state, however, it is still important to consider what naval forces can do relative to other forces before establishing and evaluating one's force structure and specific strategies. In simple terms, naval forces can, on the one hand, undertake military operations and, on the other, as a function of these military capabilities, deter war, exert diplomatic pressure, and police one's maritime borders and areas of the sea important to one's commerce and movement. Analysts have divided these roles into a large number of subcategories (Booth, 1977; Luttwak, 1974; Cable, 1981, 1985; Till, 1984; Moineville, 1983; Gorshkov, 1976), but to grasp clearly what has happened to naval forces and naval warfare since 1945, it may be more important to limit these categories.

The crucial factors affecting naval roles in contemporary strategy include: (1) nuclear weapons, (2) long-range and accurately guided aircraft, ballistic missiles, and air breathing (cruise) missiles, (3) sophisticated sensors of enormous range and power, (4) automation extending human ability to control with greater precision and speed equipment and forces, and (5) techniques of quieting or changing the configuration of military platforms or projectiles (e.g., submarines, planes, missiles) so as to be less susceptible to detection. In addition to these factors, technical in character and with impacts far beyond naval roles, two other critical factors, should be signalled: (1) the wide dispersion of sophisticated weapons and (2) the uncertainty of forward basing and access. Taken together, these elements have and will shape the employment of naval force alone and in conjunction with other forces and, as importantly, the basic concepts of strategy.

The advent and development of nuclear weapons capability raise several key issues for naval forces and warfare. The most obvious issue arises from the ability to deliver, with increasing accuracy, nuclear warheads from relatively secure platforms, a matter which has engaged the attention of navies since the beginning of the nuclear age. Delivery by aircraft from carriers, by ballistic missiles from submarines, and by cruise missiles from a variety of surface and sub-surface platforms have been responses to the nuclear mission, with the submarine-delivered weapons being the least controversial because of that platform's higher degree of survivability and thus ability to contribute to a secure second strike. Even though the development of the highly accurate and powerful submarine-launched D–5 missile system is seen by some as potentially contributing to a war winning first-strike capability and hence "instability," the numbers and variety of forces on both sides make this exceedingly improbable, even if one assumed substantial reduction of forces as a result of strategic arms agreements. A combination of hardening, mobility, cloaking, and trajectory paths of forces, sea-borne or otherwise, makes a disarming first strike a very risky option indeed. The issue of how to use naval forces in a nuclear deterrent or warfighting mode raises, however, broader concerns about the general nature of warfare and naval roles.

In simple terms, strategic planners and analysts have asked whether the nuclear capabilities of the superpowers guarantee that any general conflict between them will quickly escalate to a nuclear exchange either in the general theatre or on their homelands, thus rendering irrelevant the traditional naval role of delivering to and sustaining ground forces in the theatre of battle and consequently of maintaining the lines of communication. Moreover, the coupling of nuclear weapons and accurate sensors makes naval surface forces themselves subject to nuclear bombardment. The conclusion of this line of reasoning for the United States is that, in large part, surface naval forces should be structured and sized for contingencies unrelated to general deterrence or general conflict with the Soviet Union, that is, "peacetime" missions, Third World conflicts, and so on (Beatty, 1987; Brooks, 1977, 1984).

The reply to this view arises from a general assessment of the nuclear balance and the geostrategic posture of the two superpowers. It is argued that the very existence of secure second-strike capabilities on both sides, as well as the total inexperience with nuclear war, make the early—or late—use of such weapons unpromising as a rational strategy and potentially catastrophic in its global implications. Should the existence of these capabilities preserve the relative immunity of the Soviet heartland and the continental United States, major struggles elsewhere (e.g., Central Europe, Southern Asia) are still possible, but the very risk of nuclear escalation to the intercontinental level may forestall the use of nuclear weapons within those theatres. Some believe that the recently-concluded intermediate nuclear forces (INF) treaty points in this direction and there is evidence that strategic planners on both sides are considering the possibility of relatively protracted conventional warfare and hence of conventional deterrence (*Discriminate Deterrence,* 1988; MccGwire, 1987b).

All this implies that, although extended nuclear deterrence is not moribund, it no longer carries the same weight in strategic thinking as in earlier decades. McGeorge Bundy remarked as early as the 1960s that the real utility of nuclear weapons is to prevent their use by the other side. If true, both pre-war and intra-war nuclear deterrence may be considered to be aimed primarily at reducing the possibility that nuclear weapons will ever be used in combat. This does not dispose of the problem but it certainly shapes the way one approaches naval forces, including one's basic strategic concepts. As will be discussed later, U.S. maritime strategy is premised on this view, as indeed are many recent NATO developments that seek to raise the nuclear threshold.

Even if the actual use of nuclear weapons in a conflict involving the superpowers becomes increasingly remote, other non-nuclear developments both extend the range and power of naval forces and increase their vulnerability. Even at the conventional level naval forces can deliver controlled, accurate, potent firepower both against other navies and against targets at considerable distance across the shore. Again, the issues themselves are simple to state but complex to manage in practice.

The recommissioning of the four high-speed endurance Iowa-class battleships, each armed with thirty-two Tomahawk and sixteen Harpoon cruise missiles, provides the U.S. fleet with considerable punch in potential crises and contingencies. The apparently successful bid by the Reagan administration to obtain fifteen postwar-built aircraft carriers, armed with an increased night/

all-weather strike capability, airborne early warning, and over-the-horizon targeting of adversary forces, also increased the reach and power of a sea-based attack. Ticonderoga-class Aegis cruisers provide what is generally judged to be the best anti-air missile system, as well as a highly capable anti-submarine warfare system, and is belatedly providing an anti-ship capability. Like a battleship, cruisers are armed with Harpoon and Tomahawk missiles, as well as a vertically launched anti-submarine rocket. Destroyers are similarly armed, and construction has begun on the Arleigh Burke class of Aegis guided missile destroyers. The multi-function, phased-array (fixed antenna) radar that is the heart of the Aegis system clearly provides an unparalleled command and control system. Both the cruiser and destroyer are designed to provide anti-air (AAW) and anti-submarine (ASW) defense for other surface forces and to serve as screening ships for carrier battlegroups. Also being added to the fleet ships are towed long-range acoustic detection arrays that are far less vulnerable than the seafloor sound surveillance system (SOSUS). The combination of these ships and aircraft, as well as submarine forces, constitutes the battlegroups. This combination points not only to the potency of the gathered forces but also to the issue of vulnerability.

The range and accuracy of sensors and of weapons, as well as the ability to control forces with speed and accuracy, give the contemporary naval force great power but also dictate that they be combined in order to defend against precisely the same kinds of threats from an adversary. Moreover, as naval forces move in close to land, additional land-based air support is integral to both fleet defense and offense. Even against a non-Soviet threat, the nature and spread of modern weaponry requires a degree of sophistication and combination of forces that can approach the level required for general conflict. Although naval power has the kind of flexibility and mobility often desired by national command authorities to signal deterrence, intimidate, or project power, it can be easily appreciated that the cost entailed by modern technology makes the effectiveness of such a force distinctly a great power operation—with strains on their national treasuries as well.

The fate of the frigate *Stark* is instructive. The *Oliver Hazard Perry* class of ships like the *Stark* consists of high speed vessels designed primarily for anti-submarine warfare but also intended to provide some anti-air defense for amphibious and replenishment groups and convoys. Such a ship is armed with a Harpoon anti-ship missile, and it has a weapons and electronic system to allow it to detect and intercept Exocet-type missiles. But it is typically not part of a battlegroup. The maintenance and correct operation of its systems, as well as the quality of its command, are crucial to its survival and its ability to perform its mission. Equipment failures or command errors can negate its strengths.

It should not be assumed that naval warfare problems are proliferating only on the surface. Longer detection ranges from both on-board and off-board sensors improved real-time communications with submerged submarines, new sea mines, improved techniques to quiet the submarines, and longer range anti-ship and land attack capabilities. All these point to both the power that a submarine can deliver *and* the increasing difficulty of anti-submarine warfare.

When enormous strength confronts enormous strength, the result can be stalemate. But stalemate may have many forms. Mutual nuclear deterrence can be seen as a kind of stalemate. So too, however, can the trench warfare of World War I. And so too can mutual sea denial. But when a continental power undertakes struggle with a maritime power, mutual sea denial is not stalemate but victory for the continental power. The ability of the maritime state to neutralize or to destroy the air, surface, and submarine threat of the continental state is an absolute precondition for its projection of power and support of allies. Hence under the stability of nuclear deterrence, unless you can assume a conventional force on the land periphery of the continental power that is also robust enough to engineer stalemate, the maritime power must strive not for mutual sea denial but for superiority—or in Mahanian terms, command of the seas. It should be obvious that the difficulty of this task has increased. Both the logic of command of the sea and the problematical character of this command animate the U.S. maritime strategy—and the debate among strategic analysts.

Achieving command of the sea vis-à-vis a superpower adversary in moments of general crisis is not the only problem that has been rendered difficult by technical developments. "Peacetime" and contingency operations, as noted earlier, have also been complicated by the spread of technology. The argument that navies are particularly useful in these latter circumstances but that the required sophistication—and cost—are substantially less than for a navy sized and shaped for general war has lost some of its weight. More restrictive rules of engagement in peacetime, lesser willingness of the public and its representatives in less than wartime circumstances to accept risk and loss, terrorist actions of some states and movements, along with the spread of technology, heighten the demands on naval forces in terms of relative sophistication and operational practices.

These demands are further increased if the growing difficulty of forward basing is considered. Alfred Thayer Mahan argued that the translation of those elements favoring a maritime orientation into actual seapower depended on the creation of a merchant navy and a naval force and on the acquisition of a basing structure. Already the decline of the American merchant marine has compounded the difficulties in planning supply and replenishment operations in wartime, but the uncertain character of advanced basing and access to foreign facilities has made even crisis and contingency planning problematical at best.

Technology has indeed analytically reduced the requirements for numbers of merchant ships and bases. But this has, in turn, made retention and protection of the remaining ships and facilities more demanding and necessary.

Larger container vessels can move greater cargo, and the longer reach of our warships untethers them from many ports. It can easily be grasped, however, that the remaining merchant marine is more important because each unit is of higher value. Now that construction and operation of these ships are largely under foreign flags, the control of these assets for U.S. national purposes is far less certain. At the same time, restrictions for political reasons on U.S. bases—not only naval facilities but also the supporting land-based air facilities—complicate all the planning factors relative to cost, distance, and time in a projected naval operation. At the same time, the synergistic effect of combining carrier air, surface attack vessels, amphibious assault forces, *and* proximate land-based air is considerably diminished if forward bases disappear or are restricted in use.

The reflections presented thus far demonstrate that it is possible to *think* of strategy in the abstract. It is not possible, however, to develop strategies or naval operations in the abstract. One may define the general character of strategy, broad principles of warfare, and general uses of naval power, but, as conceptual tissues that connect actual political ends and existing forces, military strategies and naval operations are quite concrete. It is now time to see how the world's largest navy has adjusted to the realities of the post-World War II era in terms of both missions and strategies.

POLITICAL-MILITARY TRANSFORMATIONS AND STRATEGIC THOUGHT: THE RISE OF THE MARITIME STRATEGY

In 1945, U.S. naval superiority was absolute—the fruit of victorious war. In the late 1940s and in the 1950s, the strategic significance of this dominance was persistently debated. In the 1960s, the role of the Navy as a secure second-strike capability and as an instrument of the Flexible Response doctrine became primary. But in the 1970s the U.S. Navy sank to the nadir of its post-World War II strength, and its utility as a tool for peacetime management or for general warfighting was questioned. The 1980s saw a massive increase of naval strength and a renewed maritime strategy both to justify the buildup and to guide the development of campaign plans and warfare scenarios.

The advent of nuclear weapons and, by the mid-1950s, the enunciation of the doctrine of Massive Retaliation raised serious questions about the role of the navy in a direct confrontation with the Soviet Union. No one doubted its efficacy in a limited war such as Korea or in support of operations in Lebanon—but these were virtually uncontested and thus, from the point of view of general deterrence and warfighting, untested. In any case, if U.S. relations with the Soviet Union were to be defined in nuclear terms, the conventional capabilities of the Navy were largely irrelevant. On the other hand, the nuclear striking capabilities of the carrier air wing *was* relevant and it was in this area that naval authorities sought justification in the budgetary battles, especially with the Air Force. Indeed, this capacity became a defined element of the Strategic Integrated Operating Plan (SIOP).

With the developments in submarine-launched ballistic missiles (SLBM), beginning with the *Polaris,* the role of the SLBM force was secured and has remained a consistent element in naval missions. While retaining a nuclear-strike capability, the carrier battle force was removed from the SIOP. But the doctrine of Flexible Response and the concern for "Third World" contingencies articulated in the early 1960s—not to mention the decisive role of the Navy in the Cuban missile crisis—appeared to insure a continuing and major naval role. Vietnam, like Korea, demonstrated the advantage of a secure and, at least on the sea, uncontested naval presence.

The general defense build-down growing out of Vietnam, however, coupled with the aging of the American fleet and the impressive buildup of Soviet naval capacities, most particularly submarines and naval aviation, reduced naval capabilities to their lowest post-World War II levels and introduced a profound element of strategic insecurity into naval thinking. The twin problems of reduced forces and increased threat led Admiral Elmo Zumwalt in the early 1970s to establish the Office of Navy Net Assessment—something utterly unnecessary in the immediate post-war period given the dimensions of U.S. dominance. The point to which the Navy had come was clear in the 1978 Defense Guidance which defined the Navy in a purely defensive role.

By the late Carter administration, modest increased funding for the Navy was proposed and serious evaluation of how to directly confront the Soviet threat was begun, most particularly under the leadership of Admiral Thomas Hayward. At the same time, debate as to whether early, massive, or certain nuclear exchanges would ensue in the event of an American-Soviet clash began to develop. The nature of the strategic nuclear balance, reevaluations of the conventional balance in Europe, and developments in Soviet doctrinal thought combined to produce a lively debate on the shape of an hypothesized U.S.-Soviet confrontation. The fluidity of the strategic debate and the massive infusion of money into the defense budget under the first Reagan administration generated a renaissance in naval thinking and the shaping of what came to be known as the "maritime strategy."

In the first instance the maritime strategy as enunciated by the early 1980s derived from a twin assessment. First, as Soviet SLBMs increased their range they would most likely be deployed close to Soviet territorial waters (the "bastions") and a significant proportion of Soviet attack submarines and land-based air would be dedicated to defense of these bastions; second, that U.S. attack submarines and general ASW capabilities could reinforce this defensive tendency by an aggressive anti-SSBN (ballistic missile submarine) campaign that would at one and the same time put significant Soviet assets at risk and, by forcing the concentration of Soviet forces closer to home, diminish the threat to the major western sea lines of communication. It was equally understood that should the Soviet ballistic fleet be configured geographically (e.g., under ice) or technologically (e.g., quieter) to escape detection and targeting and should a smaller proportion of mobile Soviet strategic assets be submarine deployed, the relative effectiveness of an anti-SSBN campaign would be reduced and other avenues to compel a Soviet defensive posture would have to be sought. Nonetheless, technology and doctrine appeared to reinforce the viability of the initial strategy through the late 1980s and the beginning of the 1990s.

The maritime strategy also meant, as will be described, that control of certain key land-air areas adjacent to the seas would be critical to maintain command of the air and therefore control of the sea lines of communication. It was felt that carrier airpower, as well as land-based power, and the positioning of elements of the Marine Corps would be able to maintain this posture, for instance in Norway.

The issue of control of important land areas points to one of the most significant aspects of the developing strategy. Although it was clearly assumed that the maritime strategy would assist the Navy in its competition for budget dollars, it is equally true that the basic concepts thrust well beyond traditional Navy campaign thinking.

The maritime strategy was conceived not as a self-contained employment of naval forces but as a component of a broader national and alliance strategy. Indeed, the designation of the strategy as "maritime" rather than "naval" was meant to communicate that it was a combined arms strategy for the maritime theatres, not simply a strategy for the employment of submarines and carrier battle forces. Combined arms, put simply, means using all of the forces available to the commander in the theatre in such a manner that attack on one element of the force exposes the enemy to counter from another element. U.S. and allied forces will play essential roles in stopping a Soviet thrust into northern Norway and in sinking the Soviet Navy. In budget battles it is relatively easy to partition the threat and to decide which platform performs which missions. In global war games, as in war, the one who brings to the battle whatever forces are required to achieve superiority generally wins.

Aside from the combined arms aspect of the maritime strategy, there are a number of other critical assumptions. Those assumptions are capsulated by the words "forward," "conventional," "global," "coalition," and "deterrent."

A forward strategy is consistent with both political and military exigencies. In the case of NATO, the political commitment is the mutual defense of the territory of all member states, including those areas separated by water or non-alliance countries from the other members—Norway and the Northern islands. Militarily, to maintain the lines of communication between Europe and the United States and to prevent the Warsaw Pact from turning the northern flank demands a forward posture. As Vice Admiral H. C. Mustin, former Commander, Striking Fleet Atlantic, recently observed: "The loss of northern Norway would be a determining factor in the battle of the Atlantic as would the loss of Iceland; the loss of Greenland would be severe; losing control of the Baltic Straits would allow the Soviet Baltic Fleet access to the Norwegian Sea."

Furthermore, the shortage of maritime forces dictates that those forces be used at decisive places and moments. Although many allied forces are configured for convoy protection in the central Atlantic Ocean, the ability to execute this role depends on the control of northern Norway. By seizing northern Norway, the Soviets would effectively control the Norwegian Sea, increase substantially the risks in the central Atlantic, and jeopardize the air defense of the United Kingdom and thus degrade Britain's ability to provide air support for the central region. Studies indicate that the air battle in north Norway might be decided in the first ten days and the land battle in the first fifteen to thirty days of war. Prudential allocation of resources thus demands that the United States explore campaign options as far forward as possible.

A forward strategy implies the early movement and deployment of forces. Again the situation in Norway, for example, could require the early emplacement of marines to forestall a Warsaw Pact amphibious assault and the early movement of submarines and carriers to fix and destroy Soviet air and submarine power as far north as possible. The inability to act early and decisively would allow the Soviets to concentrate their force and would make U.S. support for Europe more problematical.

If the maritime strategy is part and parcel of the national and NATO forward strategy, it is also intended to contribute to conventional deterrence. Naval forces, particularly the sea-launched ballistic missile force, continue as a major component of the nuclear deterrent. But unless the West maintains a credible ability to defeat the Soviet wartime strategy at both the conventional and nuclear levels, the Soviets may well decide under certain circumstances that a perhaps territorially limited but rapid, massive strike on their periphery could lead to successful war termination below the nuclear threshold. The ability to strike important Soviet targets from various points around the Soviet periphery may well affect their calculation as to whether to make war.

If one looks again at the Soviet political-military perspective, it is clear that, if they believe that circumstances warrant war, the battle should be geographically limited and conducted in such a way as to limit damage to themselves while rapidly overwhelming their adversary. The campaign should be characterized by the highest degree possible of clear control and exact timing. It must be precisely the West's aim to persuade the Soviets that they cannot with any degree of certainty look forward to this desired outcome. Instead, they must face a possibly global, protracted conflict in which crucial elements of their military capabilities and political control are put at jeopardy. In other terms, the West must have the ability to reconfigure the conflict. Conceptually, it should be emphasized that this is not entirely new. Those who choose to deter by early reliance on an intercontinental nuclear strike are also in effect threatening global—and cataclysmic—war as the price for a Soviet thrust into the central front of Europe. This capability, and hence threat, remains. Credibility not only at this level but also across the board is strongly reinforced if the Soviets understand that they cannot confine the battle to the central front even at the conventional level. A genuine threat in the north and south of Europe, and as far away as the Pacific with the prospect of an adversary mobilized for prolonged conflict, should strengthen the Western position simply by making it difficult for the Soviets to clearly discern an acceptable war termination position.

It should be patently obvious that such a forward, global, conventional strategy is underpinned by a credible assured nuclear destruction capability. In addition, geography, politics, and resources dictate that this strategy be both a joint and combined arms effort. It is preeminently a design for integrating forces into combined campaigns. And most crucially it is a coalition strategy.

A union or a convergence of perspective and planning on the part of NATO and non-NATO states provides the ideal precondition for such a deterrent posture. Peace may never in fact be utterly indivisible, but the deterrence of general war with the Soviets may come close.

Obviously, those charged with naval responsibility will be sensitive to the attitudes of the states within the maritime areas of operation and particularly at the so-called choke points. But the fact that even the maritime campaigns cannot be executed solely with naval forces, and that the object of U.S. strategy is to complicate Soviet planning across many theatres, means that a fundamental understanding among a wide range of states is necessary. The links, for instance, among the European central front, the northern and southern flanks, and the Caribbean and Florida straits should be explicated and understood. Furthermore, the geopolitics of a state that is both European and Asian must be part of U.S. strategic thinking. Political understanding and military cooperation among the states in the Pacific basin may be nearly as important a factor in general deterrence as the U.S. defense posture in Europe.

The maritime strategy may therefore most fruitfully be viewed as the maritime aspect of a much broader forward strategy—a military posture that flows from the nature of the Soviet threat and the exigencies of the containment policy. The NATO position and the maritime campaigns designed to serve that position are defensive and deterrent in intent. Defense, however, does not require, nor will genuine deterrence allow, a geographically restricted strategy and "Maginot line" mentality. Whether at the nuclear or the conventional level, the Soviets must understand that their warfighting strategies cannot succeed and their political aspiration must necessarily be kept within limits.

In a real sense, the maritime aspects of the forward strategy are the most deterrent and the least provocative in nature. It has been noted many times that, although war cannot be won at sea, the failure to achieve victory in the maritime theatres could lose the war. This also means that no conventional attack from the sea can in itself be as threatening, for instance, to Soviet control within its own borders and the Warsaw Pact countries as the reinforcement of the central front. Soviet naval forces may be destroyed, its bases in Kola and elsewhere may come under attack, its strategic reserves at sea may be degraded, and its ability to turn the flanks may be halted. All of these prospects may give the Soviets serious pause before undertaking war and will complicate their ability to concentrate at the decisive center. Neither side, however, is under any illusion that U.S. abilities at these points can overthrow Soviet power. Moreover, the ability to move maritime forces with some dispatch either in or out of an area reinforces their particularly deterrent qualities.

ISSUES AND DEBATES CONCERNING THE U.S. MARITIME STRATEGY

The resources devoted to the buildup of the U.S. fleet, the type of forces purchased, and the strategic concepts developed for the employment of the fleet have aroused discussion and debate. A number of the issues are apparent from what has been discussed above, but four points should be signalled: (1) the cost of the buildup relative to spending on land and land-based air forces designated for the Central European front, (2) the early employment in wartime of the fleet in forward operations versus missions directly designed for maintaining the sea lines of communication and convoy protection, (3) the conscious policy of putting the Soviet ballistic missile fleet at risk, and (4) the concentration on the carrier force relative to attack submarines (Mearsheimer, 1986; Brooks, 1986).

The issues are transparent but not easily resolved, for they involve not only technical assessments but also political judgments and projections. For instance, the question of whether to put one's marginal defense increase—or in normal times one's marginal defense decrease—in the U.S. conventional posture on the Central European front or in maritime forces deployable for European and global contingencies or in other force commitments will only be resolved by arguments about the division of labor among coalition partners, congressional attitudes, and probable versus possible threats. In addition, a straight strategic judgment will have to be made on how to "win" on the central front.

Some of the critics most sanguine about halting a Soviet advance on the central front with conventional forces are the harshest in their criticism of the expenditure of resources on naval, especially carrier forces. They contend that marginal resource increases could be better applied on the European central front. The consequent naval role would be maintenance of the sea lines of communication across the Atlantic with heavy emphasis on convoy escort.

Proponents of the maritime strategy often accept the critics' basic premise but turn the point. It is accepted that conventional deterrence and defense are possible but that the necessary weight of the ground force will have to be increasingly fielded by the Europeans because of political-economic calculations on both sides of the Atlantic and on strategic grounds as well.

On the broadest conceptual level, geography dictates that the things necessary for immediate defense be in place, that the things that take the longest time to bring to the battle be closest to the battle, and that the means to sustain the battle be preserved. In general, this would mean that European allies should concentrate on the development of heavy ground forces which take time to ferry across the Atlantic and which are potentially escalatory if sent to a theatre during a crisis. Without reducing the current U.S. commitment in theatre, the ability of European allies to provide for initial forward defense on the ground and in the air should be a top priority. Inter- and intra-theatre lift to permit flexible use of these forces anywhere in Europe should be a goal. The United States, it is argued, cannot assume full responsibility for these forces because of the size of the forces required and the need for U.S. forces to look after global interests and responsibilities.

In the naval realm, the forces that meet the above prescription are small ships (such as minesweepers, diesel submarines, and intercoastal ferries) that are not readily transferred across the Atlantic. In addition, European allies should contribute to control of the seas adjacent to their littorals so that power projection forces can be applied. As the size of the Navy required for near sea control by most NATO members is consistent with their definition of their global responsibilities, no change in force structure is contemplated by this observation. Finally, interoperability between allies defending forward on land, sea, and air, and power projection forces coming to their support is a critical concern.

At the same time, although defenders of the maritime strategy accept that one could concentrate on maintaining the Atlantic sea lines of communication, they note that the precondition of successfully ferrying goods across the Atlantic is control of the channel ports and the access points between Greenland, Iceland, Norway, and the United Kingdom in order to forestall a reload capability on the part of Soviet submarines. As noted earlier, however, such control is crucially related to command of the Norwegian sea, airspace, and land littoral. Already this requires a naval force considerably beyond that envisaged by the critics.

Moreover, argue the maritime strategists, control of these access points allows U.S. naval forces in conjunction with ground forces, including air, in the northern and southern European theatres and with the combined alliance naval capabilities to plan and fight a sequenced campaign threatening Soviet forces and targets on their flank and thereby lessening the weight of their continuing advance. At this stage in the discussion, critics question whether the United States and its allies in fact, even under the most optimistic assumptions dispose of sufficient forces to have this effect. The proponents argue that it is as much the proper union and concentration of forces that is crucial—and that this is related to an accepted strategic perspective.

A final point related to the size, structure, and posture of naval forces concerns the global dimension of the maritime strategy. This is most clearly focused on the question of why, in terms of general deterrence and war-fighting vis-à-vis the Soviets and given the strategic focus that the USSR still gives to Europe, the United States would put such heavy weight on a Pacific strategy. As discussed above, at the critical center of the maritime strategy is the fact that deterrence is reinforced if the Soviets understand, should they choose war, that they *may* not be able to limit the conflict to a single theatre and that a Central European conflict will entail pressure in Asia as well. The maritime strategy proponents also argue that, if you consider the growing defense industrial support capacity in Japan and other Pacific rim countries, a new strategic map emerges, one with America in the middle instead of "at the left edge." Instead of envisioning sea lines of communication running solely from the United States' East Coast to NATO–Europe, for some key war materials, these supply lines could now stretch across the United States, across the vast Pacific to countries such as Japan which could augment NATO's defense-industrial capacity in a major NATO–Warsaw Pact conflict. The defense of the Japanese islands, as well as the seas surrounding and approaching those islands, thus become critical issues whether from the point of view of deterrence or battle. Finally, the very fact that the Pacific and Asia are looming larger in U.S. political and economic considerations dictates in the minds of the maritime strategists that, in the distribution of defense resources, forces oriented to Asia will have increasing claim. Although it does not follow that heightened economic interests in a region entail greater defense commit-ments, there is no question that this argument will be used to sustain the claims of the Commander-in-Chief, Pacific, and be associated with the general logic of the maritime strategy.

Perhaps the most contentious aspect of the maritime strategy has been the proposed prosecution of an active anti-SSBN campaign, the logic of which has been discussed above. In many regards, this issue may be less central than it was once held to be. The ability of the Soviet SSBN fleet to deploy deep under the ice and in coastal and near coastal defensive zones sustained by mine barriers coupled with substantial improvements in their attack sub-marines means that, although a threat to that force may reinforce the defensive posture of Soviet naval power in general, a concentrated campaign against the SSBNs may be too costly in terms of our own attack submarines and unnecessary in terms of keeping Soviet forces well beyond the critical global access or choke points and the sea lines of communication.

This development does, however, raise the final issue: the relative invest-ment of resources in U.S. attack submarines versus carriers. This is not an easy problem. Control of the sea, the airspace, and adjacent land areas in crucial maritime theatres (e.g., Norway, Turkey) constitutes the precondition both for maintaining the sea lines of communication and for ultimately bringing to bear pressure on Soviet forces and military and economic elements crucial to the maintenance of those forces. Robust carrier task forces are central to this mission. At the same time, however, the Soviet submarine threat has grown apace. As Admiral A.H. Trost, Chief of Naval Operations, has expressed it:

The Soviet Union has placed increased emphasis on closing the gap in undersea warfare through an aggressive and effective submarine quieting program and an intensive ASW research effort. Without increased emphasis on a variety of advanced ASW research programs in support of battle group operations and construction of the Seawolf class submarine, the U.S. could lose the technological advantages in this area crucial to the maintenance of maritime superiority and support for national military strategy (Polmar, 1987; Trost, 1987; CNO Posture Statement, 1987).

The inability to prosecute a successful anti-submarine campaign against the Soviets will in itself defeat the intent of the maritime strategy. The proper balance of forces is thus likely to be a continuing source of debate.

It should be apparent that, however one comes down on the issues related to the U.S. maritime strategy, the articulation of the strategy has itself focused strategic analysis on the central trends in the context and character of naval power raised in the early pages of this discussion. Both the analysis and changes in the external world will thus necessarily make the maritime strategy an evolving set of concepts and guides for campaign planning.

CONCLUSION: MARITIME STRATEGY, FORCE STRUCTURE, AND NATIONAL ROLES

The maritime strategy as articulated in the 1980s is most accurately seen as a set of concepts for employing joint forces in maritime theatres in support of U.S. national policy and strategy and of alliance, including NATO, commitments. A critical supposition of these concepts is that both deterrence and warfare have fundamentally a coalition character.

These general concepts are being translated into a variety of campaign options for the maritime theatres so that U.S. and allied forces can be exercised under a range of scenarios. The exercise of such options is considered the essence of readiness—reinforcing deterrence by demonstrating the ability to concentrate and to deploy forces flexibly in warfighting situations.

Strategy should shape the size and structure of one's forces. In this sense, all strategic concepts are force builders. At any time, however, strategy needs to be determined by the forces in being. Otherwise, it represents dangerous wishful thinking. The maritime elements of national and coalition strategy begin with the forces in being or reasonably projected.

The articulation and exercise of those elements of strategy should in turn provide the basis for force developments. It is hoped that this evaluation will keep strategy and force characteristics in harmony with each other and with the actual geopolitical and technological environment.

It can be persuasively argued that by the mid-1980s, a balance between naval forces and strategic concepts was being achieved. The combination of Soviet military doctrine, the size and sophistication of the U.S. fleet, and the increased joint and allied perspective of planners—all these allowed the articulation of a global deterrent and general warfighting posture that took into account the nuclear context of modern conflict but was not paralyzed by the vision of a short, cataclysmic nuclear war. The impressive increase of naval forces and the renaissance of strategy and campaign thought induced in naval leadership a confidence not seen since the halcyon days of victory in World War II.

Yet there were darkening clouds on the horizon. The rapid buildup and modernization of the fleet required substantial support to maintain and to exercise, but, by 1988, the politics of fiscal austerity was in full swing. The prospect of an undermanned and inadequately maintained fleet, albeit at a higher force level, seemed real indeed. Moreover, technological advances by the Soviets, particularly in submarine warfare and fourth-generation aircraft, made the forward defenses more challenging, if still, it was felt, achievable. The cost of maintaining U.S. superiority at sea was clearly going to be high, but the scramble for money among the several services in a fiscally constrained environment was intensifying. Despite developments in naval thought, it was clear that as a nation there was still little clarity in U.S. national priorities and, consequently, in the strategic perspective by which to judge force structures and levels, as well as the concepts according to which those forces would be used.

Moreover, there were increasing arguments that U.S. naval strategy and forces were geared toward the least probable conflict—a direct Soviet-American confrontation—whereas naval forces had become the primary military instrument of power management in an era of violent peace. The reasonable response was that the requirements of deterrence and survival required priority attention to the central balance and that, in any case, since a nation gets only one Navy, the force was optimized to execute both general war and "peacetime" missions.

As a starting point, this counter-argument was plausible enough—but it was also clear that certain forces were *not* favored because of the coalition assumptions of a general war-oriented strategy—for instance, mine warfare forces—and that systematic thought about power management strategies was inchoate. Of course, the increasing demographic and fiscal constraints made the necessary intellectual exercise appear painful indeed. Two things however, were clear enough: the proper role of the Navy would continue to be debated and naval power would continue to be called on regularly by national leaders intent on securing global interests.

REFERENCES

Barnett, Roger W. 1987. The Maritime Continental Debate Isn't Over. *U.S. Naval Institute Proceedings* (June): 28–34.

———. 1987. U.S. Maritime Strategy: Sound and Safe. *Bulletin of the Atomic Scientists* (September): 30–33.

Beatty, Jack. 1987. In Harm's Way. *The Atlantic Monthly,* May, pp. 37–46, 48–49, 52–53.

Booth, Ken. 1977. *Navies and Foreign Policy*. New York: Crane, Russak.

———. 1985. *Law, Force and Diplomacy at Sea*. Boston: George Allen & Unwin.

Brooks, Linton F. 1984. Escalation and Naval Strategy. *U.S. Naval Institute Proceedings,* (August): 33–37.

———. 1986. Naval Power and National Security: The Case for the Maritime Strategy. *International Security* (Fall): 58–88.

———. 1987. The Nuclear Maritime Strategy. *U.S. Naval Institute Proceedings* (April): 33–39.

Cable, James. 1981. *Gunboat Diplomacy 1919–1979,* 2nd ed., New York: St. Martin's Press.

———. 1985 editor, *Diplomacy at Sea*. London: MacMillan.

Discriminate Deterrence--Report of the Commission on Integrated Long-term Strategy, delivered to the Secretary of Defense and the Assistant to the President for National Security Affairs, on 11 Jan. 1988, Washington: U.S. Government Printing Office, January.

Dunn, Keith A. and William O. Staudenmaier. 1984. *Strategic Implications of the Continental-Maritime Debate*. New York: Praeger.

Eccles, Henry E. 1979. Strategy—the Theory and Application. *Naval War College Review* (May-June): 11–21.

Friedman, Norman. 1986. "The Battle Group and US Naval Strategy." *Defense Science 2002+,* 46–51.

———. 1985. "US Maritime Strategy." *International Defense Review* no. 7: 1071–1075.

Froggett, S. J. 1987. The Maritime Strategy: Tomahawk's Role. *U.S. Naval Institute Proceedings* (February): 51–54.

George, James L., ed. 1985. *The U.S. Navy: the View from the Mid-1980s*. Boulder, Colo.: Westview Press.

Gorshkov, S. G. *The Sea Power of the State*. Annapolis, MD: Naval Institute Press, 1976.

Gray, Colin S. 1986. *Maritime Strategy, Geopolitics, and the Defense of the West*. New York: National Strategy Information Center.

Hall, John V. 1982. *Why the Short-War Scenario is Wrong for Naval Planning*. Alexandria, Va: Naval Studies Group, Center for Naval Analyses.

Handler, Joshua. 1987. Waging Submarine Warfare. *Bulletin of the Atomic Scientists* (September): 40–43.

Hanks, Robert J. 1985. *American Sea Power and Global Strategy*. Washington, D.C.: Pergamon-Brassey's.

Kelley, P. X., and Hugh K. O'Donnell. 1986. The Amphibious Warfare Strategy. *U.S. Naval Institute Proceedings* (Maritime Strategy Supplement) (January): 18–29.

Komer, Robert W. 1984. *Maritime Strategy or Coalition Defense?* Cambridge, Mass.: Abt Books.

Lehman, John F., Jr. 1986. The 600-Ship Navy. *U.S. Naval Institute Proceedings.* (Maritime Strategy Supplement), (January): 30–40.

Luttwak, Edward N. 1974. *The Political Uses of Sea Power.* Baltimore: The Johns Hopkins University Press.

Mackay, S. V. 1987. Maritime Strategy: an Allied Reaction, *U.S. Naval Institute Proceedings* (April): 82–89.

Mahan, Alfred T. 1897. *Interest of America in Sea Power, Present and Future.* Boston, Mass: Little Brown.

MccGwire, Michael. 1987a. *Military Objectives in Soviet Foreign Policy.* Washington, DC: The Brookings Institution.

———. 1987. The Changing Role of the Soviet Navy. *Bulletin of the Atomic Scientists,* (September): 34–39.

Mearsheimer, John J. 1986. A Strategic Misstep: the Maritime Strategy and Deterrence in Europe. *International Security* (Fall): 3–57.

Moineville, Hubert. 1983. *Naval Warfare Today and Tomorrow.* Oxford: B. Blackwell.

Polmar, Norman. 1987. *The Ships and Aircraft of the U.S. Fleet.* 14th ed., Annapolis, Md: Naval Institute Press.

Posen, Barry R. 1987. U.S. Maritime Strategy: a Dangerous Game. *Bulletin of the Atomic Scientists* (September): 24–28.

Posture Statement of the Chief of Naval Operations, *Report to the Congress, Fiscal Year 1988.* 1987. Arlington, Vir: Navy Internal Relations Activity, Print Media Division.

Swartz, Peter M. 1987a. *Addendum to "Contemporary U.S. Naval Strategy: a Bibliography".* Annapolis, Md: U.S. Naval Institute.

———. 1987b. The Maritime Strategy in Review. *U.S. Naval Institute Proceedings,* (February): 113–116.

———. 1986. Contemporary U.S. Naval Strategy: a Bibliography. *U.S. Naval Institute Proceedings* (Maritime Strategy Supplement) (January): 41–47.

Till, Geoffrey et al. 1984. *Maritime Strategy and the Nuclear Age.* 2nd ed. New York: St. Martin's Press.

Trost, Carlisle A. H. 1987. Looking Beyond the Maritime Strategy. *U.S. Naval Institute Proceedings,* (January): 13–16.

Ullman, Harlan and Thomas H. Etzold. 1985. *Future Imperative: National Security and the U.S. Navy in the Late 1980s.* Washington: Georgetown University, Center for Strategic and International Studies.

U.S. Congress. Senate. Committee on Armed Services. 1985. *Department of Defense Authorization for Appropriations for FY 85. Part 8.* Washington D.C.: U.S. Government Printing Office. Part 8: Sea power and force projection hearings. See especially: pp. 3851–3900.

———. House. Committee on Armed Services. Seapower and Strategic and Critical Materials Subcommittee. 1986. *The 600-Ship Navy and the Maritime Strategy: Hearings.* Washington: U.S. Government Printing Office.

———. 1986. *The 600-Ship Navy: Report.* Washington, D.C.: U.S. Government Printing Office.

U.S. Navy Department. *Department of the Navy Report to the Congress Fiscal Year . . .* Alexandria, Va: Navy Internal Relations Activity (annual).

U.S. Office of the Chief of Naval Operations. 1979. *The Maritime Balance Study: the Navy Strategic Planning Experiment.* Washington, D.C.

————. 1979. *The Maritime Balance Study: the Navy Strategic Planning Experiment; Excecutive Summary*. Washington, D.C.

Watkins, James D. 1986. The Maritime Strategy. *U.S. Naval Institute Proceedings* (Maritime Strategy Supplement), (January): 2–17.

West, F. J., Jr. 1985. Maritime Strategy and NATO Deterrence. *Naval War College Review* (September-October): 5–19.

Wood, Robert S. 1987. The Conceptual Framework for Strategic Development at the Naval War College--text of statement before the Senate Armed Services Committee on 13 January 1987. *Naval War College Review* (Spring): 4–16.

————. 1986. Maritime Strategy for War in the North. *Journal of Defense and Diplomacy,* (September): 17–24.

————. and John P. Hanley. Jr. 1985. The Maritime Role in the North Atlantic. *Naval War College Review* (November-December): 5–18.

9

On Conventional Weapons Proliferation

MICHAEL BRZOSKA

ARMS PRODUCTION AND ARMS TRANSFERS

No military force is entirely supplied from domestic arms industries. All countries are arms importers, but only some are arms exporters.

The two most important military powers, the United States and the Soviet Union, import only a few weapons systems and components for weapons systems built in other countries. They could produce the whole spectrum of weapons systems but choose to buy some weapons abroad in order to create "two-way streets" in arms trade with countries that are importers of their weapons. In the West, there is often political controversy over what the United States should be obliged to buy from its allies. Since this question is more political than economic, it is often bundled up with other inter-alliance problems, like coordination of arms procurement and differences in military style.

Major reasons for the great powers' independence in arms procurement are the size of the military budgets of the United States and the USSR, the strength of their arms industries, and, above all, their extensive efforts in research and development (R&D). An estimated 80 percent of worldwide military R&D spending is by the United States and the Soviet Union—a much higher percentage than their 60 percent share of world military spending (SIPRI, 1986, pp. 231, 302).

Below the United States and the Soviet Union is a group of industrialized countries able to produce many, but not all, of the weapons their domestic armed forces want. Even the procurement budgets of France, the United Kingdom, or the Federal Republic of Germany are too small to finance the whole range of arms industrial activities. Their military R&D efforts are insufficient to remain on top of scientific advances in more than a few areas. There are various ways in which these and other states in Western Europe,

Canada, and Australia try to cope with the problem of limited domestic demand. All of them have direct implications for arms trading.

One way is to agree on a division of labor within a military alliance. This is the pattern within the Warsaw pact. The Soviet Union produces about 90 percent of the weapons deployed within the alliance. The smaller countries specialize—Bulgaria and Romania in small arms, Czechoslovakia in small arms and small aircraft, and Poland in some types of ships. They export such weapons to the Soviet Union and import major weapons from the Soviet Union. In addition, they try to export those weapons in which they specialize. Within NATO, there is no agreement on division of labor, though smaller states also have to specialize within narrow fields of expertise if they want to compete at all. Canada, for example has specialized in the production of small aircraft, some types of ships, and electronics; Norway in electronics and missiles; and the Netherlands in small aircraft and electronics. They can then try to trade such goods for all the other weapons their respective armed forces demand. As in the Warsaw Pact, there is extensive inter-alliance trade, and an interest in selling from specialized production lines to the world market.

Another way to try to cope with limited domestic demand that is more applicable for states interested in producing a broader range of weapons is to freely import arms production technology, preproducts, and components, but to tell the armed forces to procure final products at home. This is the option exercised by larger NATO members such as France, the United Kingdom, the Federal Republic of Germany, and Italy, but also smaller neutral countries like Sweden, Yugoslavia, and Switzerland. In these cases, the trade in finished weapon systems is not very extensive. Instead, there is a lot of trade in arms production technology, in the form of license and co-production agreements, and components for weapon systems.

A third option is to scale down efforts and to produce no weapons or only very few weapons under foreign licenses, without trying to specialize much. Among the larger industrialized states only Japan has favored this option.

In all of the countries in the second group, arms production is less than optimal from an economic viewpoint. Only if large production runs can be achieved through large exports can arms production be economically viable. Otherwise, it remains dependent on the willingness of local governments to subsidize the difference between actual costs and what it would cost to import such weapons systems (SIPRI, 1971, ch. 14).

The same economic dilemma confronts a third group of countries that experienced a dramatic increase in arms exports in the late 1970s and early 1980s: countries in the Third World but also in the European southern periphery.[1] In many of these countries, there is not only limited demand but also no large and diversified industrial base. These countries—with the exception of Israel—find it very difficult to follow the lead of the larger West

European arms producers and to become competitive in at least some high technology areas, or even to be able to produce many weapon systems under foreign license. India, Argentina, or Egypt have invested large amounts of money without much achievement. But the situation is different when the aim has not been to emulate the most modern technology, but rather to produce less advanced, easier to use weapons (Brzoska and Ohlson, 1986). Brazil has been particularly successful in exporting such weapons.

Despite the buildup of arms production in the Third World, and some export success, the countries of the Third World remain—with some exceptions like Brazil—totally dependent on the supply of weapons from the industrialized states. Their imports are the backbone of the arms trade, much larger than the imports of the industrialized countries. The various arms trade statistics show an average share of about 70 percent for Third World imports.[2] It is this proliferation of weapons to Third World countries on which the rest of this chapter will focus. Issues of inter-alliance arms trade, of cooperation and co-production among industrialized countries, will not be dealt with in detail.

The three groups of countries exhibit different behavior in the arms market. The United States and the Soviet Union, superpowers with worldwide strategic interests, are using arms transfers as instruments of leverage, as parts of their foreign policy. For the other large industrialized states, the motive to maintain a strong and fairly independent arms industry dominates. For Third World countries, the main issue is to get a foothold in a highly competitive market. Of course, not only the supply, but also the demand for weapons has to be considered, as well as the interplay of demand and supply. Another section of this chapter will summarize some of the more important effects of arms transfers within recipient countries and for international relations. At the end, a look is taken at arms transfer control and at research deficits. First, however, a short overview of the post-war evolution of the structure and some current and possible future trends in the proliferation of conventional weapons is given; the push and pull of arms transfers are seen in a historical perspective.

PHASES AND STRUCTURE

Until the early 1960s, most arms were transferred within military alliances, from patrons to clients. Weapons transferred were mainly surplus weapons, many from World War II. Weapons were mostly given for free. Arms transfers were part of the construction of military alliances, including the ring of containment built by the United States on the borders of the Soviet Union, and Soviet efforts to destroy that ring. Thus, the first transfer of Soviet weaponry outside its bloc after World War II was to Egypt. (For early reviews of conventional weapons proliferation, see Leiss and Kemp, 1970, SIPRI, 1971, and Harkavy, 1975.)

The emergence of many new nations in Africa and Asia in the early 1960s, balance-of-payments problems in the United States, and the economic revival of Western Europe slowly changed this structure. The United States began to ask its allies to pay for the arms they received. This further motivated the stronger West European nations to broaden their arms production activities. At the same time, they expanded their efforts to sell weapons. The Soviet Union tried to woo many nations into its camp via the continued free transfer of arms and became, in the mid-1960s, the most important supplier of weapons to the Third World, surpassing the United States for the first time. The position of the importers of weapons got better and worse at the same time; with more suppliers from both east and west, they had more choice, but at the same time they had to pay either in money or with political allegiance.

During the 1960s, the ground was laid for the large expansion of the arms trade during the 1970s. But it took other factors to enable the arms trade to increase by a factor of 2 within a decade (see Figures 9.1 and 9.2). First, there was the rise in the price of oil and some other raw materials. This gave some states in the Third World unprecedented amounts of financial resources. Second, with lots of money available in some Third World states that could only invest part of it, and uncertain economic prospects in the industrialized countries, great amounts of finance at cheap terms became available to other Third World countries, originally not favored by increases in prices of raw materials, in the form of credits on international financial markets. A good part of the debt incurred in the 1970s—estimates range around 10 percent (Brzoska, 1983)—was used to buy weapons. Third, the October War in the Middle East provided a strong stimulus for rearmament throughout that conflict-torn and newly enriched region. Fourth, arms transfers were riding on the crest of a procurement cycle in many Third World countries. Those armed forces that had received World War II-weapons in the 1950s and early 1960s were in dire need of replacements. Fifth, the economic crisis in many industrialized countries that paralleled the oil price increase raised their economic interest in making money from arms transfers. "Arms for oil" became a catchword, not only in Western Europe, but also in the Soviet Union, which greatly increased its sales of weapons for hard currency. In the United States, the situation was also affected by the end of the Vietnam War, which left some production capacities unoccupied. The companies looked for work abroad. Sixth, both the United States and the Soviet Union changed their attitudes toward arms transfers as a policy instrument. The United States, influenced by the Vietnam experience, formulated a policy of arms transfers to friendly regionally dominant states in preference to direct military involvement—often called the Nixon Doctrine (Sorley, 1983; Klare, 1985). Although such regional powers were expected to pay for the weapons they received, they were to be treated preferentially and with the full backing of the U.S. government. The Soviet Union, eager not to destroy advances in detente with the United States, while at the same time trying to exploit the weak post-

Figure 9.1
Sources of Arms Transfers of Major Weapons

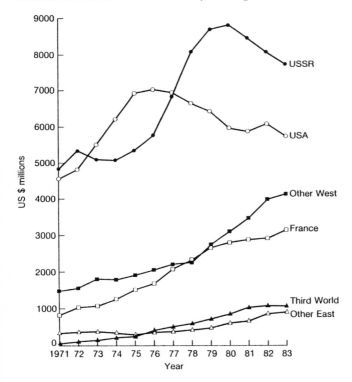

Figure 9.2
Destinations of Arms Transfers of Major Weapons

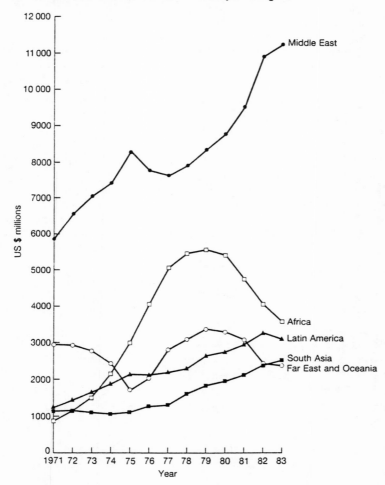

Vietnam international position of the United States, also raised the importance of arms transfers as an instrument of its foreign policy (Krause, 1985).

In addition to the large increase in volume, important structural changes became manifest in the 1970s. First, the Third World segment of the arms market became much more important, as transfers to the Third World grew rapidly, while the trade among industrialized countries stagnated. Second, used or outdated weapons were hardly traded anymore. Those states that could pay demanded more sophisticated weapons. In some cases they even contributed financially to the development of new weaponry, as when Iran partly financed the development of the F-14 aircraft in the United States. Third, more and more customers demanded arms production technology in addition to weapon systems. Many of them wanted to build up domestic arms industries with foreign help so that they could become more independent in the long run. Fourth, the financing of the arms trade changed. While military aid remained available for many poor countries, countries at war, and strategically important allies of the great powers, in general weapons had to be paid for, either in cash or via credit financing. In the late 1970s, credit financing became the most common form of arms transfer payment.

The expansive phase of the 1970s was still marked by the elements of a hierarchic system, despite the use of the arms trade by Western countries to recycle money paid for oil and by Eastern suppliers to gain hard currency. Especially the French government, and following it the West German and the Italian governments, looked at arms transfers primarily in a commercial way. But their market shares were small. Both superpowers and most recipients continued to attach much political weight to arms transfer decisions. In the early 1970s, the post-war structure of the arms market—dominated by the United States and the Soviet Union as suppliers with mainly political aims in their arms transfer policies—reached its highest stage. As the 1970s moved ahead, some of the elements that have come to dominate the different structure of the arms market in the 1980s such as increased production in the Third World, increased competition among producers, and a less hierarchical structure, became clearly visible.

In the late 1970s, the arms trade began to stagnate. Several factors contributed to this trend. First, raw material prices, including those for oil, fell drastically. Second, accumulated debt became a heavy burden in many Third World countries. Third, government deficits that were allowed to rise in the 1970s—partly to finance increasing arms budgets—had to be cut in order to stabilize economies that had gotten out of fiscal and, consequently, monetary, control. Fourth, international financial institutions like the International Monetary Fund and the World Bank for the first time took an interest in the military spending in several of the debtor states and tried to persuade some countries, such as Peru, Zaire, and Morocco, to spend less on weapons. All these factors limited arms purchasing power throughout most of the Third World. In addition, domestic arms production in Third World countries has become a factor to be reckoned with. Some countries in the Third World now produce a fair share of their weaponry domestically, and some have even become exporters of weapons.

Another factor contributing to the stagnating demand for arms imports in the 1980s was that, after the extensive purchases of the 1970s, many armed forces expressed no need for new weapons. Some, like Libya's forces, even had not integrated the weapons bought earlier. The procurement cycle of the 1970s had come to an end.

Still, effective demand stagnated and did not fall. It was fueled by several conflicts, for example the Iraq-Iran War. In some countries, for example Saudi Arabia, buildups of armed forces had been initiated in the 1970s and were moving into their hardware-expensive phases. In addition, the United States and the Soviet Union, faced with clients that could not pay for weapons, were more willing again to increase their military aid.

While demand slowed, supply increased. The arms trade in the 1980s is marked by tough competition among suppliers. The ongoing economic crisis in many East and West European countries further stimulated efforts to sell weapons. New suppliers, both form Europe—Spain and Greece—and from the Third World, entered the market.

Some structural changes were notable. First, the United States and the Soviet Union, which were not willing to fully enter the race for orders and to abandon their political approach to arms transfers, lost market shares. While in the late 1970s their combined share in arms transfers to the Third World stood at over 70 percent, by the mid-1980s it had fallen to less than 60 percent (SIPRI, 1986). For the whole world, the share has fallen to around 50 percent (US ACDA, 1987). This trend was reinforced by the desire of many recipients to get weapons without political strings attached—and therefore preferably not from the United States or the Soviet Union. Second, two tiers of the market for complete weapons systems developed. In one section new weapon systems are bought by rich Third World States. In another section poor states are buying old or simple weapons, often from other Third World countries or from private arms dealers. The business of updating weapons has also gained in importance. The Chinese arms industry has specialized in offering their Soviet-type armored vehicles and aircraft integrated with Western (British, Israeli, U.S) electronics. Third, arms production technology partly substituted for the trade in complete weapon systems. Third World customers are demanding and receiving work shares in the production of weapon systems they purchase and licenses and components for the weapons they want to produce. Fourth, more recipients are demanding large offsets in order to lessen the economic burdens of arms imports. These offsets often take the form of civilian or military goods that have to be imported by the weapon exporter (Neuman, 1985). Fifth, the grey and black markets have become more important. Many of the new exporters rely on the services of private dealers to enter the highly competitive market. The same is true for established arms producers that do not want to be caught dealing with problematic customers, like Iran, and prefer to have intermediaries.

The stagnation in the arms market in the 1980s is explained largely by short-term economic and long-term procurement factors on the side of the recipients. It is therefore possible that the volume of arms transfers will increase again, if and as economic conditions improve and weapons get outdated. In addition, weapons are used in conflicts. The number and intensity of Third World conflicts has not decreased in the 1980s (Sivard, 1986). But there are some structural influences on arms transfers, including domestic arms production, the economic differentiation among Third World countries, and political developments within Third World countries, that might preclude a return to an arms market with high growth rates. Domestic arms production in Third World countries is growing, despite severe problems in many cases. The gap between many poor and some rich Third World states will increase and with it the differentiation in the arms market. Only some countries will be able to buy more expensive modern weapon systems. Many Third World countries, especially in Latin America, have returned to civilian government after long periods of military rule. If this trend continues, it means that less weapons may be bought by the respective states and that chances for regional accords among Third World states may rise.

There is no reason to assume a reduction in supply. A U.S.–Soviet agreement on how to handle their rivalry in the Third World, which might put a cap on military aid and thereby lower the supply of weapons, seems far away. But even if there will continue to be numerous customers who, owing to lack of financial resources, will be happy to receive weapons for free from the United States or the Soviet Union, the share of the two superpowers in the arms market will continue to fall. The arms market is getting more and more commercialized. The shares of suppliers are more and more determined by their industrial and financial capacity. Still, the two superpowers will remain dominant because of their worldwide political interests and because so much of new weapons development is concentrated in these two countries.

SUPERPOWER ARMS TRANSFER MANAGEMENT

The United States and the Soviet Union have remained the dominant suppliers. Their shares in the arms trade are much higher than their shares in the trade of other goods—much more so for the Soviet Union than for the United States. For them, the trade in arms is not like the trade in other goods; rather, it is dominated by political motives.

Both in the United States and the Soviet Union, arms transfers are used as an instrument of foreign policy. There are other arms suppliers which use arms transfers as a foreign policy instrument, like France in Africa, but on a much more limited scale.[3] The precise role of arms transfers depends on the the availability and perceived usefulness of other instruments, such as economic and military measures. Within the range of foreign policy instruments available, arms transfers fall between more coercive ones, like the show of force or direct military intervention, and less coercive ones like economic assistance or diplomatic exchanges. One aspect that makes arms transfers an often used instrument is that they are frequently easier to supply than other goods or services asked for.

Arms transfers can be used as foreign policy instruments in many ways. First, weapons can be allowed to be transferred. Second, weapons can be given for free as military aid. Third, the transfer of weapons and spare parts can be stopped. Arms transfers, military assistance, and arms boycotts both directly affect the military capabilities of the recipients and are political signals. Such signals can be directed toward the recipients—expressing some support, strong support, or dissatisfaction—toward other countries in the recipient's region, and toward the other superpower, or toward all of these.

Arms transfers are used to help accomplish a large number of foreign policy goals. One goal is to make and support allies and friends. A second is to exchange arms for military assets which recipients offer in exchange, like base rights, overflight rights, and the right to conduct intelligence gathering. A third is to change a client's political behavior, for example, in the fields of human rights; nuclear non-proliferation; crisis management; or conduct of an ongoing war—or to convince the client not to change behavior.

Arms transfers are intended to be instruments of supplier leverage. But they can also, as diplomatic and political signals, bind the supplier. They imply a commitment to the recipient state, the recipient's policies and acts. They can lead to an escalation in the commitment. Clients can wring more and more concessions both in weapons and in more coercive foreign policy actions from suppliers through reverse leverage.

There is another important implication of arms transfers on the superpower level. Superpowers can be drawn further into conflict with each other owing to commitments coming from the arms transfers—up to direct confrontation. This danger is greatest in the Middle East in the confrontation between Syria and Israel. Both the United States and the Soviet Union are aware of this danger and have behaved so as to preclude such a direct confrontation. Thus, both superpowers, while heavily arming their clients in the Middle East, have not given them sufficient military power to substantially change the current balance of forces, since this would threaten the direct military intervention of the patron of the losing side. In another region, the Soviet Union has refrained from giving fighter aircraft to Nicaragua, although they were asked to, whereas the United States had not given fighter aircraft to Honduras until 1986, when the administration decided to supply F-5s.

Another way to avoid direct confrontation is to use what has been frequently employed in the supply of warring states: the use of dependent third countries (Neuman, 1986). Nicaragua is receiving few weapons from the Soviet Union directly, but many from East European allies of the Soviet Union. The Afghan rebels are receiving Egyptian and Pakistani arms, but few from the United States. Third country transfers are also a way to support both sides in a conflict.

Thus, East European countries became important suppliers of Iraq in late 1980 and 1981, when the Soviet Union was courting Iran. The U.S. government supported the sale of British Tornado fighter aircraft to Saudi Arabia in 1985, when it became clear that a direct sale of F-15s from the United States would be strongly opposed by Congress.

Although there are many common features of U.S. and Soviet arms export policy, there are also important differences. For the Soviet Union, arms transfers are a more important instrument, both because of its political-military-industrial apparatus and because of its lack of alternatives.

The Soviet Union has large stocks of weapons. Old weapons are seldomly discarded but are normally stored. In addition, it is the Soviet style to manufacture large numbers of a given weapon system. The decision-making process is concentrated close to the center of power, the Central Committee of the Communist party and the Defense Council. The State Committee of Foreign Economic Relations which is staffed mostly with military officers administers arms transfers. The Soviet Union can supply large quantities of weapons at comparatively short notice, as when large numbers of weapons were sent to Ethiopia in 1977 and to Syria in 1982. Many Soviet weapons are older and of simple design. They are often easier to use and more rugged than weapons of Western origin. Prices are often low. Together with the quantitative aspect, these qualities make Soviet weapons especially attractive to poor countries and combatants in war.

Arms transfers are a very important instrument of Soviet foreign policy. This results partly from the Soviet Union's lack of capacity in the economic sphere. Two countries, Cuba and Vietnam, are absorbing a large part of the funds which the Soviet Union is prepared to spend on economic development of Third World countries. Its technology is not very much in demand in the Third World. Even political allies like Syria and Libya prefer Western industrial technology. It is no wonder, then, that about half of all Soviet exports to Third World countries are exports of weapons compared with less than 8 percent for the United States.

The United States has a less flexible political-military-industrial apparatus but a wider spectrum of alternatives. Lead times between orders and deliveries for U.S. weapons are often very long. The procedures for immediate shipments during crises are not very developed. If the U.S. president does not invoke his authority for emergency shipments, a long political process ensues before weapons can be delivered, which involves the Departments of State and Defense and Congress, if not the White House (Grimmett, 1982; Hammond et al., 1983). Government officials in both the United States and potential recipient countries tend to see this—especially the participation of Congress—as a complication, while Congress has over time strengthened its role in decision-making over arms transfers. Although up to early 1986 only one arms transfer request by the U.S. government had been voted down by Congress (a sale to Jordan in 1985), arms transfer packages were often changed and sometimes abandoned in anticipation or because of congressional opposition. Such opposition regularly came up when arms transfers to Saudi Arabia, Jordan, and Kuwait were proposed. It was also voiced when arms were delivered to countries violating human rights. Another reason for opposition was the proposal to introduce new weapon systems into a region, as when the Reagan administration proposed to send F-16 aircraft to Venezuela in 1981. There are also some specific legal requirements, which have been debated at times, such as that military assistance is not to be given to countries trying to build a nuclear bomb (famous case: Pakistan) or cooperating militarily with South Africa (a provision aimed at Israel).

The role of arms transfers, military aid, and arms boycotts has been hotly debated in the United States (Cahn et al., 1977; Pierre, 1979; Hammond et al., 1983; Sorley, 1983; Klare, 1984). Not much is known about internal debate in the Soviet Union (Kozyrev, 1985), but the twists and turns of Soviet policy on arms exports suggest that there is also discussion there. In any case, there is large disagreement in the West about the intentions behind Soviet arms export policy (Pajak, 1981; Albrecht 1983; Krause, 1985).

Generally speaking, discussion centers on two questions: the goals of arms transfer policy, and the success of arms transfers as a foreign policy instrument.

With respect to the first question, the debate does not have much to do with arms transfers themselves. It is a discussion about the Third World policies of the respective superpower in general. Thus, the debate, for instance, about whether Saudi Arabia should receive Airborne Warning and Control Systems (AWACS) was actually over the U.S. commitment to conservative Arab states versus its commitment to Israel. The position in the debate over military assistance to the Contras fighting the Nicaraguan government depends on the view of the threat the Nicaraguan government presents to the United States. Some observers see a consistent pattern behind Soviet arms exports designed to drive the United States out of the Third World, while others see only a series of exploited opportunities. The evidence in Soviet arms transfers is not conclusive; rather, such positions are derived from a more general understanding of Soviet Third World policy.

The second question hinges on a very difficult empirical concept in the area of foreign policy, namely, that of success and its causes. It is generally impossible to know what would have happened had the instrument of arms transfers not been used the way it was used.

Some examples suffice to illustrate this point here. (1) In the 1970s, the United States allowed the unlimited supply of conventional weapons to Iran. In fact, the U.S.–Iranian relationship was largely built on the arms link. When the Shah fell, partly because of the close U.S.-Iranian military link which had offended many Iranians, the United States lost an important ally in the Middle East. The new Islamic government regarded the United States, which had been so closely connected with the Shah, as its enemy number one. (2) The

Soviet Union's most important ally in the Middle East from the late 1950s to the early 1970s was Egypt, to whom the Soviets gave large amounts of military aid. In the early 1970s, however, when Egypt began preparations for an attack on Israel against the Soviet Union's wishes, political frictions developed and Soviet advisers were asked to leave the country in 1972. Although deliveries of weapons and spare parts continued until 1975, Egypt now turned to the West. (3) After 1977, the Carter administration stopped the transfer of most types of arms to Argentina because of human rights violations by Argentinian authorities. The Argentinian armed forces were built up during the following years, with weapons supplied from Western Europe and the domestic arms industry. When in 1982 the Argentinian armed forces took the Falkland/ Malvinas Islands from the United Kingdom, the United States did not have much leverage to influence Argentinian behavior through arms transfer policy. (4) The Soviet Union gave substantial military aid to the armed forces of Grenada in the early 1980s. Partly because of fears of possible future consequences of the Grenadian–Soviet military cooperation, the United States invaded Grenada and put a right-wing anti-Soviet government in power.

As these examples show, it is very difficult to assess whether or not the use of arms transfers as a foreign policy instrument was successful. Views will depend on the definition of foreign policy goals and assumptions about possible alternative courses of events. Such views can be divided into three clusters. The first prefers arms transfers over other foreign policy instruments as one that is both less committed and more directly related to force and power than alternative means (Sorley, 1983). A second view is prepared to use sales, but with restraints as dominant consideration and with careful calibration according to customers and circumstances (Cahn et al., 1977; Hammond et al., 1983). A third view opposes arms transfers, either because of their effects on recipient countries or because of their identification with the hegemonic U.S. role in the world (Kaldor and Eide, 1979).

Both the United States and the Soviet Union make frequent use of arms transfers as a foreign policy instrument, but the importance of arms transfer policy has been different at different times in post-war history, reflecting changing views of the Third World; success and failures of arms exports policies; and changing superpower relations.

In the United States, arms transfers became a preferred foreign policy instrument during the Nixon administration. This was partly a result of the problems encountered with the direct use of force in Vietnam and partly an answer to the evolution of Third World powers. The large increase in U.S. orders, however, was viewed critically by both Congress and the general public. Congress expanded its oversight over arms transfers in 1975, and incoming President Carter vowed to reduce arms transfers. In 1977, via Presidential Directive 13, strict rules for a limitation of U.S. arms transfers were laid down. The main objectives were to refuse to deliver weapons to states violating human rights, to refrain from introducing weapon systems in a region first, and to keep a ceiling on yearly arms sales. Although some of these regulations were soon revoked, for example, to continue the close arms transfer relationship with Iran, U.S. arms transfers decreased. The Reagan administration did not agree with the aims of the Carter administration's arms export policy and revoked the earlier limitations. But arms transfers have not regained the importance they had during the Nixon years, partly because of congressional opposition and partly because of the use of other instruments such as the direct use of military force.

Soviet weapons exports grew in the late 1950s and early 1960s after a pessimistic view on the possibility of Communist revolutions in the Third World under Stalin had given way to a much more optimistic assessment under Khrushchev. In the late 1960s, Soviet policy again became more cautious after some disappointments. In Ghana and Indonesia, for example, socialist governments were overthrown by local armed forces that had been equipped by the Soviet Union. Soviet arms exports were expanded again in the mid- and late 1970s, in response to the perceived post-Vietnam American weakness and the prosperous arms market where it was possible to earn the money needed to import Western technology. In the 1970s, hard currency earnings from arms exports became more important than military aid which had dominated Soviet arms transfers earlier. In the 1980s, Soviet arms exports decreased again. One reason was that it became much more difficult to make money from arms exports. Another was that many Soviet customers that had received large amounts of weapons in the 1970s, like Libya and Ethiopia, were not ready to take more.

U.S. and Soviet arms transfers were out of phase most of the time. When U.S. arms transfers were increasing, as in the early 1970s, Soviet arms transfers were stagnating; when Soviet arms transfers increased, as in the late 1970s, American arms exports decreased. Part of this pattern stems from periodically changing internal assessments of the usefulness of arms transfers, and part of it is a reaction to earlier behavior of the other superpower. Only in the 1980s did arms exports for both superpowers lag behind—when arms transfers from primarily economically motivated suppliers became much more important.

THE ECONOMICS OF ARMS TRANSFERS

Although foreign policy considerations dominate U.S. and Soviet decision-making on arms transfers, economic interests also influence them. For other suppliers, economic interests are much more important, depending on the extent of national involvement in international affairs and the size of the respective arms industry. Thus, for France, a country with a large arms industry that employs 300,000 people and is heavily dependent on arms exports, economic motives weigh very heavily, though in the case of Black African states where France is still the guardian of the status quo, France pursues a restrictive policy in order to maintain control (Kolodziej, 1982). For Italy, another country with a large and very export-dependent arms industry, economic motives are almost the only ones.

There are various economic motives for extensive arms exports on various levels of the nation-state. First, there is the obvious level of the companies and factories. If they are privately owned, or state owned but run as private enterprises, as most major arms producers in France and Italy are, their objective is to make profit. Since arms exports will increase business and thus normally profits, arms producers will generally push for more exports. As studies of bureaucratic behavior have shown, the same thing is true for factories that are state-owned but not profitmaking. Here the managers have a clear interest in expanding their businesses and thus their responsibilities.

Second, there is the level of regional and sectoral policy. Governments can steer arms production, including arms exports, much easier than they can steer other industrial production which is not under their control. They are therefore tempted to use arms exports to support unprosperous regions and specific industries with economic problems. In West Germany, for instance, the economy of the northern part of the country did not grow as well as that of the South in the 1970s and the 1980s. This was partly due to a crisis in shipbuilding. Although West German governments were generally restrictive with respect to arms transfers, they freely allowed the export of ships, mainly to aid the ailing shipbuilding industry in northern Germany.

Third, there is the national level. Various considerations can play a role here—to increase employment; to bolster current accounts; and to receive foreign contributions to finance technological advances. On the national level, there is one important consideration, which, while it looks like an economic motive, really is a strategic one. It is to lower the cost of domestic arms production, or, in extreme cases, to make local production possible at all. Arms exports serve the strategic aim of having a broad domestic arms industry. France, for example, would find it very costly, even impossible, to produce the broad range of weapons that are manufactured in France without the extensive income from arms exports (Kolodziej, 1987). In Italy, few sectors of the arms industry would be viable without arms exports.

Arms exports thus have considerable economic and strategic benefits. But they also have disadvantages. One disadvantage is that they make a country's foreign policy dependent on economic considerations. For example, before the French socialists came to power in 1982, they had announced that they would decrease French arms exports. After a few weeks in power, they found the economic and strategic costs of reduced arms exports too high for a change in policy and instead initiated a drive to increase arms exports. Moreover, extensive arms exports, like intensive arms production, skews industrial production in a way that is disadvantageous for economic productivity (Rothschild, 1973). Arms production requires advanced skills and production methods that are not very useful for civilian production. Countries with extensive arms production find it more difficult in the long run to maintain a good standing in the civilian end of the world market than countries with less arms production. As the combination of welfare and security embodied in arms production and exports is sought after by more and more states, overproduction becomes a major problem. This tendency of overproduction is also built into domestic arms production, because of the necessity to stay with advancing scientific knowledge and follow-on imperatives (Kaldor, 1982).

In some of the mostly economically motivated supplier countries, there is extensive discussion about arms transfers. Several issues are debated. First, objections are raised to the sustaining of combatants. The denial of transfers to countries at war or close to war is part of the legislation of almost all West European states. This restriction is another element that distinguishes these arms suppliers from the superpowers, which are very often to be found supplying one side in a crisis or during war. Still, arms often find their way to places where they are being used. Weapons from a large number of countries were delivered to Iran and Iraq during their war in the 1980s. Second, there is sometimes opposition to the supply of weapons to certain specific countries. Opposition was voiced when French weapons were exported to Libya when France was at the same time supporting the Chadian government in fighting Libyan-supported groups. Third, the delivery of weapons to states violating human rights is sometimes opposed. The Thatcher government in Britain, for instance, has been under heavy attack because of arms deliveries to Chile. Only a few states, such as Austria, have regulations limiting arms exports to governments violating human rights. Fourth, there is debate about whether it makes sense to sell weapons to countries that are at the same time receiving economic aid. Thus, in West Germany, Parliament cut economic aid to India when the Indian government ordered Mirage-2000 fighter aircraft in France. Fifth, the morality of arms transfers to the Third World is questioned. In France, the United Kingdom, and the Federal Republic of Germany, for instance, the established churches have voiced criticism over arms exports.

Among the more economically oriented producers, France is the most important one, with a share of more than 10 percent in the world arms trade (Figure 9.1). This position was reached in a slow growth process that began in the late 1950s. In the 1960s, South Africa and Israel were the most important recipients. After an arms embargo against Israel in 1968, the trade with Arab states was expanded. In the 1980s, the Middle East was by far the most important region for French arms exports (Kolodziej, 1987).

The United Kingdom had been the second most important arms exporter to the Third World until the late 1950s, when that role was taken over by the Soviet Union. From the early 1970s on, French arms exports also exceeded British transfers. The major reasons for Britain's loss in market share were its decreased worldwide political importance and the concentration of its industry on very advanced products not well suited for the export market.

The Thatcher government tried to reverse the trend with some success in the 1980s (Pearson, 1983).

West Germany adopted a very restrictive arms export policy in the early 1970s after some scandals shook the Republic in the 1960s. Because of domestic economic problems, restrictions were eased step by step beginning in the mid-1970s. Still, West Germany was more restrictive than, for example, France and the United Kingdom, which exercised few limitations on arms transfers in the 1980s (Pearson, 1985).

The Italian arms industry greatly expanded in the 1970s as a response to the growing arms market. Many U.S. production licenses were used. There were hardly any export restrictions beyond those imposed by the United States. In the 1980s, with the slump in the arms market, the Italian arms industry entered a prolonged crisis.

Other European arms producers, including Spain, Greece, Yugoslavia, Romania, and Bulgaria, tried to jump on the bandwagon of increased arms imports in the 1970s. One tendency among these new exporters was that they did not look too closely at the customers' credentials. In addition, since their industrial capabilities were limited, they concentrated on the production of less advanced weaponry. Several of the newcomers had high growth rates when they began to export weapons, but sales were greatly reduced in the 1980s when the market did not grow as much as it had in the 1970s.

Another group of traditional arms producers' sales were not greatly affected by either the boom or the slump. These are small industrial countries, like Sweden, Switzerland, Canada, and the Netherlands, that specialize in the production of certain weapon systems.

Finally, it should be mentioned that two states refuse to sell or give weapons to the Third World. These are Norway and Japan. Japan is afraid of reviving its militarist image, whereas in Norway the possible negative effects of arms transfers to the Third World is judged higher than possible economic gains. But as recent transfers of high-tech goods to the Soviet Union have shown, many critical items, for instance computers and machinery, are coming from these countries and can have military significance.

THIRD WORLD EXPORTERS

Some countries in the Third World have been able to change their role from recipients to exporters. Most prominent among them are Israel and Brazil. Israel exports a wide range of both outdated Soviet-type weapons captured during its various wars with Arab countries and modern equipment built in Israel (Klieman, 1985). Brazil's arms exports consist mainly of armored vehicles, aircraft, and rocket artillery of simple design. Other Third World exporters that entered the arms market in the late 1970s and early 1980s were South Korea, Chile, and Singapore. All produce some weapons domestically, using foreign technology as the basis. Other Third World countries that have substantial arms industries, like India, Argentina, and South Africa, also tried to export weapons on a greater scale but were not very successful (Brzoska and Ohlson, 1986).

Two factors favor Third World arms exports. One is that there are very few restrictions on them. (Israel, for example did not allow weapon exports to the Arab countries in its vicinity.) Therefore, it is not surprising to find that most arms transfers from Third World countries were directed to crisis or war areas, especially where Western European suppliers were reluctant to deliver. Almost the whole range of Third World arms suppliers can be found in the list of suppliers to the Iraq-Iran War, and many as suppliers to both sides. The second factor favoring Third World arms exports is the nature of weapons produced in several countries. They are designed much more for the use of Third World armed forces—rugged and simple to use—than many weapons coming from the countries mainly developing weapons for a war in Europe. At the same time, some Third World producers, like the Brazilian, Israeli, and Singaporean arms manufacturers, are using very modern technology for their simplified designs, so that their weapons can by no means be called outdated. There are also technological counter-examples. Third World producers that tried to make technological steps too fast, like India and Argentina, sometimes could not convince many prospective customers of the value of their products.

Third World arms production has remained dependent on technological inputs from the major industrial countries. The United States and the Soviet Union have been reluctant to part with arms technology and licenses to produce weapons. They have also tried to restrict Third World country exports—with limited success, since West European suppliers are very willing to sell arms production technology and to substitute for the superpowers.

One factor that is only seldom important is price. In general, Third World arms production is comparatively costly because of short production runs and the dearth of supporting industries that are necessary for arms production. Only when simple designs are used, or when labor is an important cost factor, as in the production of ammunition, are Third World producers generally cheaper than producers from industrialized countries.

Observers do not agree about whether arms exports from Third World countries will or can expand in the future (Neuman, 1984; Brzoska and Ohlson, 1986). Third World arms production is fraught with technical and financial problems. It seems improbable that many more countries can start arms production since this requires an industrial base. On the other hand, there is obviously much room for substitution of arms imports by domestic production, with arms exports a logical extension of arms production. Much will depend on the behavior of the more established suppliers from industrialized countries—for example, whether they will change their designs and regulations to more directly compete with Third World exporters.

PUSH AND PULL

As outlined, arms suppliers have numerous interests in the transfer of weapons. They use persuasive measures to try to convince potential customers of the benefits of importing arms from them. These can take the form of diplomatic overtures, selling campaigns, arms fairs, commissions, fees and bribes, and so on (Sampson, 1977; Pierre, 1982).

Obviously, recipients also have interests in purchasing weapons, primarily to be armed against external enemies, and secondly to be armed against internal opponents. Quite different weapons are required for the latter—counter-insurgency weapons like small aircraft, armored vehicles, and tear-gas grenades. There is a little noticed section of the arms trade dealing in such weapons (Klare, 1979). Arms imports can also be an internal political symbol of power. Governments can buy modern weapon systems to impress internal opponents or to keep the military in its barracks content. Finally, weapons can be symbols of a state's international relations, signalling where alliances and allegiances lie.

The importance of pull factors is seen in the regional distribution of weapons imports in the Third World (Figure 9.2). More than half of all weapons imported by Third World countries go to the Middle East, that is, both the most conflict-prone and resource-rich region. During the late 1970s, Africa's importance as an arms-importing region increased dramatically—as a function both of conflicts (Western Sahara War, Conflicts in the Horn) and high oil incomes in some countries (Algeria, Libya).

There is considerable controversy over the relative importance of supply and demand factors. Different views on this point have, for instance, differing implications for the position one adopts on arms transfer restraint (Cahn et al., 1977, introduction). If the push factors are most important, then limitations have to start in the supplying countries. If the pull factors are most important, then restraint must come from the recipient side.

In fact, demand and supply are very difficult to distinguish and are often closely related. Push and pull reinforce each other in the perception of mutual benefits. Arms suppliers will praise their weapons and try to convince customers disposed toward acquisition. The situation gets even more obvious where the military rules, as it did in more than half of all the Third World countries in many years in the 1970s and 1980s (Sivard, 1986). Here there is no obvious check on the acquisition interests of the military from a parliament or a civilian government.

Mutual reinforcement of supply and demand goes far beyond arms transfers. It derives from doctrinal development, training, and military education, all of which are centered in the major industrial countries, the United States, the Soviet Union, and, to some extent, the former colonial powers. In this broader sense, the arms transfers system has remained very hierarchical, with the United States and the Soviet Union on top, where arms production technology is most advanced; where military doctrines are developed and taught; and where most of the general staff officers of Third World nations go for at least some of their advanced courses (Kaldor and Eide, 1979; Kaldor, 1982).

ARMS TRANSFER EFFECTS

Arms are supplied and received because of mutually perceived benefits. But in fact, interests between suppliers and recipients often differ. In addition, the actual consequences of arms transfers are not always identical to the perceived ones. Since there are many effects of arms transfers, it is possible only to give some idea of the problems involved.

First, on the military level, arms transfers are designed to increase the military power of the recipient armed forces. Sometimes this is not what happens. The weapons supplied may be too complicated, too technologically advanced, unsuitable for the purpose at hand, or simply too numerous for the armed forces to use.

Second, on the bilateral political level, there are the issues of dependence and leverage. For suppliers with foreign policy interests in their arms transfers, it is important that transfers give leverage to achieve the desired aims. This leverage can take different forms. The first is the direct negotiation leverage inherent in the power to give or not give weapons in exchange for something sought. The second form of leverage comes with a longer and broader arms transfer relation. Once an armed force is built around certain types of weapon systems, there is a strong need for spare parts, modernization kits, and replacements. A third form of leverage is less obvious, though often the strongest one. It comes with training, doctrinal discussions, and the general association between the supplying and recipient countries' armed forces, and might be called cultural leverage (Kaldor, 1982). Recipient countries very often try to avoid any of these types of leverage which make them dependent on the good will of the recipient, except when they are interested in reverse leverage. One way to counter dependence is to buy from suppliers without foreign policy aims; another is to build up domestic arms production. But even where such measures were not taken, or not very successful, Third World states at times have been prepared to take the risks and costs of a change in suppliers in order to avoid dependence.

The United States has experienced this in its Latin American arms export policy, where European suppliers stepped in from the late 1960s, when the United States tried to impose its ideas about arms restraint on Latin American states. The Soviet Union experienced it in Egypt, Somalia, and Sudan in the 1970s. All the armed forces that changed suppliers had some problems and extra costs because of the changeover. In many cases, the fighting abilities of the armed forces decreased dramatically because of the lack of spare parts. In the 1980s, with the highly competitive market, short-run dependence on the supply of spare parts and ammunition has become a less important problem. Even Iran was able to receive lots of ammunition and spare parts for the weapons in its arsenal during the war with Iraq despite a Western embargo and the Soviet tilt toward Iraq.

Third, with respect to international relations, the effects of arms transfers on war and peace are important to discuss. Often arms are supplied in order to create or strengthen perceived military balances in Third World regions. The Camp David accords between Egypt, Israel, and the United States, for example, included large arms transfers to the Egyptian and Israeli forces. But it is nearly impossible to impartially assess whether there is a balance or an imbalance and it is far from certain that military balances in Third World regions guarantee peace. The British government, which had allowed substantial arms transfers to Argentina prior to April 1982, found that weapons exported can be put to use even against the supplier. Although this was an exceptional case, weapons are often used in ways not intended by the original supplier, both by governments to which they were originally supplied and to succeeding governments that may be of completely different political orientation. Iran, for example, has used quite a lot of the material supplied in the 1970s in the Iraq-Iran War. Only a few supporters of the argument that balances are strengthening peaceful international relations are prepared to extend their favorable assessment to nuclear weapons in the possession of Third World governments. Another issue is the question of whether arms transfers escalate crises and lead to war. Here, again, the available evidence is not conclusive (Harkavy, 1985). A generally accepted statement, however, is that the transfer of modern weapons has made Third World wars bloodier.

Fourth, on the economic level, it is obvious that arms purchases are diverting funds from economic development. The acquisitions that have to be paid for in hard currency are especially burdensome since many Third World countries have great difficulties in earning it. About 6 percent of all imports by Third World countries and 20 percent of their imports of technologically comparable goods—machinery and transportation goods—in the mid-1980s consisted of arms (U.S. Arms Control and Disarmament Agency, 1985). In addition, arms transfers can have follow-on costs and effects that were not reckoned with at the time of the purchase. In some recipient countries, military expenditures are a substantial burden for the economy. The large arms credit expansion in the late 1970s and early 1980s has put an additional burden on many Third World economies (Deger, 1986).

ARMS TRANSFERS CONTROL

There are various restraints in the international transfer of conventional weapons. Some restraint is exercised unilaterally by supplying countries, either for specific foreign policy reasons or for more general considerations. Of course, there is also unilateral recipient restraint, partly because governments decide that enough weapons have been acquired and partly because of financial limitations. In addition, there are some restraints on a wider base. Thus, the United States and the Soviet Union exercise some implicit restraint in not delivering weapons that might lead to their direct military involvement in wars (Neuman, 1986). Some multilateral arms boycotts were in effect at the time of writing, like the mandatory arms embargo against South Africa declared by the U.N. security council in 1977, or a joint U.S.–European Economic Community arms embargo against Libya, declared after terrorist incidents in 1985. No multilateral recipient control regimes are in effect, although a number of Latin American countries announced their intention to have such a regime in the declaration of Ayacucho from 1974. This initiative did not lead to any regulated control on arms transfers, but it was renewed in the mid-1980s in the Lima declaration of 1985.

The existing level of restraint and control is viewed as insufficient by many, though not by all, observers and decision-makers (Betts, 1980). Most Western and Warsaw Pact states are on record as favoring more restraint of the arms trade and as saying they would not attempt to destroy a regulation if it was globally exercised.[4] Various reasons are given for this attitude. One that is especially relevant on the level of the superpowers is that it would decrease the danger of escalation of a local crisis or war into an East-West military confrontation. Second, control might deescalate current crises in some regions. A third reason given is that restraint will decrease the role of the military in Third World politics and thus have a positive influence on democratic political development in Third World states. Fourth, fewer resources would be taken away from productive uses in Third World economies, thereby enhancing the chances for economic development.

The wish for more agreed restraint and control of the proliferation in conventional weapons is not universal, however. Neither the United States nor the Soviet Union is willing to give away an important instrument of foreign policy if there are no substitutes guaranteeing their positions in the world. The economically oriented suppliers are afraid of far-reaching problems for their domestic arms industries.

But most objections against arms transfer control regimes have come from the recipients. Those that aspire to some regional power status are afraid that they will be decisively crippled in military terms in comparison with the industrialized countries. In the extreme, they view it as a continuation of colonial attitudes by the big powers, which are trying to increase their military domination (Subrahmanyam, 1972). In any case, it is seen as an unbalanced approach that greatly favors those states producing armaments over those that are importing them. Until the first U.N. special session in 1978, Third World states were reluctant even to talk about this subject. In 1978, it was agreed to study the idea within the framework of the United Nations, but nothing concrete has resulted so far (United Nations, 1982, 1985; Brandt, 1981; Palme, 1983).

Consequently, most of the activity to achieve more agreed restraint of the arms trade has come from the suppliers, especially the big powers trying to sort out their regional interests. In the early 1950s, the Tripartite Agreement between the United States, the United Kingdom, and France limited arms transfers to the Near East. In the late 1970s, the Carter administration, keen on limiting arms transfers, initiated the Conventional Arms Transfer (CAT) talks with the Soviet Union. The Soviet Union showed more enthusiasm than many critics of the Carter approach had assumed. After some discussion, it was agreed to discuss restraint region by region, but there was no agreement about which regions would be discussed first. After some internal debate, the U.S. government stopped this exercise again (Blechman et al., 1982; Pierre, 1982; Hammond, et al., 1983).

There are different opinions about whether the CAT talks could have led to anything. In one view, the approach was wrong, burdening the arms transfer agenda. Instead of focusing on regions and thereby having the whole issue of U.S.–Soviet competition in Third World regions intrude, negotiations should have centered on some especially dangerous weapons, like ballistic missiles and offensive bomber aircraft. Another view—that in the internal discussion in the United States the administration carried the day—held such limitations worthless if they were not embedded in understandings of the real conflict that was not about specific weapons but about U.S.–Soviet rivalry in the Third World. A second problem concerned the inclusion of more parties than the Soviet Union in CAT talks. Because of the increasing importance of the Western European suppliers, many thought it fruitless to limit U.S. and Soviet transfers since they would readily be replaced by deliveries from other suppliers. Others, whose opinions guided the negotiations, argued that these suppliers, which did not show much enthusiasm about being included, should be dealt with later, since the focus in the early phase should be on U.S.–Soviet problems.

Preparations for the CAT talks brought out a number of problems that any attempt at further restraint would face, but also gave hints at new avenues. The increasing number of suppliers and the decreasing importance of the superpowers in conventional weapons transfers makes it very difficult for them to control the volume of the arms trade. But this does not mean that they could not attack the specific problems rising out of their rivalry in a bilateral approach. The CAT talks preparations also showed that economically motivated suppliers would have to restructure their domestic arms industries in order to ease the economic pressure to export, for instance, through greater cooperation in arms production (Franko, 1979). In addition, if the aim were to control the volume of the trade, the inclusion of the recipient states would be unavoidable, since it would be possible for them to get the weapons they wanted somewhere. In summary, the CAT talks exercise demonstrated that many levels of control stem from the various interests in more agreed restraint in the arms trade. Partial approaches seem much more realistic than holistic ones.

Although there is room for measures taken by the suppliers, the structure

232   MICHAEL BRZOSKA

of the arms trade in the 1980s has further shifted responsibility for more restraints toward the recipient countries. They have shown no great willingness to start such a process so far, but strong economic pressure might force them to consider the arguments more seriously. The objection that there is an inherent imbalance between arms producers and arms importers could be dealt with by limiting not only arms imports, but also arms production; or by discussing levels of military spending. The other argument, that the military dominance of the big powers would increase further if the Third World disarmed, would lose credibility if the big military alliances would also start to disarm.

But all such good ideas and arguments about conventional transfer restraint run counter to the current trends in the arms market. The current trend is toward greater commercialization, depoliticization, and diversity in the arms market. All these factors make control of the volume and composition of the arms trade more difficult and less likely.

FUTURE RESEARCH PATHS

The arms trade is a multifaceted phenomenon deeply rooted in internal politics in recipient and supplying countries, in bilateral and international relations. Therefore, it is difficult to imagine that there can be much more than a description of events and partial analytical connections with other phenomena. Still, it is the objective of scientific inquiry and the hope of many decision-makers that some aggregating concepts, some strong propositions, and some unifying ideas can be developed. Some such concepts and parts of theories were used above, such as the concept of dependency and the differentiation of suppliers according to motivations, none of which is unchallenged and can claim universal applicability.

A first task of research on arms transfers has to remain the observation of the marketplace. The available data bases are still not good enough for the research needed. Especially important empirical deficits are the data about the financing of the arms trade; about grey and illegal markets; about components (Klare, 1983); about small arms; and about offsets (Neuman, 1985). The data must provide the basis for a constant interpretation of the marketplace since there is always change that has to be recorded. Interpretation must and will focus on different aspects, including implications for national foreign policies—for example, of the United States.

A second task is to continue testing some assumptions, even if there is a strong hunch that there can be no conclusive answers. Examples of connections that have to be looked at again and again are the relations between arms transfers and superpower rivalry; arms transfers and military balances and wars; arms transfers and Third World warfare (Harkavy, 1985); arms transfers and dependency; and arms transfers and Third World internal politics. There also is still room for more comparative studies on the effects of arms transfers in both the supplying and recipient countries; a specific lacuna is the relation to cultural phenomena (Kaldor, 1982). Only if such studies could accumulate more conclusive evidence would it be possible to come up with more arms trade theory. While this seems a very distant proposition, it should not be beyond the aims of research.

NOTES

1. The Third World is defined here as the countries on the South American, African, and Asian (except Japan) continents, regardless of their stage of economic development or their political orientation.

2. There are two major arms trade statistical series. One is maintained by the U.S. government. Part of it is published in two regular series: the U.S. Arms Control and Disarmament Agency's *World Military Expenditures and Arms Transfers*, and Richard Grimmett's *Trends in Conventional Arms Transfers to the Third World by Major Suppliers*. (Grimmett is a specialist at the Library of Congress's Congressional Research Service.) The other arms trade data base is maintained by the Stockholm International Peace Research Institute (SIPRI). It is built exclusively from open sources and covers only the trade in major weapons. Lists of transfers are published annually in the SIPRI Yearbooks. Long-term data are given in Brzoska and Ohlson (1987). Descriptions and critical assessments of the data can be found in Neuman and Harkavy (1979) and Brzoska (1982). For a methodologically new approach, see Sherwin and Laurence (1979).

3. Almost all suppliers use arms transfers as instruments of diplomacy in the sense that they are part of bilateral political relations. But so are almost all major economic transactions, like the sale of factories or commercial aircraft. This use is different from the use as an instrument of foreign policy in the sense that specific foreign policy goals are pursued via arms transfers.

4. Declarations to this effect can be found in the statements of governments to the First U.N. Special Session on Disarmament in 1978 (United Nations, 1978). For a declaration of the position of the Reagan administration, see Buckley (1981). An exposition of the Soviet position is given in Kozyrev (1985).

REFERENCES

Albrecht, Ulrich. 1983. Soviet Arms Exports. Pp. 361–70 in Stockholm International Peace Research Institute, *World Armaments and Disarmament. SIPRI Yearbook 1983*. London: Taylor and Francis.

Betts, Richard K. 1980. The Tragicomedy of Arms Trade Control. *International Security* 5:80–110.

Blechman, Barry M., Janne Nolan, and Alan Platt. 1982. Pushing Arms. *Foreign Policy* 46:138–54.

Brandt, Willy, chairman. 1981. *A Programme for Survival*. London: Pan Books.

Brzoska, Michael. 1982. Arms Transfer Data Sources. *Journal of Conflict Resolution* 26:77–108.

———. 1983. The Military Related External Debt of Third World Countries. *Journal of Peace Research* 20:271–277.

———, and Thomas Ohlson, eds. 1986. *Arms Production in the Third World*. London: Taylor and Francis.

———, and Thomas Ohlson. 1987. *Third World Arms Imports*. London: Oxford University Press.

Buckley, James L. 1981. Arms Transfers and the National Interest. *Current Policy*, no. 279. U.S. Department of State, Bureau of Public Affairs, Washington, D.C.

Cahn, Anne, Joseph Kruzel, Peter M. Dawkins, and Jacques Huntzinger. 1977. *Controlling Future Arms Trade*. New York: McGraw-Hill.

Cannizzo, Cindy, ed. 1980. *The Gun Merchants: Politics and Policies of the Major Arms Suppliers*. New York: Pergamon Press.

Deger, Saadet. 1986. *Military Expenditure in Third World Countries: The Economic Effects*. London and Boston: Routledge and Kegan Paul.

Franko, Lawrence G. 1979. Restraining Arms Exports to the Third World: Will Europe Agree? *Survival* 21:14–25.

Grimmett, Richard F. Annual. *Trends in Conventional Arms Transfers to the Third World by Major Suppliers*. Library of Congress. Congressional Research Service, Washington, D.C.

———. 1982. *Executive-Legislative Consultation on US Arms Sales*. Congress and Foreign Policy Series No. 7. Washington, D.C.: U.S. Government Printing Office.

Hammond, Paul Y., David J. Louscher, Michael D. Salomone, and Norman A. Graham. 1983. *The Reluctant Supplier: U.S. Decision-making for Arms Sales*. Cambridge, Mass.: Oelgeschlager, Gunn and Hain.

Harkavy, Robert E. 1975. *The Arms Trade and International Systems*. Cambridge, Mass.: Ballinger.

———. 1985. Arms Resupply During Conflict: A Framework for Analysis. *Jerusalem Journal of International Relations* 77:5–41.

Kaldor, Mary. 1982. *The Baroque Arsenal*. London: Andre Deutsch.

———, and Asbjorn Eide, eds. 1979. *The World Military Order: The Impact of Military Technology on the Third World*. London: Macmillan.

Klare, Michael T. 1979. *Supplying Repression*. Washington, D.C.: Institute for Policy Studies.

———. 1983. The Unnoticed Arms Trade: Exports of Conventional Arms-Making Technology. *International Security* 8:68–90.

———. 1984. *American Arms Supermarket*. Austin: University of Texas Press.

Klieman, Arie S. 1985. *Israel's Global Reach: Arms Sales as Diplomacy*. Washington, D.C.: Pergamon-Brassey.

Kolodziej, Edward A. 1982. Security Interests and French Arms Transfer Policy in Sub-Saharan Africa. Pp. 125–52 in Bruce E. Arlinghouse, *Arms for Africa*. Lexington, Mass.: Lexington Books.

———. 1987. *Making and Marketing Arms: The French Experience and Its Implications for the International System*. Princeton, N.J.: Princeton University Press.

Kozyrev, Alexei. 1985. *The Arms Trade: A New Level of Danger*. Moscow: Progress Publisher.

Krause, Joachim. 1985. *Soujetische Militärhilfe an die Dritte Welt*. Baden-Baden: Nomos.

Leiss, Amelia, and Geoffrey Kemp, eds. 1970. *Arms Transfers to Less Developed Countries*. Cambridge, Mass.: Center for International Studies, Massachusetts Institute of Technology.

Neuman, Stephanie G. 1984. International Stratification and Third World Military Industries. *International Organization* 38:167–98.

———. 1985. Coproduction, Barter and Countertrade: Offsets in the International Arms Market. *Orbis* 29:183–214.

———. 1986. *Military Assistance in Recent Wars. The Dominance of the Superpowers.* Washington Papers 122. New York: Praeger.

———, and Robert E. Harkavy, eds. 1979. *Arms Transfers in the Modern World.* New York: Praeger Special Studies.

Pajak, Roger F. 1981. Soviet Arms Transfers as an Instrument of Influence. *Survival* 23:165–73.

Palme, Olof, chairman. 1983. *Common Security.* London: Pan Books.

Pearson, Fred S. 1983. The Question of Control in British Defence Sales Policy. *International Affairs* 28:211–38.

———. 1985. Of Leopards and Cheetahs. *Orbis* 29:165–82.

Pierre, Andrew J., ed. 1979. *Arms Transfers and American Foreign Policy.* New York: New York University Press.

———. 1982. *The Global Politics of Arms Sales.* Princeton, N.J.: Princeton University Press.

Rothschild, Kurt W. 1973. Military Expenditures, Exports and Growth. *Kyklos* 26:804–14.

Sampson, Anthony. 1977. *The Arms Bazaar.* London: Hodder and Stoughton.

Sherwin, Ronald G., and Edward J. Laurence. 1979. Arms Transfers and Military Capability: Measuring and Evaluating Arms Transfers. *International Studies Quarterly* 23:360–89.

Sivard, Ruth. Annual. *World Military and Social Expenditures.* Leesburg, Va.: WMSE Publications.

Sorley, Lewis. 1983. *Arms Transfers Under Nixon: A Policy Analysis.* Lexington, Ky.: University of Kentucky Press.

Stockholm International Peace Research Institute (SIPRI). Annual. *Armaments and Disarmament. SIPRI Yearbook.* London: Oxford University Press (until 1985: Taylor and Francis).

———. 1971. *The Arms Trade with the Third World.* Stockholm: Almqvist and Wicksell.

Subrahmanyam, K. 1972. *Perspectives in Defense Planning.* New Delhi: Abhinav Publications.

Tower, John, chairman. 1987. *Report of the President's Special Review Board.* Washington, D.C.: U.S. Government Printing Office.

United Nations. 1978. *Report of the Preparatory Committee of the Special Session of the General Assembly Devoted to Disarmament.* A/S–10/1–5. New York: United Nations.

———. 1982. *The Relationship Between Disarmament and Development.* E.82.1X.1. New York: United Nations.

———. 1985. *Study on Conventional Disarmament.* E.85.1X.2. New York: United Nations.

United States Arms Control and Disarmament Agency. Annual. *World Military Expenditures and Arms Transfers.* Washington, D.C.: U.S. Government Printing Office.

PART IV

SUBCONVENTIONAL
CONFLICT

10

On Low-Intensity Conflict
and National Security Policy:
A Comparative Analysis

RICHARD SHULTZ

INTRODUCTION

As with any field of study, international security studies seeks to establish a commonly accepted set of concepts, methods, and approaches. Many of the topics in security studies have a long history, but the field itself is only embryonic. Consequently, a sound conceptual basis for the field has yet to be established. One example is "spectrum of conflict," a term frequently utilized in the American national security community. The objective is to establish a conceptual framework or typology that identifies the different forms of conflict/war via a three-level classification, based on the intensity of engagement.

Disagreement exists over the parameters of these categories. There is general agreement that *high-intensity conflict* includes theatre and strategic nuclear warfare. *Mid-intensity conflict* involves limited or general conventional warfare; however, it might also cover conflict with battlefield nuclear, chemical, and biological weapons, blurring the boundaries a bit. Special operations/ unconventional warfare measures might also be utilized, although these are more frequently identified with the third category. Defining the parameters of *low-intensity conflict* (LIC) has engendered the most disagreement and confusion. According to a senior Department of Defense official in the Reagan administration, "the central and most vexing aspect of low intensity conflict is its ambiguity. The threat is seldom clear" (Armitage, 1986). Listing the various forms of conflict and military operations equated with LIC bears this out: special operations, unconventional warfare, guerrilla war, revolutionary insurgency, resistance forces, international and state-sponsored terrorism, internal defense, advisory assistance, psychological operations, foreign internal war, urban insurrection, revolt and revolution, and coup d'etat.

This ambiguity has presented Pentagon planners with a serious dilemma.

The Reagan administration became increasingly concerned about threats to U.S. interests at the low end of the conflict spectrum. After much discussion, the following definition of LIC was forged, unfortunately in an all-encompassing manner (U.S. Army Training and Doctrine Command, 1986):

A limited politico-military struggle to achieve political, social, economic, and psychological objectives. It is often protracted, and ranges from diplomatic, economic, and psychological pressures to terrorism and insurgency. LIC is generally confined to a geographic area, and it is often characterized by constraints on the weaponry, tactics and level of violence.

There are obvious problems with this definition. It covers every conceivable form of competition, conflict, and war below the conventional level. As a result, it greatly complicates development of doctrine, organization, and capabilities for responding to low-intensity threats.

This chapter examines how Western states have understood and developed the means to respond to low-intensity conflict. First, it is necessary to outline the parameters of LIC. This will be followed by an investigation of the American experience since 1945. Next, we examine the ways LIC has been addressed by other Western governments. Finally, we will look at the lessons that can be drawn and what they suggest about what course the field should follow.

LOW-INTENSITY CONFLICT: CONCEPTUAL DIMENSION

The term *low-intensity conflict* was added to the lexicon of the U.S. national security community during the 1970s. It refers to conflicts that are, in terms of U.S. involvement, limited in scope and generally unconventional in approach. (For the other parties involved, the conflict is often neither low intensity nor limited in scope.) One of the first attempts to identify the parameters of LIC and its possible implications was undertaken by RAND in 1976. The RAND report saw LIC as a class of conflict that included guerilla war, civil war, terrorism, military intervention, spheres of influence, skirmishes, communal wars, and peasant revolutions (Tanham et al., 1978).

In many ways, this repeats an effort undertaken nearly a decade earlier by Harry Eckstein to categorize types of conflict occurring in the Third World. Under the rubric of "internal war" he subsumed "revolution, civil war, revolt, rebellion, uprising, guerrilla warfare, mutiny, jacquerie, coup d'etat and insurrection." For Eckstein, internal war "stands for the genus of which the others are species" (Eckstein, 1965).

Perhaps the most complex and often misunderstood manifestation of LIC is "revolutionary insurgent warfare"—what communist states refer to as "wars of national liberation" or "People's Wars." Beginning in the late 1940s, this was the principal form of LIC that concerned the British and French. By the end of the 1950s, it became an important national security issue for the United States as well. Widely used against colonial rule, the strategy of revolutionary insurgent warfare can also be employed against post-colonial regimes, as we will discuss below.

Irregular guerrilla tactics are just an element of revolutionary insurgent warfare, not synonymous with it. Nevertheless, the two terms have been frequently used interchangeably, especially in the United States. This confusion, and the fact that from the late 1940s to the early 1970s revolutionary insurgencies constituted the major form of LIC of concern to Western powers, makes a closer look necessary.

Guerrilla warfare has been employed throughout history. The comprehensive work by Robert Asprey, *War in the Shadows: The Guerrilla in History,* describes how guerrillas hindered Alexander the Great during his campaign in Persia. Asprey notes how guerrillas plagued Hannibal during his epic march from Spain to northern Italy and the Roman army in its pacification of Spain (Asprey, 1975). The military history of the United States is also dotted with involvement in guerrilla conflicts during the War of Independence, the Civil War, and struggles against various Indian tribes. At the turn of the century, the U.S. Army faced guerrilla challenges in the Philippines and Mexico.

None of these cases, however, was equivalent to today's revolutionary insurgent warfare. Revolutionary insurgent warfare employs ancient military tactics in conjunction with political and psychological techniques in order to transfer governmental power as a prelude to the transformation of the social structure. Unconventional military tactics are combined with political and psychological operations to establish a competing political and ideological structure. The roots of this strategy can be traced to the Chinese Communists during the 1930s, refined by their Vietnamese counterparts in the 1940s and 1950s. They frequently referred to it as "People's War."

In the West the French were among the first to grasp the meaning of revolutionary warfare and to articulate a counter-strategy. Many French analysts served in Indochina where, according to Bernard Fall, "they learned their Mao Tse-tung the hard way" (Trinquier, 1964, Preface). Roger Trinquier's *Modern Warfare* is perhaps the most succinct statement by a French officer about this form of conflict. Another French analyst, Colonel Bonnet, advanced the following equation to describe revolutionary warfare (Paret, 1964, p. 16):

RW (Revolutionary Warfare) $= G$ (Guerrilla Tactics) $+ P$ (Political and Psychological Activities)

Bonnet and other French officers concluded that in revolutionary warfare military tactics are secondary to the central strategic objective achieved through political and psychological means. The principal goal is to destroy the legitimacy of the target government through establishment of a counter-ideology and counter-institutions. It is the central importance of political warfare and psychological operations that differentiates revolutionary warfare from other forms of irregular combat.

The British specialist, Sir Robert Thompson, drew similar conclusions: "in revolutionary war the aim is always political.... (T)he revolutionary party seeks to gain control over the population first before it can defeat the opposing military forces" (Thompson, 1970, pp. 5, 16). Thompson is perhaps the best known of the British specialists, including Duncanson (1968), Clutterbuck (1966), and Kitson (1971), who studied revolutionary warfare in the years immediately following WW II. Some Americans drew similar conclusions, most notably Tanham (1967), Lansdale (1972), Pike (1972), Fall (1966), Yarborough (1968), and Stilwell (1961).

Drawing on theoretical literature and the practical application of revolutionary warfare, one can identify a number of general tenets of this strategy. Revolutionary warfare involves the use of an illegal political organization and, until its final stages, irregular military forces. A critical role is assigned to political and psychological measures that are aimed at both the indigenous population and groups, states, and organizations in the international arena. During the initial stage of an insurgency, stress is placed on the primacy of propaganda, psychological warfare, and political action. Through these activities the insurgent leaders hope to advance to a point where they may seriously challenge for state power. The vanguard party concentrates on the formation of a competing or counter-ideology. This does not call for the redressing of particular problems, but instead challenges the regime's basic legitimacy and right to govern. The ideology contains justification and guidance for revolutionary war.

While movements employing this strategy have generally followed some variant of Marxism-Leninism, the ideology in practical terms blends the "idealistic" elements of communism with attention to resolution of indigenous economic, social, and political inequalities. The insurgents (and those states that support them) focus their propaganda and political action on indigenous targets plus international actors. A second and related element is mass mobilization. To accomplish this, insurgent movements employ a host of programs and communications techniques. For example, within the vanguard party one of its major committees has responsibility for proselytizing. The objectives are to attract elements of the population, attack the enemy through psychological warfare, and utilize indoctrination to maintain allegiance. The practitioners of revolutionary warfare also employ negative incentives. If those parts of the population inclined to support the government can be intimidated to remain neutral, this is a victory. To accomplish this, various tactics may be utilized, ranging from threats to the use of terrorism.

A larger objective is to establish a political-military infrastructure or organization. The classical statement on this issue is Lenin's *What Is to Be Done?* The adaptation of Leninism to the strategy of revolutionary warfare resulted in an expansion in the size of the revolutionary organization. This is especially true of the hierarchy of mass organizations. They become part of a political structure controlled by the vanguard party which serves as a shadow government. In the regional and international arenas, this shadow government seeks to become recognized as the legitimate alternative to the existing regime.

The final elements of the strategy include military-paramilitary tactics and the acquisition of external assistance. During the early stages, the insurgents rely on hit-and-run operations. In addition, terrorist tactics may be directed against government officials and elements of the population. Other forms of irregular combat including sabotage, hostage-taking, and related activities are also utilized. Larger unit conventional tactics are added as the insurgency grows.

Although several insurgencies have imitated the Chinese-Vietnamese prototype, different approaches have also been developed. In Latin America the Cuban revolution established the Foco model, subsequently adopted by other revolutionary movements in the region. The Foco approach calls for a small insurgent organization and military units that can quickly seize power. Political action is subordinated to and follows military operations (Guevara, 1961; Debray, 1967).

The Foco strategy was generally unsuccessful, leading to development of an urban insurgent variant (Evans, 1984). Its distinguishing characteristics included a small, highly organized, and clandestine cellular organization, with mobilization of mass organizations quite limited, if not eschewed entirely, and tactics focused on use of various forms of violence associated with terrorism. The goal was to incite the government to overreact and discredit itself (Moss, 1971; Russell, et al., 1979).

As decolonialization came to an end, French and British concern with colonial low-intensity conflict died out. With the withdrawal of the United States from Vietnam, some in the United States likewise argued that the use of revolutionary insurgent strategy was on the wane in the Third World (Johnson, 1973). However, a new type of LIC then began to emerge. It took the form of international terrorism which, in the 1970s and 1980s, increasingly included state sponsorship. This resulted in the re-tasking or creation of special units by the United States, Britain, and Israel to respond to this new threat. The French also became involved in still another LIC mission in the form of contingency operations to insure the security of France's former African colonies.

In the 1980s, LIC once again came to include counter-insurgency for the United States. In Nicaragua, guerrillas combined the Maoist, Foco, and urban approaches into a new hybrid and eventually rekindled U.S. concern. Another LIC mission took the form of assistance and advisory support to Third World anti-Communist movements in countries ruled by Marxist-Leninist regimes.

To summarize, while the term low-intensity conflict has engendered a significant degree of conceptual confusion, an examination of U.S., British, French, and Israeli policies during the post-World War II period allows us to develop a four-part typology:

- *Counterinsurgency*
  Assisting friendly governments to prevent or defeat Communist insurgent movements backed by the USSR, its allies, and surrogates. Elements include foreign internal defense, civil affairs, security assistance, and psychological operations (PSYOPS).
- *Terrorism Counteraction*
  Offensive and defensive measures against international terrorist groups and states that directly or indirectly sponsor/support these activities. Elements include strike operations, rescue, PSYOPS, and political and economic measures.
- *Anti-Communist Resistance*
  Assisting Third World anti-Communist resistance movements in countries ruled by Marxist-Leninist regimes (with the aid of the Soviet bloc). Elements include unconventional warfare, PYSOPS, security assistance, and measures to assist a resistance movement to evolve into a popular political organization in a country and in international arenas.
- *Contingency Operations*
  Sensitive military operations characterized by the rapid projection or employment of forces in conditions that are politically delicate. These include strikes, raids, rescues, demonstrations/shows of force, and related short-term operations requiring speed, flexibility, precision, surprise, special capabilities, and effective C^3.

THE AMERICAN EXPERIENCE: UNCONVENTIONAL WAR, COUNTERINSURGENCY AND LOW INTENSITY CONFLICT

The Early Post-World War II Years

The Truman administration was the first to confront a Communist guerrilla insurgency in the post-World War II period. A military mission was deployed in Greece to assist in equipping and training the Greek Army, but no attempt was made to draw counterinsurgency lessons and develop doctrine. During the Korean War, Special Operations Forces (SOF) were employed and gained a permanent status within the American military. Their activities included partisan warfare, deep infiltration, and related behind-the-lines operations (Paddock, 1982). Their purpose, however, was to support conventional operations. The Korean War was fought primarily in a conventional fashion. Unconventional warfare actions carried out by SOF units were considered ancillary to the conventional mission.

Following Korea, the national security community paid little attention to the challenge of revolutionary insurgency. U.S. doctrine for counter-insurgency remained sketchy and undeveloped. For instance, during the late 1950s the capstone Army field manual, *Field Service Regulations and Operations* (FM100–5), did not address counter-guerrilla missions. However, other Army publications in the 1950s began to recognize some of the unique features of counterinsurgency operations, although there appears to have been no acceptance of the idea that special preparation was required for such missions. The prevailing view was that "all types of attack [can] be executed by organizations and forces comprising the over-all defense structure" (U.S. Department of the Army, 1953). As General Curtis LeMay said: "the dog that can deal with the cat can also deal with the kittens" (Olsen, 1986). Furthermore, organizing partisan guerrilla forces was the only form of LIC under consideration and was now envisioned within a NATO–Warsaw Pact conflict.

Lack of concern with revolutionary war was reflected in the Eisenhower administration's doctrine of Massive Retaliation. There were, however, exceptions as with the coups in Iran and Guatemala. Other covert actions were carried out in Tibet and Indonesia, and in the late 1950s the plan to destabilize Cuba was initiated. These actions were directed against existing governments and were under CIA auspices (Prados, 1986). The Eisenhower administration also sent assistance and advisers to the Philippines to help counter the Huk insurgency. These U.S. efforts were ad hoc and had little effect on doctrine and force structure.

The Kennedy Administration and Counterinsurgency

With the election of John F. Kennedy, a critic of Massive Retaliation and an advocate of the need to develop doctrine and capabilities to respond to guerrilla threats, the prevailing attitude was challenged. He attempted to carry out a "revolution from above" in the U.S. armed forces and national security bureaucracy. "President Kennedy's first few months in office were the crucible for the policies that came to be called counterinsurgency" (Blaufarb, 1977, p. 52).

Kennedy immediately made clear his concern with revolutionary insurgency. This was further heightened by Khrushchev's speech of January 6, 1961, which declared Soviet determination to "encourage and support wars of national liberation" (Blaufarb, 1977). The speech was distributed at the first session of the National Security Council as required reading (Hilsman, 1967). At the meeting Kennedy directed the secretary of defense to place additional emphasis on developing counter-guerrilla forces (Krepinevich, 1986). In addition to speaking out on the subject, including a major address to the Congress in May 1961, Kennedy involved himself directly in reorienting the services for counterinsurgency (COIN) missions. For example, he worked directly with General William Yarborough, the director of the Special Warfare School at Fort Bragg, to upgrade the Special Forces training program.

Furthermore, Kennedy was of the view that COIN was not solely a military responsibility. To this end, he took steps to establish COIN requirements for the appropriate non-military elements of the national security apparatus. This included the Department of State, the Agency for International Development

(AID), the Central Intelligence Agency (CIA), and the U.S. Information Agency. The administration established a Special Group Counterinsurgency at the National Security Council (NSC) level to be the authority responsible for COIN requirements, policy, and interagency coordination. The group, chaired by General Maxwell Taylor, included: chairman of the Joint Chiefs of Staff (JCS), director of the CIA, deputy undersecretary of state for political affairs, deputy secretary of defense, special assistant to the president for national security affairs, director of the U.S. Information Agency (USIA), AID administrator, and attorney general.

With these initiatives, President Kennedy provided general direction for the development of policy and strategy. However, the translation of this guidance into concrete programs proved extremely difficult. Opposition developed in both the military and non-military sectors. The Army was particularly resistant to change. For instance, JCS chairman and former Army chief of staff, General Lyman L. Lemnitzer, reportedly stated that the administration had "oversold" the importance of COIN and that too much emphasis on counter-guerrilla measures would impair the ability of the South Vietnamese Army to meet a conventional assault, like the attack on Korea (Hilsman, 1967, p. 416). This view was held by other members of the JCS, as well as many senior officers (Krepinevich, 1986).

Army resistance can be seen in how COIN was treated in the mainstream doctrinal statements. With the exception of FM31–32, *U.S. Counterinsurgency Forces* (1963), the counterinsurgency mission was tasked to the entire Army. According to one Army report, "the whole subject of counterinsurgency/ counter-guerrilla warfare is a matter of major importance to the whole army and its doctrine and combat development system" (U.S. Department of the Army, USCONARC, 1962). Apparently, COIN was to be integrated into conventional war planning and doctrine. Accordingly, FM31–16, prepared by the Infantry Combat Development Agency at Fort Benning, was to "provide guidance for all infantry and airborne commanders and where applicable, staffs of the brigade, battalion and rifle company when they have the primary mission for conducting counterguerrilla operations." This guidance also applied to "mechanized infantry and armor units" (U.S. Department of the Army, 1963, p. 2). The end result was that the services, and particularly the Army, came to emphasize a military response to guerrilla insurgency set within the context of their conventional missions.

The U.S. experience in Vietnam bears this out. A number of studies have documented the fact that the war was fought primarily in a conventional way (Krepinevich, 1986; Hunt and Shultz, 1982; The Pentagon Papers, 1971; Summers, 1981). Counterinsurgency strategy created problems for the U.S. military establishment, which approached war in a fundamentally different way. As the conflict intensified during 1964–1965 and the enemy employed both revolutionary warfare and mobile conventional tactics, the U.S. military adopted an attrition strategy, and counterinsurgency/pacification was relegated primarily to the South Vietnamese (Shultz, 1979).

There is no question that as the insurgents added mobile conventional tactics to their strategy of revolutionary warfare the United States and South Vietnam required diverse military capabilities. However, this did not negate the need for the political, social, economic, developmental, and psychological aspects of an integrated COIN strategy. After the Tet offensive, the United States sought to implement a Vietnamization-pacification strategy that contained many COIN measures. However, the United States was moving to withdraw from Vietnam. It was a "race against the clock," and the degree to which the Vietnamization-pacification strategy stabilized the situation is still debated (Lewy, 1978; Thayer, 1985; Palmer, 1984; Hunt and Shultz, 1982).

The 1970s: Decreasing Concern with LIC

As the Nixon administration sought to negotiate an end to U.S. involvement in Vietnam, it articulated a new LIC policy. As part of the Nixon Doctrine, the United States would no longer assume primary responsibility for providing the forces for the defense of a nation threatened by revolutionary insurgency. At most, it would contribute military and economic assistance (Hartley, 1975). When asked directly about COIN doctrine, Nixon stated that, while there was "a future for American counterinsurgency tactics" this was true "only in the sense . . . where one of our friends in Asia asks for advice or assistance, under proper circumstances." The president cautioned that "where we must draw the line is in becoming involved heavily with our personnel, doing the job for them, rather than helping them do the job for themselves" (Nixon, 1974, p. 1).

By the mid-1970s, the concept articulated by Nixon became the basis for Army doctrine. The 1974 edition of FM100–20, *Internal Defense and Development*, drew a clear distinction between U.S. Army responsibility and that of the host country (U.S. Department of the Army, 1974). Political developments soon eclipsed such documents. Successive administrations paid less attention to low-intensity conflicts, with the exception of international terrorism, resulting in drastic cuts in LIC organization and capabilities (Sarkesian and Scully, 1981; Barnett, Tovar, and Shultz, 1985). By 1975, appropriations for Special Operations Forces (SOF) declined to under $100 million. Even in the Reagan administration the SOF budget increased slowly until a significant jump in 1983 to over $200 million. In the 1970s, parallel reductions in the CIA paramilitary assets played an important role in COIN and related activities (Godson, 1981).

The Reagan Administration: Increased Attention to SOF/LIC

The election of President Reagan in many ways marked a return to the policy initiated by President Kennedy in 1961. A new emphasis was placed on threats at the lower end of the conflict spectrum, which has been a major preoccupation at the highest policy levels as reflected in both the rhetoric of senior officials and appropriations for SOF. However, there was disagreement over what constitutes the major LIC threats and missions. Spending on SOF did not necessarily improve the U.S. ability to conduct LIC activities. Finally, bureaucratic resistance and organizational impediments had a significant impact on strategy formulation and policy implementation.

Officials' comments reflected the differences within the administration and national security bureaucracy. For the president, non-Communist resistance movements were of particular concern (Rosenfeld, 1986). Other administration members focused on counterinsurgency and counter-terrorism. Members of the administration, as well as senior military officers, asserted that defining the parameters of LIC remained a vexing problem. Some believed that "debating the definition of low intensity warfare" was for "small minds." but one could also argue that a prerequisite for appropriate policy and strategy is an understanding of the parameters of the threat (U.S. Department of Defense, 1986, p. 7).

In 1986, the Joint Low-Intensity Conflict Project, in its Final Report, brought some clarity to the matter of defining LIC parameters. The primary missions were to include counterinsurgency, anti-Communist insurgency (or resistance), terrorist counteraction, contingency operations, and peacekeeping (Joint Low-Intensity Conflict Project, 1986). The ultimate impact of the report on policy, doctrine, organization, and capabilities remains unclear, however.

Military command and control and interagency coordination had been perennial problems. The Reagan administration took steps to develop organizations and capabilities to respond effectively to LIC threats. However, this policy appeared difficult for many within the services and relevant government agencies to accept as either necessary or viable. To remedy this situation, the administration initiated a number of steps. The Army's First Special Operations Command at Fort Bragg was established to unify all Army Special Operations Forces.

In addition, the Air Force's First Special Operations Wing of the 23rd Air Force was created. Finally, a multiservice Joint Special Operations Agency (JSOA), which was to report directly to and advise the JCS, was instituted to direct attention to LIC doctrine, strategy, planning, budget, resource development and allocation, training, and command and control. Headed by a major general, it was activated in January 1984 to assume responsibility for all aspects of Special Operations. However, JSOA has proven ineffective. According to Major General Wesley Rice, former head of JSOA, "I had many responsibilities but I had little authority. . . . As a two-star general, I had little clout in a town of three- and four-star generals" (New York Times, September 6, 1986).

There remains a strong impetus within the military to subsume LIC missions within the existing command structure. The services view conventional war as the major contingency they face. The effect on SOF is to task it to support this mission. Consequently, an important portion of SOF revitalization, has been directed towards force readiness and equipment to meet CINC (commander-in-chief) plans and service responsibilities for conventional war. In this general war scenario, SOF would be deployed behind Soviet and East European lines in Europe. LIC missions are accorded secondary priority. Spending money, therefore, is not necessarily an indication of progress. There are still shortfalls in doctrine, personnel, and equipment.

Opposition also exists within civilian agencies that have a role in LIC missions. In the intelligence community there is strong resistance to paramilitary operations. Under Carter the paramilitary mission of the CIA was downgraded (Godson, 1981; Shackley, 1981). When the Reagan administration chose to employ this capability, it found not only shortfalls, but also an institutional opposition to the paramilitary function (Blair, 1983; Tovar, 1983). Similar opposition exists in other civilian agencies.

What impact did these developments have on the Reagan administration policy? Despite the revitalization efforts, the U.S. response to the primary LIC missions identified previously—counterinsurgency, anti-Communist resistance, and counter-terrorism—remains disjointed and ad hoc. Evidence of this is summarized below:

Counterinsurgency

- Recent studies conclude that the United States is not yet prepared to work with Third World military and internal security forces facing insurgency (Hosmer and Tanham, 1986; Waghelstein, 1985; Hosmer, 1985).
- SOF does not have as a first priority civic action, nation-building, PSYOPS, security assistance, or advisory support missions related to counterinsurgency (Decker, 1984).
- The Army continues to train Third World forces to fight an American-style conventional war and to rely on U.S. equipment and support (e.g., El Salvador).
- The Reagan administration did not achieve significant improvement in SOF ability to accomplish political-military counterinsurgency tasks in LIC. Shortfalls in equipment, language skills, area and cultural orientation, human intelligence (Humint), and strategy continue (Hosmer and Tanham, 1986; Dean, 1986).
- Bureaucratic and organizational commitment to conventional warfare continues to hamper developments in LIC (Krepinevich, 1986).

Resistance

- Many of the problems that plague counterinsurgency preparation also affect the U.S. ability to support anti-Communist resistance movements. The United States has not developed the means to assist these movements in creating political and military structures and strategies that can effectively prosecute a protracted political-military struggle (Ra'anan et al., 1985).

- The United States presently does not have a corps of experts, who know local cultural and physical environments, to develop doctrine, strategy, and assistance programs that would provide political-military training and advice (Hosmer and Tanham, 1986; Christian, 1985; Rosenfeld, 1986; Dickey, 1986).

- Even when the United States is providing military support, the equipment arrives in a sporadic fashion, is often inappropriate, and is siphoned off by governments where the resistance is based.

Counterterrorism

- Most SOF revitalization for LIC went into building up the "black" or counter-terrorist (CT) assets. However, even here there are still shortfalls (Russell, 1986; Livingstone, 1985; Shultz, 1986).

- In 1985, when the White House wanted to send Navy SEALs to free the *Achille Lauro* hostages, the mission encountered serious problems. The plane assigned was not in shape to make the trip. After trying three planes, the SEALs finally took off. However, they arrived too late. Serious airlift problems reportedly also limited the U.S. SOF/CT response during the TWA crisis during 1985.

Congress and SOF/LIC: Military Reform Legislation

By 1985, members of Congress became impatient with administration efforts. Senator William S. Cohen summed up congressional concern: "We are not prepared for unconventional conflict . . . and it shows." A "new form of warfare has emerged, a form of warfare that we have not properly understood, and that we have not effectively deterred" (*New York Times,* September 6, 1986; *The Times*—London, August 4, 1986). Congressman Earl Hutto asserted that "We have no national policy" for LIC. "We have no national strategy. We have no joint doctrine" (U.S. Department of Defense, 1986, p. 149).

Following Senate and House hearings, the Congress enacted legislation to enhance Special Operations Forces and other capabilities to respond to LIC threats. This included establishment of a unified Special Operations Forces Command headed by a four-star flag or general officer. The purpose was to raise the visibility and importance of SOF and the ability of its CINC to interact more effectively with the services, other CINCs, and civilian agencies. The legislation also created an assistant secretary of defense for special operations and low-intensity conflict. At the National Security Council level, an interagency board for SOF/LIC was to be established headed by a deputy assistant to the president for national security affairs.

Conclusion

We have examined how different administrations sought to address low-intensity conflict problems. The U.S. experience and preparation have clearly varied widely from one administration to another. Within the services and civilian bureaucracy there has been resistance, at times quite significant, to the development of policy, strategy, and capabilities for LIC.

THE FRENCH APPROACH TO REVOLUTIONARY WARFARE AND CONTINGENCY OPERATIONS

Since World War II the French have been actively engaged in low-intensity conflict. However, the specific LIC situation has varied with changing French interests and foreign policy objectives. After 1945, France sought to re-establish its colonial interests in the Third World in direct confrontation with the forces of revolutionary nationalism. In Indochina and then Algeria it found itself involved in protracted insurgent struggles. To meet these challenges French military planners developed counterinsurgency strategies for defeating guerrilla insurgents. They called their approach Guerre Revolutionaire or Revolutionary war.

The French Military and Guerre Revolutionaire

In many ways the French were in the forefront of counterinsurgency (Paret, 1964; Trinquier, 1964; Lacheroy et al., 1957; Hogard, 1957; Ximenes, 1957; Chassin, 1953). According to one analyst, many of the principles of this warfare were honed by the French military long before the decolonialization conflicts of the post-war period and have their origins in the pacification of Algeria during the first half of the 1800s (Martin, 1985). Here we are concerned with the form these principles took as the French sought to counter Mao Tse-tung's "People's War."

During the early 1950s, French officers, many of whom were stationed in Indochina, were among the foremost advocates of counterinsurgency strategy. Their ideas were influenced by both earlier French experiences in colonization and the strategy and tactics of the Vietminh. During the war against the Vietminh, a number of these officers wrote about "People's War" and how to counter it. For instance, General Lionel-Max Chassin (Chassin, 1952), General C. Nemo, and Colonel Charles Lacheroy (Nemo, 1952; Lacheroy, 1954) wrote important works on Guerre Revolutionaire. However, it was among the junior officers that the most vocal proponents of counterinsurgency emerged. They served in Indochina as platoon leaders, intelligence officers, and so on. Perhaps the most notable was Trinquier, with his book *Modern Warfare: A French View of Counterinsurgency* (Trinquier, 1964).

French doctrine can be divided into irregular combat tactics and psychological-political operations. Irregular tactics emphasize light forces, mobility, offensive tactics, and surprise. These forces were to project power and gain control over a rural area where the Vietminh had established a political-military infrastructure. Once an area was pacified, a fortified base was established as a source of supplies and to ensure the security of that region. Then control would be extended into a contiguous region, as small mobile forces launched attacks from the base. This has frequently been referred to as the oil spot technique. The French sought to implement this strategy, although French planners disagreed over its viability.

Mao and other leading theorists and practitioners stress the importance of political and psychological operations. The advocates of Guerre Revolutionaire took this aspect seriously. The French objective was to break the linkages between the guerrillas and the local/rural populace. French COIN doctrine asserted that military operations were to be paralleled by social, economic, and administrative actions to undercut the insurgent cause. Consequently, the French military found itself involved in what U.S. military doctrine terms civic action. The objective was to attract, protect, educate, and economically assist the local population, drawing them away from the insurgents. French officers found themselves managing agricultural projects, directing local commerce and trade, running schools, hospitals, and related social institutions, as well as training local defense forces (Paret, 1964). In effect, the training and integration of local elements into French forces served a dual purpose. It was an important aspect of the psychological dimension of COIN doctrine, and it offset shortages in French personnel. In Algeria the French military also sought to initiate and implement a series of socio-economic reform measures (Trinquier, 1964; Heggoy, 1972; Vidal-Nasquet, 1963; Tillion, 1961; Ambler, 1966). While conceptually sound, these measures fell within the context of colonialism, a major flaw, and thus proved inadequate in the face of revolutionary nationalism.

There was also a dark side to French COIN strategy: the use of manipulation, intimidation, and torture to break up the insurgent organization or infrastructure. In the words of Trinquier, "terrorism will then compel any reluctant citizens to give the required information" (Trinquier, 1964, p. 109). These techniques were utilized in Algeria. They greatly undermined the image of the military in France and internationally.

After the Algerian conflict, French interest in this form of LIC came to an end. As the French withdrew from such conflicts, the United States viewed revolutionary war as a serious aspect of the East-West conflict. Many of the COIN principles developed by the French had an impact on American specialists. The Army translated and disseminated such studies as Lacheroy's analysis of the Vietminh use of irregular tactics (Lacheroy, 1954, 1957); Sonyris's discussion of COIN principles (Sonyris, 1957); Ximenes's contributions on how to access the stages of revolutionary warfare (Ximenes, 1957); and Hogard's analysis of the five-stage COIN model (Hogard, 1957). The parallels between U.S. and French doctrine are significant (McCuen, 1966). However, there are important differences, particularly in the use of more draconian tactics.

Contingency Operations in Africa

If French LIC doctrine after 1945 focused almost exclusively on COIN, since then it has followed a more heterogeneous pattern. Contingency operations have included large-scale intervention with mechanized infantry in Chad, aerial strikes against the Polisario guerrillas, airborne rescue in Zaire, and internal security actions in Niger and the Central African Republic (Martin, 1985). These and related actions require technological sophistication in power projection, specialized forces, forward deployed supplies and bases, and domestic political support.

Following decolonialization, France sought to maintain ties with its former African colonies. The security arrangements involved defense agreements to ensure security and stability. These accords have resulted in the French playing a key role in the external and internal policymaking of these states. Two general forms of intervention have resulted. To insure domestic stability France has undertaken actions to resolve internal crises. In 1973 it intervened to halt a mutiny in Niger (Martin, 1985, p. 127). During 1979, steps were taken to help remove Emperor Bokassa in the Central African Republic (Martin, 1985, pp. 127–28). However, by the 1980s this kind of intervention was on the wane.

The second pattern, clearly predominant today, is intervention to assist against external threats. Given the fact that such situations frequently require both a rapid and carefully calibrated use of force, the requirements for effective crisis management are substantial.

During the 1960s, French intervention forces were forward deployed in various states in or on the periphery of Africa. At its peak, this included over 60,000 troops dispersed in 100 African garrisons (Martin, 1981; Lelloche and Moisi, 1979; Chaigneau, 1984). By 1980 this was reduced to approximately 10,000, and the force structure had undergone important changes.

With new airlift/transport capabilities, the forward deployment of troops became less necessary. Those that remained deployed in Africa were now to provide logistical assistance for intervention forces airlifted directly from France. Indigenous troops, organized and trained by French military advisers, were to replace some French forces. Advanced airstrike capabilities were also developed. These included the in-flight refuelable Jaguar and Mirage aircraft which provided France with the ability to direct long-range strike capabilities to Africa. They were used, for example, against Polisario guerrillas in the Western Sahara during the late 1970s. By the 1980s, advanced technologies gave the Air Force precision-guided ordinance. The Air Force also provided French forces deployed on the ground with tactical operational support, reconnaissance, and other intelligence-related information (Martin, 1985; Pons, 1981).

In sum, airpower can be used for independent missions and as part of joint intervention operations like that in Chad in the early 1980s. After Libyan troops occupied half of the country, through military operations and diplomatic actions the French were able to successfully assist Chad in reducing the Libyan threat (Yost, 1983). By 1987, Chad was able to successfully defend itself against a similar challenge.

With respect to French ground forces, African interventions have been carried out through special units. Key elements are the Eleventh Airborne Division (approximately 16,000 troops) and the Ninth Marine Infantry Division (approximately 9,000 troops). The Eleventh Airborne is composed of paratroop infantry, artillery and armor, helicopter, light aviation, and C^3 components. Ground intervention forces also include the Foreign Legion Operational Group and Thirty-First Demi-Brigade, which specializes in helicopter and amphibious missions (Martin, 1985, p. 134).

The mission of these ground forces is to be prepared to deploy rapidly for direct action missions in Africa. They are also employed in training, advising, and security assistance missions for crisis-prevention purposes. The speed with which France can react can be seen in the 1978 operation in Zaire's Shaba province. Within forty-eight hours the first French elements arrived in Shaba, and shortly thereafter the rebels of the Front National de Liberation du Congo were expelled and a large number of European civilians evacuated (Mangold, 1979; Pons, 1981).

The use of French LIC capabilities has not been affected by the kinds of domestic political opposition that emerged to oppose counterinsurgency actions in the 1950s. However, contingency missions are structured to avoid protracted intervention. The goal is to deploy rapidly to defuse the crisis and then withdraw. While not politically contentious, the development and maintenance of such intervention capabilities is quite costly. The expense has raised budgetary concerns, and cost affects the size of French intervention forces (Kolodziej and Lokolutu, 1982; Martin, 1981 and 1985). Herein lies a primary constraint on French involvement in future LIC missions.

Conclusion

During the early post-war period, the French were involved against revolutionary insurgent movements. The record was mixed, although a sophisticated and controversial counterinsurgency doctrine was developed. The second period, which continues today, has seen France develop doctrine and capabilities for various LIC contingency missions. Displaying speed, surprise, flexibility, and technical sophistication, French intervention forces have been used to ensure the stability of a number of its former African colonies. These have included both internal security maintenance and protection against external threats.

BRITISH LIC OPERATIONS: COUNTERINSURGENCY AND COUNTER-TERRORISM

British involvement in low-intensity conflict has a long history. During World War I, Colonel T. E. Lawrence organized Arab forces into an irregular guerrilla army that contributed to the defeat of the Turks. Lawrence sought to codify his experience in *The Seven Pillars of Wisdom* (Lawrence, 1935). During World War II British Army planners established a substantial number of special operations forces (SOF)—the Commandos and Special Air Service (SAS)—and employed them to conduct raids, sabotage, and other behind-the-lines strike operations, as well as to organize resistance forces (Foot, 1966, 1976). Following the war, however, most of these SOF capabilities were demobilized. Inside the British Army there was opposition to SOF and the way these units operated outside traditional military procedures (Foot, 1970).

As with the French, the British came to be involved in LIC as a result of imperial commitments. Through the 1960s, they faced various forms of revolutionary insurgency. This led to the development of counterinsurgency doctrine and capabilities, and a mixed record of achievement.

During this time, the United Kingdom had to cope with the twofold and quite dissimilar missions of counterinsurgency in the Third World and conventional war in Europe. By the early 1970s, the missions in the Third World ended. However, SOF units were then redirected and given a new LIC mission, as the British faced the challenge of terrorism.

British Counterinsurgency Doctrine and Policy

The first low-intensity conflict for post-war Britain took place in Palestine against the Jewish underground. The Army did poorly in understanding the cause and operations of the opposition. The British command approached the problem in a traditional military manner and lacked a clear view of the political context in which the conflict took place (Charters, 1985; Snyder, 1964; Hamilton, 1981). COIN doctrine and capabilities were not developed. Only with the "Emergency in Malaya" were these matters seriously addressed.

During 1948 the Communist-led guerrilla forces in Malaya stepped up paramilitary and terrorist actions to such an extent that the situation was declared a rebellion. Although the emergency did not end until 1960, the insurgent forces were effectively defeated by 1954 (Paget, 1967; Clutterbuck, 1966; Komer, 1972; Short, 1975). During the initial period the British response was less than adequate. The British appear to have underestimated the extent of the threat. According to one officer who served in Malaya, "by the spring of 1950, though we had survived two dangerous years, we were undoubtedly losing the war" (Clutterbuck, 1966 pp. 55–56). Unified command and control was lacking, intelligence was inadequate, and conventional military forces were having a difficult time responding to irregular insurgent tactics.

This was the situation when General Sir Harold Briggs assumed command as director of operations. He believed insurgent strength and ability to carry out operations derived from support obtained from Chinese squatter communities. He argued that this linkage had to be destroyed. The "Briggs Plan" was based on this assumption (Paget, 1967, pp. 56–57). Resettlement of the Chinese and civic action programs (including schools, dispensaries, public services, and land ownership) were directed toward this end. Other parts of the counterinsurgency program included a unified and integrated command/ control structure, deployment of military units prepared in counter-guerrilla/ jungle warfare tactics, improved intelligence and psychological operations, and insurgent food-denial actions (Komer, 1972; Dougherty, 1962). These all made an important contribution to the defeat of the insurgents. Other significant facts included steady progress toward and granting of Malayan independence in 1957 and guerrilla tactics that increasingly relied on terrorism (Paget, 1967; Muros, 1962).

Out of the Malayan experience general counterinsurgency principles or guidelines resulted (Thompson, 1970; Kitson, 1971; Clutterbuck, 1966). The first dealt with the command and control structure for formulating and carrying out policy objectives. The central idea was that a joint committee of military, civilian, and police elements, headed by a single director, was vital. The goal was to maintain strict political control over all military and non-military actions. Once established, the system worked successfully in Malaya. The application of this principle in Kenya proved more difficult. The Mau Mau uprising was underway for some time before a joint committee structure was established. Even then its day-to-day direction of the emergency took time to hone (Kitson, 1957). Likewise, an effectively structured joint command and control system took time to evolve in Northern Ireland (Clutterbuck, 1973; Evelegh, 1978; Mansfield, 1980).

A second principle required the British Army to carry out civic action, internal security assistance, and unconventional military operations. This necessitated adaptation of these skills to a rural environment, including jungle, mountain, and desert conditions, in Malaya, Kenya, Borneo, and Oman. However, in Northern Ireland troops had to be trained for irregular urban warfare.

Although the regular Army adopted the development of counterinsurgency doctrine and skills, during the Malayan Emergency elements of the Special Air Service (SAS) also became involved in jungle operations. In the 1950s, and 1960s, the SAS was utilized in various COIN actions. In 1959, they successfully defeated a large insurgent force in Oman (O'Neill, 1980; Jeapes, 1980; Tremayne, 1977). They likewise served with distinction in Borneo (Dickens, 1983; Warner, 1971). During the 1960s, SAS forces were integrated into COIN doctrine (Charters, 1985). Formal tasks included intelligence collection and surveillance, training of indigenous forces, and strike operations (e.g., ambush, sabotage, harassment, and assassination).

Early on, the British saw the importance of intelligence and political-psychological operations. In Malaya a Combined Intelligence Staff was established to facilitate the intelligence process (Short, 1975; Komer, 1972; Clutterbuck, 1966). The objective was to establish an all-source data base through the integration of military, police, and civilian intelligence organizations. A single integrated intelligence entity, first in Malaya and then in other COIN missions, was seen as an essential ingredient.

The British also came to realize during the Malayan Emergency that psychological operations (PSYOPS) were integral to COIN. Throughout the 1950s and 1960s, this was seen as primarily a civilian responsibility. In Malaya the Psychological Warfare Section was headed and staffed by civilians, with nominal military representation. The Army's role in PSYOPS changed significantly in Northern Ireland. In the early 1970s, as the IRA began to win the "war of ideas," the Ministry of Defense (MOD) took steps to establish effective counter-propaganda tactics. This included training programs in various aspects of PSYOPS and public relations (Clutterbuck, 1981; Charters, 1985, 1977).

Counter-Terrorism: The LIC Mission of the 1970s and 1980s

With the end of its imperial responsibilities, the British need for COIN doctrine and capabilities came to an end. The exception, of course, has been Northern Ireland. However, even in this situation, the tactics of the IRA increasingly became confined to urban terrorism in Northern Ireland (Alexander and O'Day, 1984). In conjunction with the escalation of international terrorism, the United Kingdom recognized the need to maintain counterterrorist assets.

The Special Air Service was re-tasked to prepare for counterterrorism missions. The way in which the London Balcombe Street siege (1975), Mogadishu rescue (1977), and Iranian Embassy incident (1980) were handled suggests that SAS has successfully adapted to the CT mission. They have developed the skills and been provided with new weapons and related special equipment to meet the threat of international terrorism. However, as far as can be determined, this has been confined to defensive/reactive measures. British policy has not involved offensive measures to combat terrorism. This excludes the offensive use of special assets against the IRA.

Conclusion

As with the French, following World War II the primary form of LIC for the British was counterinsurgency. The British Army developed doctrine and capabilities accordingly. The degree of success was limited, but in general, it would seem that the Army and its civilian counterparts were able to adapt to revolutionary insurgent challenges.

Unlike the French, following decolonialization the British did not develop elaborate security agreements with the governments of former colonies. Initially, this seemed to invite demobilization of SAS units. However, in the 1970s terrorism provided SAS with a new mission and became the justification for its retention. Thus far, its performance has been successful.

LOW-INTENSITY CONFLICT AND THE ISRAELI DEFENSE FORCE

When the Israeli Defense Force (IDF) was formally established, many of its officers had a significant background in military matters. The modus operandi of pre-independence units was in low-intensity/irregular operations. This was, in part, due to the efforts of Captain Charles Wingate, a British officer who assisted in the formation of these units. The need for special military operations grew out of the Arab Revolt in the latter half of the 1930s. The objective was to prepare the Haganah, created to protect the Jewish population, to attack the bases of forces carrying out strikes against Jewish settlements. Wingate's goal was to establish forces and doctrine utilizing the elements of surprise, mobility, and irregular tactics (Luttwak and Horowitz, 1975; Sykes, 1959).

Although Wingate left Palestine in 1939, his concept had a strong impact on Haganah military thinking, as reflected in the Palmach, the shock or strike units of Haganah (Rothenberg, 1978). Palmach units played an important role in efforts against the British and striking back against Arab attacks. It emphasized special operations. This approach was also advocated by the Irgun, a splinter Jewish military organization (Allon, 1971; Bauer, 1973). Following independence, both of these special units played an important part in the conflict between the new Jewish state and Arab regimes. Ever since, the IDF has had to prepare for both conventional and low-intensity operations. As we know, this requires very different approaches to the conduct of military actions (Luttwak and Horowitz, 1975; Rothenberg, 1978; Handel, 1973).

Independence and the Establishment of the Israeli Defense Force

The Palmach was an elite military unit that stressed initiative, improvisation, and semi-independence. The prime minister and other senior officials were concerned about separate elite forces. Ben Gurion moved to demobilize the Palmach in 1948 (Cohen, 1978; Kimche and Kimche, 1960; Barzohar, 1966). He sought a unified military establishment that would be integrated into the entire society. In effect, the IDF was part of the nation-building process.

Although the objective was to create an IDF that could defend Israel against a conventional attack, the early military problems did not take this form. By 1950, the government was faced with increasing cross-border guerrilla strikes (Rothenberg, 1978). The use of conventional units proved disappointing. As a result, in 1953 the senior IDF leadership concluded that it was necessary to reestablish special operations forces to conduct contingency operations.

The first special unit—Unit 101—was headed by a young Ariel Sharon. Shortly after its creation, Unit 101 was combined with IDF paratrooper forces (Luttwak and Horowitz, 1975; Rothenberg, 1985). The goal was to combine the strike capacity of Unit 101 with the discipline of the IDF. The result was Unit 202, a force that established a remarkable record and gained considerable prestige inside Israel. Over the next decade the force grew to six brigades and was assigned the missions of coordination in a conventional battle and strike contingency operations (Rothenberg, 1978; Luttwak and Horowitz, 1975). The latter involved strikes against Palestine Liberation Organization (PLO) units and bases. As the PLO escalated its use of guerrilla and terrorist actions, the paratroopers were used for retaliation and pre-emption in the West Bank, Lebanon, and Jordan (Perlmutter, 1969). Israel also began to rely on airpower for actions against both PLO bases and Arab states directly assisting the PLO.

Internal Defense and Counterinsurgency

Although the 1967 war was a great victory for Israel, it also resulted in military problems. PLO leaders believed they could use the occupied territories of the West Bank and Gaza Strip to carry out a "people's war" modeled on the Chinese-Vietnamese approach. By conducting a "protracted popular war of national liberation," the PLO asserted it could succeed where the Arab armies failed (O'Neill, 1978). Israel responded with internal defense and counterinsurgency actions. This new PLO strategy met with little success. According to one specialist, "as things turned out, a combination of factors— sound Israeli counterinsurgency practices, a poor physical environment, insurgent disunity, organizational deficiencies, and differences within the Arab states—undermined what success the Fedayeen had enjoyed in 1968–1969" (O'Neill, 1978). With respect to Israeli COIN, both active and passive measures were used to secure the border areas. Cross-border operations against the PLO were carried out by paratroopers and Sayeret units (reconnaissance units developed for special occasions). These actions had a demoralizing impact on PLO guerrilla forces, significantly reducing the number of missions initiated (Alon, 1980; Rothenberg, 1985). Pacification of the occupied territories of the West Bank and Gaza, which included the use of force, economic incentives, and good intelligence activities further limited PLO effectiveness. The PLO expulsion from Jordan during the latter part of 1970 constituted the final blow to the PLO strategy.

Israeli Special Operations in the 1970s

During the 1970s, Israeli special units were tasked to respond against two threats: (1) international terrorist incidents conducted against its officials and citizens abroad and (2) the PLO use of the southern part of Lebanon to carry out operations against Israel. The first mission has, in part, been turned over to Israeli intelligence (Gazit and Handel, 1980). This has led to a number of defensive and offensive measures outside Israel, conducted independently or in coordination with special military units. The most famous instance was the successful raid on Entebbe.

As the PLO expanded and fortified its bases in Lebanon, the IDF directed SOF capabilities against this threat. From the mid-1970s until the 1982 intervention, the PLO mounted various guerrilla and terrorist actions from bases in Lebanon. Israel countered with special operations forces, including the paratroopers and Sayeret. However, as the size, military capabilities, and defensive fortification of PLO bases in Lebanon increased, the use of contingency strikes by small special operations units became increasingly difficult. Israel came to rely on airstrikes to compensate.

By the end of the decade, senior IDF planners came to believe that the problem in Lebanon could only be addressed through a major conventional force intervention. In 1978, the IDF undertook such an initiative. However, international political pressure led to an early withdrawal. In 1982, a more ambitious intervention was undertaken, halting only as the IDF reached Beirut and under significant pressure from the United States.

During the occupation of southern Lebanon, the IDF employed special operations units, primarily Sayeret, to strike against guerrilla forces. IDF general-purpose forces continue to be plagued by irregular military operations directed against it, which had a demoralizing effect on both regular and reserve forces. In addition, public support for Israeli special operations and involvement in protracted low-intensity conflicts came to an end with the protracted operation in Lebanon.

Conclusion

The Israeli Defense Force is generally considered an outstanding conventional army, and it has had a comparable record in low-intensity conflict. Its experience includes counterinsurgency and internal defense, as well as contingency and counterterrorism missions. The IDF has developed special operations forces that, in conjunction with the intelligence services, have compiled a successful record in LIC. They had the backing of the Israeli public, an important ingredient in a democracy, until the protracted occupation in Lebanon.

SUMMARY

Since World War II, the United States, France, Britain, and Israel have been involved in different types of low-intensity conflict. These missions are characterized by the interaction of a number of dimensions of LIC, including political, psychological, civic action, intelligence, irregular combat, and technological elements. As we have seen, the importance of each will vary depending on which LIC mission is being considered. For instance, advanced technologies are more germane to contingency operations which require speed, flexibility, precision, surprise, special capabilities, and sophisticated C^3. On the other hand, counterinsurgency is less technology intensive. Each of the four low-intensity missions is affected by the political dimension in two critical ways. The nature of the conflicts themselves is highly political, a fact that has to be taken into account in planning appropriate strategies. Strict civilian political control over these missions is required, which necessitates a close working relationship between non-military and military organizations. This is especially true for counterinsurgency strategy, but it is also the case for the other LIC missions. Beyond the operational context, it is also a truism that domestic political opposition has greatly affected previous U.S., British, French, and Israeli planning and involvement in LIC activities. Disenchantment at home with French policy in Algeria in the late 1950s and U.S. policy in Vietnam in the 1960s and 1970s had an important impact, even though the insurgents were not winning on the battlefield. The same political dynamic affected the Israeli occupation of Lebanon. Finally, political disagreement between the U.S. Congress and the Reagan administration has limited assistance to anti-Communist resistance forces. In sum, the more protracted the conflict, the more likely that political disagreements at home will influence policy.

LIC missions have also resulted in antagonisms within the military and non-military organizations involved. This has been the case more in the United States than in the other three countries examined here. Within the American military services and civilian bureaucracies there has been resistance, at times quite strong, to development of policy, strategy, and capabilities for certain LIC missions. This is due both to organizational routines that prescribe certain ways of "doing business" and to institutional memory of what happened when previous policies changed. On the former one can cite U.S. Army resistance to missions outside conventional conflict, whereas the latter can be seen in the opposition by CIA professionals to paramilitary covert actions in the 1980s.

Finally, in each of the case studies we saw that as foreign policy goals and interests changed, so did the need to be able to conduct LIC missions. As France and Britain withdrew from the colonial world, there was no longer a need for COIN strategy and capabilities. Following Vietnam, one could argue that de facto this was also true for the United States. In addition, as the perception of LIC threats changed, each of the four countries sought to develop the necessary capabilities to respond. Counter-terrorism is a case in point.

Because of space limitations, this study has focused on a broad overview of how four democratic or open systems have approached LIC since World

War II. Much remains to be examined and assessed. Here we have introduced concepts and issues, and covered broad strategy and policy trends. We have not addressed how closed systems like the USSR view and prepare for involvement in LIC (Collins, 1987; Shultz, 1988; Ra'anan et al., 1985). We likewise have not examined these issues as they relate to countries in the developing world. In effect, much remains to be considered in this area of international security studies.

REFERENCES

Alexander, Yonah, and Alan O'Day, eds. 1984. *Terrorism in Ireland*. New York: St. Martin's Press.

Allon, Yigel. 1971. *The Making of Israel's Army*. New York: Bantam Books.

Alon, H. 1980. *Countering Palestinian Terrorism in Israel: Towards a Policy Analysis of Countermeasures*. Santa Monica, Calif.: RAND.

Ambler, John. 1966. *The French Army in Politics 1945–1962*. Columbus: Ohio State University Press.

Armitage, Richard L. 1986. Statement by the Assistant Secretary of Defense (International Security Affairs) before the Subcommittee on Readiness, Committee on Armed Services, U.S. Senate.

Asprey, Robert. 1975. *War in the Shadows,* 2 vols. Garden City, N.Y.: Doubleday and Co.

Barnett, Frank, B. Hugh Tovar, and Richard Shultz, eds. 1985. *Special Operations in U.S. Strategy*. Washington, D.C.: National Defense University Press.

Barzohar, Michael. 1966. *The Armed Prophet: A Biography of Ben Gurion*. London: Arthur Baker.

Bauer, Yehuda. 1973. *From Diplomacy to Resistance*. New York: Atheneum.

Blair, Arthur, et al. 1983. Unconventional Warfare: A Legitimate Tool of Foreign Policy. *Conflict,* no. 1:59–82.

Blaufarb, Douglas. 1977. *The Counterinsurgency Era*. New York: Free Press.

Chaigneau, Pascal. 1984. *La Politique Militaire de la France en Afrique*. La Documentation Francaise.

Charters, David. 1985. From Palestine to Northern Ireland: British Army Adaptation to Low Intensity Operations. In David Charters and Maurice Tugwell, eds., *Armies in Low Intensity Conflict: A Comparative Study of Institutional Adaptation to New Forms of Warfare*. Ottawa: Department of National Defense.

———. 1977. Intelligence and Psychological Warfare Operations in Northern Ireland. *RUSI Journal,* September 22–26.

Chessin, L. M. 1953. Guerre en Indochine. *Revue de Militaire Nationale* (July):11–22.

———. 1952. *La Conquete de la Chine par Mao Tse-Toung*. Paris: Mimeographed.

Christian, Shirley. 1985. *Nicaragua: Revolution in the Family*. New York: Random House.

Clutterbuck, Richard. 1966. *The Long, Long War: Counterinsurgency in Malaya and Vietnam*. New York: Praeger.

———. 1981. *The Media and Political Violence*. London: Macmillan.

———. 1973. *Protest and the Urban Guerrilla*. London: Cassell.

Cohen, Eliot. 1978. *Commandos and Politicians*. Cambridge, Mass.: Harvard University Center for International Affairs.

Collins, John. 1987. *Green Berets, SEALS, and Spetsnaz: U.S. and Soviet Special Military Operations*. New York: Pergamon-Brassey's.

Dean, David, ed. 1986. *Low Intensity Conflict and Modern Technology*. Montgomery, Ala.: Air University Press.

Debray, Regis. 1967. *Revolution in Revolution*. New York: Monthly Review Press.

Decker, David. 1984. *U.S. Army Special Operations in Low Intensity Conflict: Today/ Tomorrow*. Unpublished Manuscript.

Dickens, Peter. 1983. *SAS—The Jungle Frontier*. London: Arms and Armor Press.

Dickey, Christopher. 1986. *With the Contras*. New York: Simon and Schuster.

Dougherty, James. 1962. The Guerrilla War in Malaya. In Franklin Osanka, ed., *Modern Guerrilla Warfare*. New York: Free Press of Glencoe.

Duncanson, Dennis. 1968. *Government and Revolution in Vietnam*. London: Oxford University Press.

Eckstein, Harry. 1965. On the Etiology of Internal Wars. *History and Theory*, no. 2:1–30.

Evans, Ernst. 1984. Revolutionary Movements in Central America: The Development of a New Strategy. In Howard Wiarda, ed., *Rift and Revolution*. Washington, D.C.: American Enterprise Institute.

Evelegh, Robin. 1978. *Peace-Keeping in a Democratic Society: The Lessons of Northern Ireland*. Montreal: McGill-Queens University.

Fall, Bernard. 1966. *Vietnam Witness 1953–1966*. New York: Praeger.

Foot, M.R.D. 1976. *Resistance: An Analysis of European Resistance to Nazism, 1940–1945*. London: Eyre Methuen.

———. 1966. *SOE in France*. London: H. M. Stationery Office.

———. 1970. Special Operations, 1 and 11. In Michael Elliot-Bateman, ed., *The Fourth Dimension of Warfare, Volume 1: Intelligence, Subversion, Resistance*. Manchester: Manchester University Press.

Gazit, Schlomo, and Michael Handel. 1980. Insurgency, Terrorism, and Intelligence. In Roy Godson, ed., *Intelligence Requirements for the 1980s: Counterintelligence*. New York: National Strategy Information Center.

Godson, Roy, ed. 1981. *Intelligence Requirements for the 1980s: Covert Action*. New York: National Strategy Information Center.

Guevara, Che. 1961. *Guerrilla Warfare*. New York: Vintage Books.

Hamilton, Nigel. 1981. *Monty: The Making of a General*. London: Hamilton.

Handel, Michael. 1973. *Israel's Political-Military Doctrine*. Cambridge, Mass.: Harvard University Center for International Affairs.

Hartley, A. 1975. *American Foreign Policy in the Nixon Era*, Adelphi Papers, no. 110. London: International Institute for Strategic Studies.

Heggoy, Alf. 1972. *Insurgency and Counterinsurgency in Algeria*. Bloomington, Ind.: Indiana University Press.

Hilsman, Roger. 1967. *To Move a Nation*. Garden City, N.Y.: Doubleday and Co.

Hogard, J. 1957. Guerre Revolutionaire et Pacification. *Revue Militaire d'Information* (January):7–24.

Hosmer, Stephen, 1985. *Constraints on U.S. Strategy in Third World Conflict*. Santa Monica, Calif.: RAND.

————, and George Tanham. 1986. *Countering Covert Aggression*. Santa Monica, Calif.: RAND.

Hunt, Richard, and Richard Shultz, eds. 1982. *Lessons from an Unconventional War*. New York: Pergamon.

Jeapes, Toney. 1980. *SAS: Operation Oman*. London: Kimber.

Johnson, Chalmers. 1979. *Autopsy on People's War*. Los Angeles, Calif.: University of California Press.

Joint Low-Intensity Conflict Project. 1986. *Final Report—Analytical Review of Low Intensity Conflict*. Fort Monroe, Va.: U.S. Army Training and Doctrine Command.

Kimche, Jon, and David Kimche. 1960. *Both Sides of the Hill: Britain and the Palestine War*. London: Secker and Warburg.

Kitson, Frank. 1971. *Low Intensity Operations*. Harrisburg, Pa.: Stackpole.

————. 1957. The Turning Tide. In *The Unquiet Peace: Stories from the Post War Army*. London: Wingate.

Kolodziej, Edward, and Bokanga Lokolutu. 1982. Security Interests and French Arms Transfer Policy in Sub-Saharan Africa. In Bruce Arlinghaus, ed., *Arms for Africa*. Lexington, Mass.: D. C. Heath.

Komer, R. W. 1972. *The Malayan Emergency in Retrospect: Organization of a Successful Counterinsurgency*. Santa Monica, Calif.: RAND.

Krepinevich, Andrew. 1986. *The Army and Vietnam*. Baltimore, Md.: Johns Hopkins University Press.

Lacheroy, Charles, et al. 1957. Guerre du Viet-Minh. *Revue Militaire d'Information* (February-March):25–41.

————. 1954. *Une Armee du Viet-Minh*. Paris: Mimeographed.

Lansdale, Edward. 1972. *In the Midst of War*. New York: Harper and Row.

Lawrence, T. E. 1935. *The Seven Pillars of Wisdom*. London: Jonathan Cape.

Lelloche, Pierre, and Dominique Moisi. 1979. French Policy in Algeria: A Lonely Battle Against Destabilization. *International Security*, no. 4:108–33.

Lewy, Guenter. 1978. *America in Vietnam*. New York: Oxford University Press.

Livingstone, Neil, ed. 1985. *Fighting Back: Winning the War Against Terrorism*. Lexington, Mass.: Lexington Books.

Luttwak, Edward, and Dan Horowitz. 1975. *The Israeli Army*. London: Allen Lane.

McCuen, John. 1966. *The Art of Counterrevolutionary Warfare*. Harrisburg, Pa.: Stackpole Press.

Mangold, Peter. 1979. Shaba 1 and 11. *Survival*, no. 3:107–15.

Mansfield, Don. 1980. The Irish Republican Army and Northern Ireland. In Bard O'Neill, William Heaton, and Donald Alberts, eds., *Insurgency in the Modern Age*. Boulder, Colo.: Westview Press.

Martin, Michael L. 1985. From Algeria to N'Djamena: France's Adaptation to Low Intensity Conflict in Historical Perspective. In David Charters and Maurice Tugwell, eds., *Armies in Low Intensity Conflict: A Comparative Study of Institutional Adaptation to New Forms of Warfare*. Ottawa: Department of National Defense.

————. 1981. *Warriors to Managers: The French Military Establishment Since 1945*. Chapel Hill: University of North Carolina Press, 1981.

Moss, Robert. 1971. *Urban Guerrilla Warfare*. Adelphi Papers, no. 79. London: International Institute for Strategic Studies.

Muros, Ralph. 1962. Communist Terrorism in Malaya. In Franklin Osanka, ed. *Modern Guerrilla Warfare*. New York: Free Press of Glencoe.

Nemo, C. 1952. *En Indochine: Guerilla et Contre-Guerilla*. Paris: Mimeographed.

Nixon, Richard. 1974. *Public Papers of the Presidents*. Washington, D.C.: U.S. Government Printing Office.

Olsen, William. 1986. *Low Intensity Conflict and the Principles and Strategies of War*. Carlisle Barracks, Pa.: U.S. Army War College, Strategic Studies Institute.

O'Neill, Bard. 1978. *Armed Struggle in Palestine: A Political-Military Analysis*. Boulder, Colo.: Westview Press.

————. 1980. Revolutionary War in Oman. In Bard O'Neill, William Heaton, and Donald Alberts, eds., *Insurgency in the Modern Age*. Boulder, Colo.: Westview Press.

Paddock, Alfred. 1982. *U.S. Army Special Warfare*. Washington, D.C.: National Defense University Press.

Paget, Julian. 1967. *Counter-Insurgency Campaigning*. London: Faber and Faber.

Palmer, Bruce. 1984. *The 25-Year War: America's Military Role in Vietnam*. Lexington: University of Kentucky Press.

Paret, Peter. 1964. *French Revolutionary Warfare from Indochina to Algeria*. New York: Praeger.

Perlmutter, Amos. 1969. *Military and Politics in Israel*. London: Cass.

Pike, Douglas. 1970. *Viet Cong*. Cambridge, Mass.: MIT Press.

Pons, Jacque. 1981. Lessons of Modern History: The French Experience. In Sam Sarkesian and William L. Scully, eds., *U.S. Policy and Low Intensity Conflict*. New Brunswick, N.J.: Transaction Books.

Prados, John. 1986. *Presidents' Secret Wars*. New York: William Morrow and Co.

Ra'anan, Uri, Robert L. Pfaltzgraff, Richard Shultz, Ernst Halperin, and Igor Lukes, eds. 1985. *Hydra of Carnage*. Lexington, Mass.: Lexington Books.

————, et al. 1985. *Third World Marxist-Leninist Regimes: Strengths, Vulnerabilities, and U.S. Policy*. New York: Pergamon-Brassey's

Rosenfeld, Stephen. 1986. The Guns of July. *Foreign Affairs* 64, no. 4:698–714.

Rothenberg, Gunther. 1978. *The Anatomy of the Israeli Army*. London: Batsford.

————. 1985. The Israeli Defense Forces and Low-Intensity Conflict. In David Charters and Maurice Tugwell, eds., *Armies in Low Intensity Conflict: A Contemporary Study of Institutional Adaptation to New Forms of Warfare*. Ottawa: Department of National Defense.

Russell, Charles et al. 1979. The Evolution of Revolutionary Warfare: From Mao to Marighella and Meinhoff. In Robert Kupperman and Darrell Trent, eds., *Terrorism: Threat, Reality, Response*. Stanford, Cal.: Hoover Institution Press.

Russell, James A. 1986. SOF: They Can't Get There from Here. *Military Logistics Forum*. April. 41–49.

Sarkesian, Sam, and William L. Scully, eds. 1981. *U.S. Policy and Low Intensity Conflict*. New Brunswick, N.J.: Transaction Books.

The Senator Gravel Edition. 1971. *The Pentagon Papers: The Defense Department History of United States Decisionmaking on Vietnam*. Boston: Beacon Press.

Shackley, Theodore. 1981. *The Third Option*. New York: Reader's Digest Press.

Short, Anthony. 1975. *The Communist Insurrection in Malaya, 1948–1960*. London: Muller.

Shultz, Richard. 1986. Can Democratic Regimes Use Military Force in the War Against Terrorism? The US Confrontation with Libya. *World Affairs* 148, no. 205–16.

————. 1979. Coercive Force and Military Strategy. *Western Political Quarterly,* no. 4:444–66.

————. 1988. *The Soviet Union and Revolutionary Warfare: Principles, Practices and Regional Comparisons.* Stanford, Calif.: Hoover Institution Press.

Snyder, William P. 1964. *The Politics of British Defense Policy.* Columbus: Ohio State University Press.

Sonyris, A. 1957. Les Conditions de la Parade et de la Riposte a la Guerre Revolutionaire. *Revue Militaire d'Information* (February–March):93–111.

Stilwell, Richard. 1961. *The Army's Role in Counterinsurgency.* Declassified U.S. Army Report.

Summers, Harry G. 1981. *On Strategy: The Vietnam War in Context.* Carlisle Barracks, Pa.: U.S. Army War College, Strategic Studies Institute.

Sykes, Charles. 1959. *Wingate.* London: Collins.

Tanham, George. 1967. *Communist Revolutionary Warfare.* New York: Praeger.

————, et al. 1978. United States Preparation for Future Low-Level Conflict. *Conflict,* no. 1–2:1–19.

Thayer, Thomas. 1985. *War Without Fronts: The American Experience in Vietnam.* Boulder, Colo.: Westview Press.

Thompson, Robert. 1970. *Revolutionary Warfare in World Strategy.* New York: Taplinger Publishing Co.

Tillion, Germaine. 1961. *France and Algeria.* New York: Alfred A. Knopf.

Tovar, B. Hugh. 1983. Covert Action. In Roy Godson, ed., *Intelligence Requirements for the 1980s: Elements of Intelligence.* New York: National Strategy Information Center.

Tremayne, Penelope. 1977. End of a Ten Years War. *RUSI Journal* (March):44–48.

Trinquier, Roger. 1964. *Modern Warfare.* New York: Praeger.

U.S. Army Training and Doctrine Command, 1986. *Pamphlet 525–44, U.S. Army Operational Concept for Low-Intensity Conflict,* Army Training and Doctrine Command, Fort Monroe, Va.

U.S. Department of the Army. 1963. *FM 31–16, Counterguerrilla Operations.* Washington, D.C.: U.S. Government Printing Office.

————. 1974. *FM 100–20, Internal Defense and Development: U.S. Army Doctrine.* Washington, D.C.: U.S. Government Printing Office.

————. 1953. *Operations Against Airborne Attack, Guerrilla Action and Infiltration.* Washington, D.C.: U.S. Government Printing Office.

U.S. Department of the Army, USCONARC, Historical Division. 1962. Special Warfare Board Final Report. In *Summary of Major Events and Problems, HQ USCONARC, FY 1962,* Vol. 16, Enclosure 5, Section VII.

U.S. Department of Defense. 1986. *Proceedings of the Low Intensity Warfare Conference.* Washington, D.C.: U.S. Department of Defense.

Vidal-Naquet, Pierre. 1963. *Torture.* Baltimore, Md.: Penguin Books.

Waghelstein, John. 1985. Post-Vietnam Counterinsurgency Doctrine. *Military Review* (May):42–49.

Warner, Phillip. 1971. *The Special Air Service.* London: Kimber.

Ximenes. 1957. Guerre Revolutionaire. *Revue Militaire d'Information* (February–March):9–22.

Yarborough, William. 1968. Needed—A New Approach to Counter-insurgency. Unpublished manuscript.

Yost, David. 1983. French Policy in Chad and the Libyan Challenge. *Orbis* 26, no. 4:965–98.

11

On Terrorism and Counterterrorism

MARTHA CRENSHAW

Terrorism is scarcely a new issue. In the nineteenth century the Russian Czars complained of the sympathy which revolutionary terrorists enjoyed in Europe. British officials resented the sanctuary afforded Irish republicans by the United States, and in the 1880–1914 period anarchist terrorism was suspected of being an international conspiracy. More recently, the Algerian FLN in the 1950s used terrorism to attract international attention to the struggle for independence. Yet only in the past two decades has terrorism emerged as a prominent issue of international security, because it has threatened the safety of civil aviation, the institutions of diplomacy, and the interests of the United States and Western Europe.

Contemporary terrorism involves transnational processes of violence—attacks on foreign nationals or on foreign territory, sanctuary in third countries, and linkages across national borders among sub-state actors. However, is terrorism genuinely a feature of international politics or is it a spillover of civil violence? Terrorism may be a form of domestic conflict with international consequences, but if its purpose is to change the international system, it directly challenges world security.

In the 1980s terrorism rapidly became a priority for public policy, but the systematic study of terrorism is just beginning. Many positions on the issue are based on fixed preconceptions and random observations, not rigorous theoretical and empirical analysis. Approaching the issue of terrorism objectively has proven particularly troublesome.

PROBLEMS OF DEFINITION

Some scholars, such as Paul Wilkinson (1974), insist that the concept of terrorism be evaluative. He argues that academic objectivity should not override questions of morality. Other researchers (e.g., Hutchinson, 1972) have tried to isolate the concept of terrorism from moral judgments. In practice, however, evaluations of terrorism reflect opinions about the legitimacy of the objectives of its users. In the West, it is often equated with any violence performed by left revolutionary or national liberation movements. The Third World, however, regards state repression and imperialism as terrorism.

Intellectual confusion also plagues efforts to define terrorism. Distinguishing terrorism from other forms of low-level political violence, especially guerrilla warfare, insurgency, revolution, or partisan resistance, is problematic. The boundaries are imprecise and hard to specify. Ambiguity is evident, for example, in analyses of mass-based nationalist or revolutionary movements that practice a broad repertoire of violent tactics.

The existence of "many terrorisms," each context-dependent, rather than a single homogeneous phenomenon further complicates definition (Wilkinson, 1986) as well as formulation of theoretical generalizations. Groups as varied as the Japanese Red Army, the Popular Front for the Liberation of Palestine (PFLP), the Secret Army for the Liberation of Armenia, the Front de Libération du Québec, the Tupamaros of Uruguay, and the Italian Red Brigades have all resorted to actions commonly labeled as international terrorism. A recent directory lists well over 500 guerrilla and terrorist organizations worldwide (Janke, 1983).

Terrorism also encompasses diverse forms of violence. Some terrorist organizations, such as the Basque Euzkadi ta Akatasuna (ETA), usually restrict themselves to domestic operations, whereas others, such as the PFLP, are innovators in the development of international tactics. (The first hijacking in which terrorists demanded the release of prisoners was the 1968 seizure of an El Al aircraft by the PFLP.) Bell (1978) holds that the distinction between national and international terrorism is meaningless, since changes in the distribution of power at the national level are often more consequential for international politics than the hijackings and diplomatic kidnappings conventionally referred to as international. Wilkinson (1986) agrees, arguing that terrorism against foreign targets or involving cross-national cooperation is merely an extension of domestic politics. However, the State Department and the RAND Corporation retain this distinction and focus their recordkeeping efforts on the external dimensions of terrorism.

Conceptual Foundations

Well-specified, logical definitions that clearly identify the attributes of terrorism are scarce. Schmid (1983, pp. 5–118) attempts to extract a core definition, reflecting what appears to be the scholarly consensus but noting differences of opinion. The following discussion draws in part on his analysis.

First, the identity and motives of perpetrators of terrorist activity are irrelevant. As Freedman (1986, p. 56) notes, "the methods of terrorism are not the monopoly of any cause or political philosophy." States may therefore practice terrorism, and the analysis of sub-state terrorism must include radicals of both right and left. Terrorism may be used to defend the status quo as much as to defy it. It may be a tool of social control as much as an instrument of disruption.

The victims of terrorism are noncombatants (Schmid, 1983, pp. 81–83). They are often (not always) civilians, but as non-combatants they are unprepared to defend themselves at the time of the assault. Violence against military targets can be considered terrorism only if other conditions are met.

The relationship between the physical victim of terrorism and the target is critical. Wilkinson (1974, pp. 13–14, and 1986, pp. 54–55) refers to the arbitrariness and indiscriminacy of terrorism. Thornton (1964) refers to symbolism in order to emphasize that the victims are instrumental to a broader purpose. Victims are selected to manipulate the attitudes of audiences and to influence government decisions. Assassination, kidnapping, and sabotage are not in themselves terrorism but may be the means of terrorism (cf. Rapoport, 1971). Terrorism may appear random, but it is actually systematic and deliberate.

Terrorist violence is extranormal, as Thornton (1964) describes it. Many authors stress cruelty (Wilkinson, 1974 and 1986) or atrocity (Rapoport, 1977). Perceptions of the brutality of particular forms of violence may be culturally relative (nineteenth-century Russian terrorists thought terrorism more humane than popular insurrections since it risked fewer lives), but the distinctiveness of terrorism remains. The weapon is often novel, the time and place unexpected, the agents anonymous, and the preparation for the act clandestine. Most importantly, terrorism is a deliberate rejection of the moral code and behavioral norms of the political system it attacks.

It is difficult to define terrorism without referring to the intentions behind it. Gurr (1979) attempts to formulate a neutral definition dependent on empirically observable facts. However, when Schmid (1983, pp. 101–03) argues that terrorism cannot be reduced to its component parts (i.e., that kidnapping or hijacking per se is not terrorism), he explicitly takes into account the intentions of the terrorists and the circumstances of their actions. That terrorists intend to produce psychological effects is clear from their methods. The pattern of activity, not the single incident, enables the observer to classify an act as terrorist. An audience interprets terrorist actions as meaningful only in the context of the goals of their perpetrators.

APPROACHES AND UNITS OF ANALYSIS

The complex and diverse reality of terrorism is another source of confusion. Analysts often talk past each other because they concentrate on different levels of analysis or facets of the process of terrorism—the terrorist incident, individual practitioners of terrorism, the terrorist organization as actor, or government policy toward terrorism (Gurr, 1987). Historical or theoretical comprehensiveness is rare.

Terrorist Incidents

Studies of the terrorist incident include analyses on both macroscopic and microscopic levels. Macroscopic analysts use aggregate data and quantitative methods in search of global or regional trends and patterns. The ITERATE data set held by the Interuniversity Consortium for Political and Social Research (Michigan) is probably the most widely used. The Rand Chronology of International Terrorism is also available (see Fowler, 1981).

These studies may concern processes of contagion in terrorist incidents, whether in the aggregate or broken down by type (Midlarsky, Crenshaw, and Yoshida, 1980; Heyman, 1980; Hamilton and Hamilton, 1983). The diffusion of terrorism appears to follow structured patterns, based on international hierarchies or geographical contiguity. Different types of terrorism spread at different rates. The ease with which bombings can be imitated, for example, heightens their contagiousness. Contagion processes may be least reversible in open, democratic societies and more likely to be halted with repression than reform (Hamilton and Hamilton, 1983).

Hostage-taking is the type of incident most frequently analyzed. The RAND Corporation has provided statistical analyses of the attributes, including outcomes, of embassy takeovers (Jerkins, 1981) and international hostage episodes (Jenkins, Johnson, and Ronfeldt, 1977). Baumann (1973) analyzed diplomatic kidnappings in Latin America. Aston (1982) concentrated on hostage-taking in Western Europe, with a case study of the 1972 Munich Olympics incident.

The microscopic approach focuses on the progress of an individual incident or type of incident, through individual case studies or comparisons. The inherent logic and dynamics of hostage-taking, involving interaction between terrorists and governments, have been studied from the perspectives of game theory and aggregate statistics (Corsi, 1981), public choice or rational actor models (Sandler, Tschirhart, and Cauley, 1983), bargaining theory (Baldwin, 1976) and historical case study (Wohlstetter, 1974). Knutson (1980) studied the psychological aspects of negotiations primarily from the point of view of the terrorist. An early analysis by Bell (1972) linked the tactic of assassination specifically to international politics. His study also emphasized the lack of novelty in attacking diplomats since the cases he analyzed were the assassinations of British and United Nations officials by the Jewish resistance organization Lehi (or the Stern Gang) in Palestine in 1948.

Individual Terrorists

Because terrorists are so few in number, it seems plausible that some set of characteristics would distinguish them from the wider population. One approach is the background profile, detailing the social, economic, and political circumstances of the participants (Russell and Miller, 1977; Jäger, Schmidtchen, and Süllwold, 1981; Eubank and Weinberg, 1987). These studies of social background are usually on a country basis, as cross-national comparisons become difficult.

Psychological analysis of motivation, individual propensities toward violence, and the interactions among members of terrorist organizations are important areas of research (Knutson, 1981; Ferracuti, 1982; Post, 1984; Crenshaw, 1986). The idea that terrorism is the result of mental pathology or a specific terrorist personality is not widely credited. Terrorists are not necessarily violence-prone individuals, but early socialization into patterns of violent reaction to frustration may be critical. Like other political extremists, they are likely to see the world in stark terms of good and evil, and to feel morally justified in their actions. The importance of the group to individual behavior is central, as pressures toward solidarity and cohesion reinforce the individual's dependence on the community of believers.

The Terrorist Organization

Terrorism is the activity of a political organization, and a majority of studies focus on the organization as actor—its structure, ideology, collective goals, and strategy. Descriptive case studies of single groups or, less frequently, comparisons among groups predominate. Prominent opposition organizations employing terrorism on an international scale, such as the Palestinian resistance, the Uruguayan Tupamaros, the German Red Army Fraction, and the Italian Red Brigades, have been covered extensively (see, for example, Furet, Liniers, and Raynaud, 1985; Halperin, 1976; Lodge, ed., 1981; Cobban, 1984; O'Neill, 1978). Attempts to generalize across groups include studies of organizational politics (Crenshaw, 1985) and statistical analysis of the relevance of group size and intergroup cooperation to forms of terrorism (Oots, 1986). The RAND Corporation has developed a conceptual framework for the analysis of terrorist groups in order to permit the construction of a computerized data base containing information on the characteristics of twenty-nine contemporary organizations (Cordes, Jenkins, and Kellen, 1985).

Typologies are usually based on the political purposes of terrorist organizations. Wilkinson (1974) classifies terrorism as revolutionary, sub-revolutionary, and repressive. Schmid and de Graaf (1982, p. 60) propose three categories: insurgent, vigilante, and regime. Insurgent terrorism in turn is classified as social-revolutionary, separatist, or single-issue.

Terrorism has also been analyzed as strategic behavior, based on conceptions of collective rationality. DeNardo (1985) uses mathematical models to demonstrate how terrorism is selected as an alternative for opposing the state. He explains the logic of revolutionary strategic thought. Freedman (1986) defines terrorism as a problem in military strategy. He sees dependence on terrorism as a sign of strategic failure; in contrast, tactical or adjunct terrorism is more likely to be effective in gaining indirect influence, though not direct control.

Combatting Terrorism

The most popular dimension of terrorism is its cure, which naturally preoccupies governments. Their strong prescriptive orientation drives analysts to focus on current events and on policy recommendations, often to the exclusion of theoretical explanation.

International terrorism as an issue has been taken most seriously in the United States. American policy toward terrorism, generally viewed in terms of crisis management, is a major topic. Much of the work of the RAND Corporation concerns U.S. policy. Evans (1979) surveyed the American foreign policy response to international terrorism, whereas Farrell (1982) examined the government's organizational efficiency. Shultz (1980) provided an overview of American policy, with a focus on its operational aspects. Kupperman and Trent (1979) criticized the government's administrative capacity to cope with catastrophic terrorism, a possibility that interests many researchers. Terrorist exploitation of nuclear devices is especially alarming (Beres, 1979; Blair and Brewer, 1977; Rosenbaum, 1977; Schelling, 1982). Dealing with hostage negotiations is also the subject of policy analysis (e.g., Mickolus, 1976). American policy has also been criticized from a European point of view (Freedman et al., 1986).

Israeli policy has attracted attention. Alon (1980) expresses doubts about the wisdom of emphasizing the threat of terrorism, given the few casualties it produces compared to other disasters. Maoz (1981) applies a formal decision analysis framework to the Israeli decision to intervene during the 1976 Entebbe crisis.

The general problem which terrorism poses for liberal democracy has been treated by Bell (1978), Wilkinson (1986), and Wardlaw (1982). Wilkinson's work emphasizes the defense of democracy, with special attention to British policy in Northern Ireland. Bell is skeptical in rejecting the advocacy and special pleading that accompany most policy recommendations. He warns that the cure may be worse than the disease if coercive measures are adopted in haste and with the expectation that they will end terrorism. Wardlaw also argues for a moderate response.

The legal dimensions of dealing with terrorism have concerned experts since the early 1970s. The articles in Evans and Murphy (1978) and the detailed analysis by Murphy (1985) deal comprehensively with this subject. Crelinsten, Laberge-Altmejd, and Szabo (1978) also directed studies of different national legal systems.

INTERPRETATIONS OF TERRORISM

The study of terrorism is so new that it is unrealistic to expect a comprehensive explanatory theory. Some authors feel that general theories are impossible (Laqueur, 1977; Wilkinson, 1974, 1986). The literature often lacks theoretical self-consciousness, but progress toward greater logic and rigor is apparent. A number of what can be termed partial or mid-level theories now exist. Other "theories" are actually sets of implicit hypotheses that have been derived from clusters of disconnected statements and ad hoc observations. Most descriptive or polemical accounts are based on unexplained assumptions about cause and effect. Existing schools of thought differ as to the nature and seriousness of the threat of terrorism, its sources or origins, its implications for international order, and the appropriate response.

State Sponsorship and Cold War Conflict

The explanation most recently advanced is that international terrorism is not primarily the work of small oppositional movements but a tool of state policy, particularly of the Soviet Union and its allies (Cline and Alexander, 1984, 1985, 1986; Goren, 1984; Livingstone and Arnold, eds., 1986; Netanyahu, ed., 1986; Ra'anan, Pfaltzgraff, Shultz, Halperin, and Lukes, eds., 1986; Sterling, 1981). In this view, terrorism poses a major threat to U.S. national security. The Soviet Union is said to support the Irish Republican Army, the ETA, the RAF, the Red Brigades, and Turkish terrorists in order to weaken NATO. The Palestine Liberation Organization (PLO) is regarded as the linchpin of Soviet anti-Israeli and anti-American policy in the Middle East.

Advocates of the Cold War view stop short of claiming that the Soviet Union controls a global conspiracy, but assert that many terrorist groups would end their activities if the Soviet Union withdrew its support (Livingstone and Arnold, 1986, p. 21). According to late CIA Director William J. Casey (1986, pp. 11–12),

International terrorism is inconceivable apart from the financial support, military training, and sanctuary provided to terrorists by certain states. To seek the causes of terrorism in the behavior of societies victimized by terrorism is thus to look in the wrong place. Rather, these causes are to be found in the convictions and expectations of the terrorists themselves and in the activities of those states that find it in their interest to support international terrorism—the Soviet Union and its satellite states in Eastern Europe, Libya, Syria, Iran, Iraq, North Korea, the People's Democratic Republic of Yemen, Cuba, and Nicaragua.

To Benjamin Netanyahu, Israel's permanent representative to the United Nations, "...communist totalitarianism and Islamic radicalism have between them inspired virtually all of contemporary terrorism. The practical outgrowth of these ideological and religious forces ... are states and groups which, taken together, form a worldwide network of terror" (1986, p. 3). States support terrorism, with or without intermediaries or proxies, because conventional warfare has become too dangerous and expensive. However, the cooperation of terrorist organizations in this network is though to be motivated by ideological affinity as much as strategic considerations.

The proponents of this view urge Western leaders to recognize terrorism as a threat to Western civilization and to react with appropriate defensive measures (Cline and Alexander, 1985). Western states are portrayed as apathetic and reluctant. The "national will" to fight terrorism's causes is absent, according to Casey (1986, p. 15). Sterling (1986, p. 54) asserts that "the primary reason for our having arrived at this very unhappy state in the development of international terrorism in our time is this perverse unwillingness on the part of the Western powers to face ... reality...." Netanyahu (1986, p. 6) criticizes the lack of courage and moral clarity and the weakness and disunity on which terrorism thrives. Academic inquiry is also cited as impeding effective response: "semantic confusion over the precise definition of terrorism ... has hindered formulation of national and military policy by nations of the free world" (Cline and Alexander, 1985, p. xii).

This view is attractive because it provides a simple monocausal explanation, free of the complexities that often make more detailed studies confusing and ambiguous. It elevates terrorism to the status of a major threat to international stability and Western interests, thus requiring a vigorous hardline response. It explains why Americans are among the preferred victims of terrorists and why terrorism occurs more frequently in democracies than in Communist states. It dismisses time-consuming and expensive scholarly inquiries into psychological motivation or social conditions as not only unnecessary but harmful.

The problems with this approach are legion. It is based on limited and imprecise evidence, oversimplifies reality, and in doing so neglects facts that contradict its assumptions, such as the rivalry between Syria and Arafat, conflicts within the PLO, and antagonism between Iran and the Soviet Union. Domestic sources of terrorism are ignored. The astounding assertion that the IRA would not exist without Soviet support is not accepted by any experts on the Irish case. Terrorism from the right, whether insurgent or state sponsored, is unaccounted for. This approach is at best a partial theory—no one disputes the fact that states do become involved in terrorism—masquerading as a comprehensive explanation.

Proxy or Surrogate Warfare: A New Mode of Conflict

More nuanced and moderate than the Cold War view is the argument that terrorism is a new mode of international conflict, practiced by states and non-states acting autonomously. Jenkins (1975) has long held that terrorism has become a form of surrogate warfare that exceeds the bounds of conventional international conflict because terrorist organizations and some states see no reason to play by the rules of a system that excludes them. Recognizing the trend toward the use of terrorist tactics by governments that are too weak to mount a conventional military challenge, Jenkins (1984, p. 3) argues that

we may be on the threshold of an era of armed conflict in which limited conventional warfare, classic guerrilla warfare, and international terrorism will coexist, with both government and subnational entities employing them individually, interchangeably, sequentially, or simultaneously, as well as being required to combat them.

Jenkins downgrades the importance of terrorism to U.S. national security. Allowing terrorism to determine American foreign policy gives too much power to the terrorists (1984, p. 6). Attempts to isolate states that support terrorism are frustrated by the fact that responsibility for such assistance is widespread. Both Spain and Italy charge France with harboring terrorists, and kidnapping or assassination teams have reportedly been sent abroad by the governments of Yugoslavia, Chile, Argentina, Israel, and South Korea. Jenkins warns that definitions of terrorism that are too sweeping or policies that appear selfishly motivated are unlikely to produce useful results.

Wilkinson (1986) holds similar views of terrorism as an indirect means of warfare, a recourse of the weak to change the distribution of power and the established boundaries of the international system. Third World states and transnational organizations, not the Soviet Union, are seen as the primary challengers. Motivations grow from a variety of beliefs, ideologies, regimes, conflicts, and strategic and tactical conditions. Insurgents motivated by genuine grievances fully understand the utility of bringing international pressure to bear on their opponents. The Palestinian problem, rather than Soviet opportunism, is the major cause of international terrorism.

Wilkinson is optimistic about the strengths of liberal democracy in combatting terrorism. He emphasizes the necessity of maintaining the rule of law and democratic values, rather than the lack of moral fiber in the West. He notes that terrorism is of limited value as a revolutionary strategy in democracies and that international terrorism (especially as compared to full-scale war) is much less of a problem than internal terrorism. Wardlaw (1982) also warns against exaggeration of the threat and overreaction.

Theorists of international politics have rarely turned their attention directly to terrorism. However, Hedley Bull (1971) argued that terrorism is a form of internationalization of civil violence. Only its worldwide nature is new, being "one of a number of signs of the emergence in the twentieth century of a single, global political system, of which the global diplomatic system or system of states is only part" (p. 29). When civil factions become violent international actors, or when international actors resort to violence in an effort to avoid responsibility for their actions, they undermine the principles of sovereignty and mutual adherence to rules on which the international order is based. These developments imply a return to the medieval idea of private war (p. 31). His assessment of the potential consequences of uncontrolled international terrorism is pessimistic.

Superpower Behavior

Stohl (1987, 1984) extends the analysis of state terrorism to include both superpowers. States, not insurgents, are the most frequent and effective employers. Both superpowers use terrorism, which includes coercive diplomacy, covert operations (whether practiced by agents of the state or intermediaries), and surrogate activity, defined as assistance to other states or actors employing terrorism. Surrogate terrorism may involve direct support or merely acquiescence in the terrorism of others, such as U.S. aid to the internal security agencies of repressive regimes. The motivation for terrorism is not ideological but opportunistic; terrorism results from cost-benefit calculations of advantage. Totalitarian states are not more likely to resort to such tactics than are democracies. In fact, the United States, through its interventionist policies in the Third World, is the chief offender (1984, p. 52). Observable differences in behavior are due to the structure of the international system, where the Soviet Union finds allies in insurgent organizations and the United States in established states. Neither side is restricted by moral considerations, although in democracies the potential cost of public disapproval can be a constraint. The answer to terrorism, according to this analysis, is to delegitimize it regardless of the initiator. Ignoring the terrorism of one's friends undermines political credibility. The use of military force is unlikely to be effective.

This interpretation is simultaneously too broad and too narrow. The definition of terrorism is too inclusive to permit distinction between terrorism and other examples of violent coercion. Narrowness results from a concentration on state policy that excludes violent opposition to the status quo, the dimension of private war that Bull stresses. However, it is relevant to note that states can be far more destructive than non-states and that covert operations are not alien to the foreign policies of democracies.

Violence as Communication

No study of terrorism is complete without a passing reference to the role of the media in encouraging terrorism. Schmid and de Graaf (1982) develop a systematic theory of the symbiotic relationship between media and terrorists. They emphasize that the international system provides access to publicity and media attention only to the powerful. Insurgent terrorism is a form of violent communication, linked to the rise of the mass media and the development of a Western information order. Terrorism communicates otherwise ignored grievances. Publicity is not always essential—dealing with the government may be sufficient in a hostage-seizure—but most often terrorism is the result of a flaw in social communication systems. The mass media possess enormous powers of social control, yet access to them is denied to those without political or financial resources because Western and especially American interests dominate the world information order. The violent drama of terrorism is useful to commercial elites in capitalist systems while dissident groups gain the ability to appeal directly to the public, bypassing the parliamentary systems that have failed them. The answer to terrorism is to "lower the threshold of communication" by insuring equality of access to the media. This access is in itself a form of power; if granted to aggrieved minorities it would diminish terrorism. For this to happen, public control must replace commercialization.

Publicity is the admitted goal of many insurgent terrorist organizations, although this is not usually the case with states or right-wing extremists. However, the chance to air political opinions before the public is unlikely to substitute for violence as an attention-getting mechanism. The practical obstacles to establishing an open communications system are also formidable. Furthermore, terrorism coexists with public control of the media (in Britain and France, for example).

POLICY RESPONSES

Defining the Threat

Although the destructiveness of terrorism pales in comparison to other forms of violent conflict, the number of international terrorist incidents appears to be increasing steadily (U.S. Department of State, 1986). The year 1985 saw a 30 percent increase over 1984, with a total of 782 international incidents that killed over 800 people. The 597 incidents with over 300 killed in 1984 was a 20 percent increase over the average of the preceding four years. Uninvolved or bystander casualties are also growing, and indiscriminacy stirs public fears. Many high-casualty attacks occurred in the West, including the June 1985 bombing of an Air India flight en route from Canada that caused 329 deaths. In 1986 a rash of bombing attacks in Paris raised concerns.

Terrorism has also acquired status on the policy agenda because of state support. In 1985, the U.S. government considered only 12 percent of international incidents to be state-supported, the vast majority by Middle Eastern governments. However, state support is thought to be connected to the growing lethality of terrorism. If terrorism is not the spillover of civil violence but a new form of international conflict, its power to disrupt is enhanced. To some American policymakers, the role of the Soviet Union as a sponsor of terrorism lifts the threat to an acute level. To other Western governments, however, claims of Soviet support are not only unpersuasive but a reason for denying the seriousness of terrorism. American complaints are dismissed as ideological or self-interested.

In general, terrorism is a threat not to military and economic capabilities but to prestige. Gilpin (1981, pp. 30–34) defines prestige as the reputation for power in international affairs, equivalent to authority within the state, and as such dependent on other actors' perceptions of a state's willingness and ability to use power. As the "currency" of international politics, it is critical to the ordering and functioning of the international system. With sufficient prestige, states can determine the outcomes of international interactions without resorting to the open display of power. A decline in prestige matters deeply, since its diminution in one encounter weakens the state's bargaining position in the next. National leaders must fear that yielding to pressure will be perceived as evidence of weakness (Gilpin, 1981, p. 32). Great powers have more to lose than small powers if they appear impotent before the terrorist challenge, whether issued by states or non-states. Schelling (1966, p. 124) explained the logic of this sensitivity:

It is often argued that "face" is a frivolous asset to preserve, and that it is a sign of immaturity that a government can't swallow its pride and lose face. It is undoubtedly true that false pride often tempts a government's officials to take irrational risks or to do undignified things—to bully some small country that insults them, for example. But there is also the more serious kind of "face,"... consisting of other countries' beliefs (their leaders' beliefs, that is) about how the country can be expected to behave. It relates not to a country's "worth" or "status" or even "honor," but to its reputation for action. If the question is raised whether this kind of "face" is worth fighting over, the answer is that this kind of face is one of the few things worth fighting over.

A government unable to assure the safety of diplomats, military personnel, and tourists suffers a loss of international prestige, as well as a blow to domestic authority.

For the United States, national prestige is linked to world order responsibilities. Terrorism violates the traditional rules that govern both peace and war. Because terrorists have singled out Americans—a targeting pattern that was brought home with violence in Iran and Lebanon at the beginning of the 1980s—national interest and world order concerns have merged. Creating an international environment in which terrorism is not acceptable is in the U.S. interest. This difference in scope of responsibilities and interests partially explains why the issue often divides the United States and its European allies.

Policy Options

A report on terrorism from the Center for Strategic and International Studies (1985, p. 15) makes the point that "governments without policies are perceived to be either indifferent or ineffectual." A general policy of opposing terrorism need not narrow options for the sake of an ideal of consistency or on the assumption that terrorism is an undifferentiated threat. At each instance of terrorism, governments should consider the full range of instruments at their disposal and tailor them to the circumstances at hand. No single approach has been or is likely to be fully successful.

In practice, responses to terrorism have varied. The first task of all governments is prevention, which involves both physical protection and the apprehension of terrorists. Apprehending and punishing terrorists has also been considered essential to upholding the rule of law. Governments face more difficult problems when terrorists seize hostages and demand concessions. Whether to apply sanctions to the state supporters of terrorism is another troubling issue. But most controversial is the decision to use military force. Through all of these choices runs the question of pursuing these ends through unilateral or multilateral means. To what extent is international cooperation required for any counterterrorist options to be effective? Since 1972 the United States has urged greater international cooperation. However, some observers (Bass, Jenkins et al., 1981) note that the United States missed an opportunity to take advantage of the consensus against terrorism that emerged from the Iran hostage crisis. By the 1980s, interest in comprehensive and universal agreements had declined, although the United States remained keenly interested in securing the cooperation of its NATO allies.

Security from Terrorism

Problems in erecting physical barriers to terrorist attacks are multiple. It is difficult to reduce vulnerability. Improving security in one field or at one facility may only deflect terrorism onto softer targets. At a certain point physical protection measures impede the conduct of diplomacy and interfere with commerce and travel. Making embassies into heavily guarded fortresses is incompatible with the open diplomacy that American authorities have tried to project, reflecting the public relations qualities of modern diplomacy. Security is also financially costly. In 1986, for example, the United States passed legislation providing for over $4 billion to improve embassy security during the next five years.

The complement to physical protection is anticipation of threats in time to prevent them. Successful interception depends on intelligence that is not only accurate and timely but extremely specific. Such warnings are rare.

Logically, a multilateral response in this area is desirable. The vulnerability of diplomatic premises, aviation and maritime facilities, and nuclear materials cannot be dealt with unilaterally because much of the responsibility for protecting them rests largely with the national authorities of the countries where they are located. Furthermore, anticipating threats depends on exchanges of information among governments, since terrorism may be imported as much as domestic.

On the positive side, informal and formal cooperation at the operational or technical level is widespread. Cooperation through INTERPOL has grown since 1984, when its General Assembly removed restrictions on sharing information on terrorism. In 1976, the European Community established the "Trevi" system of working groups on terrorism (see Hill, 1986, pp. 89–91), an institutional framework for cooperation among Ministries of the Interior, police forces, and security services. The U.S. State Department maintains an anti-terrorism assistance program for training and supplying foreign security services. Domestic agencies, such as the Federal Aviation Administration, assist in improving foreign airport security. U.S. authorities also have the power to issue travel advisories warning of unsafe airports abroad, a form of coercive diplomacy that is used as a last resort. The International Atomic Energy Agency also concluded a convention on protecting special nuclear material from theft.

Apprehension and Punishment

Governments usually want not only to prevent terrorism but also to seize and punish its perpetrators. This goal directly invites international legal cooperation, since one factor that makes modern international terrorism possible is the mobility of terrorists. The problem is not so much that they may find sanctuary in hospitable states but that national borders can be easily crossed. Success in this area depends not only on locating terrorist offenders but also on the willingness of the states where terrorists are apprehended either to extradite or to punish.

Treaties have usually concentrated on outlawing specific terrorist actions, such as hijackings or diplomatic kidnappings. Six counter-terrorist conventions have been adopted under the auspices of the United Nations: three anti-hijacking agreements negotiated by the International Civil Aviation Organization (the Tokyo, Hague, and Montreal Conventions, respectively); the Convention on the Prevention and Punishment of Crimes Against Internationally Protected Persons, Including Diplomatic Agents; and the International Convention Against the Taking of Hostages. In addition, there are three regional conventions. The Organization of American States preceded the United Nations in outlawing attacks on diplomats. The Council of Europe negotiated the European Convention on the Suppression of Terrorism, which the European Community also attempted to incorporate. The U.N. General Assembly and the Western summit conferences have condemned terrorism generally, which reinforces the moral authority behind legal proscriptions.

These treaties suffer from a number of problems: neither signature to, ratification of, nor compliance with the treaties is ensured. France has refused to ratify the European conventions. Some states fear terrorist retaliation should they extradite to a state likely to be extremely punitive or should they impose stiff penalties. No treaty provides for sanctions against states that fail to comply with the law (excepting the 1978 Bonn Declaration of Western heads of states, which is not binding in international law).

Murphy (1985) criticizes the disaggregation of the phenomenon on which the international law approach is based. He argues that terrorism should be defined universally and made an international crime. He also notes that the complexity of the international legal system and its relationship to different national laws impedes cooperation, even when states are willing.

The principle of sovereignty also hinders agreement, because it justifies the persistence of the political offense exception. States reserve the right to grant asylum to persons accused of committing offenses that are political in the eyes of the government to which the appeal is made. Extradition is never automatic, even within the European Community. Only in 1986 did London win a revision of the U.S.-U.K. bilateral extradition treaty (there is no extradition from the United States without such prior formal agreement) to exclude acts of terrorism from the category of political crimes. Opposition came not from the State or Justice departments but from Congress.

On a global level, the issue of punishing non-state terrorists is highly divisive. In the aftermath of the 1972 Munich Olympics incident, the United States proposed a draft U.N. convention to counter terrorism. Most Third World nations refused even to consider a definition of terrorism that did not refer to its causes, which they named as oppression and imperialism. In the post-colonial international system, the high value accorded national self-determination and the difficulty of isolating means from ends in politics have undermined efforts to delegitimize terrorism. The United States is accused of trying to suppress all movements of national liberation and of hypocrisy in singling out revolutionary violence as terrorism while dismissing the much more destructive actions of right-wing authoritarian regimes. The fact that the Soviet Union and its allies have traditionally supported revolutionary movements and regimes draws the dispute over national liberation into the East-West conflict.

No-concessions Versus Negotiations

The seizure of hostages in order to make political demands on foreign governments is an innovation of the post-1968 wave of international terrorism, which began with diplomatic kidnappings in Latin America and hijackings in the Middle East. By the mid-1980s in Lebanon, hostage-taking reached epidemic proportions.

Most governments seem to have dealt with demands on a case-by-case basis, although the trend in the 1970s was toward resistance since acquiescence appeared to encourage more terrorism. An important factor in shifting attitudes was a change in the direction of terrorist demands. Often states whose nationals were seized were actually third parties in the bargaining process, because demands for the release of prisoners or the payment of ransom were addressed to the host government. West Germany, for example, argued for concessions when the West German ambassador to Guatemala was kidnapped. German authorities insisted that the Guatemalan government's failure to protect diplomats required securing the ambassador's release. However, when the Red Army Faction began to kidnap German politicians and industrialists, Germany switched to refusal. The perception that being "soft" on terrorism was an electoral liability for a socialist party influenced the decision.

American adherence to a no-concessions policy was rhetorically consistent from the late 1960s onward. Before the wave of international terrorism, however, the U.S. government followed a "safe-release" policy, for example, in Cuba in 1958 when Castro rebels kidnapped American Marines (see Wohlstetter, 1974). It was extremely rare for the United States to be the direct object of demands for payment of ransom, release of prisoners, or safe passage. (Jenkins, et al., 1977, noted only three instances between 1968 and 1975.) In addition, the United States acquiesced in concessions made by host governments in order to secure the release of American citizens.

The turning point toward a firmer policy came under the Nixon administration in 1973, when American diplomats were seized by Palestinians in Khartoum. Nixon's refusal to give in to demands for, among other things, the release of Sirhan Sirhan led to the deaths of the hostages at the hands of the Black September organization. In the Iranian hostage crisis, however, Carter attempted to negotiate. In part as a result of Carter's perceived ineffectiveness, the centerpieces of Reagan's declaratory policy were no-concessions and swift retribution.

Consistency in refusing to concede to terrorists is obviously difficult to maintain. Even Israel, equally firm in its hard-line policies, has occasionally relented. At Entebbe in 1976, Israel was prepared to concede until information was acquired that made a military rescue feasible. One problem is that, as the RAND Corporation (Bass et al., 1981, pp. 5–6) has noted, the evidence that the no-concessions policy works is "meager and unconvincing: changes in American policy have not correlated with the number of U.S. officials kidnapped, there is no evidence that concessions encourage future terrorism, and there is sufficient precedent for terrorists to believe that the policy will be relaxed in particular cases." Hostage-taking episodes have only become longer and more complex as governments have resisted compromise. Their incidence has not decreased.

Governments seem to fear that the deaths of hostages will result in a loss of public support. Media attention to the families of hostages reinforces this perception. Individual leaders may also be susceptible to psychological pressures that make it painful for them to resist when lives are at stake. Such pressures, combined with false expectations of a successful outcome, may have prompted some American officials to agree to swap arms for hostages.

Military Force

Frustration over the ineffectiveness of a passive if uncompromising policy increased the temptation to use military force against terrorists. After the 1972

Munich Olympics incident—when hostages were killed in part as a result of police inefficiency—most Western governments began to develop specialized elite intervention units. The precedent was set in 1976 when Israel intervened at Entebbe (Maoz, 1981). The Israeli purpose was to escape being caught between two equally unpleasant alternatives: either give in, which would result in the fall of the government and international loss of prestige, or refuse and allow the hostages to be killed, risking public anger.

The Entebbe raid succeeded beyond all expectation, but subsequent attempts at armed rescues produced mixed results (Gazit, 1981). West Germany at Mogadishu in 1977 and Indonesia at Bangkok in 1981 were successful. The Egyptians at Larnaca in 1978 and the United States in Iran in 1980 failed. The Egyptian rescue attempt at Malta in 1985 resulted in the deaths of most of the hostages, but the outcome might not have been better without Egyptian intervention. The Israeli success at Entebbe was the exception, not the rule. The United States has not attempted a unilateral armed rescue abroad since the debacle at Desert 1, although assistance is provided to states that seek it in domestic hostage seizures or kidnappings, and the United States supports armed rescues by appropriate authorities.

The United States has, however, resorted to force in order to seize suspected terrorists. In 1985, frustration led the United States to intercept an Egyptian plane carrying Palestinians suspected of murdering a passenger on the hijacked cruise ship *Achille Lauro*. Although the interception was technically flawless, it resulted in political conflict with Italian authorities and ultimately in the release of primary suspect.

The resort to military force to rescue hostages is a limited and precise mission. The implications broaden, however, when nations retaliate against or preempt the use of terrorism. The Israeli response to terrorism was, again, a precedent for the American response. Israel endorses a policy of active retaliation against Palestinian terrorists without regard for national borders. Infiltration attempts launched from Egypt, Jordan, or Lebanon have met the same retaliation. Israel habitually responds with aerial bombing of what are suspected to be terrorist command centers. Their retaliatory or preemptive options also include forcible seizures or selective assassinations of PLO leaders in the Middle East and in Europe, and military invasion (of the Sinai in 1955 and 1956 and Lebanon since 1978). The 1982 invasion of Lebanon was nominally a response to the attempted assassination of the Israeli ambassador to London.

The Reagan administration came to power having made resolve in the face of terrorism a key campaign issue. The bombing of the Marine barracks in Beirut in 1983 initiated an internal debate over the use of force (see Motley, 1986, and Livingstone and Arnold, 1986). The issue of how to respond to terrorism provoked public dispute between the secretaries of state and defense, with George Shultz (1984) calling for the adoption of vigorous counterterrorism policies including military force, even if "evidence that can stand up in an American court of law" is lacking, public support is ambivalent, and innocent lives may be lost: "We cannot allow ourselves to become the Hamlet of nations, worrying endlessly over whether and how to respond. A great nation with global responsibilities cannot afford to be hamstrung by confusion and indecisiveness. Fighting terrorism will not be a clean or pleasant contest, but we have no choice but to play it" (p. 445). In contrast, Caspar Weinberger, strongly urged caution and restraint. Uncertainty about public reactions to military intervention clearly troubled many American decision-makers.

The United States has not found the appropriate opportunity to retaliate against non-state organizations, but Libyan involvement in anti-American terrorism clarified U.S. choices and provided a convenient target. In early 1986, U.S. military exercises in the Gulf of Sidra provoked Libyan counteraction, which in turn furnished an excuse for limited American strikes against military targets. In April 1986, after a bombing in Berlin that American intelligence services laid openly to Libya's account, President Reagan ordered American forces to conduct bombing raids against targets in Tripoli and Benghazi. Although the stated purpose of the raid was retaliation, it was suspected that the United States also wished to remove Quaddafi from power, either by killing him or by undermining his control.

Coercive Sanctions

As a policy option, military force is more appropriate to state supporters of terrorism than to underground organizations. So is the use of diplomatic and economic sanctions. During the Iran hostage crisis, Carter unsuccessfully urged collective sanctions against Iran, but American allies were reluctant. Different degrees of dependence on the Middle Eastern resources influenced Western policies, as did the argument that sanctions are ineffectual. Reagan has called for sanctions against all states that support terrorism, including Libya and Syria as well as Iran. A number of unilateral trade and foreign aid restrictions apply by law to states listed under the Export Administration Act as supporters of terrorism.

In 1986, Great Britain broke diplomatic relations with Syria after official Syrian complicity in an attempted mid-air bombing of an El Al airliner was exposed in a public trial. Attempts to persuade its European Community partners to follow suit were unsuccessful. West Germany also expelled several Libyan diplomats after similar revelations. Embarrassment has apparently resulted in Syrian adoption of less adventurous and more constructive policies, especially in Lebanon.

Economic and diplomatic sanctions are often part of a campaign of public condemnation. Their value is symbolic. However, an advantage of economic sanctions is that they may be undertaken as part of "quiet diplomacy" and need not be as dramatic, costly, or irreversible as military coercion. The problem is to find measures less costly to their initiators than to their objects and more painful to governments than to their citizens. Furthermore, the costs of collective sanctions must be distributed equally among allies.

POLICY DOCTRINE

The intellectual basis for American policy is an extension of the theory of deterrence that has been an underpinning of American foreign policy since World War II (Hutchinson, 1975; Evans, 1979). Its principle is that denial of reward and threats of punishment will convince the states and organizations that practice terrorism to desist. Rewards or failures to punish will encourage more terrorism.

For deterrence to succeed against terrorism, a government must know what will make an action costly to an adversary and must possess the capability to manipulate those values. Terrorists must therefore be thought to operate under conditions of instrumental rationality. Communications must also be clear.

Reality may not fit these assumptions. It is difficult to deny reward to terrorists if their goals extend beyond specific demands to public recognition of their grievances. If communication of a political message is the goal (as Schmid and de Graaf, 1982, argue, for example), then governments cannot deny reward unless they prevent the act. The practical difficulties in preventing terrorism are exceptional.

Punishing non-state terrorists through military reprisals faces several obstacles. First, even if these organizations can be located, they usually lack the visible and accessible assets of states—territory, economic resources, civilian populations. Terrorist organizations appear to be easily rebuilt unless governments have long-term and effective control over the territories in which they operate. Military retaliations may even facilitate recruitment and provide free publicity for the cause. Furthermore, military strikes must be extremely precise and discriminate not only to be effective in influencing the calculations of terrorists but to be acceptable to domestic public opinion.

If a government cannot decide how to punish or what kind of punishment would be sufficiently painful, then the credibility of the threat is beside the point. In fact, constantly threatening swift and sure retribution while doing nothing erodes credibility. It was this impasse that the Reagan administration fretted over from 1981 to 1986, while at the same time trying to remove the problem through secret negotiations.

The revelation of open state sponsorship of terrorism in the 1980s simplified matters. The presumption of state responsibility improves the applicability of the theory of deterrence. States are conventional adversaries. If not always rational, at least they can be located and possess tangible assets. Freedman (1986, pp. 70–76) agrees that state sponsorship is a clear challenge to international security, but he contends that the need to justify a policy of military retaliation may lead to an exaggeration of the threat. The necessity of generating popular support for risky measures (essentially to maintain superior motivation vis-à-vis the adversary) encourages overestimation of the adversary's level of hostility and offensive capability.

The use of force against terrorists may also be a signal to other would-be adversaries of one's determination to punish, even if that punishment is asymmetrical, and to recalcitrant allies, unwilling to collaborate in a collective defense, that the result of going it alone may be escalation and loss of control. Roberts (1987, p. 22) notes that "the very threat of international disorder implicit in the April 1986 U.S. raid on Libya may, paradoxically, have spurred other states to take the matter of non-violent sanctions more seriously—which they did, for example, at the Tokyo summit" in May.

The consequences of forceful responses for international stability may exceed those of terrorist violence. The first risk is escalation. Israeli retaliation against the PLO led to conflicts with Syria and Egypt and costly intervention in Lebanon. The 1970 Jordanian civil war, precipitated by the hijackings of the Popular Front for the Liberation of Palestine, threatened to draw in Syria and Israel, and with them their respective superpower allies. The First World War began with a response to a terrorist assassination. Fear of escalation or heightened international tension was one obstacle to American retaliation against Iran during the hostage crisis. Brzezinski (1983) recommended retaliatory strikes to support a military response and to camouflage what he expected to be a failed rescue mission. The Soviet invasion of Afghanistan made this course of action too risky. The Reagan administration's unwillingness to attack either Iran or Syria for involvement in terrorism results from similar caution.

The resort to force may also jeopardize relations with allies or neutrals. Carter and Brzezinski were sensitive to the danger of jeopardizing relations with Middle Eastern nations and allowing the Soviet Union to gain influence. The seizure of the *Achille Lauro* hijackers temporarily cooled U.S. relations with Egypt and Italy. The 1986 bombing of Libya deepened divisions within the Atlantic Alliance. France and Spain refused overflight permission to American bombers. Only the British government was firm in support of U.S. policy (and was rewarded with the conclusion of a bilateral extradition treaty that restricted the use of the political offense exception by IRA members).

When force appears to succeed, public doubt over the wisdom of military intervention quickly recedes. But when rescues or retaliatory strikes fail, domestic political consequences can be fatal. Freedman (1986, p. 73) points out the "high premium on success" involved in decisions to use force. Fear of failure may lead to overreaction as well as to deception.

There is no evidence that using force deters terrorists. It is always difficult to know when deterrence has succeeded, especially when dealing with terrorists motivated by psychological pressures or rivalries among groups as much as the intolerability of the status quo. Terrorist actions are not solely responses to government moves. When terrorists do react, they are as likely to be provoked to more terrorism as to desist. Yet in confronting terrorism there are few demonstrably effective alternatives and none so appealingly straightforward and immediately rewarding as the use of military force. Diplomatic successes are rare, and covert operations that succeed in preventing specific terrorist actions or in purchasing the release of hostages cannot be publicized. The arguments in favor of the military option are political rather than military, and domestic as much as international. If terrorism continues—and so far it has appeared to follow an unpredictable momentum of its own—state use of force may become as routinized as the resort to terrorism.

CONCLUSIONS

Terrorism raises a number of questions about international politics. In what ways do the sources of terrorist violence lie in the processes, rules, and power structure of the international system? What are its consequences for international order? What are the implications for national security policies and for the long-term control of terrorism?

Terrorism against foreign targets has become habitual for non-states that perceive outside actors as responsible for their dissatisfaction. Such organizations seem motivated by the belief that seizing political power at the national level requires change at the international level. Terrorism has also become a method of blocking the pursuit of foreign policy objectives, of weakening commitments, and of preventing the peaceful resolution of disputes. In the Middle East, terrorism is often coercive intimidation, meant to protest French support for Iraq or American assistance to Lebanon or Israel. States eager to avoid the risks of open attack also use terrorism as a clandestine instrument of foreign policy. Both states and non-states are able to justify the recourse to terrorism by claiming to act in the interest of anti-colonialism and national liberation.

Global interdependence facilitates international terrorism because commercial and diplomatic linkages have created multiple convenient targets, provided terrorists with mobility and anonymity, and sometimes impeded international cooperation because of the economic concerns of threatened states. The expansion of the global arms trade and technical progress in weaponry and explosives aids terrorists. A worldwide communications network furnishes instantaneous publicity. A developed, commercialized, industrialized world with prosperous citizens who travel frequently, watch television, and elect their leaders presents terrorists with infinite opportunities for disruption.

What are the effects of terrorism? Attacks on diplomats and on civilians are no longer exceptions. The distinction between peace and war and between acceptable and unacceptable targets of violence has been blurred. But whether the result has been to strengthen or weaken the rules of the system remains an open question. In many ways, terrorism has gradually produced unity among victims, despite the slow progress of international cooperation. Yet at the same time terrorism has produced a sense of helplessness and frustration, which in turn has strengthened the temptation to use military force. The suspicion that state adversaries secretly practice terrorism deepens mistrust. States targeted by terrorists find the passivity of their allies irritating. Allies who think the threat is exaggerated are alarmed and dubious. Terrorism has demonstrated the power to disrupt the regional peace process in the Middle East and to undermine the American commitment to restoring order in Lebanon. Yet it has not altered the global balance of power or the distribution of major resources within the system.

The implications for national security policies are ambiguous. First, governments should not confuse the outcomes of terrorism with the effects of counterterrorist measures. It is difficult to judge the results of government policies. Governments confront a policy dilemma because, although a subtle and nuanced response may be best, public opinion is widely perceived as forcing governments into active counterterrorism. A "grand policy" (Dror, 1983) on terrorism may not be feasible, but ad hoc responses may not satisfy the public. To escape this dilemma, governments may engage in covert negotiations which they later disavow. In consequence, democratic accountability in foreign policy is jeopardized.

Another issue for governments is whether or not to pursue international cooperation, and if so with what scope: only within the Western alliance, on East-West terms, or linking North and South? Will the use of military force increase or reduce the potential for international cooperation? Does American hegemony obstruct efforts to organize the international community? Is it possible for governments to make the international environment inhospitable for terrorists? Is there any assurance that a concerted international response would control terrorism?

Scholarly inquiry should investigate not only the sources and consequences of terrorism, but also the determinants of counterterrorist policies. In particular, leaders' perceptions of the threat of terrorism and the role of public opinion in influencing policy decisions deserve analysis. The effectiveness of policies toward terrorism should be evaluated: What has worked to reduce terrorism? Are nonviolent or noncoercive options feasible? Can trends in terrorism be charted over time, especially patterns of innovation and escalation? Studies should identify incentives for as well as obstacles to international cooperation.

On a more abstract level, scholars should ask how terrorism fits into existing theories of international politics. Too often terrorism has been regarded as an issue unlike any other, without context or reference points. Instead, the case of terrorism should be used to test the explanatory power and applicability of general theories of power, conflict, and change in world politics.

REFERENCES

Alexander, Yonah, and John M. Gleason, eds. 1981. *Behavioral and Quantitative Perspectives on Terrorism*. New York: Pergamon.

Alon, Hanan. 1980. *Countering Palestinian Terrorism in Israel: Toward a Policy Analysis of Countermeasures*. Santa Monica, Calif.: RAND.

Arblaster, Anthony. 1977. Terrorism: Myths, Meaning and Morals. *Political Studies* 25:413–24.

Aston, Clive. 1982. *A Contemporary Crisis: Political Hostage-Taking and the Experience of Western Europe*. Westport, Conn.: Greenwood Press.

Baldwin, David A. 1976. Bargaining with Airline Hijackers. Pp. 404–29 in I. William Zartman, ed., *The 50% Solution*. Garden City, N.Y. Doubleday.

Bass, Gail, Brian M. Jenkins, Konrad Kellen, and David Ronfeldt. 1981. *Options for U.S. Policy on Terrorism*. Santa Monica, Calif.: RAND.

Baumann, Carol Edler. 1973. *The Diplomatic Kidnappings: A Revolutionary Tactic of Urban Terrorism*. The Hague: Nijhoff.

Bell, J. Bowyer. 1972. Assassination in International Politics: Lord Moyne, Count Bernadotte, and Lehi. *International Studies Quarterly* 16:59–82.

———. 1975. *Transnational Terror*. Washington, D. C.: American Enterprise Institute.

———. 1977. Trends on Terror: The Analysis of Political Violence. *World Politics* 19:476–88.

———. 1978. *A Time of Terror: How Democratic Societies Respond to Revolutionary Violence*. New York: Basic Books.

Beres, Louis Rene. 1979. *Terrorism and Global Security: The Nuclear Threat*. Boulder, Colo.: Westview Press.

Blair, Bruce G., and Garry D. Brewer. 1977. The Terrorist Threat to World Nuclear Programs. *Journal of Conflict Resolution* 21:379–403.

Brzezinski, Zbigniew. 1983. *Power and Principle: Memoirs of the National Security Adviser 1977–1981*. New York: Farrar, Straus and Giroux.

Bull, Hedley. 1971. Civil Violence and International Order. Pp. 27–36 in *Civil Violence and the International System*. Part II. Violence and International Security. Adelphi Papers, no. 83. London: International Institute for Strategic Studies.

Casey, William J. 1986. The International Linkages—What Do We Know? Pp. 5–15 in Uri Ra'anan, Robert L. Pfaltzgraff, Jr., Richard H. Shultz, Ernst Halperin, and Igor Lukes, eds., *Hydra of Carnage*. Lexington, Mass.: Lexington Books.

Center for Strategic and International Studies. 1985. *Combating Terrorism: A Matter of Leverage*. Washington, D.C.: Georgetown University.

Cline, Ray S., and Yonah Alexander. 1984. *Terrorism: The Soviet Connection*. New York: Crane Russak.

Cobban, Helena. 1984. *The Palestine Liberation Organisation*. Cambridge, Mass.: Cambridge University Press.

Cordes, Bonnie, Brian M. Jenkins, and Konrad Kellen. 1985. *A Conceptual Framework for Analyzing Terrorist Groups*. Santa Monica, Calif.: RAND.

Corsi, Jerome R. 1981. Terrorism as a Desperate Game: Fear, Bargaining and Communication in the Terrorist Event. *Journal of Conflict Resolution* 25:47–86.

Crelinsten, Ronald D., Danielle Laberge-Altmejd, and Denis Szabo.1978. *Terrorism and Criminal Justice: An International Perspective*. Lexington, Mass.: Lexington Books.

Crenshaw, Martha. 1985. An Organizational Approach to the Analysis of Political Terrorism. *Orbis* 29:465–89.

———. 1986. The Psychology of Political Terrorism. Pp. 379–413 in Margaret G. Hermann, ed., *Political Psychology: Contemporary Problems and Issues*. San Francisco: Jossey-Bass.

DeNardo, James. 1985. *Power in Numbers: The Political Strategy of Protest and Rebellion*. Princeton, N.J.: Princeton University Press.

Dror, Yehezkel. 1983. Terrorism as a Challenge to the Democratic Capacity to Govern. Pp. 65–90 in Martha Crenshaw, ed., *Terrorism, Legitimacy, and Power: The Consequences of Political Violence*. Middletown, Conn.: Wesleyan University Press.

Eubank, William Lee, and Leonard Weinberg. 1987. Italian Women Terrorists. *Terrorism: An International Journal* 9:241–62.

Evans, Alona E., and John F. Murphy, eds. 1978. *Legal Aspects of International Terrorism*. Lexington, Mass.: Lexington Books.

Evans, Ernest. 1979. *Calling a Truce to Terror: The American Response to International Terrorism*. Westport, Conn.: Greenwood Press.

Farrell, William R. 1982. *The U.S. Government Response to Terrorism: In Search of an Effective Strategy*. Boulder, Colo.: Westview Press.

Ferracuti, Franco. 1982. A Sociopsychiatric Interpretation of Terrorism. *Annals of the American Academy of Political and Social Science* 463:129–40.

Fowler, William W. 1981. *Terrorism Data Bases: A Comparison of Missions, Methods, and Systems*. Santa Monica, Calif.: RAND.

Freedman, Lawrence. 1986. Terrorism and Strategy. Pp. 56–76 in Lawrence Freedman, et al., *Terrorism and International Order*. Chatham House Special Paper. London: Routledge and Kegan Paul.

Freedman, Lawrence, Christopher Hill, Adam Roberts, R.J. Vincent, Paul Wilkinson, and Philip Windsor. 1986. *Terrorism and International Order*. Chatham House Special Paper. London: Routledge and Kegan Paul.

Furet, Francois, Antoine Liniers, and Philippe Raynaud. 1985. *Terrorisme et démocratie*. Paris: Fayard.

Gazit, Schlomo. 1981. Risk, Glory, and the Rescue Operation. *International Security* 6:111–35.

———, and Michael Handel. 1980. Insurgency, Terrorism, and Intelligence. Pp. 125–47 in Roy Godson, ed., *Intelligence Requirements for the 1980s: Counterintelligence*. New Brunswick, N.J.: Transaction Books.

Gilpin, Robert. 1981. *War and Change in World Politics*. Cambridge, Mass.: Cambridge University Press.

Goren, Roberta. 1984. *The Soviet Union and Terrorism*. London: Allen and Unwin.

Gurr, Ted Robert. 1979. Some Characteristics of Political Terrorism in the 1960s. Pp. 23–49 in Michael Stohl, ed., *The Politics of Terrorism*. New York: Marcel Dekker.

———. 1987. Methodologies and Data for the Analysis of Oppositional Terrorism. In Michael Stohl and Robert O. Slater, eds., *Current Perspectives on International Terrorism*. New York: St. Martin's Press.

Halperin, Ernst. 1976. *Terrorism in Latin America*. Beverly Hills, Calif.: Sage.

Hamilton, Lawrence C., and James D. Hamilton. 1983. Dynamics of Terrorism. *International Studies Quarterly* 27:39–54.

Heyman, Edward. 1980. The Diffusion of Transnational Terrorism. Pp. 190–244 in Richard H. Schultz, Jr., and Stephen Sloan, eds., *Responding to the Terrorist Threat: Security and Crisis Management*. New York: Pergamon.

Hill, Christopher. 1986. The Political Dilemmas for Western Governments. Pp. 77–100 in Lawrence Freedman, et al., eds. *Terrorism and International Order*. London: Routledge and Kegan Paul.

Hutchinson, Martha Crenshaw. 1972. The Concept of Revolutionary Terrorism. *Journal of Conflict Resolution* 16:383–96.

———. 1975. Transnational Terrorism and World Politics. *Jerusalem Journal of International Relations* 1:109–29.

Jäger, Herbert, Gerhard Schmidtchen, and Lieselotte Süllwold. 1981. *Analysen zum Terrorismus: Lebenslauf-Analysen*. Opladen, FRG: Westdeutscher Verlag.

Janke, Peter. 1983. *Guerrilla and Terrorist Organisations: A World Directory and Bibliography*. New York: Macmillan.

Jenkins, Brian M. 1975. International Terrorism: A New Mode of Conflict. Pp. 13–49 in David Carlton and Carlo Schaerf, eds., *International Terrorism and World Security*. New York: Halsted Press.

———. 1981. *Embassies Under Seige: A Review of 48 Embassy Takeovers, 1971–1980*. Santa Monica, Calif.: RAND.

———. 1984. *The Lessons of Beirut: Testimony Before the Long Commission*. Santa Monica, Calif.: RAND.

———, Janera Johnson, and David Ronfeldt. 1977. *Numbered Lives: Some Statistical Observations from 77 International Hostage Episodes*. Santa Monica, Calif.: RAND.

Knutson, Jeanne N. 1980. The Terrorists' Dilemmas: Some Implicit Rules of the Game. *Terrorism: An International Journal* 4:195–222.

———. 1981. Social and Psychodynamic Pressures Toward a Negative Identity: The Case of an American Revolutionary Terrorist. Pp. 105–50 in Yonah Alexander and John M. Gleason, eds., *Behavioral and Quantitative Perspectives on Terrorism*. New York: Pergamon.

Kupperman, Robert, and Darrell Trent. 1979. *Terrorism: Threat, Reality, Response*. Stanford, Calif.: Hoover Institution Press.

Laqueur, Walter. 1977. *Terrorism*. Boston: Little, Brown.

Livingstone, Neil C., and Terrell E. Arnold, eds. 1986. *Fighting Back: Winning the War Against Terrorism*. Lexington, Mass.: Lexington Books.

Lodge, Juliet, ed. 1981. *Terrorism: A Challenge to the State*. New York: St. Martin's Press.

Maoz, Zeev. 1981. The Decision to Raid Entebbe: Decision Analysis Applied to Crisis Behavior. *Journal of Conflict Resolution* 25:677–707.

Mickolus, Edward F. 1976. Negotiating for Hostages: A Policy Dilemma. *Orbis* 19:1309–1325.

Midlarsky, Manus I., Martha Crenshaw, and Fumihiko Yoshida. 1980. Why Violence Spreads: The Contagion of International Terrorism. *International Studies Quarterly* 24:262–98.

Motley, James Barry. 1986. Target America: The Undeclared War. Pp. 59–84 in Neil C. Livingstone and Terrell E. Arnold, eds., *Fighting Back: The War Against Terrorism*. Lexington, Mass.: Lexington Books.

Murphy, John F. 1985. *Punishing International Terrorists: The Legal Framework for Policy Initiatives*. Totowa, N.J.: Rowman and Allenheld.

Netanyahu, Benjamin, ed. 1986. *Terrorism: How the West Can Win*. New York: Farrar, Straus and Giroux.

O'Neill, Bard E. 1978. *Armed Struggle in Palestine: A Political-Military Analysis*. Boulder, Colo.: Westview Press.

Oots, Kent L. 1986. *A Political Organization Approach to Transnational Terrorism*. Westport, Conn.: Greenwood Press.

Post, Jerrold M. 1984. Notes on a Psychodynamic Theory of Terrorist Behavior. *Terrorism: An Interdisciplinary Journal* 7:241–56.

Rapoport, David C. 1971. *Assassination and Terrorism*. Toronto: Canadian Broadcasting Corporation.

———. 1977. The Politics of Atrocity. Pp. 46–61 in Yonah Alexander and Seymour Maxwell Finger, eds., *Terrorism: Interdisciplinary Perspectives*. New York: John Jay Press.

Roberts, Adam. 1987. Terrorism and International Order. Pp. 7–25 in Lawrence Freedman, et al., *Terrorism and International Order*. London: Routledge and Kegan Paul.

Rosenbaum, David M. 1977. Nuclear Terror *International Security* 1:140–61.

Russell, Charles A., and H. Bowman Miller. 1977. Profile of a Terrorist. *Military Review* 58:21–34.

Sandler, Todd, John T. Tschirhart, and Jon Cauley. 1983. A Theoretical Analysis of Transnational Terrorism. *American Political Science Review* 77:36–54.

Schelling, Thomas C. 1966. *Arms and Influence*. New Haven, Conn.: Yale University Press.

———. 1982. "Thinking About Nuclear Terrorism." *International Security* 6:61–77.

Schmid, Alex P. 1983. *Political Terrorism: A Research Guide*. New Brunswick, N.J.: Transaction Books.

———, and Janny de Graaf. 1982. *Violence as Communication: Insurgent Terrorism and the Western News Media*. Beverly Hills, Calif.: Sage.

Shultz, George P. 1984. Terrorism in the Modern World. *Terrorism: An International Journal* 7:431–37.

Shultz, Richard H., Jr., 1980. The State of the Operational Art: A Critical Review of Anti-Terrorist Programs. Pp. 18–58 in Richard H. Shultz, Jr., and Stephen Sloan, eds., *Responding to the Terrorist Threat: Security and Crisis Management*. New York: Pergamon.

Sterling, Claire. 1981. *The Terror Network*. New York: Reader's Digest Press.

———. 1986. The State of the Art. Pp. 49–56 in Uri Ra'anan et al., eds., *Hydra of Carnage*. Lexington, Mass.: Lexington Books.

Stohl, Michael. 1984. International Dimensions of State Terrorism. Pp. 43–58 in Michael Stohl and George A. Lopez, eds., *The State as Terrorist: The Dynamics of Governmental Violence and Repression*. Westport, Conn.: Greenwood Press.

———. 1987. States, Terrorism, and State Terrorism: The Role of the Superpowers. In Michael Stohl and Robert O. Slater, eds., *Current Perspectives on International Terrorism*. New York: St. Martin's Press.

Thornton, Thomas P. 1964. "Terror as a Weapon of Political Agitation." Pp. 71–99 in Harry Eckstein, ed., *Internal War: Problems and Approaches*. New York: Free Press.

U.S. Department of State. 1986. *Patterns of Global Terrorism: 1985*. Washington, D.C.

Walter, Eugene Victor. 1969. *Terror and Resistance: A Study of Political Violence*. New York: Oxford University Press.

Wardlaw, Grant. 1982. *Political Terrorism*. London: Cambridge University Press.

Wilkinson, Paul. 1974. *Political Terrorism*. New York: John Wiley.

————. 1986. *Terrorism and the Liberal State*. New York: New York University Press.

Wohlstetter, Roberta. 1974. Kidnapping to Win Friends and Influence People. *Survey* 20:1–40.

PART V

ARMS CONTROL AND CRISIS MANAGEMENT

12

On Strategic Arms Control and International Security

PATRICK M. MORGAN

Insecurity is characteristic of life in the international system, inherent in the lack of authoritative management and the absence of common moral, cultural, and behavioral restraints on the use of force. States fear force may be used against them but are reluctant to part with the possibility of using force for their own benefit.

Insecurity is a serious burden in statecraft, while military forces and war are costly and dangerous. This invites attention to the possibility of cooperation among states to ease the burden and limit the dangers and costs. Such cooperation could take many forms and be directed at a wide range of objectives. Cooperation aimed precisely at limiting the costs and harmful consequences of military forces is what we refer to as "arms control."

Arms control is not new. Elements of it appear in the records of systems of autonomous states (Friedman, 1972; Bond, 1974; Burns, 1977). Arms control impulses paralleled the origin of the nation-state. The Catholic Church in medieval Europe attempted to limit warfare, and chivalry can be seen as an elaborate arms control endeavor. The breakdown of the Church and the savagery of the wars of religion promoted the elaboration of international law, with its extensive rules for warfare, and led to the restrained mode of warfare that predominated in the seventeenth and eighteenth centuries (Keen, 1965; Liddell Hart, 1947). The nineteenth century saw the introduction of international conventions to restrain warfare, including provisions allowing noncombatants (the Red Cross) to assist the wounded (see Towle, 1983). The twentieth century brought still further conventions, treaties, and eventually a theory, of sorts, of arms control.

Despite its long pedigree, the significance of arms control was quite limited until well after 1945. Then its importance sharply increased because of several novel developments. First, arms control began to receive attention at the highest levels in the greatest states. Second, arms control endeavors were extended, in an unprecedented fashion, to the most important and sensitive military forces. Finally, arms control was assigned a higher degree of responsibility for national and international security than ever before.

We lack a true theory of arms control. We can see this by comparing what we have with what a theory should provide. The theory of arms control should address or have some bearing on the following questions:

1. What is arms control?
   If we don't insist on too much precision, there is a good deal of consensus in the field on how to define the subject.

2. How is it related to the nature of international politics?
   Thinking about this issue has been limited and amorphous; the question has not been consistently addressed.

3. Is it better than the alternatives?
   We need to know if arms control is worth time and effort in view of its potential effects, feasibility, and probability of success in comparison with other measures. This question has often been addressed but with no conclusive results.

4. Under what circumstances can it come about and be maintained?
   This question has received much attention. There is considerable agreement about some conditions as prerequisites for arms control, and continuing debate about others. However, recent developments call into question much of what we thought we knew.

5. If a government seeks arms control, what should it do?
   The answer is unclear. The field is full of suggestions as to what might be done and debates about what ought to be done.

DEFINITION

The most influential definition of arms control is a functional one. Nearly thirty years ago, Schelling and Halperin proposed that arms control included "all the forms of military cooperation between potential enemies in the interest of reducing the likelihood of war, its scope and violence if it occurs, and the political and economic costs of being prepared for it" (Schelling and Halperin, 1985, p. 2). They had in mind measures to stabilize nuclear deterrence, ease nuclear arms race pressures, reduce the likelihood that any nonnuclear war would escalate, and increase the chances of stopping any nuclear war as quickly as possible.

The definition is quite serviceable, though a bit too limited. Its authors did not confine their analysis to cooperation between enemies and included unilateral measures as well, and there is no reason why arms control cannot be undertaken among friends. It also seems clear that arms control is ultimately intended to contribute to security. Thus, a more inclusive definition would be:

measures, directly related to military forces, adopted by governments to contain the costs and harmful consequences of the continued existence of arms (their own and others), within the overall objective of sustaining or enhancing their security (Morgan, 1986, p. 285).

Definitions are one thing, expectations and practices another. Over the course of the strategic arms control negotiations, other goals or functions have been suggested. Many people came to assume that arms control should at least put an end to the growth and further modernization of nuclear arsenals, the viewpoint emphasized in the nuclear freeze campaign. Others expected significant *reductions* in nuclear arsenals, the position adopted by the Reagan administration (and initially by the Carter administration as well). By contrast, neither reductions nor a freeze were deemed essential by those who initially developed the conception of arms control; they noted it might sometimes be associated with more arms, not less.

Next, strategic arms control has been assigned various political functions. It has been described as registering the readjustments in the power and political influence of the superpowers (Wolfe, 1979), and as a dialogue for setting the rules of the game and managing the entire superpower competition. It has been called an index of the American-Soviet political relationship (Mandelbaum, 1987), and therefore public opinion and the media in the West treat the negotiations as a good sign, their absence as evidence that things are not going well. Newhouse argues that arms control assists the political leaders in both nations in coping with their own military establishments and controlling their national security policy processes (Newhouse, 1973).

Negotiations have also been seen as educational. For a while, SALT was said to be about informing the Soviets of the virtue of stabilizing mutual assured destruction (MAD). Analysts have described the various negotiations as broadening each side's understanding of the other, providing more predictability about future military capabilities so as to prevent overreactions. In this sense, the negotiations themselves can be considered a confidence-building measure (Nye, 1986).

There has been some interest in strategic arms control for its possible contribution to inhibiting horizontal proliferation of nuclear weapons. The idea is that by curbing their own nuclear appetites the superpowers would help legitimize the non-proliferation regime, living up to their obligations under the Nuclear Non-proliferation Treaty.

Finally, critics have called strategic arms control a sham. Its true function has been to legitimize and deflect attention from each side's continued military programs. Alva Myrdal was a well-known proponent of this view. Developing countries have said much the same, especially in assessments of the non-proliferation treaty. Nuclear freeze advocates often claimed that arms control had been captured by the arms race and the national security establishment (Miller, 1984).

That strategic arms control has numerous political overtones is now taken for granted, though this is often deplored. There is less confidence than in the past that negotiations have any great educational benefit. Thus far, strategic arms control has contributed little or nothing to preventing nuclear proliferation. The question as to whether the entire endeavor is fraudulent is still open. One response is that the expectations have been too high; it is not a fraud, it just can do much less than observers have thought it would.

ARMS CONTROL AND INTERNATIONAL POLITICS

The modern theory of arms control was laid out in a flurry of writings in 1959–1961 (Shelling and Halperin, 1985; Bull, 1961; Brennan, 1961; Wohlstetter, 1959; Brodie, 1959. See also Freedman, 1981; Kaplan, 1983; Miller, 1984; Kruzel, 1986.) It was a logical extension of deterrence theory. If deterrence theory told us how to avoid war in the nuclear age, arms control theory was about how to make deterrence stable and cheaper and about what we might do to survive if it failed.

All this was in reaction to the arrival of *mutual* nuclear deterrence and the ICBM. Mutual deterrence meant both sides were deeply at risk and national security could not be fully assured unilaterally. Arms control analysis postulated the existence of a mutual interest in stability amidst such interdependence. ICBMs brought with them a continuous vulnerability to almost instantaneous attack on a terminal scale, with potential advantages to the side that attacked first, and this put a premium on finding ways to enhance deterrence stability.

As this suggests, the theory was intended to be "policy relevant" from the start. Its ideas about how arms control fit into international politics were as follows. First, nuclear weapons (and other arms) were not about to disappear, because they reflected enduring political disagreements among states. Comprehensive disarmament was impractical. This meant that arms control was a pretty conservative and pragmatic approach; disarmament, by contrast, was really a radical idea requiring the transformation of world affairs (Garnett, 1979; Kruzel, 1981). In an arms control perspective, military forces are necessary and legitimate (Blechman, 1984).

Next came the assumption that nuclear weapons changed international politics. They produced an overriding interest in avoiding war, allowing cooperation for arms control purposes despite political conflicts. This was a crucial intellectual breakthrough, coming as it did in the midst of the Cold War.

From there it was just a matter of suggesting the forms that cooperation could take—crisis management, limiting wars, containing proliferation, and so on. Most striking was the idea that each side would do well to avoid tampering with the survivability and effectiveness of the other side's deterrent.

Then it was only a short step to the view that not only preemptive-strike forces but even defensive systems would be counterproductive.

Theorists stressed that arms control could be pursued by unilateral actions as well as in conjunction with others, and that cooperation could be informal and tacit in nature, involving no negotiated treaties. This broadened the range of possible arms control activities considerably.

Such thinking shared with nuclear deterrence theory the objective of describing rational behavior in the nuclear age so policymakers could act accordingly, particularly where rationality dictated a counterintuitive course of action. Of course, that meant ascribing to the enemy a substantial degree of rationality also.

Little effort was made to give these ideas a larger theoretical or empirical foundation. On the empirical side, arms control thinking was an offshoot of deterrence theory, which was itself a historical and nonempirical (George and Smoke, 1974). Thus, "in arguing for arms control, those who wrote in 1960 saw no necessity to consult a historical record" (Graubard, 1980, p. V).

As for a broader theoretical foundation, arms control falls in the family of phenomena that call for an explanation of cooperation under anarchy (see World Politics, 1985). There are several possible ways to proceed. Perhaps nuclear weapons override anarchy, altering international politics in the way arms control analysts initially suggested. This would mean that there is no political requirement or prerequisite for arms control; "linkage" does not apply. Sooner or later the logic of mutual nuclear deterrence will prevail; mutual vulnerability and the need to cooperate to manage it successfully are *facts,* not just policies.

The best evidence in support of this approach would be if the superpowers more or less ignored the tenor of their political rivalry in their arms control dealings. There is now a widely shared view that this has not happened, that there are political preconditions for strategic arms control—that linkage is unavoidable. If so, it appears there are some standard aspects of international politics that nuclear weapons do not supersede, and the problem of explaining how the cooperation necessary for arms control comes about remains unsolved.

As an illustration, the early arms control analysts failed to anticipate the "bargaining chip" approach. Here the political conflict leads to the view that the other side must be forced into signing an equitable agreement, that is, cooperation must be induced rather than simply occurring, by pressing for new or additional strategic forces unless one receives an appropriate concession in the negotiations. This view gives leverage to those in intragovernmental politics who want more arms by allowing them to claim that a military buildup is good for arms control. This in turn may undermine, not enhance, cooperation, especially by encouraging a pace in technological change in weapons that outruns arms control agreements.

Arms control advocates have sometimes assumed that experience was the key to cooperation—the experience of successful negotiations and workable agreements, of continued arms race burdens, of the futility of seeking nuclear superiority, and so on. There is little evidence to sustain this position. The burden of strategic forces is not consistently increasing, and it is well within the resources of the superpowers to handle. Past failures to achieve strategic superiority do not seem to have eliminated interest in trying to achieve it in some quarters. As for the effects of negotiations, expecting the experience to deepen understanding is much like the "spillover" effect anticipated in early integration theory. Nothing of the sort occurred. The initial SALT agreements were followed by a deterioration in US-Soviet relations. Agreements turned into sources of contention, suspicion, and misunderstanding complete with charges of cheating and bad faith.

Another possible approach is to assert that cooperation occurs when anarchy is modified by the presence of a hegemonic state, a perspective now debated in international political economy. Those who see a hegemon as vital are opposed by others who think cooperation can continue even as a hegemon declines; still others see cooperation as partly compatible with anarchy (Keohane, 1984; *World Politics,* 1985).

It is now customary in the field to treat parity as a prerequisite for serious strategic arms control, which is to deny that hegemony is useful. The significant agreements that have been reached were under conditions of hegemonic decline, when American strategic superiority had disappeared. Hegemony may be bad for the cooperation required in arms control, whatever its effects in political economy. This raises the interesting possibility, as yet unexplored, that the conditions in international politics that facilitate some important forms of cooperation might diminish the chances of others. Alternatively, one could treat strategic arms control as a manifestation of an emerging duopolistic superpower hegemony, cooperation that ensures their joint preeminence at everyone else's expense. This is, of course, what some other states have feared the negotiations might come to.

Still another possibility is to treat arms control as a facet of the rising *interdependence* in the international system. Nuclear deterrence is cited as a major manifestation of interdependence, and the SALT/START process has sometimes been treated as a "regime." However, the effects of interdependence are not clear. It might lead to increased frictions among states and, as a result, a greater effort by governments to insulate their societies from its effects (Holsti, 1980). With regard to strategic forces, this would mean the appearance of attempts to escape from mutual deterrence. The alleged Soviet effort to develop a nuclear warwinning capability and the American Strategic Defense Initiative (SDI) program would be quite understandable, as would the way SALT failed to prevent, and even contributed to, the decline of detente. This would mean that arms control is not necessarily enhanced by interdependence; instead, interdependence may tend to undermine it.

In the case of SDI, the Reagan administration has suggested using arms control to make a smooth transition out of nuclear deterrence, reducing interdependence. Aside from the view that this is not technically possible (SDI won't work), the standard criticism of this idea is that nuclear deterrence is good for us. The fear is that nuclear deterrence is really what prevents another world war, that the absence of nuclear weapons would make the world "safe" for conventional conflicts (Howard, 1983, p. 22; Questor, 1986, p. 8; Schelling, 1985–1986; Forsberg, 1987). The theory of arms control would therefore depend on one's conception of the relationship between nuclear deterrence and the absence of great power warfare.

Interdependence is also problematic as a basis for arms control because this reinforces the expectation that linkage is unavoidable, with strategic arms control dependent on superpower political relations. The trouble with this idea is that nuclear deterrence is sought precisely because those relations are so poor, and one of the original attractions of arms control thinking was the prospect that the management of deterrence might be insulated from politics. Now we would have to reject this notion not only on the basis of the SALT experience but on theoretical grounds as well.

A final, and currently influential, approach to a theory of arms control depicts it not as a truly cooperative endeavor but as an arena of continuing U.S.-Soviet conflict. Inhibited from engaging in open warfare, the superpowers carry on their military (and political) competition in surrogate ways, including arms control negotiations. Agreements are a product, and a measure, of the military strength, political leverage, will, and skill each can bring to bear. Each seeks unilateral advantages. Each tries to use the negotiations and any agreements to gain an edge in other facets of their competition, and vice versa. Agreements are the outcomes of political struggles that reflect temporary intersections of national interests. An agreement basically consists of "registering and codifying an existing balance of forces" (Burt, 1986, p. 200. See also Osgood, 1986; Gray, 1984).

Arms control agreements are therefore just like many of the others that states reach within the international system. They do not transform relationships or mitigate political competition. The cooperation involved is quite limited. They reflect interdependence only in the traditional sense that no state fully controls its security. Thus,

American and Soviet interests are essentially competitive and... superpower cooperation is the exception rather than the rule.... Only if they perceive mutual advantage will the two superpowers sometimes seek to coordinate policy and be willing to subordinate immediate notions of gain to a larger objective from which each believes it will derive some greater good (Blacker, 1987, p. 122).

Many people are not apt to be comfortable with this position over the long run. It implies that arms control arrangements will come and go, be made and unmade as technology, superpower relations, and leaders change. Many will want arms control to be less transient, less fluid and political, and to embody, instead, a realization that in the nuclear age we must rise above politics as usual.

ARMS CONTROL VERSUS THE ALTERNATIVES

If the objective of arms control is simply to ease the burdens of the strategic arms competition while the American-Soviet political struggle continues, then no real alternative to it is apparent. However, there is skepticism that this goal is feasible (see Burt, 1981). There are those who also doubt that it would be beneficial since research and the development of new weapons systems often work to increase the stability of deterrence, crisis stability, and the possibility of limiting any nuclear war (Adelman, 1984–1985).

If the objective of enhancing national security is added, then strategic arms control is the subject of much debate. As previously noted, in some quarters arms control is seen as a sham. It rationalizes the huge arsenals that are the real threat to security. From another perspective, the conservative critique of arms control has been that the goal of security was eclipsed in the 1970s by the pursuit of arms control for its own sake. Agreements permitted a Soviet strategic advantage to emerge while dampening Western defense efforts. The United States was moving to institutionalize a flawed perspective on national security (MAD) while the Soviets were trying to evade it. Arms control became divorced from strategy (Nitze, 1986; Burt, 1986, 1981; Luttwak, 1978).

This view is attacked by those who see the record as one of considerable accomplishment (Slocombe, 1984). A frequent argument is that nuclear weapons are of no value for anything but deterrence and mutual deterrence is inescapable. Security lies in recognizing this fact and in working to stabilize deterrence cooperatively, rejecting warfighting strategies and hypothetical strategic defenses (Drell, 1980, 1986; Kattenburg, 1985; Committee on Foreign Affairs, 1982). Often this is coupled with the assertion that the contributions of arms control, while valuable, should not be overestimated (Friedberg, 1984).

Can arms control lead the way in improving East-West relations? The consensus view is that it probably has to be a part of detente but cannot by itself generate or sustain it. Arms control was oversold on this score during SALT, and our expectations should now be lower (Friedberg, 1984; Kruzel, 1986).

The general skepticism in the field about what to expect from strategic arms control makes it appear to be of very marginal value in preventing horizontal proliferation as well, though it is a staple of the literature on nonproliferation that strategic arms reductions are very much needed.

How does arms control stack up in comparison with the alternatives? Many people still strongly favor general nuclear disarmament either alone (Kennan, 1982) or in conjunction with a complete adjustment in the global political system (Kim, 1984, and other World Order Modelling Project analysts). Very few who espouse such views regularly work in the field of security studies. Many security analysts now think that a nuclear-disarmed world would be extremely dangerous. The advantages of having even a few nuclear weapons would be so great that the temptation to secretly develop them would be almost irresistible. Suspicion that this was what rivals were up to would be endemic, breeding fear and instability (Intriligator and Brito, 1987; Questor, 1986; Garnett, 1979).

The opposite alternative is seeking security by unilaterally arming. The Soviet Union has been frequently described as driven by this perspective (for example, Payne, 1982; Nitze, 1986). Crisis stability and deterrence have been held to require a usable American military superiority, because "forces that do not lend themselves to politically intelligent employment in war are probably insufficient to deter" (Gray, 1980, p. 136).

There has also been an attack on the idea that unrestrained strategic arms competition is necessarily destabilizing and ruinous, and on the notion that very large nuclear arsenals are extremely dangerous. Analysts have pointed out that the so-called arms race has not continuously spiraled upward, that it has not brought the superpowers closer to war (Osgood, 1986), and that enormous arsenals lend great stability to deterrence (Intriligator and Brito, 1987; Schelling, 1985–1986), such as by easing fears of a "breakout."

The Reagan administration seemed bent on achieving superiority when it listed the ability to "prevail" as one goal for American forces. However, it soon retreated to the Reagan dictum that "a nuclear war cannot be won and should never be fought." It was evident that the reaction at home and abroad to an explicit war-winning posture would be too much to handle. The administration eventually resumed the pursuit of arms control. Evidently, arms control was more attractive, more durable, as an approach to security than most observers were willing to suggest at the beginning of the decade.

The only other alternative route to the objectives assigned to arms control is political settlement, starting with detente and then moving well beyond it. This has usually been dismissed as unrealistic in the large sense, feasible only as a modest degree of detente. The relationship between detente and arms control is taken up in the next section. Here we need only note that there was a distinct shift in the field, and in broader public policy debates, by the early 1980s toward the view that detente was necessary, that detente and arms control should work in conjunction, and that arms control could not supply "technological solutions to what are essentially political problems" (Blacker, 1987, p. 175).

WHAT MAKES ARMS CONTROL POSSIBLE?

We can begin with examples of the numerous statements in the literature that politics matters in arms control.

One necessary condition of arms control success is that negotiating states must have already reached some form of political accommodation (Kruzel, 1981, p. 153). No arms control process will be effective unless a stable political relationship exists between the United States and the Soviet Union (Lodal, 1980, p. 170).
So long as political rivalry and hostility are not abated there can be no sufficient basis for an arms control process to accomplish anything more substantial than a registration of the facts of military competition (Gray, 1984, p. 160).

This was what nearly everyone concluded on the basis of the SALT experience.

The argument has been elaborated in various ways. Tension feeds pressures for elaborate verification. Such verification is very difficult to negotiate, and it magnifies the significance of suspected or perceived violations. Tension strengthens the position of those opposed to arms control, so that building the necessary domestic political consensus is more difficult. That leads to trade-offs; more military research, larger defense budgets, and new weapons are supported within each government to get a consensus but these steps offset or undermine the arms control process. In the end each side's confidence in arms control is weakened, and criticism of the whole process is provoked.

Another version, associated with conservative critics of SALT and the early Reagan administration, was that the political nature of the Soviet Union made it an unsuitable negotiating partner. Pipes and others described the Soviet system as fundamentally militarist (Pipes, 1980). Cited were Moscow's imperial ambitions, its ideological rejection of the concept of stability, its predisposition to reject mutual vulnerability and define security as military superiority (Nitze, 1986; Gray, 1980). Also noted was a Soviet penchant for extreme secrecy and a negotiating style that eschews flexibility and the trading of concessions in favor of probing for every possible weak point and loophole (Luttwak, 1978; Gray, 1984). From this perspective, arms control progress required a marked shift in the Soviet political system itself and in its policies. This was translated by the Reagan administration into linking arms control to a change in Soviet policies on human rights, Nicaragua, Afghanistan, Poland, and so on.

This version of the political prerequisites has been vigorously disputed. Specialists have insisted that the USSR is not driven to seek military superiority and is seriously interested in arms control (Garthoff, 1978, 1985; Payne, 1980; Holloway, 1980, 1983). Some studies detect a growing sector of civilian security analysts in the USSR who are sophisticated proponents of arms control and have more influence than previously (Gottemoeller, 1986; Sloan, 1986).

Attention has also been given to the domestic political necessities in the United States. Steven Miller has catalogued the chief domestic hurdles for arms control: the difficult process of fashioning a stance within the government, the perils in the Senate ratification process, the intrusions of electoral politics, the disruptions introduced when administrations change, and the domestic political reverberations of Soviet actions. He thinks these were as responsible as anything else for the sag in arms control by the early 1980s, and their cumulative effect is to make it very difficult to go beyond quite modest agreements (Miller, 1984).

Robert Hoover has examined U.S. decision-making in six arms control episodes. Analysts frequently use either a bureaucratic politics or a presidential leadership model to explain arms control decisions. The case studies, however, suggest that both models are only sometimes applicable and that many other factors come into play, especially when the president does not seize control of the whole process (Hoover, 1986).

Analysts have repeatedly found that the American political system neglects *strategy*, which cripples U.S. participation in arms control negotiations (Luttwak, 1978; Kruzel, 1981). Colin Gray argues that the American government oversells arms control efforts in search of short-term domestic political benefits, leading to domestic pressure for American concessions to get agreements. (The same thing happens with U.S. allies.) This also cripples the U.S. ability to "arm to parley" and curbs American reactions to Soviet cheating (Gray, 1984).

Another view is that American and Soviet decision-making processes are only occasionally synchronized to a sufficient degree. A recent example is the Steinbruner point that a long Soviet military buildup, implementing decisions a decade or more old, slowed by the early 1980s just as the United States initiated its own buildup. The mismatch was reinforced by the contrast in decision styles. In Moscow broad doctrinal and posture questions are raised and settled only rarely, and policies flow deductively from then on, whereas Washington periodically makes its big decisions on specific weapons programs with larger questions and strategy only worked out inductively. These differences distort each country's view of what the other is up to (Steinbruner, 1985).

Existing assessments of the relationship between arms control and politics are of little assistance in interpreting developments in the second half of the Reagan administration. The press for major agreements that emerged could be seen as invalidating the conclusion that important political accommodations must precede or accompany strategic arms control. After all, there were no breakthroughs on the "trouble spots" in the Third World in advance of the negotiations, no jump in U.S.–Soviet economic relations, no wholesale Soviet adherence to the Helsinki Accords. In fact, the greatest movement in U.S.–Soviet relations was in arms control. We might soon be back to the view that strategic arms control *can* be insulated from the political rivalry to some extent, and to the idea that it can be the engine driving the superpowers toward detente.

On the other hand, we could stress the following: the Gorbachev domestic reforms including *glasnost,* the release of dissidents with permission for some to emigrate, a Soviet willingness to leave Afghanistan, three Reagan-Gorbachev summits, and a modest *glasnost* in Soviet military affairs—the congressional delegation's visit to the Krasnoyarak radar, the journalists' tour of a Soviet nuclear testing site, and more Soviet flexibility on verification. These may add up to detente. If so, then perhaps the consensus in the field is supported.

There is also a problem with highlighting domestic political impediments to arms control. It is clear that strong congressional pressures (see Committee on Foreign Affairs, 1982; Fascell, 1987) helped move the administration to pursue arms control with more vigor. In addition, the president and a few top advisers dispensed with much of the bureaucracy (including the Joint Chiefs) in proposing at Reykjavik some breathtaking arms control steps. This can be taken as a sign that the political difficulties, inside and outside the government, are not all that serious (the key is that the top officials be strongly committed and take an active role), particularly (as was said of Nixon) when the president has excellent credentials as a conservative anti-communist.

But we might conclude instead that what has happened is due to proponents of arms control having pulled themselves together politically. Momentum was built up by the nuclear freeze campaign, and the spadework by the many organizations like the Physicians for Social Responsibility was finally paying off. The arms control supporters in Congress are now much better organized. Sam Nunn and Les Aspin have skillfully exercised the leverage of their positions with the Armed Services Committee. One could add, with a nod to Steinbruner, that the defense buildup is over, and this makes the administration more inclined to see arms control in a favorable light.

What about other prerequisites for arms control? There is still no agreement on the utility of bargaining chips and negotiating from strength. Since 1969 U.S. administrations have pleaded, with great success, for programs (ABM, B-1, M-X, Cruise Missiles, Pershing II) that Moscow would dislike and seek to forestall through concessions. Critics charge that the Soviets cannot be successfully pressured this way, and that such systems pick up so much momentum that they become difficult to trade, undermining the arms control process they were supposed to facilitate.

It seems likely that the experience of the 1980s will be seen as lending much more support to the negotiating-from-strength view. That NATO deployed the GLCMs and Pershings will be given much of the credit for moving the USSR to the zero option. There is widespread agreement that SDI has moved Moscow to take sharp cuts in offensive systems seriously. These days, arms control supporters who normally dislike the bargaining chip view have been regularly proposing that SDI be treated as one, traded for Soviet concessions on offensive systems.

Attention has also been given to alleged technological prerequisites. A standard view is that a mature arms system lends itself better to arms restraints than an emerging technology, and there are recurring suggestions that attempts be made to curb military R & D with this idea in mind. Verification problems can be severe until the testing stage, and the United States is reluctant to forego its advantage in this area which has been used to offset Soviet quantitative superiority (in missiles, throw-weight, etc.). For its part, the Soviet Union dislikes arrangements that would allow U.S. possession of technology it has yet to match. It is also apparent that technological change frequently has outrun negotiations, sometimes, it has been charged, by design. Thus, the technological "windows of opportunity" for arms control are intermittent. (A recent example is ASAT).

Technological developments have outmoded the SALT approach in various ways. The proliferation of "grey area" systems adds forces with potential strategic missions that fall outside the SALT limits—the Soviet Backfire bomber, U.S. cruise missiles,and the Pershing II. Improvements in warhead accuracies have made the distinction between missiles with good hard-target-kill capabilities and those that did not, based on missile size, less applicable. Technology has brought cruise missiles and mobile ICBMs that pose serious verification problems. It has also revived interest in strategic defenses, threatening the ABM Treaty.

These and related difficulties do not appear to pose insuperable barriers. A lot depends on what sort of arms control is contemplated. (See the excellent discussion in Bajusz 1986–1987). For instance, the problem of coping with hard-target-kill systems that threaten ICBM survivability could be eased considerably with deep cuts in land-based missiles. For those whose main concern is deterrence stability via large arsenals and who see the exact numbers as relatively unimportant, cruise missiles and mobile ICBMs may be quite acceptable because they cancel the value of attacking first (Schelling, 1985–1986, 1987). Technological change that enhances targeting enemy forces can also be used to improve verification capabilities.

A final condition for arms control suggested by some analysts is a shared strategic perspective (or national perspectives that are sufficiently congruent). A definitive conclusion on this subject eludes us. It was apparent in SALT that the two sides had differing *political* objectives and divergent *strategic* conceptions (see Wolfe, 1979). Agreements were reached nonetheless. But it cannot be denied that the differences played a large part in making SALT a failure. Clearly, agreements can be reached that serve the different objectives of the parties simultaneously, but the value attached to agreements varies with one's strategic perspective (Wolfe, 1979, pp. 250–51), and thus the commitment to them of the parties may be far from equal. On the other hand, when the Reagan administration installed a strategy said to be much closer to the Soviet view, the two governments still held quite divergent positions on the value of SALT II, strategic defenses, and the like.

WHAT IS TO BE DONE?

The literature is exceedingly rich in suggestions both as to possible arms control measures and how to proceed. Numerous examples of "what should be done" analyses could be cited on proliferation (Dunn, 1982), a nuclear test ban (Doty, 1987), arms control in space (Bhupendra, 1984), a nuclear weapons freeze (Miller, 1984), the better control of all nuclear operations (May and Harvey, 1987), and so on. A significant number of recent works probe deeply into all aspects of verification (for example, Potter, 1985; Krass, 1985, Tsipis, 1986). There is renewed interest in the problem of whether and how a nuclear war could be terminated (Cimbala, 1986; Ball, 1981; Knorr, 1985).

When it comes to priorities, however, the field is in disarray (or creative disagreement). One cleavage is between those who think the foremost goal must be to reaffirm the SALT II limits and preserve the ABM Treaty (such as Blacker, 1987) and others, including the Reagan administration, who are willing to depart from these agreements to move in a new direction. Another is between those who want to see nuclear arsenals cut sharply and new systems forbidden (Feiveson et al., 1987) and those who see such a focus as misplaced. Intriligator and Brito (1987) see large arsenals as stabilizing; the real problems lie in the possibility of accidents, pressures for proliferation, ASAT systems, and further technological developments that add to preemption capabilities. Our arms control agenda, they feel, should be adjusted accordingly. Steinbruner (1985) sees cutting arsenals as less important than forestalling big new weapons systems. Bertram (1978) and Schelling (1985–1986) argue that the capabilities of weapons (are they destabilizing or not?) are much more important than their numbers or whether they are new.

Recently, there has been an upsurge of concern about the present and potential vulnerability of C^3I systems. This concern is reflected in fears that unless something is done soon to curb anti-satellite weapons development the door will be open to a host of dangerous developments, a tack that has been taken by various members of Congress. Seventeen analysts have jointly produced a long list of recommendations, ranging from hardening C^3I and upgrading crisis communication facilities to deep cuts in strategic offensive forces (Ball, 1987).

The Reagan administration chose steep cuts in missile systems as its top priority. Until recently, this was considered unfeasible by most analysts. Thus, the response has been lukewarm in the field, with some support (Perle, 1987) offset by fears for extended deterrence or of the possibility that this will just shift the arms competition to other areas (Sloss, 1987). Hence, the proposal has been made that parallel cuts occur in conventional forces as well (Forsberg, 1987).

In going after sweeping, bold agreements, the administration was also at odds with the prevailing wisdom (an exception being Drell, 1980). The reaction to the fading of SALT was to assert that large agreements were inappropriate. They were too complex to negotiate smoothly or behind which to build domestic support. Their pursuit raised excessive expectations, which were ultimately harmful to the arms control cause. It was better to lower horizons, narrow the scope of negotiations, and go for specific, precise results (Stanley Foundation, 1986).

Some went further, suggesting that less effort be put into formal agreements in favor of informal understandings. Coming from the administration (Adelman, 1984–1985), this suggestion might be taken as a ploy for evading negotiations born of its suspicion about the whole arms control process. But for Schelling (1985–1986) it reflected his view that negotiations often lead to preoccupation with details that do not matter while the point of the enterprise is lost. For Miller (1984) it was a way around the domestic political impediments to the arms control process. For Nye, the point was to retain formal agreements and simply be more alert to the many unilateral steps available to reduce the chances of a nuclear war (Nye, 1986).

Disagreement along the same lines continues about SDI. The Reagan administration refused to sacrifice SDI research, adding at Reykjavik the argument that strategic defenses would be vital to guard against cheating if we were ever to do away with nuclear weapons. In the field there is very little support for SDI other than as a hedge against Soviet research and as a bargaining chip (Osgood, 1986). In many quarters there is exasperation with the administration for pursuing a project that is technically unpromising and potentially destabilizing (for example, Lebow, 1986), and that would trade the stability of deterrence for the impossible dream of eliminating nuclear weapons (Schlesinger, 1987).

SDI has helped draw greater attention to the interplay between arms control and extended deterrence, and to the larger subject of involving allies in strategic arms control negotiations. It is widely believed that, as strategic arms control has numerous implications for allies' security and the old distinction between strategic and non-strategic nuclear weapons has broken down, the superpower negotiating format is becoming increasingly awkward. The close connection between START and the INF talks, the close consultation with allies that the INF talks required, and the planned increases in allied nuclear forces all seem to point toward the need for a multilateral negotiating forum. No one, however, has a ready answer for the fear that adding more cooks will spoil the broth.

CONCLUSION

No conclusive steps forward on a theory of arms control seem to have been made since the early 1960s. The supposed "lessons" of the 1970s that led to a retreat from the theory have not been borne out by the experience of the 1980s. Arms control turned out not to be dead or in deep trouble. The domestic political barriers in the United States have been significantly lowered. That detente is a prerequisite is not fully confirmed. It seems that sweeping agreements are more feasible than was thought. On numerous other matters there is little consensus in the field.

PATRICK M. MORGAN

The Reagan administration has pretty much done without the dominant perspectives of the field, initially by putting arms control efforts aside and denigrating past agreements, then by turning to SDI and a new conception of what strategic arms control should be about, and finally by pursuing agreements of unprecedented scope. Analysts have failed both to shape such developments and, with the exception of the first, to anticipate them. Strategic arms control remains basically a pragmatic operation with shallow roots in either strategy or theory.

An agenda for the field would therefore begin with the need to take up more systematically the problem of defining, in a theoretical sense, the role of arms control in international politics. Without such a perspective in hand, it is quite difficult for analysts to assess the importance of specific developments, whether in U.S.–Soviet relations or in other areas of the international system, for the prospects for arms control. Our answers to questions about what can be and should be done are now too often driven by a relatively shallow reading of recent events, and by references to past experience without the intellectual framework necessary to identify which aspects of that experience can be considered significant and which can be largely discounted. Many analysts have confined their calls for a better analytical perspective to the level of national strategy, citing the need to link American (and Western) arms control thinking and proposals to a better sense of what our national purposes are in the area of security. The field of security studies should seek to go further than this in devising a theoretical appreciation of arms control.

Next, we need to better integrate the study of arms control with the rest of the field of security studies in much the same way, as it is often said, that arms control needs to be integrated with national security policymaking. Many of the differing perspectives on strategic arms control can be traced back to divergent attitudes toward nuclear deterrence, the utility of military power, and the definition of national security in the nuclear age. It is impossible to have a separate theory of arms control that would be of any real assistance on either the intellectual or policy issues that are part of the subject.

Finally, recent experience suggests that the question of how arms control and politics interact needs to be reopened. The domestic politics of arms control is a subject worthy of further investigation, particularly with respect to the impact that a reform-minded general secretary or a visionary president can have. The relationship between strategic arms control and detente is still not clear. The political interplay among allies is certain to loom larger in the dynamics of arms control efforts in the future. Finally, it is not impossible that a general weariness with the seemingly endless security burdens of the superpowers may supersede cynical acceptance of things as they are as the most important facet of the political context within which arms control is pursued.

REFERENCES

Adelman, Kenneth L. 1984–1985. Arms Control With and Without Agreements. *Foreign Affairs*. 63, no. 2 (Winter): 240–63.

Bajusz, William. 1984–1987. Deterrence, Technology and Strategic Arms Control. *Adelphi Papers*, no. 215. London: International Institute for Strategic Studies.

Ball, Desmond. 1981. Can Nuclear War Be Controlled? *Adelphi Papers*, no. 169. London: International Institute for Strategic Studies.

————, et al., eds. 1987. *Crisis Stability and Nuclear War*. Ithaca, N.Y.: Cornell University Peace Studies Program.

Bertram, Christoph. 1978. Arms Control and Technological Change: Elements of a New Approach. *Adelphi Papers*, no. 146. London: International Institute for Strategic Studies.

Bhupendra, Jasani, ed. 1984. *Space Weapons—The Arms Control Dilemma*. London: Taylor and Francis.

Blacker, Coit. 1987. *Reluctant Warriors: The United States, The Soviet Union and Arms Control*. New York.: W. H. Freeman.

Blechman, Barry M. 1984. Do Negotiated Arms Limitations Have a Future? In Charles W. Kegley and Eugene R. Wittkopf, eds., *The Global Agenda: Issues and Perspectives*. New York.: Random House.

Bond, James. 1984. *The Rules of Riot: Internal Conflict and the Law of War*. Princeton N.J.: Princeton University Press.

Brennan, Donald, ed. 1961. *Arms Control, Disarmament and National Security*. New York: George Braziller.

Brodie, Bernard. 1959. *Strategy in the Missile Age*. Princeton, N.J.: Princeton University Press.

Bull, Hedley. 1961. *The Control of the Arms Race: Disarmament and Arms Control in the Missile Age*. New York: Praeger.

Burns, Richard Dean. 1977. *Arms Control and Disarmament, A Bibliography*. Santa Barbara: ABC-CLIO.

Burt, Richard. 1981. The Relevance of Arms Control in the 1980s. *Daedalus* 110, no. 1 (Winter 1981): 159–77.

————. 1986. Defense Policy and Arms Control: Defining the Problem. Pp. 187–210 in Bernard F. Halloran, ed., *Essays on Arms Control and National Security*. Washington, D.C.: Arms Control and Disarmament Agency. The article originally appeared in 1982.

Cimbala, Stephen J., ed. 1986. *Strategic War Termination*. New York: Praeger.

Committee on Foreign Affairs, House of Representatives. 1982. *Strategic Arms Control and U.S. National Security Policy*. Washington, D.C.: U.S. Government Printing Office.

Doty, Paul. 1987. A Nuclear Test Ban. *Foreign Affairs* 65, no. 4, (Spring): 750–69.

Drell, Sidney D. 1980. Arms Control: Is There Still Hope? *Daedalus* 109, no. 4 (Fall): 177–88.

————. 1986. What Has Happened to Arms Control? In Catherine McArdle Kelleher et al., eds. *Nuclear Deterrence: New Risks, New Opportunities*. Washington, D.C.: Pergamon-Brassey.

Dunn, Lewis A. 1982. *Controlling the Bomb*. New Haven, Conn: Yale University Press.

Fascell, Dante B. 1987. Congress and Arms Control. *Foreign Affairs* 65, no. 4 (Spring): 730–49.

Feiveson, Harold A., Richard H. Ullman, and Frank von Hippel. 1987. Reducing U.S. and Soviet Nuclear Arsenals. Pp. 311–24 in Len Ackland and Steven McGuire, eds., *Assessing the Nuclear Age*. Chicago: University of Chicago Press.

Forsberg, Randall. 1987. Abolishing Ballistic Missiles: Pros and Cons. *International Security* 12, no. 1 (Summer): 190–96.

———. 1987. Parallel Cuts in Conventional Forces. Pp. 285–93 in Len Ackland and Steven McGuire, eds., *Assessing the Nuclear Age*. Chicago: University of Chicago Press.

Freedman, Lawrence. 1981. *The Evolution of Nuclear Strategy*. New York: St. Martin's Press.

Friedberg, Aaron L. 1984. What SALT Can (and Cannot) Do. Pp. 121–28 in Bernard F. Halloran, ed., *Essays on Arms Control and National Security*. Washington, D.C.: Arms Control and Disarmament Agency. The article originally appeared in 1979.

Friedman, Leon. 1972. *The Law of War, A Documentary History*. Vol. 1. New York.: Random House.

Garnett, John. 1979. Disarmament and Arms Control Since 1945. Pp. 187–217. Lawrence Martin, ed., *Strategic Thought in the Nuclear Age*. Baltimore: Johns Hopkins University Press.

Garthoff, Raymond L. 1978. Mutual Deterrence and Strategic Arms Limitation in Soviet Policy. *International Studies* 3, no. 1, (Summer): 112–47.

———. 1985. *Detente and Confrontation*. Washington, D.C.: Brookings Institution.

George, Alexander, and Richard Smoke. 1974. *Deterrence in American Foreign Policy: Theory and Practice*. New York: Columbia University Press.

Gottemoeller, Rose E. 1986. Soviet Arms Control Decision Making Since Brezhnev. Pp. 86–113 in Roman Kolkowicz and Ellen Propper Mickiewicz, eds., *The Soviet Calculus of Nuclear War*. Lexington, Mass.: Lexington Books.

Graubard, Stephen R. 1980. Preface to the Issue: 'U.S. Defense Policy in the 1980s'. *Daedalus* 109, no. 4 (Fall): V–XV.

Gray, Colin S. 1980. Strategic Stability Reconsidered. *Daedalus* 109, no. 4 (Fall): 135–54.

———. 1984. Arms Control: Problems. Pp. 154–69 in R. James Woolsey, ed., *Nuclear Arms: Ethics, Strategy, Politics*. San Francisco: ICS Press.

Holloway, David. 1980. Military Power and Political Purpose in Soviet Policy. *Daedalus* 109, no. 4 (Fall): 13–30.

———. 1983. *The Soviet Union and the Arms Race*. New Haven, Conn.: Yale University Press.

Holsti, K. J. 1980. Change in the International System: Interdependence, Integration, and Fragmentation. In Ole Holsti et al., eds., *Change in the International System*. Boulder, Colo.: Westview Press.

Hoover, Robert A. 1986. Strategic Arms Limitation Negotiations and U.S. Decision Making. Pp. 93–114 in Wolfram Hanrieder, ed., *Technology, Strategy and Arms Control*. Boulder, Colo.: Westview Press.

Howard, Michael. 1983. *The Causes of Wars*. London: Unwin Paperbacks.

Intriligator, Michael, and Dagobert Brito. 1987. Arms Control: Problems and Prospects.

Institute on Global Conflict and Cooperation Research Paper, no. 2. San Diego: University of California.

Kaplan, Fred. 1983. *The Wizards of Armageddon*. New York: Simon and Schuster.

Kattenburg, Paul M. 1985. MAD Is the Moral Position. Pp. 77–84 in Charles W. Kegley, Jr., and Eugene R. Wittkopf, eds., *The Nuclear Reader*. New York: St. Martin's Press.

Keen, M. H. 1965. *The Laws of War in the Late Middle Ages*. London: Routledge and Kegan Paul.

Kennan, George. 1982. *The Nuclear Delusion*. New York: Pantheon Books.

Keohane, Robert. 1984. *After Hegemony: Cooperation and Discord in the World Political Economy*. Princeton, N.J.: Princeton University Press.

Kim, Samuel. 1984. *The Quest for a Just World Order*. Boulder, Colo.: Westview Press.

Knorr, Klaus. 1985. Controlling Nuclear War. *International Security* 9, no. 4 (Spring): 79–98.

Krass, Allen. 1985. *Verification, How Much Is Enough?* Lexington, Mass.: Lexington Books.

Kruzel, Joseph J. 1981. Arms Control and American Defense Policy: New Alternatives and Old Realities. *Daedalus* 110, no. 1. (Winter 1981): 137–57.

———. 1986. Arms Control: What's Wrong with the Traditional Approach. Pp. 235–50 in Paul R. Viotti, ed., *Conflict and Arms Control: An Uncertain Agenda*. Boulder, Colo.: Westview Press.

Lebow, Richard Ned. 1986. Assured Strategic Stupidity: The Quest For Ballistic Missile Defense. Pp. 65–92 in Wolfram Hanrieder, ed., *Technology, Strategy and Arms Control*. Boulder, Colo.: Westview Press.

Liddell Hart, B. H. 1947. *The Revolution in Warfare*. New Haven, Conn.: Yale University Press.

Lodal, Jan M. 1980. Deterrence and Nuclear Strategy. *Daedalus* 109, no. 4 (Fall): 155–75.

Luttwak, Edward. 1978. Why Arms Control Has Failed. *Commentary* (January): 19–28.

Mandelbaum, Michael. 1987. Uncertainty of the Status Quo. Pp. 285–93 in Len Ackland and Steven McGuire, eds., *Assessing the Nuclear Age*. Chicago: University of Chicago Press.

May, Michael M., and John R. Harvey. 1987. Nuclear Operations and Arms Control. Pp. 704–35 in Ashton Carter et al., eds., *Managing Nuclear Operations*. Washington, D.C.: Brookings Institution.

Miller, Steven E., ed. 1984. *The Nuclear Weapons Freeze and Arms Control*. Cambridge, Mass.: Ballinger.

———. 1984. Politics Over Promise: Domestic Impediments to Arms Control. *International Security* (Spring): 67–90.

Morgan, Patrick. 1986. Elements of a General Theory of Arms Control. In Paul Viotti, ed., *Conflict and Arms Control: An Uncertain Agenda*. Boulder, Colo.: Westview Press.

Newhouse, John. 1973. *Cold Dawn: The Story of SALT*. New York: Holt, Rinehart and Winston.

Nitze, Paul. 1986. Assuring Strategic Stability in an Era of Detente. Pp. 91–120 in Bernard F. Halloran, ed., *Essays on Arms Control and National Security*. Washington, D.C.: Arms Control and Disarmament Agency. The article originally appeared in 1976.

Nye, Joseph. 1986. Arms Control and the Prevention of War. Pp. 255–72 in Edward F. Halloran, ed., *Essays on Arms Control and National Security*. Washington, D.C.: Arms Control and Disarmament Agency.

Osgood, Robert E. 1986. Arms Control, A Skeptical Appraisal and a Modest Proposal. *Foreign Policy Briefs*, Johns Hopkins Foreign Policy Institute. Washington, D.C.

Payne, Samuel B. 1980. *The Soviet Union and SALT*. Cambridge, Mass.: MIT Press.

Perle, Richard. 1987. Reykjavik as a Watershed in U.S.-Soviet Arms Control. *International Security* 12, no. 1 (Summer): 175–78.

Pipes, Richard. 1980. Militarism and the Soviet State. *Daedalus* 109, no. 4 (Fall): 1–12.

Potter, William C., ed. 1985. *Verification and Arms Control*. Lexington, Mass.: Lexington Books.

Questor, George. 1986. *The Future of Nuclear Deterrence*. Lexington, Mass.: Lexington Books.

Schelling, Thomas. C. 1985–1986. What Went Wrong with Arms Control? *Foreign Affairs* 64, no. 2, (Winter):219–33.

———. 1987. Abolition of Ballistic Missiles. *International Security* 12, no. 1 (Summer):179–83.

———, and Morton Halperin. 1985. *Strategy and Arms Control*, 2nd ed. Washington, D.C.: Pergamon-Brassey.

Schlesinger, James. 1987. Reykjavik and Revelations: A Turn of the Tide? *Foreign Affairs: America and the World 1986* 65, no. 3: 423–46.

Sloan, Anne T. 1986. Soviet Positions on Strategic Arms Control and Arms Policy: A Perspective Outside the Military Establishment. Pp. 115–41 in Roman Kolkowicz and Ellen Propper Mickiewicz, eds., *The Soviet Calculus of Nuclear War*. Lexington, Mass.: Lexington Books.

Slocombe, Walter B. 1984. Arms Control: Prospects. Pp. 184–89 in R. James Woolsey, ed., *Nuclear Arms: Ethics, Strategy, Politics*. San Francisco: ICS Press.

Sloss, Leon. 1987. A World Without Ballistic Missiles. *International Security* 12, no. 1 (Summer): 184–89.

Stanley Foundation. 1986. Redefining Arms Control. Report of a Vantage Conference, May 1–3, 1986. Muscatine, Iowa: Stanley Foundation.

Steinbruner, John. 1985. Arms Control. *Foreign Affairs* 63, no. 5 (Summer): 1036–49.

Towle, Phillip. 1983. *Arms Control and East-West Relations*. New York.: St. Martin's Press.

Tsipis, Kosta, et al., eds. 1986. *Arms Control Verification*. Washington, D.C.: Pergamon-Brassey.

Wohlstetter, Albert. 1959. The Delicate Balance of Terror. *Foreign Affairs* (January).

Wolfe, Thomas W. 1979. *The SALT Experience*. Cambridge, Mass.: Ballinger.

World Politics. 1985. October. The issue is devoted to cooperation under anarchy.

13

On Nuclear Proliferation[1]

WILLIAM C. POTTER

OVERVIEW OF THE PROBLEM

Five nations—the United States, the Soviet Union, Great Britain, France, and China—are known to possess nuclear weapons in their military arsenals. India detonated a single nuclear device in 1974 but has not conducted further tests or developed nuclear weapons. Although no other states have demonstrated the ability to construct and detonate a nuclear explosive, an increasing number of states have advanced to the nuclear "twilight zone" in which absence of operational nuclear weapons is more a function of political will than of technical know-how. One prominent analyst suggests that for many countries a time schedule rather than a formal nuclear or non-nuclear designation best describes nuclear weapons status (Schelling, 1976). If a country can manufacture or deploy a nuclear bomb within a short period (e.g., during a crisis), other states have to regard it as having a nuclear option. Israel is most frequently cited in this connection, but Pakistan, South Korea, South Africa, and Taiwan are candidates in terms of their perceived security incentives and probable possession of or access to requisite technical skills and nuclear materials. Indeed, if one chooses to emphasize technical capabilities, one can identify over a dozen non-nuclear weapon states with nuclear power reactors in operation, each capable of generating enough by-product plutonium annually for over a dozen nuclear weapons.[2] Five of these countries are not parties to the 1968 Non-Proliferation Treaty (Argentina, Brazil, Israel, Pakistan, and South Africa), and others, though formal parties to the treaty, are "pariah" states or are plagued by domestic and regional security problems (e.g., Taiwan and South Korea).

Capability does not imply the likelihood that it will be exercised. Germany and Japan are representatives of a larger body of states with very sophisticated nuclear technologies which for political reasons have chosen to forego nuclear weapons. Over 100 states have formally renounced their intention of acquiring nuclear weapons by ratifying the Non-Proliferation Treaty (NPT). These states also have pledged under Article III of the NPT to accept international safeguards for the explicit purpose of preventing diversion of nuclear material and technology from peaceful use to the production of nuclear weapons. The adequacy of these safeguards is subject to much debate and most likely would not deter a state determined to obtain nuclear explosives. Support for the non-proliferation objectives of the NPT is nevertheless widespread, as is the belief that international safeguards are a useful, if imperfect, means to deter the diversion of nuclear materials.

Until recently, most attention has been directed toward containing the spread of nuclear weapons to additional national governments. A growing proliferation concern, however, is that subnational or transnational groups, including terrorist organizations, could attain the capability to manufacture a nuclear explosive from stolen plutonium or highly enriched uranium (see Leventhal and Alexander, 1986, 1987). Much of the requisite technical knowledge for bomb design is available in the public literature. There is a growing cadre of individuals familiar with nuclear technology who could help assemble a crude nuclear bomb. The principal impediment, it is generally assumed, is acquisition of the nuclear material. This is a major obstacle for would-be nuclear terrorists since most nuclear power reactors use uranium well below the level of enrichment required for weapons.[3] The spent fuel produced by these reactors is also unsuitable because it is highly radioactive and normally contains plutonium isotopes that are undesirable for weapons purposes. It is unlikely that a terrorist organization, without access to costly and sophisticated reprocessing or enrichment facilities, could safely obtain the necessary nuclear material. This situation could change, however, if reprocessing and recycling of plutonium were introduced as a major part of the nuclear power fuel cycle. This is one of the fears expressed by those opposed to the commercial development of a plutonium-dependent breeder reactor program.

Mention should also be made of the problems associated with the global spread of nuclear energy facilities and the potential they present as surrogate nuclear weapons in time of war. The implications of the destruction of nuclear energy facilities in war are not well understood and until recently received surprisingly little attention in the public literature (Ramberg, 1984). What is known suggests that nuclear energy plants pose some of the same threats as nuclear bombs. As the 1986 disaster at Chernobyl dramatically demonstrated, they pose the danger of releasing highly radioactive nuclear products over a wide area, even in the absence of a nuclear explosion. They have the unusual property of conferring nuclear destructive power not to the host of the nuclear installation but to any party able to target it with the proper conventional weapons. Although destruction would not be an easy task given the normal containment of commercial nuclear reactors in structures made of reinforced concrete designed to withstand the impact of a jetliner, it is made possible by conventional penetrating weapons able to burrow through yards of concrete before releasing their charge. Israel's attack on Iraq's nuclear facility demonstrated that this is a real policy option. It also underscored the "lightning rod effect" that vulnerable reactors share with poorly defended nuclear forces. Both present a tempting first-strike target.

THE CONSEQUENCES OF PROLIFERATION

Implicit in almost all discussions of nuclear proliferation is the assumption that it is undesirable. That is the perspective in this analysis. It is important, however, to make explicit the logic underlying this perspective and to recognize alternative assessments. Although U.S. decision-makers and scholars have generally viewed proliferation negatively, there is a minority view. Fred Iklé once suggested that the spread of nuclear weapons might actually reduce the risk of nuclear war by making the superpowers less likely to intervene in local conflicts (Iklé, 1966).[4] Morton Kaplan described a theoretical "unit veto" international system in which deterrence results when each actor possesses the capability to destroy any other actor (Kaplan, 1957). A similar argument is that the spread of nuclear weapons may create regional balances that approximate the relatively stable U.S.-Soviet strategic relationship (Brito and Intriligator, 1983; Waltz, 1981). It has been suggested that the possible existence of Israeli nuclear weapons had a moderating effect on Arab decision-makers in 1973 and that "an overtly nuclearized Middle East strategic balance might facilitate a future political settlement between the Arabs and Israelis" (Dunn, 1977, p. 12; see also Feldman, 1982, and Rosen, 1976). Nuclear proliferation from this perspective induces governments to behave in a more prudent fashion. It is also suggested that nuclear weapons may act as a great equalizer, enabling middle-range states to achieve minimal deterrence against the superpowers. Finally, there is the view which denies that nuclear weapons have had any major impact, good or bad, on international politics. Possession of nuclear weapons, it is argued, does not induce more prudent behavior; it merely reinforces existing patterns of international conduct (Organski, 1968, pp. 334–47).

These arguments can be challenged on a number of grounds. The argument that nuclear weapons would create regional balances analogous to the U.S.-Soviet relationship ignores the fact that, to the extent that a deterrence relationship characterizes U.S.-Soviet relations, it is probably more delicate than stable and represents a theoretical goal not yet violated rather than a description of the actual relationship. Moreover, conditions usually cited as responsible for stability in U.S.–Soviet relations (e.g., invulnerable second-strike forces, established systems of command and control, domestic political stability, and relative satisfaction with the status quo) are conspicuously absent in most potential Nth country strategic situations. In their stead are apt to be small and vulnerable nuclear forces with tenuous systems of command and control. The existence of nuclear weapons under these circumstances, rather than enhancing deterrence stability, would serve as an incentive for preemptive attack and promote crisis instability. As illustrated by the Israeli raid on Iraq's nuclear facility, the danger of preemption can be acute even for a state that is perceived by its adversary to have embarked on a nuclear weapons program.

Even if new nuclear forces were modeled after the U.S. and Soviet strategic arsenals, the probability of their use would rise through the greater opportunity for mechanical accidents, unauthorized demonstration, strategic miscalculation, and the escalation of conventional conflict to nuclear war. Indeed, the record of U.S. and Soviet experience with nuclear weapons provides few reasons for optimism regarding nuclear safety or nuclear restraint.

A further problem posed by proliferation is that negotiating meaningful international restraints will probably be more difficult. Negotiating restraints between even two relatively equal nuclear powers is very difficult. An increase in the number of nuclear armed states would almost certainly compound the problems, even if the proliferators did not partake directly in the negotiating process. The planned modernization of British and French nuclear forces currently has this effect.

Identification of the major hazards of proliferation does not by itself answer the question of whether potential gains from a vigorous anti-proliferation effort outweigh the political costs. That requires additional information about the non-proliferation objectives of policymakers and their place in the broader scheme of domestic and foreign policy strategy. One can also argue that the question is academic. Some analysts contend that the real issue is not *if* the dam will burst but *when* and *in what fashion*. In any case, the risks of proliferation are substantial. Although it may be impractical to halt permanently or reverse the process of nuclear proliferation, there appears to be merit in the argument that the fewer the number of proliferators and the longer the delay in proliferation, the better (Wohlstetter, 1977a).

PROLIFERATION DETERMINANTS

One of the most influential essays on nuclear non-proliferation adopts as its guiding principle Florence Nightingale's admonition that "Whatever else hospitals do they should not spread disease" (Wohlstetter, 1976, p. 1). Retarding the spread of nuclear weapons, however, implies some knowledge of its causes. Although prescriptions for non-proliferation abound, surprisingly little is known about the conditions affecting national decisions to "go nuclear" or to acquire the capabilities to do so. Even more tenuous is our knowledge of how attempts to fill these prescriptions by means of exhortation, example, rewards, and/or punishment may affect other significant foreign policy objectives.

Table 13.1 provides a list of factors often cited as proliferation determinants.[5] This list distinguishes among hypothesized national prerequisites (i.e., necessary conditions), underlying pressures and constraints, and more transitory situational variables.

National Prerequisites

The ability to predict national postures toward proliferation based on national economic wealth, scientific expertise, and technological skills has been eroded by the increased accessibility on a global scale of both nuclear technology and fissile material. This has led some analysts to abandon the notion of indigenous prerequisites or necessary conditions for proliferation. There is, for example, the school of thought which substitutes "technological imperative" for national technical prerequisites. According to this perspective, once a nation acquires the physical ability to manufacture nuclear weapons it will inevitably do so.[6] Herbert York's commentary in reference to reports of a Japanese atomic weapons program in World War II illustrates this viewpoint:

...the Japanese story completes the set, that every nation that might plausibly have started nuclear weapons programs did so: Germany, Great Britain, the United States, the Soviet Union, France, and we now know, Japan. So the case has been weakened for those who have argued that governments, or more precisely, generals, emperors, and presidents can hold back from this decision and say "No." The decision to develop nuclear weapons is but a general technological imperative (Shapely, 1978, p. 155).

An alternative and less deterministic conception emphasizes the "synergistic link" between civilian nuclear power and nuclear weapons and assumes that national energy needs, international commerce in nuclear technology, and technology diffusion pressures are critical "contextual variables" that affect the calculus of the nuclear weapons decision (Kegley et al., 1980). These are also among the factors singled out by advisers to the Ford and Carter administrations as critical elements that could be manipulated to influence the balance of proliferation incentives and constraints abroad and to create a more proliferation-resistant international nuclear regime (see Wohlstetter et al., 1977b; Nye, 1978).

UNDERLYING PRESSURES AND CONSTRAINTS

One method to sort out the different pressures and constraints on the decision to demonstrate a nuclear explosive capacity is to group them according to the relative importance of internal or external considerations and

Table 13.1
Hypothesized Proliferation Determinants

Determinants	Orientation	Illustrative Sources[a]
I. *National Prerequisites*		
Economic wealth	Internal	Bull (1961)
		Schwab (1969)
Latent capacity		Meyer (1984)
Scientific and technological expertise		Barnaby (1969)
II. *Underlying Pressures*		
Deterrence	External	Beaton and Maddox (1962)
		Donnelly (1984)
		Dunn and Kahn (1976)
		Epstein (1977)
		Greenwood (1977)
		Meyer (1984)
		Molander and Nichols (1985)
		OTA (1977)
		Quester (1973)
		Rosecrance (1964)
		Schoettle (1976)
Warfare advantage and defense	External	(same as for Deterrence)
Weapon of last resort	External	Dunn and Kahn (1976)
		Haselkorn (1974)
		Harkavy (1977)
		OTA (1977)
Coercion	External	Dunn and Kahn (1976)
International status/ prestige	External	(same as for Deterrence)
Assertion of autonomy and influence	External	Beaton and Maddox (1962)
		Epstein (1977)
		Kapur (1979)
		Meyer (1984)
		OTA (1977)
		Rosecrance (1964)
		Schoettle (1976)
Economic spillover	Internal	Beaton and Maddox (1962)
		Dunn and Kahn (1976)
		Epstein (1977)
		Greenwood (1977)

Table 13.1 continued

Determinants	Orientation	Illustrative Sources[a]
		Meyer(1984)
		OTA (1977)
		Quester (1973)
		Rosecrance (1964)
Domestic politics	Internal	Donnelly (1984)
		Dunn and Kahn (1976)
		Kapur (1979)
		Meyer (1984)
		OTA (1977)
Technological momentum	Internal	Dunn and Kahn (1976)
		Rosecrance (1964)
		Scheinman (1964)
III. *Underlying Constraints*		
Military reaction by other states	External	Dunn and Kahn (1976)
		Epstein (1977)
		Greenwood (1977)
		Meyer (1984)
		OTA (1977)
		Quester (1973)
The strategic credibility gap	External	Dunn and Kahn (1976)
		Epstein (1977)
		Greenwood (1977)
		OTA (1977)
		Quester (1973)
		Rosecrance (1964)
Absence of perceived threat	External	Quester (1973)
		Rosecrance (1964)
International and legal commitments and norms	External	Council on Foreign Relations (1986)
		Donnelly (1984)
		Epstein (1977)
		Greenwood (1977)
		Meyer (1984)
		Quester (1973)
Economic and political sanctions	External	Dunn and Kahn (1976)
		Epstein (1977)
		Greenwood (1977)
		OTA (1977)
Unauthorized seizure	Internal	Dunn and Kahn (1976)
		Greenwood (1977)
		Meyer (1984)
		OTA (1977)

Table 13.1 continued

Determinants	Orientation	Illustrative Sources[a]
Economic costs	Internal	Dunn and Kahn (1976) Greenwood (1977) OTA (1977) Quester (1973)
Public opinion	Internal	Dunn and Kahn (1976) Greenwood (1977) OTA (1977) Quester (1973)
Bureaucratic politics	Internal	Betts (1980) Kapur (1979) Rosecrance (1964)
IV. *Situational Variables*		
International crisis	External	Dunn and Kahn (1976)
Weakening of security guarantees	External	Dunn and Kahn (1976) Greenwood (1977) Lefever (1979) OTA (1977) Rosecrance (1964) Willrich (1976)
Increased accessibility of nuclear materials	Internal/ External	Dunn and Kahn (1976) Ford/Mitre (1977) Meyer (1984) Wohlstetter et al. (1979)
Vertical proliferation	External	Kapur (1979) Schwab (1969)
Domestic crisis and leadership change	Internal	Council on Foreign Relations (1986) Dunn and Kahn (1976) Kapur (1979)

[a] Source: This table draws on the categorizations provided by Kegley et al. (1980), p. 235, and Meyer (1984), pp. 64 and 102.

of military or political-economic objectives. This yields four broad clusters of proliferation incentives and disincentives, labeled here as factors of international security, international politics, domestic security, and domestic politics (see Figure 13.1).

Figure 13.1
Underlying Pressures and Constraints on Proliferation

	Domestic	External
Military	Domestic Security	International Security
Political-economic	Domestic Political	International Political

International Security Incentives

Deterrence of Adversaries. A desire to deter external threats is often cited as an underlying international security incentive for proliferation. One finds arguments that the acquisition of nuclear weapons can afford a measure of deterrence against nuclear attack or blackmail by a superpower, conventional attack, and prospective acquisition of nuclear weapons by a regional rival (Dunn and Kahn, 1976; Epstein, 1977; Office of Technology Assessment, 1977; Lefever, 1979; and Greenwood, Feiveson, and Taylor, 1977).

Warfare Advantage. Nuclear weapons may also be sought as a means of achieving an advantage in war should deterrence fail. U.S. and British interest in the development of the atomic bomb, for example, can be attributed in large measure to their determination to wage war successfully against Germany. Small and middle-range powers might seek tactical nuclear weapons to help defend themselves in the absence of credible security guarantees by a superpower. Nuclear weapons, it has been suggested, might even be a stabilizing factor that would enable "any nation not now a nuclear power, and not harboring ambitions for territorial aggrandizement, to walk like a porcupine through the forest of international affairs: no threat to its neighbors, too prickly for predators to swallow" (Sandoval, 1976, p. 19). Although Taiwan and South Africa are most often thought of as potential proliferators interested in the tactical nuclear arms, debates in Switzerland and Sweden have in the past also centered on the role of battlefield nuclear weapons in a policy of armed neutrality.

Weapon of Last Resort. Related to "defense against invasion" is the motivation to possess a weapon of last resort—to be used only on the brink of total destruction and defeat. The rationale could be psychological and punitive ("if we are going to go, we'll take someone with us"), and tactical in the sense of being able to threaten convincingly escalation to a level in which the benefits to be achieved by the "victor" would be outweighed by the costs of "total victory."

Coercion. Nuclear blackmail, intimidation of non-nuclear regional adversaries, and even use of nuclear weapons in a "preventive first strike" may be perceived as desirable by leaders of certain "crazy states" as well as those facing a long-term deterioration of their security vis-à-vis non-nuclear opponents (Dror, 1971).

International Security Disincentives

Hostile Reactions of a Military Nature by Adversaries and Allies. The anticipated hostile response of an adversary might range from the threat of military action to overt military operations designed to destroy an incipient nuclear weapons force and production capability. A country contemplating proliferation may also be dissuaded by fear of provoking an adversary to follow suit, resulting in a costly race without any increase in security. Hostile allied responses might take the form of a reduction or severance of established security guarantees and the disruption of the supply of important conventional armaments.

The Strategic Credibility Gap. The difficulty of obtaining the technical components of a credible nuclear deterrent (e.g., secure second-strike forces, effective systems of command and control, and reliable delivery vehicles) may diminish the attraction of nuclear weapons. An embryonic and poorly defended nuclear force, it can be urged, serves as an incentive for a preemptive strike and a source of crisis instability.

Absence of Perceived Security Threat. Absence of a hostile international environment, or more precisely, the perception of it by a nation's leadership could be a disincentive. Even in a threatening international milieu, security guarantees from a powerful ally might reduce the pressure to develop an independent nuclear deterrent.

International Political Incentives

Increased International Status. Nuclear weapons are a symbol of scientific expertise and technological development. They are almost synonymous with great power status (although arguably not the primary cause for a great power's international standing) and are viewed by many states as a source of international prestige and autonomy. Aside from bolstering a nation's self-confidence, nuclear weapons may engender both fear and respect from neighbors and adversaries.

Studies indicate that prestige and influence are particularly important incentives for potential Third World proliferators (Kapur, 1979; Poulose, 1979). Nuclear weapons may appear as a useful lever in North-South politics and as a means of commanding the attention of the industrialized states and prompting greater economic assistance and political support. As one study notes, "the developing states probably did not overlook the fact that India's economic aid from the Western industrial states was increased by some $200 million less than a month after its nuclear explosion" (Greenwood, 1977, p. 51).

Increased Autonomy. A nuclear weapons capability may be sought to enhance intra-alliance influence and international freedom of action and to exert greater influence on regional security arrangements and in international political forums (Office of Technology Assessment, 1977, p. 94; Greenwood, 1977). Development of the French *force de frappe,* for example, has been explained this way (Dunn and Kahn, 1976, pp. 3–4).

International Political Disincentives

International Norms. The third Non-Proliferation Treaty (NPT) Review Conference in 1985 affirmed "its determination to strengthen further the barriers against the proliferation of nuclear weapons and other nuclear explosive devices to additional States" (Final Document, 1985, Annex 1, p. 2). Moreover, well over 100 nations remain parties to the NPT, which explicitly states that proliferation would seriously increase the danger of nuclear war. This norm is also embodied in the Treaty of Tlatelolco (Redick, 1981) and the safeguard statutes of the International Atomic Energy Agency, and is reflected in the efforts of politically diverse states such as the Soviet Union and the United States to restrict exports of sensitive nuclear technology and fuel cycle components (see Potter, 1985). Although some countries may assume treaty membership and a public non-proliferation stance to conceal their real nuclear weapons ambitions, such international treaty commitments are usually not undertaken lightly or easily repudiated. It may even be that "the political commitments involved in the acceptance of the NPT and IAEA safeguards are as important as the accompanying physical constraints" (Greenwood, 1977).

Economic and Political Sanctions by Other States. Fear of reprisals may serve as another disincentive. This concern is apt to be greatest among nations that depend heavily on the superpowers for economic assistance and technological aid. Would-be proliferators also run the risk of censure and sanctions by international organizations.

Domestic Security Incentives and Disincentives

The literature on nuclear proliferation does not indicate any domestic security incentives for acquiring a nuclear weapons capability. The risk of unauthorized seizure of nuclear weapons, however, may be a domestic security disincentive, especially for countries subject to frequent political upheavals and domestic turmoil (Kapur, 1980).

Several scenarios involving unauthorized acquisition of nuclear weapons have been suggested. One involves the seizure of all or part of a nation's nuclear weapons by revolutionary groups or terrorists for the purpose of political blackmail (Office of Technology Assessment, 1977, p. 98). Another identifies the military as a possible threat in a "nuclear coup d'etat" (Dunn, 1978; see also Spector, 1987).

Domestic Political Incentives

Economic Spillover. The economic potential of peaceful nuclear explosions (PNEs) was heralded in the 1950s as part of President Eisenhower's "Atoms for Peace" program. The U.S. government and industry spent over $200 million to explore use of nuclear explosions in excavations of canals and harbors, production of oil from shale, and gas and oil stimulation. Although most U.S. analysts became convinced that PNEs were not cost-effective and/ or posed significant environmental hazards, many potential proliferators at least profess the view that PNEs have substantial economic promise. This is sometimes cited as an incentive to develop a nuclear explosive capability.

Bureaucratic and Domestic Politics. The literature on nuclear proliferation tends to emphasize rational decision-making and the maximization of national interests. One can discern, however, domestically oriented pressures to go nuclear which may be difficult to justify from a national perspective. These include pressures from various industrial, scientific, and military groups that would stand to benefit from an expensive nuclear program; broad-based public support for an independent nuclear force; and pressure from politicians anxious to divert attention from other domestic and foreign policy failures.

Technological Momentum. Development of nuclear weapons may also result from technological momentum in which the technological feasibility of the project takes precedence over the military or political necessity of the task and in which a formal decision to go ahead may in fact be lacking. The phenomenon of "technological creep" may also be in effect, in which significant progress is achieved by incremental advances in different fields without a formal decision to develop a nuclear explosive. It is reported, for example, that lower level French scientists and bureaucrats took major steps toward developing nuclear weapons before being directed to do so by the national leadership (Office of Technology Assessment, 1977, p. 100).

Domestic Political Disincentives

Cost. The economic cost may be prohibitive, not just the actual expenditures but also the opportunity costs of diverting monetary and personnel resources from other projects (Dunn and Kahn, 1976). However, perceived costs may diminish with the growth of civilian nuclear power and "the concurrent decline in the incremental cost associated with a weapons program" (Office of Technology Assessment, 1977, p. 96; see also Graham, 1983).

Public Opinion. Adverse domestic opinion may also serve as a constraint. In Japan, West Germany, Sweden, and Canada, for example, public opposition could have a decided effect on nuclear weapon decisions. The fear of adverse public opinion, on the other hand, might be marginal for many non-democratic developing nations.

Bureaucratic Politics. The play of bureaucratic politics may be a disincentive. Competition for scarce resources could produce an alignment of bureaucratic actors opposed to the creation of new institutions and potential competitors. The military, for example, might oppose a nuclear weapons program perceived as likely to interfere with the funding of preferred weapons systems or to shift the distribution of the military fiscal pie. Here, one can also include any opposition to the acquisition of nuclear weapons by key individuals owing to their personal philosophical convictions (Nehru is the most frequently cited example) or calculations of self-interest.

SITUATIONAL VARIABLES

Regardless of the role they attribute to national prerequisites for proliferation (i.e., *necessary* conditions), most analyses of nuclear weapons choice imply the operation of two sets of *sufficient conditions:* (1) the balance between underlying proliferation incentives and disincentives and (2) the presence of one or more situational factors that might precipitate a decision to go nuclear whenever incentives outweigh constraints. The most widely cited potential "trigger events" are summarized below.

International Crisis. A variety of international crisis situations have been identified as possible precipitants. Most commonly mentioned is nuclearization of another state, particularly a neighbor or regional rival. An action-reaction dynamic is assumed to operate in which one nation's decision to go nuclear intensifies an adversary's sense of insecurity and simultaneously reduces the psychological and political barriers to proliferation. A widely shared nuclear taboo, for example, might be weakened, altering the balance in the domestic debate over possessing nuclear weapons (Wohlstetter et al., 1979, pp. 138–39; Dunn and Kahn, 1976, p. 8). More generally, a crisis may provide the opportunity to forge a new bureaucratic consensus in support of a decision to go nuclear (Dunn and Overholt, 1977, p. 11).

Weakening of Security Guarantees. Credible alliance guarantees by the superpowers are often credited with reducing proliferation incentives (Betts, 1980). Consequently, any diminution of those guarantees, or the perceived collapse of the superpowers' nuclear umbrellas, might lead to a decision to acquire nuclear weapons.

Increased Accessibility of Necessary Technology and Material. A necessary but not sufficient condition for proliferation is access to nuclear technology and material. For some would-be proliferators, increased availability of these resources might trigger a decision.

Vertical Proliferation. The failure of the superpowers to implement their promise in the NPT to undertake effective measures to halt the nuclear arms race has been a major complaint of non-nuclear parties to the NPT. The failure to negotiate a Comprehensive Test Ban and the accelerated U.S.–Soviet arms race in space has further increased this concern. This could bolster the case of *N*th country advocates of an independent nuclear force option.

Domestic Crisis and Leadership Change. It is sometimes suggested that domestic events might trigger a decision to go nuclear. These include political crises in which the leadership might attempt to capitalize on a nuclear weapons decision to restore popular confidence in the government, and a change in political leadership in favor of individuals committed to a nuclear weapons program (Dunn and Kahn, 1976, pp. 8–9).

THE TYPICAL PROLIFERATOR

The literature on determinants of proliferation consists primarily of case studies that emphasize the country-specific attributes of past and potential proliferators.[7] This literature yields an extensive list of variables that may influence a nation's nuclear weapons posture but provides little insight into the relative explanatory power of these variables. A preliminary comparative analysis is summarized in Table 13.2, with potential proliferation determinants applied to thirteen past and potential proliferators (see Potter, 1982, pp. 145–76).

Although the limited number of countries examined makes generalization hazardous, several hypotheses are suggested. One is the predominance of international over domestic pressures and constraints. Indeed, only in France was a domestic factor, bureaucratic momentum, identified as a primary underlying pressure for acquisition of nuclear weapons. The role of domestic factors as a primary disincentive is also rare. The only cases are India before Nehru's death (his personal philosophical opposition) and the Soviet Union in 1940 (opposition by entrenched senior scientists to nuclear research proposals of younger colleagues with less institutional power). In contrast, international factors appear as primary pressures in every case and as primary constraints in seven of the nine countries in which major underlying constraints were discerned. Our analysis also indicates that the primary incentives to acquire nuclear weapons have remained relatively unchanged over time.[8] Future studies might therefore profit from a closer examination of historical examples.

Although proliferation disincentives have also remained fairly constant—by far the most significant one being the anticipated reaction of other states—the absence of major or persisting political or security disincentives for the first five nuclear weapons states is highlighted by our comparative analysis. Stated somewhat differently, the major potential proliferators today, in contrast to the first members of the nuclear weapons club, appear to attach more importance to the anticipated political and military reactions of other states. Their greater sensitivity to external factors is not surprising given their lower ranking on most indices of international power.

Were it not for the case of France and, to a much lesser degree, India, one

Table 13.2
Summary of Proliferation Determinants

Country	Underlying Pressures		Underlying Constraints		Most likely Precipitants
	Primary Determinant	*Secondary Factor*	*Primary Determinant*	*Secondary Factor*	
Argentina	5,6	8	10,12,14	13,15	19
Brazil	5,6		10,12,14	13,15	19
Canada[a]	2		12,13	6,16,17	
France	5,6,9		19	16	
India	5,6	1,8,9	10,14	10,11,13,14,16	19,20,24
Israel	1,3	2,6	10,14	17	19,20,24
PRC	1,5,6			10,16,18	
Pakistan	1,2,6	8	10,14	11	19,21,22
South Korea[a]	1,2	6	10,14	15	21
Taiwan[a]	1,2,3,6	5	10,14	11	21,24
United Kingdom[a] (World War II)	2	7			20
(post-war)	5,6	9			20
United States[a]	2	9	18[b]		20
USSR[a]	1	9			19

Table 13.2 continued

Key:

1 Deterrence	13 International norms
2 Warfare advantage and defense	14 Economic and political sanctions
3 Weapon of last resort	15 Unauthorized seizure
4 Coercion	16 Economic costs
5 Status/prestige	17 Public opinion
6 Autonomy/influence	18 Bureaucratic politics
7 Economic spillover	19 Nuclearization of other states
8 Domestic politics	20 International crisis
9 Technological momentum	21 Weakening of security guarantees
10 Military reaction by other states	22 Increased accessibility of know-how/material
11 Strategic credibility gap	23 Vertical proliferation
12 Absence of perceived threat	24 Domestic crisis/leadership change

would be tempted to emphasize the existence of an acute security threat as the major factor that discriminates between necessary conditions (e.g., technical know-how and availability of fissile material and weapon fabrication facilities) and the determining or sufficient condition to "go nuclear." The perception of an acute security threat and the desire to achieve deterrence and/or warfare advantages were the major underlying pressures to acquire nuclear weapons for the United States, the Soviet Union, Great Britain (through 1945), China, and Israel. The change in threat perception (from crisis and severe military danger to relative security) also largely accounts for the reversal in Canadian interest in nuclear weapons. One can even argue that, although the post-war British decision to develop nuclear weapons was not directly stimulated by international security concerns, the atomic explosion in 1952 was simply the fulfillment of a task whose decision and momentum were established during the war (Rosecrance, 1964, p. 300).

One might infer that "near nuclear" states like Brazil and Argentina which are relatively free from international security challenges will be less inclined to opt for nuclear weapons than threatened states such as Pakistan, South Korea, and Taiwan. A difficulty with this interpretation—although on balance it is still probably correct—is that it discounts the example of France, where international security considerations were of secondary importance, and perhaps also India (depending on when one dates the Indian nuclear decision). It also probably does not attach sufficient importance to psychological and non-rational bureaucratic political determinants—dimensions which most proliferation studies inadequately tap. It is not coincidental that the two studies which stand out in their efforts to focus on bureaucratic politics—by Kapur and Scheinman—find considerations other than international security important in Indian and French nuclear decisions (Kapur, 1976; Scheinman, 1964).

It is possible to interpret our findings as consistent with the perspective that no *typical N*th country exists in terms of the mix of underlying pressures, constraints, and precipitating factors. However, this obscures the fact that a small number of variables appear to be of primary importance in nuclear weapon decisions. What appears to vary most is not the proliferation motivations or constraints, but the sequence in which political decisions to "go nuclear" precede, follow, or coincide with technological developments. In the French and Indian cases, technological developments preceded and paved the way for political decisions. The reverse sequence appears to have occurred in the Soviet Union and the People's Republic of China. Illustrative of a third pattern, in which technology and politics go hand in hand, are the cases of the United States and Great Britain during World War II.[9]

These different patterns and the very different levels of nuclear weapons capability sought and achieved by nations highlight the need to specify what is meant by "going nuclear." In particular, it may be useful to define this concept in a fashion that facilities the observation and measurement of po-

Figure 13.2
Ladder of Nuclear Weapons Capability

8   Secure C^3 and second-strike capability

7   Test thermonuclear explosion

6   Stockpile of atomic weapons

5   Test atomic explosion

4   Bomb in the basement

3   Access to unsafeguarded fissile material

2   Possession of research or power reactors

1   Nuclear weapons technical know-how and manufacturing capability

Although not included in the ladder because of difficulty in locating its hierarchical position, possession of a nuclear weapons delivery system is a critical component of a state's nuclear capability.

For alternative nuclear capability ladders, see Lewis A. Dunn and William H. Overholt, "The Next Phase in Nuclear Proliferation Research," in William H. Overholt, ed., *Asia's Nuclear Future* (Boulder, Colo.: Westview Press, 1977), p. 4, and Kathleen Bailey, "When and Why Weapons," *Bulletin of the Atomic Scientists* (April 1980): 43.

tentially meaningful differences in nuclear weapons behavior. In other words, to explain or influence a nation's nuclear weapons posture, it may be necessary to describe more carefully the dependent variable.

Traditionally, the acid test for going nuclear has been detonation of a single atomic explosion. The emphasis has been on the divide between nuclear and non-nuclear rather than on the disparities among those who have crossed the divide in terms of the number of subsequent detonations, the size of the nuclear arsenal, the availability of invulnerable and reliable delivery systems, and the articulation of a strategic doctrine.

An alternative means to conceptualize "going nuclear" is to think in terms of a range of nuclear decisions rather than a discrete event. Figure 13.2 provides such a conception for the thirteen states in our survey. At one end of the continuum, or ladder, are the two superpowers in possession of vast arsenals, reliable second-strike delivery vehicles, and sophisticated command, control, and communications (C^3) systems. At the other end are those states, such as South Korea, which probably have the technical know-how and industrial infrastructure to build and to detonate a nuclear device. In between, one finds the bulk of the states in our survey, some resting at readily identifiable heights such as India, and others, like Israel, more difficult to locate precisely.

A ladder of nuclear capability, similar to the one shown in Figure 13.2, may be of assistance in associating consequences of proliferation with specific stages of vertical proliferation. It may also direct attention to points along the vertical proliferation continuum which are most subject to external influence. A more adequate graphic representation of the process of going nuclear, however, should also depict the manner in which technical capabilities intersect with military and political pressures. An admittedly crude effort to do so is presented in Figure 13.3. Although one can quarrel with the precise location on the two axes of some states, the graph calls attention to the two dimensions of going nuclear—technical capabilities and the balance of military, political, and economic pressures and constraints. By compiling similar plots for different points in time, one can also capture the dynamic nature of the proliferation process.

STRATEGIES FOR CONTROL

Many strategies have been proposed to deal with proliferation. Most can be distinguished in terms of their emphasis on affecting the *demand* for versus the *supply* of weapons. Demand-oriented approaches are intended to reduce the incentives and to strengthen the disincentives to acquire nuclear weapons. Supply-oriented approaches, on the other hand, are designed to make it more difficult for a party seeking nuclear weapons to obtain them. The general characteristics and strengths and weaknesses of these approaches are discussed below, in an effort to assess their relative utility.[10]

DEMAND POLICIES

Reducing Incentives

International security concerns represent the principal nuclear incentives for many states. Among strategies often proposed to reduce security incentives to acquire nuclear weapons are the provision of conventional arms, superpower security guarantees, arms control measures, and fuel supply assurances.

1. Arms Transfers. Using arms transfers as an instrument of non-proliferation policy is founded on the premise that states with enough arms will gain confidence in their ability to defend themselves and have less reason to covet nuclear arms. Advocates of this approach can point to recent breakthroughs in conventional weapons technology providing increased accuracy and firepower which may enable advanced conventional weapons to assume certain military missions previously reserved for nuclear arms.

The arms transfer approach is the subject of considerable debate. States

Figure 13.3
Dual Dimensions of Proliferation for 1986

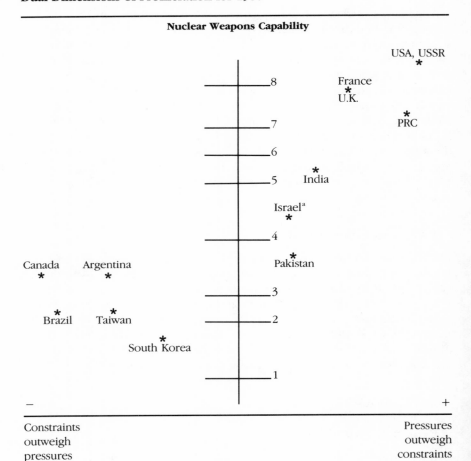

Nuclear Weapons Capability

USA, USSR
★

France
★
U.K.

PRC
★

India
★

Israel[a]
★

Pakistan
★

Canada   Argentina
★   ★

Brazil   Taiwan
★   ★

South Korea
★

8

7

6

5

4

3

2

1

−   +

Constraints   Pressures
outweigh   outweigh
pressures   constraints

[a]The testimony of Mordecai Vanunu in October 1986 suggests that Israel may have accumulated a substantial stockpile of nuclear weapons, some of which rely partly on nuclear fusion, without actually testing the weapons. See "Revealed: The Secrets of Israel's Nuclear Arsenal," *Sunday Times* (London), October 5, 1986.

most frequently mentioned as possible targets for a selective arms transfer strategy are Taiwan, South Korea, Pakistan, and Israel. For those and other countries, however, the goal of nonproliferation may come into conflict with other foreign policy objectives, including that of limiting regional arms races. The tension between containing nuclear proliferation and slowing conventional arms transfers has been called the "dove's dilemma" (Dunn, 1981; Husbands, 1980).

The use of conventional arms as a nonproliferation tactic entails risks. An influx of arms may increase regional instability by emboldening the recipient to assume a more belligerent posture and/or encouraging the recipient's adversary to escalate the arms race (perhaps even to the nuclear level) or to strike preemptively before the military balance has been changed. Arms transfers can also exacerbate the supplier's relations with other countries in the region without satiating the recipient's appetite for nuclear arms. The possibility exists, moreover, that even if security pressures were reduced, other compelling proliferation incentives would remain. There is also the risk that, although the leaders of proliferation-prone countries may accept the logic of the arms transfers/non-proliferation linkage and the implied dependence, they may not be able to fulfill their end of the bargain because of domestic politics and intra-governmental opposition.

Perhaps the most serious deficiency of most proposals to use arms transfers as an instrument of nonproliferation policy is the tendency to focus on narrow considerations of one Nth country's security dilemma in isolation from broader regional and international political issues. As one perceptive analyst points out, "most of the restraints on the potential use of arms transfers to ease proliferation pressures in Taiwan, South Korea, Pakistan, and South Africa result from U.S. policy goals rather than a desire to limit arms sales or aid." (Husbands, 1980, p. 42).

The preceding discussion does not point to a resolution of the dove's dilemma. Although the risks associated with arms transfers are great, they may be preferable to the introduction of nuclear weapons into a conflict-prone region. Before a determination of these relative risks can be made, it is essential, at a minimum, that an analysis be undertaken of (1) the Nth country's security perceptions and incentives to go nuclear; (2) its conventional defense capabilities and the impact arms transfers will have on them; and (3) its near-term capabilities to acquire nuclear weapons. Unless a judgment can be made that the Nth country's proliferation incentives are principally security-related, can be alleviated by the infusion of more arms, and can be translated into an operational nuclear weapons capability, an arms transfer non-proliferation strategy is apt to entail great risks but hold little prospect of success.

2. Security Guarantees. Another approach often discussed in conjunction with arms transfers is the extension of security guarantees by one or more of the nuclear weapons states. These guarantees may be in the form of the deployment in the Nth country of the guarantor's troops, military facilities, and weaponry (including nuclear arms and their delivery vehicles), formal alliances, or less formal commitments to ensure the territorial integrity of the Nth country.

The success of security guarantees, from a nonproliferation standpoint, has been mixed. On the one hand, security assurances from nuclear powers have been a prerequisite for many states to adhere to the NPT and to justify their decisions in the face of domestic opposition. Security guarantees appear to have been especially important for South Korea and Taiwan. Firm U.S. security assurances, on the other hand, have not kept Israel from moving to the threshold of nuclear weapons status. The formal American security commitment to Pakistan has also proved ineffective as a nonproliferation strategy. Moreover, American nuclear guarantees and the NATO umbrella failed to deter Great Britain and France from developing their own nuclear arsenal.

Although security guarantees may be successful in specific situations, the general applicability of the approach is constrained by a number of factors. Among the most important are the reluctance of potential guarantors to extend security guarantees that may entangle them in the *N*th country's foreign and domestic policy problems and the unwillingness of many *N*th countries to accept security guarantees if they entail the loss of control of certain aspects of their own domestic and external policies. The utility of security guarantees may also be compromised if they are directed against allies or states with whom the prospective guarantor seeks improved relations. At the end of 1979, for example, the United States judged it necessary to terminate its defense treaty with the Republic of China in the interest of improving relations with the People's Republic of China.

The difficulty of providing credible security guarantees should also be mentioned. Credibility is not something that can be produced by a treaty signature or solemn pledge. It results from past performances and the perception of strong and enduring common interests (Dowty, 1974, p. 21).

Finally, the use of security guarantees is subject to two caveats raised previously on arms transfers: (1) security-oriented approaches are irrelevant for *N*th countries whose primary motives for acquiring nuclear weapons are other than security; and (2) security guarantees must not be viewed in isolation from broader foreign policy objectives, some of which may be at odds with the extension of security commitments.

3. Arms Control Measures. International and regional arms control measures represent another approach. They tend to be directed at both the security and prestige motivations of potential proliferators and to emphasize the obligations of the nuclear powers under Article VI of the NPT to work for a cessation of the nuclear arms race at an early date and for nuclear disarmament. Among the more frequently proposed arms control measures are adoption of a comprehensive test ban (CTB) and creation of nuclear-free zones.

Proponents of a CTB cite both political and technical ways this would serve the cause of non-proliferation. Politically, they argue, a CTB would reduce the incentives to acquire nuclear weapons by demonstrating the nuclear powers' commitment to Article VI of the NPT (pursuit of "negotiations in good faith on effective measures relating to the cessation of the nuclear arms race at an early date"). Failure to make progress on the CTB front, it is argued, underscores the discriminatory aspect of the NPT and undermines the effectiveness of the nonproliferation regime (Blechman, 1981; Caldwell, 1980; Drell, 1978; York and Greb, 1979). The technical argument is that non-nuclear nations could not confidently develop a nuclear explosive without nuclear testing. A corollary is that in the absence of testing, design of an explosive would have to be more conservative and would require more fissionable material per weapon.

Those who oppose a CTB generally maintain that there is little, if any, connection between the arms race behavior of the superpowers and non-proliferation. In addition, they cite a litany of perceived adverse effects likely to accompany a comprehensive test ban. This list includes difficulties in verifying Soviet compliance with a CTB; problems of assuring the reliability of existing nuclear weapons without an ongoing testing program; the need to make weapons safer and more secure against accidents and misuse; the need to study the effects of nuclear explosives (e.g., in designing a ballistic missile defense system); the potential peaceful uses of nuclear explosives; the danger of losing trained personnel; and the problem of nuclear powers who refuse to take part in test ban negotiations (see Brennan, 1976; May, 1976).

It is not feasible here to assess the competing charges of proponents and critics of a CTB. However, there is much to Dan Caldwell's observation that "neither the claims of the ardent proponents nor the dire predictions of the hardline opponents accurately depict the most likely effect that a comprehensive test ban would have on proliferation [i.e., very little]. In all probability, the 'near' nuclear states" would remain ambiguously non-nuclear (Caldwell, 1980, p. 31).

If one assumes that a CTB would not affect near-nuclear states such as Israel, South Africa, and Pakistan, its major promise lies in making the superpowers' call for nuclear restraint more credible to other states, thereby reducing the political excuse, if not the primary incentive, to pursue a nuclear weapons program.[11] For parties that signed, the CTB would also raise the political costs of "going nuclear."

Nuclear-free zones constitute another arms control approach. Most nuclear-free zone proposals have been initiated by non-nuclear weapon states of the region concerned. Proposals tend to share the general objective of promoting regional peace and stability and the more specific goal of removing the region from competition between nuclear weapon states.

The idea of nuclear-free zones grew out of the German question in the 1950s and first found formal expression in the so-called Rapacki Plan to denuclearize Central Europe. Subsequent proposals have been made for the South Pacific, the Middle East, Mediterranean, Nordic countries, South Asia, Africa, the Balkans, and the Indian Ocean. The approach was also reflected in the Antarctic Treaty of 1959, the Outer Space Treaty of 1967, and the Seabed Treaty of 1971. The most significant nuclear-free zone in existence is provided by the 1967 Treaty for the Prohibition of Nuclear Weapons in Latin America, commonly known as the Treaty of Tlatelolco. The current status of the Tlatelolco regime and nonproliferation in Latin America illustrates both the potential and the problems of a nuclear-free zone approach.

Under the Treaty, currently in force for twenty-two Latin American states, parties have pledged to keep their territories entirely free of nuclear weapons. The Treaty also established an international agency to ensure compliance and a control system that includes application of International Atomic Energy Agency (IAEA) safeguards to all nuclear activities of the parties. The significance of this agency is diluted by the absence as full parties of the region's prime proliferation candidates, Argentina and Brazil.[12]

A major problem with the Treaty involves peaceful nuclear explosions (PNEs). Although most Latin American states have interpreted the Treaty as not permitting indigenously produced PNE, this interpretation has not been shared by Argentina and Brazil and is advanced as a major justification for their failure to adhere to the Treaty. Both states maintain that the key factor distinguishing a PNE from a weapon is the intent of the user.

It is difficult to judge the applicability of the Tlatelolco experience to other regions. Progress toward the Latin American nuclear-free zone was certainly facilitated by the coincidence of a number of circumstances: (1) the establishment of a legal instrument in advance of military-technological momentum (i.e., nuclear technology was not well established in Latin America in the 1960s); (2) the strong leadership and tenacity of Mexican Under-Secretary Garcia Robles; (3) the stimulus of the Cuban missile crisis in October 1962 (at which time the initial proposal for the Latin American nuclear-free zone was introduced); (4) the shared cultural and legal traditions of the region, as well as commonly held perceptions of a regional identity; and (5) the relative absence of superpower competition in the region (Redick, 1981, p. 100).

It is unlikely that these circumstances will be duplicated elsewhere. Perhaps most difficult to obtain will be a region relatively free of superpower competition and confrontation. The slow progress toward completion of the Treaty of Tlatelolco system, and the recent Treaty of Raratonga, nevertheless suggest the possibility of a nuclear-free zone if it enjoys general support of states in the region, is based on a genuine search for a common interest, and does not significantly alter the regional balance of power.

4. Fuel Supply Assurances. Although insecurity appears to be the dominant motive for most states pursuing nuclear weapons, a number of non-proliferation approaches focus on alternative motivations. One that has received considerable attention (especially after the 1974 Indian nuclear explosion) and is designed primarily to reduce incentives for premature use of plutonium and the development of nationally controlled sensitive technologies is the provision of nuclear fuel supply assurances.

Although there is little evidence that fuel supply assurances have had much bearing on national decisions to go nuclear, the concept of assured supply has been fundamental to the nonproliferation regime that has evolved since the mid-1950s. The logic is clearly presented in a report of the Atlantic Council's Nuclear Fuels Policy Working Group:

Supply alone, on an *ad hoc* basis, unaccompanied by assurances of its dependability on reasonable terms, would not have had the intended deterrent effect on the development of independent and potentially uncontrolled sources of nuclear materials and equipment. In normal markets, this assurance is supplied largely by the traditions of the market itself, and the self-interest of the supplier in maintaining his profitable supply arrangements. In the case of nuclear materials and equipment, the security sensitivity of the products, the absence of any orderly market tradition and the limited number of suppliers combined to make a new form of governmentally assured supply essential, if the objective of deterring independent sources was to be realized (*Nuclear Power and* . . . , 1978, p. 122).

The logic was endorsed by the International Nuclear Fuel Cycle Evaluation, which concluded that "assurance of supply and assurance of non-proliferation are . . . complementary and that greater assurance of supply can . . . contribute to non-proliferation objectives by reducing the pressures for a world-wide spread of enrichment and reprocessing facilities" *(INFCE, 1980, p. 122)*.

A number of methods have been proposed to remove security of supply as a driving force for the acquisition of nationally controlled sensitive technologies. These include both market mechanisms and governmental control measures and range from the removal of all political restrictions on purchases of enriched or natural uranium fuels and reliance on a competitive market for protection against interruptions of supply to bilateral and multinational fuel cycle arrangements in which accession to full-scope safeguards would be a precondition for fuel supply guarantees. (See *INFCE*, 1980, pp. 125–32; *Nuclear Nonproliferation* . . . , *1980;* Yager, 1981, pp. 41–82.)

The International Nuclear Fuel Cycle Evaluation noted both safety net arrangements such as cross guarantees and an international nuclear fuel bank as possible short- to medium-term supply guarantee mechanisms. A competitive market, however, was identified as the preferred long-term solution to fuel supply problems *(INFCE, 1980, p. 130)*. A number of market-oriented approaches have received considerable attention recently (Greenwood and Haffa, 1981; Baker, 1979; Lovins et al., 1980). Most approaches emphasizing market incentives, however, tend to be attuned more closely to supplier rather than consumer concerns. In particular, they ignore consumers' fears that uranium supplies will be suspended for political reasons or that supply contracts will be unilaterally amended and new conditions applied retroactively.

More generally, non-proliferation strategies that emphasize fuel supply assurances appear to be more appropriate for relatively low-risk Nth countries that may move unintentionally up the nuclear weapons capability ladder (see Figure 13.2) than for states actively pursuing nuclear weapons because of security considerations. This does not mean that efforts to establish reliable, long-term fuel supply assurances should be abandoned. Such assurances are probably both attainable and necessary. Measures that restore stability, predictability, and security to the fuel supply market, however, should not be regarded as treatment for the underlying causes of proliferation.

Strengthening Disincentives

To strengthen disincentives means to raise the perceived costs of acquiring nuclear weapons. A frequently proposed means to accomplish this task is to threaten to impose, and to impose, sanctions.

Sanctions can take a variety of forms, from low-level economic and political penalties such as the delay of economic assistance and diplomatic protest to the use of force. Sanctions often suggested include termination of nuclear assistance and trade, imposition of a multilateral trade embargo, termination of military assistance and the supply of conventional arms, a ban on private investment, and withdrawal of prior security guarantees.

The effectiveness of sanctions depends on the nature of the incentives for an Nth country to go nuclear, the economic and political vulnerability of the proliferator, and the degree of support from the international community for specific sanctions. The nature of the Nth country's proliferation motives is critical since some motives, such as perceived threats to national survival, may not be susceptible to influence by any form of sanction but might be reduced by security guarantees. Moreover, some domestic pressures to proliferate might actually be intensified rather than reduced by sanctions that produce a nationalist reaction. Unilateral action by a great power may work well in selected cases where overwhelming leverage can be exerted (e.g., U.S. success in inducing South Korea to rescind its order for a French reprocessing plant), but unilateral sanctions against other Nth countries are apt to be futile. For Brazil, Argentina, and South Africa, for example, even multilateral sanctions probably could only raise the cost but not prevent implementation of a decision to produce nuclear weapons.

SUPPLY POLICIES

Supply-oriented approaches to non-proliferation tend to focus on means to prevent the misuse of civil nuclear energy facilities for military purposes.

International Safeguards

According to Article III, A, 5 of its statute, the International Atomic Energy Agency (IAEA) is mandated

To establish and administer safeguards designed to ensure that special fissionable and other materials, services, equipment, facilities, and information made available by the Agency or at its request or under its supervision or control are not used in such a way as to further any military purpose; and to apply safeguards, at the request of the parties, to any bilateral or multilateral arrangement, or at the request of a State, to any of that State's activities in the field of atomic energy.

No authority is granted the agency to recover diverted material or to provide physical security for nuclear materials or facilities. The IAEA Statute and its safeguards systems do not prohibit states from acquiring fissile material or making nuclear weapons. India did not technically violate any IAEA safeguards agreement when it exploded a nuclear device. The safeguards are simply intended to ensure that specific facilities, projects, and nuclear material are not diverted from peaceful to military uses.

The effectiveness of international safeguards is a subject of considerable controversy. Critics point in particular to the non-universal scope of the NPT and its safeguards requirements; provisions of the NPT which tend to discriminate against non-nuclear weapon states (NNWS) party to the treaty by requiring "full-scope" safeguards for non-parties; the IAEA's commitment to non-intrusive safeguards and its unwillingness to insist on strict safeguards compliance; and problems regarding the physical security of nuclear material which is left exclusively to individual states (Rochlin, 1979; Fischer and Szasz, 1985). The point is also sometimes made that, although the safeguards system is useful in helping to build confidence in the non-proliferation regime, it does not prevent nations from moving within days or less of having nuclear explosives without violating existing safeguards. As Henry Rowen notes, "It is not a violation of the NPT to have possession of nuclear explosive materials nor is it a violation to do experiments on rapidly crushing materials at very high pressures, i.e. to build the non-nuclear components of nuclear explosives" (Rowen, 1977, Pp. 5–6). Because Article X.1 of the NPT gives parties the right to withdraw from the treaty on three months notice, a state concerned that detection of safeguard violations is imminent can withdraw.

Although much of the criticism of the existing safeguards system comes from those who believe it needs to be strengthened, one can also discern resistance to the upgrading of IAEA safeguards if that entails further spending by the agency. This resistance comes primarily from developing countries and involves the difficulty of striking a balance between nuclear safeguards and the transfer of nuclear technology for peaceful purposes. A number of developing countries worry that safeguards may come to dominate the IAEA's program to the detriment of the agency's technical assistance functions.

There is widespread recognition that the international safeguards system is imperfect and needs improvement. Among the partial remedies often suggested are technological improvements such as advanced material accounting systems (Mabry, 1981), augmenting IAEA funding, staffing, and technical competence at a rate commensurate with the global expansion of civilian nuclear energy production (Office of Technology Assessment, 1977, p. 80), closing the gap between the NPT and non-NPT safeguards regime (e.g., standardizing bilateral safeguard measures), (Mabry, 1981), and moving toward compulsory full-scope and universal safeguards (Epstein, 1976, p. 160). The last recommendation is the most contentious and would require the greatest change in the existing system, although it has been advocated by some major suppliers, including the Soviet Union.

Export Controls

Export restrictions on sensitive technologies represent perhaps the most hotly disputed approach. At the heart of the dispute are disagreements over the efficacy of technology denial measures and their justifiability under the terms of the NPT.

Proponents of export restraints on technologies such as enrichment and reprocessing plants generally do not regard controls as a potential solution to the problem of proliferation, but see them as a means of slowing the spread of nuclear weapons capabilities and thereby buying time for the development of safer fuel cycle components and a stronger international nonproliferation regime. Underlying this approach, which is embodied in the 1978 U.S. Nuclear Non-Proliferation Act (NNPA), is the principle that some nuclear technologies should be denied even under safeguards.

Outside the U.S. Congress, it is difficult to find strong support today for the NNPA. Many of its critics do not dispute the need for export restraints, but regard the rigidity of the 1978 Act and its imposition of new conditions on most of America's nuclear trading partners (in some cases retroactively) as counterproductive. U.S. attempts to gain nonproliferation leverage through denial of nuclear materials, it is argued, "only tightens near-term supply conditions and increases uncertainties abroad, adding to the pressure to decide in favor of the very activities the United States is trying to restrain" (Smith and Rathjens, 1981, p. 887). A nonproliferation strategy emphasizing technology denial, in other words, may reduce confidence among importing states about access to materials and technology and give impetus to nuclear autarky. The failure to consider nuclear export policy within a broader foreign policy context and the indiscriminate application of export controls have aggravated U.S. relations with critical non-nuclear weapons states without seriously affecting the weapons programs of overt nuclear aspirants.

For other critics, opposition to nuclear export restraints is more fundamental. Many Third World states, for example, regard U.S. export legislation and the activities of the Nuclear Suppliers Group as concerted efforts to flout the nuclear assistance provisions of the NPT. They are also inclined to view such restrictive measures as serving suppliers' economic interests rather than nonproliferation goals (see Walker and Lonnroth, 1983). At a more abstract level, Third World opposition also appears to be based on the premise that export restraints perpetuate the status quo and the "have-not" status of most Third World countries.

Efforts to regulate nuclear exports have generally been directed at two groups: the "first-tier" nuclear suppliers capable of providing the entire range of advanced civilian nuclear technology, facilities, and services, and "second-tier" suppliers with a more limited range of nuclear exports. A "third-tier" of nuclear suppliers has begun to emerge: developing states with advanced nuclear technologies. Argentina and India have already assumed the role of third-tier nuclear suppliers, and Brazil, Taiwan, Pakistan, and South Korea may well attempt to emulate them in the future (Dunn, 1984; Potter, forthcoming). From a nonproliferation standpoint, this situation is troubling since many third-tier suppliers are not NPT parties. The prospects for coopting third-tier suppliers into future nuclear suppliers group arrangements seems slim given their suspicions about export restraints. India, for example, has expressed no interest in joining the suppliers group, although it has also taken the stance that it will not export sensitive technology.

More generally, nonproliferation proposals involving supplier cooperation and coordination must overcome enormous political and economic obstacles. At a minimum, nuclear-exporting countries will have to perceive sufficient shared interests and dangers to overcome economic rivalries and the inclination to view nuclear exports as a source of political influence and prestige. Export controls must also be sufficiently flexible and sensitive to consumer state concerns so as not to stimulate the development of national nuclear industries, including enrichment and reprocessing facilities. In other words, not only must the opportunity costs of controls be perceived by the supplier states as equitably distributed, but the perception must also exist among importers that "controls do not unreasonably hinder diffusion of the benefits of civilian nuclear energy—either in terms of energy supply or cost" (Office of Technology Assessment, 1977, p. 75). These are difficult conditions to satisfy. As a consequence, as one U.S. government study points out, "the political viability of export controls for more than the short term is very much in doubt" (Office of Technology Assessment, 1977, p. 76).

Technical Measures

The potential impact of technical measures on proliferation is restricted by the widespread availability of the material and technical wherewithal to make nuclear weapons. The lack of a "technical fix" for the problem of proliferation is reflected in the findings of both the International Nuclear Fuel Cycle Evaluation (INFCE) and the U.S. Nonproliferation Alternative Systems Assessment Program (NASAP). Although these two massive studies differ substantially in their operating assumptions and specific recommendations, they generally agree that technical measures by themselves can have only a limited impact on the full range of proliferation risks, particularly those above the level of subnational seizure threats. Nevertheless, many proliferation analysts continue to search for technical ways of increasing fuel cycle proliferation resistance.

Technical measures aimed at making it more difficult for national governments or subnational groups to divert nuclear material generally fall into one of three categories. They are: (1) measures to reduce the presence and quantities of pure plutonium or highly enriched uranium in the fuel cycle; (2) measures to use radioactivity to protect those materials from diversion; and (3) measures to guard the materials by means of physical barriers.[13] While these "technical fixes" vary in their economic costs, environmental hazards, and impact on existing safeguards procedures, most studies conclude that all would likely be much more effective against theft by subnational actors than diversion by national governments. This finding suggests the hazards of relying extensively on technical approaches if it obscures what is generally regarded as the greater danger of national proliferation and the need to reduce the political and security pressures for acquisition of nuclear weapons.

MANAGING PROLIFERATION

The primary focus of the nonproliferation strategies discussed in the preceding section is prevention of proliferation. They pay little attention to managing the proliferation process in order to moderate its most threatening characteristics. Both demand and supply approaches, for example, do not appear to be very helpful in reducing the risk of an inadvertent or unintended war initiated by a nuclear weapons novice. One alternative and controversial strategy that has been proposed to deal with this contingency is the provision by existing nuclear weapon states of technical assistance to Nth countries, designed to influence the characteristics of their future nuclear forces and strategic doctrine (Dunn and Kahn, 1976, p. 144; Jones, 1984, pp. 248–50). Technical assistance could be provided to improve early warning system and command and control reliability, weapons safety, and force survivability. The existing nuclear powers could also attempt to influence doctrine and reinforce the nuclear taboo by encouraging the assessment of nuclear war outcomes and the study of deterrence theory.

Unfortunately, although such assistance might promote development of a more secure Nth country nuclear force and reduce the risk of war by accident, miscalculation, unauthorized use, or preemption, it might also have several counterproductive effects. Assistance that reduces the danger of preemptive attack by increasing force survivability, for example, might remove what otherwise would be a compelling proliferation disincentive. Efforts to improve weapons reliability and safety and command and control performance also run the risk of making nuclear forces more usable. An additional danger is that such assistance would be perceived by other potential *N*th countries as a reward for going nuclear.

The risks of attempting to influence *N*th country nuclear postures and policy to reduce the probability of inadvertent or unintended war illustrates the basic tension that exists between efforts to manage proliferation and attempts to retard it. The proper nonproliferation emphasis, moreover, is apt to vary from case to case and to depend on such factors as the anticipated proliferation impact of a given country, other national security policy objectives, the means available for retarding a particular *N*th country's movement toward nuclear weapons, and the means available for influencing the characteristics of that state's nuclear program at the margin.

Careful consideration of the means available for retarding or managing proliferation is itself a necessary first step toward adoption of an effective nonproliferation strategy. There is a need, in other words, to assess nonproliferation measures, not only in terms of the extent to which they address the most important proliferation problems (however they are defined), but also with respect to their relevance for problems that are susceptible to manipulation, prevention, and cure. From this perspective, the source of past U.S. nonproliferation policy difficulties was principally one of misconception, not implementation. Far too much emphasis was placed on supply-oriented approaches in pursuit of the improbable task of restructuring the domestic nuclear energy programs of other countries. Inadequate attention, on the other hand, was given to the implementation of fuel supply assurances—a less pivotal factor with respect to nuclear weapons decision-making, but one over which the United States could have exercised significant influence.

Two additional proliferation problem areas appear to be susceptible to manipulation and treatment, if not prevention: nuclear theft and terrorism by non-state actors and vertical proliferation. Most applicable to the first problem are domestic safeguards and more diversion-resistant fuel cycle technologies. The limited effectiveness of safeguards and so-called technological fixes with respect to national proliferation should not detract from their potential utility as a means of curbing subnational proliferation threats. Similarly, although superpower-initiated arms control measures such as CTB may have only a limited direct impact on the decision-making calculus of potential *N*th countries, this should not obscure their potential for moderating vertical proliferation and restoring the credibility and acceptability of other nonproliferation measures, some of which may be necessarily discriminatory. A failure to moderate U.S.-Soviet arms competition, on the other hand, can only increase pressures in both the United States and the Soviet Union to subordinate nonproliferation policy objectives to other foreign policy goals defined more narrowly in East-West terms. One likely consequence of this kind of preoccupation is the reliance on security guarantees and conventional arms transfers not as measures to reduce proliferation incentives, but as enticements to resist the advances of the other superpower. Potential nonproliferation measures utilized in this fashion may whet rather than satiate the appetites of potential Nth countries for nuclear weapons by emphasizing security threats and the perceived utility of weapons.

CONCLUSION

It would be convenient to conclude this chapter by identifying a single culprit responsible for proliferation and a simple nonproliferation remedy in need only of faithful implementation. What is most apparent, however, is the multicausal nature of the spread of nuclear weapons and the need to tailor nonproliferation measures to specific cases.

This does not mean that patterns are non-existent or that we should abandon efforts to model the proliferation process. Indeed, Stephen Meyer's careful application of quantitative methods to explore the correlates of proliferation is a useful reminder of an underutilized approach to test contending proliferation hypotheses. Particularly noteworthy is his demonstration of the inadequacy of the "technological imperative" model to account for the scope or pace of past proliferation. This is consistent with our survey of thirteen past and potential proliferators, which reveals the predominance of international political and security incentives and constraints.

The relationship between the growth of nuclear power and nonproliferation is still evolving. Unfortunately, the relationship to date has been an antagonistic one. This has led even sophisticated observers sometimes to pose the necessity of choice between "the avoidance of nuclear weapons spread and the provision of additional energy sources" (Quester, 1979, p. 566). To pose the dilemma in this fashion, however, is to exaggerate the technological component of the proliferation problem. More to the point is Richard Rosecrance's observation over two decades ago that the dispersion of nuclear weapons is "eminently a problem in strategy and politics" (Rosecrance, 1964, p. 314). To this one might add that no nonproliferation policy is a substitute for a sound foreign policy and that major nonproliferation successes are probably attainable only at substantial cost to other domestic and foreign policy goals.

NOTES

1. For more extensive discussion, see Potter, 1982.
2. For relevant information see "Nuclear Power Status..." 1986; Spector, 1987; *Nuclear Proliferation...*, 1985, pp. 501–28.
3. Natural uranium is 99 percent U-238 and 0.7 percent U-235. The concentrate of the isotope U-235 must be increased (i.e., enriched) to about 3 percent for use in most power reactors and to about 90 percent for weapons. Many research reactors, however, use highly enriched uranium and are a potential target for diversion.
4. Iklé later became an advocate of nonproliferation. See Iklé, 1979.

5. Table organization based on Table 7.1 in Kegley, Raymond, and Skinner, 1980, pp. 231–36.

6. See Meyer, 1984, for discussion of this school of thought and a sophisticated effort to test its explanatory power.

7. Major exceptions are Beaton and Maddox (1962), Rosecrance (1944), Dunn and Kahn (1976), and Meyer (1984).

8. A partial exception is the absence of political prestige and influence incentives in the nuclear weapons decisions during the Second World War.

9. Meyer (1984) attempts to quantify the requisites for an atomic weapons manufacturing capability and lists the dates when different states acquired that capability.

10. A useful survey of means to check proliferation is Dunn (1982). See also *Blocking the Spread*... (1984).

11. A number of near nuclear powers (e.g., Brazil, India, and South Africa) which have refused to ratify the NPT are nevertheless parties to the Limited Test Ban Treaty whose preamble commits parties to subscribe to a CTB.

12. Argentina has signed and announced its intention to ratify, Brazil has signed and ratified, but under the treaty's complex implementation conditions is not yet a full party to the accord. See Redick (1981), pp. 106–107.

13. For discussion of those technical measures, see *Reprocessing*... (1980); *Nuclear Nonproliferation and*... (1980), Vol. 1, pp. 143–48 and Vol. 2, pp. 2–35; and Potter (1982), pp. 217–21.

REFERENCES

Baker, Steven J. 1979. Why Not a Nuclear Fuel Cartel? Pp. 152–56 in William H. Kincade and Jeffrey D. Porro, eds. *Negotiating Security: An Arms Control Reader*. Washington, D.C.: The Arms Control Association and the Carnegie Endowment for International Peace.

Barnaby, C. F. 1969. The Development of Nuclear Energy Programs. Pp. 16–35 in Barnaby, ed., *Preventing the Spread of Nuclear Weapons*. London: Souvenir.

Beaton, Leonard, and John Maddox. 1962. *The Spread of Nuclear Weapons*. New York: Praeger.

Betts, Richard K. 1980. Incentives for Nuclear Weapons. Pp. 116–44 in Joseph A. Yager, ed., *Nonproliferation and U.S. Foreign Policy*. Washington, D.C.: Brookings Institution.

Blechman, Barry M. 1981. The Comprehensive Test Ban Negotiations: Can They Be Revitalized? *Arms Control Today* (June).

Blocking the Spread of Nuclear Weapons: American and European Perspectives. 1986. New York: Council on Foreign Relations.

Brennan, Donald G. 1976. A Comprehensive Test Ban: Everybody or Nobody. *International Security* (Summer): 92–117.

Brito, Dagobert L., and Michael D. Intriligator. 1983. Proliferation and the Probability of War: Global and Regional Issues. Pp. 135–44 in Brito et al., *Strategies for Managing Nuclear Proliferation*. Lexington, Mass.: Lexington Books.

Bull, Hedley. 1961. *The Control of the Arms Race*. New York: Praeger.

Caldwell, Dan. 1980. CTB: An Effective SALT Substitute. *Bulletin of the Atomic Scientists* (December).

Council on Foreign Relations. 1986. *Blocking the Spread of Nuclear Weapons: American and European Perspectives,* New York: Council on Foreign Relations.

Donnelly, Warren. 1984. An Assessment of the Proliferation Threat of Today and Tomorrow. A Congressional Research Service Report prepared for Senator William Proxmire.

Dowty, Alan. 1974. *The Role of Great Power Guarantees in International Peace Agreements.* Jerusalem: Hebrew University.

Drell, Sidney D. 1978. The Case for the Test Ban. *The Washington Post,* July 4.

Dror, Yehezkel. 1971. *Crazy States.* Lexington, Mass.: Lexington Books.

Dunn, Lewis A. 1977. The Proliferation Policy Agenda: Taking Stock. *Report of the World Peace Foundation Conference on Managing in a Proliferation-Prone World.* Dedham, Mass.

———. 1978. Military Politics, Nuclear Proliferation, and the Nuclear Coup d'Etat. *Studies* (May):31–50.

———. 1981. Some Reflections on the Dove's Dilemma. *International Organization* (Winter):181–92.

———. 1982. *Controlling the Bomb.* New Haven, Conn.: Yale University Press.

———. 1984. The Emerging Nuclear Suppliers: Some Dimensions of the Problem." In Rodney Jones, Cesare Merlini, Joseph Pilat, and William Potter, eds., *The Nuclear Suppliers and Nonproliferation.* Lexington, Mass.: Lexington Books.

———, and Herman Kahn. 1976. *Trends in Nuclear Proliferation, 1975–1995.* Croton-on-Hudson, N.Y.: Hudson Institute.

———, and William H. Overholt. 1977. The Next Phase in Nuclear Proliferation Research. In Overholt, ed., *Asia's Nuclear Future.* Boulder, Colo.: Westview Press.

Epstein, William. 1976. *The Last Chance.* New York: Free Press.

———. 1977. Why States Go—and Don't Go—Nuclear. Pp. 16–28 in *The Annals of the American Academy of Political and Social Science* (March).

Feldman, Shai. 1982. *Israeli Nuclear Deterrence.* New York: Columbia University Press.

Final Document, Third Non-Proliferation Treaty Review Conference. 1985.

Fischer, David, and Paul Szasz. 1985. *Safeguarding the Atom: A Critical Appraisal.* London: Taylor and Francis.

Ford/Mitre Study. 1977. *Nuclear Power Issues and Choices.* Cambridge, Mass.: Ballinger.

Graham, Thomas. 1983. The Economics of Producing Nuclear Weapons in Nth Countries. Pp. 9–28 in Dagobert L. Brito et al., eds., *Strategies for Managing Nuclear Proliferation.* Lexington, Mass.: Lexington Books.

Greenwood, Ted. 1977. Discouraging Proliferation in the Next Decade and Beyond. Pp. 25–122 in Greenwood et al., *Nuclear Proliferation: Motivations, Capabilities, and Strategies for Control.* New York: McGraw-Hill.

———, Harold Feiveson, and Theodore Taylor. 1977. *Nuclear Proliferation: Motivations, Capabilities,and Strategies for Control.* New York: McGraw-Hill.

———, and Robert Haffa, Jr. 1981. Supply-Side Non Proliferation. *Foreign Policy* (Spring): 125–40.

Harkavy, Robert. 1977. *Israel's Nuclear Weapons: Spectre of Holocaust in the Middle East.* Denver: University of Denver Press.

Haselkorn, Avigdor. 1974. Israel—An Option to a Bomb in the Basement. In Robert

Lawrence and Joel Larus, eds., *Nuclear Proliferation Phase II*. Lawrence: University Press of Kansas.

Husbands, Jo. 1980. Arms Transfers and Nuclear Proliferation: Policy Implications of the "Doves Dilemma." Paper delivered at the Annual Meeting of the International Studies Association, Los Angeles.

Ikle, Fred C. 1966. Nth Countries and Disarmament. *Bulletin of the Atomic Scientists* (December).

———, 1979. Introduction. In Albert Wohlstetter et al., *Swords from Plowshares*. Chicago: University of Chicago Press.

INFCE Summary Volume. 1980. Vienna: IAEA.

Jones, Rodney. 1984. Small Nuclear Forces and U.S. Security Policy. In Jones, ed. *Small Nuclear Forces and U.S. Security Policy*. Lexington, Mass.: Lexington Books.

Kaplan, Morton A. 1957. *System and Process in International Politics*. New York: John Wiley.

Kapur, Ashok. 1976. *India's Nuclear Option*. New York: Praeger.

———. 1979. *International Nuclear Proliferation: Multilateral Diplomacy and Regional Aspects*. New York.: Prager.

———. 1980. A Nuclearizing Pakistan: Some Hypotheses. *Asian Survey* (May): 495–516.

Kegley, Charles, Gregory Raymond, and Richard Skinner. 1980. A Comparative Analysis of Nuclear Armament. In Patrick McGowan and Charles Kegley, eds., *Threats, Weapons, and Foreign Policy*. Beverly Hills, Calif.: Sage Publications.

Lefever, Ernst. 1979. *Nuclear Arms in the Third World*. Washington, D.C.: Brookings Institution.

Leventhal, Paul, and Yonah Alexander, eds. 1986. *Nuclear Terrorism: Defining the Threat*. Washington, D.C.: Pergamon-Brassey.

———, and Yonah Alexander, eds. 1987. *Preventing Nuclear Terrorism*. Lexington, Mass.: Lexington Books.

Lovins, Amory, L. Hunter Lovins, and Leonard Ross. 1980. Nuclear Power and Nuclear Bombs. *Foreign Affairs* (Summer): 1137–77.

Mabry, Ralph. 1981. The Present International Nuclear Regime. In Joseph Yager, ed. *International Cooperation in Nuclear Energy*. Washington: D.C.: Brookings Institution.

May, Michael. 1976. Do We Need a Nuclear Test Ban? *Wall Street Journal,* June 28.

Meyer, Stephen. 1984. *The Dynamics of Nuclear Proliferation*. Chicago: University of Chicago Press.

Molander, Roger, and Robbie Nichols. 1985. *Who Will Stop the Bomb?* New York: Facts on File Publications.

Nuclear Nonproliferation and Civilian Nuclear Power. 1980. Report of the Nonproliferation Alternative Systems Assessment Program. Vols. 1–7. Washington, D.C.: U.S. Department of Energy.

Nuclear Power and Nuclear Weapons Proliferation. 1978. Report of the Atlantic Council's Nuclear Fuels Policy Working Group, Vol. 1. Boulder, Colo.: Westview Press.

Nuclear Power Status at the End of 1985. 1986. *IAEA Bulletin*. Summer.

Nuclear Proliferation Factbook, 4th ed., 1985. Washington, D.C.: U.S. Government Printing Office.

Nye, Joseph S. 1978. Nonproliferation: A Long-Term Strategy. *Foreign Affairs* (April): 601–23.

Office of Technology Assessment (OTA). 1977. *Nuclear Proliferation and Safeguards*. New York: Praeger.

Organski, A.F.K. 1968. *World Politics*, 2nd ed. New York: Alfred A. Knopf.

Potter, William C. 1985. Nuclear Proliferation: U.S.-Soviet Cooperation. *The Washington Quarterly* (Winter): 141–54.

———. 1987. *Nuclear Power and Nonproliferatioin: An Interdisciplinary Perspective*. Cambridge, Mass.: Oelgeschlager, Gunn and Hain.

———, ed. Forthcoming. *The Emerging Nuclear Suppliers and Nonproliferation*.

Poulose, T. T. 1979. Nuclear Proliferation: A Third World Perspective. *The Round Table* (April).

Quester, George. 1973. *The Politics of Nuclear Proliferation*. Baltimore: Johns Hopkins University Press.

———. 1979. Nuclear Proliferation: Linkages and Solutions. *International Organization* (Autumn).

Ramberg, Bennett. 1984. *Nuclear Power Plants as Weapons for the Enemy*. Berkeley: University of California Press.

Redick, John R. 1981. The Tlatelolco Regime and Nonproliferation in Latin America. *International Organization* (Winter): 103–34.

Reprocessing, Plutonium Handling, Recycle. 1980. Report of INFCE Working Group 4. Vienna: IAEA.

Rochlin, Gene I. 1979. *Plutonium, Power, and Politics*. Berkeley: University of California Press.

Rosecrance, Richard. 1964. International Stability and Nuclear Diffusion. In Rosecrance, ed., *The Dispersion of Nuclear Weapons*. New York: Columbia University Press.

Rosen, Steven. 1976. Nuclearization and Stability in the Middle East. *Jerusalem Journal of International Relations* (Spring): 1–32.

Rowen, Henry S. 1977. How to Develop Nuclear Power While Limiting Its Dangers: Proposed Changes in the International Nuclear System. Mimeo, August 23.

Sandoval, R. Robert. 1976. Consider the Case of the Porcupine: Another View of Nuclear Proliferation. *Bulletin of the Atomic Scientists* (May).

Scheinman, Lawrence. 1964. *Atomic Energy Policy in France Under the Fourth Republic*. Princeton, N.J.: Princeton University Press.

Schelling, Thomas C. 1976. Who Will Have the Bomb? *International Security* (Summer). Pp. 77–91.

Schoettle, Enid C.B. 1976. Arms Limitations and Security Policies Required to Minimize the Proliferation of Nuclear Weapons. Pp. 102–31 in David Carlton and Carlo Schaerf, eds., *Arms Control and Technological Innovation*. New York: Halsted Press.

Schwab, G. 1969. Switzerland's Tactical Nuclear Weapon Policy. *Orbis* (Fall): 900–14.

Shapely, Deborah. 1978. Nuclear Weapons History: Japan's Wartime Bomb Prospects Revealed. *Science* (January 13):152–57.

Smith, Gerard, and George Rathjens. 1981. Reassessing Nuclear Nonproliferation Policy. *Foreign Affairs* (Spring):875–94.

Spector, Leonard S. 1987. *Going Nuclear*. Cambridge, Mass.: Ballinger.

Walker, William, and Mans Lonnroth. 1983. *Nuclear Power Struggles: Industrial Competition and Proliferation Control*. Boston: George Allen and Unwin.

Waltz, Kenneth N. 1981. The Spread of Nuclear Weapons: More May Be Better. *Adelphi Papers,* no. 71. London: International Institute For Strategic Studies.

Willrich, Mason. 1966. Guarantees to Non-Nuclear Nations. *Foreign Affairs* (July): 683–92.

Wohlstetter, Albert, et al. 1976. "Moving Toward Life in a Nuclear Armed Crowd?" Report to the U.S. Arms Control and Disarmament Agency. Los Angeles: Pan Heuristics. A revised version (1979) published as *Swords from Plowshares*. Chicago: University of Chicago Press.

———. 1977a. *The Spread of Nuclear Bombs: Predictions, Premises, Policies*. Los Angles: Pan Heuristics.

———, et al. 1977b. Moving Toward Life in a Nuclear Armed Crowd? In Nuclear Energy Policy Study Group. *Nuclear Power Issues and Choices*. Cambridge, Mass.: Ballinger.

———, et al. 1979. *Swords from Plowshares*. Chicago: University of Chicago Press, 1979.

Yager, Joseph A. 1981. *International Cooperation in Nuclear Energy*. Washington, D.C.: Brookings Institution.

York, Herbert, and G. Greb. 1979. The Comprehensive Nuclear Test Ban. La Jolla: California Seminar on Arms Control and Foreign Policy.

14

On International Crises and National Security

CHARLES F. HERMANN

INTRODUCTION

Crises often act as sudden and profound change agents in international affairs. They may become catalysts transforming peace to war or trigger a major escalation in existing hostilities. More generally, crises can lead to the demise or reformulation of a complete international system or some of its components. The changes induced by crises can be beneficial, leading to high levels of political and economic integration, promoting detente. Confronted with a crisis, policymakers can react with greater initiative and innovation or they can become overwhelmed and perform far less effectively than normal.

The potential force of crises as agents of change in foreign policy and world affairs has made them the topic of extensive study. When do crises lead to war or other severely dysfunctional outcomes? Can crises be detected and averted? Can crises be managed so as to reduce the risk of undesirable outcomes and increase the likelihood of benefit? There is no absence of candidate situations to examine in order to explore these and similar questions. In fact, the media bombard us relentlessly with reports of international situations designated crises by some group of policymakers, journalists, commentators, academics, or affected citizens. Some seem to have no lasting consequences for more than a few people and fade from the memories of most of us as quickly as they arise. Others have profound effects and become the objects of repeated examination and debate.

Ponder the diversity of a very small sample of events labeled crises by various observers that have become the focus of attention, at least briefly, in recent years. In early April of 1982, the military forces of Argentina seize the Falkland/Malvinas Islands challenging British possession of those South Atlantic islands that Argentina has declared to be part of its own territory. The British issue extremely strong warnings and begin preparations for a military invasion to retake the islands if the Argentines do not leave voluntarily. Meanwhile, the United States, fearing a military clash between two of its allies, initiates intense negotiations in an attempt to avert war.

Throughout 1981 and early 1982, the war in southern Lebanon intensifies with Israel actively supporting the Phalange against the Palestine Liberation Organization (PLO). Escalation steadily increases with airstrikes by Israel and PLO attacks against northern Israeli settlements. On June 3, 1982, the fuse is lit with the assassination of the Israeli ambassador to Britain by PLO agents. Israel invades Lebanon.

On the night of September 1, 1983, a Korean Air Lines flight 007 from New York City to Seoul, Korea, deviates significantly from the established northern Pacific air route. It passes over Kamchatka Peninsula, which contains a number of the Soviet Union's sensitive military installations. When it crosses into Soviet territory again over Sakhalin Island, it is shot down by a Soviet SU-15 killing all 269 people on board. In the tense aftermath, the United States charges the Soviet Union with barbaric behavior, and the Soviet Union counters that the crew of the Korean aircraft was engaged in an espionage mission for the United States.

An Italian cruise ship, the *Achille Lauro,* is seized by a group of terrorists while sailing in the Mediterranean in October 1985. After killing one American passenger, the hijackers eventually agree to allow the ship to dock in Alexandria, Egypt, in return for safe passage out of the country. American military aircraft, however, intercept the Egyptian airliner in flight and force it to land in Italy where the hijackers are arrested. Egypt protests to the United States for its own act of air piracy while the United States appeals unsuccessfully for the extradiction of the ship hijackers to stand trial in this country for allegedly killing an American citizen.

At Chernobyl in the Soviet Union at 1:23 A.M. on April 26, 1986, an explosion occurs in a nuclear power generator. During a prolonged and intense fire, radioactive material vents into the atmosphere and forms a toxic cloud that drifts over parts of Eastern and Western Europe as well as the Soviet Union before dissipating. Alarmed governments initiate varied actions in attempts to protect citizens, agricultural produce, and wildlife. They demand information, explanations, and assurances from the Soviet Union.

In violation of an anti-dumping arrangement with the United States, Japanese companies sell computer chips to third countries who then supply them for the U.S. market. In 1987, angry American officials initiate boycotts against the selected products of the Japanese companies involved while members of Congress demand even harsher actions. In a climate of growing economic tension between Japan and the United States, the prospect of a trade war and a broad pattern of protectionism appear more likely.

During the same years from which these examples were drawn, many other incidents occurred and could have been added to greatly enlarge the list. One source or another has labeled each of these episodes a crisis and to the participants directly involved in any of them, each must have seemed a demanding, non-routine situation calling for special concentration of effort and abilities. From the perspective of scholarship and, more specifically, national security studies and world affairs, there emerges a fundamental issue. Are all of these, or some subset, or some subset, representative of a larger, coherent class of phenomena? Do they share certain common characteristics? By studying past episodes of a certain kind, can we learn something about the consequences of future crises if certain things are done or avoided?

As happens often in the social sciences where terms are adopted that appear frequently in everyday parlance and have broad and imprecise meaning, we risk being unable to define the concept so as both to preserve common understanding and to provide necessary precision. The problem of definition strongly affects the answers to basic research questions and the prospects for a better understanding of crises. Defining the set of situations carelessly or too broadly almost ensures that extremely different episodes that have very different antecedents and dynamics will be lumped together and thus defeat the effort to strengthen our knowledge of crises. The thoughtful person must exercise extreme caution in assessing insights drawn from comprehensive chronologies of crises that provide only a post hoc definition constructed after the episodes have been collected—or worse, no definition at all.

Although occasional pitfalls resulting from poorly defined crises continue to occur, many analysts both inside and outside government exercise more care. They appropriately specify and limit the set of situations they examine according to the class of problems they seek to understand. Because the problems differ and their associated levels of analysis change, the definitions of crisis vary. As a consequence, there is not one definition of crisis but many. Recognizing this condition is one of the essential prerequisites for interpreting the contemporary literature on crises and the findings emerging from them. It is necessary to sort out studies that define crises in one way for one purpose from those that define them in other ways for other purposes, as well as to recognize that occasionally one encounters a study using an undifferentiated "grab bag," all-inclusive approach. The task of keeping types of crises differentiated is complicated because some actual events may appropriately fit in more than one definition. The Cuban missile crisis of 1962, often included in studies by Western analysts, is an example. Only by comparing research using similar definitions of crisis, however, is it possible to make sense of the findings—at times contradictory—emerging from the substantial body of literature.

As a means of sorting out the alternative kinds of definitions of crises and their distinctive purposes, this chapter employs three levels of analysis—the international system, actor confrontations, and internal decision-making. This division was used by Snyder and Diesing (1977) in their landmark study, as well as by the author (Hermann and Brady, 1972) in an earlier effort to sort the findings emerging from crisis research.

Systemic crises focus fundamentally on the question of system transformation. A system can be conceptualized as a collective structure composed of units whose recurrent interactions are regulated or governed by some sort of norms, laws, comparative capabilities, or interdependencies. A systemic crisis is one with the potential to disrupt, destroy or transform the system. In international politics, modern systems have consisted of nation-states and other international actors. The events leading to the outbreak of major wars have been a frequent kind of system crisis.

Actor confrontation crises involve two or more interacting parties. Whereas systemic crises concern the fate of the system as a whole, crises between actors focus on the relative consequences for each party to the crisis. Typically, actor confrontation crises involve a challenge by one actor to the established, status quo position of another party. The fundamental dynamic of such crises is bargaining—direct or tacit. Although any instrument of statecraft can presumably be used in issuing a challenge, military instruments have figured prominently in either the challenge or the response to such international crises.

Finally, we have decision-making crises. These examine the task of reaching and implementing choices within a single government or other policymaking unit. The members of the government perceive, not always correctly, the emergence of an acute situation that can cause them, or their policy, harm. The individual and organizational means of coping with the crisis problem becomes the object of study. With respect to international crises defined from this perspective, the concern is with the quality of foreign and national security policymaking under such conditions. It is entirely possible that an episode may generate a decision-making crisis in only one country or international actor.

These alternative perspectives enable us to sort out the illustrative episodes reviewed in the beginning of this section. The Chernobyl nuclear power station accident can be viewed as a potential systemic crisis in which the system in question is some kind of ecological one that could be upset by the introduction of massive amounts of radioactive material into the atmosphere. (As catastrophic as that accident was, it does not now seem to have been of such magnitude as to threaten a major global ecological system.) The other example that bears review from a systemic perspective is the American reprisals against the Japanese computer companies. If the action had touched off—in a way it appears not to have done—an abrupt rejection by many international actors of existing norms of international trade in favor of far more protectionist policies, then a systemic crisis in the post-war international economic system would be at hand.

When the Argentines challenged British control of the Malvinas/Falkland Islands or when the Israelis challenged the PLO movement into southern Lebanon, we appear to have excellent examples of actor confrontation crises. In both cases periods of intense bargaining ensued. Some of it occurred in the form of diplomatic negotiations (using third parties), and some of it involved tacit negotiations through military moves.

The appearance over the Soviet Union of an intruder aircraft that turned out to be the Korean Air Line Flight 007 and the means of coping with the international response that followed the destruction of the airliner likely created a decision-making crisis for the Soviet Union's top political and military leaders. Similarly, the hijacking of the *Achille Lauro* triggered decision-making crises in several capitals, including the United States.

Notice that some of these illustrative episodes might be plausibly included in more than one approach to crises; others lack such scope. Thus, the Israeli invasion of Lebanon can be regarded as a potential sub-system crisis (Israel and its Arab neighbors). Such would particularly be the case if Israel had been able to eliminate the PLO, as some of its leaders hoped, and had thereby enabled Israel to have a much stronger influence over the future of Lebanon. It certainly can be examined as a decision-making crisis for several countries including Israel. On the other hand, as tragic as the destruction of the Korean airliner was, it would be hard to characterize it as a systemic crisis. In sum, what we can say about crises depends directly on the specification of the class of phenomena to be inscribed by that term. When grouped according to one or another definition, however, useful knowledge becomes possible.

One other definitional issue deserves attention. Some research has included as a defining characteristic of crisis that the policymakers recognize a high potential of war or military escalation (e.g., Brecher, 1978). In the context of international security scholarship, this might be a practical boundary to impose on the domain of crisis studies. But the insistence on this requirement as a necessary condition for a crisis should not be accepted lightly for a least two reasons. First, the stipulation of a future state (i.e., war) as contrasted with keying on presently existing attributes of a situation inevitably requires greater judgment (regardless of whether the judgment is made by policymakers in the situation or analysts), reducing the utility of the material for "real time" analysis and forecasting. This is particularly so if the requirement for estimating risk of war is from the involved policymakers' perceptions. Second, some crises that have little immediate likelihood of escalating to war or greater violent conflict can have profound national security consequences.

Research at each level of analysis associated with a definition of crisis involves lines of inquiry intended to have implications for national security policy. After examining the major question of concern and the main direction of recent research at each level, we will review an applied area of policy research that can be derived from that level. For systems, we will explore deterrence stability in crises; for actor confrontations, we will examine crisis forecasting; and for decision-making, attention will be directed to crisis management.

INTERNATIONAL SYSTEMIC CRISES

The Interplay of Crisis and System

Two major lines of inquiry can be detected in research on crises from a systemic perspective. The first treats the international system as the context and potential source of explanation for crises. The second examines the effect of crises on the system as a totality. In other words, the distinction is whether crisis is the dependent variable influenced by the system or the other way around.

Although various kinds of international political systems have been described (e.g., Kaplan, 1957; Bozeman, 1960; Rosecrance, 1963; Luard, 1976; Holsti, 1977), the studies concerned with how international systems affect crises have generally compared balance of power or multipolar systems with bipolar systems. Polarity has been understood primarily in terms of military power and political alignment. Waltz (1964) hypothesized that bipolar systems trigger more crises than multipolar systems because of the much more constant confrontation in the bipolar between always opposing forces in which any attempted gain by one side is immediately challenged as a potential loss by the other. Waltz (1964) also proposed that in a bipolar system crises are more likely to become a substitute for war rather than as the catalyst for the initiation of war, which is more likely in a multipolar system. Snyder and Diesing (1977) concur that bipolarity tends to make crises a surrogate for war. "From this perspective, although they are still dangerous, crises are more functional than dysfunctional. Their systemic function is to resolve without violence, or with only minimal violence, those conflicts that are too severe to be settled by ordinary diplomacy and that in earlier times would have been settled by war" (Snyder and Diesing, 1977, p. 455). They suggest that, although the surrogate function can be derived from the structure of power in the respective international systems, another systemic property—the structure of military technology (currently nuclear weapons)—may also account for crises replacing wars in the system.

The primary systemic interest of Snyder and Diesing (1977) is to explore the international system's effect on crisis bargaining. They suggest that in multipolar systems, where the support of allies for one of their members in a crisis is less certain than in a bipolar system, bargaining will occur as much among allies as between adversaries. The bargaining in one arena will have considerable influence on the interaction in the other and on the ultimate crisis outcome. Detente also operates differently in the two systems according to Snyder and Diesing. In a multipolar system detente between adversaries may be the opening for an eventual realignment or alliance. Detente cannot have the same consequence in a bipolar system without leading to a system transformation, although detente can facilitate and alter the nature of crisis bargaining in a bipolar system.

In contrast to these considerations of the effects of systems on crises are those that focus on system stability and instability and view crises as major change agents—as one means of leading to the termination, modification, or transformation of the system. System stability entails the ability to retain within acceptable limits variables or structural features essential for continuation of the system's distinctive relationship among key actors. A crisis consists of a sudden shock to the system that may cause the limits to be exceeded or may reduce the system's ability to withstand future stress and shocks. The aftermath of a system-transforming crisis may be the loss of actors and their roles in the system. For example, after World War I Austro-Hungary, Germany, and Russia were profoundly different in their systemic roles. From the systems perspective, however, it is not so much the change of actors as the alteration of the relationships governing their interaction. McClelland (1972) envisions the international system in terms of patterns of interaction that can be characterized in terms of the volume and diversity of information exchanged. Systemic crises from McClelland's perspective disrupt the established pattern of information distribution and can lead to uncertainty and the adaptation of new modes of interaction. The phases of a crisis—and presumably its effects on the system—can be monitored through the changing pattern of information exchange.

In another effort to examine system transformation, Rosecrance (1963) identifies nine historical systems between 1740 and 1960 and considers the elements maintaining their relative stability for a period followed by instability and transformation. System stability is viewed as a dynamic balance between the disruptive and regulatory elements to be found in any system. Rosecrance regards the disruptive challenges to a system emerging primarily from within its component units, and when these disruptions can no longer be absorbed by the system's established regulatory processes and the flexibility of the environment, major system change occurs. At these crucial junctures, "in some manner or other the modes, objectives, and techniques of diplomacy change" (Rosecrance, 1963, p. 7). Thus, in a fashion akin to McClelland, Rosecrance views system change to be evident in the pattern of interaction. Crises per se do not appear as a major construct in Rosecrance's (1963) analysis, but some of the more abrupt breakdowns in a system's ability to absorb disruptive challenges—for example, events triggering revolutions and wars—can be recognized as such.

It is precisely rapid increases in the demands made on control and regulatory capabilities of the international system that comprise a major feature of systemic crises according to Young (1967). Thus, in Young's view the impact of a crisis depends on the nature of both the crisis and the system's regulatory capabilities. "A set of events that would constitute a severe crisis for a system with little homeostatic control would not even be perceived as a crisis for a system with better regulatory processes" (Young, 1971, p. 11). Such observations invite questions: What kind of systemic regulatory mechanisms reduce the dysfunctional effects of what kinds of crises? Although some general reflection has been devoted to such issues of system maintenance and regulatory mechanisms (e.g., Waltz, 1979), no extensive work appears to have yet been done.

Not all crises need be dysfunctional for a system, particularly if it has the capacity to learn and strengthen or modify its capabilities as a result of a crisis. Furthermore, a crisis may be damaging only to a component or subsystem but not have an adverse effect on the system as a whole. Hopmann and King (1980) suggest that the Cuban missile crisis of 1962 contributed to detente between the Soviet Union and the United States as policymakers on both sides learned from the crisis to find means of limiting their competition.[1] The leadership of the European Community has clearly used crisis as a means of forcing national governments to take further integrative steps or risk collapse of a subsystem producing beneficial results for them. The role of crises as a means of promoting new forms of cooperation has been considered more generally in integration theory (e.g., Genco, 1980; Morse, 1973, especially chap. 6).

In reviewing the literature on crisis effects on systems, one finds an emerging nomenclature and some suggestive ideas and hypotheses but relatively little systematic research. As Zinnes (1980, p. 16) states in her review: "There have indeed been attempts to study system transformation. But these attempts have not gone very far." The difficulty of defining key system variables in a manner that permits their identification in a variety of historical systems and then the problem of collecting data over a sufficiently long time period undoubtedly constitute a significant hurdle.

Crisis Stability in the Deterrence Subsystem

A great deal of current attention to the issue of crisis and system stability focuses not on the total international system, but on a very specific subsystem—the strategic nuclear relationship between the United States and the Soviet Union. That a relationship manifesting systemic properties exists in the strategic nuclear posture of both sides seems clear. Both countries, among other objectives, seek to deter a nuclear attack by the other against their homeland or other vital assets. Although many complexities are involved in the full operation of nuclear deterrence, the basic concept is well established. Deterrence involves the threat of punishing nuclear retaliation with weapons intended to be able to survive the adversary's most advantageous initial attack. To be effective, both sides must recognize the credibility of the threat and believe that the policymakers and weapon systems have a high likelihood of performing as declared. There have been continuous challenges to the strategic nuclear deterrence system. Both sides have made almost continuous modifications in their respective forces and governing policies. They have responded in part to advances (actual or anticipated) in technology, changes in resources, altering alliance conditions, varying perceptions of the other side, arms control proposals and agreements, and crises and other provocations. So far, deterrence appears to have worked, and in this instance appearances or perceptions of success are important. By their words and actions, there is reason to believe that the leadership of both countries sees no substantial possibility of trying to achieve objectives through a major military assault on the other or of engaging in provocative actions that carry a high risk of triggering military hostilities. Many analysts appear prepared to suggest that the likelihood of one side initiating war against the other under normal, current circumstances is extremely low. Thus, the deterrence subsystem appears to have demonstrated substantial stability.

The urgent problem concerns the stability of deterrence under conditions of a military crisis. The argument has been made that the crisis stability of the system has been declining in recent years. (For example, see Ball, 1987; Lebow, 1987; Hermann, 1987a, b.) The concern is whether both sides have introduced features that might cause a shift in the perceptions of policymakers about the possible advantage of striking first if nuclear war suddenly seemed almost inevitable. Associated with the heightened sense of impending nuclear war is either a belief that one's own retaliatory forces are extremely vulnerable to a first attack and/or a belief that there might be a decisive advantage in striking first. These beliefs produce a cycle of preemptive attack thinking. If war seems nearly certain and we might suffer much less by attacking first, should we not do so? If the other side makes the same calculations, are they not likely to initiate an attack soon? If they are going to attack, is that not a compelling reason why we should launch before they do? Such reasoning would make the deterrence system extremely unstable, and the linchpin is the changed estimate of the inevitability of war that might occur in an acute crisis involving the superpowers.

Both the United States and the Soviet Union have introduced changes in their strategic systems and their thinking about them in recent years that could contribute to the formation of beliefs in a sharply escalating situation that would produce crisis instability. These changes have occured in weapon system characteristics, preparedness and mobilization practices, the command and control of nuclear weapons, and strategic plans.

Weapons System Characteristics. Certain weapons systems on both sides may be less valuable as retaliatory weapons because of their declining ability to survive an adversary's first strike. Land-based missiles such as U.S. Minuteman and MX or Soviet SS-18s and 19s are becoming increasingly vulnerable through improvements in warhead accuracies and increasing numbers of warheads on each launcher. Whether either side could really decimate the other's fixed-site, land-based missiles in an initial strike matters less for stability than the policymakers perceptions of their own system's vulnerability under conditions of crisis.

Mobilization Practices. Despite the absence of worldwide strategic alerts by the United States in recent years, such force generation could reasonably be expected in an acute crisis. In an era of satellite surveillance and other electronic intelligence, such actions would be instantly known to the other side. In the past, the Soviet Union reportedly never put its strategic forces on a worldwide alert in response to U.S. actions, but in the era of greater strategic parity that has come into existence since 1973 such mutual mobilization seems more likely in the future. Each side's cautionary defensive steps will appear to the other side as potential moves toward preemption in a manner reminiscent of the crisis before World War I. Furthermore, once the forces of both sides are at a high state of alert, the first one moving to a lower state of readiness will be at a significant disadvantage. This fact will make de-escalation difficult and dangerous.

Command and Control. Throughout the era of nuclear deterrence, the emphasis has been on efforts to ensure the survivability of second-strike weapons systems through concealment, mobility, hardening, and so on. Recent studies (e.g., Bracken, 1983; Blair, 1985; Lebow, 1987) have revealed that the command and control systems far more than the weapons themselves would be vulnerable targets in an initial strike. If the system to control the retaliatory response were lost, it would matter very little that the weapons themselves survived. The C^3I vulnerability poses very significant problems for crisis stability in the relatively near future and according to some analysts may never be more than partially correctible.

Strategic Plans. The evolution of strategic plans designed to guide the use of nuclear forces has also introduced pressure on crisis stability. Two proposals discussed, but apparently not adopted as declared doctrine by either side at present, are Launch Under Attack and Nuclear Decapitation. Launch Under Attack calls for the launching of nuclear retaliatory forces while the enemy's initial attack is still underway and before most of the defender's forces designated for response have been destroyed. Presumably, this would require a "hair trigger" posture in crisis and possibly some prior release by the president or general secretary of the authority to use nuclear weapons. It also entails the instant launching of an attack based primarily on the integrated computer analysis of radar and other electronic surveillance information that large numbers of enemy missiles are inbound. With virtually no opportunity for any time-consuming validity checks, the possibilities of errors likely increase.

Crisis instability would also be adversely affected by a decapitation strategy in which one side seriously entertained the possibility of a first strike, not against missiles or C^3I, but instead against the human chain of command that can authorize the use of strategic nuclear weapons. If the few highest authorities with the authority to approve the use of strategic weapons could be eliminated almost simultaneously in a very swift attack, the retaliatory system would be decapitated. Steinbruner (1981–1982) suggests that a preemptive decapitation strike would reduce the damage of any retaliatory response because of the lack of necessary and timely coordination. To prevent the sudden elimination of all officials with the power to authorize the use of nuclear weapons, the logical response would appear to be the broad delegation of such power at the beginning of any crisis. Thus, the tight control, "single finger on the button," safeguard would be lost. Whether the knowledge that an adversary had initiated such a dispersal of authority would create caution or despair is difficult to determine. What is clearer is that it would make the possibility of accidental war in a crisis more likely and that expectation has an adverse effect on stability.

Not all recent developments with respect to strategic nuclear arsenals have reduced the stability of the deterrent system in crisis. In other areas there have been improvements as compared to conditions prevailing earlier in the Cold War, but they may have been offset by the modifications described above. Although the exploration of crisis effects on general international system stability has received only modest attention, this one application receives considerable attention. Various proposals have been advanced for enhancing crisis stability either by avoiding crises or by managing them in ways to limit the risk (Allison et al., 1985; Bleckman, 1985; Ball et al., 1987; Lebow, 1987).

CRISES AS CONFRONTATIONS BETWEEN ACTORS

For our purposes, then, a crisis is a period of conflict between two or more states when one side has challenged the other on a defined or definable issue, and a decision must be reached on the reaction to the challenge (Buchan, 1966, p. 20).

Typically, the immediate cause of a crisis is an attempt by one state to coerce another by an explicit or implicit threat of force. The first act of severe coercion may be called the *challenge;* technically it starts the crisis by posing a distinct possibility of war.... Once a challenge is given, it must be *resisted* by the challenged party in order for a crisis to occur.... The collision of challenge and resistance produces a *confrontation,* which is the core of the crisis [emphasis in the original] (Snyder and Diesing, 1977, pp. 11, 13–14).

The scholarship that views crises in terms of a period of sharp confrontation between two or more (but usually two) parties emphasizes the nature of the bargaining between those involved and the factors that may influence the nature of that interaction. Diplomacy, as the classical instrument of verbal negotiation, and military forces, used as tacit signalling devices for conveying the commitment and resolve, become central elements of study. One might wonder whether bargaining in crises differs significantly from the vast array of other situations in which actors with differing interests negotiate. Snyder and Diesing (1977, pp. 23–27) suggest that crisis bargaining has certain distinguishing features:

Crisis bargaining typically involves the distribution, or more likely the redistribution, of some good or resource that is mutually sought;

Crisis bargaining gives prominence to coercion and threats of the use of force.

Crisis bargaining involves a high degree of emotional content.

Crisis bargaining usually occurs under some sense of time urgency.

Crisis bargaining entails high stakes.

Crisis bargaining creates for the involved parties a sense of only limited control over the course of events.

The authors stop short of suggesting these are necessary conditions for bargaining to be in a crisis mode. They have gone further than most analysts, however, in suggesting how crisis bargaining may impose different conditions than exist in other settings. If we assume, as most research in this area does, that bargaining under conditions of crisis imposes distinctive requirements, then it is necessary to articulate those features, as Snyder and Diesing have, and to examine their consequences.

Analysts using the actor confrontation perspective on crisis have frequently relied on one of two methods for their investigation. They have often used either a series of comparative case studies or the structure of the theory of games. Substantively, a question shared by analysts adopting the confrontation perspective is what produces different bargaining outcomes. Researchers applying the theory of games generally address the conditions in which a stable solution can be found. Other researchers have focused on such issues as types of strategy, third-party intervention, and the conditions governing escalation.

Schelling (1960, 1966) has been instrumental in introducing the concepts and structure of the theory of games to the examination of international politics. He has encouraged world affairs analysts to recognize the varying structures present in different international conflicts, the implications of interdependent choices on conflict outcomes, and the seeming parallelism between certain simple games and recurrent problems in conflict bargaining among nations. More recently, some scholars (e.g., Brams, 1985; Powell, 1987) have sought to systematically apply game theory to crisis situations in order to determine when selection of certain choices by the players might lead to stable solutions or outcomes and when a kind of game contains a dominant or best strategy for either player. Brams (1985, especially ch. 2), for example, has interpreted two deterrence crises—the Cuban missile crisis and the alert crisis during the 1973 Yom Kippur War—in terms of familiar two-person games. Part of the task is to modify the game structure or conditions to provide a better representation of the actual crisis. In this instance, Brams offers a way to move from the usual static structure of such games to one involving a sequence of moves. He also shows the implications of alternative perspectives on the crises and possible alternative preferences of the players.

Subsequently, Brams and Kilgour (1987) have structured the game so that players can select degrees of cooperation or resistance. The game assumes that both parties have escalated their conflict (i.e., created a crisis), and the task is to determine whether an outcome can be found which stabilizes the situation without further severe escalation. Conditions that produce crisis stability, such as one player valuing the cooperative outcome or use of only mild threats of escalation, are identified.

Whereas Brams concentrated primarily on the elaboration of one basic game (the so-called Chicken configuration named after the supposed practice of racing cars directed toward one another from opposite directions), Snyder and Diesing (1977) used game theory structure to construct a typology of nine different crisis situations. Each one was represented as a 2 x 2 outcome matrix. The nine situations portrayed different preference orderings by the two participants of the four possible game outcomes (yield, win, compromise, or breakdown/war). All crises are viewed as following three phases: an initial challenge and response, a confrontation, and a resolution (characterized by one of the four outcomes). The games are compared to sixteen historical crises. The authors reason that certain outcomes are more likely in different situations or crisis structures. The small number of historical cases limits the ability of the actual crises to confirm expected outcomes (e.g., only two of the sixteen cases resulted in war, although three of the nine games had that as the dominant outcome), but conclusions about bargaining and information processing are reached. In general, these researchers observed that across the types of situations, coercion increased in the initial phase (perhaps to be expected by definition), but afterward bargainers in the historical cases tended to behave cautiously—to limit the magnitude of their coercive moves, to avoid major commitments, and to minimize steps entailing serious risks.

Another project offers on intriguing parallel to the Snyder and Diesing study. Leng's Behavioral Correlates of War Project (e.g., 1983, 1984, 1987) seeks to determine when militarized disputes between nations (crises) end in war and when they do not. He has gradually developed an empirically defined typology of crisis bargaining situations based on dimensions of the dispute. (A recent version is Leng, 1987.) Event data from actual historical crises are used to test the outcomes hypothesized for different types of disputes (e.g., Leng, 1983, 1984). Although differing in some important respects from Snyder and Diesing (e.g., no emphasis on game theory; use of quantitative analysis), Leng clearly shares major concerns with the other two scholars. Leng and Walker (1982) actually performed a comparative analysis. They found only partial support for the Snyder-Diesing expectations concerning bargaining strategies that corresponded to the initial authors' crisis structures. They did find, however, shifts in bargaining strategy from one phase to another. In terms of avoiding war, Leng tends to find support for a reciprocal, tit-for-tat strategy, such as proposed by Axelrod (1984). The Leng and Walker observations on their study are instructive in this regard.

Some of the conclusions of Snyder and Diesing (1977) also confirm observations by Young (1968) who examined fifteen crisis bargaining hypotheses in four confrontations between the United States and the Soviet Union between 1948 and 1962. Young found constraints on the use of violence and coercion in the superpower crises, much like Snyder and Diesing reported after examining more diverse types of crises between 1898 and 1962. It is important to recognize that neither set of crisis situations was large, nor can we be certain about what larger class of crises they may represent.

Despite the evidence that, once in a crisis, policymakers often exercise caution in the use of force and coercion, we have noted at the outset that threats of force may be one of the hallmarks of the early stages of crisis bargaining. Thus, a strategy of coercive bargaining lies close to the heart of many studies (e.g., George et al. 1971; Williams, 1976; Lauren, 1979). George and his associates identify a strategy of coercive diplomacy, which though not necessarily limited to crisis bargaining, could often be expected to arise in such situations. Coercive diplomacy entails the use of force in a demonstrative fashion intended to alter the enemy's will (rather than his capabilities) by signalling the initiator's resolve and ability to inflict more severe punishment in the future unless the adversary modifies his position in a certain fashion. It is a form of tacit communication, but the physical behavior is often accompanied by diplomatic communication designed, among other things, to specify the action the adversary must take to avoid future punishment. Reviewing three crises in which the United States was interpreted as engaging in coercive diplomacy (Laos, 1961; Cuba, 1962; Vietnam, 1965), George and his associates (1971) searched for the presence of eight conditions that they postulated increase the likelihood of such a strategy being successful. The conditions hypothesized to favor success are:

1. Strength of initiator's motivation.
2. Symmetry of motivation favoring the initiator.
3. Clarity of initiator's objectives.
4. Sense of urgency necessary to achieve initiator's objective.
5. Adequate domestic support for initiator.
6. Usable military options.
7. Opponent's fear of unacceptable escalation.
8. Clarity concerning precise terms of settlement.

Although the authors do not contend that these eight conditions are equally important for success or that they include all the necessary conditions for effective coercive diplomacy, they demonstrate that most were present in the successful cases of Laos and Cuba, and most were missing from the threatened escalation in Vietnam in 1965.

If conditions for coercive diplomacy do not prevail, neither party is able to pursue an alternative strategy that forces the other to yield, and both remain firm in their resolve, third-party intervention may be a means of breaking the deadlock or preventing a spiraling to much higher levels of hostility. Young (1967, 1971), who has contributed considerably to the study of intermediaries in international crisis negotiations, suggests that the role of such actors (i.e., international organizations, nonaligned states, and non-engaged allies) is limited during the early upswing phase of a crisis. It may be more effective subsequently—perhaps when the parties realize the likelihood of deadlock or further escalation, or when one party is looking for a face-saving way to yield. Young (1967) draws a major distinction between a third party's ability to assist in regulating or terminating the crisis and reaching substantive agreement on the underlying issues. Note also should be made of the role of smaller states, which by geography or alignment may be delicately balanced on the edge of crisis involvement. Pearson (1981) suggests most such small states will strive to maintain neutrality, and only economically well-developed minor parties will attempt to mediate major power crises that could impinge on them.

The central focus of the actor confrontation approach to crisis is the problem of how nations might interact to achieve something of what they want, or a least avoid disaster, after having had a head-on collision concerning vital conflicting interests. Although there are not as yet any very clear answers, it appears to be an area of research marked by considerable activity and invention. A strong case can be made that there has been continuing evolution since Schelling's (1960) path-breaking *Strategy of Conflict*. Researchers seem confident that there are alternative strategies for different stages of crisis bargaining and in different types of crisis situations. A diversity of methods and approaches is being applied but with sufficient commonality of purpose that the insights can be shared. It would seem reasonable to expect continued progress on the effects of types of crisis bargaining under various conditions and theoretically grounded prescriptions for averting war or stopping escalation.

Crisis Forecasting

A potential policy application of crisis studies with roots in the actor confrontation perspective is crisis forecasting and monitoring. The purpose is to provide some kind of early warning of emerging crises to the policy community. Unlike most academic studies which adopt the confrontation perspective, crisis forecasters have relatively little interest in understanding the bargaining process within a crisis. Nevertheless, most forecasting efforts share the following features with the actor confrontation approach:

• Assume that crises typically begin with some triggering event or events (i.e., a challenge).
• View crises, once initiated, as following a pattern involving certain stages or phases.
• Focus primarily on dyads of interacting actors in the world system.

As in Leng's work on militarized disputes, efforts at forecasting have depended heavily on the collection and use of event data. Edward Azar, who pioneered the collection of event data, scaled events that one nation initiated to another according to their relative intensity of cooperation or conflict. Using his Conflict and Peace Data Bank (COPDAB), Azar (1974, 1975) conducted several pilot forecasting studies.

Another early leader in event data collection and analysis was Charles McClelland. As we have seen, McClelland was concerned with crises in the international system, but he also sought the means to examine more discrete interaction patterns that evolved in specific crises. His ideas for tracing the sequence of interactions in a crisis are set forth in an early essay (McClelland, 1961). His World Event/Interaction Survey (WEIS) data coding system was adapted for an extremely ambitious crisis forecasting and monitoring project sponsored by the U.S. Defense Department's Advanced Research Projects Agency (DARPA) in the 1970s. The project envisioned using a sophisticated computer system to forewarn of crises, with event data as indicators. Parallel to the forecasting development was the design of a crisis management tool that would enable policymakers to compare the characteristics of an emerging crisis with the profiles of past crises together with the nature of previous decisions. (For an accessible description of these activities, see Young, 1977, and Hopple and Rossa, 1981.) Despite a substantial investment, by social science standards no workable system was completed. It has been suggested that policymakers lacked confidence in the quality of the event data on which the system was dependent. In addition, it may be that the theoretical understanding of the factors associated with the antecedents and triggers of various kinds of crises has not evolved to the point where major, stable indicators for monitoring could be identified.[2] Certainly, more recent efforts to consider the problem of crisis forecasting have been sensitive to the issue of better development of the theoretical underpinnings. (See Hermann and Mason, 1980; Raphael, 1982.)

Some may doubt whether systematic forecasting of certain kinds of international crises is a realistic objective. Whether it ever becomes so may well depend on continuing research on the actor confrontation perspective with its attention to the various structures of crises and their implications.

DECISION-MAKING CRISES

We now move to a third level for a different perspective on crisis. This level of analysis examines a nation, government, or other decision unit experiencing a crisis. Typically, analysts adopting this approach are concerned about the quality of the decision. How does the nature of a decision made under conditions of crisis differ from that reached in non-crisis? The decision-making approach in its fullest application embraces the occasion for decision, the collection and analysis of information, the formulation of any options and their advocacy, as well as the implementation of any decision after the choice, including any monitoring for effects and feedback.

Understandably, what constitutes a crisis from this perspective shifts to focus on the decision-maker's problem. Definitions tend to be constructed in terms of the properties of the situation facing the unit making the decision, usually as perceived by them. My own definition (Hermann, 1969) has focused on the interaction of high threat to the basic goals of the decision unit members, short time before the situation likely evolves in a manner undesired by the decision unit members, and surprise to these individuals (or the lack of expectation) that the particular situation would arise. Brecher (1978) has stipulated a situation involving threat, finite time, and a high probability of hostilities. Whatever the specific properties contained in a definition, the emphasis is from the perspective of a particular decision-making unit. This focus creates the possibility of one entity alone being in a crisis in contrast with the actor confrontation perspective where at least two entities must both be involved. Which perspective one takes depends on the research question being asked.[3]

In a recent review, Holsti (forthcoming) proposes that crisis decision-making can itself be subdivided into four levels of analysis: the nation-state, organization, small group, and individual. He makes a strong case that the questions, variables, and judgments about decision results vary among these levels. Although the four-way division is theoretically constructive, actual research entailing consideration of crises does not appear to be ongoing at each level. A realist view of international politics encourages viewing the nation-state as a single rational actor pursuing its national interests. Allison (1971) has suggested how this perspective creates a distinctive approach to decision-making. It is not one, however, in which crisis has figured as a prominent concept for analysis. For this reason, the remainder of this survey will concentrate on the organizational, small group, and individual levels of decision-making.

Organizational Decision-Making

Case studies and general speculative analysis on organizational decision-making suggest that the configuration of an organization can influence the quality of decision in a crisis. In his examination of the Cuban missile crisis from an organizational perspective, Allison (1971) illustrated the tendency of organizations to rely on standard operating procedures. Organizations normally develop a limited number of routines to respond to the range of problems they expect to encounter. Stating quite a similar feature differently, Thompson (1967) suggested that organizations have a certain "technology," which characterizes that organization's treatment of problems. The organization's technology is expected to produce a given effect. The difficulty arises when the situation with which the organization must deal does not conform to its technology or standard operating procedure. Unfortunately, crises often fall in this class. In such circumstances, the organization may tend to apply one of its standard procedures inappropriately or to become immobilized.

Another dimension of organizations in crisis concerns the volume and quality of information. Crises are likely to be situations involving considerable uncertainty about what is happening and about effects—particularly in the early stages. Thus, the task of sorting out rumor and misinformation as well as estimating the reliability and meaning of information—almost always a problem in foreign affairs—may become more acute in a crisis. The Conflict and Integration Project at Stanford University under Robert North pioneered the study of foreign policy crisis decision-making and concentrated on the collection and systematic analysis of textual data from one of the most severe crises of the twentieth century—the weeks preceding the outbreak of World War I. One of the major associates of that project analyzed organizational communication in crisis. Holsti (1972) demonstrates that in August of 1914 there was communication overload—information substantially in excess of what the key foreign ministries could process. He suggests that "some of the behavioral consequences of a situation such as the 1914 crisis are likely to include disregard for some messages, filtering of incoming information, errors, and the like" (Holsti, 1972, p. 118).

My own survey of organizations in crisis suggests a phenomenon which I call "contraction of authority" (Hermann, 1963), which may compound difficulties such as communication overload. In a crisis the power or authority for making decisions tends to move to the highest levels of the organization and to consist of a small group of the chief officer's most trusted associates, regardless of their formal areas of responsibility (in terms of fit with the domain of the crisis problem). Given the highly threatening nature of a crisis, it is not unreasonable that a leader would surround himself with his most trusted advisers. The persons at higher levels of most organizations tend to be generalists, not specialists. Secrecy and the natural process of groups under threat may cause them to shunt off much of the rest of the organization. This contraction can create severe bottlenecks in passing information from the organization's experts and those outside the organization to the decision-makers. It encourages the kind of gatekeeping and inappropriate filtering of data to which Holsti referred. Of course, modern organizations, and certainly national security organizations, have elaborate computer-based systems for information management. They also monitor much more information than in 1914.

The picture emerging from these organizational analyses tends to suggest that the quality of organizational decision-making may decline in a crisis. This conclusion, is premature. However, Milburn (1972) and Crozier (1964) are among those that find crises may liberate creative energies in an organization. Crises may provide the justification to enable people to cut through the inertia and drag that often characterize bureaucracies in routine situations. Crises, according to Crozier (1964, p. 197) "continually create a new demand for authoritarian reformer figures in the midst of bureaucratic routine." Whereas Crozier's observation relates to the presence or absence of certain kinds of individuals who can assume leadership in a crisis, March and Simon (1958) note that some organizations can build-in slack in human and other resources, so that in the press of crises their overall performance need not deteriorate. Organizations designed to deal with emergencies and natural disasters (e.g., fire departments, hospital emergency rooms) exhibit these protective qualities (see Rosenthal, 1984). They may also have decision rules to establish priorities for action in a crisis. (E.g., the State and Defense departments' priority levels for cable traffic can be used to reduce overload in a crisis.) In a thorough examination of two Israeli government decisions in crisis, Brecher (1980) found little evidence of the organizational patterns that would reduce the quality of decisions. Whether these findings can be explained by the presence or absence of certain organizational properties (e.g., slack, certain types of personalities, preestablished crisis decision rules) must be systematically considered in future studies.

Small Groups

Some of the research on small group decision-making has been of single cases of decisions that happened to be crises (e.g., Paige, 1968), although the authors did not necessarily set out to design a study that would enable one to determine if the observed activities in crises differed from more routine situations. The International Crisis Behavior Project under the direction of Michael Brecher may contribute significantly to overcoming this obstacle by an examination of 278 separate crises in the twentieth century, a subset of which will be the subject of book-length case studies using a common framework. (See Brecher, Wilkenfeld, and Moser, forthcoming.)

At present, perhaps the most significant study of small group decision-making in crisis stems from the theoretical work of Janis (1972) on groupthink. (Also see subsequent empirical investigations of Janis's theory by Tetlock, 1979.) Groupthink occurs when the desire to maintain the decision group's cohesion leads its members to such strong concurrence-seeking tendencies that each person's effective participation is impaired. "Concurrence-seeking and the various symptoms of groupthink to which it gives rise can be best understood as a mutual effort among the members of the group to maintain self-esteem, especially when they share responsibility for making vital decisions that pose threats of social disapproval and self-disapproval" (Janis, 1972, p. 203). Groupthink is hypothesized to lead to "a deterioration of mental efficiency, reality-testing, and moral judgment" (Janis, 1972, p. 9). Again, groupthink is not specifically a response to crisis and may arise in other circumstances. But some of the conditions hypothesized to trigger its occurrence are likely in a crisis (e.g., external threat, insulation of the decision group from others).

It is noteworthy that groupthink postulates very different dynamics for group decision-making than does bureaucratic politics. The latter envisions a group composed of members from different bureaucratic agencies or ministries. Members often put the differing interests of their own agency ahead of any common governmental or national interests that presumably the inter-agency decision group is charged to maintain. In the absence of a predominant authority, the conflict among these competing interests often leads to compromises, trade-offs, and log-rolls, with the result that the decision bears little resemblance to any member's preferences or a coherent position. In bureaucratic politics, the absence of loyalty to the decision group produces conflicts, compromises, and potentially poor decisions. In groupthink, excessive loyalty to the decision group may lead to covering over disagreements and avoiding challenges to the group consensus, with the result that the quality of the decision may suffer.

Clearly, both conditions cannot occur simultaneously in the same group. Moreover, an argument can be made, with support from case studies and laboratory experiments, that group decisions are not always of poor quality and inferior to individual decisions. Again we see the need for the study of possible intervening variables that establish whether one or the other or neither of these conditions is likely in a group. It may be that bureaucratic politics prevail less frequently in crisis decisions, where strong executive authority with the ability to rule among competing bureaucratic interests is more likely to be present. In some circumstances, however, no leader may have such commanding authority, as in the early period of Brezhnev's rule, or the leader simply may not elect to exercise such power.

Individual Decision-Making

The final decision-making level of analysis focuses on the individual, either as an isolated policymaker acting alone or as a member of a larger decision unit. A great deal of literature exists on the personal qualities of the individual that may affect his or her performance in public policy. With respect to crisis, however, the key factor is the effect of individual physiological and psychological stress. Considerable research exists that assumes international crises automatically create individual stress in those persons who must deal with the problem. Therefore, the very substantial literature in psychology, social psychology, medicine, and elsewhere on the effects of stress on individual decision-making can be invoked. (For reviews of this literature, see George, 1986; Holsti, forthcoming; Hermann and Brady, 1972.) The effects of substantial stress have been shown to be deleterious to individual performance on a variety of tasks related to decision-making. The number of alternatives recognized as providing possible means of coping with the problem declines;

the ability to search for new information and options becomes ineffective; the capacity to think beyond the immediate present to possible future consequences erodes; in general, cognitive processing is impeded. It is not difficult to conclude that one or a group of policymakers suffering from severe stress will engage in poorer quality decision-making than they would under less stressful conditions.

On reflection, however, it does not seem reasonable to assume that every crisis automatically triggers severe stress in every policymaker or that the consequences will necessarily be an erosion of judgment. We need a better understanding of the linkage between crisis and stress.

A distinction between the personal experience of stress and the source of stress (i.e., the stressor) seems useful. Stress can then be understood as a syndrome within the individual of (a) various signals of some sort of imminent danger to the person's well-being and (b) a variety of defensive and protective reactions, both physical and psychological, designed to reduce the sense of danger. Some responses may be automatic and common to all people; others may be learned and highly personalized. Furthermore, in responding to certain kinds of stressors, an outside observer might judge some responses of the stressed person to be highly appropriate (e.g., pumping more adrenalin through he body); others (e.g., fainting) might be regarded as less effective.

But how might a crisis act as a stressor for an individual policymaker? If the crisis severely threatens some goal of the collectivity of which the individual is a part and the person has internalized that goal, then he or she may be subjected to stress. That is, that person may no longer see the crisis as threatening some governmental policy existing separately from the self, but rather as a direct danger to a part of the self. ("I created that policy and fought to get our government to adopt it; now those foreigners are trying to destroy my policy which is an integral part of me.")

If such a representation of the relationship between an international crisis and stress is correct, then a number of conditions must be determined to exist before we can know whether and what stress effects a crisis may create for an individual.

- Has the policymaker personally internalized that goal or object which the crisis threatens?
- What is the individual's tolerance for stress? (Moderate levels of stress may actually improve performance, but if the stress becomes too severe performance will drop off sharply. Individuals appear to vary in how much stress they can experience before their performance declines.)
- For how long does the stress continue without diversion or interruption? (Fatigue and related factors will eventually affect all individuals.)
- What are the patterns of learned coping techniques for stress which the individual is likely to display?
- Do the learned stress-coping techniques reinforce or conflict with the automatic responses of the body?

In the study of foreign policy, we need to learn how to answer such questions. After that, we still will face the challenge of how to determine the status of such determining factors for actual individual policymakers.

In summary, it should be noted that studies of crisis decision-making are extensive.[4] In general, they share a concern with the quality of decision-making in crisis. Most analysts conducting decision-making studies fifteen to twenty years ago likely assumed that crises had an extremely negative effect on the quality of decision-making. Certainly, some cases of crisis and isolated laboratory experiments offer support for that conclusion. A fuller examination of the research that has emerged, however, suggests a more cautious conclusion. At each level of decision-making where there has been active research, the possibility of intervening or control variables that can influence the impact of a crisis on decision seems plausible. At the organization level, some candidate control variables have been identified. At the small group level, mediators may be necessary to determine what theory best applies (including the possibility that neither of the most prominent current ones is applicable). At the level of the individual, where much attention has been paid to the effects of stress, we need to identify the variables that determine the link between crisis and the individual and the conditions that generate various coping mechanisms in different individuals. Even, however, with the present state of knowledge about the quality of decision-making in crisis, there is the basis for consideration of crisis management.

Crisis Management

This area of inquiry explicitly seeks to design studies that offer prescriptions intended to improve the performance of policymakers in dealing with crises. It is probably unwise to conclude that all research on international crises automatically fits in this category as sometimes appears to be assumed (e.g., Gilbert and Lauren, 1980). It is possible to generate policy prescriptions from any of the levels of crisis study—system, actor confrontation, or decision-making—but decision-making seems most congenial because the research is designed to explore the issue from the perspective of the policymaker and seeks to address the problem of effects on decision quality. Indeed, many of the studies in crisis decision-making have as a stated purpose the creation of recommendations for the conduct of crises (e.g., Williams, 1976).

As Milburn (1972) notes, many recommendations for management of a crisis derive almost entirely from the value premises of the researcher that may not be explicit. In addition, some recommendations seem to demonstrate little sensitivity to the environment likely to prevail in various complex policy situations or to offer advice that likely is unfamiliar to those who have previously experienced any kind of crises. Fortunately, important contributions to crisis management exist that avoid these limitations.

In recommendations to enhance the quality of decision-making in a crisis, it is necessary to establish explicit criteria that yield observable indicators as to what constitute better decisions. Various standards have been proposed. One possibility is simply to use non-crisis decisions as reference points. Do major characteristics of the decision process in crisis (e.g., search for options, consideration of conflicting information) appear to be at least as adequate according to the precepts of decision theory as in non-crisis decisions? Another common standard is whether war is avoided. (For examples, see the essays in the East-West symposium volume edited by Frei, 1978.) Although strongly challenged in some early crisis studies, rationality or utility-maximizing standards are frequently used and a case can be made that they may be appropriate (Stein, 1978; Oneal, 1984). Oneal (1982, p. 46) has made a systematic effort to use "creative adaptation" as a standard of performance by which he means "the reversal of an initially disadvantageous crisis action short of war which protects and promotes the national values, interests, and goals threatened in the crisis." Each of these standards may be more or less appropriate in different circumstances, but it is important to determine what the criteria for good performance are in any set of crisis management recommendations. The next step is to establish that the analyst can demonstrate a linkage between the recommended crisis action and movement toward the stated standard.

The work on crisis management can be divided into two basic groups: those proposals concerned with crisis avoidance or prevention, and those concerned with coping more effectively once a crisis occurs.

One of the most creative analysts who has explored means of crisis prevention is Alexander George. Within this approach, he (e.g., George, 1983) has devoted considerable attention to the possibility of agreements among nations, and particularly the superpowers, for codes of international conduct that might limit the behaviors between adversaries that often trigger crises. It is possible to design more focused proposals if one specifies a certain kind of crisis as Lebow (1987) does with respect to characteristics of deterrence subject to destabilization in crisis. Another crisis prevention example results from a recent international agreement. In 1987, the United States and the Soviet Union agreed to create Nuclear Risk Reduction Centers in Moscow and Washington intended to exchange information and perform other activities that would reduce the likelihood of accidental wars.

As one would expect, a variety of proposals for coping with crisis or crisis management emerged from the crisis decision-making studies. Hermann and Hermann (1975) propose a system for monitoring high-level policy-makers for symptoms of acute stress. George (1972) proposes the introduction of a respected individual advocating an alternative perspective in any decision group whenever they quickly start to reach consensus on a single option without serious examination of any alternatives. Allison and associates (1985) urge that nuclear alerts not be used for political signalling in crises to avoid sharp escalations. The time is ripe for a critical assessment of the numerous proposals for both crisis avoidance and crisis coping in which the criteria for quality decision-making and the evidence for and against each prescription is examined with respect to different types of crises.

SUMMARY AND CONCLUSIONS

This chapter has suggested that the level of analysis and the fundamental questions of interest have resulted in different definitions of crisis that, at times, generate conflicting findings and insights. Each of the three major levels of crisis study has been concerned primarily with different questions:

Systemic crises—When do crises lead to destabilization of the system?

Actor confrontation crises—What bargaining strategies produce successful outcomes without war?

Decision-making crises—What effects do crises have on the quality of decisions?

Not every study shares the central question associated with its particular level of analysis, but most address the basic issue in one way or another. It has also been suggested that each level or perspective on crisis currently has a companion area of explicitly policy-oriented research. At the system level it is the effects of crisis on deterrence stability; at the actor confrontation level it is crisis forecasting and monitoring; and at the decision-making level it is crisis management.

It seems clear that research is continuing at all three of these levels, with only limited attention to the work and insights produced from other perspectives. As the opening of this chapter implied with the sample of recent crisis situations, international crises will continue to be a major feature of international politics and pose challenges for national security policy.

Future study at each of the different levels of crisis research, however, will need to address possible international changes affecting the nature of crises, their likelihood of occurrence, and their consequences. Among the possible changes worthy of exploration are crises that involve other than military forms of coercion in their initial stages, but nonetheless pose threats to basic national survival goals. Deliberate attempts to manipulate the international financial markets might be an illustration. Situations such as these highlight the need for further examination of the conditions under which a nation in crisis might threaten to use force for limited political objectives and encounter other actors who may elect to use powerful non-military instruments in response. The international environment for regulating crises may also be undergoing change as the world responds to crisis actions by non-national actors, such as by small groups of terrorists. The evidence of increased interest by the United States in ad hoc multilateral diplomacy in addition to, or as a substitute for, formal international organizations suggests another change in the regulatory system. Nowhere, however, is the evidence of change more dramatic then in the factors affecting the stability of deterrence in crisis. The pace of technology and the corresponding adjustment in policies to those changes reveal how the conditions for crisis and their effects can change quickly.

NOTES

1. There is disagreement over whether repeated experience with crises reduces or increases the risk of war. Wright (1965) postulates that the probability of war is constant for each crisis, so the overall likelihood of war increases with the number of crises. McClelland (1961) suggests that the policymakers can learn from crisis experience, and, therefore, each time they avoid war they should be better able to avert war in future crises. Waltz (1964) proposes that the structure of the system influences the relationship between crisis and war.

2. One wonders whether the project managers or their clients were attracted by an analogy with the U.S. Air Force's early warning systems for detecting an enemy bomber or missile attack on the United States. If so, the parallel breaks down in part because our understanding of both the physical indicators of missile launches and their consequences are much greater than for potential crisis-triggering events.

3. For this reason it is puzzling to have Snyder and Diesing (1977, pp. 491–92) observe: "Some analysts have included shortness of decision time as one of the defining characteristics of crisis. We reject this interpretation because most of the cases we studied did not involve really short decision time." Such a statement would appear to imply that there is an implicit true definition of crisis which analysts must discover. Definitions are not right or wrong, but they do have consequences. Empirical evidence as well as everyday experience suggests that decision-makers respond differently to situations in which they have very limited time compared to those where considerably more time for decision is available. Hence, if we want to study the impact of certain kinds of situations on decision-making, time may be an essential property. If, however, eliminating all situations offering extended decision time excludes some confrontation situations that scholars wish to study for bargaining purposes, then clearly they need a different definition. It does not follow that one formulation can be defended as capturing what "really are" crises, but rather that definitions vary with the questions we seek to explore.

4. For more complete review of the crisis decision making literature, see Tanter (1978), Lamontagne, 1985: Brecher et al. (forthcoming), and Holsti (forthcoming).

REFERENCES

Allison, G. T. 1971. *Essence of Decision: Explaining the Cuban Missile Crisis*. Boston: Little, Brown.

———, A. Carnesale, and J. Nye, Jr., eds. 1985. *Hawks, Doves and Owls*. New York: W. W. Norton.

Axelrod, Robert. 1984. *The Evolution of Cooperation*. New York: Basic Books.

Azar, Edward E. 1975. Behavioral Forecasts and Policymaking: An Events Data Approach. Pp. 215–39 in Charles W. Kegley, Jr., Gregory A. Raymond, Robert M. Rood, and Richard A. Skinner, eds., *International Events and the Comparative Analysis of Foreign Policy*. Columbia: University of South Carolina Press.

————, James P. Bennett, and Thomas J. Sloan. 1974. Steps Toward Forecasting International Interactions. *Papers of the Peace Science Society International* 23:27–67.

Ball, Desmond, et al. 1987. *Crisis Stability and Nuclear War*. Ithaca, N.Y.: Peace Studies Program.

Blair, Bruce G. 1985. *Strategic Command and Control: Redefining the Nuclear Threat*. Washington, D.C.: Brookings Institution.

Bleckman, Barry M. 1985. *Preventing Nuclear War*. Bloomington: Indiana University Press.

Bozeman, Adda B. 1960. *Politics and Culture in International History*. Princeton, N.J.: Princeton University Press.

Bracken, P. 1983. *Command and Control of Nuclear Forces*. New Haven, Conn.: Yale University Press.

Brams, Steven J. 1985. *Superpower Games*. New Haven, Conn.: Yale University Press.

————, and D. Marc Kilgour. 1987. Threat Escalation and Crisis Stability: A Game-Theoretic Analysis. *American Political Science Review* 81:833–50.

Brecher, Michael, ed. 1978. *Studies in Crisis Behavior*. New Brunswick, N.J.: Transaction Books.

————. 1980. *Decisions in Crisis: Israel, 1967–1973*. Berkeley: University of California Press.

————, Jonathan Wilkenfeld, and Sheila Moser. Forthcoming. *Crises in the Twentieth Century*. New York: Pergamon Press.

Buchan, Alastair. 1966. Crisis Management: The New Diplomacy. *The Atlantic Papers*. Boulogne-sur-Seine, France: Atlantic Institute.

Crozier, Michael. 1964. *The Bureaucratic Phenomenon*. Chicago: University of Chicago Press.

Frei, Daniel, ed. 1978. *International Crises and Crisis Management*. Westmead, England: Saxon House.

Genco, Stephen J. 1980. Integration Theory and System Change in Western Europe: The Neglected Role of Systems Transformation Episodes. Pp. 55–82 in Ole R. Holsti, Randolph M. Siverson, and Alexander L. George, eds., *Change in the International System*. Boulder, Colo.: Westview Press.

George, Alexander L. 1972. The Case for Multiple Advocacy in Making Foreign Policy. *American Political Science Review* 48:751–85.

————. 1986. The Impact of Crisis-Induced Stress on Decision Making. Pp. 529–52 in Alexander L. George, ed., *Images and Risks of Nuclear War*. Washington D.C.: National Academy Press.

————, David K. Hall, and William R. Simons. 1971. *The Limits of Coercive Diplomacy: Laos, Cuba, Vietnam*. Boston: Little, Brown.

Gilbert, Arthur N., and Paul G. Lauren. 1980. Crisis Management: An Assessment and Critique. *Conflict Resolution* 24:641–64.

Hermann, Charles F. 1987a. Trends Toward Crisis Instability: Increasing the Danger of Nuclear War. In Steve Cimbala, ed., *Challenges to Deterrence in the 1990s*. New York: Praeger.

————. 1987b. Enhancing Crisis Stability: Correcting the Trend Toward Increasing Instability. In Gilbert R. Winham, ed., *New Issues in Crisis Management*. Boulder, Colo.: Westview Press.

————. 1969. International Crisis as a Situation Variable. Pp. 409–21 in James N.

Rosenau, ed., *International Politics and Foreign Policy*. 2nd ed. New York: Free Press.

———. 1963. Some Consequences of Crisis Which Limit the Viability of Organizations. *Administrative Science Quarterly* 8:61–82.

———, and Linda P. Brady. 1972. Alternative Models of International Crisis Behavior. Pp. 281–303 in Charles F. Hermann, ed., *International Crises: Insights from Behavioral Research*. New York: Free Press.

———, and Robert E. Mason. 1980. Identifying Behavioral Attributes of Events That Trigger International Crises. Pp. 189–210 in Ole R. Holsti, Randolph M. Siverson, and Alexander L. George, eds., *Change in the International System*. Boulder, Colo.: Westview Press.

Hermann, Margaret G., and Charles F. Hermann. 1975. Maintaining the Quality of Decision Making in Foreign Policy Crises: A Proposal. In Alexander L. George, ed., *Towards More Soundly Based Foreign Policy: Making Better Use of Information*. Report to the Commission on the Organization of Government for the Conduct of Foreign Policy, Appendix D. Washington, D.C.: U.S. Government Printing Office.

Holsti, Kalevi J. 1977. *International Politics: A Framework for Analysis,* 3rd ed. Englewood Cliffs, N.J.: Prentice-Hall.

Holsti, Ole R. Forthcoming. Crisis Decision-Making. In Robert Jervis, Philip Tetlock, and Charles Tilly, eds., *Contributions of Behavioral and Social Science to the Prevention of Nuclear War,* Vol. 1.

———. 1972. *Crisis, Escalation, War*. Montreal, Canada: McGill-Queen's University Press.

Hopmann, P. Terrence, and Timothy D. King. 1980. From Cold War to Detente: The Role of the Cuban Missile Crisis and the Partial Nuclear Test Ban Treaty. Pp. 163–88 in Ole R. Holsti, Randolph M. Siverson, and Alexander L. George, eds., *Change in the International System*. Boulder, Colo.: Westview Press.

Hopple, Gerald W., and Paul J. Rossa. 1981. International Crisis Analysis: Recent Developments and Future Directions. Pp. 65–98 in Terrence P. Hopmann, Dina A. Zinnes, and J. David Singer, eds., *Cumulation in International Relations Research*. Monograph Series in World Affairs, University of Denver, Vol. 18.

Janis, Irving L. 1972. *Victims of Groupthink*. Boston: Houghton Mifflin.

Kaplan, Morton. 1957. *System and Process in International Politics*. New York: John Wiley.

Lamontagne, Gilles. 1985. Empirical Research Project on International Crisis: Theoretical Orientation, Progression of Research and Future Outlook. Unpublished paper, Montreal, Quebec, Canada.

Lauren, Paul Gordon, ed. 1979. *Diplomacy: New Approaches in History, Theory, and Policy*. New York: Free Press.

Lebow, Richard N. 1987. *Nuclear Crisis Management: A Dangerous Illusion*. Ithaca, N.Y.: Cornell University Press.

Leng, Russell J. 1983. Coercive Bargaining in Recurrent Crises. *Conflict Resolution* 27:379–419.

———. 1982. Crisis Bargaining: Confrontation, Coercion, and Reciprocity. *Conflict Resolution* 26: 571–91.

———. 1984. Reagan and the Russians: Crisis Bargaining Beliefs and the Historical Record. *American Political Science Review* 78:338–55.

―――. 1987. Structure and Action in Militarized Disputes. Pp. 187–202 in C. F. Hermann, C. W. Kegley, Jr., and J. N. Rosenau, eds., *New Directions in the Study of Foreign Policy*. Boston: Allen and Unwin.

―――, and Stephen Walker. 1982. Comparing Two Studies of Crisis Bargaining: Confrontation Coercion and Reciprocity. *Journal of Conflict Resolution* 27:379–419.

Luard, Evan. 1976. *Types of International Society*. New York: Free Press.

McClelland, Charles A. 1961. The Acute International Crisis. *World Politics* 14:182–204.

―――. 1972. The Beginning, Duration and Abatement of International Crises: Comparisons in Two Conflict Arenas. Pp. 83–105 in Charles F. Hermann, ed., *International Crises*. New York: Free Press.

March, James G., and Herbert A. Simon. 1958. *Organizations*. New York: John Wiley.

Milburn, Thomas W. 1972. The Management of Crisis. Pp. 259–77 in Charles F. Hermann, ed., *International Crises*. New York: Free Press.

Morse, Edward L. 1973. *Foreign Policy and Interdependence in Gaullist France*. Princeton, N.J.: Princeton University Press.

Oneal, John R. 1984. The Appropriateness of the Rational Actor Model in the Study of Crisis Decision Making. An unpublished paper, Department of Political Science, Vanderbilt University.

―――. 1982. *Foreign Policy Making in Times of Crisis*. Columbus: Ohio State University Press.

Paige, Glenn, D. 1968. *The Korean Decision: June 24–30, 1950*. New York: Free Press.

Pearson, Frederic S. 1981. *The Weak State in International Crisis*. Washington, D.C.: University Press of America.

Powell, Robert. 1987. Crisis Beginning, Escalation, and MAD. *American Political Science Review* 81: 717–36.

Raphael, Theodore D. 1982. Integrative Complexity Theory and Forecasting International Crisis: Berlin 1946–1962. *Conflict Resolution* 26:423–50.

Rosecrance, Richard N. 1963. *Action and Reaction in World Politics: International Systems in Perspective*. Boston: Little, Brown.

Rosenthal, Uriel. 1984. *Disasters, Riots and Hostage-Takings: Crisis Decision-Making in The Netherlands*. Amsterdam: DeBataafsche Leeun.

Schelling, Thomas C. 1966. *Arms and Influence*. New Haven, Conn.: Yale University Press.

―――. 1960. *The Strategy of Conflict*. New York: Oxford University Press.

Snyder, Glenn H., and Paul Diesing. 1977. *Conflict Among Nations: Bargaining, Decision Making, and System Structure in International Crises*. Princeton, N.J.: Princeton University Press.

Stein, Janice. 1978. Can Decision-Makers Be Rational and Should They Be? Evaluating the Quality of Decisions. Pp. 316–39 in Michael Brecher, ed., *Studies in Crisis Behavior*. New Brunswick, N.J.: Transaction Books.

Steinbruner, J. D. 1981–1982. Nuclear Decapitation. *Foreign Policy* 45:16–28.

Tanter, Raymond. 1978. International Crisis Behavior: An Appraisal of the Literature. Pp. 340–74 in Michael Brecher, ed., *Studies in Crisis Behavior*. New Brunswick, N.J.: Transaction Books.

Tetlock, P. E. 1979. Identifying Victims of Groupthink from Public Statements of Decision Makers. *Journal of Personality and Social Psychology* 37:1314–24.

Thompson, James. 1967. *Organizations in Action*. New York: McGraw-Hill.

Waltz, Kenneth N. 1964. Stability of a Bipolar World. *Daedalus* 43:883–84.

Waltz, Kenneth N. 1979. *Theory of International Politics*. New York: Random House.

Williams, Phil. 1976. *Crisis Management*. New York: John Wiley.

Wright, Quincy. 1965. *A Study of War,* 2nd ed. Chicago: University of Chicago Press.

Young, Oran R. 1967. *The Intermediaries: Third Parties in International Crises*. Princeton, N.J.: Princeton University Press.

———. 1968. *The Politics of Force: Bargaining During International Crises*. Princeton, N.J.: Princeton University Press.

Young, Robert A., ed. 1977. Special Issue on International Crisis: Progress and Prospects for Applied Forecasting and Management. *International Studies Quarterly* 21.

Zinnes, Dina A. 1980. Prerequisites for the Study of System Transformation. Pp. 3–22 in Ole R. Holsti, Randolph M. Siverson, and Alexander L. George, eds., *Change in the International System*. Boulder, Colo.: Westview Press.

A Core Collection of Reference Books on Arms Control, Disarmament, International Security, National Security, and Peace

STEPHEN E. ATKINS

Acquisition of a core collection of reference books on arms control, disarmament, international security, national security, and peace depends on obtaining materials from a myriad of international publishers. Although a dozen or so private and public publishers dominate publishing in these fields, there are important sources from a variety of institutes and small presses. Together, they produce enough reference books to fulfill the research needs of the scholar, the student, and the general public. But it is almost impossible for selectors in libraries, institutes, and think tanks to determine quality reference books from the mass of materials flooding the publishing market. The purpose of this chapter is to recommend the best of these reference books to form a core collection for libraries at universities, institutes, and think tanks.

Reference material comes in various formats. The most useful for beginning and advanced researchers and the general public are bibliographies. Bibliographies provide lists of books, reports, and articles on a specific topic. Another valuable format is the annual or yearbook. This type of reference source deals with a specific subject over a limited timespan, normally a year. Databooks, handbooks, and sourcebooks are other reference books that provide various kinds of in-depth information for the benefit of researchers. Guidebooks serve as a research guide for the study of a particular subject. Finally, there are directories which give researchers places to make contacts with other researchers or find new materials. Each of these formats is popular with both publishers and the readers of their publications, because all provide information unavailable elsewhere.

ARMS CONTROL AND DISARMAMENT

Bibliographies on arms control and disarmament appear at irregular intervals, but they constitute an invaluable reference source. The best bibliography in the arms control and disarmament field remains Richard Dean Burns's *Arms Control and*

Disarmament: A Bibliography (Santa Barbara, Calif.: ABC-Clio, 1977. 430 pp.). Although this work is beginning to become dated, it is still the most valuable retrospective bibliography in the field. Most of its entries are on American contributions to arms control and disarmament literature, but the value of this book resides in its comprehensiveness.

Another brief but still useful bibliography is Dan Caldwell's *Bibliography on Contemporary Arms Control and Disarmament* (Providence, R.I.: Center for Foreign Policy Development, 1983. 47 pp.). This book contains 609 citations on arms control and disarmament books and articles from a variety of English-language sources. It is stronger on journal and newspaper articles than on books.

A look at international disarmament issues can be obtained in the *Repertory of Disarmament* (Geneva, Switzerland: Palais de Nations, 1982. 449 pp.). This bibliography is a product of the United Nations Institute for Disarmament Research (UNIDIR). UNIDIR has attempted to make this a comprehensive bibliography dealing with international disarmament issues, but Western European sources predominate.

British contributions to disarmament literature appear in Lorna Lloyd and Nicholas A. Sims's *British Writing on Disarmament from 1914 to 1978: A Bibliography* (London: Francis Pinter, 1979. 171 pp.). The authors believe that British efforts on disarmament have been underrepresented in earlier bibliographies, and this book is an attempt to provide a complete bibliography of British efforts in the disarmament field. While it includes significant books, articles, and government reports, the strength of this bibliography resides in references to pamphlets and position papers.

A more recent bibliography on a more specific topic is *Strategic Nuclear Arms Control Verification: An Annotated Bibliography, 1977–1984* (Washington, D.C.: American Association for the Advancement of Science, 1985. 90 pp.) This book, edited by Richard A. Scribner and Robert Travis Scott, covers a total of 333 articles, books, and reports. It is an important source for arms control researchers on the subject of nuclear arms control verification.

Only a few annuals and yearbooks are published in the arms control and disarmament field, but they make up in quality for the lack of quantity. The Stockholm Peace Research Institute (SIPRI) produces the top yearbook in this field, the *World Armaments and Disarmament: SIPRI Yearbook* (London: Taylor and Francis, 1967– $31.00). This yearbook attracts an international cast of arms control and disarmament experts, and their contributions make this yearbook an eagerly awaited publication each year.

Another particularly useful annual is the U.S. Arms Control and Disarmament Agency's *World Military Expenditures and Arms Transfers* (Washington, D.C.: U.S. Arms Control and Disarmament Agency. 1974–   ). It is a compilation of data on world military expenditures and arms transfers for 145 countries over a ten-year period. Data from this source are best utilized for comparison over time.

The Carnegie Endowment for International Peace initiated a series of annual reports on the spread of nuclear weapons in 1984. Leonard S. Spector's *The Spread of Nuclear Weapons* (New York: Vintage, 1984– $5.95 [pb.]) is the series title, but other annuals in this series have been published under different titles. All of them provide detailed analyses on the nuclear programs of all countries with the potential to develop nuclear weapons. This source is invaluable in determining trends in nuclear proliferation.

A number of databooks, handbooks, and sourcebooks provide background information for researchers on arms control and disarmament. Two publications from the U.S. Arms Control and Disarmament Agency (ACDA), *Arms Control and Disarmament Agreements: Texts and Histories of Negotiations* (Washington, D.C.: U.S. Arms Control and Disarmament Agency, 1982. 290 pp.), and *Documents on Disarmament, 1984* (Washington, D.C.: U.S. Arms Control and Disarmament Agency, 1986. 964 pp.) give the texts of major arms control and disarmament agreements. The latter is an annual publication; the latest edition is cited. These two publications present the official American positions on various types of arms control agreements along with historical background.

A similar type of sourcebook is by Jozef Goldblat. His *Agreements for Arms Control: A Critical Survey* (London: Taylor and Francis, 1982. 2 vols.), and *Arms Control Agreements: A Handbook* (New York: Praeger, 1983. 328 pp.) cover much the same territory as the ACDA sourcebooks, but with increased coverage of international bilateral and multilateral arms control agreements. Together with the ACDA sourcebooks, these reference works provide complete texts of all arms control agreements in effect since 1945.

A basic handbook on various aspects of research in arms control is Dennis Menos's *Arms Control Fact Book* (Jefferson, N.C.: McFarland, 1985. 140 pp.). It contains sections on the international arms control system, an analysis of organizations active in arms control and disarmament, and general statistical data on arms control. This useful reference tool is most valuable for the novice researcher.

A different type of handbook is *The Disarmament Catalogue* (New York: Pilgrim Press, 1982. 209 pp.). This publication is a direct action handbook in opposition to the prevailing U.S. government's attitude toward the feasibility of nuclear war. Although this publication lists a variety of resources for peace studies including audiovisual materials, checklists of books, and disarmament organizations, its main purpose is to serve as a reference source to promote disarmament.

A new reference source on arms control issues is *Arms Control Handbook: A Guide to the History, Arsenals and Issues of U.S.-Soviet Negotiations* (Washington, D.C.: Heritage Foundation, 1987. 175 pp.) The conservative think tank, the Heritage Foundation, has produced this handbook to provide its assessment of the arms control process. It has up-to-date information on the military strategic balance between the United States and the Soviet Union, and background material on past arms control negotiations. Despite its hardline conservative viewpoint, this handbook can be recommended for both the general reader and the specialist.

Finally, there is a most unusual reference work from Canada on classification of arms control verification proposals. This source originates from the Operational Research and Analysis Establishment of the Canadian Department of National Defence. A. Crawford's *Compendium of Arms Control Verification Proposals* (Ottawa, Canada: Operational Research and Analysis Establishment, Department of National Defense, 1982. 2nd edition. 485 pp.) studies 296 arms control verification proposals in arms control literature for similarities and differences of approach and content. The result is a reference source unrivaled in the field.

Only a few guidebooks are worthy of inclusion in an arms control collection, but these few are all of high quality. Jozef Goldblat's *Nuclear Non-Proliferation: A Guide to the Debate* (London: Taylor and Francis, 1985. 95 pp.) is a study of the non-proliferation policies of the fifteen leading candidate states for the acquisition of nuclear weapons. This guidebook serves as a solid introduction to future trends in non-proliferation.

Teena Mayers, formerly with the U.S. Arms Control and Disarmament Agency, presents a guide to understanding arms control issues in her *Understanding Nuclear Weapons and Arms Control: A Guide to the Issues* (Washington, D.C.: Pergamon-Brassey, 1986. 3rd ed. 121 pp.). Among its virtues is a balanced presentation of arms control issues, but it also includes a considerable amount of statistical data. This guidebook remains a quality reference source from a respected authority in the field.

Another reference book on nuclear proliferation issues is Ann Florini's *Nuclear Proliferation: A Citizen's Guide to Policy Choices* (New York: United Nations Association of the United States of America, 1983. 48 pp.). This guidebook is intended to inform the American public on the dangers of nuclear proliferation. It is also to be used as a resource for the formation of direct action groups to lobby on non-proliferation issues. The result is an illustrated and readable booklet of moderate length which is full of reference materials.

INTERNATIONAL SECURITY

Only a few bibliographies on international security are of benefit to security specialists. By far the best is the *Quarterly Strategic Bibliography* (Boston: American Security Council Foundation, 1975– $84.00). This quarterly bibliography from the American Security Foundation lists articles on security and strategic issues from 175 periodicals, congressional documents, monographs, and reports. Since it appears at regular intervals and carries an array of diverse materials, this publication is the most comprehensive security bibliography in the field.

Two other bibliographies of a lesser stature but still worth noting are Colin Gordon's *The Atlantic Alliance: A Bibliography* (London: Francis Pinter, 1978. 216 pp.) and Michael Underdown's *Threat Perception: A Bibliography and Introductory Essay* (Parkville, Australia: Program in Public Policy Studies, University of Melbourne, 1982. 131 pp.). Gordon's bibliography has 3,000 English-language references on the history and organization of the North Atlantic Treaty organization (NATO) from its beginnings in 1949 to around 1977. Journal articles and government papers dealing with the analysis of threat perception and crisis management fill Underdown's bibliography. Neither bibliography is definitive, but they contain enough material to help any researcher starting on a research project on these topics.

There are no outstanding international security annuals, but several provide enough material to be of value. The best is *Annual of Power and Conflict* (London: Institute for the Study of Conflict, 1972– $100.00). It is a product of the authoritative Institute for the Study of Conflict (ISC), London. Sources of political instability, subversive and terrorist movements in more than 120 countries are covered in this annual. Although this publication remains the top annual in its field, it has a slow publication cycle.

Another important annual is the *International Security Yearbook* (New York: St. Martin's Press, 1984– $11.95). This yearbook presents an empirical and objective analysis of the events of the past year that influence Western security. It is published under the auspices of the Georgetown University Center for Strategic and International

Studies, Washington, D.C., and it is a quality reference source from this prestigious institute.

Four annuals of regional interests are *Asian Security* (London: Brassey's Defence, 1979– $29.95), *The Middle East Annual* (Boston: G.K.Hall, 1980– $92.00), *Middle East Contemporary Survey* (New York: Holmes and Meier, 1976– $198.00), and *Southeast Asian Affairs* (Singapore: Institute of Southeast Asian Studies, 1974– $25.00). Each of these annuals presents an analysis of contemporary affairs in its region. Together, these publications give a good overview of politics, economic, and military affairs in these strategic areas.

There are a few solid databooks, handbooks, and sourcebooks. One of the better examples is *Border and Territorial Disputes* (London: Longman, 1982. 406 pp.). This publication traces current unresolved border and territorial issues between states around the world. More than 70 present or potential situations have been isolated because of their territorial and/or political significance.

Two publications of a similar type are *Arms Production in the Third World* (London: Taylor and Francis, 1986. 391 pp.) and Nicole Ball's *Third-World Security Expenditure: A Statistical Compendium* (Stockholm, Sweden: Swedish National Defence Research Institute, 1983. 248 pp.). Both publications study arms production and security expenditures of Third World countries. The first uses data acquired from SIPRI's computerized data bases on the production and trade in major conventional weapons. Ball uses the U.N. reporting matrix to analyze the military expenditures of forty-eight Third World states. Together, these sourcebooks provide the researcher with statistical data for further research on Third World security concerns.

Another type of sourcebook is Alex P. Schmid's *Soviet Military Interventions Since 1945* (New Brunswick, N.J.: Transaction Books, 1985. 223 pp.). This surveys about fifty cases of alleged Soviet interventions in the post-1945 era. Ten cases have been isolated for a more in-depth treatment. The epilogue, in which the author uses charts on the various types of interventions, represents this publication's most unique contribution.

A documentary record of the Israeli-Palestinian Conflict is in *Documents on the Israeli-Palestinian Conflict, 1967–1983* (London: Cambridge University Press, 1984. 247 pp.). The International Center for Peace in the Middle East, an Israeli think tank, published this sourcebook in response to requests from the Israeli Knesset for a documentary history of the Middle East conflict. This book consists of key documents and statements from the respective parties to the conflict from 1967 to 1983; these documents are difficult to find in any other source.

Finally, Michael Kidron's unique sourcebook, *The State of War Atlas: Armed Conflict—Armed Peace* (New York: Simon and Schuster, 1983. $19.95), depicts the changing international military order since 1945. The author identified nearly 300 wars since World War II and analyzes them by means of forty maps. This combination of pictorial representation and statistical data makes this handbook as valuable to the scholar as to the general public.

Several of the guidebooks are exceptional values for understanding research trends in international security subjects. Two of the better guidebooks are Bruce R. Kuniholm's *The Palestinian Problem and United States Policy: A Guide to Issues and References* (Claremont, Calif.: Regina Books, 1986, 157 pp.) and his *The Persian Gulf and United States Policy: A Guide to Issues and References* (Claremont, Calif.: Regina Books, 1984. 220 pp.). These guidebooks combine essays on the subject matter followed by a bibliography of sources on the same subject. Both the Palestinian question and the Persian Gulf security are key international security problems about which these guidebooks provide some much needed information.

Two guides to the nuclear arms race are Christy Campbell's *Nuclear Facts: A Guide to Nuclear Weapon Systems and Strategy* (London: Hamlyn, 1984. 192 pp.) and Sandra Sedacca's *Up in Arms: A Common Cause Guide to Understanding Nuclear Arms Policy* (Washington, D.C: Common Cause, 1984. 130 pp.). Campbell's book analyzes each of the nuclear powers and makes projections on each country's future strategic and technological developments. Sedacca's book seeks to give the average American citizen information about the terminology, the strategies and tactics, and the argument of the nuclear arms debate. Either as a duo or separately, these guidebooks provide information on trends in the nuclear arms race.

The top directory in international security studies in the *Directory Guide of European Security and Defense Research* (Leuven, Belgium: Leuven University Press, 1985. 376 pp.). Information and reference material on over 200 research centers in nineteen European countries are covered in this research directory. The editors believe that increased communication and cooperation among European research centers will stimulate research on defense, disarmament, and security subjects. This directory gives the addresses and research specialties of most European security and defense institutes. Such information allows American scholars to contact these research centers.

NATIONAL SECURITY

Most of the bibliographies on national security subjects are oriented more toward military than defense topics. The top bibliographical source is *Current Military Literature: Comment and Abstracts and Citations of Important Articles from International Military and Defence Periodicals* (Oxford, England: Military Press, 1983– $135.00). This British bibliography appears six times a year, and it is intended as a research aid for persons interested in military warfare and strategic problems. An impressive list of military journals is scanned for this publication.

Another bibliography of the same type is *Aerospace/Defense Markets & Technology* (Cleveland, Ohio: Predicasts, 1983– $850.00). This quarterly publication contains abstracts from nearly 100 aerospace and defense-related periodicals. It is an excellent source for finding information on the development and testing of new military technology. The biggest drawback of this bibliography is its high cost.

A more traditional bibliography is Brian Champion's *Advanced Weapon Systems: An Annotated Bibliography of the Cruise Missile, MX Missile, Laser and Space Weapons and Stealth Technology* (New York: Garland, 1985. 206 pp.). This annotated bibliography of weapon systems has been complied by Canadian librarians from the University of Alberta, and it consists of citations from a variety of influential military and scientific journals. Although the material in this type of publication ages quickly, this bibliography has a number of valuable citations of interest to scholars in national security studies.

Finally, there is Ruth Leger Sivard's *World Military and Social Expenditures* (Leesburg, Va.: World Priorities, 1975– $5.00). This annual is an accounting of the use of world resources for social and military purposes. It has a statistical approach with numerous graphs and charts. The appearance of this annual is always eagerly awaited by scholars in the field because of the authoritative nature of its statistics.

The rate of change in defense, military technology, and weapons systems has produced several high-quality annuals. Jane's Publishing specializes in the production of annuals filled with evaluations of current military and security affairs. Among their significant publications are *Jane's Fighting Ships* (London: Jane's Publishing, 1898– $112.50), *Jane's Infantry Weapons* (London: Jane's Publishing, 1973– $112.50), *Jane's Military Communications* (London: Jane's Publishing, 1980– $140.00), *Jane's Military Vehicles and Ground Support Equipment* (London: Jane's Publishing, 1980– $137.00), and *Jane's Weapon Systems* (London: Jane's Publishing, 1969– $125.00). All of the annuals are characterized by an encyclopaedic coverage of the subject. These annuals are the most up-to-date authoritative reference works on military subjects on the market.

A serious rival to the Jane's annuals in prestige is the *RUSI and Brassey Defence Yearbook* (Oxford, England: Brassey's Defence Publishers, 1896– $53.12). It is a product of the Royal United Services Institute for Defence Studies (RUSI), London. This yearbook provides up-to-date information about international defense trends.

Other important annuals are the *American Defense Annual* (Lexington, Mass.: Lexington Books, 1985– $20.00) and *Defense and Foreign Affairs Handbook* (Washington, D.C.: Defense and Foreign Affairs, 1976– $82.00). The *American Defense Annual* is part of a series published under the auspices of the Mershon Center at Ohio State University explaining the operations of the American defense establishment. It also specializes in current changes in U.S. defense strategy. Nearly 200 countries' defense policies and foreign affairs are considered in the **Defense and Foreign Affairs Handbook**. While general statistical information is provided on each country, the major feature is the information on the defense structure, including Army and Navy orders of battle.

A Canadian research institute, the Russian Research Center of Nova Scotia and Dalhousie University, produces the *Soviet Armed Forces Review Annual* (Gulf Breeze, Fla.: Academic International Press, 1976– price varies). American, British, and Canadian military specialists evaluate the Soviet Air Force, Army, Navy, and strategic rocket forces. This annual combines authoritative analysis with a mass of statistical data useful for any type of research on the Soviet armed forces.

A new annual is John Laffin's *War Annual* (London: Brassey's Defence Publishers, 1986– $24.95). His approach is to analyze all the wars in progress during a particular year. By such an analysis, the background, course, conduct and possible conclusion of each war can be ascertained. Combining both currency of information and prediction makes this book a welcome reference source.

Databooks, handbooks and sourcebooks are a growth industry in national security studies. While none of these reference works stands out as superior, all make contributions. One of the better is Christy Campbell's *War Facts Now* (Glasgow, Scotland: Fontana Paperbacks, 1982. 304 pp.). Facts and figures about all aspects of modern warfare are the specialty of this handbook. The author is the managing editor of Jane's Publishing, and he uses these resources to concentrate on an analysis of modern warfare and future weapon trends.

Another resource of considerable interest is John M. Collins's *U.S.–Soviet Military Balance, 1980–1985* (Washington, D.C.: Pergamon-Brassey, 1985. 360 pp.). This publication provides the reader with an account of the changes in the U.S.–Soviet military balance of forces since 1980. The author is a senior analyst on national security and military affairs for the Congressional Research Service. He utilizes his position to document the growing military strength of the Soviet Union over the five-year period.

A similar source is David C. Isby's **Armies of NATO's Central Front** (London: Jane's Publishing, 1985. 479 pp.). Capabilities, deployments, and tactics of NATO forces in Central Europe are featured in this sourcebook. Each NATO defense force is analyzed for its potential defense effectiveness in case of hostilities with the Warsaw Pact. No study of NATO strategy and tactics can ignore the material in this book.

The best sourcebook on U.S. nuclear weapon capabilities is in the first volume of the **Nuclear Weapons Databook** (Cambridge, Mass.: Ballinger, 1984– $38.00 each). This volume is entitled **U.S. Nuclear Forces and Capabilities,** and it is part of a projected eight-volume study of all aspects of the production and the deployment of nuclear weapons worldwide. Volume one is a comprehensive study of U.S. nuclear forces and their tactical capabilities. It features solid analysis with in-depth information of American weapons and equipment. Volume two, **U.S. Nuclear Weapons Production Complex,** deals with the civilian-military defense industry weapons procurement system.

James N. Constant's **Fundaments of Strategic Weapons: Offense and Defense Systems** (The Hague: The Netherlands: Martinus Nijhoff, 1981. 2 vols.) is another approach for a sourcebook. It covers the technology, evolution, functions, costs, societal impacts, and limitations of modern strategic weapon systems. Considerable expertise is required to understand the scientific principles involved in this publication. It remains the best textbook source of information on strategic weapons.

Several others sourcebooks are available for specialized topics. Among these are **Air Forces of the World** (Geneva, Switzerland: Interavia, 1985. 827 pp. $300.00), Christopher Chant's **Naval Forces of the World** (London: Winchmore Publishing Services, 1984. 192 pp.), Christopher F. Foss's **Artillery of the World** (New York: Scribner's, 1981. 3rd ed. 176 pp.), John Jordan's **Soviet Warships: The Soviet Surface Fleet 1960 to the present** (Annapolis, Md.: Naval Institute Press, 1983. 128 pp.), Chris McAllister's **Military Aircraft Today** (London: Batsford, 1985. 168 pp.), Martin Streetly's **World Electronic Warfare Aircraft** (London: Jane's Publishing, 1983. 127 pp.), and **Weyers Warships of the World** (Annapolis, Md.: Nautical and Aviation Publishing, 1983. 57th ed. 730 pp.).

There are also a number of useful guidebooks for national security studies. Two related guidebooks from the same publishers are Kenneth A. Bertsch's **The Nuclear Weapons Industry** (Washington, D.C.: Investor Responsibility Research Center, 1984. 405 pp.) and Linda Shaw's **Stocking the Arsenal: A Guide to the Nation's Top Military Contractors** (Washington, D.C.: Investor Responsibility Research Center, 1985. 207 pp.). Both publications deal with defense industry subjects, and they provide information difficult to find in any other source.

A different type of guidebook is **Defense Dollars and Sense: A Common Cause Guide to the Defense Budget Process** (Washington, D.C.: Common Cause, 1983. 90 pp.). The processes of the American defense budget are scrutinized in this guidebook published under the auspices of Common Cause. Each step of the defense budget process is examined for cost-benefit to the United States. This guidebook is a major assessment and critique of the defense budget infrastructure.

Another guidebook of value is James F. Dunnigan's *A Quick and Dirty Guide to War: Briefings on Present and Potential Wars* (New York: Morrow, 1985. 415 pp.). Current and potential wars and violent political conflicts are the focus of this publication. By surveying the political, ethnic, and economic makeups of these military hotspots, the authors believe that the reader can have a better comprehension of the possibility of the outbreak of hostilities in these localities.

Bill Gunston, the former technical editor of *Flight International* and the assistant compiler of several Jane's publications, and Doug Richardson have made careers of compiling illustrated guidebooks on military aviation. All of these guidebooks have their uses, but the most significant is Gunston's *An Illustrated Guide to Future Fighters and Combat Aircraft* (London: Salamander, 1984. 159 pp.) and Richardson's *An Illustrated Survey of the West's Modern Fighters: Technical Details of Today's Most Advanced Fighting Aircraft* (London: Salamander, 1984. 207 pp.). While Gunston concentrates on the technologies of military aircraft now in the process of development for the period after 1990, Richardson surveys trends in attack aircraft, tactical fighters, and air-superiority interceptors among members of the Western Alliance.

A guidebook on the study of the MX controversy is Robert A. Hoover's *The MX Controversy: A Guide to Issues and References* (Claremont, Calif.: Regina Books, 1982. 116 pp.). The debate over the MX missile system during the six years of three presidential administrations is summarized in this guidebook. Besides analysis of the MX controversy, this book has a bibliography of 360 documents, pamphlets, books, and articles on the subject.

Paul Rodgers's *Guide to Nuclear Weapons, 1984–85* (Bradford, England: School of Peace Studies, 1984. 124 pp.) is a survey of nuclear weapons in the world's military arsenals. This publication from Bradford University School of Peace Studies is an excellent source for guidance on further study on nuclear weapons.

Two other valuable guidebooks are Norman Polmar's *Guide to the Soviet Navy* (Annapolis, Md.: Naval Institute Press, 1983. 3rd ed. 465 pp.) and William C. Green's *Soviet Nuclear Weapons Policy: A Research and Bibliographic Guide* (Boulder, Colo.: Westview Press, 1987. 399 pp.). Polmar has gathered information from a variety of sources on the operational capacity, personnel requirements, and ships of the Soviet Navy. Although this publication resembles other guides on Soviet naval data, its strength is in its evaluation of the strategic uses of Soviet naval forces. Green's contribution is a research guide to Western and Soviet literature on Soviet nuclear weapons policy. Besides essays on aspects of Soviet nuclear strategy, there is a lengthy annotated bibliography of recent publications on the subject.

There are three major national security directories. Two of them are products of the Swiss defense publisher Interavia. Both *Interavia ABC Aerospace Directory* (Geneva, Switzerland: Interavia, 1936– $222.00) and *International Defense Directory* (Geneva, Switzerland: Interavia, 1984– $245.00) provide information on the international aerospace industries and the international defense industries. Researchers interested in information about the respective industries will find these directories of interest.

The other directory is *Jane's Spaceflight Directory* (London: Jane's Publishing, 1986. 453 pp.). This directory is an encyclopedia of information on space programs in operation in 1986. Each of the Jane's publications provides a mass of material, and this book is no exception.

PEACE

Peace reference books are almost as plentiful as books in the other fields, but they are divided between basic information sources and direct action guides. The best bibliography is Berenice A. Carroll's *Peace and War: A Guide to Bibliographies* (Santa Barbara, Calif.: ABC-Clio, 1983. 580 pp.). This publication is a bibliography of bibliographies, and as such it is a serious attempt to achieve bibliographical control over the literature on peace and war. Bibliographies are included from 1785 through 1980, and annotations have been added for the benefit of the reader.

Another worthy bibliography is *Bibliography on World Conflict and Peace* (Boulder, Colo.: Westview Press, 1979. 2nd ed. 168 pp.). This bibliography started out as a booklet for teachers and students in the field of conflict and peace studies, but it has been expanded, until now it covers most peace materials published in North America and Europe. The original method of material selection was based on a definition of conflict and peace prepared by the Committee on the Sociology of World Conflicts, but a change in criteria for the second edition has meant a more varied selection of topics.

The only peace annual of merit is the *Unesco Yearbook on Peace and Conflict Studies* (Westport, Conn.: Greenwood Press, 1980– $30.00). This yearbook is published under the auspices of Unesco, and it contains articles from a wide variety of contributors dealing with the issues of peace and conflict. Its emphasis is on providing teachers and researchers on peace and conflict studies with basic information. An ongoing weakness of this publication is a three-year delay in its publication cycle.

Most of the databooks, handbooks, and sourcebooks on peace have a distinct orientation toward direct action politics. Two exceptions are reference books on peace-keeping activities. The first publication is *Basic Documents on United Nations and Related Peace-Keeping Forces* (Dordrecht, the Netherlands: Martinus Nijhoff, 1985. 273 pp.). Essential documents relating to the peace-keeping efforts of the United Nations have been compiled in this sourcebook. Some thirteen peace-keeping operations have been undertaken by the United Nations since 1956, and documents on each mission are contained in this publication.

The other publication is the *Peacekeeper's Handbook* (New York: Pergamon Press, 1984. 439 pp.). This handbook is a ready reference source for the planning and conducting of peace-keeping operations. It is a product of the International Peace Academy (IPA), which is an educational institute designed for dispute settlement and conflict management. The text of this handbook reflects the academic orientation of the IPA.

The remainder of the materials are direct action handbooks. Barry Popkess's *The Nuclear Survival Handbook: Living Through and After a Nuclear Attack* (New York: Collier Books, 1980. 345 pp.) is the most objective. He has complied a survival handbook in both American and British versions to educate the general public on surviving a nuclear attack. All the post-attack hazards—nuclear, biological, environmental, and social consequences—are treated in depth.

Three other handbooks are more subjective. These are *Keeping the Peace: A Woman's Peace Handbook* (London: Women's Press, 1983. 161 pp.), *Waging*

Peace: A Handbook for the Struggle to Abolish Nuclear Weapons (San Francisco: Harper and Row, 1982), and *Working for Peace: A Handbook of Practical Psychology and Other Tools* (San Luis Obispo, Calif.: Impact Publishers, 1985. 270 pp.). The first publication contains essays from representatives of the various women's peace groups on woman's role in keeping the peace. Waging peace is the theme of an educational and informational handbook for those who are concerned about the political struggle of preventing nuclear war. Working for peace concerns the personal and interpersonal psychological principles of peace as explained by specialists from a variety of disciplines.

There are several excellent guidebooks on peace issues. Perhaps the best is *Peace Resource Book: A Comprehensive Guide to Issues, Groups, and Literature, 1986* (Cambridge, Mass.: Ballinger, 1986. 416 pp.). This guidebook is the much expanded successor to the *American Peace Directory, 1984*. As a product of the Institute for Defense and Disarmament Studies, Cambridge, Massachusetts, it is intended as a handy guide for activists, organizations, journalists, teachers, and students interested in learning more about peace.

A different type of guidebook is *Nucleography: An Annotated Resource Guide for Parents and Educators on Nuclear Energy, War, and Peace* (Berkeley, Calif.: Nucleography, 1982. 110 pp.). This publication is an annotated resource guide dealing with nuclear technology and its impact on society. Each entry has been judged to be a valuable resource in teaching or learning about nuclear energy, war and/or peace.

Finally, there is Crispin Phillips's *The Nuclear Casebook: An Illustrated Guide* (Edinburgh, Scotland: Polygon Books, 1983. 47 pp.). Two British medical doctors, who are affiliated with the Medical Campaign Against Nuclear Weapons, have produced this illustrated guide to the medical effects of the use of nuclear weapons. The result is an effective treatise on the horrors of nuclear war. This guidebook is an effective use of illustrations and statistics to argue a cause.

The best peace directory is *World Directory of Peace Research Institutions* (Paris: Unesco, 1981. 4th ed. 213 pp.). A total of 313 international peace organizations are listed along with types of organization, specialities, addresses, types of publication, number of researchers, and annual budgets. This directory is the best source of its type available, but it needs more frequent updates.

The core reference books described in this chapter constitute a reference collection of benefit to researchers, students, teachers, and the general public. Many of these books are now out of print, but a number of them reappear with updated material in later editions. Any subject specialist or acquisition librarian would be able to acquire most of these materials. The cost of such a collection is between $5,000 and $7,500, with serials running in the neighborhood of $2,500. This price for such a collection will continue to increase as more reference books appear on the market and publishing costs continue to escalate. But collections of this type are heavily used by patrons concerned with the problems of arms control, disarmament, international security, national security, and peace. My experience as an administrator of this type of collection indicates that the demand for such material is so active that it is difficult to keep the reference books from disappearing off the shelves.

Index

ABM Treaty, 72, 74, 76, 122, 311, 312
Acheson, Dean, 37
Achille Lauro incident, 250, 285, 288, 358, 361
Adelphi Papers, 65
AD–70, 170
Advanced Research Projects Agency, U.S. Department of Defense (DARPA), 372
AFCENT, 177
Afghanistan: indirect U.S. support for rebels in, 218; Soviet invasion of, 288
Ailleret, Gen. Charles, 116
Airborne Warning and Control Systems (AWACS), 220
Aircraft carriers. *See* Naval forces
Aircraft shelter program, for NATO, 174
Alexander the Great, 241
Algeria: arms purchases by, 227; French involvement in, 251, 252, 261; terrorism in, 269
Alliances: arms transfers within, 211, 218; conflict of interests in, 182; credibility of, 38, 331; destructive capacity between, 139; formation processes, 20; and polarization, 19–20; responding to attacks within, 37, 47, 141; for use of nuclear weapons, 113–15, 339–40. *See also* Coalitions; North Atlantic Treaty Organization; Warsaw Pact
Allison, G. T., 373, 379

Antarctic Treaty of 1959, 341
Anti-satellite (ASAT) weaponry, 74, 312
Anti-SSBN (ballistic missile submarine) campaign, 196, 202
Arab League, 128
Argentina: arms production, procurement, and sales by, 211, 221, 226, 229; nuclear capability of, 319, 335, 342, 344, 347. *See also* Falkland Islands conflict
Armed forces: international correlation of, 62, 66; maintaining survivability of, 36–37, 89; measuring comparability of, 165–67; reserve mobilization of, 178–79. *See also* Naval forces; Nuclear forces; Special Operations Forces
Armed neutrality, use of nuclear weapons in, 327
Arms control: alternatives to, 306–7; compliance with, 74–76; conditions for, 307–11; and crisis management, xvii; definition of, 300–302; and deterrence theory, 302, 303; efforts at, xii; history of, 299; of nuclear proliferation, 337–48; role in international politics, 302–6; suggestions for achieving, 311–13; and survivability of forces, 37; verification of, 312. *See also* Nuclear balance
Arms Control and Disarmament Agency (ACDA), 79, 233 n.2

in NATO, 143; nonproliferation of nuclear weapons in, 330, 335
Carrington, Lord, 175
Carter, Ashton B., 89
Carter, Jimmy, 67, 74, 85, 96, 152, 172, 196, 221, 231, 249, 284, 286, 288, 301
Casey, William J., 275, 276
CENTAG, 173, 178
Central Intelligence Agency (CIA), 62
Chad: conflict with Libya, 224; French involvement in, 253, 254
Chassin, Gen. Lionel-Max, 251
Chernobyl nuclear accident, 320, 358, 360
Chile: arms production in, 225; British arms transfers to, 224
China: arms production in, 216; as nuclear power, 111, 112–13, 124–28, 133, 319, 335; "People's War" in, 241; U.S. defense treaty with, 340
Churchill, Winston, 183
Clausewitz, Carl von, xii, 188
Coalitions: to defend balance of power, 15–16. See also Alliances
Cohen, William S., 250
Collins, John M., 65
Co-located Operating Bases (COBs), 174
Command: assessment of, 88–93; definition of, 86, 87–88, 100; of the sea, 194; vulnerability of, 90–91. See also C³I
Commitments: based on arms transfers, 218; and national interests, 37–38, 47
Communication, violent, 278–79
Communications, definition of, 86–87. See also C³I
Communists: resistance to, 244, 249–50, 261
Comprehensive test ban (CTB), 331, 340–41, 349
Conflict: spectrum of, 239. See also Low-intensity conflict; War
Conflict, systemic: associated with capability concentration, 16–17; and balance of power, 15–16; based on status inconsistency, 20–21; between nation-states, xii, xiv-xv, 3–27; definition of, 4; due to polarization, 19–20; expla-

nations for, 4–22; hegemonic cost-benefit model for, 8–9; leadership long cycle model for, 9–10; persistence of, xiv, 3–4; power cycle model for, 7–8; power transition model for, 5–7; and stability, 17–19; types of, 13; world-economy model for, 10–12
Conflict and Peace Data Bank (COPDAB), 372
Contingency operations, 244. See also Low-intensity conflict
Control: assessment of, 88–93; definition of, 86, 87–88, 100. See also C³I
Conventional Arms Transfer (CAT) talks, 231
Conventional Defense Imporvement (CDI) plan, 175
Conventional forces: and deterrence, 45, 46; as deterrent to "going nuclear," 337, 339; land warfare with, 161–86; and NATO forces, xvi, 148, 156, 161–86; proliferation of, 209–35; role of in nuclear age, xvi, 139–58; Soviet, 98–99, 176; of the U.S., 149–50; and warfare at sea, 187–207
Convention on the Prevention and Punishment of Crimes Against Internationally Protected Persons, Including Diplomatic Agents, 282
Core powers. See Great powers
Council of Europe, 282
Counterinsurgency, 244, 249. See also Low-intensity conflict
Counterterrorism. See Terrorism, counteraction to
Credibility, as factor in nuclear deterrence, 38–41, 43, 115, 328, 331, 340
Crelinsten, Ronald D., 274
Crisis: actor confrontation, 360, 367–72; arms control management of, xvii, 40–41, 101, 299–318; decision-making, 360, 372–80; definitions of, 359–60, 361; forecasting, 371–72; management of, 378–80; and national security decision making, xvii-xviii, 357–85; systemic, 360, 362–67
Crisis bargaining, 367–68
Crozier, Michael, 374–75

About the Contributors

STEPHEN E. ATKINS is the Arms Control Bibliographer at the University of Illinois at Urbana-Champaign Library. Included among his publications are "Serials on Arms Control," *Serials Review* (1985), "Information Sources: Arms Control, Disarmament, and International Security," *National Forum* (1986), and "Arms Control, Disarmament and Peace Newsletter," *Behavioral & Social Sciences Librarian* (1986). At present he is finishing a book on arms control, disarmament, defense, international security, military and peace materials

WILLIAM H. BAUGH is Associate Professor of Political Science at the University of Oregon. His research has focused broadly on conflict and national security issues, with particular emphasis on the US-Soviet strategic balance, formal models of arms competitions, and problems of conventional arms transfers. Among his publications are *The Politics of Nuclear Balance* (1984), as well as articles and chapters in edited collections.

MICHAEL BRZOSKA is currently Hochschulassistent at the University of Hamburg. Formerly at Stockholm International Peace Research Institute, Sweden, he is co-editor of *Third World Arms to the Third World 1971–85* (1987).

STEPHEN J. CIMBALA is Professor of Political Science of Pennsylvania State University. He has contributed to the field of national security studies for many years. His recent books include *Nuclear Strategy: Unfinished Business* (Greenwood, 1987) and *Rethinking Nuclear Strategy* (1988).

MARTHA CRENSHAW is Professor of Government at Wesleyan University in Middletown, Connecticut. Her publications include *Revolutionary Terrorism* (1978) and *Terrorism, Legitimacy, and Power* (1983). She is also the author of "The Psychology of Political Terrorism" in Margaret G. Hermann, ed., *Political Psychology* (1986).

CHARLES F. HERMANN is Director of the Mershon Center for Research and Education in National Security and Public Policy and Professor of Political Science at The Ohio State University. He has maintained a career-long interest in problems of international crisis and crisis decision-making as revealed in some of his publications including *Crisis in Foreign Policy* (1969); *International Crises* (1972); "International Crises as a Situation Variable," in J. N. Rosenau's *International Politics and Foreign Policy* (1969); "Enhancing Crisis Stability" in Winham's *New Issues in International Crisis Management* (1988); and "Crisis Stability" in the Mershon Center's *American Defense Annual, 1988–1989* (1988). In addition to the research on crisis, Hermann is involved in the comparative study of foreign policy and decision-making

EDWARD A. KOLODZIEJ is Research Professor of Political Science and Director of the European Arms Control Project at the University of Illinois, Urbana-Champaign. A frequent contributer to professional journals, he is the author of *The Uncommon Defense and Congress: 1945–1963* (1966); *French International Policy under De Gaulle and Pompidou: The Politics of Grandeur* (1974); and *Making and Marketing Arms: The French Experience and Its Implications for the International System* (1987) as well as three edited books. He is currently working on a manuscript on comparative nuclear deterrence systems.

RICHARD L. KUGLER is Director of the Strategic Concepts Development Center at the National Defense University, Department of Defense, Washington, D.C. He also is adjunct professor of international relations at George Washington University. He is author of several academic articles on NATO affairs and U.S. defense planning, and has extensive official publications.

PATRICK M. MORGAN is Professor of Political Science at Washington State University. Among his publications are *Deterrence, A Conceptual Analysis* 2nd ed. (1983), and *Theories and Approaches to International Politics* 4th ed. (1987) as well as, with Klaus Knorr, *Strategic Military Surprise* (1983). In 1987–88, he was a visiting professor at Katholeike Universiteit Leuven and the College of Europe (Bruges) in Belgium.

WILLIAM C. POTTER is Executive Director of the Center for International and Strategic Affairs, University of California, Los Angeles. He is the author of *Nuclear Power and Nonproliferation: An Interdisciplinary Perspective* (1982), the editor of *Verification and SALT: The Challenge of Strategic Deception* (1980), and the co-editor of *Soviet Decisionmaking for National Security* (1984) and *Nuclear Suppliers and Nonproliferation* (1985). He also has contributed to numerous scholarly books and journals. He is a consultant to Lawrence Livermore National Laboratory and to the U.S. Arms Control and

Disarmament Agency. His present research focuses on Soviet decision making for Chernobyl and the emerging nuclear suppliers and nonproliferation.

DAVID N. SCHWARTZ is currently with the London office of Goldman, Sachs, and Co. He was formerly the Director of Strategic Nuclear Policy in the Department of State's Politico-Military Bureau, having held various staff positions in the Bureau from 1980 to 1985. He has also worked on the Foreign Policy Staff of the Brookings Institution where he wrote *NATO's Nuclear Dilemma* (1983); co-edited *Ballistic Missile Defense* (1985); and contributed to several other Brookings studies.

RICHARD SHULTZ is Associate Professor of International Politics and a member of the International Security Studies Program of the Fletcher School of Law and Diplomacy. Among his publications are *The Soviet Union and Revolutionary Warfare; Principles, Practices and Regional Comparisons* (1988); *Guerrilla Warfare and Counterinsurgency: U.S.-Soviet Policy in the Third World* (1988); *Hydra of Carnage: The International Linkages of Terrorism* (1985); co-authored and co-edited with Uri Ra'anan, Robert L. Pfaltzgraff, Jr., Ernst Halperin, and Igor Lukes; *Dezinformatsia: Active Measures in Soviet Strategy* (1984), co-authored with Roy Godson. During 1987–1988 he was the recipient of an Earhart Foundation Research Felowship.

WILLIAM R. THOMPSON is Professor of International Relations in the Center for Politics and Policy at Claremont Graduate School. Among his recent publications are *Contending Approaches to World System Analysis, Rhythms in Politics and Economics* (Praeger, 1985), edited with Paul M. Johnson; *Seapower in Global Politics, 1494–1993* (1988), with George Modelski; and *On Global War: Historical-Structural Approaches to World Politics* (1988). He is currently engaged in projects on the historical linkages between global war and state making and the political economy of relative decline.

ROBERT S. WOOD is Chester W. Nimitz Professor of National Security and Foreign Affairs and Dean of the Center for Naval Warfare Studies at the Naval War College. He has written or contributed to eleven books including *France in the World Community* (1973), *The Foreign Policy of the Netherlands* (1978), *The U.S. Navy: The View from the Mid–1980's* (1985), and *Evolving European Defense Policies* (1987), as well as numerous articles.